# CONTEMPORARY STRATEGY ANALYSIS

## EIGHTH EDITION

## ROBERT M. GRANT

**WILEY**

*Registered office*
John Wiley & Sons Ltd, The Atrium, Southern Gate, Chichester, West Sussex, PO19 8SQ, United Kingdom

For details of our global editorial offices, for customer services and for information about how to apply for permission to reuse the copyright material in this book please see our website at www.wiley.com.

ISBN 9781119941880 (pbk)
ISBN 9781118600306 (iebk)
ISBN 9781118591086 (ebk)
ISBN 9781118591048 (ebk)
ISBN 9781118560693 (ebk)

A catalogue record for this book is available from the British Library

Set in 10/12pt ITC Garamond Std by MPS Limited, Chennai, India
Printed in Great Britain by TJ International, Padstow, Cornwall

IN ... E-BOOK

LOC... MBEDDED MEDIA

*Easily navigate your
e-book using the
chapter menu, searc...
and bookmark optio...*

...ou can save notes
...r voice annotations
...s a reminder of key
...oints.

3
CREATE
CHAPTER 1 THE CONCEPT OF S...
View

*Watch video clips to
bring the case studies
alive and expand your
understanding of the
issues.*

Ch 1 Flashcards A - 100%

Business
Strategy

*Test your understanding
with key term flashcards
and quizzes.*

WILEY

# CONTEMPORARY STRATEGY ANALYSIS

To Sue

# BRIEF CONTENTS

# CONTENTS

# PREFACE TO EIGHTH EDITION

*Contemporary Strategy Analysis* equips managers and students of management with the concepts, frameworks, and techniques needed to make better strategic decisions. My goal is a strategy text that reflects the dynamism and intellectual rigor of this fast-developing field of management and takes account of the strategic management practices of leading-edge companies.

*Contemporary Strategy Analysis* endeavors to be both rigorous and relevant. While embodying the latest thinking in the strategy field, it aims to be accessible to students from different backgrounds and with varying levels of experience. I achieve this accessibility by combining clarity of exposition, concentration on the fundamentals of value creation, and an emphasis on practicality.

This eighth edition maintains the book's focus on the essential tasks of strategy: identifying the sources of superior business performance and formulating and implementing a strategy that exploits these sources of superior performance. At the same time, the content of the book has been revised to reflect recent developments in the business environment and in strategy research and to take account of feedback from instructors.

Distinctive features of the eighth edition include a:

- broader approach to value creation that takes account of the value that is [creat]ed for stakeholders other than the firm's shareholders (Chapter 2);
- [stron]ger emphasis on the role of complementary products, especially in tech[nolo]gy-based industries (Chapters 4 and 9);
- [mor]e systematic treatment of resource and capability analysis that is struc[ture]d around a practical approach to undertaking an analysis of resources [and] capabilities;
- [mor]e integrated treatment of strategy implementation; while the book main[tain]s its emphasis on integrating strategy formulation with strategy implemen[tatio]n, Chapters 6 and 14 offer a systematic approach to strategy execution;
- [new] chapter on external growth strategies through mergers, acquisitions, and [allia]nces (Chapter 15), which are important to firms as they navigate a chal[leng]ing and unpredictable business world.

[There i]s little in *Contemporary Strategy Analysis* that is original: I have plundered [freel]y the ideas, theories, and evidence of fellow scholars. My greatest debts are to my colleagues and students at the business schools where this book has been developed and tested, notably Georgetown University and Bocconi University. I have also benefitted from feedback and suggestions from professors and students in the many other schools where *Contemporary Strategy Analysis* has been adopted. I look forward to continuing my engagement with users.

I am grateful for the professionalism and enthusiasm of the editorial, production, and sales and marketing teams at John Wiley & Sons, Ltd, especially to Steve Hardman, Deb Egleton, Claire Jardine, Peter Hudson, Kelly Simmons, Juliet Booker, and Tim Bettsworth—I couldn't wish for better support!

Robert M. Grant

# GUIDE TO WEB RESOURCES

Visit **www.contemporarystrategyanalysis.com** for access to all the teaching and learning resources available for this textbook.

## Instructors will find:

- Instructor's manual
- Case teaching notes
- PowerPoint slides
- Test bank
- Case video clips   *NEW TO THIS EDITION*

## Students will find:

- Self-test quizzes
- Author video clips
- Glossary flashcards   *NEW TO THIS EDITION*

You can also access your interactive e-book at **www.wileyopenpage.com** using the scratch code included on the inside-front cover of the printed book. Video clips, quizzes, and flashcards are embedded throughout the e-book for easy access:

Simply click on the "Play" icon located at relevant parts of the text.

Refer to the advert at the front of this book for more information.

# I
# INTRODUCTION

# 1    The Concept of Strategy   ▶

Strategy is the great work of the organization. In situations of life or death, it is the Tao of survival or extinction. Its study cannot be neglected.

—SUN TZU, *THE ART OF WAR*

To shoot a great score you need a clever strategy.

—RORY MCILROY, *GOLF MONTHLY*, MAY 19, 2011

## OUTLINE

## Introduction and Objectives

Strategy is about achieving success. This chapter explains what strategy is and why it is important to success, both for organizations and individuals. We will distinguish strategy from planning. Strategy is not a detailed plan or program of instructions; it is a unifying theme that gives coherence and direction to the actions and decisions of an individual or an organization.

The principal task of this chapter will be to introduce the basic framework for strategy analysis that underlies this book. I will introduce the two basic components of strategy analysis: analysis of the external environment of the firm (mainly industry analysis) and analysis of the internal environment (primarily analysis of the firm's resources and capabilities).

By the time you have completed this chapter, you will be able to:

- ◆ appreciate the contribution that strategy can make to successful performance, both for individuals and for organizations, and recognize the key characteristics of an effective strategy;

- ◆ comprehend the basic framework of strategy analysis that underlies this book;

- ◆ become familiar with how our thinking about business strategy has evolved over the past 60 years;

- ◆ be capable of identifying and describing the strategy of a business enterprise;

- ◆ understand how strategy is made within organizations;

- ◆ gain familiarity with the challenges of strategy making among not-for-profit organizations.

Since the purpose of strategy is to help us to win, we start by looking at the role of strategy in success.

## The Role of Strategy in Success

Strategy Capsules 1.1 and 1.2 describe the careers of two individuals, Queen Elizabeth II and Lady Gaga, who have been outstandingly successful in leading their organizations. Although these two remarkable women operate within vastly different arenas, can their success be attributed to any common factors?

For neither of these successful women can success be attributed to overwhelmingly superior resources. For all of Queen Elizabeth's formal status as reigning monarch, she has very little real power and, in most respects, is a servant of the British government led by the prime minister. Lady Gaga is clearly a creative and capable entertainer, but few would claim that she has outstanding talents as a vocalist, musician, or songwriter.

Nor can their success be attributed either exclusively or primarily to luck. Indeed, Queen Elizabeth has experienced a succession of difficulties and tragedies, while Lady Gaga has experienced setbacks (e.g., the cancelation of her first recording contract). Their ability to respond to events with flexibility and clarity of direction has been central to their success.

My contention is that common to both the 60-year successful reign of Queen Elizabeth II and the short but remarkable career of Lady Gaga is the presence of a soundly formulated and effectively implemented strategy. While these strategies did not exist as explicit plans, for both Queen Elizabeth and Lady Gaga we can observe a consistency of direction based on a clear understanding of desired goals and a keen awareness of how to maneuver into a position of advantage.

In the vast array of formal and informal activities that Elizabeth Windsor has performed as queen, she has given herself a clearly defined role in relation to the people of the UK and the Commonwealth countries. This role has combined the traditional notions of being a figurehead for the nation, a symbol of British family and cultural life, and an exemplar of service and professional dedication. Yet this constancy has also embraced flexibility to respond to the unexpected.

Lady Gaga's remarkable success in the three years up to the beginning of 2012 reflects a career strategy that uses music as her gateway, but she has then built a celebrity status by combining the generic tools of star creation—shock value, fashion leadership, and media presence—with a uniquely differentiated image that has captured the imagination and affection of teenagers and young adults throughout the world.

We can go further. What do these examples tell us about the characteristics of a strategy that are conducive to success? In both stories, four common factors stand out (Figure 1.1):

- *Goals that are consistent and long term*: Both Queen Elizabeth and Lady Gaga display a focused commitment to career goals that they have pursued steadfastly.
- *Profound understanding of the competitive environment*: The ways in which both Elizabeth II and Gaga define their roles and pursue their careers reveal a deep and insightful appreciation of the external environments in which they operate. Queen Elizabeth has been alert both to the changing political environment in which the monarchy is situated and to the mood and needs of the British people. Lady Gaga's business model and strategic positions show a keen awareness of the changing economics of the music business, the marketing potential of social networking, and the needs of Generation Y.
- *Objective appraisal of resources*: Both Queen Elizabeth and Lady Gaga have been adept at recognizing and deploying the resources at their disposal. Both, too, have been aware of the limits of those resources and drawn upon the resources of others—Queen Elizabeth through her family, the royal household, and a network of loyal supporters; Lady Gaga upon the variety of talents in her Haus of Gaga.
- *Effective implementation*: Without effective implementation, the best-laid strategies are of little use. Critical to the success of Queen Elizabeth and Lady Gaga has been their effectiveness as leaders and the creation of loyal, supportive organizations to provide decision support and operational implementation.

## STRATEGY CAPSULE 1.1
# Queen Elizabeth II and the House of Windsor

June 2012 marked the diamond jubilee of the reign of Queen Elizabeth II: for 60 years she had been the ruling monarch of the United Kingdom of Great Britain and Northern Ireland.

At her birth on April 21, 1926, hereditary monarchies were common throughout the world. Apart from the British Empire, 45 countries had this form of government. By 2012, the forces of democracy, modernity, and reform had reduced these to 26—mostly small autocracies such as Bahrain, Qatar, Oman, Kuwait, Bhutan, and Lesotho. Monarchies had also survived in Denmark, Sweden, Norway, the Netherlands, and Belgium, but these royal families had lost most of their wealth and privileges.

By contrast, the British royal family retains considerable wealth—the Queen's personal net worth was estimated by *Forbes* magazine at $450 million—in addition, she and her family have use of palaces and real estate owned by the nation and receive annual government funding of £7.9 million ($12 million). Despite having no political power, she has formal status as head of state, head of the Church of England, and head of the armed forces. Despite the winding down of the British Empire, the Queen retains her role as head of the Commonwealth and is head of state of 15 other countries, including Canada and Australia. In addition, she has created a strong informal role. According to her website, she "has a less formal role as Head of Nation" where she "acts as a focus for national identity, unity and pride; gives a sense of stability and continuity; officially recognises success and excellence; and supports the ideal of voluntary service" (www.royal.gov.uk).

How has Queen Elizabeth been able to retain not just the formal position of the monarchy but also its status, influence, and wealth despite the challenges of the past 60 years? These challenges include the social and political changes which have swept away most of the privileges conferred by hereditary status (including the exclusion of most hereditary lords from the House of Lords, Britain's upper chamber of Parliament) and the internal challenges presented by such a famously dysfunctional family—including the failed marriages of most of her family members and the controversy that surrounded the life and death of her daughter-in-law, Diana, Princess of Wales.

At the heart of Elizabeth's sustaining of the British monarchy has been her single-minded devotion to what she regards as her duties to the monarchy and to the nation. Throughout her 60-year reign she has cultivated the role of leader of her nation—a role that she has not compromised by pursuit of personal or family interests. In pursing this role she has recognized the need for political neutrality—even when she has personally disagreed with her prime ministers (notably

These observations about the role of strategy in success can be made in relation to most fields of human endeavor. Whether we look at warfare, chess, politics, sport, or business, the success of individuals and organizations is seldom the outcome of a purely random process. Nor is superiority in initial endowments of skills and resources typically the determining factor. Strategies that build on these four elements almost always play an influential role.

Look at the "high achievers" in any competitive area. Whether we review the world's political leaders, the CEOs of the Fortune 500, or our own circles of friends with Margaret Thatcher's "socially divisive" policies and Tony Blair's commitment of British troops to Iraq and Afghanistan).

Her leadership embodies a set of values—both British and Christian—which are directed toward sustaining British traditions and promoting British influence, British culture, and British values within the wider world. The Commonwealth provides a key focus for her promotion of British influence: she has made multiple visits to each of the 54 Commonwealth nations, including 26 to Canada and 16 to Australia.

Maintaining her popularity with the British people and the status of the royal family has required adaptation to the wrenching changes of her era. Recognizing the growing unacceptability of hereditary privilege and the traditional British class system, she has repositioned the royal family from being the leader of the ruling class to an embodiment of the nation as a whole. To make her and her family more inclusive and less socially stereotyped she cultivated involvement with popular culture, with ordinary people engaged in social service and charitable work, and, most recently, endorsing the marriage of her grandson William to Kate Middleton—the first member of the royal family to marry outside the ranks of the aristocracy.

In broadening the popular appeal of the monarchy, she has been adept at exploiting new media. Television has provided an especially powerful medium for communicating both with her subjects and with a wider global audience. The Queen's web page appeared in 1997, in 2009 she joined Twitter, and in 2010 Facebook. Throughout her reign, her press and public relations strategy has been carefully managed by a group of top professionals who report to her private secretary.

While respecting tradition and protocol, she adapts in the face of pressing circumstances. The death of her daughter-in-law, Diana, created difficult tensions between her responsibilities as a grandmother and her need to show leadership to a grieving nation. In responding to this time of crisis she departed from several established traditions: including bowing to the coffin of her ex-daughter-in-law as it passed the palace.

In pursuing her role of monarch, Elizabeth has drawn upon the resources available to her. First and foremost of these has been the underlying desire of the British people for continuity and their inherent distrust of their political leaders. By positioning herself above the political fray and emphasizing her lineage—including the prominent public role of her mother until her death in 2002—she reinforces the legitimacy of herself, her family, and the institution they represent. She has also exploited her powers of patronage, using her formal position to cultivate informal relationships both with political leaders such as Nelson Mandela and with individuals such as the Australian entertainer Rolf Harris, who obtained the rare privilege of painting her portrait.

The success of Elizabeth's 60-year reign is indicated by the popular support for her personally and for the institution of the monarchy. Outside of Northern Ireland, the UK lacks any significant republican movement; republicanism is also weak in Canada and Australia.

and acquaintances, those who have achieved outstanding success in their careers are seldom those who possessed the greatest innate abilities. Success has gone to those who managed their careers most effectively, typically by combining these four strategic factors. They are goal focused; their career goals have taken primacy over the multitude of life's other goals—friendship, love, leisure, knowledge, spiritual fulfillment—which the majority of us spend most of our lives juggling and reconciling. They know the environments within which they play and tend to be fast learners in terms of recognizing the paths to advancement. They know themselves well in

## STRATEGY CAPSULE 1.2
# Lady Gaga and the Haus of Gaga

Stefani Joanne Angelina Germanotta, better known as Lady Gaga, is the most successful popular entertainer to emerge in the 21st century. Since releasing her first album, *The Fame*, in 2008 she has certified record sales of 42 million,[a] swept leading music awards including Grammy, MTV, and Billboards, completed a 201-concert world tour that grossed $227.4 million (the highest for any debut artist), and topped *Forbes Celebrity 100* list for 2011.

Since dropping out of NYU's Tisch School of the Arts in 2005, she has shown total commitment to advancing her musical career and developing her Lady Gaga persona. After initially working as a songwriter, she developed her own musical act and image. Her debut album and its follow up, *The Fame Monster*, yielded a succession of number-one hits during 2009 and 2010.

Gaga's music is a catchy mix of pop and dance, well suited to dance clubs and radio airplay. It features good melodies, Gaga's capable singing voice, and her reflections on society and life, but it is hardly exceptional or innovative: music critic Simon Reynolds described it as: "ruthlessly catchy, naughties pop glazed with Auto-Tune and undergirded with R&B-ish beats."[b]

However, music is only one element in the Lady Gaga phenomenon—her achievement is not so much as a singer or songwriter as in establishing a persona which transcends pop music. Like David Bowie and Madonna before her, Lady Gaga is famous for being Lady Gaga. To do this requires a multi-media, multi-faceted offering that comprises an integrated array of components including music, visual appearance, newsworthy events, a distinctive attitude and personality, and a set of values with which fans can identify.

Key among these is visual impact and theatricality. Her hit records were heavily promoted by the visually stunning music videos that accompanied them. *Paparazzi* and *Bad Romance* each won best video awards at the 2009 and 2010 Grammies; the latter is the second-most-downloaded YouTube video of all time. Most striking of all has been Lady Gaga's dress and overall appearance, which have set new standards in eccentricity, innovation, and impact. Individual outfits—her plastic bubble dress, meat dress, and "decapitated-corpse dress"—together with weird hairdos, extravagant hats, and extreme footwear (she met President Obama in 16-inch heels)—are as well known as her hit songs. The range of visual images she projects is so varied that her every appearance creates a buzz of anticipation as to her latest incarnation.

terms of both strengths and weaknesses. Finally, they implement their career strategies with commitment, consistency, and determination. As the late Peter Drucker observed: "we must learn how to be the CEO of our own careers."[1]

There is a downside, however. Focusing on a single goal may lead to outstanding success but may be matched by dismal failure in other areas of life. Many people who have reached the pinnacles of their careers have led lives scarred by poor relationships with friends and families and stunted personal development. These include Howard Hughes and Jean Paul Getty in business, Richard Nixon and Joseph Stalin in politics, Elvis Presley and Marilyn Monroe in entertainment, Mike Tyson and O. J. Simpson in sport, and Bobby Fischer in chess. Fulfillment in our personal lives is likely to require broad-based lifetime strategies.[2]

More than any other star, Lady Gaga has developed a business model that recognizes the realities of the post-digital world of entertainment. Like Web 2.0 pioneers such as Facebook and Twitter, Gaga has followed the model: first build market presence, and then think about monetizing that presence. Her record releases are accompanied, sometimes preceded, by music videos on YouTube. With 45 million Facebook fans, 15.8 million Twitter followers, and 1.9 billion YouTube views (as of November 16, 2011), Famecount crowned her "most popular living musician online." Her networking with fans includes Gagaville, an interactive game developed by Zynga, and The Backplane, a music-based social network.

Her emphasis on visual imagery reflects the ways in which her fame is converted into revenues. While record royalties are important, concerts are her primary revenue source. Her 2012 Born This Way Ball Tour promises to make her one of the world's highest-earning entertainers. Other revenue sources—product placement in videos and concerts, merchandizing deals, and her appointment as Polaroid's creative director—also link closely with her visual presence.

A distinctive feature of Gaga's market development is the emphasis she gives to building relations with her fans. The devotion of her fans—her "Little Monsters"—is based less on their desire to emulate her look as upon empathy with her values and attitudes. They recognize Gaga's images more as social statements of non-conformity than as fashion statements. In communicating her experiences of alienation and bullying at school and her values of individuality, sexual freedom, and acceptance of differences—reinforced through her involvement in charities and gay rights events—she has built a global fan base that is unusual in its loyalty and commitment. The sense of community is reinforced by tools such as the "Monster Claw" greeting and the "Manifesto of Little Monsters." As "Mother Monster," Gaga is spokesperson and guru for this community.[c]

Lady Gaga possesses talents as a singer, musician, and songwriter; however, her most outstanding abilities lie in her showmanship and theatricality. Modeled on Andy Warhol's "Factory," The Haus of Gaga is her creative workshop and augments her own capabilities. It includes manager Troy Carter, choreographer and creative director Laurieann Gibson, fashion director Nicola Formichetti, hair stylist Frederic Aspiras, stylist and designer Anna Trevelyan, fashion photographer Nick Night, makeup artist Tara Savelo, marketing director Bobby Campbell, and others involved in designing and producing songs, videos, concert sets, photo shoots, and the whole range of Gaga's public appearances.

**Notes:**
[a]http://en.wikipedia.org/wiki/List_of_best-selling_music_artists, accessed 14 Nov. 2011.
[b]Quoted in http://en.wikipedia.org/wiki/Lady_Gaga, accessed 14 November, 2011.
[c]I have drawn extensively upon Mauro Sala's BSc thesis, *The Strategy of Lady Gaga*, Bocconi University, Milan, June 2011.

**FIGURE 1.1** Common elements in successful strategies

These same ingredients of successful strategies—clear goals, understanding the competitive environment, resource appraisal, and effective implementation—form the key components of our analysis of business strategy.

## The Basic Framework for Strategy Analysis

Figure 1.2 shows the basic framework for strategy analysis that we shall use throughout the book. The four elements of a successful strategy shown in Figure 1.1 are recast into two groups—the firm and the industry environment—with strategy forming a link between the two. The firm embodies three of these elements: goals and values ("simple, consistent, long-term goals"), resources and capabilities ("objective appraisal of resources"), and structure and systems ("effective implementation"). The industry environment embodies the fourth ("profound understanding of the competitive environment") and is defined by the firm's relationships with competitors, customers, and suppliers.

This view of strategy as a link between the firm and its industry environment has close similarities with the widely used **SWOT framework**. However, as I explain in Strategy Capsule 1.3, a two-way classification of internal and external forces is superior to the four-way SWOT framework.

The task of business strategy, then, is to determine how the firm will deploy its resources within its environment and so satisfy its long-term goals, and how it will organize itself to implement that strategy.

### Strategic Fit

Fundamental to this view of strategy as a link between the firm and its external environment is the notion of **strategic fit**. This refers to the consistency of a firm's strategy, first, with the firm's external environment and, second, with its internal environment, especially with its goals and values and resources and capabilities. A major reason for the decline and failure of some companies comes from their having a strategy that lacks consistency with either the internal or the external environment. The decline of Nokia (which lost over 90% of its stock market value in the four years up to July 2012) may be attributed to a strategy which failed to take account of a major change in its external environment: the growing consumer demand for smartphones. Other companies struggle to align their strategies to their internal resources and capabilities. A critical issue for Nintendo will be whether it possesses

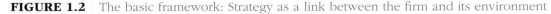

**FIGURE 1.2**  The basic framework: Strategy as a link between the firm and its environment

## STRATEGY CAPSULE 1.3
# What's Wrong with SWOT?

Distinguishing between the external and the internal environment of the firm is common to most approaches to strategy analysis. The best-known and most widely used of these approaches is the "SWOT" framework, which classifies the various influences on a firm's strategy into four categories: Strengths, Weaknesses, Opportunities, and Threats. The first two—strengths and weaknesses—relate to the internal environment; the last two—opportunities and threats—relate to the external environment.

Which is better, a two-way distinction between internal and external influences or the four-way SWOT taxonomy? The key issue is whether it is sensible and worthwhile to classify internal factors into strengths and weaknesses and external factors into opportunities and threats. In practice, such distinctions are difficult.

Is Alex Ferguson a strength or a weakness for Manchester United Football Club? As the world's most experienced and successful soccer coach, he is a strength. As a 70-year-old man who has no obvious successor, he is a weakness.

Is global warming a threat or an opportunity for the world's automobile producers? By encouraging higher taxes on motor fuels and restrictions on car use, it is a threat. By encouraging consumers to switch to fuel-efficient and electric cars, it offers an opportunity for new sales.

The lesson here is that classifying external factors into opportunities and threats, and internal factors into strengths and weaknesses, is arbitrary. What is important is to carefully identify the external and internal forces that impact the firm, and then analyze their implications.

In this book I will follow a simple two-way classification of internal and external factors and avoid any superficial categorization into strengths or weaknesses, and opportunities or threats.

---

the financial and technological resources to continue to compete head-to-head with Sony and Microsoft in the market for video game consoles.

The concept of strategic fit also relates to the internal consistency among the different elements of a firm's strategy. Effective strategies are ones where functional strategies and individual decisions are aligned with one another to create a consistent strategic position and direction of development. This notion of internal fit is central to Michael Porter's conceptualization of the firm as an **activity system**. Porter states that "Strategy is the creation of a unique and differentiated position involving a different set of activities."[3] The key is how these activities fit together to form a consistent, mutually reinforcing system. Ryanair's strategic position is as Europe's lowest-cost airline providing no-frills flights to budget-conscious travelers. This is achieved by a set of activities which fit together to support that positioning (Figure 1.3).

The concept of strategic fit is one component of a set of ideas known as **contingency theory**. Contingency theory postulates that there is no single best way of organizing or managing. The best way to design, manage, and lead an organization depends upon circumstances—in particular the characteristics of that organization's environment.[4]

**FIGURE 1.3** Ryanair's activity system

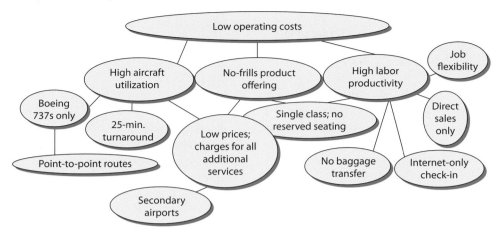

## A Brief History of Business Strategy

### Origins and Military Antecedents

Enterprises need business strategies for much the same reason that armies need military strategies—to give direction and purpose, to deploy resources in the most effective manner, and to coordinate the decisions made by different individuals. Many of the concepts and theories of business strategy have their antecedents in military strategy. The term *strategy* derives from the Greek word *strategia*, meaning "generalship." However, the concept of strategy did not originate with the Greeks: Sun Tzu's classic, *The Art of War*, from about 500 BC is regarded as the first treatise on strategy.[5]

Military strategy and business strategy share a number of common concepts and principles, the most basic being the distinction between strategy and tactics. Strategy is the overall plan for deploying resources to establish a favorable position; a tactic is a scheme for a specific action. Whereas tactics are concerned with the maneuvers necessary to win battles, strategy is concerned with winning the war. Strategic decisions, whether in military or business spheres, share three common characteristics:

- they are important
- they involve a significant commitment of resources
- they are not easily reversible.

Many of the principles of military strategy have been applied to business situations. These include the relative strengths of offensive and defensive strategies; the merits of outflanking over frontal assault; the roles of graduated responses to aggressive initiatives; the benefits of surprise; and the potential for deception, envelopment, escalation, and attrition.[6] At the same time, there are major differences between business competition and military conflict. The objective of war is (usually) to defeat the enemy. The purpose of business rivalry is seldom so aggressive: most business enterprises limit their competitive ambitions, seeking coexistence rather than the destruction of competitors.

The tendency for the principles of military and business strategy to develop along separate paths indicates the absence of a general theory of strategy. The publication of Von Neumann and Morgenstern's *Theory of Games* in 1944 gave rise to the hope that a general theory of competitive behavior would emerge. During the subsequent six decades, **game theory** has revolutionized the study of competitive interaction, not just in business but in politics, military conflict, and international relations as well. Yet, as we shall see in Chapter 4, game theory has achieved only limited success as a practical and broadly applicable general theory of strategy.[7]

## From Corporate Planning to Strategic Management

The evolution of business strategy has been driven more by the practical needs of business than by the development of theory. During the 1950s and 1960s, senior executives experienced increasing difficulty in coordinating decisions and maintaining control in companies that were growing in size and complexity. While new techniques of discounted cash flow analysis allowed more rational choices over individual investment projects, firms lacked systematic approaches to their long-term development. **Corporate planning** (also known as *long-term planning*) was developed during the late 1950s to serve this purpose. Macroeconomic forecasts provided the foundation for the new corporate planning. The typical format was a five-year corporate planning document that set goals and objectives, forecasted key economic trends (including market demand, the company's market share, revenue, costs, and margins), established priorities for different products and business areas of the firm, and allocated capital expenditures. The diffusion of corporate planning was accelerated by a flood of articles and books addressing this new science.[8] The new techniques of corporate planning proved particularly useful for guiding the diversification strategies that many large companies pursued during the 1960s.[9] By the mid-1960s, most large US and European companies had set up corporate planning departments. Strategy Capsule 1.4 provides an example of this formalized corporate planning.

During the 1970s and early 1980s, confidence in corporate planning was severely shaken. Not only did diversification fail to deliver the anticipated synergies but the oil shocks of 1974 and 1979 ushered in a new era of macroeconomic instability, while increased international competition intensified as Japanese, Korean, and Southeast Asian firms stepped onto the world stage. The new turbulence meant that firms could no longer plan their investments and resource requirements three to five years ahead—they couldn't forecast that far ahead.

The result was a shift in emphasis from planning to strategy making, where the focus was less on the detailed management of a company's growth path as on market selection and positioning the company relative to its competitors in order to maximize the potential for profit. This transition from corporate planning to what became called *strategic management* involved a focus on competition as the central characteristic of the business environment, and on performance maximization as the primary goal of strategy.

This emphasis on strategy as a quest for performance directed attention to the sources of profitability. During the late 1970s and into the 1980s, attention focused on sources of profit within the industry environment. Michael Porter of Harvard Business School pioneered the application of industrial organization economics to

**STRATEGY CAPSULE 1.4**
## Corporate Planning in a Large US Steel Company, 1965

The first step in developing long-range plans was to forecast the product demand for future years. After calculating the tonnage needed in each sales district to provide the "target" fraction of the total forecast demand, the optimal production level for each area was determined. A computer program that incorporated the projected demand, existing production capacity, freight costs, etc. was used for this purpose.

When the optimum production rate in each area was found, the additional facilities needed to produce the desired tonnage were specified. Then the capital costs for the necessary equipment, buildings, and layout were estimated by the chief engineer of the corporation and various district engineers. Alternative plans for achieving company goals were also developed for some areas, and investment proposals were formulated after considering the amount of available capital and the company debt policy. The vice president who was responsible for long-range planning recommended certain plans to the president and, after the top executives and the board of directors reviewed alternative plans, they made the necessary decisions about future activities.

*Source:* H. W. Henry, *Long Range Planning Processes in 45 Industrial Companies* (Englewood Cliffs, NJ: Prentice-Hall, 1967): 65.

analyzing the profit potential of different industries and markets.[10] Other studies examined the impact of market share and experience in determining how profits were distributed between the different firms in an industry.[11]

During the 1990s, the focus of strategy analysis shifted from the sources of profit in the external environment to the sources of profit within the firm. Increasingly the resources and capabilities of the firm became regarded as the main source of competitive advantage and the primary basis for formulating strategy.[12] This emphasis on what has been called the **resource-based view of the firm** represented a substantial shift in thinking about strategy. Rather than firms pursuing similar strategies, as in seeking attractive markets and favorable competitive positions, emphasis on internal resources and capabilities has encouraged firms to identify how they are *different* from their competitors and design strategies that exploit these differences.

During the 21st century, new challenges have continued to shape the principles and practice of strategy. Digital technologies have had a massive impact on the competitive dynamics of many industries, creating winner-take-all markets and standards wars.[13] Disruptive technologies[14] and accelerating rates of change have meant that strategy has become less and less about plans and more about creating options of the future,[15] fostering strategic innovation,[16] and seeking the "blue oceans" of uncontested market space.[17] The complexity of these challenges have meant that being self-sufficient is no longer viable for most firms—they increasingly depend upon other firms through outsourcing and strategic alliances.

The 2008–2009 financial crisis has had a major impact on firm strategy, encouraging new thinking about the purpose of business. Disillusion with the excesses and unfairness of market capitalism has renewed interest in corporate social responsibility, ethics, sustainability, and the role of legitimacy in long-term corporate success.[18]

**FIGURE 1.4**  Evolution of strategic management

Figure 1.4 summarizes the main developments in strategic management since the mid-20th century.

## Strategy Today

### What Is Strategy?

In its broadest sense, strategy is the means by which individuals or organizations achieve their objectives. Table 1.1 presents a number of definitions of the term strategy. Common to most definitions is the notion that strategy is focused on achieving certain goals; that it involves allocating resources; and that it implies some consistency, integration, or cohesiveness of decisions and actions.

Yet, as we have seen, the conception of firm strategy has changed greatly over the past half-century. As the business environment has become more unstable and unpredictable, so strategy has become less concerned with detailed plans and more about guidelines for success. This is consistent with the examples that began this chapter. Neither Queen Elizabeth nor Lady Gaga appears to have had any detailed strategic plan, but both possessed clear ideas of what they wanted to achieve and how they would achieve it. This shift in emphasis from strategy as plan to strategy as direction does not imply any downgrading of the role of strategy. The more

**TABLE 1.1**  Some definitions of strategy

- Strategy: a plan, method, or series of actions designed to achieve a specific goal or effect.
  —*Wordsmyth Dictionary* (http://www.wordsmyth.net)

- The determination of the long-run goals and objectives of an enterprise, and the adoption of courses of action and the allocation of resources necessary for carrying out these goals.
  —Alfred Chandler, *Strategy and Structure*
  (Cambridge, MA: MIT Press, 1962)

- Strategy is the pattern of objectives, purposes, or goals and the major policies and plans for achieving these goals, stated in such a way as to define what business the company is in or is to be in and the kind of company it is or is to be.
  —Kenneth Andrews, *The Concept of Corporate Strategy*
  (Homewood, IL: Irwin, 1971)

- Lost Boy:          "Injuns! Let's go get 'em!"
  John Darling:     "Hold on a minute. First we must have a strategy."
  Lost Boy:          "Uhh? What's a strategy?"
  John Darling:     "It's, er . . . it's a plan of attack."
  —Walt Disney's *Peter Pan*

turbulent the environment, the more must strategy embrace flexibility and responsiveness. But it is precisely in these conditions that strategy becomes more, rather than less, important. When the firm is buffeted by unforeseen threats and where new opportunities are constantly appearing, then strategy becomes the compass that can navigate the firm through stormy seas.

## Why Do Firms Need Strategy?

This transition from strategy as plan to strategy as direction raises the question of why firms (or any type of organization) need strategy. Strategy assists the effective management of organizations, first, by enhancing the quality of decision making, second, by facilitating coordination, and, third, by focusing organizations on the pursuit of long-term goals.

*Strategy as Decision Support*    Strategy is a pattern or theme that gives coherence to the decisions of an individual or organization. But why can't individuals or organizations make optimal decisions in the absence of such a unifying theme? Consider the 1997 "man versus machine" chess epic in which Garry Kasparov was defeated by IBM's "Deep Blue" computer. Deep Blue did not need strategy. Its phenomenal memory and computing power allowed it to identify its optimal moves based on a huge decision tree.[19] Kasparov—although the world's greatest chess player—was subject to *bounded rationality*: his decision analysis was subject to the cognitive limitations that constrain all human beings.[20] For him, a strategy offered guidance that assisted positioning and helped create opportunities. Strategy improves decision making in several ways:

- It simplifies decision making by constraining the range of decision alternatives considered and acts as a *heuristic*—a rule of thumb that reduces the search required to find an acceptable solution to a decision problem.

- The strategy-making process permits the knowledge of different individuals to be pooled and integrated.
- It facilitates the use of analytic tools—the frameworks and techniques that we will encounter in the ensuing chapters of this book.

*Strategy as a Coordinating Device*   The central challenge of management is coordinating the actions of different organizational members. Strategy acts as a communication device to promote coordination Statements of strategy are a means by which the CEO can communicate the identity, goals, and positioning of the company to all organizational members. The strategic planning process acts as a forum in which views are exchanged and consensus developed; once formulated, strategy can be translated into goals, commitments, and performance targets that ensure that the organization moves forward in a consistent direction.

*Strategy as Target*   Strategy is forward looking. It is concerned not only with how the firm will compete now but also with what the firm will become in the future. A key purpose of a forward-looking strategy is not only to establish a direction for the firm's development but also to set aspirations that can motivate and inspire members of the organization. Gary Hamel and C. K. Prahalad use the term **strategic intent** to describe this desired strategic position: "strategic intent creates an extreme misfit between resources and ambitions. Top management then challenges the organization to close the gap by building new competitive advantages."[21] The implication is that strategy should be less about fit and resource allocation and more about stretch and resource leverage.[22] Jim Collins and Jerry Porras make a similar point: US companies that have been sector leaders for 50 years or more—Merck, Walt Disney, 3M, IBM, and Ford—have all generated commitment and drive through setting "Big, Hairy, Ambitious Goals."[23] Striving, inspirational goals are found in most organizations' statements of vision and mission. One of the best known is that set by President Kennedy for NASA's space program: "before this decade is out, to land a man on the moon and return him safely to Earth."

## Where Do We Find Strategy?

A company's strategy can be found in three places: in the heads of managers, in their articulations of strategy in speeches and written documents, and in the decisions through which strategy is enacted. Only the last two are observable.

Strategy has its origins in the thought processes of entrepreneurs and senior managers. For the entrepreneur the starting point of strategy is the idea for a new business. In most small companies, strategy remains in the heads of business proprietors: there is little need for any explicit statement of strategy. For large companies statements of strategy are found in board minutes and strategic planning documents, which are invariably confidential. However, most companies—public companies in particular—see value in communicating their strategy to employees, customers, investors, and business partners. Collis and Rukstad identify four types of statement through which companies communicate their strategies:

- The mission statement describes organizational purpose; it addresses "Why we exist."

- A statement of principles or values states "What we believe in and how we will behave."
- The vision statement projects "What we want to be."
- The strategy statement articulates the company's competitive game plan, which typically comprises statements of objectives, business scope, and advantage.[24]

These statements are typically found on the corporate pages of companies' websites. More detailed statements of strategy—including qualitative and quantitative medium-term targets—are often found in top management presentations to analysts, which are typically included in the "for investors" pages of company websites.

Detailed information on business scope (the products with which and the markets where the firm competes) and advantage (how it competes) can be found in a company's annual reports. For US corporations, the description of the business that forms Item 1 of the 10-K annual report to the Securities and Exchange Commission (SEC) is particularly informative about strategy.

Strategy Capsule 1.5 provides statements of strategy by McDonald's, the global fast-food giant, and Nokia, the world's largest supplier of wireless handsets.

Ultimately, strategy becomes enacted in the decisions and actions of an organization's members. Indeed, checking strategy statements against the actual decisions and behaviors is essential to close the gap between rhetoric and reality. As a reality check upon grandiose and platitudinous sentiments of vision and mission, it is useful to ask:

- Where is the company investing its money? Notes to financial statements provide detailed breakdowns of capital expenditure by region and by business segment.
- What technologies is the company developing? Identifying the patents that a company has filed (using the online databases of the US and EU patent offices) indicates the technological trajectory it is pursuing.
- What new products have been released, major investment projects initiated, and top management hired? These strategic decisions are typically announced in press releases.

To identify a firm's strategy it is necessary to draw upon multiple sources of information in order to build an overall picture of what the company says it is doing and what it is actually doing. We will return to this topic when we discuss *competitive intelligence* in Chapter 4.

## Corporate and Business Strategy

Strategic choices can be distilled into two basic questions:

- Where to compete?
- How to compete?

The answers to these questions define the two major areas of a firm's strategy: **corporate strategy** and **business strategy**.

## STRATEGY CAPSULE 1.5

# Statements of Company Strategy: McDonald's and Nokia

## MCDONALD'S CORPORATION PLAN TO WIN

Our entire System is unified by McDonald's Plan to Win—a clear set of actions involving the Company, our franchisees and our suppliers. This Plan is aimed at making McDonald's our customers' favorite place and way to eat by implementing the key drivers of an exceptional customer experience—people, products, price, place and promotion.

It's about having well-trained, friendly *people* working in our restaurants and the right *products* at a range of affordable prices. It's also about showcasing our restaurants as *places* that are clean, contemporary and welcoming, as well as creating promotions and marketing activities that resonate with key customer groups.

McDonald's Plan to Win is designed to support our strategy of growing sales at existing restaurants, rather than growing simply by opening more restaurants. Implementation of the Plan enables us to align our human and financial resources with our strategy for growth, and eliminate activities that are not focused on our customers or our restaurants.

*Source:* McDonald's Corporation *Summary Annual Report*, 2003, p. 5

## NOKIA: OUR VISION AND STRATEGY

*Nokia's mission is simple*: Connecting People. Our goal is to build great mobile products that enable billions of people worldwide to enjoy more of what life has to offer. Our challenge is to achieve this in an increasingly dynamic and competitive environment . . .

*Regaining leadership in the smartphone space.* To help us achieve our mission, Nokia has formed a strategic partnership with Microsoft that will, we hope, see us regain lost ground in the smartphone market. Together, we intend to build a global ecosystem that surpasses anything currently in existence. The Nokia–Microsoft ecosystem will deliver differentiated and innovative products with unrivalled scale in terms of product breadth, geographical reach and brand identity.

*Connecting the next billion.* In feature phones, Nokia's strategy is to leverage its innovation and strength in growth markets to connect even more people to their first internet and application experience. By providing compelling, affordable and localized mobile experiences, particularly to emerging markets, our ambition is to bring the next billion online . . .

*Source:* Reproduced from http://www.nokia.com/global/about-nokia/about-us/about-us/ with permission from Nokia

Corporate strategy defines the scope of the firm in terms of the industries and markets in which it competes. Corporate strategy decisions include choice over diversification, vertical integration, acquisitions, and new ventures, and the allocation of resources between the different businesses of the firm.

Business strategy is concerned with how the firm competes within a particular industry or market. If the firm is to prosper within an industry, it must establish a

**FIGURE 1.5** The sources of superior profitability

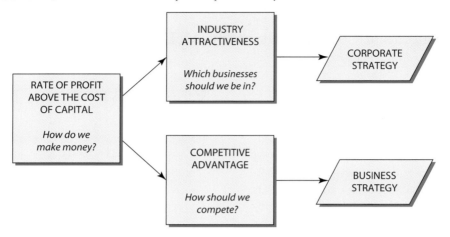

competitive advantage over its rivals. Hence, this area of strategy is also referred to as *competitive strategy*.

The distinction between corporate strategy and business strategy corresponds to the organizational structure of most large companies. Corporate strategy is the responsibility of the top management team and the corporate strategy staff. Business strategy is primarily the responsibility of divisional management.

This distinction between corporate and business strategy also corresponds to the primary sources of superior profit for a firm. As we have noted, the purpose of strategy is to achieve superior performance. Basic to this is the need to survive and prosper, which in turn requires that over the long term the firm earn a rate of return on its capital that exceeds its cost of capital. There are two possible ways of achieving this. First, by choosing to locate within industries where overall rates of return are attractive (corporate strategy). Second, by attaining a position of advantage vis-à-vis competitors within an industry, allowing it to earn a return that exceeds the industry average (Figure 1.5).

This distinction may be expressed in even simpler terms. The basic question facing the firm is "How do we make money?" The answer to this question corresponds to the two basic strategic choices we identified above: "Where to compete?" ("In which industries and markets should we be?") and "How should we compete?"

As an integrated approach to firm strategy, this book deals with both business and corporate strategy. However, my primary emphasis will be on business strategy. This is because the critical requirement for a company's success is its ability to establish competitive advantage. Hence, issues of business strategy precede those of corporate strategy. At the same time, these two dimensions of strategy are intertwined: the scope of a firm's business has implications for the sources of competitive advantage, and the nature of a firm's competitive advantage determines the range of businesses it can be successful in.

## Describing Strategy

These same two questions—"Where is the firm competing?" and "How is it competing?"—also provide the basis upon which we can describe the strategy that a firm is pursuing. The *where* question has multiple dimensions. It relates to the products the firm supplies, the customers it serves, the countries and localities where it operates, and the vertical range of activities it undertakes.

Thus, Coca-Cola's strategy can be described in terms of these *where* and *how* choices. With regard to *where*:

- Coca-Cola competes in the soft drinks industry, where it supplies concentrate for its branded soda drinks (such as Coca-Cola, Sprite, Fanta, Tab, and Fresca) and supplies non-carbonated drinks (such as Minute Maid, Hi-C and Five Alive fruit juices, and Dasani bottled water).
- Geographically, Coca-Cola competes worldwide; its "big five" markets are the US, Mexico, Brazil, Japan, and China.
- In terms of vertical scope, Coca-Cola's main activities are product development, brand management, and the manufacture and distribution of concentrate. The production and distribution of its soft drinks are undertaken by its sister company, Coca-Cola Enterprises, and franchised local bottlers.

With regard to *how*, Coca-Cola pursues a differentiation strategy where it relies on brand image developed through heavy advertising and promotion. It seeks market share leadership through its mass marketing and through close relationships with the leading bottlers in every country where it does business.

However, strategy is not simply about "competing for today"; it is also concerned with "competing for tomorrow." This dynamic concept of strategy involves establishing objectives for the future and determining how they will be achieved. Future objectives relate to the overall purpose of the firm (mission), what it seeks to become (vision), and how it will meet specific performance targets.

In the case of Coca-Cola, this dynamic dimension of its strategy is outlined in terms of vision ("to refresh the world, to inspire moments of optimism and happiness, and to create value and make a difference"), mission (goals in relation to its six Ps: people, portfolio, planet, partners, profit, and productivity), and specific objectives (such as increasing system revenue to $200 billion by 2020 and doubling volume in terms of servings).[25]

These two dimensions of strategy—the static and the dynamic—are depicted in Figure 1.6. As we shall see in Chapter 8, reconciling these two dimensions of strategy—what Derek Abell calls "competing with dual strategies"—is one of the central dilemmas of strategic management.[26]

## How Is Strategy Made? The Strategy Process

How companies make strategy and how they should make strategy are among the most hotly debated issues in strategic management. The corporate planning undertaken by large companies during the 1960s was a highly formalized approach to strategy making. Strategy may also emerge through adaptation to circumstances. In our opening discussion of Queen Elizabeth and Lady Gaga, I discerned a consistency and pattern to their career decisions that I identified as strategy, even though there is no evidence that either of them engaged in any systematic strategy making. Similarly, most successful companies are not products of grand designs. In August

**FIGURE 1.6**   Describing firm strategy: Competing in the present, preparing for the future

**Strategy as Positioning**
- *Where are we competing?*
  - -Product market scope
  - -Geographical scope
  - -Vertical scope
- *How are we competing?*
  - -What is the basis of our competitive advantage?

*COMPETING FOR THE PRESENT*

**Strategy as Direction**
- *What do we want to become?*
  - -Vision statement
- *What do we want to achieve?*
  - -Mission statement
  - -Performance goals
- *How will we get there?*
  - -Guidelines for development
  - -Priorities for capital expenditure, R & D
  - -Growth modes: organic growth, M & A, alliances

*PREPARING FOR THE FUTURE*

2011, Apple surpassed Exxon Mobil to become the world's most valuable company. Apple's success was based upon a strategy of creating consumer electronic products that integrated hardware, software, and design aesthetics to create a user experience characterized by accessibility and intuitive functionality. Apple began with Steve Jobs' recognition of the revolutionary potential of personal computing and the vision of creating a personal computer that would be cheap and easy to use. However, the strategy that would eventually make Apple one of the most successful companies of all time was a product of insight, intuition, experimentation, and events.

So, what does this mean for strategy making by companies and other types of organizations? Should managers seek to formulate strategy through a rational systematic process, or is the best approach in a turbulent world to respond to events while maintaining some sense of direction in the form of goals and guidelines?

## Design versus Emergence

Henry Mintzberg is a leading critic of rational approaches to strategy design. He distinguishes intended, realized, and emergent strategies. **Intended strategy** is strategy as conceived of by the top management team. Even here, intended strategy is less a product of rational deliberation and more an outcome of negotiation, bargaining, and compromise among the many individuals and groups involved in the strategy-making process. However, **realized strategy**—the actual strategy that is implemented—is only partly related to that which was intended (Mintzberg suggests only 10–30% of intended strategy is realized). The primary determinant of realized strategy is what Mintzberg terms **emergent strategy**—the decisions that emerge from the complex processes in which individual managers interpret the intended strategy and adapt to changing circumstances.[27]

According to Mintzberg, rational design is not only an inaccurate account of how strategies are actually formulated but also a poor way of making strategy: "The notion that strategy is something that should happen way up there, far removed from the details of running an organization on a daily basis, is one of the great fallacies of conventional strategic management."[28] The emergent approaches to strategy making permit adaptation and learning through a continuous interaction between strategy formulation and strategy implementation in which strategy is constantly being adjusted and revised in the light of experience.

The debate between those who view strategy making as a rational, analytical process of deliberate planning (the *design school*) and those who envisage strategy making as an emergent process (the *emergence* or *learning school* of strategy) has centered on the case of Honda's successful entry into the US motorcycle market during the early 1960s.[29] The Boston Consulting Group lauded Honda for its single-minded pursuit of a global strategy based on exploiting economies of scale and learning to establish unassailable cost leadership.[30] However, subsequent interviews with the Honda managers in charge of its US market entry revealed a different story: a haphazard, experimental approach with little analysis and no clear plan.[31] As Mintzberg observes: "Brilliant as its strategy may have looked after the fact, Honda's managers made almost every conceivable mistake until the market finally hit them over the head with the right formula."[32]

In practice, strategy making almost always involves a combination of centrally driven rational design and decentralized adaptation. The design aspect of strategy comprises a number of organizational processes through which strategy is deliberated, discussed, and decided. In larger companies these include board meetings and a formalized process of strategic planning supplemented by more broadly participative events, such as strategy workshops. I will discuss processes of strategic planning more fully in Chapter 6.

At the same time, strategy is being continually enacted through decisions that are made by every member of the organization—by middle management especially. The decentralized, bottom-up process of strategy emergence often precedes more formalized top-down strategy formulation. Intel's historic decision to abandon memory chips and concentrate on microprocessors was initiated in the decisions taken by business unit and plant managers that were subsequently promulgated by top management as strategy.[33]

In all the companies I am familiar with, strategy making combines design and emergence—a process that I have referred to as "planned emergence."[34] The balance between the two depends greatly upon the stability and predictability of the organization's business environment. The Roman Catholic Church and La Poste, the French postal service, inhabit relatively stable environments; they can plan activities and resource allocations in some detail quite far into the future. For WikiLeaks, Zimbabwe Banking Corporation, or Somali pirate gangs, strategic planning will inevitably be restricted to a few guidelines; most strategic decisions must be responses to unfolding circumstances.

As the business environment becomes more turbulent and less predictable, so strategy making becomes less about detailed decisions and more about guidelines and general direction. Bain & Company advocates the use of strategic principles— "pithy, memorable distillations of strategy that guide and empower employees"—to combine consistent focus with adaptability and responsiveness.[35] McDonald's strategy statement in Strategy Capsule 1.5 is an example of such strategic principles. Similarly, Southwest Airlines encapsulates its strategy in a simple statement: "Meet customers' short-haul travel needs at fares competitive with the cost of automobile travel." Kathy Eisenhardt and Don Sull make a similar argument when they advocate "simple rules" as the basis for successful strategies in fast-moving businesses. For example, Lego evaluates new product proposals by applying a checklist of rules: "Does the product have the Lego look?" "Will children learn while having fun?" "Does it stimulate creativity?"[36]

We shall return to the role of rules and principles to guide an organization's evolution and coordinate the decisions of its many members in our final chapter, where we explore some of the implications of complexity theory for strategic management.

## The Role of Analysis in Strategy Formulation

Despite the criticism of rational, analytical approaches to strategy formulation by Henry Mintzberg and others, the approach of this book is to emphasize analytic approaches to strategy formulation. This is not because I wish to downplay the role of intuition, creativity, or spontaneity—these qualities are essential ingredients of successful strategies. Nevertheless, whether strategy formulation is formal or informal, whether strategies are deliberate or emergent, systematic analysis is a vital input into the strategy process. Without analysis, strategic decisions are susceptible to power battles, individual whims, fads, and wishful thinking. Concepts, theories, and analytic tools are complements of, and not substitutes for, intuition and creativity. Their role is to provide frameworks for organizing discussion, processing information, and developing consensus.

This is not to endorse current approaches to strategy analysis. Strategic management is still a young field and the existing toolbox of concepts and techniques remains woefully inadequate. Our challenge is to do better. If existing analytical techniques do not adequately address the problems of strategy making and strategy implementation under conditions of uncertainty, technological change, and complexity, we need to augment and extend our analytical toolkit. In the course of this book, you will encounter concepts such as *real options, tacit knowledge, hypercompetition, complementarity,* and *complexity* that will help you address more effectively the challenges that firms are facing in today's turbulent business environment. We must also recognize the nature of *strategy analysis.* Unlike many of the analytical techniques in accounting, finance, market research, or production management, strategy analysis does not generate solutions to problems. It does not offer algorithms or formulae that tell us the optimal strategy to adopt. The strategic questions that companies face (like those that we face in our own careers and lives) are simply too complex to be programmed.

The purpose of strategy analysis is not to provide answers but to help us understand the issues. Most of the analytic techniques introduced in this book are frameworks that allow us to identify, classify, and understand the principal factors relevant to strategic decisions. Such frameworks are invaluable in allowing us to come to terms with the complexities of strategy decisions. In some instances, the most useful contribution may be in assisting us to make a start on the problem. By guiding us to the questions we need to answer and by providing a framework for organizing the information gathered, strategy analysis places us in a superior position to a manager who relies exclusively on experience and intuition. Finally, analytic frameworks and techniques can improve our flexibility as managers. The analysis in this book is general in its applicability; it is not specific to particular industries, companies, or situations. Hence, it can help increase our confidence and effectiveness in understanding and responding to new situations and new circumstances. By encouraging an in-depth understanding of fundamental issues concerning competitive advantage, customer needs, organizational capabilities, and the basis of competition, the concepts, frameworks, and techniques in this book will encourage rather than constrain innovation and flexibility.

## Strategic Management of Not-For-Profit Organizations

When strategic management meant top-down, long-range planning, there was little distinction between business corporations and not-for-profit organizations: the techniques of forecast-based planning applied equally to both. As strategic management has become increasingly oriented toward the identification and exploitation of sources of profit, it has become more closely identified with for-profit organizations. So, can the concepts and tools of corporate and business strategy be applied to not-for-profit organizations?

The short answer is yes. Strategy is as important in not-for-profit organizations as it is in business firms. The benefits I have attributed to strategic management in terms of improved decision making, achieving coordination, and setting performance targets (see the section "Why Do Firms Need Strategy?" above) may be even more important in the non-profit sector. Moreover, many of the same concepts and tools of strategic analysis are readily applicable to not-for-profits—albeit with some adaptation. However, the not-for-profit sector encompasses a vast range of organizations. Both the nature of strategic planning and the appropriate tools for strategy analysis differ among these organizations.

The basic distinction here is between those not-for-profits that operate in competitive environments (most non-governmental, non-profit organizations) and those that do not (most government departments and government agencies). Among the not-for-profits that inhabit competitive environments we may distinguish between those that charge for the services they provide (most private schools, non-profit-making private hospitals, social and sports clubs, etc.) and those that provide their services free—most charities and NGOs (non-governmental organizations). Table 1.2 summarizes some key differences between each of these organizations with regard to the applicability of the basic tools of strategy analysis.

Among the tools of strategy analysis that are applicable to all types of not-for-profit organizations, those which relate to the role of strategy in specifying organizational goals and linking goals to resource-allocation decisions are especially important. For businesses, profit is always a key goal since it ensures survival and fuels development. But for not-for-profits, goals are typically complex. The mission of Harvard University is to "create knowledge, to open the minds of students to that knowledge, and to enable students to take best advantage of their educational opportunities." But how are these multiple objectives to be reconciled in practice? How should Harvard's budget be allocated between research and financial aid for students? Is Harvard's mission better served by investing in graduate or undergraduate education? The strategic planning process of not-for-profits needs to be designed so that mission, goals, resource allocation, and performance targets are closely aligned. Strategy Capsule 1.6 shows the strategic planning framework for the US State Department.

Similarly, most of the principles and tools of strategy implementation—especially in relation to organizational structure, management systems, techniques of performance management, and choice of leadership styles—are common to both for-profit and not-for-profit organizations.

In terms of the analysis of the external environment, there is little difference between the techniques of industry analysis applied to business enterprises and those relevant to not-for-profits that inhabit competitive environments and charge for their services. In many markets (theaters, sports clubs, vocational training) for-profits

**TABLE 1.2** The applicability of the concepts and tools of strategic analysis to different types of not-for-profit organization

| | Organizations in competitive environments that charge users | Organizations in competitive environments that provide free services | Organizations sheltered from competition |
|---|---|---|---|
| *Examples* | Royal Opera House Guggenheim Museum Stanford University | Salvation Army Habitat for Humanity Greenpeace Linux | UK Ministry of Defence European Central Bank New York Police Department World Health Organization |
| *Analysis of goals and performance* | Identification of mission, goals, and performance indicators and establishing consistency between them is a critical area of strategy analysis for all not-for-profits | | |
| *Analysis of the competitive environment* | Main tools of competitive analysis are the same as for for-profit firms | Main arena for competition and competitive strategy is the market for funding | Not important. However, there is interagency competition for public funding |
| *Analysis of resources and capabilities* | Identifying and exploiting distinctive resources and capabilities critical to designing strategies that confer competitive advantage | | Analysis of resources and capabilities essential for determining priorities and designing strategies |
| *Strategy implementation* | The basic principles of organizational design, performance management, and leadership are common to all organizational types | | |

---

### STRATEGY CAPSULE 1.6
# US State Department Strategic Plan, 2007–2012

## MISSION

Advance freedom for the benefit of the American people and the international community by helping to build and sustain a more democratic, secure, and prosperous world composed of well-governed states that respond to the needs of their people, reduce widespread poverty, and act responsibly within the international system.

## STRATEGIC GOALS

SG 1: Achieving Peace and Security

SG 2: Governing Justly and Democratically

SG 3: Investing In People

SG 4: Promoting Economic Growth and Prosperity

SG 5: Providing Humanitarian Assistance

SG 6: Promoting International Understanding

SG 7: Strengthening Consular and Management Capabilities

## OPERATIONALIZING THE GOALS

These strategic goals were translated into a set of strategic priorities which were then operationalized through Mission Strategic Plans, Country Operational Plans, Bureau Strategic Plans, and a Department Performance Plan. Each of these plans was subject to an annual review.

*Source:* US Department of State and US Agency for International Development, *Strategic Plan for Fiscal Years 2007–2012.*

and not-for-profits may be in competition with one another. Indeed, for these types of not-for-profit organizations, the pressing need to break even in order to survive may mean that their strategies do not differ significantly from those of for-profit firms.

In the case of not-for-profits that do not charge users for the services they offer (mostly charities), competition does not really exist at the final market level: different homeless shelters in San Francisco cannot really be said to be competing for the homeless. However, these organizations compete for funding—raising donations from individuals, winning grants from foundations, or obtaining contracts from funding agencies. Competing in the market for funding is a key area of strategy for most not-for-profits.

The analysis of resources and capabilities is important to all organizations that inhabit competitive environments and must deploy their internal resources and capabilities to establish a competitive advantage; however, even for those organizations that are monopolists—many government departments and other public agencies—performance is enhanced by aligning strategy with internal strengths in resources and capabilities.

## Summary

This chapter has covered a great deal of ground—I hope that you are not suffering from indigestion. If you are feeling a little overwhelmed, not to worry: we shall be returning to most of the themes and issues raised in this chapter in the subsequent chapters of this book.

The key lessons from this chapter are:

- Strategy is a key ingredient of success both for individuals and organizations. A sound strategy cannot guarantee success, but it can improve the odds. Successful strategies tend to embody four elements: clear, long-term goals; profound understanding of the external environment; astute appraisal of internal resources and capabilities; and effective implementation. These four elements form the primary analytic components of this book.

- Strategy is no longer concerned with detailed planning based upon forecasts; it is increasingly about direction, identity, and exploiting the sources of superior profitability.

- To describe the strategy of a firm (or any other type of organization) we need to recognize where the firm is competing, how it is competing, and the direction in which it is developing.

- Developing a strategy for an organization requires a combination of purpose-led planning (rational design) and a flexible response to changing circumstances (emergence).

- The principles and tools of strategic management have been developed primarily for business enterprises; however, they are also applicable to guiding the development and decision making of not-for-profit organizations, especially those that inhabit competitive environments.

Our next stage is to delve further into the basic strategy framework shown in Figure 1.2. As I have noted, the elements of this framework—goals and values, the industry environment, resources and capabilities, and structure and systems—comprise the basic components of strategy analysis. The next part of the book devotes separate chapters to each. We then deploy these tools in the analysis of competitive advantage (Part III), in the formulation and implementation of business strategies in different industry contexts (Part IV), and then in the development of corporate strategy (Part V). Figure 1.7 shows the framework for the book.

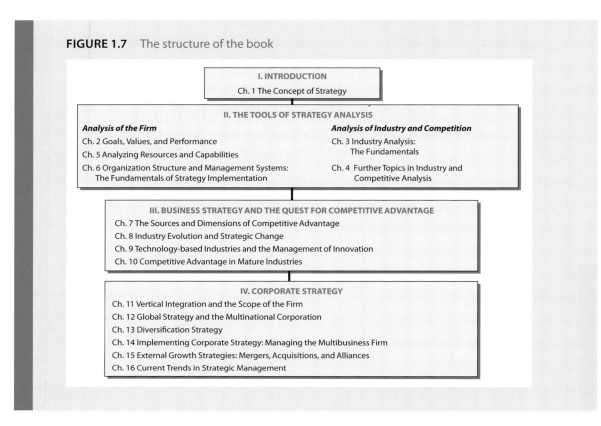

**FIGURE 1.7**   The structure of the book

**I. INTRODUCTION**
Ch. 1 The Concept of Strategy

**II. THE TOOLS OF STRATEGY ANALYSIS**

*Analysis of the Firm*

Ch. 2 Goals, Values, and Performance

Ch. 5 Analyzing Resources and Capabilities

Ch. 6 Organization Structure and Management Systems:
The Fundamentals of Strategy Implementation

*Analysis of Industry and Competition*

Ch. 3 Industry Analysis:
The Fundamentals

Ch. 4 Further Topics in Industry and
Competitive Analysis

**III. BUSINESS STRATEGY AND THE QUEST FOR COMPETITIVE ADVANTAGE**

Ch. 7 The Sources and Dimensions of Competitive Advantage

Ch. 8 Industry Evolution and Strategic Change

Ch. 9 Technology-based Industries and the Management of Innovation

Ch. 10 Competitive Advantage in Mature Industries

**IV. CORPORATE STRATEGY**

Ch. 11 Vertical Integration and the Scope of the Firm

Ch. 12 Global Strategy and the Multinational Corporation

Ch. 13 Diversification Strategy

Ch. 14 Implementing Corporate Strategy: Managing the Multibusiness Firm

Ch. 15 External Growth Strategies: Mergers, Acquisitions, and Alliances

Ch. 16 Current Trends in Strategic Management

Quizzes and flashcards to test yourself further are available in your interactive e-book at
**www.wileyopenpage.com**

## Self-Study Questions

1. In relation to the four characteristics of successful strategies in Figure 1.1, assess the US government's strategy toward Iraq during 2002–12.

2. The discussion of the evolution of business strategy (see the section "From Corporate Planning to Strategic Management") established that the characteristics of a firm's strategic plans and its strategic planning process are strongly influenced by the volatility and unpredictability of its external environment. On this basis, what differences would you expect in the strategic plans and strategic planning processes of Coca-Cola Company and Facebook Inc.?

3. I have noted that a firm's strategy can be described in terms of the answers to two questions: "Where are we competing?" and "How are we competing?" Applying these two questions, provide a concise description of Lady Gaga's career strategy (see Strategy Capsule 1.2).

4. Using the framework of Figure 1.6, describe the strategy of the university or school you attend.

5. What is your career strategy for the next five years? To what extent does your strategy fit with your long-term goals, the characteristics of the external environment, and your own strengths and weaknesses?

# Notes

1. P. F. Drucker, "Managing Oneself," *Harvard Business Review* (March/April 1999): 65–74.
2. Stephen Covey (in *The Seven Habits of Highly Effective People*, New York: Simon & Schuster, 1989) recommends that we develop lifetime mission statements based on the multiple roles that we occupy: in relation to our careers, our partners, our family members, our friends, and our spiritual lives.
3. M. E. Porter, "What is Strategy?" *Harvard Business Review* (November/December 1996): 61–78.
4. Major contributions to contingency theory include F. E. Fiedler's *Leader Attitudes and Group Effectiveness* (Urbana, IL: University of Illinois Press, 1958); and A. H. Van De Ven and R. Drazin's "The concept of fit in contingency theory" (*Research in Organizational Behavior* 7: 333–65, 1985).
5. Sun Tzu, *The Art of Strategy: A New Translation of Sun Tzu's Classic "The Art of War,"* trans. R. L. Wing (New York: Doubleday, 1988).
6. See R. Evered, "So What Is Strategy?" *Long Range Planning* 16, no. 3 (June 1983): 57–72; and E. Clemons and J. Santamaria, "Maneuver Warfare," *Harvard Business Review* (April 2002): 46–53.
7. On the contribution of game theory to business strategy analysis, see F. M. Fisher, "Games Economists Play: A Non-cooperative View," *RAND Journal of Economics* 20 (Spring 1989): 113–24; C. F. Camerer, "Does Strategy Research Need Game Theory?" *Strategic Management Journal* 12 (Winter 1991): 137–52; A. K. Dixit and B. J. Nalebuff, *The Art of Strategy: A Game Theorist's Guide to Success in Business and Life* (New York: W. W. Norton, 2008).
8. For example, D. W. Ewing, "Looking Around: Long-range Business Planning," *Harvard Business Review* (July/August 1956): 135–46; and B. Payne, "Steps in Long-range Planning," *Harvard Business Review* (March/April 1957): 95–101.
9. H. I. Ansoff, "Strategies for diversification," *Harvard Business Review* (September/October, 1957): 113–124.
10. M. E. Porter, *Competitive Strategy* (New York: Free Press, 1980).
11. See Boston Consulting Group, *Perspectives on Experience* (Boston: Boston Consulting Group, 1978) and studies using the PIMS (Profit Impact of Market Strategy) database, for example R. D. Buzzell and B. T. Gale, *The PIMS Principles* (New York: Free Press, 1987).
12. R. M. Grant, "The Resource-based Theory of Competitive Advantage: Implications for Strategy Formulation," *California Management Review* 33 (Spring 1991): 114–135; D. J. Collis and C. Montgomery, "Competing on Resources: Strategy in the 1990s," *Harvard Business Review* (July/August 1995): 119–128.
13. E. Lee, J. Lee, and J. Lee, "Reconsideration of the Winner-Take-All Hypothesis: Complex Networks and Local Bias," *Management Science* 52 (December 2006): 1838–48; C. Shapiro and H. R. Varian, *Information Rules* (Boston: Harvard Business School Press, 1998).
14. C. Christensen, *The Innovator's Dilemma* (Boston: Harvard Business School Press, 1997).
15. P. J. Williamson, "Strategy as options on the future," *Sloan Management Review* 40(3, 1999): 117–126.
16. C. Markides, "Strategic innovation in established companies," *Sloan Management Review* (June 1998): 31–42.
17. W. C. Kim and R. Mauborgne, "Creating new market space," *Harvard Business Review* (January/February 1999): 83–93.
18. Robert Peston, *The New Capitalism* (London: Hodder & Stoughton, 2010).
19. "Strategic Intensity: A Conversation with Garry Kasparov," *Harvard Business Review* (April 2005): 105–13.
20. The concept of bounded rationality was developed by Herbert Simon ("A Behavioral Model of Rational Choice," *Quarterly Journal of Economics* 69 (1955): 99–118.
21. G. Hamel and C. K. Prahalad, "Strategic Intent," *Harvard Business Review* (May/June 1989): 63–77.
22. G. Hamel and C. K. Prahalad, "Strategy as Stretch and Leverage," *Harvard Business Review* (March/April 1993): 75–84.
23. J. C. Collins and J. I. Porras, *Built to Last: Successful Habits of Visionary Companies* (New York: HarperCollins, 1995).
24. D. J. Collis and M. G. Rukstad, "Can You Say What Your Strategy Is?" *Harvard Business Review* (April 2008): 63–73.
25. http://www.thecoca-colacompany.com/ourcompany/mission_vision_values.html, accessed August 2, 2012).
26. D. F. Abell, *Managing with Dual Strategies* (New York: Free Press, 1993).
27. H. Mintzberg, "Patterns of Strategy Formulation," *Management Science* 24 (1978): 934–48; "Of Strategies: Deliberate and Emergent," *Strategic Management Journal* 6 (1985): 257–72.
28. H. Mintzberg, "The Fall and Rise of Strategic Planning," *Harvard Business Review* (January/February 1994): 107–14.
29. The two views of Honda are captured in two Harvard cases: Honda [A] and [B] (Boston: Harvard Business School, Cases 384049 and 384050, 1989).
30. Boston Consulting Group, *Strategy Alternatives for the British Motorcycle Industry* (London: Her Majesty's Stationery Office, 1975).
31. R. T. Pascale, "Perspective on Strategy: The Real Story Behind Honda's Success," *California Management Review* 26, no. 3 (Spring 1984): 47–72.
32. H. Mintzberg, "Crafting Strategy," *Harvard Business Review* (July/August 1987): 70.

33. R. A. Burgelman and A. Grove, "Strategic Dissonance," *California Management Review* 38 (Winter 1996): 8–28.

34. R. M. Grant, "Strategic Planning in a Turbulent Environment: Evidence from the Oil and Gas Majors," *Strategic Management Journal* 14 (June 2003): 491–517.

35. O. Gadiesh and J. Gilbert, "Transforming Corner-office Strategy into Frontline Action," *Harvard Business Review* (May 2001): 73–80.

36. K. M. Eisenhardt and D. N. Sull, "Strategy as Simple Rules," *Harvard Business Review* (January 2001): 107–16.

# II

# THE TOOLS OF STRATEGY ANALYSIS

# 2 Goals, Values, and Performance

The strategic aim of a business is to earn a return on capital, and if in any particular case the return in the long run is not satisfactory, then the deficiency should be corrected or the activity abandoned for a more favorable one.

—ALFRED P. SLOAN JR., PRESIDENT AND THEN CHAIRMAN OF
GENERAL MOTORS, 1923 TO 1956.[1]

Profits are to business as breathing is to life. Breathing is essential to life, but is not the purpose for living. Similarly, profits are essential for the existence of the corporation, but they are not the reason for its existence.

—DENNIS BAKKE, FOUNDER AND FORMER CEO, AES CORPORATION

## OUTLINE

## Introduction and Objectives

Our framework for strategy analysis (Figure 1.2) comprises four components: the firm's goals and values, its resources and capabilities, its structure and management systems, and its industry environment. The chapters that form Part II of this book develop these four components of strategy analysis. We begin with goals and values of the firm and, by extension, the performance of the firm in attaining its goals.

As the opening quotations to this chapter indicate, there is fierce debate over the appropriate goals for business enterprises. In this chapter we will consider the extent to which the firm should pursue the interests of its owners, of its stakeholders, and of society as a whole. Our approach will be pragmatic. While acknowledging that firms possess multiple goals and, as reflected in their statements of mission and vision, that each firm has a unique purpose, we focus upon a single goal: the quest for value. This I interpret as the pursuit of profit over the lifetime of the firm. Hence, the focus of our strategy analysis is upon concepts and techniques that are concerned with identifying and exploiting the sources of profitability available to the firm. Our emphasis on profitability and value creation also means that we will draw upon some of the tools of financial analysis for the purposes of performance appraisal, performance diagnosis, and target setting.

Although profitability is the most useful indicator of firm performance, we shall acknowledge that firms are motivated by goals other than profit. Indeed, the companies that are most successful in generating profits over the long run are typically those motivated by other goals. Profit is the lifeblood of the organization, but it is not a goal that inspires organizational members to outstanding achievement. Moreover, for a firm to survive and generate profit over the long run requires responsiveness to the requirements of its social, political, and natural environments.

By the time you have completed this chapter, you will be able to:

- recognize that, while every firm has a distinct purpose, the common goal for all firms is creating value, and appreciate how the definition of value informs the debate over shareholder versus stakeholder goals for the firm;

- understand the relationship between profit, cash flow, and enterprise value;

- use the tools of financial analysis to appraise firm performance, diagnose the sources of performance problems, and set performance targets;

- appreciate how a firm's values, principles, and pursuit of corporate social responsibility can help define its strategy and support its creation of value;

- understand how real options contribute to firm value and the role of options thinking in strategy analysis.

## Strategy as a Quest for Value

There is more to business than making money. For the entrepreneurs who create business enterprises, personal wealth appears to be a less important motivation than the wish for autonomy, the desire for achievement, and lust for excitement. Almost 80 years ago, the economist Joseph Schumpeter observed: "The entrepreneur–innovator's motivation includes such aspects as the dream to found a private kingdom, the will to conquer and to succeed for the sake of success itself, and the joy of creating and getting things done."[2] Business enterprises are creative organizations which offer individuals unsurpassed opportunity to make a difference in the world. Certainly, making money was not the goal that inspired Henry Ford to build a business that precipitated a social revolution:

> I will build a motor car for the great multitude … It will be so low in price that no man making good wages will be unable to own one and to enjoy with his family the blessing of hours of pleasure in God's great open spaces … When I'm through, everyone will be able to afford one, and everyone will have one.[3]

Each entrepreneur is inspired by a goal that is personal and unique—family cars for the multitude (Henry Ford), bringing the power of personal computing to the individual (Steve Jobs), reducing deaths from infection after surgery (Johnson & Johnson), or revolutionizing vacuum cleaning (James Dyson). In the case of established companies, Cynthia Montgomery argues that "forging a compelling organizational purpose" is the ongoing job of company leaders and the "crowning responsibility of the CEO."[4] Organizational purpose is articulated in companies' statements of mission and vision:

- Google's mission is "to organize the world's information and make it universally accessible and useful."
- "The IKEA vision is to create a better everyday life for the many people. We make this possible by offering a wide range of well-designed, functional home furnishing products at prices so low that as many people as possible will be able to afford them."
- "SAP strives to define and establish undisputed leadership in the emerging market for business process platform offerings and accelerate business innovation powered by IT for companies and industries worldwide."

Within this vast variety of organizational purposes, there is a common denominator: the desire, and the need, to create value. Value is the monetary worth of a product or asset. Hence, we can generalize by saying that the purpose of business is, first, to create value for customers and, second, to appropriate some of that customer value in the form of profit—thereby creating value for the firm.

Value can be created in two ways: by production and by commerce. Production creates value by physically transforming products that are less valued by consumers into products that are more valued by consumers—turning clay into coffee mugs, for example. Commerce creates value not by physically transforming products but by repositioning them in space and time. Trade involves transferring products from individuals and locations where they are less valued to individuals and locations where they are more valued. Similarly, speculation involves transferring products from a point in time where a product is valued less to a point in time where it is valued more. Thus, the essence of commerce is creating value through arbitrage across time and space.[5]

The difference between the value of a firm's output and the cost of its material inputs is its **value added**. Value added is equal to the sum of all the income paid to the suppliers of factors of production. Thus:

$$\text{Value Added} = \text{Sales revenue from output} - \text{Cost of material inputs}$$
$$= \text{Wages/Salaries} + \text{Interest} + \text{Rent} + \text{Royalties/License fees}$$
$$+ \text{Taxes} + \text{Dividends} + \text{Retained profit}$$

## Value for Whom? Shareholders versus Stakeholders

The value added created by firms is distributed among different parties: employees (wages and salaries), lenders (interest), landlords (rent), government (taxes), and owners (profit). In addition, firms also create value for their customers to the extent that the satisfaction customers gain exceeds the price they pay (they derive **consumer surplus**). It is tempting, therefore, to think of the firm as operating for the benefit of multiple constituencies. This view of the business enterprise as a coalition of interest groups where top management's role to balance these different—often conflicting—interests is referred to as the **stakeholder approach to the firm**.[6]

The idea that the corporation should balance the interests of multiple stakeholders has a long tradition, especially in Asia and continental Europe. By contrast, most English-speaking countries have endorsed shareholder capitalism, where companies' overriding duty is to produce profits for owners. These differences are reflected in international differences in companies' legal obligations. In the US, Canada, the UK, and Australia, company boards are required to act in the interests of shareholders. In most continental European countries, companies are legally required to take account of the interests of employees, the state, and the enterprise as a whole.

There is an ongoing debate as to whether companies should operate exclusively in the interests of their owners or should also pursue the goals of multiple stakeholders. During the 1990s, "Anglo-Saxon" shareholder capitalism was in the ascendant—many continental European and Asian companies changed their strategies and corporate governance to reflect shareholder interests. However, during the 21st century, shareholder value maximization has become tainted by its association with short-termism, financial manipulation, excessive CEO compensation, and the failures of risk management that precipitated the 2008–2009 financial crisis.

Clearly, companies have legal and ethical responsibilities to employees, customers, society, and the natural environment. However, companies that adopt a stakeholder approach and seek to pursue the combined interests of multiple stakeholders face major problems in formulating and implementing their strategies. Taking account of multiple goals and specifying tradeoffs between them vastly increases the complexity of decision making.[7] Michael Jensen argues that, for all practical purposes, "multiple objectives is no objective."[8] The complexities of balancing the interests of different stakeholder groups can result in top management decision making becoming bogged down in political wrangling, indecisiveness, and lack of accountability.[9]

To simplify our analysis of strategy formulation I make the assumption that the primary goal of strategy is to maximize the value of the enterprise through seeking to maximize profits over the long term. Having extolled the virtues of business enterprises as creative institutions, how can I justify this unedifying focus on money making? I have three justifications:

- *Competition*: Competition erodes profitability. As competition increases, the interests of different stakeholders converge around the goal of survival. Survival requires that, over the long term, a firm earn a rate of profit that covers its cost of capital; otherwise, it will not be able to replace its assets. When weak demand and fierce international competition depress return on capital, few companies have the luxury of sacrificing profits for other goals.

- *The market for corporate control*: Management teams that fail to maximize the profits of their companies tend to be replaced by teams that do. In the "market for corporate control," companies that underperform financially suffer a declining share price, which attracts acquirers—both other public companies and private equity funds. Despite the admirable record of British chocolate maker Cadbury in relation to employees and local communities, its dismal return to shareholders between 2004 and 2009 meant that it was unable to resist acquisition by Kraft Foods. In addition, activist investors— both individuals and institutions—pressure boards of directors to dismiss CEOs who fail to create value for shareholders.[10]

- *Convergence of stakeholder interests*: There is likely to be more community of interests than conflict of interests among different stakeholders. Profitability over the long term requires loyalty from employees, trusting relationships with suppliers and customers, and support from governments and communities. Indeed, the instrumental theory of stakeholder management argues that pursuit of stakeholder interests is essential to creating competitive advantage, which in turn leads to superior financial performance.[11] As Michael Jensen observes: "In order to maximize value, corporate managers must not only satisfy, but enlist the support of, all corporate stakeholders—customers, employees, managers, suppliers, local communities." Empirical evidence shows that firms which take account of a broader set of interests, including that of society, achieve superior financial performance.[12]

Hence, the issue of whether firms should operate in the interests of shareholders or of all stakeholders matters more in principle than in practice. According to Jensen: "enlightened shareholder value maximization … is identical to enlightened stakeholder theory." We shall return to this issue later in this chapter when we consider explicitly the social and environmental responsibilities of firms.

## What Is Profit?

Thus far, I have referred to firms' quest for profit in general terms. It is time to look more carefully at what we mean by **profit** and how it relates to value creation.

Profit is the surplus of revenues over costs available for distribution to the owners of the firm. But if profit maximization is to be a realistic goal, the firm must know what profit is and how to measure it; otherwise, instructing managers to maximize profit offers little guidance. What is the firm to maximize: total profit or rate of profit? Over what period? With what kind of adjustment for risk? And what is profit anyway—accounting profit, cash flow, or economic profit? These ambiguities become apparent once we compare the profit performance of companies. Table 2.1 shows that ranking companies by profitability depends critically on what profitability measure is used.

## Accounting Profit and Economic Profit

A major problem of *accounting profit* is that it combines two types of returns: the normal return to capital, which rewards investors for the use of their capital, and **economic profit**, which is the surplus available after all inputs (including capital) have been paid for. Economic profit is a purer measure of profit which is a more precise measure of a firm's ability to generate surplus value. To distinguish economic profit from accounting profit, economic profit is often referred to as *rent* or *economic rent*.

A widely used measure of economic profit is **economic value added (EVA)**, devised and popularized by the consulting firm Stern Stewart & Company.[13] Economic value added is measured as follows:

$$\text{EVA} = \text{Net operating profit after tax (NOPAT)} - \text{Cost of capital}$$

where,

$$\text{Cost of capital} = \text{Capital employed} \times \text{Weighted average cost of capital (WACC)}.$$

Economic profit has two main advantages over accounting profit as a performance measure. First, it sets a more demanding performance discipline for managers. At many capital-intensive companies seemingly healthy profits disappear once cost of capital is taken into account. Second, it improves the allocation of capital between the different businesses of the firm by taking account of the real costs of more capital-intensive businesses (Strategy Capsule 2.1).

**TABLE 2.1**   The performance of some of the world's leading companies in terms of different profitability measures, 2010

| Company | Market capitaliza-tion[a] ($ billion) | Net income[a] ($ billion) | ROS[b] (%) | ROE[c] (%) | ROA[d] (%) | Return to share-holders[e] (%) |
|---|---|---|---|---|---|---|
| ExxonMobil | 354 | 30.5 | 15.2 | 20.7 | 17.5 | 10.1 |
| Apple | 338 | 14.0 | 31.2 | 29.3 | 29.0 | 53.1 |
| PetroChina | 226 | 22.9 | 10.6 | 15.3 | 11.7 | −8.4 |
| General Electric | 155 | 11.6 | 12.7 | 9.8 | 18.9 | 23.9 |
| JPMorgan Chase | 108 | 17.4 | 28.5 | 9.9 | 11.8 | 2.3 |
| Wal-Mart Stores | 196 | 30.5 | 5.9 | 23.5 | 14.1 | 3.2 |
| Volkswagen | 64 | 9.1 | 7.5 | 32.9 | 3.6 | 123.2 |

*Notes:*
[a]Shares outstanding × closing price of shares on October 28, 2011.
[b]Return on sales = Pretax profit as a percentage of sales revenues.
[c]Return on equity = Net income as a percentage of year-end shareholder equity.
[d]Return on assets = Operating income as a percentage of year-end total assets.
[e]Dividend + share price appreciation during 2010.

STRATEGY CAPSULE 2.1

# Economic Value Added at Diageo plc.

At Guinness-to-Johnny-Walker drinks giant Diageo, EVA transformed the way in which Diageo measured its performance, allocated its capital and advertising expenditures, and evaluated its managers.

Taking account of the costs of the capital tied up in slow-maturing, vintage drinks such as Talisker and Lagavulin malt whisky, Hennessey cognac, and Dom Perignon champagne showed that these high-margin drinks were often not as profitable as the company had believed. The result was that Diageo's advertising expenditures were reallocated toward Smirnoff vodka, Gordon's gin, Baileys, and other drinks that could be sold within weeks of distillation.

Once managers had to report profits after deduction of the cost of the capital tied up in their businesses,

they took measures to reduce their capital bases and make their assets work harder. At Diageo's Pillsbury food business, the economic profit of every product and every major customer was scrutinized. The result was the elimination of many products and efforts to make marginal customers more profitable. Ultimately, EVA analysis resulted in Diageo selling Pillsbury to General Foods. This was followed by the sale of Diageo's Burger King chain to Texas Pacific, a private equity group.

Value-based management was extended throughout the organization by making EVA the primary determinant of the incentive pay earned by 1400 Diageo managers.

**Sources:** John McGrath, "Tracking Down Value," *Financial Times Mastering Management Review* (December 1998); www.diageo.com.

## Linking Profit to Enterprise Value

There is also the problem of time. Once we consider multiple periods of time, then profit maximization means maximizing the net present value of the stream of profits over the lifetime of the firm.

Hence, profit maximization translates into maximizing the value of the firm. The value of the firm is calculated in the same way as any other asset: it is the *net present value* (NPV) of the returns that the asset generates. The relevant returns are the cash flows to the firm. Hence, firms are valued using the same *discounted cash flow* (DCF) methodology that we apply to the valuation of investment projects. Thus, the value of an enterprise ($V$) is the sum of its free cash flows ($C$) in each year $t$, discounted at the enterprise's cost of capital ($r$).[14] The relevant cost of capital is the weighted average cost of capital ($r_{e+d}$) that averages the cost of equity ($r_e$) and the cost of debt ($r_d$):

$$V = \sum_t \frac{C_t}{(1 + r_{e+d})^t}$$

where C is measured as:

Net operating profit + Depreciation − Taxes − Investment in fixed and working capital

Thus, to maximize its value, a firm must maximize its future net cash flows while managing its risk to minimize its cost of capital.

This value-maximizing approach identifies cash flow rather than profit as the relevant performance measure for the value-maximizing firm. In practice, valuing companies by discounting economic profit gives the same result as by discounting net cash flows. The difference is in the treatment of the capital consumed by the business. The cash flow approach deducts capital at the time when the capital expenditure is made; the EVA approach follows the accounting convention of charging capital as it is consumed (through charging depreciation). In principle, a full DCF approach is the most satisfactory approach to valuing companies. In practice, for DCF analysis to be meaningful requires forecasting cash flows several years ahead, since cash flow for a single year is a poor indicator of underlying profitability (for instance profitable, fast-growing companies often have negative free cash flows). If financial forecasts can only be made for a few years out, then profit (net of depreciation) may offer a better basis for valuation than cash flow does.

The practical difficulties associated with DCF analysis have resulted in a search for alternative approaches to maximizing firm value that avoid the problems of forecasting cash flows or profits far into the future. McKinsey & Company argues that enterprise value depends upon three key variables: return on invested capital (ROIC), weighted average cost of capital (WACC), and growth of operating profit. Hence, creating enterprise value requires increasing ROIC, reducing WACC, and increasing the rate of growth of profits.[15]

## What's Wrong with Shareholder Value Maximization?

How does maximizing the value of the firm (enterprise value) relate to the much-lauded goal of maximizing shareholder value? In 1958, Modigliani and Miller laid the foundations of modern financial theory by showing that the value of a company (the NPV of its stream profit) equals the market value of its securities: equity and debt.[16] Shareholder value is equal to enterprise value minus the value of the firm's debt. For most companies, maximizing enterprise value and maximizing shareholder value are roughly equivalent (i.e., they imply similar management decisions).

Shareholder value maximization may be interpreted in two ways:

- in terms of intrinsic value, shareholder value is the NPV of the stream of profits that accrue to owners (i.e., after the deduction of interest payments) discounted at the cost of equity;
- in terms of market value, shareholder value is the current stock market value of the firm's shares.[17]

So long as the stock market is reasonably efficient in valuing firm's future returns, current stock market valuation is a good indicator of intrinsic value. Hence, maximizing net profits over the life of the firm should also mean maximizing the stock market value of the firm. However, the experience of the past two decades suggests when top management focuses upon stock market value rather than profit over the life of the firm undesirable consequences follow. If stock markets are myopic, management may be encouraged to maximize short-term profits to the detriment of long-run profitability. This in turn may tempt top management to boost short-term earnings through financial manipulation rather than by growing the firm's operating profits. Such manipulation may include adjustments to financial structure, earnings smoothing, and the use of asset sales to flatter short-term reported profits. Hence, for shareholder value maximization to be aligned with the interests of long-term interests of shareholders and other stakeholders, it is vital that managers focus their attention not on their company's share price but on driving the profits that ultimately those share prices depend upon.

Our emphasis in this book will be on maximizing enterprise value rather than maximizing shareholder value. This is partly for convenience: distinguishing debt from equity is not always straightforward, due to the presence of preference stock and convertible debt, while junk bonds share the characteristics of both equity and debt. More importantly, focusing on the value of the enterprise as a whole supports our emphasis of the fundamental drivers of firm value in preference to the distractions and distortions that result from a preoccupation with stock market valuation.

## Putting Performance Analysis into Practice

Our discussion so far has established that, while every business enterprise has a distinct purpose, profit earnings over the life of the business—enterprise value—is the best common indicator of the success of the business as a value-creating entity and offers the best guide to the selection of strategies for achieving business purpose.

So, how do we apply these principles to appraise and develop business strategies? There are four key areas where our analysis of profit performance can guide strategy: first, in appraising a firm's (or business unit's) performance; second, in diagnosing the sources of poor performance; third, in selecting strategies on the basis of their profit prospects; and, finally, setting performance targets.

### Appraising Current and Past Performance

The first task of any strategy formulation exercise is to assess the current situation. This means identifying the current strategy of the firm and assessing how well that strategy is doing in terms of the financial performance of the firm. The next stage is diagnosis—identifying the sources of unsatisfactory performance. Thus, good strategic practice emulates good medical practice: first, assess the patient's state of health, and then determine the causes of any sickness.

*Forward-Looking Performance Measures: Stock Market Value*    If our goal is to maximize profit over the lifetime of the firm, then to evaluate the performance of a firm we need to look at its stream of profit (or cash flows) over the rest of its life. The problem, of course, is that we can only make reasonable estimates of these a few years ahead. For public companies stock market valuation represents the best available estimate of the NPV of future cash flows. Thus, to evaluate the performance of a firm in value creation we can compare the change in the market value of the firm relative to that of competitors over a period (preferably several years). Clearly, stock market valuation is an imperfect performance indicator—particularly in terms of its sensitivity to new information and its vulnerability to market psychology and disequilibrium—but it is the best indictor we have of intrinsic value.

*Backward-Looking Performance Measures: Accounting Ratios*    Because of the volatility of stock market values, evaluations of firm performance for the purposes of assessing the current strategy or evaluating management effectiveness tend to use accounting measures of performance. These are inevitably historical: financial reports appear at least three weeks after the period to which they relate. That said, many firms offer *earnings guidance*—forecasts of profit for the next 12 months (sometimes longer).

The McKinsey valuation framework identifies three drivers of enterprise value: rate of return on capital, cost of capital, and profit growth (see page 40). Among these, return on capital is the key indicator of the invested firm's effectiveness in generating profits from its assets. Hence, ROIC and its equivalent, return on capital employed (ROCE), or its closely related rate of return indicators, such as return on equity (ROE) and return on assets (ROA), are valuable performance indicators. Different profitability measures are related—the longer the period under consideration, the more they tend to converge.[18] Over shorter periods, the key issues are, first, to be aware of the limitations and biases inherent in any particular profitability measure and, second, to use multiple measures of profitability so that their consistency can be judged. The greatest of these limitations concerns the use of historical measures of performance to indicate the success of the firm in creating future profits. Table 2.2 outlines some widely used performance indicators.

**TABLE 2.2** Profitability ratios

| Ratio | Formula | Comments |
|---|---|---|
| Return on Invested Capital (ROIC) | $$\frac{\text{Operating profit before interest after tax}}{\text{Fixed assets} + \text{Net current assets}}$$ | ROIC measures the return on the capital invested in the business. ROIC is also known as return on capital employed (ROCE). The numerator is operating profit or earnings (EBIT), and can be pre-tax or post-tax. The denominator can also be measured as equity plus debt. |
| Return on Equity (ROE) | $$\frac{\text{Net income}}{\text{Shareholders' equity}}$$ | ROE measures the firm's success in using shareholders' capital to generate profits that are available for remunerating investors. Net income is often measured net of income from discontinued operations and before any special items. |
| Return on Assets (ROA) | $$\frac{\text{Operating profit}}{\text{Total assets}}$$ | The numerator should correspond to the return on all the company's assets—e.g., operating profit, EBITDA (earnings before interest, tax, depreciation, and amortization), or EBIT (earnings before interest and tax). |
| Gross margin | $$\frac{\text{Sales} - \text{Cost of bought-in goods and services}}{\text{Sales}}$$ | Gross margin measures the extent to which a firm adds value to the goods and services it buys in. |
| Operating margin | $$\frac{\text{Operating profit}}{\text{Sales}}$$ | Operating margin and net margin measure a firm's ability to extract profit from its sales, but for appraising firm performance, these ratios reveal little because margins vary greatly between sectors according to capital intensity (see Table 2.1). |
| Net margin | $$\frac{\text{Net income}}{\text{Sales}}$$ | |

**Notes:**
Few accounting ratios have standard definitions, hence, it is advisable to be explicit about how you have calculated the ratio you are using. A general guideline for rate of return ratios is that the numerator should be the profits that are available to remunerate the owners of the assets in the denominator.
Profits are measured over a period of time (typically over a year). Assets are valued at a point of time. Hence, in rate of return calculations, assets, equity, and capital employed should to be averaged between the beginning and end of the period.

Interpreting probability ratios requires benchmarks. Comparisons over time tell us whether a profitability ratio is improving or deteriorating. Interfirm comparisons tell us how a firm is performing relative to a competitor, relative to its industry average, or relative to firms in general (e.g., relative to the Fortune 500, S&P 500, or FT 500). Another key benchmark is cost of capital. ROIC and ROCE should be compared with WACC, and ROE compared with the cost of equity capital.

## Performance Diagnosis

If profit performance is unsatisfactory, we need to identify the sources of poor performance so that management can take corrective action. The main tool of diagnosis is disaggregation of return on capital in order to identify the fundamental *value drivers*. A starting point is to apply the Du Pont Formula to disaggregate return on invested capital into sales margin and capital turnover. We can then further disaggregate both sales margin and capital productivity into their component items (Figure 2.1). This points us toward the specific activities that are the sources of poor performance.

Strategy Capsule 2.2 compares the performance of UPS with that of FedEx. By disaggregating the overall return on assets, we can begin to pinpoint the sources of

**FIGURE 2.1**  Disaggregating return on capital employed

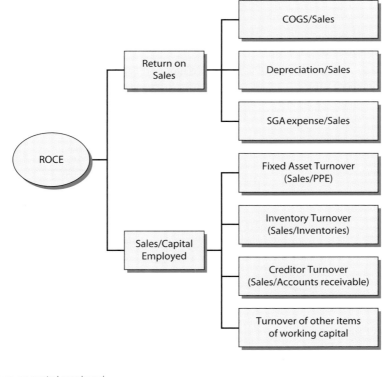

**Notes:**
ROCE: Return on capital employed.
COGS: Cost of goods sold.
PPE: Property, plant, and equipment.

For further discussion, see T. Koller *et al.*, *Valuation*, 5th edn (Chichester: John Wiley & Sons, Ltd, 2010).

## STRATEGY CAPSULE 2.2
# Diagnosing Performance: UPS vs. FedEx

Between 2006 and 2011, United Parcel Service (UPS), the world's leading package delivery company, has earned about double the return on invested capital as its closest rival, FedEx Corporation. What insights can financial analysis offer into the sources of this performance differential?

Disaggregating the companies' return on capital employed into sales margin and capital turnover shows that differences in ROCE can be attributed almost entirely to differences in return on sales—asset productivity (as indicated by capital turnover) is almost identical for the two companies. Disaggregation of capital turnover points to no significant differences between the two companies in the productivity with which individual assets are managed. See Figure 2.2.

However, disaggregation of ROS highlights major differences in the cost structure of the two companies:

UPS is more labor intensive with a much higher ratio of employee costs to sales. FedEx has much higher costs in terms of fuel, maintenance, depreciation, and "other."

These cost differences reflect differences in the composition of the two companies' business. UPS is more heavily involved in ground transportation (UPS has 100,000 vehicles; FedEx has 50,000), which tends to be more labor intensive. FedEx is more oriented toward air transportation (UPS has 527 aircraft; FedEx has 688). For FedEx, its express delivery segment was much less profitable than its ground delivery segment. However, the differences in business mix do not appear to completely explain the wide discrepancy in fuel, maintenance, and other costs between FedEx and UPS. The suspicion is that UPS has superior operational efficiency.

**FIGURE 2.2** Analyzing why UPS (U) earns a higher return on capital employed (ROCE) than FedEx (F)

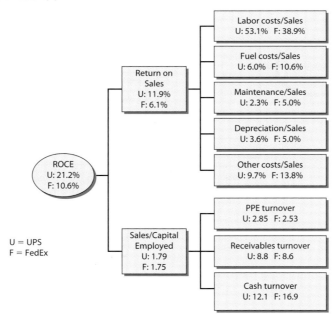

UPS's superior profitability. If we then combine the financial data with qualitative data on UPS's business strategy, its operations, its product strategy, the organizational issues it has faced, and the conditions in the world logistics and express delivery market, we can begin to diagnose why it has outperformed FedEx.

## Can Past Performance Guide Strategies for the Future?

A probing diagnosis of a firm's recent performance—as outlined above—provides a useful input into strategy formulation. If we can establish why a company has been performing badly then we have a basis for corrective actions. These corrective actions are likely to be both strategic (i.e., focused on the medium to long term) and operational (focused on the short term). The worse a company's performance, the greater the need to concentrate on the short term. For companies teetering on the brink of bankruptcy—several of the world's airlines and some automotive companies—long-term strategy takes a back seat; survival is the dominant concern.

For companies that are performing well, financial analysis allows us to understand the sources of superior performance so that strategy can protect and enhance these determinants of success. For example, in the case of UPS (see Strategy Capsule 2.2), financial analysis points to the efficiency benefits that arise from being the US's biggest package delivery company and having an integrated system of collection and delivery that optimizes operational efficiency. The superior profitability of UPS's international business points to its ability to successfully enter foreign markets and integrate overseas operations within its global system.

However, analyzing the past only takes us so far. The world of business is one of constant change and the role of strategy is to help the firm to adapt to change. The challenge is to look into the future and identify factors that threaten performance or create new opportunities for profit. In making strategy recommendations to UPS, our financial analysis can tell us some of the reasons why UPS has been doing well up until now, but the key to sustaining UPS's performance is to recognize how its industry environment will be changing in terms of customer requirements, competition, technology, and energy costs and to assess UPS's capacity to adapt to these new conditions. While financial analysis is inevitably backward looking, strategic analysis allows us to look forward and understand some of the critical factors impacting a firm's success in the future.

## Setting Performance Targets

We noted in Chapter 1 that an important role for strategic planning systems is to drive corporate performance through setting performance goals then monitoring results against targets. To be effective, performance targets need to be consistent with long-term goals, linked to strategy, and relevant to the tasks and responsibilities of individual organizational members. Company goals need to be actionable. A key problem of the stakeholder view is the difficulty of interpreting the goal of pursuing the interests of all stakeholders. Even the more precise goal of maximizing enterprise value may have little meaning outside the executive suite. Broad corporate goals need to be translated into specific objectives that are meaningful to managers further down the organization. The key is to establish performance targets that match the variables over which different managers exert influence. Thus, for the CEO, it may make sense to set the overall goal of maximizing enterprise value. For the chief operating officer and divisional heads, it makes sense to set more specific financial goals (such as maximizing ROCE on existing assets and investing in projects whose rate of return exceeds the cost of capital). More specific operating targets are preferable for functional, departmental, and unit managers. Thus, in a retailing company, store managers might be given targets with regard to sales per square foot and gross margins. Warehouse managers might be required to achieve target levels of inventory turns. Purchasing managers might be required to reduce the cost of goods purchased as a percentage of sales revenue. The chief financial officer might be required to minimize the average cost of capital and reduce cash balances.

The same procedure that we used to disaggregate return on capital for appraising past performance can be used to set performance targets appropriate to different levels and functions within the organization. Figure 2.3 uses the same breakout of the drivers of return on capital as Figure 2.1. The difference is that Figure 2.3 provides a basis for identifying the financial and operating ratios appropriate to managers at the different levels and in the different functions of the company.

*Balanced Scorecards*   The problem with any system of performance management is that the performance goals are long term (e.g., maximizing profits over the lifetime of the company), but to act as an effective control system performance targets need to be monitored over the short term. The problem with the above financially based approach of disaggregating profitability into its constituent ratios is that the short-term pursuit of financial targets is unlikely to result in long-term profit maximization. One

**FIGURE 2.3**   Linking value drivers to performance

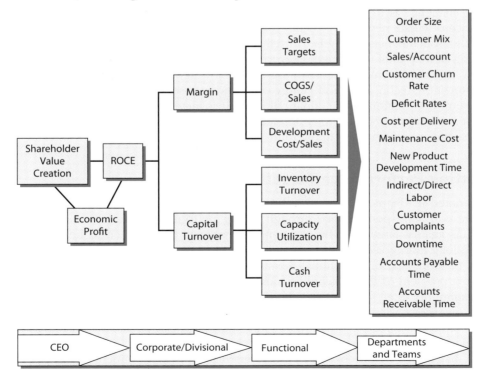

solution to this dilemma is to link the overall corporate goal of value maximization to strategic and operational targets to ensure that the pursuit of financial goals is not at the expense of the longer-term strategic position of the company. The most widely used method for doing this is the **balanced scorecard** developed by Robert Kaplan and David Norton.[19] The balanced scorecard methodology provides an integrated framework for balancing financial and strategic goals and cascading performance measures down the organization to individual business units and departments. The performance measures included in the balanced scorecard derive from answers to four questions:

- How do we look to shareholders? The financial perspective is composed of measures such as cash flow, sales and income growth, and return on equity.
- How do customers see us? The customer perspective comprises measures such as goals for new products, on-time delivery, and defect and failure levels.
- What must we excel at? The internal business perspective relates to internal business processes such as productivity, employee skills, cycle time, yield rates, and quality and cost measures.
- Can we continue to improve and create value? The innovation and learning perspective includes measures related to new product development cycle times, technological leadership, and rates of improvement.

By balancing a set of strategic and financial goals, the scorecard methodology allows the strategy of the business to be linked with the creation of shareholder value while providing a set of measurable targets to guide this process. Figure 2.4 shows the balanced scorecard for a US regional airline.

**FIGURE 2.4**   Balanced scorecard for a regional airline

| Simplified Strategy Map | Performance Measures | Targets | Initiatives |
|---|---|---|---|
| **Financial** — Increase Profitability, Lower Cost, Increase Revenue | • Market Value<br>• Seat Revenue<br>• Plane Lease Cost | • 25% per year<br>• 20% per year<br>• 5% per year | • Optimize routes<br>• Standardize planes |
| **Customer** — More Customers, On-time Flights, Low Prices | • FAA on-time arrival rating<br>• Customer ranking<br>• No. customers | • First in industry<br>• 98% satisfaction<br>• % change | • Quality management<br>• Customer loyalty program |
| **Internal** — Improve turnaround time | • On Ground Time<br>• On-Time Departure | • <25 Minutes<br>• 93% | • Cycle time optimization program |
| **Learning** — Align Ground Crews | • % Ground crew stockholders<br>• % Ground crew trained | • Year 1, 70%<br>• Year 4, 90%<br>• Year 6, 100% | • Stock ownership plan<br>• Ground crew training |

**Source:** Reproduced from www.balancedscorecard.org with permission.

*Rethinking Performance Targets*   Financial value drivers and balanced score-cards are systematic techniques of performance management based upon the assumption that, if overall goals can be disaggregated into precise, quantitative, time-specific targets, each member of the organization knows what is expected of him or her and is motivated toward achieving the targets set. However, a mounting body of evidence points to the unintended consequences of managing through performance targets. In particular, many of the companies that are the most effective long-term generators of profit and are best at creating shareholder value place little emphasis on financial goals. Why does the pursuit of profit so often fail to realize its goal? First, profit goals will only guide effective management action if managers know what determines profit. Obsession with profitability and shareholder return can blinker managers' perception of the real drivers of superior performance: in the case of Enron it helped fuel the destruction of all shareholder value.[20] Conversely, if companies focus their attention on the strategic drivers of competitive advantage, this can ultimately lead to superior long-term profitability. The general point—illustrated by the case of Boeing (Strategy Capsule 2.3)—is that *obliquity*, pursuing our goals indirectly, is often superior to a direct approach.[21]

There is also the danger that whenever broad, long-term goals are translated into time-specific performance metrics the performance targets become divorced from

---

## STRATEGY CAPSULE 2.3
# The Pitfalls of Pursuing Shareholder Value: Boeing

Boeing was one of the most financially successful members of the Dow Jones Industrial Index between 1960 and 1990. Yet Boeing gave little attention to financial management. CEO Bill Allen was interested in building great planes and leading the world market with them: "Boeing is always reaching out for tomorrow. This can only be accomplished by people who live, breathe, eat and sleep what they are doing." At a board meeting to approve Boeing's biggest ever investment, the 747, Allen was asked by non-executive director Crawford Greenwalt for Boeing's financial projections on the project. In response to Allen's vague reply, Greenwalt buried his head in his hands. "My God," he muttered, "these guys don't even know what the return on investment will be on this thing."

The change came in the mid-1990s when Boeing acquired McDonnell Douglas and a new management

team of Harry Stonecipher and Phil Condit took over. Mr Condit proudly talked of taking the company into "a value-based environment where unit cost, return on investment, and shareholder return are the measures by which you'll be judged."

The result was lack of investment in major new civil aviation projects and diversification into defense and satellites. Under Condit, Boeing relinquished market leadership in passenger aircraft to Airbus, while faltering as a defense contractor due partly to ethical lapses by key executives. When Condit resigned on December 1, 2003, Boeing's stock price was 20% lower than when he was appointed.

*Source:* Adapted from John Kay, "Forget how the Crow Flies," *Financial Times Magazine* (January 17, 2004): 17–27, with permission.

the ultimate objective—as the Buddhist teaching warns us: "Mistaking the finger pointing at the moon for the moon itself." The widespread adoption of performance targets in the public sector has resulted in the propensity for agencies to "game the system" through neglecting what has not been targeted, manipulating data, and achieving targets but not improving the underlying performance that performance indicators are intended to reflect.[22]

## Beyond Profit: Values and Corporate Social Responsibility

At the beginning of this chapter, I argued that, while every company has a distinct organizational purpose, the common goal for every business enterprise is to create value, and the best indicator of value creation is profit over the lifetime of the company—or, equivalently, maximizing enterprise value. Although the corporate scandals of the 21st century—from Enron in 2001 to Lehman Brothers in 2008—have discredited the pursuit of profit, in particular the principle of shareholder value maximization, I have justified the goal of long-run profit maximization as the most appropriate and practical goal for the firm.

This justification was based largely on the alignment which I perceived, first, between profits and the interests of society (reflecting Adam Smith's principle of the "invisible hand" which guides self-interest toward the common good) and, second, between the pursuit of stakeholder interests and earning profit over the long-term ("enlightened value maximization"). But what about when the pursuit of profit is not consistent with the social good or where it conflicts with ethics? How are such inconsistencies and conflicts to be managed? Is it sufficient to follow Milton Friedman's dictum that:

> There is one and only one social responsibility of business—to use its resources and engage in activities designed to increase its profits so long as it stays within the rules of the game, which is to say, engage in open and free competition without deception or fraud.[23]

Under this approach, it is the role of government to intervene in the economy where the pursuit of profit conflicts with the interest of society, using taxes and regulations to align profit incentives with social goals and legislation to criminalize unethical behavior. Conversely, others have argued that business enterprises should take the initiative to establish principles and values that extend beyond the limits of the law, and introduce strategies that are explicitly oriented toward the interests of society. Let us discuss each of these areas in turn.

### Values and Principles

A sense of purpose—as articulated in statements of mission and vision—is often complemented by beliefs about how this purpose should be achieved. These organizational beliefs typically comprise a set of **values**—in the form of commitments to certain ethical precepts and to different stakeholder interests—and a set of principles to guide the decisions and actions of organizational members. Strategy Capsule 2.4 summarizes Shell's values and business principles.

## STRATEGY CAPSULE 2.4
# Royal Dutch Shell's Values and Principles

### OUR VALUES

Shell employees share a set of core values—honesty, integrity and respect for people. We also firmly believe in the fundamental importance of trust, openness, teamwork and professionalism and pride in what we do.

### PRINCIPLES

1　Economic. Long-term profitability is essential to achieving our business goals and to our continued growth…

2　Competition. Shell companies support free enterprise. We seek to compete fairly and ethically and within the framework of applicable competition laws…

3　Business integrity. Shell companies insist on honesty, integrity and fairness in all aspects of our business…

4　Political activities. Shell companies act in a socially responsible manner within the laws of the countries in which we operate in pursuit of our legitimate commercial objectives…

5　Health, safety, security and the environment. Shell companies have a systematic approach to health, safety, security and environmental management in order to achieve continuous performance improvement.

6　Local communities. Shell companies aim to be good neighbors by continuously improving the ways in which we contribute directly or indirectly to the general wellbeing of the communities within which we work…

7　Communication and engagement. Shell companies recognize that regular dialogue and engagement with our stakeholders is essential. We are committed to reporting of our performance by providing full relevant information to legitimately interested parties…

8　Compliance. We comply with all applicable laws and regulations of the countries in which we operate.

**Source:** Extracted from Royal Dutch Shell plc General Business Principles, 2008 with permission from Shell International.

At one level, statements of values and principles may be regarded as instruments of companies' external image management. Yet, to the extent that companies are consistent and sincere in their adherence to values and principles, these ideals can be a critical component of organizational identity and an important influence on employees' commitment and propensity to collaborate. To the extent that values are shared among organizational members, they form a central component of organizational culture.

The evidence that commitment to values and principles influences organizational performance is overwhelming. McKinsey & Company places "shared values" at the center of its "7-S framework."[24] Jim Collins and Jerry Porras argue that "core values" and "core purpose"—the organization's most fundamental reasons for being—unite to form an organization's "core ideology" which "defines an organization's timeless character" and is "the glue that holds the organization together."[25] They argue that when core ideology is put together with an "envisioned future" for the enterprise the result is a powerful sense of strategic direction that provides the foundation for long-term success.

## Guidelines for Corporate Social Responsibility

The debate over the social responsibilities of companies has been both contentious and confused. Underlying the debate are different conceptions of the public corporation: "the property conception," which views the firm as a set of assets owned by the shareholders, and the "social entity conception," which views the firm as the community of individuals that is sustained and supported by its relationships with its social, political, economic, and natural environment.[26] While the "firm as property" view implies that management's sole responsibility is to operate in the interests of shareholders, the "firm as social entity" implies a responsibility to maintain the firm within its overall network of relationships and dependencies.

However, even from a pure efficacy viewpoint, it is clear that both poles of the spectrum of opinions are untenable. The proponents of the view that the sole purpose of the business enterprise is to make profit fail to recognize that to survive and earn profit an organization must maintain social legitimacy. The near-elimination of investment banks during the financial crisis of 2008-2009—including the transformation of Goldman Sachs and other investment banks into commercial banks—was caused less by their commercial failure as by a collapse of legitimacy. The phone hacking scandal that resulted in the closure of a British newspaper owned by Rupert Murdoch's News Corporation represented less than 1% of News Corp's revenues. However, in the five weeks after the scandal broke in July 2011, News Corp's market capitalization declined by 25%—a loss of $11 billion.

At the other end of the spectrum, the argument that the primary responsibility of business enterprises should be the pursuit of social goals is likely to be similarly dysfunctional. To extend Adam Smith's observation that it "is not from the benevolence of the butcher, the brewer or the baker, that we expect our dinner, but from their regard to their own interest,"[27] it is likely that if the butcher becomes an animal rights activist, the brewer joins the Temperance League, and the baker signs up to Weight Watchers none of us has much hope of getting dinner.

Somewhere in the middle of this spectrum therefore lies a region of sustainability where business enterprises are aligned with the requirements of their social and natural environment but have not lost touch either with their business purpose or with the need for financial viability. A number of contributions to the management literature have allowed us to define more precisely this intermediate region of sustainability and to outline the considerations that should guide the pursuit of social responsibility.

The key consideration here is survival through adaptation. The efficacy argument for **corporate social responsibility (CSR)** views the firm as embedded within an ecosystem of its social and natural environments, implying a congruence between the interests of the firm and those of the supporting ecosystem. Thus, according to former Shell executive Arie de Geus, long-living companies are those that build strong communities, have a strong sense of identity, commit to learning, and are sensitive to the world around them. In short, they recognize they are living organisms whose lifespans depend upon effective adaptation to a changing environment.[28]

This view of the firm jointly pursuing its own interests and those of its ecosystem has been developed by Michael Porter and Mark Kramer into guidelines for a focused and pragmatic approach to CSR.[29] Putting aside ethical arguments (what they call "the moral imperative"), they identify three reasons why CSR might also be in the interests of a company: the *sustainability* argument—CSR is in firms' interests due to a mutual interest in sustaining the ecosystem; the *reputation* argument—CSR enhances a firm's reputation with consumers and other third parties; and the *license-to-operate* argument—to conduct their businesses firms need the support of the constituencies upon which they depend. The critical task, in selecting which CSR initiatives firms should pursue is to identify specific intersections between the interests of the firm and those of society (i.e., projects and activities that create competitive advantage for the firm while generating positive social outcomes)—what they term *strategic CSR*.

In a subsequent article, Porter and Kramer develop their analysis of this intersection between corporate and social interests, which they call *shared value*: "creating economic value in a way which also creates value for society."[30] Shared value, they argue, is not about redistributing the value already created; it is about expanding the total pool of economic and social value. For example, fair trade is about the redistribution of value by paying farmers a higher price for their crops—in the case of Ivory Coast cocoa growers, it increases their incomes by 10–20%. By contrast, efforts by the major buyers to improve the efficiency of cocoa growing through improved growing methods, better quality control, and improved infrastructure can increase growers' incomes by 300%. Creating shared value involves reconceptualizing the firm's boundaries and its relationship with its environment. Rather than seeing itself as a separate entity which transacts with the external environment, the firm recognizes that it is co-dependent upon and intimately involved with its environment and the organizations and individuals it comprises. This offers three types of opportunity for shared value creation: reconceiving products and markets, redefining productivity within the value chain, and building local clusters of suppliers, distributors, and related businesses at the places where the firm does business.

This notion of shared value is embedded in **the bottom of the pyramid** initiatives—the potential for multinational companies to create profitable business and promote social and economic development through serving the world's poor—especially the four billion people living off less than $2 a day.[31] Again, the key is a switch of perception: rather than viewing the poor as victims or a burden, if multinationals recognize them as potential consumers, resilient workers, and creative entrepreneurs then a whole world of opportunity opens up.

## Beyond Profit: Strategy and Real Options

So far, we have identified the value of the firm with the net present value (NPV) of its profit earnings (or free cash flows). But NPV is not the only source of value available to the firm. The simple idea that an option—the choice of whether to do something or not—has value has important implications for how we value firms. In recent years, the principles of option pricing have been extended from valuing financial securities to valuing investment projects and companies. The resulting field of **real option analysis** has emerged as one of the most important developments in financial theory over the past decade, with far-reaching implications for strategy analysis. The technical details of valuing real options are complex. However, the underlying principles are intuitive. Let me outline the basic ideas of real options theory and what they mean for strategy analysis.

Consider the investments that Royal Dutch Shell is making in joint-venture development projects to produce hydrogen for use in fuel cells. The large-scale use of fuel cells in transportation vehicles or for power generation seems unlikely within the foreseeable future. Shell's expenditure on these projects is small, but almost certainly these funds would generate a higher return if they were used in Shell's core oil and gas business. So, how can these investments—indeed, all of Shell's investments in renewable energy—be consistent with shareholder interests?

The answer lies in the option value of these investments. Shell is not developing a full-scale fuel cell business, and nor is it developing commercial-scale hydrogen production plants: it is developing technologies that could be used to produce hydrogen if fuel cells become widely used. By building know-how and intellectual property in this technology, Shell has created an *option*. If economic, environmental, or political factors restrict hydrocarbon use and if fuel cells advance to the point of technical and commercial viability, then Shell could exercise that option by investing much larger amounts in commercial-scale hydrogen production.

In a world of uncertainty, where investments, once made, are irreversible, flexibility is valuable. Instead of committing to an entire project, there is virtue in breaking the project into a number of phases, where the decision of whether and how to embark on the next phase can be made in the light of prevailing circumstances and the learning gained from the previous stage of the project. Most large companies have a "phases and gates" approach to product development in which the development process is split into distinct "phases," at the end of which the project is reassessed before being allowed through the "gate." Such a phased approach creates the options to continue the project, to abandon it, to amend it, or to wait. Venture capitalists clearly recognize the value of growth options. In September 2009, Twitter—which earned almost no revenue and burnt cash at the rate of about $10 million a month—raised over $100 million in investment, implying a company valuation of $1 billion. These investors were buying an option on Twitter's ability to find a way of monetizing its massive online presence and thereby establish a profitable business. The emphasis that venture capitalists place on *scalability*—the potential to scale up or replicate a business should the initial launch be successful—similarly acknowledges the value of growth options. Strategy Capsule 2.5 addresses the calculation of real option values.

## Strategy as Options Management

For strategy formulation, our primary interest is how we can use the principles of option valuation to create shareholder value. There are two types of real option: growth options and flexibility options. *Growth options* allow a firm to make small initial investments in a number of future business opportunities but without committing to them. *Flexibility options* relate to the design of projects and plants that permit adaptation to different circumstances—flexible manufacturing systems allow different product models to be manufactured on a single production line. Individual projects can be designed to introduce both growth options and flexibility options. This means avoiding commitment to the complete project and introducing decision points at multiple stages, where the main options are to delay, modify, scale up, or abandon the project. Merck, an early adopter of option pricing, notes, "When you make an initial investment in a research project, you are paying an entry fee for a right, but you are not obligated to continue that research at a later stage."[32]

## STRATEGY CAPSULE 2.5
# Calculating Real Option Value

Application of real option value to investment projects and strategies has been limited by the complexity of the valuation techniques. Yet, even without getting into the mathematics needed to quantify option values, we can use the basic principles involved to understand the factors that determine option values and to recognize how projects and strategies can be designed in order to maximize their option values.

The early work on real option valuation adapted the Black–Scholes option-pricing formula developed for valuing financial options to the valuation of real investment projects.[a] Black–Scholes comprises six determinants of option value, each of which has an analogy in the valuation of a real option:

1  Stock price = The NPV of the project: a higher NPV increases option value

2  Exercise price = Investment cost: the higher the cost, the lower the option value

3  Uncertainty: for both financial and real options, uncertainty increases option value

4  Time to expiry: for both financial and real options, the longer the option lasts, the greater its value

5  Dividends = Decrease in the value of the investment over the option period: lowers option value

6  Interest rate: a higher interest rate increases option value by making deferral more valuable.[b]

However, the dominant methodology used for real option valuation is the binomial options pricing model. By allowing the sources of uncertainty and key decision points in a project to be modeled explicitly, the technique offers a more intuitive appreciation of the sources of option value. The analysis involves two main stages:

1  Create an event tree that shows the value of the project at each development period under two different scenarios.

2  Convert the event tree into a decision tree by identifying the key decision points on the event tree, typically the points where commitments of new funds to the project are required or where there is the option to defer development. Incremental project values at each stage can then be calculated for each decision point by working back from the final nodes of the decision tree (using a discount factor based upon the replicating portfolio technique). If the incremental project value at the initial stage exceeds the initial investment, proceed with the first phase, and similarly for each subsequent phase.[c]

***Notes:***

[a]See: F. Black and M. Scholes, "The Pricing of Options and Corporate Liabilities," *Journal of Political Economy* 81 (1993): 637–54.

[b]See: K. J. Leslie and M. P. Michaels, "The Real Power of Real Options," *McKinsey Quarterly Anthology: On Strategy* (Boston: McKinsey & Company, 2000). See also A. Dixit and R. Pindyck, "The Options Approach to Capital Investment," *Harvard Business Review* (May/June 1995): 105–15.

[c]This approach is developed in T. Copeland and P. Tufano, "A Real-world Way to Manage Real Options," *Harvard Business Review* (March 2004). See also T. Copeland, Developing Strategy Using Real Options (Monitor Company, October 2003).

In developing strategy, our main concern is with growth options. These might include:

- Platform investments. These are investments in core products or technologies that create a stream of additional business opportunities.[33] 3M's investment in nanotechnology offers the opportunity to create new products across a wide range of its businesses, from dental restoratives and drug-delivery systems to adhesives and protective coatings. Google's search engine and the huge internet traffic it draws has offered a platform for a large number of initiatives—not just search products but also a wide array of other software products and internet services (e.g., Gmail, Chrome, Android, Google+).[34]

- Strategic alliances and joint ventures, which are limited investments that offer options for the creation of whole new strategies.[35] Virgin Group has used joint ventures as the basis for creating a number of new businesses: with Stagecoach to create Virgin Rail, with AMP to create Virgin Money (financial services), with Deutsche Telecom to form Virgin Mobile. Shell has used joint ventures and alliances as a means of making initial investments in wind power, biodiesel fuel, solar power, and other forms of renewable energy.

- Organizational capabilities, which can also be viewed as options offering the potential to create competitive advantage across multiple products and businesses.[36] Apple's capability in combining hardware, software, aesthetics, and ergonomics to create products of exceptional user-friendliness has given it the option to expand into several new product areas: MP3 audio players, smartphones, tablet computers, and interactive TV.

## Summary

Chapter 1 introduced a framework for strategy analysis that provides the structure for Part II of this book. This chapter has explored the first component of that framework—the goals, values, and performance of the firm.

We have explored in some depth the difficult, and still contentious, issue of the appropriate goals for the firm. While each firm has a specific business purpose, common to all firms is the desire, and the necessity, to create value. How that value is defined and measured distinguishes those who argue that the firms should operate primarily in the interests of owners (shareholders) from those who argue for a stakeholder approach. Our approach has been pragmatic: in practice there is widespread convergence between shareholder and stakeholder interests and, where they diverge, the pressure of competition limits the scope for pursuing stakeholder interests at the expense of profit, hence my conclusion that long-run profit—or its equivalent, enterprise value—is appropriate both as an indicator of firm performance and as a guide to strategy formulation. We explored the relationships between value, profit, and cash flow and saw how the failings of shareholder value maximization resulted primarily from its misapplication.

The application of financial analysis to the assessment of firm performance is an essential component of strategic analysis. Financial analysis creates a basis for strategy formulation, first, by appraising overall firm performance and, second, by diagnosing the sources of unsatisfactory performance. Combining financial analysis and strategic analysis allows us to establish performance targets for companies and their business units.

Finally, we looked beyond the limits of our useful, yet simplistic, profit-oriented approach to firm performance and business strategy. We looked, first, at how the principles of corporate social responsibility could be incorporated within a firm's strategy to enhance its creation of both social and shareholder value. Second, we extended our analysis of value maximization to take account of the fact that strategy creates enterprise value not only by generating profit but also by creating real options.

Quizzes and flashcards to test yourself further are available in your interactive e-book at **www.wileyopenpage.com**

## Self-Study Questions

1.  Table 2.1 compares companies according to different profitability measures.

    a.  Which two of the six performance measures do you think are the most useful indicators of how well a company is being managed?

    b.  Is return on sales or return on equity a better basis on which to compare the performance of the companies listed?

    c.  Several companies are highly profitable yet have delivered very low returns to their shareholders. How is this possible?

2.  India's Tata Group is a diversified group. Some of its largest companies are: Tata Steel, Tata Motors, Tata Consultancy Services (IT), Tata Power (electricity generation), Tata Chemicals, Tata Tea, Indian Hotels, and Tata Communications. How do you think Tata Group's recent adoption of EVA as a performance management tool is likely to influence the way in which it allocates investment among the companies listed above?

3.  With regard to Strategy Capsule 2.2, what additional data would you seek and what additional analysis would you undertake to investigate further the reasons for UPS's superior profitability to FedEx?

4.  The CEO of a chain of pizza restaurants wishes to initiate a program of CSR to be funded by a 5% levy on the company's operating profit. The board of directors, fearing a negative shareholder reaction, is opposed to the plan. What arguments might the CEO use to persuade the board that CSR might be in the interests of shareholders, and what types of CSR initiatives might the program include to ensure that this was the case?

5.  Nike, a supplier of sports footwear and apparel, is interested in the idea that it could increase its stock market value by creating options for itself. What actions might Nike take that might generate option value?

# Notes

1. A. P. Sloan, *My Years at General Motors* (New York: Doubleday, 1963).
2. J. A. Schumpeter, *The Theory of Economic Development* (Cambridge, MA: Harvard University Press 1934).
3. See www.abelard.org/ford.
4. C. A. Montgomery, "Putting Leadership Back into Strategy," *Harvard Business Review* (January 2008): 54–60.
5. In this chapter, I use the term *value* in two distinct senses. Here I am referring to *economic value*, which is worth as measured in monetary units. I shall also be discussing values as moral principles or standards of behavior.
6. T. Donaldson and L. E. Preston, "The stakeholder theory of the corporation," *Academy of Management Review* 20 (1995): 65–91.
7. J. Figuero, S. Greco, and M. Ehrgott, *Multiple Criteria Decision Analysis: State of the Art Surveys* (Berlin: Springer, 2005).
8. M. C. Jensen, "Value Maximization, Stakeholder Theory, and the Corporate Objective Function," *Journal of Applied Corporate Finance* 22 (Winter 2010): 34.
9. M. B. Lieberman and N. Balasubramanian ("Measuring Value Creation and Its Distribution among Stakeholders of the Firm," Anderson School, UCLA, June 2007) outline a method for estimating aggregate stakeholder value through calculating the sum of consumer and producer surplus. However, the complexity and multiple assumptions of their method render it impractical as a management tool.
10. J. Helwege, V. Intintoli, and A. Zhang, "Voting with Their Feet or Activism? Institutional Investors' Impact on CEO Turnover," *Journal of Corporate Finance* (forthcoming 2012).
11. T. M. Jones, "Instrumental Stakeholder Theory: A Synthesis of Ethics and Economics," *Academy of Management Review* 20 (1995): 404–37.
12. M. Orlitzky, F. L. Schmidt, and S. L. Rynes, "Corporate Social and Financial Performance: A Meta-Analysis," *Organization Studies* 24 (Summer 2003): 403–41.
13. See www.sternstewart.com. See also J. L. Grant, *Foundations of Economic Value Added*, 2nd edn (New York: John Wiley & Sons, Ltd, 2003).
14. The cost of equity capital is calculated using the capital asset pricing model: Firm X's cost of equity = the risk-free rate of interest + a risk premium. The risk premium is the excess of the stock market rate of return over the risk-free rate multiplied by Firm X's beta coefficient (its measure of systematic risk). See T. Koller, M. Goedhart, and D. Wessels, *Valuation: Measuring and Managing the Value of Companies*, 5th edn (Hoboken, NJ: John Wiley & Sons, Inc., 2010), Chapter 11.
15. T. Koller, M. Goedhart, D. Wessels, *Valuation: Measuring and Managing the Value of Companies*, 5th edn (Hoboken, NJ: John Wiley & Sons, Inc., 2010).
16. F. Modigliani and M. H. Miller, "The Cost of Capital, Corporation Finance, and the Theory of Investments," *American Economic Review* 48 (1958): 261–97.
17. This distinction is made by K. Kaiser and S. D. Young, "Blue Line Management: What Value Creation Really Means," Insead Working Paper 2009/37/FIN/AC.
18. J. A. Kay and C. Meyer, "On the Application of Accounting Rates of Return," *Economic Journal* 96 (1986): 199–207.
19. R. S. Kaplan and D. P. Norton, "The Balanced Scorecard: Measures that Drive Performance," *Harvard Business Review* (January/February 1992): 71–9; R. S. Kaplan and D. P. Norton, "Using the Balanced Scorecard as a Strategic Management System," *Harvard Business Review* (January/February 1996): 75–85.
20. S. Chatterjee, "Enron's Incremental Descent into Bankruptcy: A Strategic and Organizational Analysis," *Long Range Planning* 36 (2003): 133–49.
21. J. Kay, *Obliquity* (London: Profile Books, 2010).
22. G. Bevan and C. Hood, "What's Measured Is What Matters: Targets and Gaming in the English Public Health Care System," *Public Administration* 84 (2006): 517–538.
23. M. Friedman, *Capitalism and Freedom* (Chicago: University of Chicago Press, 1963).
24. L. Bryan, "Enduring Ideas: The 7-S Framework," *McKinsey Quarterly* (March 2008).
25. J. Collins and J. Porras, "Building Your Company's Vision," *Harvard Business Review* (September/October 1996): 65–77.
26. W. T. Allen, "Our Schizophrenic Conception of the Business Corporation," *Cardozo Law Review* 14 (1992): 261–81.
27. A. Smith, *An Inquiry into the Nature and Causes of the Wealth of Nations*, 5th edn (London: Methuen & Co., 1905), Chapter 2.
28. A. de Geus, "The Living Company," *Harvard Business Review* (March/April 1997): 51–9.
29. M. E. Porter and M. R. Kramer, "Strategy and Society: The Link between Competitive Advantage and Corporate Social Responsibility," *Harvard Business Review* (December 2006): 78–92.
30. M. E. Porter and M. R. Kramer, "Creating Shared Value," *Harvard Business Review* (January 2011): 62–77.
31. C. K. Prahalad and S. L. Hart, "The Fortune at the Bottom of the Pyramid," *strategy + business* 26 (2002): 54–67; T. London and S. L. Hart, "Reinventing Strategies for Emerging Markets: Beyond the Transnational Model," *Journal of International Business Studies* 35 (2004): 350–370.
32. N. Nichols, "Scientific Management at Merck: An Interview with CFO Judy Lewent," *Harvard Business Review* (January/February 1994): 89–105.

33. B. Kogut and N. Kulatilaka, "Options Thinking and Platform Investments: Investing in Opportunity," *California Management Review* (Winter 1994): 52–69.

34. A. Gower and M. A. Cusamano, "How Companies Become Platform Leaders," *Sloan Management Review* (Winter 2008): 28–35.

35. T. Chi, "Option to Acquire or Divest a Joint Venture," *Strategic Management Journal* 21 (2000) 665–87.

36. B. Kogut and N. Kulatilaka, "Capabilities as Real Options," *Organization Science* 12 (2001) 744–58; R. G. McGrath, W. Furrier, and A. Mendel, "Real Options as Engines of Choice and Heterogeneity," *Academy of Management Review* 29 (2004): 86–101.

# 3 Industry Analysis: The Fundamentals

> When a management with a reputation for brilliance tackles a business with a reputation for poor fundamental economics, it is the reputation of the business that remains intact.
>
> —WARREN BUFFETT, CHAIRMAN, BERKSHIRE HATHAWAY

> The reinsurance business has the defect of being too attractive-looking to new entrants for its own good and will therefore always tend to be the opposite of, say, the old business of gathering and rendering dead horses that always tended to contain few and prosperous participants.
>
> —CHARLES T. MUNGER, CHAIRMAN, WESCO FINANCIAL CORP

## OUTLINE

## Introduction and Objectives

In this chapter and the next we explore the external environment of the firm. In Chapter 1 we observed that profound understanding of the competitive environment is a critical ingredient of a successful strategy. We also noted that business strategy is essentially a quest for profit. The primary task for this chapter is to identify the sources of profit in the external environment. The firm's proximate environment is its industry environment; hence our environmental analysis will focus on the firm's industry surroundings.

Industry analysis is relevant both to corporate-level and business-level strategy.

◆ Corporate strategy is concerned with deciding which industries the firm should be engaged in and how it should allocate its resources among them. Such decisions require assessment of the attractiveness of different industries in terms of their profit potential. The main objective of this chapter is to understand how the competitive structure of an industry determines its profitability.

◆ Business strategy is concerned with establishing competitive advantage. By analyzing customer needs and preferences and the ways in which firms compete to serve customers, we identify the general sources of competitive advantage in an industry—what we call *key success factors*.

By the time you have completed this chapter, you will be able to:

◆ appreciate that the firm's industry represents the core of its external environment and understand that its characteristics and dynamics are essential components of strategy analysis;

◆ recognize the main structural features of an industry and understand how they impact the intensity of competition and overall level of profitability in the industry;

◆ apply industry analysis to explain the level of profitability in an industry and predict how profitability is likely to change in the future;

◆ develop strategies that (a) position the firm most favorably in relation to competition and (b) influence industry structure in order to enhance industry attractiveness;

◆ define the boundaries of the industry within which a firm is located;

◆ identify opportunities for competitive advantage within an industry (key success factors).

## From Environmental Analysis to Industry Analysis

The business environment of the firm consists of all the external influences that impact its decisions and its performance. Given the vast number and range of external influences, how can managers hope to monitor, let alone analyze, environmental conditions? The starting point is some kind of system or framework for organizing information. Environmental influences can be classified by source, for example, into political, economic, social, and technological factors—what is known as *PEST analysis.* PEST analysis and similar approaches to macro-level environmental scanning can be useful in keeping a firm alert to what is happening in the world. The danger, however, is that continuous, systematic scanning and analysis of such a wide range of external influences is costly and may result in information overload.

The prerequisite for effective environmental analysis is to distinguish the vital from the merely important. To do this let us return to first principles in order to establish what features of a firm's external environment are relevant to its decisions. For the firm to make a profit it must create value for customers. Hence, it must understand its customers. Second, in creating value, the firm acquires goods and services from suppliers. Hence, it must understand its suppliers and manage relationships with them. Third, the ability to generate profitability depends on the intensity of competition among firms that vie for the same value-creating opportunities. Hence, the firm must understand competition. Thus, the core of the firm's business environment is formed by its relationships with three sets of players: customers, suppliers, and competitors. This is its industry environment.

This is not to say that macro-level factors such as general economic trends, changes in demographic structure, or social and political trends are unimportant for strategy analysis. These factors may be critical determinants of the threats and opportunities a company will face in the future. The key issue is how these more general environmental factors affect the firm's industry environment (Figure 3.1). Consider the threat of global warming. For most companies this is not an important strategic issue (at least, not for at least a decade). However, for those businesses most directly affected by changing weather patterns—farmers and insurance companies—and those subject to carbon taxes and environmental regulations—electricity generators and automobile producers—global warming is a vital issue. For these businesses, the key is to analyze the strategic implications of global warming for their particular industry. In the case of the automobile makers, what will be the impact on consumers and their preferences?

Will regulatory changes force a switch from private to public transportation? With regard to competition, will there be new entry by manufacturers of electric vehicles? Will the need for increased R & D cause the industry to consolidate?

If strategy is about identifying and exploiting sources of profit, then the starting point for industry analysis is the simple question "What determines the level of profit in an industry?"

In the last chapter we learned that for a firm to make profit it must create value for the customer. Value is created when the price the customer is willing to pay for

**FIGURE 3.1**   From environmental analysis to industry analysis

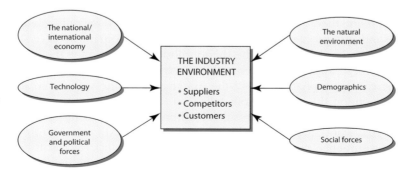

a product exceeds the costs incurred by the firm. But customer value does not translate directly into profit. The surplus of value over cost is distributed between customers and producers by the forces of competition. The stronger competition is among producers, the more of the surplus is received by customers as *consumer surplus* (the difference between the price they actually pay and the maximum price they would have been willing to pay) and the less is received by producers (as *producer surplus* or *economic rent*). A single supplier of umbrellas outside the Gare de Lyon on a wet Parisian morning can charge a price that fully exploits commuters' desire to keep dry. As more and more umbrella sellers arrive, so the price of umbrellas will be pushed closer to the wholesale cost.

However, the profit earned by Parisian umbrella sellers, or any other industry, does not just depend on the competition between them. It also depends upon their suppliers. If an industry has a powerful supplier—a single wholesaler of cheap, imported umbrellas—that supplier may be able to capture a major part of the value created in the local umbrella market.

Hence, the profits earned by the firms in an industry are determined by three factors:

- the value of the product to customers
- the intensity of competition
- the bargaining power of industry members relative to their suppliers and buyers.

Industry analysis brings all three factors into a single analytic framework.

## Analyzing Industry Attractiveness

Table 3.1 shows the profitability of different US industries. Some industries consistently earn high rates of profit; others fail to cover their cost of capital. The basic premise that underlies industry analysis is that the level of industry profitability is neither random nor the result of entirely industry-specific influences: it is determined by the systematic influences of the industry's structure. The pharmaceutical industry and the automobile industry not only supply very different products but also have very different structures, which make one highly profitable and the other a nightmare of price competition and weak margins.

Small markets can offer particular profit opportunities if they can be dominated by a single firm. Strategy Capsule 3.1 gives examples of such niche markets.

The underlying theory of how industry structure drives competitive behavior and determines industry profitability is provided by industrial organization (IO) economics. The two reference points are the theory of monopoly and the theory of perfect competition; these form end points of the spectrum of industry structures. While a monopolist can appropriate in profit the full amount of the value it creates, under perfect competition the rate of profit falls to a level that just covers firms' cost of capital. These outcomes are the result of differences in industry structure (Table 3.2). In the real world, industries fall between these two extremes. During the 1990s (before the resurgence of the Apple Mac and entry of Linux), Microsoft held a near monopoly of the market for PC operating systems. Foreign exchange trading is close

**TABLE 3.1** The profitability of US industries, 2000–2010

| Industry[1] | Median ROE (%)[2] | Leading companies |
|---|---|---|
| Tobacco | 33.5 | Philip Morris Intl., Altria, Reynolds American |
| Household and Personal Products | 27.8 | Procter & Gamble, Kimberly-Clark, Colgate-Palmolive |
| Pharmaceuticals | 20.5 | Pfizer, Johnson & Johnson, Merck |
| Food Consumer Products | 20.0 | PepsiCo, Kraft Foods, General Mills |
| Food Services | 19.9 | McDonald's, Yum! Brands, Starbucks |
| Medical Products and Equipment | 18.5 | Medtronic, Baxter International, Boston Scientific |
| Petroleum Refining | 17.6 | ExxonMobil, Chevron, ConocoPhillips |
| Mining, Crude Oil Production | 16.3 | Occidental Petroleum, Devon Energy |
| Securities | 15.9 | KKR, BlackRock, Charles Schwab |
| Chemicals | 15.7 | Dow Chemical, DuPont, PPG Industries |
| Aerospace and Defense | 15.7 | Boeing, United Technologies, Lockheed Martin |
| Construction and Farm Equipment | 14.5 | Caterpillar, Deere, Illinois Tool Works |
| IT Services | 14.1 | IBM, Computer Sciences, SAIC |
| Specialty Retailers (non-apparel) | 13.9 | Home Depot, Costco, Lowe's |
| Communications Equipment | 13.1 | Cisco Systems, Motorola, Qualcomm |
| Healthcare Insurance and Managed Care | 13.1 | United Health Group, WellPoint, Aetna |
| Commercial Banks | 12.4 | Bank of America, JPMorgan Chase, Citigroup, |
| Engineering, Construction | 12.3 | Fluor, Jacobs Engineering, KBR |
| Computers, Office Equipment | 12.1 | Hewlett-Packard, Apple, Dell Computer |
| Diversified Financials | 12.0 | General Electric, Fannie Mae |
| General Merchandisers | 11.6 | Wal-Mart, Target, Sears Holdings |
| Energy | 11.4 | AES, AEP, Constellation Energy, |
| Pipelines | 11.1 | Plains All American Pipeline, Enterprise Products, ONEOK |
| Utilities: Gas and Electric | 10.6 | Execon, Southern, NextEra |
| Packaging and Containers | 10.2 | Ball, Crown Holdings, Owens-Illinois |
| Automotive Retailing and Services | 9.8 | AutoNation, Penske, Hertz |
| Food and Drug Stores | 9.6 | CVS, Kroger, Walgreens |
| Insurance: Property and Casualty | 9.5 | Berkshire Hathaway, AIG, Allstate |
| Insurance: Life and Health | 8.7 | MetLife, Prudential, Aflac |
| Hotels, Casinos, Resorts | 8.5 | Marriott International, Caesars, Las Vegas Sands |
| Metals | 8.2 | Alcoa, US Steel, Nucor |
| Semiconductors and Electronic Components | 7.7 | Intel, Texas Instruments, Jabil Circuit |
| Forest and Paper Products | 7.3 | International Paper, Weyerhaeuser, Domtar |
| Food Production | 5.2 | Archer Daniels Midland, Tyson Foods, Smithfield Foods |
| Telecommunications | 5.8 | Verizon, AT&T, Sprint Nextel |
| Motor Vehicles and Parts | 4.4 | GM, Ford, Johnson Controls |
| Entertainment | 3.9 | Time Warner, Walt Disney, News Corp. |
| Airlines | −11.3 | AMR Corporation, United Airlines, Delta Air Lines |

**Notes:**
[1]Industries with fewer than five firms were excluded (with the exception of tobacco). Also omitted were industries that were substantially redefined during the period.
[2]Median ROE for each industry averaged across the 11 years (2000–2010).

**Source:** Data from Fortune 500.

---

**STRATEGY CAPSULE 3.1**

## Chewing Tobacco, Sausage Skins, and Slot Machines: The Joys of Niche Markets

**UST** is a subsidiary of Altria, the largest tobacco company in the US, which supplies "smokeless tobacco" (chewing tobacco and snuff) with brands such as Skoal, Copenhagen, and Red Seal. In 2010, Altria earned an operating margin of 52% on its sales of smokeless tobacco. Before it was acquired by Altria, UST was the most profitable company in the S&P 500, with an average ROCE (operating profit as percentage of capital employed) of 63% during 2003–2008. What's the secret of UST's profitability? It accounts for 55% of the US market for smokeless tobacco, and its long-established brands, its distribution through thousands of small retail outlets, and government restrictions on advertising tobacco products create formidable barriers to entry into this market.

**Devro plc**, based in the Scottish village of Moodiesburn, is the world's leading supplier of collagen sausage skins ("casings"). "From the British 'Banger' to the Chinese Lap Cheong, from the French Merguez

to the South American Chorizo, Devro has a casing to suit all product types." Its overall world market share is around 60%. During 2009–2010, its ROCE averaged 18.7%, significantly above the average for UK (FTSE 100) companies.

**International Game Technology** (IGT) based in Reno, Nevada is the world's dominant manufacturer of slot machines for casinos. IGT maintains its 70% US market share through close relations with casino operators and a continuous flow of new products. With heavy investment in R & D, new product saturation, tight control over distribution and servicing, and a policy of leasing rather than selling machines, IGT offers little opportunity to rivals. During 2007–2011, IGT earned an average ROE of 23.1% and ROCE of 19.0%, despite severe recession in the US casino industry.

*Sources:* www.altria.com, www.devro.com, and www.igt.com.

---

**TABLE 3.2**  The spectrum of industry structures

|  | Perfect Competition | Oligopoly | Duopoly | Monopoly |
|---|---|---|---|---|
| Concentration | Many firms | A few firms | Two firms | One firm |
| Entry and exit barriers | None | Significant |  | High |
| Product differentiation | Homogeneous product (commodity) | Potential for product differentiation |  |  |
| Information availability | No impediments to information flow | Imperfect availability of information |  |  |

to being perfectly competitive, while most manufacturing and service industries are oligopolies: they are dominated by a small number of major companies.

### Porter's Five Forces of Competition Framework

Table 3.2 identifies four structural variables influencing competition and profitability. In practice there are many features of an industry that determine the intensity of competition and the level of profitability. The most widely used framework for classifying

**FIGURE 3.2**   Porter's five forces of competition framework

and analyzing these factors was developed by Michael Porter of Harvard Business School.[1] Porter's five forces of competition framework views the profitability of an industry (as indicated by its rate of return on capital relative to its cost of capital) as determined by five sources of competitive pressure. These five forces of competition include three sources of "horizontal" competition: competition from substitutes, competition from entrants, and competition from established rivals; and two sources of "vertical" competition: the power of suppliers and the power of buyers (Figure 3.2).

The strength of each of these competitive forces is determined by a number of key structural variables, as shown in Figure 3.3.

## Competition from Substitutes

The price that customers are willing to pay for a product depends, in part, on the availability of substitute products. The absence of close substitutes for a product, as in the case of gasoline or cigarettes, means that consumers are comparatively insensitive to price (demand is inelastic with respect to price). The existence of close substitutes means that customers will switch to substitutes in response to price increases for the product (demand is elastic with respect to price). The internet has provided a new source of substitute competition that has proved devastating for a number of established industries. Travel agencies, newspapers, and telecommunication providers have all suffered severe competition from internet-based substitutes.

The extent to which substitutes depress prices and profits depends on the propensity of buyers to substitute between alternatives. This, in turn, depends on their price-performance characteristics. If city-center to city-center travel between Washington and New York is 50 minutes quicker by air than by train and the average traveler values time at $30 an hour, the implication is that the train will be competitive at fares of $25 below those charged by the airlines. The more complex the product and the more difficult it is to discern performance differences, the lower

**FIGURE 3.3**   The structural determinants of the five forces of competition

the extent of substitution by customers on the basis of price differences. The failure of low-priced imitations of leading perfumes to establish significant market share reflects consumers' difficulty in recognizing the performance characteristics of different fragrances.

## Threat of Entry

If an industry earns a return on capital in excess of its cost of capital, it will act as a magnet to firms outside the industry. If the entry of new firms is unrestricted, the rate of profit will fall toward its competitive level. Increased health awareness in the US has encouraged increasing demand for fruit juice and smoothies. However, low entry barriers have resulted in about 4,000 new juice and smoothie bars being established since 2000 resulting in market saturation and a high rate of business failures.[2] Why is it that my wife, a psychotherapist, earns much less than our niece, a recently qualified medical doctor? Barriers to entry are one factor. In psychotherapy there are multiple accrediting bodies and limited state licensing, hence the entry barriers to psychotherapy are much lower than in medicine.

Threat of entry rather than actual entry may be sufficient to ensure that established firms constrain their prices to the competitive level. Only American Airlines offers a direct service between Dallas/Fort Worth and Santa Barbara, California, for example. Yet American may be unwilling to exploit its monopoly power to the full if Southwest or another airline can easily extend its routes to cover the same two cities. An industry where no barriers to entry or exit exist is contestable: prices and profits tend toward the competitive level, regardless of the number of firms within the industry.[3] Contestability depends on the absence of sunk costs—investments whose value cannot be recovered on exit. An absence of sunk costs makes an industry vulnerable to "hit and run" entry whenever established firms raise their prices above the competitive level.

In most industries, however, new entrants cannot enter on equal terms with those of established firms. A *barrier to entry* is any advantage that established firms have over entrants. The height of a barrier to entry is usually measured as the unit cost disadvantage faced by would-be entrants. The principal sources of barriers to entry are discussed below.

*Capital Requirements*   The capital costs of becoming established in an industry can be so large as to discourage all but the largest companies. The duopoly of Boeing and Airbus in large passenger jets is protected by the huge capital costs of establishing R & D, production, and service facilities for supplying these planes. Likewise with the business of launching commercial satellites: the costs of developing rockets and launch facilities make new entry highly unlikely. In other industries, entry costs can be modest. One reason why the e-commerce boom of the late 1990s ended in financial disaster for most participants is that the initial setup costs of new internet-based ventures were typically very low. Across the service sector more generally, start-up costs tend to be low. For example, start-up costs for a franchised pizza outlet begin at $150,000 for a Domino's and $638,000 for a Pizza Hut.[4]

*Economies of Scale*   The sources of high capital requirements for new entrants are also sources of scale economies. In industries that require large, indivisible investments in production facilities or technology or research or marketing, cost efficiency requires amortizing these indivisible costs over a large volume of output. The problem for new entrants is that they typically enter with a low market share and, hence, are forced to accept high unit costs. A major source of scale economies is new product development costs. Airbus's A380 superjumbo cost about $18 billion to develop and must sell about 400 planes to break even. Once Airbus had committed to the project, then Boeing was effectively excluded from the superjumbo segment of the market. In automobiles, scale economies in product development and purchasing mean that cost efficiency for a full-range automaker requires producing at least four million vehicles a year.

*Absolute Cost Advantages*   Established firms may have a unit cost advantage over entrants, irrespective of scale. Absolute cost advantages often result from the acquisition of low-cost sources of raw materials. Established oil and gas producers, such as Saudi Aramco and Gazprom, which have access to the world's biggest and most accessible reserves, have an unassailable cost advantage over more recent entrants such as Cairn Energy and BG Group. Absolute cost advantages may also result from economies of learning. Intel, AMD, and IBM's dominance of the market for advanced microprocessors for computers and video game consoles arises in part from the cost advantage they derive from their wealth of experience.

*Product Differentiation*   In an industry where products are differentiated, established firms possess the advantages of brand recognition and customer loyalty. The percentage of US consumers loyal to a single brand varies from under 30% in batteries, canned vegetables, and garbage bags, up to 61% in toothpaste, 65% in mayonnaise and 71% in cigarettes.[5] New entrants to such markets must spend disproportionately heavily on advertising and promotion to gain levels of brand awareness and brand goodwill similar to those of established companies. One study found that, compared to early entrants, late entrants into consumer goods markets incurred additional advertising and promotional costs amounting to 2.12% of sales revenue.[6]

*Access to Channels of Distribution*   For many new suppliers of consumer goods, the principal barrier to entry is likely to be gaining distribution. Limited capacity within distribution channels (e.g., shelf space), risk aversion by retailers, and the fixed costs associated with carrying an additional product result in retailers being reluctant to carry a new manufacturer's product. The battle for supermarket shelf space between the major food processors (typically involving "slotting fees" to reserve shelf space) further disadvantages new entrants. One of the most important competitive impacts of the internet has been allowing new businesses to circumvent barriers to distribution.

*Governmental and Legal Barriers*   Economists from the Chicago School claim that the only effective barriers to entry are those created by government. In taxicabs, banking, telecommunications, and broadcasting, entry usually requires a license from a public authority. From medieval times to the present day, companies and favored individuals have benefitted from governments granting them an exclusive right to ply a particular trade or offer a particular service. In knowledge-intensive industries, patents, copyrights, and other legally protected forms of intellectual property are major barriers to entry. In the pharmaceutical industry, the major players seek to delay entry by generic drug makers by extending their original patents through changes in dosage and delivery modes. Regulatory requirements and environmental and safety standards often put new entrants at a disadvantage in comparison with established firms because compliance costs tend to weigh more heavily on newcomers.

*Retaliation*   Barriers to entry also depend on the entrants' expectations as to possible retaliation by established firms. Retaliation against a new entrant may take the form of aggressive price-cutting, increased advertising, sales promotion, or litigation. The major airlines have a long history of retaliation against low-cost entrants. Southwest and other budget airlines have alleged that selective price cuts by American and other major airlines amounted to predatory pricing designed to prevent its entry into new routes.[7] To avoid retaliation by incumbents, new entrants may seek initial small-scale entry into less visible market segments. When Toyota, Nissan, and Honda first entered the US auto market, they targeted the small-car segments, partly because this was a segment that had been written off by the Detroit Big Three as inherently unprofitable.[8]

*The Effectiveness of Barriers to Entry*   Industries protected by high entry barriers tend to earn above-average rates of profit.[9] Capital requirements and advertising appear to be particularly effective impediments to entry.[10] The effectiveness of barriers to entry depends on the resources and capabilities that potential entrants possess. Barriers that are effective against new companies may be ineffective against established firms that are diversifying from other industries.[11] Google has used its massive web presence as a platform for entering a number of other markets, including Microsoft's seemingly impregnable position in browsers.

## Rivalry between Established Competitors

In most industries, the major determinant of the overall state of competition and the general level of profitability is competition among the firms within the industry. In some industries, firms compete aggressively—sometimes to the extent that prices are pushed below the level of costs and industry-wide losses are incurred. In other industries, price competition is muted and rivalry focuses on advertising, innovation, and other non-price dimensions. The intensity of competition between established firms is the result of interactions between six factors. Let us look at each of them.

*Concentration*  **Seller concentration** refers to the number and size distribution of firms competing within a market. It is most commonly measured by the *concentration ratio*: the combined market share of the leading producers. For example, the four-firm concentration ratio (CR4) is the market share of the four largest producers. In markets dominated by a single firm (for example P&G's Gillette in razor blades, Apple in MP3 players, or Altria in the US smokeless tobacco market), the dominant firm can exercise considerable discretion over the prices it charges. Where a market is dominated by a small group of leading companies (an oligopoly), price competition may also be restrained, either by outright collusion or, more commonly, by "parallelism" of pricing decisions.[12] Thus, in markets dominated by two companies, such as soft drinks (Coca-Cola and Pepsi), news weeklies (*Time* and *Newsweek*), and antivirus software (Symantec and McAfee), prices tend to be similar and competition focuses on advertising, promotion, and product development. As the number of firms supplying a market increases, coordination of prices becomes more difficult and the likelihood that one firm will initiate price-cutting increases. However, despite the frequent observation that the exit of a competitor reduces price competition, while the entry of a new competitor stimulates it, there is little systematic evidence that seller concentration increases profitability. Richard Schmalensee concludes that: "The relation, if any, between seller concentration and profitability is weak statistically and the estimated effect is usually small."[13]

*Diversity of Competitors*  The extent to which a group of firms can avoid price competition in favor of collusive pricing practices depends on how similar they are in their origins, objectives, costs, and strategies. The cozy atmosphere of the US auto industry prior to the advent of import competition was greatly assisted by the similarities of the companies in terms of cost structures, strategies, and top management mindsets. The intense competition that affects the car markets of Europe and North America today is partly due to the different national origins, costs, strategies, and management styles of the competing firms. Similarly, the key challenge faced by OPEC is agreeing and enforcing output quotas among member countries that are sharply different in terms of objectives, production costs, politics, and religion.

*Product Differentiation*   The more similar the offerings among rival firms, the more willing are customers to switch between them and the greater is the inducement for firms to cut prices to boost sales. Where the products of rival firms are virtually indistinguishable, the product is a commodity and price is the sole basis for competition. Commodity industries such as agriculture, mining, and petrochemicals tend to be plagued by price wars and low profits. By contrast, in industries where products are highly differentiated (perfumes, pharmaceuticals, restaurants, management consulting services), price competition tends to be weak, even though there may be many firms competing.

*Excess Capacity and Exit Barriers*   Why does industry profitability tend to fall so drastically during periods of recession? The key is the balance between demand and capacity. Unused capacity encourages firms to offer price cuts to attract new business. Excess capacity may be cyclical (e.g., the boom–bust cycle in the semiconductor industry); it may also be part of a structural problem resulting from overinvestment and declining demand. In these latter situations, the key issue is whether excess capacity will leave the industry. **Barriers to exit** are costs associated with capacity leaving an industry. Where resources are durable and specialized, and where employees are entitled to job protection, barriers to exit may be substantial.[14] In the European and North American auto industry, excess capacity together with high exit barriers have devastated industry profitability. Conversely, rapid demand growth creates capacity shortages that boost margins. Expanding world trade, fueled by the growth of China, pushed up charter rates of large bulk carriers ("Capesizes") from under $18,000 a day at the beginning of 2003 to a peak of $233,988 per day on June 5, 2008. With the onset of global recession and fleet expansion by ship owners, rates declined precipitously to a mere $2,773 a day by November 26, 2008.[15] On average, companies in growing industries earn higher profits than companies in slow-growing or declining industries (Figure 3.4).

**FIGURE 3.4**   The impact of growth on profitability

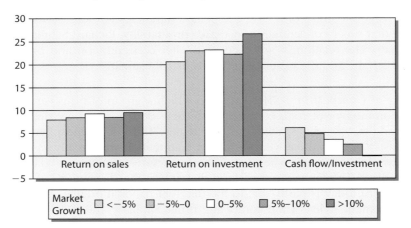

**Source:** R. D. Buzzell and B. T. Gale, *The PIMS Principles* (New York: Free Press, 1987): 56–7.

*Cost Conditions: Scale Economies and the Ratio of Fixed to Variable Costs*   When excess capacity causes price competition, how low will prices go? The key factor is cost structure. Where fixed costs are high relative to variable costs, firms will take on marginal business at any price that covers variable costs. The incredible volatility of bulk shipping rates reflects the fact that almost all the costs of operating bulk carriers are fixed. Similarly, in the airline industry the emergence of excess capacity almost invariably leads to price wars and industry-wide losses. The willingness of airlines to offer heavily discounted tickets on flights with low bookings reflects the very low variable costs of filling empty seats. "Cyclical" stocks are characterized not only by cyclical demand but also by a high ratio of fixed to variable costs, which means that fluctuations in revenues are amplified into much bigger fluctuations in profits.

Scale economies may also encourage companies to compete aggressively on price in order to gain the cost benefits of greater volume. If scale efficiency in the auto industry means producing four million cars a year, a level that is currently achieved by only five companies, the outcome is a battle for market share as each firm tries to achieve critical mass.

## Bargaining Power of Buyers

The firms in an industry compete in two types of markets: in the markets for inputs and the markets for outputs. In input markets firms purchase raw materials, components, and financial and labor services. In the markets for outputs, firms sell their goods and services to customers (who may be distributors, consumers, or other manufacturers). In both markets the transactions create value for both buyers and sellers. How this value is shared between them in terms of profitability depends on their relative economic power. Let us deal first with output markets. The strength of buying power that firms face from their customers depends on two sets of factors: buyers' price sensitivity and relative bargaining power.

*Buyers' Price Sensitivity*   The extent to which buyers are sensitive to the prices charged by the firms in an industry depends on four main factors:

- The greater the importance of an item as a proportion of total cost, the more sensitive buyers will be about the price they pay. Beverage manufacturers are highly sensitive to the costs of aluminum cans because this is one of their largest single cost items. Conversely, most companies are not sensitive to the fees charged by their auditors, since auditing costs are a tiny fraction of total company expenses.
- The less differentiated the products of the supplying industry, the more willing the buyer is to switch suppliers on the basis of price. The manufacturers of T-shirts and light bulbs have much more to fear from Wal-Mart's buying power than have the suppliers of perfumes.
- The more intense the competition among buyers, the greater their eagerness for price reductions from their sellers. As competition in the world automobile industry has intensified, so component suppliers face greater pressures for lower prices.
- The more critical an industry's product to the quality of the buyer's product or service, the less sensitive are buyers to the prices they are charged. The

buying power of personal computer manufacturers relative to the manufacturers of microprocessors (Intel and AMD) is limited by the vital importance
of these components to the functionality of PCs.

*Relative Bargaining Power*   Bargaining power rests, ultimately, on the refusal to
deal with the other party. The balance of power between the two parties to a transaction
depends on the credibility and effectiveness with which each makes this threat. The
key issue is the relative cost that each party sustains as a result of the transaction
not being consummated. A second issue is each party's expertise in managing its
position. Several factors influence the bargaining power of buyers relative to that of
sellers:

- Size and concentration of buyers relative to suppliers. The smaller the number of buyers and the bigger their purchases, the greater the cost of losing
  one. Because of their size, health maintenance organizations can purchase
  healthcare from hospitals and doctors at much lower costs than can individual patients. Empirical studies show that buyer concentration lowers prices
  and profits in the supplying industry.[16]
- Buyers' information. The better-informed buyers are about suppliers and their
  prices and costs, the better they are able to bargain. Doctors and lawyers do
  not normally display the prices they charge, nor do traders in the bazaars of
  Marrakesh or Chennai. Keeping customers ignorant of relative prices is an effective constraint on their buying power. But knowing prices is of little value if the
  quality of the product is unknown. In the markets for haircuts, interior design,
  and management consulting, the ability of buyers to bargain over price is limited by uncertainty over the precise attributes of the product they are buying.
- Ability to integrate vertically. In refusing to deal with the other party, the
  alternative to finding another supplier or buyer is to do it yourself. Large
  food-processing companies such as Heinz and Campbell Soup have reduced
  their dependence on the manufacturers of metal cans by manufacturing their
  own. The leading retail chains have increasingly displaced their suppliers'
  brands with their own-brand products. Backward integration need not necessarily occur—a credible threat may suffice.

## Bargaining Power of Suppliers

Analysis of the determinants of relative power between the producers in an industry
and their suppliers is precisely analogous to analysis of the relationship between
producers and their buyers. The only difference is that it is now the firms in the
industry that are the buyers and the producers of inputs that are the suppliers. The
key issues are the ease with which the firms in the industry can switch between different input suppliers and the relative bargaining power of each party.

Because raw materials, semi-finished products, and components are often commodities supplied by small companies to large manufacturing companies, their suppliers usually lack bargaining power. Hence, commodity suppliers often seek to
boost their bargaining power through cartelization (e.g., OPEC, the International
Coffee Organization, and farmers' marketing cooperatives). Conversely, the suppliers
of complex, technically sophisticated components may be able to exert considerable

bargaining power. The dismal profitability of the personal computer industry may be attributed to the power exercised by the suppliers of key components (processors, disk drives, LCD screens) and the dominant supplier of operating systems (Microsoft).

Labor unions are important sources of supplier power. US industries where over 60% of employees are unionized earned a return on investment that was five percentage points lower than industries where less than 35% of employees were unionized. If its employees are unionized, as in airlines and automobiles, a business's profitability is reduced.[17]

## Applying Industry Analysis to Forecasting Industry Profitability

Once we understand how industry structure drives competition, which, in turn, determines industry profitability, we can apply this analysis to forecast industry profitability in the future.

### Identifying Industry Structure

The first stage of any industry analysis is to identify the key elements of the industry's structure. In principle, this is a simple task. It requires identifying who are the main players—the producers, the customers, the input suppliers, and the producers of substitute goods—then examining some of the key structural characteristics of each of these groups that will determine competition and bargaining power.

In most manufacturing industries identifying the main groups of players is straightforward; in other industries, particularly in service industries, mapping the industry can be more difficult. Consider the US television broadcasting industry. Where do we draw the industry boundaries? Is there a single TV distribution industry or do we identify separate industries for TV airwaves broadcasting, cable TV, and satellite TV? In terms of identifying buyers and sellers we see that there the industry has quite a complex value chain that includes the producers of TV shows, the networks, and cable channels that put together program schedules, and local TV stations and cable companies that undertake final distribution. The industry has two types of buyer: viewers and advertisers. Additional complexity is created by the fact that some companies are vertically integrated across several stages of the value chain—thus, network broadcasters such as Fox and NBC are backward integrated into TV production and forward integrated into final distribution through ownership of local TV stations. We shall return to issues of industry definition later in this chapter.

### Forecasting Industry Profitability

We can use industry analysis to understand why profitability has been low in some industries and high in others but, ultimately, our interest is not to explain the past but to predict the future. Investment decisions made today will commit resources to an industry for years—often for a decade or more—hence, it is critical that we are able to predict what level of returns the industry is likely to offer in the future. Current profitability is a poor indicator of future profitability—industries such as newspapers, solar (photovoltaic) panels, and mobile phone handsets have suffered catastrophic declines in profitability. Conversely, several industries where returns were low—steel, metals mining, and several other "commodity industries"—have experienced remarkable revivals in profitability over the past decade. However, if an industry's profitability is determined by the structure of that industry then we can use observations of the structural trends in an industry to forecast the likely changes in competition and profitability. Changes in industry structure tend to be the result of fundamental shifts in customer buying behavior, technology, and firm strategies; these can often be anticipated well in advance of their impacts on competition and profitability.

To predict the future profitability of an industry, our analysis proceeds in three stages:

1  Examine how the industry's current and recent levels of competition and profitability are a consequence of its present structure.

2  Identify the trends that are changing the industry's structure. Is the industry consolidating? Are new players seeking to enter? Are the industry's products becoming more differentiated or more commoditized? Will additions to industry capacity outstrip growth of demand?

3  Identify how these structural changes will affect the five forces of competition and resulting profitability of the industry. Will the changes in industry structure cause competition to intensify or to weaken? Rarely do all the structural changes move competition in a consistent direction, typically some factors will cause competition to increase; others will cause competition to moderate. Hence, determining the overall impact on profitability tends to be a matter of judgment.

Strategy Capsule 3.2 discusses the outlook for profitability in the wireless handset industry.

## Using Industry Analysis to Develop Strategy

Once we understand how industry structure influences competition, which in turn determines industry profitability, we can use this knowledge to develop firm strategies. First, we can develop strategies that influence industry structure in order to moderate competition; second, we can position the firm to shelter it from the ravages of competition.

### Strategies to Alter Industry Structure

Understanding how the structural characteristics of an industry determine the intensity of competition and the level of profitability provides a basis for identifying opportunities for changing industry structure to alleviate competitive pressures. The first issue is to identify the key structural features of an industry that are responsible for depressing profitability. The second is to consider which of these structural features are amenable to change through appropriate strategic initiatives. For example:

● The remarkable profit revival in the world's steel industry during this century was mainly the result of rising demand from China; however, it was also

**STRATEGY CAPSULE 3.2**

# The Future of the Wireless Handset Industry

Wireless telephony has been one of the greatest growth industries of the past two decades—and almost as lucrative for the handset makers as for the service providers. During the 1990s, growth of handset sales in North America, Europe, and Japan averaged close to 50% each year and generated massive profits and shareholder value for the early leaders, Motorola and Nokia.

The current decade has witnessed a profound change in competition and margins. Despite continued demand growth (especially in emerging markets), profitability has fallen. During 2000–2005, the industry leaders—Nokia, Motorola, Sony-Ericsson, Samsung, LG, and Siemens—earned an average operating margin of 23% on their sales of mobile devices. By 2009, the top-seven suppliers (Nokia, Samsung, Apple, LG, RIM, Sony-Ericsson, and Motorola) were earning an average operating margin of 4% (although Apple was highly profitable, most of the others were loss making).

The structural changes undermining industry profitability included new entry—several Chinese and Taiwanese contact manufacturers—including HTC,

Huawei, ZTE, BenQ—introduced branded phones. As mature markets became saturated, so excess capacity emerged throughout the industry, which, in turn, reinforced the buying power of the major distributors of phones, the wireless service companies.

During 2012–2016, competition and profitability will be affected by several factors:

◆ New entry seems likely to continue. In the smartphone market, the availability of the Android platform will increase the number of firms competing in this segment.

◆ Most emerging markets, the BRIC countries in particular, are likely to become saturated.

◆ Commoditization is likely to threaten not just the low end of the market but also the smartphone market through the adoption of the Android platform.

◆ Mergers among telecom service providers will increase their buying power.

supported by the rapid consolidation of the industry, led by Mittal's merger with Arcelor, which was followed by the creation of Hebei Iron and Steel (China), Tata Steel-Corus (India/UK), and Nippon-Sumitomo (Japan).

- Excess capacity was a major problem in the European petrochemicals industry during the 1970s and 1980s. Through a series of bilateral plant exchanges, each company built a leading position within a particular product area.[18]

- In the US airline industry, the major airlines have struggled to change an unfavorable industry structure. In the absence of significant product differentiation, the airlines have used frequent-flyer schemes to build customer loyalty. Through hub-and-spoke route systems, the companies have achieved dominance of particular airports: American at Dallas/Fort Worth, US Airways at Charlotte NC, and Northwest at Detroit and Memphis. Mergers and alliances have reduced the numbers of competitors on many routes.[19]

- Building entry barriers is a vital strategy for preserving high profitability in the long run. A primary goal of the American Medical Association has been to maintain the incomes of its members by controlling the numbers of doctors trained in the US and imposing barriers to the entry of doctors from overseas.

The idea of firms reshaping their industries to their own advantage has been developed by Michael Jacobides. He begins with the premise that industries are in a state of continual evolution and that all firms, even quite small ones, have the potential to influence the development of industry structure to suit their own interests—thereby achieving what he calls *architectural advantage*.[20] Jacobides encourages firms to look broadly at their industry—to see their entire value chain and links with firms producing complementary goods and services. The key is then to identify "bottlenecks"—activities where scarcity and the potential for control offer superior opportunities for profit. Architectural advantages results from three sources:

- Creating one's own bottleneck: Apple's dominance of the music download market through iTunes is achieved through a digital rights management (DRM) strategy that effectively locks in consumers' through the incompatibility of its music files with other MP3 formats.
- Relieving bottlenecks in other parts of the value chain: Google developed Android to prevent other firms from gaining a bottleneck in operating systems for mobile devices which might have threatened Google's ability to transfer its dominance of search services from fixed to mobile devices.
- Redefining roles and responsibilities in the industries: IKEA's ability to become the world's biggest and most successful supplier of furniture was based upon a strategy which required a transfer of furniture assembly from furniture manufacturers to consumers.[21]

## Positioning the Company

Recognizing and understanding the competitive forces that a firm faces within its industry allows managers to position the firm where competitive forces are weakest. The record industry, once reliant on sales of CDs, has been devastated by the substitute competition in the form of digital downloads, piracy, and file sharing. Yet not all segments of the recorded music business have been equally affected. The old are less inclined to turn to digital downloading than younger listeners are, with the result that classical music, country, and golden oldies have become comparatively more attractive than pop and hip hop genres.

Porter describes the success of US truck-maker Paccar in sheltering itself from the bargaining power of fleet buyers. By focusing on the preferences of independent owner-operators (e.g., by providing superior sleeping cabins, higher-specification seats, a roadside assistance program) Paccar has consistently been able to earn the higher rate of return in the industry.[22]

Effective positioning requires the firm to anticipate changes in the competitive forces likely to affect the industry. Traditional book retailing has been devastated by online retailers such as Amazon and e-books. The survivors are those that have positioned themselves to avoid these powerful competitive forces, for example by creating new revenue sources such as cafes and events for which admission is charged.

# Defining Industries: Where to Draw the Boundaries

In our earlier discussion of the structure of the television broadcasting industry, I noted that a key challenge in industry analysis is defining the relevant industry. The Standard Industrial Classification (SIC) offers an official guide, but this provides limited practical assistance. Suppose Jaguar—the British-based luxury carmaker, now part of the Tata Group—is assessing its future prospects. In analyzing competition and forecasting industry profitability, should it consider itself part of the "motor vehicles and equipment" industry (SIC 371), the automobile industry (SIC 3712), or the luxury car industry? Should it view its industry as national (UK), regional (Europe), or global?

## Industries and Markets

The first issue is clarifying what we mean by the term *industry*. Economists define an industry as a group of firms that supplies a market. Hence, a close correspondence exists between markets and industries. So, what's the difference between analyzing industry structure and analyzing market structure? The principal difference is that industry analysis, notably five forces analysis, looks at industry profitability being determined by competition in two markets: product markets and input markets.

Everyday usage makes a bigger distinction between industries and markets. Typically, *industries* are identified with relatively broad sectors, whereas *markets* are related to specific products. Thus, the firms within the packaging industry compete in many distinct product markets—glass containers, steel cans, aluminum cans, paper cartons, plastic containers, and so on.

Similar issues arise in relation to geographical boundaries. From an economist's viewpoint, the US automobile industry would denote all companies supplying the US auto market, irrespective of their location. In everyday usage, the term *US auto industry* typically refers to auto manufacturers located within the US (about 14 companies), and is often restricted to US-owned automakers (Ford and General Motors).

To identify and define an industry, it makes sense to start with the idea of a market: which firms compete to supply a particular product or service? At the outset, this approach may lead us to question conventional concepts of industry boundaries. For example, what is the industry commonly referred to as *banking*? Institutions called *banks* supply a number of different products and services each comprising different sets of competitors. The most basic distinction is between retail banking, corporate (and wholesale) banking, and investment banking. Each of these can be disaggregated into several different product markets. Retail banking comprises deposit taking, transaction services, credit cards, and mortgage lending. Investment banking includes corporate finance and underwriting, trading, and advisory services (such as mergers and acquisitions).

## Defining Markets: Substitution in Demand and Supply

The central issue in defining industries is to establish who is competing with whom. To do this we need to draw upon the principle of *substitutability*. There are two dimensions to this: substitutability on the demand side and substitutability on the supply side.

Let us consider once more the market within which Jaguar competes. Starting with the demand side, are customers willing to substitute only between Jaguars and other luxury brands or are they willing to substitute between Jaguars and mass-market brands on the basis of price difference? If the former, Jaguar's relevant industry is the luxury car industry; if the latter, Jaguar is part of the auto industry. What about substitution between Jaguars and types of vehicle? If Jaguar customers are unwilling to substitute a Jaguar for a truck or a motorcycle on the basis of price, then Jaguar should not be viewed as part of the motor vehicles industry.

But this fails to take account of substitutability on the supply side. If manufacturers were able to switch their production from family sedans to luxury cars and if Jaguar could enter other parts of the automobile market, then, on the basis of supply-side substitutability, we could regard Jaguar as part of the broader automobile industry. The same logic can be used to define the major domestic appliances as an industry. Although consumers are unwilling to substitute between refrigerators and dishwashers, manufacturers can use the same manufacturing plants and distribution channels for different appliances.

The same considerations apply to geographical boundaries. Should Jaguar view itself as competing in a single global market or in a series of separate national or regional markets? The criterion here again is substitutability. If customers are willing and able to substitute cars available on different national markets, or if manufacturers are willing and able to divert their output among different countries to take account of differences in margins, then a market is global. The key test of the geographical boundaries of a market is price: if price differences for the same product between different locations tend to be eroded by demand-side and supply-side substitution, then these locations lie within a single market.

In practice, drawing the boundaries of markets and industries is a matter of judgment that depends on the purposes and context of the analysis. If Tata is considering the pricing and market positioning of its Jaguar cars, it must take a micro-level approach that defines markets in terms of individual models and individual countries. In considering decisions over investments in technology, component plants, and new products, Tata will view Jaguar as competing in the global automobile industry. The longer term are the decisions being considered, the more broadly should we define the relevant industry—substitutability is higher in the long run than in the short term.

Second, the boundaries of a market or industry are seldom clear-cut. The market in which an offering competes is a continuum rather than a bounded space. Thus, we may view the competitive market of Disneyland, Anaheim as a set of concentric circles. The closest competitor is Universal Studios Tour. Slightly more distant are Sea World and Six Flags. Further still might be a trip to Las Vegas, or a skiing weekend. Beyond these would be the broader leisure market that might include cinemas, beach vacations, and video games.

For the purposes of applying the five forces framework, industry definition is seldom critical. We define an industry "box" within which industry rivals compete, but because we include competitive forces outside the industry box, notably entrants and substitutes, the precise boundaries of the industry box are not greatly important. If we define Disneyland as competing within the broad entertainment industry, then beach and ski resorts are rivals; if we define Disneyland as competing in the theme park industry, then beach and ski resorts are substitutes.[23]

## From Industry Attractiveness to Competitive Advantage: Identifying Key Success Factors

The five forces framework allows us to determine an industry's potential for profit. But how is industry profit shared between the different firms competing in that industry? Let us look explicitly at the sources of competitive advantage within an industry. In subsequent chapters I shall develop a more comprehensive analysis of competitive advantage. My goal in this chapter is to see how we can identify the factors within the industry environment that influence a firm's ability to outperform rivals—the industry's *key success factors*.[24] In Strategy Capsule 3.3, Kenichi Ohmae, former head of McKinsey's Tokyo office, discusses key success factors in forestry and their link with strategy.

Like Ohmae, our approach to identifying key success factors is straightforward and commonsense. To survive and prosper in an industry, a firm must meet two criteria: first, it must supply what customers want to buy; second, it must survive competition. Hence, we may start by asking two questions:

- What do our customers want?
- What does the firm need to do to survive competition?

To answer the first question we need to look more closely at customers of the industry and to view them not as a source of buying power and a threat to profitability but as the *raison d'être* of the industry and its underlying source of profit. This requires that we inquire: Who are our customers? What are their needs? How do they choose between competing offerings? Once we recognize the basis upon which customers' choose between rival offerings, we can identify the factors that confer success upon the individual firm. For example, if travelers choose airlines primarily on price, then cost efficiency is the primary basis for competitive advantage in the airline industry and the key success factors are the determinants of relative cost.

The second question requires that we examine the nature of competition in the industry. How intense is competition and what are its key dimensions? Thus, in airlines, it is not enough to offer low fares. To survive intense competition during recessionary periods an airline requires financial strength; it may also require good relations with regulators and government.

A basic framework for identifying key success factors is presented in Figure 3.5. Application of the framework to identify key success factors in three industries is outlined in Table 3.3.

Key success factors can also be identified through the direct modeling of profitability. In the same way that the five forces analysis models the determinants of industry-level profitability, we can also model firm-level profitability by identifying the drivers of a firm's relative profitability within an industry. Using the same approach as in Chapter 2 (Figures 2.1 and 2.3), we can disaggregate return on capital employed into component ratios, which then point to the main drivers of superior profitability. Figure 3.6 applies this analysis to identifying success factors in retailing.

In some industries, there are well-known formulae that link operating ratios to overall profitability. Strategy Capsule 3.4 uses such a formula used in the airline industry to identify key success factors.

## STRATEGY CAPSULE 3.3
# Probing for Key Success Factors

As a consultant faced with an unfamiliar business or industry, I make a point of first asking the specialists in the business, "What is the secret of success in this industry?" Needless to say, I seldom get an immediate answer and so I pursue the inquiry by asking other questions from a variety of angles in order to establish as quickly as possible some reasonable hypotheses as to key factors for success. In the course of these interviews it usually becomes quite obvious what analyses will be required in order to prove or disprove these hypotheses. By first identifying the probable key factors for success and then screening them by proof or disproof, it is often possible for the strategist to penetrate very quickly to the core of a problem.

Traveling in the US last year, I found myself on one occasion sitting in a plane next to a director of one of the biggest lumber companies in the country. Thinking I might learn something useful in the course of the five-hour flight, I asked him, "What are the key factors for success in the lumber industry?" To my surprise, his reply was immediate: "Owning large forests and maximizing the yield from them." The first of these key factors is a relatively simple matter: purchase of forestland. But his second point required further explanation. Accordingly, my next question was: "What variable or variables do you control in order to maximize the yield from a given tract?"

He replied: "The rate of tree growth is the key variable. As a rule, two factors promote growth: the amount of sunshine and the amount of water. Our company doesn't have many forests with enough of both. In Arizona and Utah, for example, we get more than enough sunshine but too little water and so tree growth is very low. Now, if we could give the trees in those states enough water, they'd be ready in less than 15 years instead of the 30 it takes now. The most important project we have in hand at the moment is aimed at finding out how to do this."

Impressed that this director knew how to work out a key factor strategy for his business, I offered my own contribution: "Then under the opposite conditions, where there is plenty of water but too little sunshine—for example, around the lower reaches of the Columbia River—the key factors should be fertilizers to speed up the growth and the choice of tree varieties that don't need so much sunshine."

Having established in a few minutes the general framework of what we were going to talk about, I spent the rest of the long flight very profitably hearing from him in detail how each of these factors was being applied.

*Source:* Kenichi Ohmae, *The Mind of the Strategist* (New York: McGraw-Hill, 1982): 85 © The McGraw-Hill Companies Inc., reproduced with permission.

In their battle for survival, the airlines have sought to optimize as many of these factors as possible in order to improve their profitability. To enhance revenue, several airlines have withdrawn from their most intensely competitive routes; others have sought to achieve a fare premium over the cut-price airlines through superior punctuality, convenience, comfort, and services. To improve load factors, companies have become more flexible in their pricing and in allocating different planes to different routes. Most notably, companies have sought to cut costs by increasing employee productivity, reducing overheads, sharing services with other airlines, and reducing salaries and benefits.

**FIGURE 3.5**   Identifying key success factors

**TABLE 3.3**   Identifying key success factors: Steel, fashion clothing, and supermarkets

| | What do customers want? (Analysis of demand) | How do firms survive competition? (Analysis of competition) | Key success factors |
|---|---|---|---|
| Steel | Low price<br>Product consistency<br>Reliability of supply<br>Technical specifications (for special steels) | Commodity products, excess capacity, high fixed costs, excess capacity, exit barriers, and substitute competition mean intense price competition and cyclical profitability<br>Cost efficiency and financial strength are essential | Cost efficiency requires: large-scale plants, low-cost location, rapid capacity adjustment<br>Alternatively, high-technology, small-scale plants can achieve low costs through flexibility and high productivity<br>Differentiation through technical specifications and service quality |
| Fashion clothing | Diversity of customer preferences<br>Customers willing to pay premium for brand, style, exclusivity, and quality<br>Mass market is highly price sensitive | Low barriers to entry and exit, low seller concentration, and buying power of retail chains imply intense competition<br>Differentiation offers price premium, but imitation is rapid | Combining differentiation with low costs<br>Differentiation based upon style, reputation, quality, and speed of response to changing fashions<br>Cost efficiency requires manufacture in low-wage countries |
| Supermarkets | Low prices<br>Convenient location<br>Wide product range adapted to local preferences<br>Fresh/quality produce, good service, ease of parking, pleasant ambience | Intensity competition depends on number and proximity of competitors<br>Bargaining power a key determinant of cost of bought-in goods | Low costs require operational efficiency, large-scale purchases, low wages<br>Differentiation requires large stores (to allow wide product range), convenient location, familiarity with local customer preferences |

**STRATEGY CAPSULE 3.4**

# Identifying Key Success Factors by Modeling Profitability: Airlines

Profitability, as measured by operating income per available seat-mile (ASM), is determined by three factors: yield, which is total operating revenues divided by the number of revenue passenger miles (RPMs); load factor, which is the ratio of RPMs to ASMs; and unit cost, which is total operating expenses divided by ASMs. Thus:

$$\frac{Profit}{ASMs} = \frac{Revenue}{RPMs} \times \frac{RPMs}{ASMs} - \frac{Expenses}{ASMs}$$

Some of the main determinants of each of these component ratios are the following:

◆ Revenue/RPMs

- intensity of competition on routes flown
- effective yield management to permit quick price adjustment to changing market conditions
- ability to attract business customers
- superior customer service.

◆ Load factor (RPMs/ASMs)

- competitiveness of prices
- efficiency of route planning (e.g., through hub-and-spoke systems)
- building customer loyalty through quality of service, frequent-flier programs
- matching airplane size to demand for individual flights.

◆ Expenses/ASMs

- wage rates and benefit levels
- fuel efficiency of aircraft
- productivity of employees (determined partly by their job flexibility)
- load factors
- level of administrative cost.

**FIGURE 3.6** Identifying key success factors through analyzing profit drivers: The case of retailing

The usefulness of industry-level success factors in formulating strategy has been scorned by some strategy scholars. Pankaj Ghemawat observes that the "whole idea of identifying a success factor and then chasing it seems to have something in common with the ill-considered medieval hunt for the philosopher's stone, a substance that would transmute everything it touched into gold."[25] However, the existence of common success factors in an industry does not imply that firms should adopt similar strategies. In the fashion clothing business we identified a number of key success factors (Table 3.3), yet all the leading companies—Inditex (Zara), H&M, Diesel, and Mango—have adopted unique strategies to exploit these key success factors.

## Summary

In Chapter 1 we established that a profound understanding of the competitive environment is a critical ingredient of a successful strategy. Despite the vast number of external influences that affect every business enterprise, our focus is the firm's industry environment which we analyze in order to evaluate the industry's profit potential and to identify the sources of competitive advantage.

The centerpiece of our approach is Porter's five forces of competition framework, which links the structure of an industry to the competitive intensity within it and to the profitability that it realizes. The Porter framework offers a simple yet powerful organizing framework for identifying the relevant features of an industry's structure and predicting their implications for competitive behavior.

The primary application for the Porter five forces framework is in predicting how changes in an industry's structure are likely to affect its profitability. Once we understand the drivers of industry profitability, we can identify strategies through which a firm can improve industry attractiveness and position itself in relation to these different competitive forces.

As with most of the tools for strategy analysis that we shall consider in this book, the Porter five forces framework is easy to comprehend. However, real learning about industry analysis and about the Porter framework in particular derives from its application. It is only when we apply the Porter framework to analyzing competition and diagnosing the causes of high or low profitability in an industry that we are forced to confront the complexities and subtleties of the model. A key issue is identifying the industry within which a firm competes and recognizing its boundaries. By employing the principles of substitutability and relevance, we can delineate meaningful industry boundaries.

Finally, our industry analysis allows us to make a first approach at identifying the sources of competitive advantage through recognizing key success factors in an industry.

I urge you to put the tools of industry analysis to work—not just in your strategic management coursework but also in interpreting everyday business events. The value of the Porter framework is as a practical tool—in helping us to understand the huge disparity in performance between the producers of airplanes and the airlines that fly them; in allowing us to predict which e-commerce start-ups have the best potential for making money. Through practical applications, you will also become aware of the limitations of the Porter framework. In the next chapter we will see how we can extend our analysis of industry and competition.

Quizzes and flashcards to test yourself further are available in your interactive e-book at
**www.wileyopenpage.com**

## Self-Study Questions

1. From Table 3.1, select a high-profit industry and a low-profit industry. From what you know of the structure of your selected industry, use the five forces framework to explain why profitability has been high in one industry and low in the other.

2. With reference to Strategy Capsule 3.1, use the five forces framework to explain why profitability has been so high in the US market for smokeless tobacco.

3. The major forces shaping the business environment of the fixed-line telecom industry are technology and government policy. The industry has been influenced by fiber optics (greatly increasing transmission capacity), new modes of telecommunication (wireless and internet telephony), deregulation, and privatization. Using the five forces of competition framework, show how each of these developments has influenced competition in the fixed-line telecom industry.

4. The leading companies in the online travel agency industry are Expedia, Travelocity (which owns Lastminute.com), Orbitz, Priceline, Cheaptickets and a host of others. The online agents compete both with traditional travel agents (American Express, Thomas Cook, Carlson) and direct online sales by airlines, cruise lines and car rental companies. Their biggest business is selling airline tickets, where they employ the services of computerized airline reservation systems such as Sabre, Amadeus, Worldspan and Galileo. Use Porter's five forces framework to predict the likely profitability of the online travel agency industry over the next ten years.

5. Wal-Mart (like Carrefour, Ahold, and Metro) competes in several countries of the world, yet most shoppers choose between retailers within a radius of a few miles. For the purposes of analyzing profitability and competitive strategy, should Wal-Mart consider the discount retailing industry to be global, national, or local?

6. What do you think are key success factors in:

   a. the pizza delivery industry?
   b. the credit card industry (where the world's biggest issuers are: Bank of America, JPMorgan Chase, Citigroup, American Express, Capital One, HSBC, and Discover)?

## Notes

1. M. E. Porter, "The Five Competitive Forces that Shape Strategy," *Harvard Business Review* 57 (January 2008): 57–71.

2. "Drink Up," Barron's (July 23, 2012); Juice & Smoothie Bars in the US: Market Research Report (IBIS World, February 2012).

3. W. J. Baumol, J. C. Panzar, and R. D. Willig, *Contestable Markets and the Theory of Industry Structure* (New York: Harcourt Brace Jovanovich, 1982). See also M. Spence, "Contestable Markets and the Theory of Industry Structure: A Review Article," *Journal of Economic Literature* 21 (1983): 981–90.

4. "Annual Franchise 500," *Entrepreneur* (January 2009).

5. "Brand Loyalty is Rarely Blind Loyalty," *Wall Street Journal* (October 19, 1989): B1.

6. R. D. Buzzell and P. W. Farris, "Marketing Costs in Consumer Goods Industries," in H. Thorelli (ed.), *Strategy + Structure = Performance* (Bloomington, IN: Indiana University Press, 1977): 128–9.

7. In October 1999, the Department of Justice alleged that American Airlines was using unfair means in attempting to monopolize air traffic out of Dallas/Fort Worth, http://www.aeroworldnet.com/1tw05179.htm, accessed July 2, 2009.

8. M. Lieberman ("Excess Capacity as a Barrier to Entry," *Journal of Industrial Economics* 35, 1987: 607–27) argues that, to be credible, the threat of retaliation needs to be supported by incumbents investing in excess capacity so that they have the potential to flood the market.

9. See, for example, J. S. Bain, *Barriers to New Competition* (Cambridge, MA: Harvard University Press, 1956); and H. M. Mann, "Seller Concentration, Entry Barriers, and Rates of Return in Thirty Industries," *Review of Economics and Statistics* 48 (1966): 296–307.

10. J. L. Siegfried and L. B. Evans, "Empirical Studies of Entry and Exit: A Survey of the Evidence," *Review of Industrial Organization* 9 (1994): 121–55.

11. G. S. Yip, "Gateways to Entry," *Harvard Business Review* 60 (September/October1982): 85–93.

12. F. M. Scherer and D. R. Ross, *Industrial Market Structure and Economic Performance*, 3rd edn (Boston: Houghton Mifflin, 1990).

13. R. Schmalensee, "Inter-Industry Studies of Structure and Performance," in R. Schmalensee and R. D. Willig (eds), *Handbook of Industrial Organization*, 2nd edn (Amsterdam: North Holland, 1988): 976. See also M. A. Salinger, "The Concentration-Margins Relationship Reconsidered," *Brookings Papers: Microeconomics* (1990): 287–335.

14. C. Baden-Fuller (ed.), *Strategic Management of Excess Capacity* (Oxford: Basil Blackwell, 1990).

15. "Dry bulk shipping rates approach all-time low," *Financial Times* (November 27, 2008).

16. T. Kelly and M. L. Gosman, "Increased Buyer Concentration and its Effects on Profitability in the Manufacturing Sector," *Review of Industrial Organization* 17 (2000): 41–59.

17. R. D. Buzzell and B. T. Gale, *The PIMS Principles* (New York: Free Press, 1987): 67.

18. J. Bower, *When Markets Quake* (Boston: Harvard Business School Press, 1986).

19. M. Carnall, S. Berry, and P. Spiller, "Airline Hubbing, Costs and Demand," in D. Lee (ed.), *Advances in Airline Economics*, vol. 1 (Amsterdam: Elsevier, 2006).

20. M. G. Jacobides, "Creating and Capturing Value: From Innovation to Architectural Advantage,"*Business Insight* (London Business School, September 2008).

21. M. G. Jacobides, "Strategy Bottlenecks," *Capgemini Telecom and Media Insights* 63 (2010), www.capgemini.com/m/en/tl/Strategy_Bottlenecks.pdf, accessed December 17, 2011.

22. M. E. Porter, "The Five Competitive Forces that Shape Strategy," *Harvard Business Review* 57 (January 2008): 57–71.

23. For a concise discussion of market definition see Office of Fair Trading, *Market Definition* (London: December 2004), especially pp. 7–17.

24. The term was coined by Chuck Hofer and Dan Schendel (*Strategy Formulation: Analytical Concepts*, St Paul: West Publishing, 1977: 77). They define key success factors as "those variables that management can influence through its decisions and that can affect significantly the overall competitive positions of the firms in an industry."

25. P. Ghemawat, *Commitment: The Dynamic of Strategy* (New York: Free Press, 1991): 11.

# 4 Further Topics in Industry and Competitive Analysis

Economic progress, in capitalist society, means turmoil.

—JOSEPH A. SCHUMPETER, AUSTRIAN ECONOMIST, 1883–1950

## OUTLINE

## Introduction and Objectives

Last chapter was concerned with outlining Porter's five forces framework and showing how it can be applied to analyzing competition, predicting industry profitability, and developing strategy. The Porter framework is one of the most useful and widely applied tools of strategic analysis. It also has its limitations. In this chapter, we shall extend our analysis of industry and competition beyond the limits of the Porter framework.

By the time you have completed this chapter, you will be able to:

◆ recognize the limits of the Porter five forces framework, and extend the framework to include the role of complements as well as substitutes;

◆ recognize competition as a dynamic, even hypercompetitive, process, appreciate the insights that game theory offers into the dynamics of rivalry, and use competitor analysis to predict the competitive moves by rivals;

◆ segment an industry into its constituent markets, appraise the relative attractiveness of different segments and apply strategic group analysis to classify firms according to their strategic types.

## Extending the Five Forces Framework

### Does Industry Matter?

Porter's five forces of competition framework has been subject to two main attacks. Some have criticized its theoretical foundations, arguing that the "structure–conduct–performance" approach to industrial organization that underlies it lacks rigor (especially when compared with the logical robustness of game theory). Others have noted its empirical weaknesses. It appears that industry environment is a relatively minor determinant of a firm's profitability. Studies of the sources of interfirm differences in profitability have produced very different results (Table 4.1), but all acknowledge that industry factors account for a minor part (less than 20%) of variation in return on assets among firms.

Do these findings imply that industry doesn't matter and we relegate the analysis of industry and competition to a minor role in our strategic analysis? Let me offer a few thoughts.

We need to acknowledge that profitability differences within industries are greater than profitability differences between industries. In Table 3.1, the difference in return on equity (ROE) between the most and least profitable industries was 45 percentage points; yet, in computer and electronic equipment the spread in ROE between Apple and Hewlett-Packard was 131 percentage points, while in forest and paper products, the spread between Domtar and International Paper was 98 percentage points.[1]

**TABLE 4.1**  How much does industry matter?

| | Percentage of variance in firms' return on assets explained by: | | |
| --- | --- | --- | --- |
| | Industry effects (%) | Firm effects (%) | Unexplained variance (%) |
| Schmalensee (1985) | 19.6 | 0.6 | 79.9 |
| Rumelt (1991) | 4.0 | 44.2 | 44.8 |
| McGahan and Porter (1997) | 18.7 | 31.7 | 48.4 |
| Hawawini *et al.* (2003) | 8.1 | 35.8 | 52.0 |
| Roquebert *et al.* (1996) | 10.2 | 55.0 | 32.0 |
| Misangyi *et al.* (2006) | 7.6 | 43.8 | n.a. |

**Note:** "Firm effects" combine business unit and corporate effects. The rows do not sum to 100% because other sources of variance are not reported.

**Sources:** R. Schmalensee, "Do markets differ much?" *American Economic Review* 75 (1985): 341–51; R. P. Rumelt, "How much does industry matter?" *Strategic Management Journal* 12 (1991): 167–85; A. M. McGahan and M. E. Porter, "How much does industry matter, really?" *Strategic Management Journal* 18 (1997): 15–30; G. Hawawini, V. Subramanian, and P. Verdin, "Is Performance Driven by Industry or Firm-Specific Factors? A New Look at the Evidence," *Strategic Management Journal* 24 (2003): 1–16; J. A. Roquebert, R. L. Phillips, and P. A. Westfall, "Markets vs. Management: What 'Drives' Profitability?" *Strategic Management Journal* 17 (1996): 653–64; V. F. Misangyi, H. Elms, T. Greckhamer, and J. A. Lepine, "A New Perspective on a Fundamental Debate: A Multilevel Approach to Industry, Corporate and Business Unit Effects," *Strategic Management Journal* 27 (2006): 571–90.

However, the usefulness of industry analysis is not conditional upon the relative importance of inter-industry and intra-industry profitability differences. Industry analysis is important because, without a deep understanding of their competitive environment, firms cannot make sound strategic decisions. Industry analysis is not relevant just to choosing which industries to locate within, as Michael Jacobides' concept of "architectural advantage" reveals, industry analysis is also important for establishing competitive advantage within an industry.

If our industry analysis is to fulfill this promise, it needs to go beyond the confines of the Porter five forces framework. We need to go further in understanding the determinants of competitive behavior between companies, in particular using more rigorous approaches to analyze the relationship between market structure and competition. We need to disaggregate broad industry sectors to examine competition within particular segments and among particular groups of firms. But let's begin by considering the potential to extend the Porter framework.

## Complements: A Missing Force in the Porter Model?

The Porter framework identifies the suppliers of substitute goods and services as one of the forces of competition that reduces the profit available to firms within an industry. However, economic theory identifies two types of relationship between different products: *substitutes* and *complements*. While the presence of substitutes reduces the value of a product, complements increase its value: without ink cartridges my printer has very little value to me.

Given the importance of complements to most products—the value of my car depends on the availability of gasoline, insurance, and repair services; the value of

**FIGURE 4.1** Five forces, or six?

my razor depends upon the supply of blades and shaving foam—our analysis of the competitive environment needs to take them into account. The simplest way is to add a sixth force to Porter's framework (Figure 4.1).[2]

Complements have the opposite effect to substitutes. While substitutes reduce the value of an industry's product, complements increase it. Indeed, where products are close complements (as with my printer and ink cartridges), they have little or no value in isolation: customers value the whole system. But how is the value shared between the producers of the different complementary products? Bargaining power, and its deployment, is the key. During the early 1990s, Nintendo earned huge profits from its video game consoles. Although most of the revenue and consumer value was in the software, mostly supplied by independent developers, Nintendo was able to appropriate most of the profit potential of the entire system through establishing dominance over the games developers. Nintendo used its leadership in the console market and ownership of the console operating system to enforce restrictive developer licenses to software producers of games, and maintained tight control over the manufacture and distribution of games cartridges (from which Nintendo earned a hefty royalty).[3]

A similar hardware/software complementarity exists in personal computers—but here power has lain with the software suppliers—Microsoft in particular. IBM's adoption of open architecture meant that Microsoft Windows became a proprietary standard, while PCs were gradually reduced to commodity status. This is a very different situation from video games, where hardware suppliers keep proprietary control over their operating systems.

Where two products complement one another, profit will accrue to the supplier that builds the stronger market position and reduces the value contributed by the other. How is this done? The key is to achieve monopolization, differentiation, and shortage of supply in one's own product, while encouraging competition, commoditization, and excess capacity in the production of the complementary product. This is the same principle of creating a *bottleneck* that we discussed in the last chapter. In the PC sector, the hardware companies have sought to counteract the dominance of the software companies, especially Microsoft, by supporting the development of open-source software. IBM has been a major supporter of Linux;[4] Sun Microsystems is a key backer of Mozilla (which offers the Firefox browser).

## Dynamic Competition: Hypercompetition, Game Theory, and Competitor Analysis

### Hypercompetition

The Porter five forces framework is based upon the assumption that industry structure determines competitive behavior, which in turn determines industry profitability. But couldn't the relationships flow in the opposite direction: the quest for profit unleashes the competitive forces of innovation and entrepreneurship that transform industry structures? Joseph Schumpeter viewed competition as a "perennial gale of creative destruction" in which market-dominating incumbents are challenged, and often unseated, by rivals that deploy innovatory products and innovatory strategies.[5]

This view of Schumpeter (and the "Austrian school" of economics) that competition is a dynamic process in which industry structure is constantly changing raises the issue of whether competitive behavior should be seen as an outcome of industry structure or a determinant of industry structure.[6] The issue is the speed of structural change in the industry—if structural transformation is rapid, then the five forces framework does not offer a stable basis on which to predict competition and profitability.

In most industries, Schumpeter's process of "creative destruction" tends to be more of a breeze than a gale. In established industries entry occurs so slowly that profits are undermined only gradually,[7] while changes in industrial concentration tend to be slow.[8] One survey observed: "the picture of the competitive process . . . is, to say the least, sluggish in the extreme."[9] As a result, both at the firm and the industry level, profits tend to be highly persistent in the long run.[10]

But what about recent trends? Has accelerating technological change and intensifying international competition reinforced the processes of "creative destruction"? Rich D'Aveni argues that a general feature of industries today is **hypercompetition**: "intense and rapid competitive moves, in which competitors must move quickly to build [new] advantages and erode the advantages of their rivals."[11] If industries are hypercompetitive, their structures are likely to be less stable than in the past, superior profitability will tend to be transitory, and the only route to sustained superior performance is through continually recreating and renewing competitive advantage—we are experiencing an "age of temporary advantage."[12]

Despite the plausibility of this thesis and everyday observations that markets are becoming more volatile and market leadership more tenuous, systematic evidence of this trend is ambiguous. One large-scale statistical study concludes: "The heterogeneity and volatility of competitive advantage in US manufacturing industries has steadily and astonishingly increased since 1950. Industry structures are destabilizing.

These results suggest that a shift towards hypercompetition has indeed occurred."[13] Another study found that increased volatility was a feature not only of technology-intensive industries but also extended beyond manufacturing industries.[14] However, another study found a "lack of widespread evidence . . . that markets are more unstable now than in the recent past."[15]

## The Contribution of Game Theory

Central to the criticisms of Porter's five forces as a static framework is its failure to take full account of competitive interactions among firms. In Chapter 1, we noted that the essence of strategic competition is the interaction among players, such that the decisions made by any one player are dependent on the actual and anticipated decisions of the other players. By relegating competition to a mediating variable that links industry structure with profitability, the five forces analysis offers little insight into competition as a process of interactive decision making by rival firms. Game theory allows us to model this competitive interaction. In particular, it offers two especially valuable contributions to strategic management:

- It permits the framing of strategic decisions. Apart from any theoretical value of the theory of games, game theory provides a structure, a set of concepts, and a terminology that allows us to describe and understand a competitive situation in terms of:
  ○ identity of the players;
  ○ specification of each player's options;
  ○ specification of the payoffs from every combination of options;
  ○ the sequencing of decisions using game trees.
- It can predict the outcome of competitive situations and identify optimal strategic choices. Through the insight that it offers into situations of competition and bargaining, game theory can predict the equilibrium outcomes of competitive situations and the consequences of strategic moves by any one player. Game theory provides penetrating insights into central issues of strategy that go well beyond pure intuition. Simple game models (e.g., the **prisoners' dilemma**) predict cooperative versus competitive outcomes, whereas more complex games permit analysis of the effects of reputation,[16] deterrence,[17] information,[18] and commitment,[19] especially within the context of multi-period games. Particularly important for practicing managers, game theory can indicate strategies for improving the structure and outcome of the game through manipulating the payoffs to the different players.[20]

Game theory offers illuminating insights into a wide variety of competitive situations. These include the Cuban missile crisis of 1962,[21] rivalry between Boeing and Airbus,[22] NASCAR race tactics,[23] auctions of airwave spectrum,[24] the 2008 financial crisis,[25] and the reasons why evolution has conferred such magnificent tails upon male peacocks.[26] In terms of applications to competition among business enterprises, game theory points to five aspects of strategic behavior through which a firm can improve its competitive outcomes: *cooperation, deterrence, commitment, changing the structure of the game being played*, and *signaling*.

*Cooperation*   One of the key merits of game theory is its ability to encompass both competition and cooperation. A key deficiency of the five forces framework is in viewing interfirm relations as exclusively competitive in nature. Central to Adam Brandenburger and Barry Nalebuff's concept of *co-opetition* is recognition of the competitive/cooperative duality of business relationships.[27] While some relationships are predominantly competitive (Coca-Cola and Pepsi) and others are predominantly cooperative (Intel and Microsoft), there is no simple dichotomy between competition and cooperation: all business relationships combine elements of both. For all their intense rivalry, Coca-Cola and Pepsi cooperate on multiple fronts, including common policies on sales of soda drinks within schools, environmental issues, and health concerns. They may also coordinate their pricing and product introductions.[28] Exxon and Shell have battled for over a century for leadership of the world's petroleum industry; at the same time they cooperate in a number of joint ventures. The desire of competitors to cluster together—antique dealers in London's Bermondsey Market or movie studios in Hollywood—points to the common interests of competing firms in growing the size of their market and developing its infrastructure.

In many business situations, competition results in inferior outcomes for participants than cooperation. The prisoners' dilemma game analyzes this predicament (Strategy Capsule 4.1).

*Deterrence*   As we saw in Strategy Capsule 4.1, one way of changing a game's equilibrium is through deterrence. The principle behind deterrence is to impose costs on the other players for actions deemed to be undesirable. By establishing the certainty that deserters would be shot, the British army provided a strong incentive to its troops to participate in advances on heavily fortified German trenches during the First World War.

The key to the effectiveness of any deterrent is that it must be credible. The problem here is that if administering the deterrent is costly or unpleasant for the threatening party, the deterrent is not credible. When King of Shaves (owned by KMI Ltd; annual sales $90 million) entered the UK razor market, Gillette might have threatened it with a price cut. But would such a threat have been credible? Once King of Shaves had entered, Gillette's dominant market share meant that a price cut would inflict more damage on itself than on its rivals.[29] Investing in excess capacity can be an effective means of discouraging entry. Prior to the expiration of its NutraSweet patents, Monsanto invested heavily in unneeded plant capacity to deter manufacturers of generic aspartame.[30] Conversely, in compact disks, the reluctance of the dominant firm (Philips) to invest heavily in new capacity to meet growing demand encouraged a wave of new entrants.[31]

Deterrence has provided a central theme in international relations. The nuclear arms race between the US and the then Soviet Union was based on the logic of "mutual assured destruction." However, the ability for deterrence to produce a stable, peaceful equilibrium depends on the willingness of the adversaries to be deterred. A central weakness of George W. Bush's "war on terror" was that ideologically motivated terrorists are not susceptible to deterrence.[32]

*Commitment*   For deterrence to be effective it must be credible, which means being backed by commitment. Commitment involves the elimination of strategic options: "binding an organization to a future course of action."[33] When Hernán Cortés destroyed his ships on arrival in Mexico in 1519, he communicated, both

## STRATEGY CAPSULE 4.1
# The Prisoners' Dilemma

The classic prisoners' dilemma game involves a pair of crime suspects who are arrested and interrogated separately. The dilemma is that each will rat on the other with the result that both end up in jail despite the fact that if both had remained silent they would have been released for lack of evidence.

The dilemma arises in almost all competitive situations—everyone could be better off with collusion. Consider competition between Coca-Cola and Pepsi in Ukraine, where each has the choice of spending big or small on advertising. Figure 4.2 shows the payoffs to each firm.

Clearly, the best solution for both firms is for them to each restrain their advertising expenditure (the upper left cell). However, in the absence of cooperation, the outcome for both firms is to adopt big budgets (the lower right cell)—the reason being that each will fear that any restraint will be countered by the rival seeking advantage by shifting to a big advertising budget. The resulting maxi-min choice of strategies (each company chooses the strategy that maximizes the minimum payoff) is a Nash equilibrium: no player can increase his/her payoff by a unilateral change in strategy. Even if collusion can be achieved, it will be unstable because of the incentives for cheating—a constant problem for

OPEC, where the member countries agree quotas but then cheat on them.

How can a firm escape from such prisoners' dilemmas? One answer is to change a one-period game (single transaction) into a repeated game. In the above example of competition in advertising, a multi-period perspective allows the companies to recognize the futility of advertising campaigns that merely cancel one another out. In the case of supplier–buyer relations, where the typical equilibrium is a low-quality product at a low price, moving from a spot-transaction to a long-term vendor relationship gives the supplier the incentive to offer a better-quality product and the buyer to offer a price that reflects the preferred quality.

A second solution is to change the payoffs through deterrence. In the classic prisoners' dilemma, the Mafia shifts the equilibrium from the suspects both confessing to their both remaining silent by using draconian reprisals to enforce its "code of silence." Similarly, if both Coca-Cola and Pepsi were to threaten one another with aggressive price cuts should the other seek advantage through a big advertising budget, this could shift the equilibrium to the top-left cell.

**FIGURE 4.2**  Coca-Cola's and Pepsi's advertising budget: The prisoners' dilemma

| | | COCA-COLA (Payoffs in $ millions) | |
|---|---|---|---|
| | | Small Advertising Budget | Big Advertising Budget |
| PEPSI | Small Advertising Budget | 10     10 | −2     15 |
| | Big Advertising Budget | 15     −2 | 4     4 |

In each cell, the lower-left number is the payoff to Pepsi; the upper-right the payoff to Coke.

to Montezuma and his men, that there was no alternative to conquest of the Aztec empire. Once Airbus had decided to build its A380 superjumbo, it was critical to signal its commitment to the project. During 2000–2002, Airbus spent heavily on advertising the plane, even before completing the design phase, in order encourage airlines to place orders and discourage Boeing from developing a rival plane.

These commitments to aggressive competition can be described as *hard commitments*. A company may also make commitments that moderate competition; these are called *soft commitments*. For example, if a company commits to achieving certain target profit levels in the coming year, this would be a soft commitment: it would signal that, in the event of an aggressive initiative by a competitor, such as a price cut, the company would be more likely to accommodate that initiative rather than forego profitability by responding aggressively.

How different types of commitment affect a firm's profitability depend on the type of game being played. Where companies compete on price, game theory shows that they tend to match one another's price changes.[34] Hence, under price adjustments, hard commitments (such as a commitment to cut price) tend to have a negative profit impact and soft commitments (such as a commitment to raise prices) have a positive impact. Conversely, where companies compete on output, game theory shows that increases in output by one firm result in output reductions by the other.[35] Hence, under quantity adjustments, a hard commitment (e.g., a commitment to build new plants) will tend to have a positive effect on the committing firm's profitability because it will tend to be met by other firms reducing their output.[36]

*Changing the Structure of the Game*    Creative strategies can change the structure of the competitive game. A company may seek to change the structure of the industry within which it is competing in order to increase the profit potential of the industry or to appropriate a greater share of the available profit. Thus, establishing alliances and agreements with competitors can increase the value of the game by increasing the size of the market and building joint strength against possible entrants. There may be many opportunities for converting win–lose (or even lose–lose) games into win–win games. A cooperative solution was found to the 1997 bidding war between Norfolk Southern and CSX for control of Conrail, for example. The bidding war was terminated when the two firms agreed to cooperate in acquiring and dismembering Conrail.[37]

In some cases, it may be advantageous for a firm to create competition for itself. By offering second-sourcing licenses to AMD, Intel gave up its potential monopoly over its x86 microprocessors. Although Intel was creating competition for itself, it also encouraged the adoption of the x86 chip by computer manufacturers (including IBM) who were concerned about overdependence on Intel. As we shall see in Chapter 9, standards battles often involve the deliberate sacrificing of potential monopoly positions by the main contestants.

*Signaling*    Competitive reactions depend on how the competitor perceives its rival's initiative. The term *signaling* is used to describe the selective communication of information to competitors (or customers) designed to influence their perceptions and hence provoke or suppress certain types of reaction.[38] The use of misinformation is well developed in military intelligence. Ben McIntyre's book *Operation Mincemeat* describes how British Military Intelligence used a corpse dressed as a marine office and carrying fake secret documents to convince German high command that the Allied landings would be in Greece, not Sicily.[39]

The credibility of threats is critically dependent on reputation.[40] Even though carrying out threats against rivals is costly and depresses short-term profitability, exercising such threats can build a reputation for aggressiveness that deters competitors in the future. The benefits of building a reputation for aggressiveness may be particularly great for diversified companies where reputation can be transferred from one market to another.[41] Hence, Procter & Gamble's protracted market share wars in disposable diapers and household detergents' have established a reputation for toughness that protects it from competitive attacks in other markets.

Signaling may also be used to communicate a desire to cooperate. Price announcements can facilitate collusive pricing among firms.[42]

## Is Game Theory Useful?

The value of game theory to strategic management has generated lively debate. For economists this seems paradoxical—to them game theory *is* the theory of strategy. The great virtue of game theory is its rigor. In microeconomics, the game theory revolution of the past 40 years has established the analysis of markets and firm behavior on a much more secure theoretical foundation.

However, the price of mathematical rigor has been limited applicability to real-world situations. Game theory provides clear predictions in highly stylized situations involving few external variables and restrictive assumptions. The result is a mathematically sophisticated body of theory that suffers from unrealistic assumptions, lack of generality, and an analysis of dynamic situations through a sequence of static equilibriums. When applied to more complex (and more realistic) situations, game theory frequently results in either no equilibrium or multiple equilibriums, and outcomes that are highly sensitive to small changes in initial assumptions. Overall, game theory has not developed to the point where it permits us to model real business situations in a level of detail that can generate precise predictions.[43]

In its empirical applications, game theory does a better job of explaining the past than of predicting the future. In diagnosing Nintendo's domination of the video games industry in the 1980s, Monsanto's efforts to prolong NutraSweet's market leadership beyond the expiration of its patents, or Airbus's wresting of market leadership from Boeing, game theory provides penetrating insight into the competitive situation and deep understanding of the rationale behind the strategies deployed. However, in predicting outcomes and designing strategies, game theory has been much less impressive—the use of game theory by US and European governments to design auctions for wireless spectrum has produced some undesirable and unforeseen results.[44]

So, where can game theory assist us in designing successful strategies? As with all our theories and frameworks, game theory is useful not because it gives us answers but because it can help us understand business situations. Game theory provides a set of tools that allows us to structure our view of competitive interaction. By identifying the players in a game, the decision choices available to each, and the implications of each combination of decisions, we have a systematic framework for exploring the dynamics of competition. Most importantly, by describing the structure of the game we are playing, we have a basis for suggesting ways of changing the game and thinking through the likely outcomes of such changes.

Game theory continues its rapid development and, although it is still a long way from providing the central theoretical foundation for strategic management, we draw upon it in several places in this book, especially in exploring competitive dynamics in highly concentrated markets. However, our emphasis in strategy formulation will be less on achieving advantage through influencing the behavior of competitors and much more on transforming competitive games through building positions of unilateral competitive advantage. The competitive market situations with which we shall be dealing will, for the most part, be different from those considered by game theory. Game theory typically deals with competitive situations with closely matched players where each has a similar range of strategic options (typically relating to price changes, advertising budgets, capacity decisions, and new product introductions). The outcome of these games is highly dependent on the order of moves, signals, bluffs, and threats. Our emphasis will be less on managing competitive interactions and more on establishing competitive advantage through exploiting uniqueness.

## Competitor Analysis and Competitive Intelligence

In highly concentrated industries, the dominant feature of a company's competitive environment is likely to be the behavior of its closest rivals. In household detergents, Unilever's industry environment is dominated by the strategy of Procter & Gamble. The same is true in soft drinks (Coca-Cola and Pepsi), jet engines (GE, United Technologies, and Rolls-Royce), and financial information (Bloomberg and Reuters). Similar circumstances are common in local markets: the competitive environment of my local Costa coffee shop is dominated by the presence of Starbucks across the road. Game theory provides a theoretical apparatus for analyzing competitive inter-action between small numbers of rivals but, for everyday business situations, a less formal and more empirically based approach to predicting competitors' behavior may be more useful. Let us examine how information about competitors can help us to predict their behavior.

*Competitive Intelligence*   Competitive intelligence involves the systematic collection and analysis of information about rivals for informing decision making. It has three main purposes:

- to forecast competitors' future strategies and decisions;
- to predict competitors' likely reactions to a firm's strategic initiatives;
- to determine how competitors' behavior can be influenced to make it more favorable.

For all three purposes, the key requirement is to understand competitors in order to predict their responses to environmental changes and our own competitive moves. To understand competitors, it is important to be informed about them. Competitive intelligence is a growth field, with specialist consulting firms, professional associations,[45] and a flood of recent books.[46] About one-quarter of large US corporations have specialist competitive intelligence units.

The boundary between legitimate competitive intelligence and illegal industrial espionage is not always clear. The distinction between public and private information is uncertain and the law relating to trade secrets is much less precise than that which covers patents and copyrights. Well-publicized cases of information theft include the $100 million fine levied on the McLaren Mercedes Formula One team for possessing confidential technical information belonging to Ferrari and the theft by Kolon Industries of South Korea of trade secrets concerning the production of DuPont's Kevlar fiber.[47] More generally, the US National Counterintelligence Executive has alleged systematic industrial espionage by the China and Russia.[48]

*A Framework for Predicting Competitor Behavior*  Competitive intelligence is not simply about collecting information. The problem is likely to be too much rather than too little information. The key is a systematic approach that makes it clear what information is required and for what purposes it will be used. The objective is to understand one's rival. A characteristic of great generals from Hannibal to Patton has been their ability to go beyond military intelligence and to "get inside the heads" of their opposing commanders. Michael Porter proposes a four-part framework for predicting competitor behavior (Figure 4.3).

- *Competitor's current strategy*: To predict how a rival will behave in the future, we must understand how that rival is competing at present. As we noted in Chapter 1, identifying a firm's strategy requires looking at what the company says and what it does (see "Where Do We Find Strategy?" in Chapter 1). The key is to link the content of top management communication (with investors, the media, and financial analysts) with the evidence of strategic actions, particularly those that involve a commitment of resources. For both sources of information, company websites are invaluable.
- *Competitor's objectives*: To forecast how a competitor might change its strategy, we must identify its goals. A key issue is whether a company is driven by financial goals or market goals. A company whose primary goal is attaining

**FIGURE 4.3**  A framework for competitor analysis

market share is likely to be much more aggressive a competitor than one that is mainly interested in profitability. The willingness of the US automobile and consumer electronics producers to cede market share to Japanese competitors was partly a result of their preoccupation with short-term profitability. By comparison, companies like Procter & Gamble and Coca-Cola are obsessed with market share and tend to react aggressively when rivals step on their turf. The most difficult competitors can be those that are not subject to profit disciplines at all—state-owned enterprises in particular. The level of current performance in relation to the competitor's objectives determines the likelihood of strategy change. The more a company is satisfied with present performance, the more likely it is to continue with its present strategy. But if performance is falling well short of target, radical strategic change, possibly accompanied by a change in top management, is likely.

- *Competitor's assumptions about the industry*: A competitor's strategic decisions are conditioned by its perceptions of itself and its environment. These perceptions are guided by the beliefs that senior managers hold about their industry and the success factors within it. Evidence suggests that not only do these systems of belief tend to be stable over time but they also tend to converge among the firms within an industry: what J.-C. Spender refers to as "industry recipes."[49] Industry recipes may engender "blindspots" that limit the capacity of a firm—even an entire industry—to respond to an external threat. During the 1960s, the Big Three US automobile manufacturers firmly believed that small cars were unprofitable. This belief was partly a product of their overhead allocation procedures. The result was a willingness to yield the fastest-growing segment of the US automobile market to imports. The complacency of British and US motorcycle manufacturers in the face of Japanese competition reflected similar beliefs (Strategy Capsule 4.2).

- *Competitor's resources and capabilities*: Evaluating the likelihood and seriousness of a competitor's potential challenge requires assessing the strength of that competitor's resources and capabilities. If our rival has a massive cash pile, it would be unwise for our company to unleash a price war by initiating price cuts. Conversely, if we direct our competitive initiative toward our rivals' weaknesses, it may be difficult for them to respond. Richard Branson's Virgin Group has launched a host of entrepreneurial new ventures, typically in markets dominated by a powerful incumbent—British Airways in airlines, EMI in music, Vodafone in wireless telecommunications. Branson's strategy has been to adopt innovative forms of differentiation that are difficult for established incumbents to respond to.

# Segmentation and Strategic Groups

## Segmentation Analysis[50]

In Chapter 3 we noted the difficulty of drawing industry boundaries and the need to define industries both broadly and narrowly according to the types of question we are seeking to answer. Initially, it may be convenient to define industries broadly, but for a more detailed analysis of competition we need to focus on markets that

## STRATEGY CAPSULE 4.2
# Motorcycle Myopia

During the 1960s, lightweight Japanese motorcycles began to flood Britain and North America. The chairman of BSA, Eric Turner, was dismissive of this competitive challenge to the dominant position of his Triumph and BSA brands:

> The success of Honda, Suzuki, and Yamaha has been jolly good for us. People start out by buying one of the low-priced Japanese jobs. They get to enjoy the fun and exhilaration of the open road and they frequently end up buying one of our more powerful and expensive machines.
>
> (*Advertising Age*, December 27, 1965)

Similar complacency was expressed by William Davidson, president of Harley-Davidson:

> Basically, we do not believe in the lightweight market. We believe that motorcycles are sports vehicles, not transportation vehicles. Even if a man says he bought a motorcycle for transportation, it's generally for leisure time use. The lightweight motorcycle is only supplemental. Back around World War I, a number of companies came out with lightweight bikes. We came out with one ourselves. We came out with another in 1947 and it just didn't go anywhere. We have seen what happens to these small sizes.
>
> (*American Motor Cycle*, September 15, 1966)

By 1980, BSA and Triumph had ceased production and Harley-Davidson was struggling for survival. The world motorcycle industry, including the heavyweight segment, was dominated by the Japanese.

are drawn more narrowly in terms of both products and geography. This process of disaggregating industries into specific markets we call **segmentation**.

Segmentation is particularly important if competition varies across the different submarkets within an industry such that some are more attractive than others. While Sony and Microsoft battled for dominance for leadership among so-called hard-core gamers with their technologically advanced PS3 and Xbox 360 consoles, Nintendo's Wii became a surprise market share leader by focusing on a large and underserved market segment: casual and older video game players. In the cutthroat tire industry, Pirelli has achieved superior margins by investing heavily in technology and focusing on high-performance tires for sports and luxury cars.[51]

The purpose of segmentation analysis is to identify attractive segments, to select strategies for different segments, and to determine how many segments to serve. The analysis proceeds in five stages (see Strategy Capsule 4.3 for an application; Strategy Capsule 4.4 looks at vertical segmentation).

1   *Identify key segmentation variables*: Our starting point is to determine the basis of segmentation. Segmentation decisions are essentially choices about

which customers to serve and what to offer them: hence segmentation variables relate to the characteristics of customers and the product (Figure 4.4). The most appropriate segmentation variables are those that partition the market most distinctly in terms of limits to substitution by customers (demand-side substitutability) and by producers (supply-side substitutability). Price differentials are a good guide to market segments: distinct market segments tend to display sustained price differentials. Typically, segmentation analysis generates far too many segmentation variables and too many categories for each variable. For our analysis to be manageable and useful, we need to reduce these to two or three. To do this we need to (a) identify the most strategically significant segmentation variables and (b) combine segmentation variables that are closely correlated. For example, in the restaurant industry, price level, service level (waiter service/self-service), cuisine (fast-food/full meals), and alcohol license (wine served/soft drinks only) are likely to be closely related. We could use a single variable, restaurant type, with three categories—full-service restaurants, cafés, and fast-food outlets—as a proxy for all of these variables.

2 *Construct a Segmentation Matrix*: Once the segmentation variables have been selected and discrete categories determined for each, the individual segments may be identified using a two- or three-dimensional matrix. Strategy Capsule

**FIGURE 4.4**   The basis for segmentation: The characteristics of buyers and products

4.3 shows a two-dimensional segmentation matrix for the world automobile industry

3   *Analyze segment attractiveness*: Profitability within an industry segment is determined by the same structural forces that determine profitability within an industry as a whole. As a result, Porter's five forces of competition framework is equally effective in relation to a segment as to an entire industry. There are, however, a few differences. First, when analyzing the pressure of competition from substitute products, we are concerned not only with substitutes from other industries but also, more importantly, with substitutes from other segments within the same industry. Second, when considering entry into the segment, the main source of entrants is likely to be producers established in other segments within the same industry. The barriers that protect a segment from firms located in other segments are called *barriers to mobility* to distinguish them from the *barriers to entry*, which protect the industry as a whole.[52] When barriers to mobility are low, then the superior returns of high-profit segments tend to be quickly eroded. As Strategy Capsule 4.3 suggests, differences in competitive conditions between segments can make some much more profitable than others; however, these profit differentials are unlikely to be sustained over the long term.

   Segmentation analysis can also be useful in identifying unexploited opportunities in an industry. Companies that have built successful strategies by concentrating on unoccupied segments include Wal-Mart (discount stores in small towns), Enterprise Rent-A-Car (suburban locations), and Edward Jones (full-service brokerage for small investors in smaller cities). This identification of unoccupied market segments is one dimension of what Kim and Mauborgne refer to as "blue ocean strategy": the quest for uncontested market space.[53]

4   *Identify the segment's key success factors (KSFs)*: Differences in competitive structure and in customer preferences between segments result in different KSFs. By analyzing buyers' purchasing criteria and the basis of competition within individual segments, we can identify KSFs for individual segments. For example, we can segment the US bicycle market into high-price enthusiasts' bikes sold through specialist bike stores and economy bikes sold through discount stores. KSFs in the enthusiast segment are technology, reputation, and dealer relations. In the economy segment, KSFs are low-cost manufacture (most likely in China) and a supply contract with a leading retail chain.

5   *Select segment scope*: Finally, a firm needs to decide whether it wishes to be a segment specialist or to compete across multiple segments. The advantages of a broad over a narrow segment focus depend on two main factors: similarity of KSFs and the presence of shared costs. If KSFs are different across segments, a firm will need to deploy distinct strategies which may require different capabilities for different segments. Harley-Davidson's attempt to compete in sports motorcycles through its Buell brand was a failure.

   Where scale economies are important and costs can be shared across different segments, firms with a broad segment scope will tend to displace specialists. In automobiles, the ability of the large-scale automakers to use common platforms and components for specialist vehicles such as luxury cars and sports cars has resulted in the disappearance of most specialist automakers.

**STRATEGY CAPSULE 4.3**

# Segmenting the World Automobile Industry

1    Identify key segmentation variables and categories. Possible segmentation variables include: price, size, engine power, body style, buyer type (retail versus fleet), and geographical market. We can reduce the number of segmentation variables—in particular, price, size, and engine power tend to be closely correlated. Other variables clearly define distinct markets (e.g., geographical regions and individual national markets).

2    Construct a segmentation matrix. The segmentation matrix in Figure 4.5 shows geographical regions (columns) and product types (rows). These product types combine multiple segmentation variables: price, size, design, and fuel type.

3    Analyze segment attractiveness. Applying five forces analysis to individual segments points to the attractiveness of the growth markets of Asia and Latin America (especially for luxury cars) as compared with the saturated, excess capacity laden markets of Europe and North America. In these mature markets, the hybrid and electric car segments may be attractive due to fewer competitors and lack of excess capacity.

4    Identify KSFs in each segment. In sports cars, technology and design aesthetics are likely to be key differentiators. In luxury cars, quality and interior design are likely to be essential. In family compact and mini-cars, low cost is the primary basis for competitive advantage.

5    Analyze attractions of broad versus narrow segment scope. Because of the potential to share technology, design, and components across models, all product segments are dominated by full-range mass-manufactures. In terms of geographical segments, only in the biggest markets (primarily China) have nationally focused producers survived.

**FIGURE 4.5**    A segmentation matrix of the World Automobile Market

| REGIONS | | | | | | | |
|---|---|---|---|---|---|---|---|
| **PRODUCTS** | North America | Western Europe | Eastern Europe | Asia | Latin America | Australia & NZ | Africa |
| Luxury cars | | | | | | | |
| Full-size cars | | | | | | | |
| Mid-size cars | | | | | | | |
| Small cars | | | | | | | |
| Station wagons | | | | | | | |
| Minivans | | | | | | | |
| Sports cars | | | | | | | |
| Sport utility | | | | | | | |
| Pickup trucks | | | | | | | |
| Hybrids | | | | | | | |

# Vertical Segmentation: Profit Pool Mapping

Segmentation is usually horizontal: markets are disaggregated according to products, geography, and customer groups. However, as we noted in the previous chapter when we discussed Michael Jacobides' approach to industry architecture, we can also segment an industry vertically by identifying different value chain activities. Bain & Company's profit pool analysis offers a way of mapping profitability differences between different vertical activities. Bain's *profit pool mapping* involves, first, estimating the industry's total profit by applying the average margin earned by a

sample of companies in the industry to an estimate of the industry's total revenues and, second, estimating the profit at each stage of the value chain. This requires disaggregating profit data for *mixed players* (those engaged in multiple activities) and adding their segment profits to those earned by *pure players* (specialists in the single value chain activity). In the US automobile industry, downstream activities such as finance, leasing, insurance, and service and repair are much more profitable than manufacturing. In Figure 4.6 the area of each rectangle corresponds to the total profit for that activity.

**FIGURE 4.6**  The US auto industry profit pool

*Source:* Reprinted by permission of Harvard Business Review. From "Profit Pools: A Fresh Look at Strategy," O. Gadiesh and J. L. Gilbert, May/June 1998, p. 142, Copyright © 1998 by the Harvard Business School Publishing Corporation; all rights reserved.

## Strategic Groups

Whereas segmentation analysis concentrates on the characteristics of markets as the basis for disaggregating industries, strategic group analysis segments an industry on the basis of the strategies of the member firms. A **strategic group** is "the group of firms in an industry following the same or a similar strategy along the strategic dimensions."[54] These strategic dimensions might include product range, geographical breadth, choice of distribution channels, level of product quality, degree of vertical integration, choice of technology, and so on. By selecting the most important strategic dimensions and locating each firm in the industry along them, it is possible to identify groups of companies that have adopted more or less similar approaches to competing within the industry. In some industries strategic groups are readily observable, for example airlines fall into two broad strategic groups: "legacy carriers" (such as United, JAL, and British Airways) and "low-cost carriers" (such as Southwest, Ryanair, and SpiceJet). Other industries are more complex: Figure 4.7 shows strategic groups within the world automobile industry; Figure 4.8 in the petroleum industry.[55]

Most of the empirical research into strategic groups has been concerned with competition and profitability between groups—the basic argument being that mobility barriers between strategic groups permit some groups of firms to be persistently more profitable than other groups.[56] In general, the proposition that profitability differences within strategic groups are less than differences between strategic groups has not received robust empirical support.[57] This may reflect the fact that the members of a strategic group, although pursuing similar strategies, are not necessarily in competition with one another. For example, within the European airline industry, budget airlines such as easyJet, airBaltic, SkyEurope, Volare, and Ryanair pursue similar strategies, but do not, for the most part, compete on the same routes. Hence, the main usefulness of strategic group analysis is in understanding strategic positioning, recognizing patterns of competition, and identifying strategic niches; it is less useful as a tool for analyzing interfirm profitability differences.[58]

**FIGURE 4.7**   Strategic groups within the world automobile industry

*Note:* *This group is almost empty: most firms in this group are now owned by broad-line producers

**FIGURE 4.8**  Strategic groups within the world petroleum industry

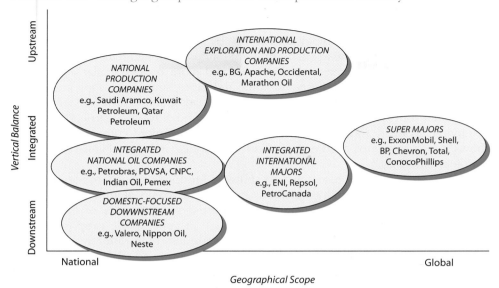

## Summary

The purpose of this chapter has been to go beyond the basic analysis of industry structure, competition, and profitability presented in Chapter 3 to consider the dynamics of competitive rivalry and the internal complexities of industries.

In terms of industry and competitive analysis, we have extended our strategy toolkit in several directions:

◆ We have recognized the potential for complementary products to add value and noted the importance of strategies that can exploit this source of value.

◆ We have noted the importance of competitive interactions between close rivals and learned a structured approach to analyzing competitors and predicting their behavior. At a more sophisticated theoretical level, we have recognized how game theory offers insights into competition, bargaining, and the design of winning strategies.

◆ We examined the microstructure of industries and markets and the value of segmentation analysis and strategic group analysis in understanding industries at a more detailed level and in selecting an advantageous strategic position within an industry.

Quizzes and flashcards to test yourself further are available in your interactive e-book at
**www.wileyopenpage.com**

## Self-Study Questions

1. HP, Canon, Epson, and other manufacturers of inkjet printers make most of their profits from their ink cartridges. Why are cartridges more profitable than printers? Would the situation be different:

   a   if cartridges were manufactured by different firms from those which make printers?
   b   if cartridges were interchangeable between different printers?
   c   if patent and copyright restrictions did not prevent other firms from supplying ink cartridges that could be used in the leading brands of printer?

2. In November 2005, six of Paris's most luxurious hotels—including George V, Le Bristol, the Ritz, and Hotel de Crillon—were fined for colluding on room rates. Regular guests showed little concern—noting that, whatever the listed rack rate, it was always possible to negotiate substantial discounts. Using the prisoners' dilemma model, can you explain why the hotels were able to collude over their listed rates but not over discounts?

3. In August 2006, Rupert Murdoch's News International announced its intention of launching a free evening newspaper, *The London Paper*, to challenge Associated Newspapers' *London Evening Standard* (daily sales 390,000). Given that the *Evening Standard* was already believed to be loss making, the new competition could be fatal for the paper. What steps might Associated Newspapers take to deter News International from launching its new paper, and if it goes ahead with the launch, what would Associated Newspapers' best response be?

4. During 2007–2009, the Nintendo Wii established leadership over the Sony PS3 and Microsoft Xbox 360 in the market for video game consoles. Unlike Sony and Microsoft, Nintendo is completely dependent upon the video games industry for its revenues. How might Nintendo use the competitor analysis framework outlined in Figure 4.3 to predict the likely reactions of Sony and Microsoft to its market success?

5. How would you segment the restaurant market in your hometown? How would you advise someone thinking of starting a new restaurant which segments might be most attractive in terms of profit potential?

## Notes

1. Data from http://money.cnn.com/magazines/fortune/fortune500/2011/industries/11/index.html.
2. A. Brandenburger and B. Nalebuff (*Co-opetition*, New York: Doubleday, 1996) propose an alternative framework, the *value net*, for analyzing the impact of complements.
3. See A. Brandenburger and B. Nalebuff, "The Right Game: Use Game Theory to Shape Strategy," *Harvard Business Review* (July/August 1995): 63–4; and A. Brandenburger, J. Kou, and M. Burnett, *Power Play (A): Nintendo in 8-bit Video Games* (Harvard Business School Case No. 9-795-103, 1995).

4. C. Baldwin, S. O'Mahony, and J. Quinn, *IBM and Linux (A)* (Harvard Business School Case No. 903-083, 2003).

5. J. A. Schumpeter, *The Theory of Economic Development* (Cambridge, MA: Harvard University Press, 1934).

6. See R. Jacobson, "The Austrian School of Strategy," *Academy of Management Review* 17 (1992): 782–807; and G. Young, K. Smith, and C. Grimm, "Austrian and Industrial Organization Perspectives on Firm-Level Competitive Activity and Performance," *Organization Science* 7 (May/June 1996): 243–54.

7. R. T. Masson and J. Shaanan, "Stochastic Dynamic Limit Pricing: An Empirical Test," *Review of Economics and Statistics* 64 (1982): 413–422; R. T. Masson and J. Shaanan, "Optimal Pricing and Threat of Entry: Canadian Evidence," *International Journal of Industrial Organization* 5 (1987): 520–535.

8. R. Caves and M. E. Porter, "The Dynamics of Changing Seller Concentration," *Journal of Industrial Economics* 19 (1980): 1–15; P. Hart and R. Clarke, *Concentration in British Industry* (Cambridge: Cambridge University Press, 1980).

9. P. A. Geroski and R. T. Masson, "Dynamic Market Models in Industrial Organization," *International Journal of Industrial Organization* 5 (1987): 1–13.

10. D. C. Mueller, *Profits in the Long Run* (Cambridge: Cambridge University Press, 1986).

11. R. D'Aveni, *Hypercompetition: Managing the Dynamics of Strategic Maneuvering* (New York: Free Press, 1994): 217–218.

12. R. A. D'Aveni, G. B. Dagnino, and K. G. Smith, "The Age of Temporary Advantage," *Strategic Management Journal* 31 (2010): 1371–85.

13. L. G. Thomas and R. D'Aveni, "The Rise of Hypercompetition in the US Manufacturing Sector, 1950–2002." Tuck School of Business, Dartmouth College, Working Paper No. 2004-11 (2004).

14. R. R. Wiggins and T. W. Ruefli, "Schumpeter's Ghost: Is Hypercompetition Making the Best of Times Shorter?" *Strategic Management Journal* 26 (2005): 887–911.

15. G. McNamara, P. M. Vaaler, and C. Devers, "Same As It Ever Was: The Search for Evidence of Increasing Hypercompetition," *Strategic Management Journal* 24 (2003): 261–78.

16. K. Weigelt and C. F. Camerer, "Reputation and Corporate Strategy: A Review of Recent Theory and Applications," *Strategic Management Journal* 9 (1988): 137–42.

17. A. K. Dixit, "The Role of Investment in Entry Deterrence," *Economic Journal* 90 (1980): 95–106; P. Milgrom and J. Roberts, "Informational Asymmetries, Strategic Behavior and Industrial Organization," *American Economic Review* 77, no. 2 (May 1987): 184–9.

18. P. Milgrom and J. Roberts, "Informational Asymmetries, Strategic Behavior and Industrial Organization," *American Economic Review* 77, no. 2 (May 1987): 184–9.

19. P. Ghemawat, *Commitment: The Dynamic of Strategy* (New York: Free Press, 1991).

20. See, for example: A. K. Dixit and B. J. Nalebuff, *Thinking Strategically: The Competitive Edge in Business, Politics, and Everyday Life* (New York: W. W. Norton, 1991); and J. McMillan, *Games, Strategies, and Managers* (New York: Oxford University Press, 1992).

21. G. T. Allison and P. Zelikow, *Essence of Decision: Explaining the Cuban Missile Crisis*, 2nd edn (Boston: Little, Brown and Company, 1999).

22. B. C. Esty and P. Ghemawat, "Airbus vs. Boeing in Superjumbos: A Case of Failed Preemption," Harvard Business School Working Paper No. 02-061 (2002).

23. D. Ronfelt, "Social Science at 190 mph on NASCAR's Biggest Superspeedways," *First Monday* 5 (February 7, 2000).

24. "Game Theory in Action: Designing the US Airwaves Auction," *Financial Times Mastering Strategy Supplement* (October 11, 1999): 4.

25. John Cassidy "Rational Irrationality," *New Yorker* (October 5, 2009).

26. J. Maynard Smith, "Sexual Selection and the Handicap Principle," *Journal of Theoretical Biology* 57 (1976): 239–42.

27. A. Brandenburger and B. Nalebuff, *Co-opetition* (New York: Doubleday, 1996).

28. T. Dhar, J.-P. Chatas, R. W. Collerill, and B. W. Gould, "Strategic Pricing between Coca-Cola Company and PepsiCo," *Journal of Economics and Management Strategy* 14 (2005): 905–31.

29. "A Sharp Act Gets an Edge," *Financial Times* (September 10, 2008).

30. *Bitter Competition: Holland Sweetener vs. NutraSweet (A)* (Harvard Business School Case No. 9-794-079, 1994).

31. A. M. McGahan, "The Incentive not to Invest: Capacity Commitments in the Compact Disk Introduction," in R. A. Burgelman and R. S. Rosenbloom (eds), *Research on Technological Innovation Management and Policy*, vol. 5 (Greenwich, CT: JAI Press, 1994).

32. D. K. Levine and R. A. Levine, "Deterrence in the Cold War and the War on Terror," UCLA Department of Economics Working Paper (2006).

33. D. N. Sull, "Managing by Commitments," *Harvard Business Review* (June 2003): 82–91.

34. Games where price is the primary decision variable are called *Bertrand models* after the 19th century French economist Joseph Bertrand.

35. Games where quantity is the primary decision variable are called *Cournot models* after the 19th century French economist Antoine Augustin Cournot.

36. F. Scott Morton, "Strategic Complements and Substitutes," *Financial Times Mastering Strategy Supplement* (November 8, 1999): 10–13.

37. R. Loving, *The Men who Loved Trains* (Bloomington, IA: Indiana University Press, 2006).

38. For a review of research on competitive signaling, see O. Heil and T. S. Robertson, "Toward a Theory of Competitive Market Signaling: A Research Agenda," *Strategic Management Journal* 12 (1991): 403–18.

39. B. Macintyre, *Operation Mincemeat: The True Spy Story that Changed the Course of World War II* (London: Bloomsbury, 2010).

40. For a survey of the strategic role of reputation, see K. Weigelt and C. Camerer, "Reputation and Corporate Strategy: A Review of Recent Theory and Applications," *Strategic Management Journal* 9 (1988): 443–54.

41. P. Milgrom and J. Roberts, "Predation, Reputation, and Entry Deterrence," *Journal of Economic Theory* 27 (1982): 280–312.

42. R. M. Grant, "Pricing Behavior in the UK Wholesale Market for Petrol," *Journal of Industrial Economics* 30 (1982): 271–92; L. Miller, "The Provocative Practice of Price Signaling: Collusion versus Cooperation," *Business Horizons* (July/August 1993).

43. On the ability of game theory to predict almost any equilibrium solution (the Pandora's Box Problem) see C. F. Camerer, "Does Strategy Research Need Game Theory?" *Strategic Management Journal*, Special Issue 12 (Winter 1991): 137–52; and F. M. Fisher, "The Games Economists Play: A Noncooperative View," *Rand Journal of Economics* 20 (Spring 1989): 113–124. Steve Postrel illustrates the point with a game theory model to explain the rationality of bank presidents setting fire to their trousers. See S. Postrel, "Burning Your Britches behind You: Can Policy Scholars Bank on Game Theory?" *Strategic Management Journal*, Special Issue 12 (Winter 1991): 153–5.

44. G. F. Rose and M. Lloyd, "The Failure of FCC Spectrum Auctions," (Washington DC: Center for American Progress, May 2006); P. Klemperer, "How not to Run Auctions: The European 3G Mobile Telecom Auctions. *European Economic Review* 46 (2002): 829–45.

45. Strategic and Competitive Intelligence Professionals; the Institute for Competitive Intelligence.

46. For example, S. Sharp, *Competitive Intelligence Advantage* (Hoboken, NJ: John Wiley & Sons, Inc., 2009); L. M. Fuld, *The Secret Language of Competitive Intelligence* (Indianapolis: Dog Ear Publishing, 2010).

47. "McLaren Docked F1 Points for Spying," *Financial Times* (September 14, 2007); "Kolon Loses $920 Million Verdict to DuPont in Trial Over Kevlar," *Washington Post* (September 15, 2011).

48. Office of the National Counterintelligence Executive, *Foreign Spies Stealing US Economic Secrets in Cyberspace: Report to Congress on Foreign Economic Collection and Industrial Espionage*, 2009–2011 (October 2011).

49. J.-C. Spender, *Industry Recipes: The Nature and Sources of Managerial Judgment* (Oxford: Blackwell, 1989). How social interaction promotes convergence of perceptions and beliefs is discussed by Anne Huff in "Industry Influences on Strategy Reformulation," *Strategic Management Journal* 3 (1982): 119–31.

50. This section draws heavily on M. E. Porter, *Competitive Advantage* (New York: Free Press, 1985): Chapter 7.

51. "Pirelli's Bet on High-performance Tires," *International Herald Tribune* (April 2, 2005).

52. R. E. Caves and M. E. Porter, "From Entry Barriers to Mobility Barriers: Conjectural Decisions and Contrived Deterrence to New Competition," *Quarterly Journal of Economics* 91 (1977): 241–62.

53. W. C. Kim and R. Mauborgne, "Blue Ocean Strategy: From Theory to Practice," *California Management Review* 47 (Spring 2005): 105–21.

54. M. E. Porter, *Competitive Strategy* (New York: Free Press, 1980): 129.

55. For more on strategic groups, see J. McGee and H. Thomas, "Strategic Groups: Theory, Research, and Taxonomy," *Strategic Management Journal* 7 (1986): 141–60.

56. A. Feigenbaum and H. Thomas, "Strategic Groups and Performance: The US Insurance Industry," *Strategic Management Journal* 11 (1990): 197–215.

57. K. Cool and I. Dierickx, "Rivalry, Strategic Groups, and Firm Profitability," *Strategic Management Journal* 14 (1993): 47–59.

58. K. Smith, C. Grimm, and S. Wally, "Strategic Groups and Rivalrous Firm Behavior: Toward a Reconciliation," *Strategic Management Journal* 18 (1997): 149–57.

# 5 Analyzing Resources and Capabilities

Analysts have tended to define assets too narrowly, identifying only those that can be measured, such as plant and equipment. Yet the intangible assets, such as a particular technology, accumulated consumer information, brand name, reputation, and corporate culture, are invaluable to the firm's competitive power. In fact, these invisible assets are often the only real source of competitive edge that can be sustained over time.

—HIROYUKI ITAMI, MOBILIZING INVISIBLE ASSETS

You've gotta do what you do well.

—LUCINO NOTO, FORMER VICE CHAIRMAN, EXXONMOBIL

## OUTLINE

## Introduction and Objectives

In Chapter 1, I noted that the focus of strategy thinking has been shifted from the external environment toward its internal environment. In this chapter, we will make the same transition. Looking within the firm, we will concentrate our attention on the resources and capabilities that firms possess. In doing so, we shall build the foundations for our analysis of competitive advantage (which began in Chapter 3 with the discussion of key success factors).

> By the time you have completed this chapter, you will be able to:
> - appreciate the role of a firm's resources and capabilities as a basis for formulating strategy;
> - identify and appraise the resources and capabilities of a firm;
> - evaluate the potential for a firm's resources and capabilities to confer sustainable competitive advantage;
> - use the results of resource and capability analysis to formulate strategies that exploit internal strengths while defending against internal weaknesses.

We begin by explaining why a company's resources and capabilities are so important to its strategy.

## The Role of Resources and Capabilities in Strategy Formulation

Strategy is concerned with matching a firm's resources and capabilities to the opportunities that arise in the external environment. So far, the emphasis of the book has been on the identification of profit opportunities in the external environment of the firm. In this chapter, our emphasis shifts from the interface between strategy and the external environment toward the interface between strategy and the internal environment of the firm—more specifically, with the resources and capabilities of the firm (Figure 5.1).

Increasing emphasis on the role of resources and capabilities as the basis for strategy is the result of two factors. First, as firms' industry environments have become more unstable, so internal resources and capabilities rather than external market focus have been viewed as comprising a more secure base for formulating strategy. Second, it has become increasingly apparent that competitive advantage rather than industry attractiveness is the primary source of superior profitability. Let us consider each of these factors.

### Basing Strategy on Resources and Capabilities

During the 1990s, ideas concerning the role of resources and capabilities as the principal basis for firm strategy and the primary source of profitability coalesced into what has become known as the *resource-based view of the firm*.[1]

**FIGURE 5.1**   Analyzing resources and capabilities: The interface between strategy and the firm

To understand why the resource-based view has had a major impact on strategy thinking, let us go back to the starting point for strategy formulation: the underlying purpose of the firm which can be answered by posing the question: "What is our business?" Conventionally, this question has been answered in terms of the market being served: "Who are our customers?" and "Which of their needs are we seeking to serve?"[2] However, in a world where customer preferences are volatile and the identity of customers and the technologies for serving them are changing, a market-focused strategy may not provide the stability and constancy of direction needed to guide strategy over the long term. When the external environment is in a state of flux, the firm itself, in terms of the bundle of resources and capabilities it possesses, may be a much more stable basis on which to define its identity.

This emphasis on resources and capabilities as the foundation of firm strategy was popularized by C. K. Prahalad and Gary Hamel in their 1990 landmark paper "The Core Competence of the Corporation."[3] The potential for capabilities to be the "roots of competitiveness," the sources of new products, and the foundation for strategy is exemplified by several companies, for example:

- Honda Motor Company is the world's biggest motorcycle producer and a leading supplier of automobiles but it has never defined itself either as a motorcycle company or a motor vehicle company. Since its founding in 1948, its strategy has been built around its expertise in the development and manufacture of engines; this capability has successfully carried it from motorcycles to a wide range of gasoline-engine products (Figure 5.2).

- Canon Inc. had its first success producing 35 mm cameras. Since then, it has gone on to develop fax machines, calculators, copy machines, printers, video cameras, camcorders, semiconductor manufacturing equipment, and many other products. Almost all of Canon's products involve the application of three areas of technological capability: precision mechanics, microelectronics, and fine optics.

- 3M Corporation expanded from sandpaper into adhesive tapes, audio and videotapes, road signs, floppy disks, and medical and household products. Its product list comprises over 30,000 separate items. Is it a conglomerate? Certainly not, claims 3M. Its vast product range rests on a foundation of core

**FIGURE 5.2** Honda Motor Company: Product development milestones

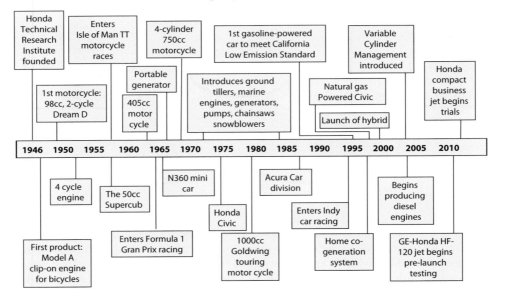

technological know-how relating to adhesives, thin-film coatings, and materials sciences supported by an outstanding ability to develop and launch new products.

In general, the greater the rate of change in a firm's external environment, the more likely it is that internal resources and capabilities rather than external market focus will provide a secure foundation for long-term strategy. In fast-moving, technology-based industries, basing strategy upon capabilities can help firms to outlive the life-cycles of their initial products. Microsoft's initial success was the result of its MS-DOS operating system for the IBM PC. However, by building outstanding capabilities in developing and launching complex software products and in managing an ecosystem of partner relationships, Microsoft extended its success to other operating systems (e.g., Windows), to applications software (e.g., Office), and to internet services (e.g., Xbox Live). Similarly, Apple's remarkable ability to combine technology, aesthetics, and ease of use has allowed it to expand beyond its initial focus on desktop and notebook computers into MP3 players (iPod), smartphones (iPhone), and tablet computers (iPad).

Conversely, those companies that when faced with radical technological change attempted to maintain their market focus have often experienced huge difficulties in building the new technological capabilities needed to serve their customers.

Eastman Kodak is a classic example. Its dominance of the world market for photographic products was threatened by digital imaging. Since 1990, Kodak invested billions of dollars developing digital technologies and digital imaging products. Yet, in January 2012, continuing losses on digital products and services forced Kodak into bankruptcy. Might Kodak have been better off by sticking with its chemical know-how, allowing its photographic business to decline while developing its interests in specialty chemicals, pharmaceuticals, and healthcare?[4]

Olivetti, the Italian manufacturer of typewriters and office equipment, offers a similar cautionary tale. Despite its early investments in electronic computing, Olivetti's attempt to recreate itself as a supplier of personal computers and printers was a failure. Might Olivetti have been better advised to deploy its existing expertise in electrical and precision engineering in other products?[5] This pattern of established firms failing to adjust to disruptive technological change within their own industries is well documented—in typesetting and in disk drive manufacturing, successive technological waves have caused market leaders to falter and have allowed new entrants to prosper.[6]

## Resources and Capabilities as Sources of Profit

In Chapter 1, we identified two major sources of superior profitability: industry attractiveness and competitive advantage. Of these, competitive advantage is the more important. Internationalization and deregulation have increased competitive pressure within most sectors; as a result, few industries (or segments) offer cozy refuges from vigorous competition. As we observed in the previous chapter (Table 4.1), industry factors account for only a small proportion of interfirm profit differentials. Hence, establishing competitive advantage through the development and deployment of resources and capabilities, rather than seeking shelter from the storm of competition, has become the primary goal of strategy.

The distinction between industry attractiveness and competitive advantage (based on superior resources) as sources of a firm's profitability corresponds to economists' distinctions between different types of profit (or *rent*). The profits arising from market power are referred to as *monopoly rents*; those arising from superior resources are *Ricardian rents*, after the 19th century British economist David Ricardo. Ricardo showed that, in a competitive wheat market, when land at the margin of cultivation earned a negligible return fertile land would yield high returns. Ricardian rent is the return earned by a scarce resource over and above the cost of bringing it into production.[7] Most of the $5.8 billion of royalties earned by Dolby Laboratories from licensing its sound reduction technologies comprises Ricardian rents, as does most of the $238 million earned in 2011 by tennis player Rafael Nadal.

Distinguishing between profit arising from market power and profit arising from resource superiority is less clear in practice than in principle. A closer look at Porter's five forces framework suggests that industry attractiveness often derives from the ownership of strategic resources. Barriers to entry, for example, are typically the result of patents, brands, know-how, or distribution channels, learning, or some other resource possessed by incumbent firms. Monopoly is usually based on the ownership of a key resource such as a technical standard or government license.

The resource-based approach has profound implications for companies' strategy formulation. When the primary concern of strategy was industry selection and positioning, companies tended to adopt similar strategies. The resource-based view, by contrast, recognizes that each company possesses a unique collection of resources and capabilities; the implication is that the key to profitability is not doing the same as other firms but rather exploiting differences. Establishing competitive advantage involves formulating and implementing a strategy that exploits a firm's unique strengths.

The remainder of this chapter outlines a resource-based approach to strategy formulation. Fundamental to this approach is a thorough and profound understanding of the resources and capabilities of a firm. Such understanding provides a basis for selecting a strategy that exploits the key resource and capabilities of an organization.

The same approach is relevant to formulating our career strategies. A sound career strategy is one that recognizes one's strengths and weaknesses and effectively exploits strengths while minimizing vulnerability to weaknesses—see Strategy Capsule 5.1 for an example. The challenge for companies is the same. For both individuals and organizations the starting point is to identify the available resources and capabilities.

## Identifying Resources and Capabilities

The first stage in the analysis of resources and capabilities is to identify the resources and capabilities of the firm—or, indeed, any organization since the analysis of resources and capabilities is as applicable to not-for-profit organizations as it is to business enterprises. It is important to distinguish between the **resources** and the **capabilities** of the firm: resources are the productive assets owned by the firm; capabilities are what the firm can do. Individual resources do not confer competitive advantage; they must work together to create organizational capability. Capability is the essence of superior performance. Figure 5.3 shows the relationships between resources, capabilities, and competitive advantage.

Our discussion of key success factors (KSFs)—the sources of competitive advantage within an industry—in Chapter 3 offers a starting point for our identification of

---

### STRATEGY CAPSULE 5.1

## Focusing Strategy around Core Capabilities: Lyor Cohen on Mariah Carey

The year 2001 was a disastrous one for Mariah Carey. Her first movie, *Glitter*, was a flop, the soundtrack was Carey's most poorly received album in a decade, her $80 million recording contract was dropped by EMI, and she suffered a nervous breakdown.

Lyor Cohen, the aggressive, workaholic chief executive of Island Def Jam records was quick to spot an opportunity: "I cold-called her on the day of her release from EMI and I said, I think you are an unbelievable artist and you should hold your head up high. What I said stuck on her and she ended up signing with us."

His strategic analysis of Carey's situation was concise: "I said to her, what's your competitive advantage? A great voice, of course. And what else? You write every one of your songs—you're a great writer. So why did

you stray from your competitive advantage? If you have this magnificent voice and you write such compelling songs, why are you dressing like that, why are you using all these collaborations [with other artists and other songwriters]? Why? It's like driving a Ferrari in first—you won't see what that Ferrari will do until you get into sixth gear."

Cohen signed Carey in May 2002. Under Universal Music's Island Def Jam Records, Carey returned to her core strengths: her versatile voice, song-writing talents, and ballad style. Her next album, *The Emancipation of Mimi*, was the biggest-selling album of 2005, and in 2006 she won a Grammy award.

***Source:*** "Rap's Unlikely Mogul," *Financial Times* (August 5, 2002). © The Financial Times, reproduced with permission.

**FIGURE 5.3**   The links between resources, capabilities, and competitive advantage

key resources and capabilities. Once we have identified the KSFs in an industry, it is a short step to identifying the resources and capabilities needed to deliver those success factors. For example:

- In budget airlines the KSF is low operating cost. This requires a standardized fleet of fuel-efficient planes; a young, motivated, non-unionized workforce; and a culture of frugality.
- In pharmaceuticals the KSF is the discovery and launch of new drugs. This requires high-quality researchers, drug-testing capability, and marketing and distribution capability.

However, as we shall see, identifying KSFs is only a starting point. To develop a comprehensive picture of an organization's resources and capabilities we need systematic frameworks for identifying and classifying different resources and capabilities.

## Identifying Resources

Drawing up an inventory of a firm's resources can be surprisingly difficult. No such document exists within the accounting or management information systems of most corporations. The corporate balance sheet provides only a partial view of a firm's resources—it comprises mainly financial and physical resources. To broaden our view of a firm's resources, we can identify three main types of resource: tangible, intangible, and human resources.

*Tangible Resources*  Tangible resources are the easiest to identify and value: financial resources and physical assets are valued in the firm's balance sheet. Yet, balance sheets tend to obscure strategically relevant information and to distort asset values. Historic cost valuation can provide little indication of an asset's market value. Disney's movie library had a balance sheet value—based on production cost less amortization—of only $1.6 billion in 2011.[8] Its total land assets (including its 28,000 acres in Florida) were valued at a paltry $1.1 billion.

However, the primary goal of resource analysis is not to value a company's assets but to understand their potential for creating competitive advantage. This requires not just balance sheet valuation but information on the composition and characteristics of the resources. With that information we can explore two main routes to create additional value from a firm's tangible resources:

- What opportunities exist for economizing on their use? Can we use fewer resources to support the same level of business or use the existing resources to support a larger volume of business?
- Can existing assets be deployed more profitably?

Strategy Capsule 5.2 discusses how Michael Eisner's turnaround of Walt Disney used both these approaches. Resource economies included consolidating administrative activities into fewer headquarters buildings and spreading the costs of movie studios over a bigger volume; redeployment of resources included

---

**STRATEGY CAPSULE 5.2**

## Resource Utilization: Revival at Walt Disney

In 1984, Michael Eisner became CEO of the Walt Disney Company. Between 1984 and 1988, Disney's sales' revenue increased from $1.66 billion to $3.75 billion, net income from $98 million to $570 million, and the stock market's valuation of the company from $1.8 billion to $10.3 billion.

The key to the Disney turnaround was the mobilization of Disney's considerable resource base. Prominent among Disney's underutilized resources were 28,000 acres of land in Florida. The acquisition of Arvida Corporation, a land development company, in 1984 assisted Disney in using its land holdings for hotels, convention facilities, residential housing, and a new theme park, the Disney-MGM Studio Tour.

To exploit its huge film library, Disney introduced videocassette sales of the Disney classics and began licensing packages of movies to TV networks. To put Disney's underutilized movie studios to work, Eisner doubled the number of movies in production while also making Disney a major producer of TV programs. Together with an expansion of animated movies, in 1988 Disney became America's leading studio in terms of box office receipts.

Above all, the new management team was exploiting Disney's most powerful and enduring asset: the affection of millions of people of different nations and different generations for the Disney name and the Disney characters. Recognition of the power of these resources allowed Disney to boost theme park admission charges, launch a chain of Disney Stores to push sales of Disney merchandise, and exploit overseas opportunities through Tokyo Disneyland and Disneyland Paris.

the exploitation of the Disney movie library releases on videocassette and then on DVD.

*Intangible Resources*   For most companies, intangible resources are more valuable than tangible resources. Yet, in companies' financial statements, intangible resources remain largely invisible—particularly in the US, where R & D is expensed.[9] The exclusion or undervaluation of intangible resources is a major reason for the large and growing divergence between companies' balance-sheet valuations (or book values) and their stock-market valuations (Table 5.1). Among the most important of these undervalued or unvalued intangible resources are brand names (Table 5.2). Interbrand values the Walt Disney brand at $29 billion; yet in Disney's balance sheet, the value of all its trademarks are a mere $1.2 billion. Brand names and other trademarks are a form of *reputational asset*: their value is in the confidence they instill in customers, suppliers, and business partners.

Like reputation, technology is an intangible asset whose value is not evident from most companies' balance sheets. Intellectual property in the form of patents, copyrights, trade secrets, and trademarks comprises technological and artistic resources where ownership is defined in law. However, some forms of technical know-how

**TABLE 5.1**   Large companies with the highest valuation ratios, March 2012

| Company | Ratio | Country of listing |
| --- | --- | --- |
| Hindustan Unilever | 31.51 | India |
| Colgate-Palmolive | 19.25 | USA |
| Yum! Brands | 17.54 | USA |
| Altria | 16.76 | USA |
| Boeing | 15.4 | USA |
| Priceline | 13.36 | USA |
| Coach | 11.9 | USA |
| Amazon | 10.88 | USA |
| BSky Broadcasting | 10.83 | UK |
| GlaxoSmithKline | 9.02 | UK |
| Tingyl | 8.49 | Hong Kong |
| Starbucks | 8.42 | USA |
| Intuitive Surgical | 7.81 | USA |
| British American Tobacco | 7.71 | UK |
| Diageo | 7.37 | UK |
| Medco Health Solutions | 6.63 | USA |
| Infosys | 6.43 | USA |
| Apple | 6.22 | USA |
| Celgene | 5.99 | USA |
| Shire | 5.89 | UK |
| Nike | 5.25 | USA |
| SAP | 5.23 | Germany |
| Coca-Cola | 5.04 | USA |
| PepsiCo | 4.96 | USA |

**Notes:**
The table shows companies from among the world's top-500 companies by market capitalization with the highest ratios of market capitalization to balance-sheet net asset value.

**Source:** Yahoo! Finance, *Financial Times*.

**TABLE 5.2**  The world's most valuable brands, 2011

| Rank | Brand | Value in 2011($ bn.) | Change from 2010 |
|------|-------|----------------------|------------------|
| 1 | Coca-Cola | 71.86 | +2% |
| 2 | IBM | 69.91 | +8% |
| 3 | Microsoft | 59.09 | −3% |
| 4 | Google | 55.32 | +27% |
| 5 | General Electric | 42.81 | +0% |
| 6 | McDonald's | 35.59 | +6% |
| 7 | Intel | 35.22 | +10% |
| 8 | Apple | 33.49 | +58% |
| 9 | Disney | 29.02 | +1% |
| 10 | Hewlett-Packard | 28.48 | +6% |
| 11 | Toyota | 27.76 | +6% |
| 12 | Mercedes Benz | 27.45 | +9% |
| 13 | Cisco | 25.31 | +9% |
| 14 | Nokia | 25.07 | −15% |
| 15 | BMW | 24.55 | +10% |
| 16 | Gillette | 23.99 | +3% |
| 17 | Samsung | 23.43 | +20% |
| 18 | Louis Vuitton | 23.17 | +6% |
| 19 | Honda | 19.43 | +5% |
| 20 | Oracle | 17.26 | +16% |

*Note:*
Brand values are calculated as the net present value of future earnings generated by the brand.
*Source:* Interbrand. Reproduced with permission from: http://www.interbrand.com/en/best-global-brands/
best-global-brands-2008/best-global-brands-2011.aspx

may be valuable but property rights may be weak or non-existent. In recent years, companies have become more attentive to the value of their intellectual property. For IBM (with the world's biggest patent portfolio), Qualcomm (with its patents relating to CDMA digital wireless telephony), and ARM (with patents relating to RISC microprocessors), intellectual property is the most valuable resource that they own.

Exploiting the profit potential of intangible assets typically involves extending the range of products over which they are exploited. Nike has extended its brand from athletic shoes to a wide range of apparel and sports equipment; Dolby Laboratories has applied its sound reduction technology to a broad variety of audio products.

*Human Resources*  Human resources comprise the skills and productive effort offered by an organization's employees. Human resources do not appear on the firm's balance sheet—for the simple reason that the firm does not own its employees; it purchases their services under employment contacts. We view human resources as part of the resources of the firm because, typically, they are stable. Although employees are free to move from one firm to another (most employment contracts require no more than a month's notice on the part of the employee), in practice most employment relationships are long term. In the US the average length of time an employee stays with an employer is 4.0 years, in Europe it is longer—8.4 years in Great Britain and 11.7 in both France and Italy.[10]

Organizations devote considerable effort to appraising their human resources: both at the hiring stage and as part of performance reviews and career planning. Human resource appraisal has become far more systematic and sophisticated. Many organizations have established assessment centers specifically for the purpose of providing comprehensive, quantitative assessments of the skills and attributes of individual employees, and appraisal criteria are increasingly based upon empirical research into the components of superior job performance. *Competency modeling* involves identifying the set of skills, content knowledge, attitudes, and values associated with superior performers within a particular job category, then assessing each employee against that profile.[11] A key research finding is the critical role of psychological and social aptitudes in determining superior work—the interest in *emotional intelligence* reflects this.[12] These findings explain the growing trend among companies to "hire for attitude; train for skills."

The ability of employees to harmonize their efforts and integrate their separate skills depends not only on their interpersonal skills but also on the organizational context. This organizational context as it affects internal collaboration is determined by a key intangible resource: the culture of the organization. The term **organizational culture** is notoriously ill defined. Sebastian Green defines organizational (or corporate) culture as "an amalgam of shared beliefs, values, assumptions, significant meanings, myths, rituals, and symbols that are held to be distinctive." The observation that companies with sustained superior financial performance are frequently characterized by strong organizational cultures has led Jay Barney to view organizational culture as a firm resource of great strategic importance that is potentially very valuable.[13]

## Identifying Organizational Capabilities

Resources are not productive on their own. A brain surgeon is close to useless without a radiologist, anesthetist, nurses, surgical instruments, imaging equipment, and a host of other resources. To perform a task, a team of resources must work together. An organizational capability is a "firm's capacity to deploy resources for a desired end result."[14] Just as an individual may be capable of playing the violin, ice-skating, and speaking Mandarin, so an organization may possess the capabilities needed to manufacture widgets, distribute them globally, and hedge the resulting foreign-exchange exposure. We use the terms *capability* and *competence* interchangeably.[15]

Our primary interest is in those capabilities that can provide a basis for competitive advantage—what have also been called *distinctive competences*.[16] Prahalad and Hamel introduced the term *core competences* to describe those capabilities fundamental to a firm's strategy and performance in that:

- they make a disproportionate contribution to ultimate customer value or to the efficiency with which that value is delivered
- they provide a basis for entering new markets.[17]

Prahalad and Hamel criticize US companies for emphasizing products over capabilities. Global leaders are those companies that develop core competences over the long term. Individual products may succeed or fail, the key is to learn from both success and failure in order to build capability.

*Classifying Capabilities*   Before deciding which organizational capabilities are "distinctive" or "core," the firms needs to take a comprehensive view of its full range of organizational capabilities. To identify a firm's organizational capabilities,

**TABLE 5.3**  A functional classification of organizational capabilities

| Functional area | Capability | Exemplars |
|---|---|---|
| CORPORATE FUNCTIONS | Financial control | ExxonMobil, PepsiCo |
| | Management development | General Electric, Shell |
| | Strategic innovation | Google, Haier |
| | Multidivisional coordination | Unilever, Shell |
| | Acquisition management | Cisco Systems, Luxottica |
| | International management | Shell, Banco Santander |
| | Corporate social responsibility | Johnson & Johnson, Danone |
| MANAGEMENT INFORMATION | Integration of IT with managerial decision making | Wal-Mart, Capital One, Cemex |
| RESEARCH AND DEVELOPMENT | Research capability | IBM, Merck |
| | New product development | Apple, 3M |
| | Fast-cycle new product development | Canon, Inditex (Zara) |
| OPERATIONS | Operational efficiency | Briggs & Stratton, UPS |
| | Continuous improvement | Toyota, Harley-Davidson |
| | Flexibility and speed of response | Four Seasons Hotels |
| DESIGN | Product design capability | Apple, Alessi |
| MARKETING | Brand management | Procter & Gamble, LMVH |
| | Building reputation for quality | Johnson & Johnson |
| | Responding to consumer requirements | L'Oréal, Amazon |
| SALES AND DISTRIBUTION | Effective sales promotion and execution | PepsiCo, Pfizer |
| | Efficient, fast order processing | L.L.Bean, Dell Computer |
| | Speed of distribution | Amazon |
| SERVICE | Customer service | Singapore Airlines, Caterpillar |

we need to have some basis for classifying and disaggregating the firm's activities. Two approaches are commonly used:

- A *functional analysis* identifies organizational capabilities within each of the firm's functional areas: Table 5.3 offers a framework for this.
- A *value chain analysis* identifies a sequential chain of the main activities that the firm undertakes. Michael Porter's generic **value chain** distinguishes between primary activities (those involved with the transformation of inputs and interface with the customer) and support activities (Figure 5.4). Porter's broadly defined value chain activities can be disaggregated to provide a more detailed identification of the firm's activities (and the capabilities that correspond to each activity). Thus, marketing might include market research, test marketing, advertising, promotion, pricing, and dealer relations.[18]

*The Nature of Capability*  Drawing up an inventory of a firm's resources is fairly straightforward. Organizational capabilities are more elusive, partly because they are idiosyncratic—every organization has features of its capabilities that are unique and difficult to capture using simple functional and value chain classifications. Consider Apple's product design and product development capabilities. Apple has a remarkable ability to combine hardware technology, software engineering, aesthetics, ergonomics, and cognitive awareness to create products with a superior user interface and unrivalled market appeal. But identifying the components of

**FIGURE 5.4**  Porter's value chain

this product design/development capability and establishing where and with whom within Apple this capability is located is no simple task. Let us explore more closely the nature and the determinants of organizational capability.

**From Resources to Capabilities: Routines and Integration**  Capabilities are based upon routinized behavior. *Routinization* is an essential step in creating organizational capability—only when the activities of organizational members become routine can tasks be completed efficiently and reliably. In every McDonald's hamburger restaurant, operating manuals provide precise directions for a comprehensive range of tasks, from the placing of the pickle on the burger to the maintenance of the milkshake machine. In practice, personnel are routinized through continuous repetition, meaning operating manuals are seldom consulted.

These **organizational routines**—"regular and predictable behavioral patterns [comprising] repetitive patterns of activity"[19]—are viewed by evolutionary economists as the fundamental building blocks of what firms do and who they are. It is through the adaptation and replication of routines that firms develop. Like individual skills, organizational routines develop through learning by doing. Just as individual skills become rusty when not used, so it is difficult for organizations to retain coordinated responses to contingencies that arise only rarely. Hence, there tends to be a tradeoff between efficiency and flexibility. A limited repertoire of routines can be performed highly efficiently with near-perfect coordination. The same organization may find it extremely difficult to respond to novel situations.[20]

Creating organizational capability is not simply a matter of allowing routines to emerge. Combining resources to create capability requires conscious and systematic actions by management. These actions include: bringing the relevant resources together within an organizational unit, designing processes, creating motivation, and aligning the activity with the overall strategy of the organization. Strategy Capsule 5.3 discusses the integration of resources to establish capability.

**The Hierarchy of Capabilities**  Whether we start from a functional or value chain approach, the capabilities that we identify are likely to be broadly defined:

## STRATEGY CAPSULE 5.3
# Integrating Resources to Build Organizational Capability

Resources are combined to create organizational capabilities; however, an organization's capabilities are not simply an outcome of the resources upon which they are based.

In sport resource-rich teams are often outplayed by teams that create strong capabilities from modest resources. In European soccer, star-studded teams (e.g., Chelsea, Real Madrid, and Manchester United) are frequently humbled by those built from limited means (e.g., Borussia Dortmund, Arsenal, and Porto). In my former hometown, Washington DC, the Redskins (NFL), Wizards (NBA), and Capitols (NHL) were among the richest teams in their leagues but consistently disappointed their long-suffering fans. Similarly in international competition: having the world's fastest sprinters is of little use in relay races if they drop the baton.

In business too we see companies with modest resources outcompeting established giants. In vacuum cleaners, the tiny British start-up Dyson Ltd. took market share leadership from the domestic appliance giant Electrolux in both the UK and the US. Hyundai Motor assembled its first car, a Ford Cortina, in 1968; by 2012, it was the world's fourth-largest producer of automobiles; in telecom equipment it was the upstart Cisco rather than established incumbents Alcatel-Lucent, Ericsson, and Siemens that led the new era of package switching; in microprocessors for mobile devices, ARM rather than Intel or Texas Instruments is the market leader.

Several factors determine the effectiveness with which resources are combined to create capabilities (Figure 5.5):

♦ *Processes*: While the academic literature has emphasized the role of routines as the foundation of capability, for practical purposes it is easier to view capabilities as comprising processes: coordinated sequences of actions through which specific productive tasks are performed. These sequences can be mapped using a flowchart.[a] For example, the process of fixing bugs in a large program developed by a computer software company involved a process of 30 distinct activities that began with problem recognition and ended with changes in software documentation.[b]

♦ *Organization structure*: For effective coordination, the individuals performing an organizational capability need to be located within the same organizational unit. The product development performance of US and European automobile manufacturers was transformed when, following Japanese practice, they created cross-functional product development teams. Organizational units may be created for the explicit purpose of developing capabilities: *communities of practice* are informal networks of employees who share their knowledge of a particular activity. At Rio Tinto, some 90 communities of practice share know-how and best practices on

manufacturing capability, marketing capability, supply chain management capability. However, our recognition that capabilities are about processes and routines suggests that broadly defined capabilities can be disaggregated into more specialist capabilities. For example, human resource (HR) management capability can be disaggregated recruitment capability, HR appraisal capability, and career development capability—among others. At the same time even broadly defined functional capabilities integrate to form wider cross-functional capabilities: new product development,

**FIGURE 5.5**   Integrating resources into capabilities

mining techniques, environmental issues, commercial activities, and more.

◆ *Motivation*: The effectiveness with which individuals combine their efforts to achieve organizational capabilities depends upon the extent to which they align their personal interests with those of the team and whether they are inspired to perform to the limit of their abilities. As we have already observed, and will continue to discover, leaders who can unify their organizational members around a clear strategic intent tend to be the most effective at combining resources with superior capabilities.

◆ *Organizational alignment*: As with so much of our strategic analysis, we come back to the issues of *fit*. The concept of organizational alignment has been applied to overall performance in relation to the consistency between environmental, strategic, and organizational factors.[c]

**Notes:**

[a]T. W. Malone, K. Crowston, J. Lee, and B. Pentland, "Tools for Inventing Organizations: Toward a Handbook of Organizational Processes," *Management Science* 45 (1999): 425–43.

[b]K. Crowston, "A Coordination Theory Approach to Organization Design," *Organization Science* 8 (1997): 157–75.

[c]T. C. Powell, "Organizational Alignment as Competitive Advantage," *Strategic Management Journal* 13 (1992): 119–134.

business development, the provision of customer solutions. What we observe therefore is a hierarchy of capabilities, for example:

● A hospital's ability to treat heart disease depends on its integration of capabilities relating to patient diagnosis, physical medicine, cardiovascular surgery, preoperative and postoperative care, as well as capabilities relating to training, information technology, and various administrative and support functions.

**FIGURE 5.6**    The hierarchy of organizational capabilities at a telecom equipment manufacturer

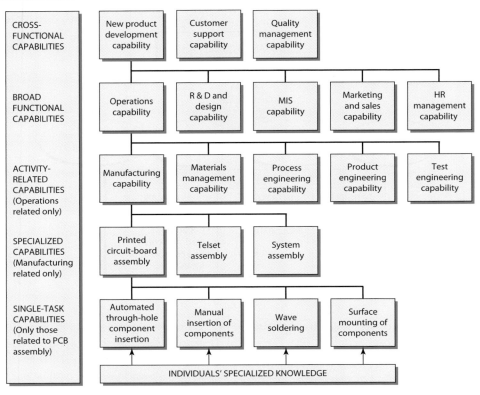

- Toyota's manufacturing ability—its system of *lean production*—integrates capabilities relating to the manufacture of components and subassemblies, supply-chain management, production scheduling, assembly, quality-control procedures, innovation management, and continuous improvement, inventory control, and various HR practices.

Figure 5.6 offers a partial view of the hierarchy of capabilities of a telecom equipment maker. As we ascend the hierarchy, capabilities become progressively more difficult to develop: higher-level capabilities require the broadest integration of know-how, typically across different functional departments. Hence, building new product development capabilities represents one of the greatest management challenges faced by many companies simply because of the vast array of technical and functional knowledge that must be integrated.[21]

## Appraising Resources and Capabilities

Having identified the principle resources and capabilities of an organization, how do we appraise their potential for value creation? There are two fundamental issues:

**FIGURE 5.7**   Appraising the strategic importance of resources and capabilities

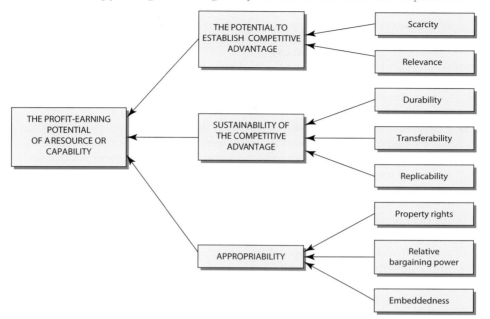

first, what is the strategic importance of different resources and capabilities and, second, what are the strengths of the focal firm, relative to its competitors' strengths, in relation to these resources and capabilities?

## Appraising the Strategic Importance of Resources and Capabilities

Strategically important resources and capabilities are those with the potential to generate substantial streams of profit for the firm that owns them. This depends on three factors: establishing a competitive advantage, sustaining that competitive advantage, and appropriating the returns from the competitive advantage. Each of these is determined by a number of resource characteristics. Figure 5.7 shows the key relationships.

*Establishing Competitive Advantage*   For a resource or capability to establish a competitive advantage, two conditions must be present:

- *Scarcity*: If a resource or capability is widely available within the industry, it may be necessary in order to compete but it will not be a sufficient basis for competitive advantage. In oil and gas exploration, technologies such as directional drilling and 3-D seismic analysis are widely available—hence they are "needed to play" but they are not "sufficient to win."
- *Relevance*: A resource or capability must be relevant to the KSFs in the market. British coal mines produced some wonderful brass bands, but these musical capabilities did little to assist the mines in meeting competition from

cheap imported coal and North Sea gas. As retail banking shifts toward automated teller machines and online transactions, so the retail branch networks
of the banks have become less relevant for customer service.

*Sustaining Competitive Advantage*    Once established, competitive advantage
tends to erode; three characteristics of resources and capabilities determine the sustainability of the competitive advantage they offer:

- *Durability*: The more durable a resource, the greater its ability to support
  a competitive advantage over the long term. For most resources, including
  capital equipment and proprietary technology, the quickening pace of technological innovation is shortening their life spans. Brands, on the other hand,
  can show remarkable resilience to time. Heinz sauces, Kellogg's cereals,
  Guinness stout, Burberry raincoats, and Coca-Cola have been market leaders
  for over a century.
- *Transferability*: Competitive advantage is undermined by competitive imitation. If resources and capabilities are transferable—they can be bought
  and sold—then any competitive advantage that is based upon them will
  be eroded. Some resources, such as finance, raw materials, components,
  machines produced by equipment suppliers, and employees with generic
  skills are transferable and can be bought and sold with little difficulty.
  Other resources and most capabilities are not easily transferred—either
  they are entirely firm specific or their value depreciates on transfer. Some
  resources are immobile because they are specific to certain locations and
  cannot be relocated. A competitive advantage of the Laphroaig distillery
  and its 10-year-old, single malt whiskey is its water spring on the Isle of
  Islay, which supplies water flavored by peat and sea spray. Capabilities,
  because they combine multiple resources embedded in an organization's
  management systems, are also difficult to move from one firm to another.
  Another barrier to transferability is limited information regarding resource
  quality. In the case of human resources, hiring decisions are typically based
  on very little knowledge of how the new employee will perform. Sellers of
  resources have better information about the performance characteristics
  of resources than buyers do. This creates a problem of *adverse selection*
  for buyers.[22] Jay Barney has shown that different valuations of resources
  by firms can result in their being either underpriced or overpriced, giving
  rise to differences in profitability between firms.[23] Finally, resources are
  complementary: they are less productive when detached from their original
  home. Typically brands lose value when transferred between companies:
  the purchase of European brands by Chinese companies—Aquascutum
  by YGM, Cerruti by Trinity Ltd., Volvo by Geely—risks the diminution of
  brand equity.
- *Replicability*: If a firm cannot buy a resource or capability, it must build it.
  In financial services, most new product innovations can be imitated easily
  by competitors. In retailing, too, competitive advantages that derive from
  store layout, point-of-sale technology, and marketing methods are easy to
  observe and easy to replicate. Capabilities based on complex organizational
  routines are less easy to copy. Federal Express's national, next-day delivery

service and Singapore Airlines' superior inflight services are complex capabilities based on carefully honed processes, well-developed HR practices, and unique corporate cultures. Even when resources and capabilities can be copied, imitators are typically at a disadvantage to initiators.[24]

- *Appropriating the returns to competitive advantage*: Who gains the returns generated by superior resources and capabilities? Typically the owner of that resource or capability. But ownership may not be clear-cut. Are organizational capabilities owned by the employees who provide skills and effort or by the firm which provides the processes and culture? In human-capital-intensive firms, there is an ongoing struggle between employees and shareholders as to the division of the rents arising from superior capabilities. As Strategy Capsule 5.4 describes, bargaining between star employees and owners over the sharing of spoils is a characteristic feature of both investment banking and professional sports. This struggle is reminiscent of the conflict between labor and capital to capture surplus value described by Karl Marx. The prevalence of partnerships (rather than shareholder-owned companies) in law, accounting, and consulting firms is one solution to this conflict over rent appropriation. The less clear are property rights in resources and capabilities, the greater the importance of relative bargaining power in determining the division of returns between the firm and its members. The more deeply embedded are individual skills and knowledge within organizational routines, and the more they depend on corporate systems and reputation, the weaker the employee is relative to the firm.

## Appraising the Relative Strength of a Firm's Resources and Capabilities

Having established which resources and capabilities are strategically most important, we need to assess how a firm measures up relative to its competitors. Making an objective appraisal of a company's resources and capabilities relative to its competitors' is difficult. Organizations frequently fall victim to past glories, hopes for the future, and their own wishful thinking. The tendency toward hubris among companies, and their senior managers, means that business success often sows the seeds of its own destruction.[25] Royal Bank of Scotland's acquisition-fuelled growth during 2000–2007 was based upon its perceived excellence in targeting and integrating acquisitions. This perception, rooted in the success of its first major acquisition, NatWest Bank, culminated in the disastrous takeovers of Citizens Bank of Ohio in 2004 and ABN Amro in 2007.[26]

**Benchmarking** is "the process of identifying, understanding, and adapting outstanding practices from organizations anywhere in the world to help your organization improve its performance."[27] Benchmarking offers a systematic framework and methodology for identifying particular functions and processes and then for comparing their performance with other companies'. By establishing performance metrics for different capabilities, an organization can rate its relative position. The results can be salutary: Xerox Corporation, a pioneer of benchmarking during the 1980s, observed the massive superiority of its Japanese competitors in cost efficiency, quality, and new-product development. More recent evidence shows wide gaps in most industries between average practices and best practices.[28]

**STRATEGY CAPSULE 5.4**

# Appropriating Returns from Superior Capabilities: Employees vs. Owners

Investment banks offer an illuminating arena to view the conflict between employees and owners to appropriate the returns to organizational capability. Historically, Goldman Sachs was widely regarded as possessing outstanding capability in relation to merger and acquisition services, underwriting new issues, and proprietary trading. These capabilities combine several resources: a high level of employee skill, IT infrastructure, corporate reputation, and the company's processes and culture. All but the first of these are owned by the company. However, the division of returns between employees and owners suggests that the former has had the upper hand in appropriating rents (Table 5.4).

In professional sport, it would appear that star players are well positioned to exploit the full value of their contribution to their teams' performance. The $27.8 million salary paid to Kobe Bryant for the 2012/13 NBA season seems likely to fully exploit his value to the Los Angeles Lakers.

Similarly with CEOs. Disney's CEO, Robert Iger, was paid $31.4 million in 2011. But determining how much Iger contributed to Disney's 2011 net income of $5,260 million as compared with that of Disney's other 156,00 employees is unknown.

The more an organizational performance can be identified with the expertise of an individual employee, the more mobile is that employee, and the more likely that the employee's skills can be deployed with another firm, then the stronger is the bargaining position of that employee.

Hence, the emphasis that many investment banks, advertising agencies, and other professional service firms give to team-based rather than individual skills. "We believe our strength lies in . . . our unique team-based approach," declares audit firm Grant Thornton. However, employees can reassert their bargaining power through emphasizing team mobility: in September 2010, most of UBS's energy team moved to Citi.

**TABLE 5.4** Profits, dividends, and employee compensation at Goldman Sachs

|  | 2008 | 2009 | 2010 | 2011 |
|---|---|---|---|---|
| Net profits | $4,440m | $13,390m | $8,354m | $4,442m |
| Dividends to ordinary shareholders | $638m | $579m | $819m | $780m |
| Total employee compensation | $20,237m | $16,190m | $15,380m | $12,200m |
| Compensation per employee | $344,900 | $498,000 | $430,000 | $366,360 |

However, benchmarking carries risks. Dan Levinthal points to the danger of looking at specific practices without taking account of interdependencies with other processes and the organizational context more broadly: "Companies should be cautious about benchmarking or imitating certain policies and practices of other firms . . . the implicit assumption in this thinking is that the policy that is benchmarked and adopted is independent of what my firm is already doing. The best human resource management practice for Nordstrom may not be the best for McDonald's. It may actually be dysfunctional."[29]

My own experience with companies points to the need for benchmarking to be supplemented by more reflective approaches to recognizing strengths and weaknesses. I find it useful to get groups of managers together to ask them to identify things that the company has done well in recent years and things that it has done badly, then to ask whether any patterns emerge.

## Developing Strategy Implications

Our analysis so far—identifying resources and capabilities and appraising them in terms of strategic importance and relative strength—can be summarized in the form of a simple display (Figure 5.8).

Our key focus is on the two right-hand quadrants of Figure 5.8. How do we exploit our key strengths most effectively? How can we address our key weaknesses in terms of both reducing our vulnerability to them and correcting them? Finally, what about our "inconsequential" strengths: are these really superfluous or are there ways in which we can deploy them to greater effect? Let me offer a few suggestions.

### Exploiting Key Strengths

The foremost task is to ensure that the firm's critical strengths are deployed to the greatest effect:

- If some of Walt Disney's key strengths are the Disney brand, the worldwide affection that children and their parents have for Disney characters, and the company's capabilities in the design and operation of theme parks, the implication is that Disney should not limit its themes park activities to six locations (Anaheim, Orlando, Paris, Tokyo, Hong Kong, and Shanghai); it should open theme parks in other locations which have adequate market potential for year-round attendance.

**FIGURE 5.8**    The framework for appraising resources and capabilities

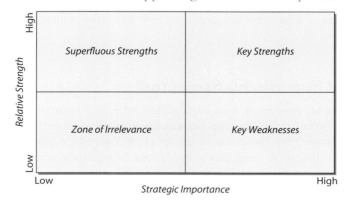

- If a core competence of quality newspapers such as the *New York Times*, the *Guardian* (UK), and *Le Monde* (France) is their ability to interpret events (especially in their home countries), can this capability be used as a basis for establishing new businesses such as customized business intelligence and other types of consulting in order to supplement their declining revenues from newspaper sales?

- If a company has few key strengths, this may suggest adopting a niche strategy. Harley-Davidson's key strength is its brand identity built on its 110-year heritage. Its strategy has been built around this single strength: a focus on super-heavyweight, traditionally styled, technologically backward motorcycles.

## Managing Key Weaknesses

What does a company do about its key weaknesses? It is tempting to think of how companies can upgrade existing resources and capabilities to correct such weaknesses. However, converting weakness into strength is likely to be a long-term task for most companies. In the short to medium term, a company is likely to be stuck with the resources and capabilities that it has inherited.

The most decisive, and often most successful, solution to weaknesses in key functions is to *outsource*. Thus, in the automobile industry, companies have become increasingly selective in the activities they perform internally. During the 1930s, Ford was almost completely vertically integrated. At its massive River Rouge plant, which once employed over 100,000 people, coal and iron ore entered at one end, completed cars exited at the other. In 2004, Ford opened its Dearborn Truck Plant on the old River Rouge site. The new plant employed 3200 Ford workers and an equal number of suppliers' employees. Almost all component production was out-sourced along with a major part of design, engineering, assembly, IT, and security. In athletic shoes and clothing, Nike undertakes product design, marketing, and overall "systems integration," but manufacturing, logistics, and many other functions are contracted out. We shall consider the vertical scope of the firm in greater depth in Chapter 11.

Clever strategy formulation can allow a firm to negate its vulnerability to key weaknesses. Consider once more Harley-Davidson. It cannot compete with Honda, Yamaha, and BMW on technology. The solution? It has made a virtue out of its outmoded technology and traditional designs. Harley-Davidson's old-fashioned, push-rod engines, and recycled designs have become central to its retro-look authenticity.

## What about Superfluous Strengths?

What about those resources and capabilities where a company has particular strengths that don't appear to be important sources of sustainable competitive advantage? One response may be to lower the level of investment into these resources and capabilities. If a retail bank has a strong but increasingly underutilized branch network, it may be time to prune its real-estate assets and invest in web-based customer services.

However, in the same way that companies can turn apparent weaknesses into competitive strengths, so it is possible to develop innovative strategies that turn apparently inconsequential strengths into key strategy differentiators. Edward Jones' network of brokerage offices and 8000-strong sales force looked increasingly irrelevant in an era when brokerage transactions were going online. However, by emphasizing personal service, trustworthiness, and its traditional, conservative investment virtues, Edward Jones has built a successful contrarian strategy based on its network of local offices.[30]

In the fiercely competitive MBA market, business schools should also seek to differentiate on the basis of idiosyncratic resources and capabilities. Georgetown's Jesuit heritage is not an obvious source of competitive advantage for its MBA programs. Yet, the Jesuit approach to education is about developing the whole person; this fits well with an emphasis on developing the values, integrity, and emotional intelligence necessary to be a successful business leader. Similarly, Dartmouth College's location in the woods of New Hampshire far from any major business center is not an obvious benefit to its business programs. However, Dartmouth's Tuck Business School has used the isolation and natural beauty of its locale to create an MBA program that features unparalleled community and social involvement that fosters personal development and close network ties.

## Choosing the Industry Context

In appraising resources and capabilities on the basis of strategic importance and relative strength we need to acknowledge that both these variables are context specific—both depend upon how we define the competitive environment of the focal firm. Consider the case of Harley-Davidson: if we view the relevant context as the world motorcycle industry, then technology is a critically important resource. If we view Harley as competing in the heavyweight-cruiser segment, then technology is less important. Similarly with the relative strength dimension—this depends critically upon which firms form our comparison set.

The choice of industry context is a matter of judgment. In general it is best to define industry context relatively broadly; otherwise, there is a risk that our resource/capability analysis becomes limited by the focal firm's existing strategy and we tend to exclude both threats from distant competitors and opportunities for radically new strategic departures.

More generally, however, we need to be alert to the limitations and weaknesses of our strategy frameworks. In the case of the Porter five forces of competition framework, the theoretical foundations of the model are largely obsolete and empirical support for the model is weak. Nevertheless, the five forces framework is a useful and revealing analytical tool. The key is to recognize that our analytical frameworks are not scientific theories: they are tools. In the case of the approach to analyzing resources and capabilities outlined here, our purpose is to make a start on identifying and understanding the resources and capabilities of organizations: the approach's value is in providing an overall picture of a firm's resource/capability profile within which more detailed analysis can then be pursued (Strategy Capsule 5.5).

**STRATEGY CAPSULE 5.5**

# Resource and Capability Analysis in Action: Ducati Motor Holding S.p.A

**TABLE 5.5**    The resources and capabilities of Ducati (prior to the acquisition by Audi)

|  | Strategic importance (1 to 10) | Ducati's relative strength (1 to 10) |
|---|---|---|
| **Resources** | | |
| Proprietary technology | Automotive technology is well-diffused throughout the industry (3) | A history of technical innovation, but few patents (6) |
| Location | Proximity to major markets, industry knowledge, and low cost inputs offer some advantages (4) | Italy is Europe's biggest motorcycle market and a center for engineering and design know-how (10) |
| Distribution | Critical to access the buyers and provide customer service (9) | Strong dealer network in Italy, weak in most other major markets (3) |
| Brand | Brand image important to buyers; scarce and costly to replicate (8) | Ducati an iconic brand with a long racing heritage (10) |
| Finance | Important for upgrading resources and capabilities (7) | Weak cash flow, parent company has limited financial resources (1) |
| **Capabilities** | | |
| Manufacturing | Capabilities with regard to efficiency, quality, flexibility are critical to cost and user satisfaction (10) | Ducati high cost due to low output (about 32,000 bikes annually); history of quality problems (2) |
| Design | Good design essential, but designs easy to replicate (6) | History of appealing and innovative designs (10) |
| Engineering | Key input into successful new product development (8) | Strong in ingenuity and innovation (8) |
| New product development | Regular launch of new models critical to market presence (10) | Despite limited resources, strong record of successful new products (9) |
| Marketing | Media advertising, promotion, and community building important, but marketing capability not rare (6) | Effective in brand promotion and online presence (8) |
| Customer service | Essential for brand reputation and sales of accessories (7) | Weak, especially outside Italy (2) |

Ducati combines sophisticated engineering with Italian design flair to produce a range of high-performance sports motorcycles. However, it inhabits an intensely competitive industry where it faces both large-scale manufacturers (Honda, Suzuki, Yamaha, BMW) and specialists (Harley-Davidson, Triumph, Piaggio, MV Agusta, and many more).

To identify resources and capabilities we can start with key success factors: what resources and capabilities are needed to compete effectively in the world motorcycle industry? We can supplement this list by considering the value chain of a typical motorcycle producer, then we can move on to appraising these resources and capabilities in terms of strategic importance and Ducati's relative strengths. Table 5.5 and Figure 5.9 show the results of this initial analysis.[31]

**FIGURE 5.9**   The resources and capabilities of Ducati Motor Holding S.p.A.

# Summary

We have shifted the focus of our attention from the external environment of the firm to its internal environment. We have observed that internal resources and capabilities offer a sound basis for building strategy. Indeed, when a firm's external environment is in a state of flux, internal strengths are likely to provide the primary basis upon which it can define its identity and its strategy.

In this chapter we have followed a systematic approach to identifying the resources and capabilities that an organization has access to and then have appraised these resources and capabilities in terms of their potential to offer a sustainable competitive advantage and, ultimately, to generate profit.

Having built a picture of an organization's key resources and capabilities and having identified areas of strength and weakness, we can then devise strategies through which the organization can exploit its strengths and minimize its vulnerability to its weaknesses. Figure 5.10 summarizes the main stages of our analysis.

In the course of the chapter, we have encountered a number of theoretical concepts and relationships; however, the basic issues of resource and capability analysis are intensely practical. The management systems of most firms devote meticulous attention to some resources and capabilities, such as the physical and financial assets that are valued on their balance sheets, to brand awareness, and to the monitoring and appraisal of human resources, but comprehensive assessment is rare. Senior managers often refer to the "core competencies" and "distinctive capabilities" of their organizations, but identification of these strengths is typically subjective and impressionistic.

**FIGURE 5.10** Summary: A framework for analyzing resources and capabilities

Because the resources and capabilities of the firm form the foundation for building competitive advantage, we shall return again and again to the concepts of this chapter. I shall also be extending the scope of our analysis. My emphasis has been on identifying, appraising, and deploying firms' existing resources and capabilities. A key challenge for companies is how they build capabilities to deal with the challenges of the future. We will address this issue in Chapter 8 when we discuss managing strategic change.

 Quizzes and flashcards to test yourself further are available in your interactive e-book at **www.wileyopenpage.com**

## Self-Study Questions

1. Many bricks-and-mortar retailers have been devastated by competition from internet retailers—book retailers and travel agents in particular. Advise either a travel agent or a traditional book retailer how it might redeploy its existing resources and capabilities to build a viable business either by repositioning within its existing industry or moving into a new area of business.

2. Microsoft's main capabilities relate to the development and marketing of complex computer software. Its greatest resource is the huge installed base of its Windows operating system, which runs on 83% of the world's personal computers. Does Microsoft's entry into video game consoles indicate that its strategy is becoming divorced from its principal resources and capabilities?

3. I have argued that the part of discrepancy between firms' stock market value and their book value reflects the fact than intangible resources are typically undervalued or not valued at all in their balance sheets. For the companies listed in Table 5.1, which types of resource are likely to be absent or undervalued in the firms' balance sheets?

4. Many companies announce in their corporate communications: "Our people are our greatest resource." In terms of the criteria listed in Figure 5.7, can employees be considered of the utmost strategic importance?

5. The chapter argues that Apple's key capabilities are product design and product development which combine hardware technology, software engineering, aesthetics, ergonomics, and cognitive awareness to create products with a superior user interface and unrivalled market appeal. How easy would it be for Samsung to replicate these capabilities of Apple?

6. Given the profile of Ducati's resources and capabilities outlined in Table 5.5 and Figure 5.9, what strategy recommendations would you offer VW?

7. Apply resource and capability analysis to your own business school. Begin by identifying the resources and capabilities relevant to success in the market for business education, appraise the resources and capabilities of your school, and then make strategy recommendations regarding such matters as the programs to be offered and the overall positioning and differentiation of the school and its offerings.

# Notes

1. The resource-based view is described in J. B.Barney, "Firm Resources and Sustained Competitive Advantage," *Journal of Management* 17 (1991): 99–120; J. Mahoney and J. R. Pandian, "The Resource-Based View within the Conversation of Strategic Management," *Strategic Management Journal* 13 (1992): 363–80; M. A. Peterlaf, "The Cornerstones of Competitive Advantage: A Resource-Based View," *Strategic Management Journal* 14 (1993): 179–92; and R. M. Grant, "The Resource-based Theory of Competitive Advantage," *California Management Review* 33 (1991): 114–35.

2. Ted Levitt ("Marketing Myopia," *Harvard Business Review*, July/August 1960: 24–47) recognized that a customer focus could result in firms defining their strategies too narrowly. Hence, he proposed that firms should define their strategies on the basis of the broad customer. For example, railroad companies should view themselves as being in the transportation business; oil companies should see themselves as energy companies. However, this fails to consider the resource implications of serving these broad customer needs. Can railroad companies enter the airline business or oil companies become successful electricity suppliers?

3. C. K. Prahalad and G. Hamel, "The Core Competence of the Corporation," *Harvard Business Review* (May/June1990): 79–91.

4. "Eastman Kodak: Failing to Meet the Digital Challenge," in R. M. Grant, *Cases to Accompany Contemporary Strategy Analysis* 8th edn (Oxford: Blackwell, 2013).

5. E. Danneels, B. Provera, and G. Verona, "Legitimizing Exploration: Olivetti's Transition from Mechanical to Electronic Technology," Management Department, Bocconi University, Milan, 2008.

6. M. Tripsas, "Unraveling the Process of Creative Destruction: Complementary Assets and Incumbent Survival in the Typesetter Industry," *Strategic Management Journal* 18, (Summer 1997): 119–42; J. Bower and C. M. Christensen, "Disruptive Technologies: Catching the Wave," *Harvard Business Review* (January/February 1995): 43–53.

7. A. Madhok and S. Li, "Ricardo Revisited: The Resource Based View, Comparative Advantage and Competitive Heterogeneity" (September 28, 2004). Available at SSRN: http://ssrn.com/abstract=611182, accessed 16 June, 2009.

8. Released theatrical productions less amortization, October 1, 2011 (Walt Disney Company, 10-K report).

9. "Why It Is So Hard to Value a Mystery?" *Financial Times* Special Report (January 7, 2008): 2.

10. *Economic Survey of the European Union*, 2007 (Paris: OECD, 2007).

11. E. Lawler, "From Job-Based to Competency-Based Organizations," *Journal of Organizational Behavior* 15 (1994): 3–15; L. Spencer and S. Spencer, *Competence at Work: Models for Superior Performance* (New York: John Wiley & Sons, Inc., 1993).

12. D. Goleman, *Emotional Intelligence* (New York: Bantam, 1995).

13. S. Green, "Understanding Corporate Culture and Its Relationship to Strategy," *International Studies of Management and Organization* 18 (Summer 1988) 6-28; J. Barney, "Organizational Culture: Can It Be a Source of Sustained Competitive Advantage?" *Academy of Management Review* 11 (1986): 656–65.

14. C. E. Helfat and M. Lieberman, "The Birth of Capabilities: Market Entry and the Importance of Prehistory," *Industrial and Corporate Change* 12 (2002) 725–60.

15. G. Hamel and C. K. Prahalad state: "the distinction between competencies and capabilities is purely semantic" (letter, *Harvard Business Review*, May/June1992: 164–5).

16. P. Selznick, *Leadership in Administration: A Sociological Interpretation* (New York: Harper & Row, 1957).

17. C. K. Prahalad and G. Hamel, "The Core Competence of the Corporation," *Harvard Business Review* (May/June1990): 79–91.

18. Porter's value chain provides the main framework of his book on *Competitive Advantage* (New York: Free Press, 1984). McKinsey & Company refers to the firm's value chain as its "business system." See C. F. Bates, P. Chatterjee, F. W. Gluck, D. Gogel, and A. Puri, "The Business System: A New Tool for Strategy Formulation and Cost Analysis," in *McKinsey on Strategy* (Boston: McKinsey & Company, 2000).

19. R. R. Nelson and S. G. Winter, *An Evolutionary Theory of Economic Change* (Cambridge, MA: Belknap, 1982).

20. As a result, specialists perform well in stable environments, while generalists do well in variable conditions: see J. Freeman and M. Hannan, "Niche Width and the Dynamics of Organizational Populations," *American Journal of Sociology* 88 (1984): 1116–45.

21. K. B. Clark and T. Fujimoto, *Product Development Performance* (New York: Free Press, 1991).

22. *Adverse selection* refers to the propensity for a market to be dominated by low-quality or risky offerings as a result of information asymmetry. This is also known as the *lemons problem*. See G. Akerlof, "The Market for Lemons: Qualitative Uncertainty and the Market Mechanism," *Quarterly Journal of Economics* 84 (1970): 488–500.

23. J. B. Barney, "Strategic Factor Markets: Expectations, Luck and Business Strategy," *Management Science* 32 (October 1986): 1231–41.

24. I. Dierickx and K. Cool ("Asset Stock Accumulation and Sustainability of Competitive Advantage," *Management Science* 35 (1989): 1504–13) point to two major disadvantages of imitation. They are subject to *asset mass*

*efficiencies* (the incumbent's strong initial resource position facilitates the subsequent accumulation of these resources) and *time compression diseconomies* (additional costs incurred by an imitator when seeking to rapidly accumulate a resource or capability e.g., "crash programs" of R & D and "blitz" advertising campaigns tend to be costly and unproductive).

25. D. Miller, *The Icarus Paradox: How Exceptional Companies Bring About Their Own Downfall* (New York: Harper-Business, 1990).

26. "Royal Bank of Scotland Investigation: the Full Story of How the 'World's Biggest Bank' Went Bust," *The Telegraph* (March 5, 2011), http://www.telegraph.co.uk/finance/newsbysector/banksandfinance/8363417/Royal-Bank-of-Scotland-investigation-the-full-story-of-how-the-worlds-biggest-bank-went-bust.html, accessed August 10, 2012.

27. "What is Benchmarking?" *Benchnet: The Benchmarking Exchange*, www.benchnet.com, accessed February 4, 2012.

28. "The Link between Management and Productivity," *McKinsey Quarterly* (February, 2006).

29. "A New Tool for Resurrecting an Old Theory of the Firm," Knowledge@Wharton, May 17, 2006 (http://knowledge.wharton.upenn.edu/article/1480.cfm, accessed February 4, 2012).

30. C. Markides, *All the Right Moves* (Boston: Harvard Business School Press, 1999).

31. This analysis of Ducati was undertaken prior to Ducati's acquisition by Audi, a subsidiary of Volkswagen AG. As part of the Volkswagen Group, Ducati's access to finance, engineering, design, technology, and several other resources and capabilities will be greatly enhanced.

# 6 Organization Structure and Management Systems: The Fundamentals of Strategy Implementation

> Ultimately, there may be no long-term sustainable advantage other than the ability to organize and manage.
>
> —JAY GALBRAITH AND ED LAWLER

> I'd rather have first-rate execution and second-rate strategy anytime than brilliant ideas and mediocre management.
>
> —JAMIE DIMON, CEO, JPMORGAN CHASE & CO.

> Many people regard execution as detail work that's beneath the dignity of a business leader. That's wrong. To the contrary, it's a leader's most important job.
>
> —LARRY BOSSIDY, FORMER CEO, HONEYWELL

## OUTLINE

## Introduction and Objectives

We spend a lot of our time strategizing: figuring out how we can best develop our careers; making plans for a summer vacation; thinking about how to improve our attractiveness to members of the opposite sex. Most of these strategies remain just wishful thinking: if strategy is to yield results, it must be backed by commitment and translated into action.

The challenges of strategy implementation are much greater for organizations than for individuals. Executing strategy requires the combined efforts of all the members of the organization. Many of those implementing strategy will have played no role in its formulation; others will find that the strategy conflicts with their own personal interests; some may not believe in the strategy. Even without these impediments, there is the simple truth that implementation tends to be neglected because it requires commitment, persistence, and hard work. "How many meetings have you attended where people left without firm conclusions about who would do what and when?" asks super-consultant, Ram Charan.[1]

We begin with the management systems through which strategy is linked to action and performance. As we shall see, formal strategic planning systems may not be particularly effective at formulating strategy; their primary value is in creating a mechanism for linking strategy to a system of implementation that involves operational planning, target setting, and resource allocation.

However, the challenge of strategy implementation goes beyond the tasks of operationalizing strategic decisions. The way in which a company organizes itself is fundamental to the effectiveness of its strategic management. Hence, a wider goal of this chapter is to introduce the concepts needed to understand the challenge of organizing and to provide a framework for designing organizational structure. Finally, we shall consider not just the role of organizational structure but also the informal aspects of an organization's social structure, namely its organizational culture.

The broad aim of this chapter is to introduce the reader to the fundamentals of strategy implementation: the basic aspects of organizational structure and systems that determine the effectiveness with which strategy is executed. In subsequent chapters we shall consider strategy implementation in particular business contexts. For example, Chapter 8 discusses the management of strategic change; Chapter 9 considers the organizational conditions conducive to innovation; Chapter 10 considers organizing to compete in mature industries; Chapter 12 examines the structure and systems of the multinational corporation; Chapter 14 deals with organizing the multibusiness company; Chapter 15 discusses the role of mergers, acquisitions, and alliances in strategy implementation.

By the time you have completed this chapter, you will be able to:

- ◆ understand how strategic planning links to operational planning, performance management, and resource allocation in implementing strategy;
- ◆ appreciate the basic principles that determine the structural characteristics of complex human organizations;
- ◆ select the organizational structure best suited to a particular business context;
- ◆ recognize how companies have been changing their organizational structures in recent years and the forces that have been driving these changes.

## From Strategy to Execution

Strategic management has conventionally been viewed as a two-stage process: first, formulation, then implementation. As we observed in Chapter 1, the notion of strategic management as a top-down process in which top management formulates then the lower levels of the organization implement has been challenged by Henry Mintzberg. His strategy-as-process view recognized that in the process of implementation the *intended strategy* is reformulated and redirected by the *emergent strategy*.[2]

The notion that strategic management can be separated into self-contained formulation and implementation stages is wrong. The intended strategy of any organization is inevitably incomplete: it comprises goals, directions, and priorities, but it can never be a comprehensive plan. It is during the implementation phase that the gaps are filled in and, because circumstances change and unforeseen issues arise, inevitably the strategy changes. At the same time, strategy formulation must take account of the conditions of implementation. The observation "Great strategy; lousy implementation" is typically a misdiagnosis of strategic failure: a strategy which has been formulated without taking account of its ability to be implemented is a poorly formulated strategy. The conventional formulation–implementation sequence is summed up in the adage "Structure follows strategy." Yet, management guru Tom Peters argues the reverse: for Domino's Pizza, with its global network of 8000 franchised outlets, or Amway, with its pyramid of commission-based, independent distributors, the structure *is* the strategy.

Clearly, strategy formulation and implementation are interdependent. Nevertheless, the fact remains that purposeful behavior requires that action must be preceded by intention. Hence, a feature of all the strategic planning systems that I have encountered is recognition that a strategy cannot be implemented until it has been formulated. In these strategy processes, formulation is linked to implementation by systems of operational planning, performance management, and resource allocation.

### The Strategic Planning System: Linking Strategy to Action

Small enterprises can operate successfully without an explicit strategy. If the business comprises a sole owner or a single family, the firm's strategy may exist only in the head of the owner-manager. Unless that owner-manager needs to write a business plan in order to attract outside financing, the strategy may never be articulated. There is no need to articulate the strategy because implementation is by the owner-manager, who knows what is in his/her own head.

Once the top management of a business comprises more than one person, strategy formulation has to become explicit. When they founded Apple Computer, Steve Jobs and Steve Wozniak each had ideas about what Apple II should be like and how it would be built and marketed. Agreeing a strategy required discussion between them. At many family firms, strategy is decided at the kitchen table.

As companies get larger, so the process of strategy making needs to be more formalized. Meetings must be held to allow managers to bring their different areas of knowledge, ideas, and perceptions together and to make decisions. Documents need to be created in order to communicate analysis and decisions from one part of the organization to another. A procedure needs to be established so that individuals and groups commit to the strategies that have been agreed.

*The Annual Strategic Planning Cycle*   Most large companies have a regular (normally annual, sometime bi-annual) strategic planning process that results in a document that is endorsed at the highest level of the company, normally the board of directors. The strategic planning process is a systematized approach that assembles information, shares perceptions, conducts analysis, reaches decisions, ensures consistency among those decisions, and commits managers to courses of action and performance targets.

Strategic planning processes vary between organizations. At some it is highly centralized. Even after the entrepreneurial start-up has grown into a large company, strategy making may remain the preserve of the chief executive. At MCI Communications, former CEO Orville Wright observed: "We do it strictly top-down at MCI."[3] At General Electric Company, Inc. and BP plc, the strategic planning process is more decentralized, driven primarily by bottom-up initiatives.

As companies mature, their strategic planning processes become more systematized and typically follow an annual cycle. Strategic plans tend to be for three to five years and combine top-down initiatives and directives and bottom-up strategy proposals. Figure 6.1 shows a typical strategic planning cycle. The principal stages are:

- The CEO typically initiates the process with some clear indications of strategic priorities—these will be influenced by the outcome of the previous performance reviews. In addition, the strategic planning unit may also offer input into the process in the form of assumptions or forecasts that provide a common basis for strategic planning by different units and levels within the organization. (Shell's 2011–2014 planning was undertaken as one of two alternative oil market scenarios: $60 a barrel and $80 a barrel.)
- On the basis of this framework of priorities and planning assumptions, the different organizational units—divisions and functional departments—create

**FIGURE 6.1**   The generic annual strategic planning cycle their strategic plans which are then presented at a series of review meetings (usually typically each involving a half-day or full day). On the basis of commentary from the CEO, CFO, and head of strategy (typically), the business plans are then revised.

Once agreed, the business plans are then integrated to create the corporate strategic plan that is then presented to the board for approval.

*The Content of Strategic Plans*   A strategic plan typically comprises the elements shown in Table 6.1.

Although strategic planning tends to emphasize the specific commitments and decisions that are documented in written strategic plans, the most important aspect of strategic planning is the strategy process: the dialog through which knowledge is shared and ideas communicated, and the consensus that is established. As General (later President) Dwight Eisenhower observed: "Plans are nothing; planning is everything." General von Moltke of Prussia made a similar point a century earlier: "No battle plan survives contact with the enemy."

Changes in strategic planning processes in recent decades have taken account of the need for flexibility and adaptation. Companies recognized the impossibility of forecasting the future and based their strategies less on medium- and long-term

**TABLE 6.1**   The contents of a strategic plan

| Main components of a strategic plan | Illustration from Royal Dutch Shell strategic plan for 2011–2014 |
| --- | --- |
| Corporate priorities: both strategic (e.g., gaining market leadership, portfolio rebalancing, competitive repositioning, new business development) and financial (e.g., sales growth, boosting profitability, debt reduction) | Goals: reinforce industry leadership, provide competitive shareholder return, help meet global energy demand in a responsible way |
| | Key differentiators: technology, project delivery capability, and operational excellence |
| | Medium-term focus: growth through upstream investment |
| Priorities of business strategies in terms of primary basis for competitive advantage (e.g., cost-reduction initiatives, innovation goals) | Upstream: focuses on exploration for new reserves with projects where technology and know-how add value, especially in Gulf of Mexico, North American tight gas, and Australian LNG. Also, selective acquisitions and exit from non-core petroleum assets |
| | Downstream: sustained cash generation by focusing on most profitable and growing businesses and exiting non-core refining capacity and selected retail positions |
| Strategic milestones: target dates for initiating or completing specific targets or for reaching certain performance goals | Project start-ups for 2012–13: Qatar gas-to-liquids plant, 2nd phase of BC-10 Brazilian oilfield, Gamusut-Kakap Malaysian oilfield |
| Resource commitments | Annual organic capital expenditure $25–$30 billion 2011–14; > 80% in upstream. Downstream investment to focus on marketing, especially in China, Brazil, and SE Asia |
| Performance targets and financial projections | Production: grow to 3.7m barrel/day by 2014 |
| | Cash flow: $43 billion by 2012 (assuming $80/barrel oil) |
| | Safety: reduce injuries from 1.3 per million hours to zero |

economic and market forecasts of the future and more on more general issues of strategic direction (in the form of vision, mission, and strategic intent) and alternative views of the future (e.g., using **scenario analysis**). Planning horizons have also shortened (two to five years is the typical planning period). The plans themselves have become less concerned with specific actions and more heavily oriented toward establishing overall performance goals.

In terms of process, strategic planning shifted from a control perspective, in which senior management used the strategic planning mechanisms as a means of controlling decisions and resource deployments by organizational units, toward a coordination perspective emphasizing dialogue, knowledge sharing, and consensus building. The result has been, first, that the strategic planning process has become increasingly informal with less emphasis on written documents and, second, that the role of strategic planning staff has diminished: responsibility for strategy making has been placed on the shoulders of line managers.[4]

*The Link with Implementation*   The strategy process achieves nothing unless the strategy is implemented. The key to strategy execution is achieved by linking the strategy process to action, through the operating plan; to motivation and accountability, through performance management; and to resource allocation, through capital budgeting. These implementation phases of the strategic planning process are shown in Figure 6.1; let us consider each of them.

## Operating Plans

Implementing a strategy requires breaking down medium-term planning into a series of short-term plans that can be a focus for action and a basis for performance monitoring. At the basis of the annual operating plan are a set of performance targets that are derived from the series of annual plans. These performance targets are both financial (sales growth, margins, returns on capital) and operational (inventory turns, defect rates, number of new outlets opened). In the section on "Setting Performance Targets" in Chapter 2, I outlined the basic *cascading* logic for goal setting: beginning with overall goals of the organization as a whole, we can disaggregate these into more specific performance goals as we move down the organization. As Chapter 1 shows, this can be based either on simple financial disaggregation or on using the balanced scorecard methodology. This approach to implementing strategy through establishing performance targets (not just for every organizational unit, but for every employee) has been widely used for over a half a century: *management by objectives* (the process of participative goal setting) was proposed by Peter Drucker in 1954.[5]

These performance targets become built into the annual operating budget. The operating budget is a pro forma profit-and-loss statement for the company as a whole and for individual divisions and business units for the upcoming year. It is usually divided into quarters and months to permit continual monitoring and the early identification of variances. The operating budget is part forecast and part target: it is set within the context of the performance targets established by the strategic plan. Each business typically prepares an operating budget for the following year that is then discussed with the top management committee and, if acceptable, approved. In some organizations the budgeting process is part of the strategic planning system: the operating budget is the first year of the strategic plans; in others, budgeting follows strategic planning.

Operational planning is more than setting performance targets and agreeing budgets; it also involves planning specific activities. As Bossidy and Charan explain: "An operating plan includes the programs your business is going to complete within one year . . . Among these programs are product launches; the marketing plan; a sales plan that takes advantage of market opportunities; a manufacturing plan that stipulates production outputs; and a productivity plan that improves efficiency."[6]

## Allocating Resources: Capital Expenditure Budgeting

Capital expenditure budgets are established through both top-down and bottom-up processes. When organizational units prepare their business plans, they will indicate the major projects they plan to undertake during the strategic planning period and the capital expenditures involved. When top management aggregates business plans to create the corporate plan, it establishes capital expenditure budgets both for the company as a whole and for the individual business units.

It is then up to the individual units to submit capital expenditure requests for specific projects. Companies have standardized processes for evaluating and approving projects. Requests for funding are prepared according to a standardized methodology, typically based on a forecast of cash flows, which are then discounted at the company's cost of capital (adjusted to take account of the project's level of risk). The extent to which the project's returns are sensitive to key environmental uncertainties is also estimated. Capital expenditure approvals take place at different levels of a company according to their size. Projects up to $5 million might be approved by a business unit head; projects up to $25 million might be approved by divisional top management; larger projects might need to be approved by the top management committee, while the biggest projects require approval by the board of directors.

## Organizational Design: The Fundamentals of Organizing

Implementing strategy is not just about strategic planning processes and linking them to goal setting, operational activities, and resource allocation. Strategy implementation encompasses the entire design of the organization. How a firm is organized determines its capacity for action. We saw in the previous chapter that the design of processes and structures are fundamental to organizational capabilities. The same is true in war: from the conquests of the Roman legions, to the one-sided outcome of the Franco-Prussian War and the Israeli victories in the Six-Day War (1967) and Yom Kippur War (1973), organizational superiority has played a critical role in military success.

Business enterprises come in many shapes and sizes. Samsung Corporation and Louie's Sandwich Bar on 32nd Street, New York share few organizational commonalities. When we include social enterprises, we expand the range of organizations even further. Yet, even giant corporations began as tiny start-ups. Strategy Capsule 6.1 summarizes some of the key developments in the development of the business corporation.

## STRATEGY CAPSULE 6.1
# The Emergence of the Modern Corporation

The large corporation, the dominant feature of the advanced capitalist economy, is of recent origin. At the beginning of the 19th century, most production, even in Britain, the most industrially advanced economy of the time, was undertaken by individuals and by families working in their own homes. In the US, the biggest business organizations in the mid-19th century were family-owned farms, especially some of the large plantations of the South.[a] The business corporation, one of the greatest innovations of modern society, resulted from two main sources: legal development and organizational innovation.

A corporation is an enterprise that has a legal identity: it can own property, enter into contracts, sue, and be sued. The first corporations were created by royal decree, notably the colonial trading companies: the British East India Company (1600), the Dutch East India Company (1602), and Hudson's Bay Company (1670). The introduction of limited liability, which protected shareholders from corporate debts, during the mid-19th century permitted large-scale equity financing.[b]

During the 19th century, most ideas about organization and management derived from the biggest organization of that time: the military. General von Moltke's organization of the Prussian army into divisions and general staff functions during the 1860s provided the basic model for large industrial corporations.[c] However, toward the end of the 19th century several organizational developments in the US formed the basis of "the second industrial revolution":

◆ *Line-and-Staff Structure*: Lack of transportation and communication meant that most companies operated in just one place. The railroad and the telegraph changed all that. In the US, the railroad companies were the first to create geographically separate operating units managed by an administrative headquarters. "Line" employees were engaged in operational tasks within operating units; "staff" comprised administrators and functional specialists located at head office. These simple line-and-staff structures developed into more complex functional structures; companies such as Sears Roebuck & Co. and Shell Transport and Trading managed numerous operating units with large functionally specialized headquarters.

◆ *The holding company* was a financial structure created by a parent company acquiring controlling equity stakes in a number of subsidiary companies. Its management structures were simple: the parent appointed the board of directors of the subsidiaries and received dividends, but otherwise there was little integration or overall managerial control. The holding company structure allows entrepreneurs such as Richard Branson and families such as the Tata family of India to control large business empires without the need for either the capital or the management structure required by an integrated corporation.

◆ *The multidivisional corporation:* During the 1920s, the multidivisional form began to replace both centralized, functional structures and loose-knit holding companies. At DuPont, increasing size and a widening product range strained the functional structure and overloaded top management. The solution devised by Pierre Du Pont was to decentralize: 10 product divisions were created, each with their own sales, R & D, and support activities. The corporate head office headed by an executive committee took responsibility for coordination, strategy, and resource allocation.[d] Soon after, General Motors, a loose holding company built by acquisition, adopted a similar structure to solve its problems of weak financial control and a confused product line. The new structure (shown in Figure 6.2) divided decision making between the division heads, each

**FIGURE 6.2**   General Motors Corporation: Organizational structure, 1921

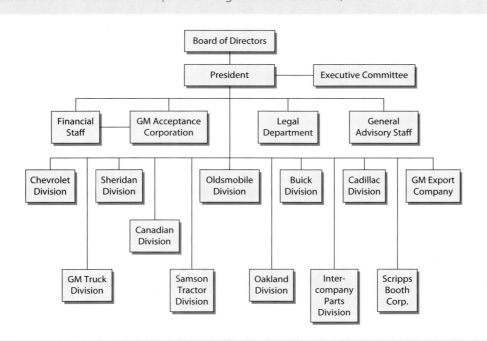

***Source:*** A. P. Sloan, *My Years with General Motors* (Orbit Publishing, 1972): 57. © 1963 by Alfred P. Sloan. © renewed 1991, Alfred P. Sloan Foundation. Reproduced with Permission.

responsible for their division's operations and performance, and the president, as head of the general office and responsible for the corporation's development and control.[e] During the next 50 years, the multidivisional structure became the dominant organizational form for large corporations.

During recent decades, international expansion has been the dominant source of corporate growth. Industry after industry has been transformed by the emergence of global giants: Arcelor Mittal in steel, AB-Inbev in beer, Toyota in automobiles, McDonald's in fast food. Yet, despite the incredible success of the shareholder-owned corporations, other business forms continue to exist. Some sectors—agriculture, retailing, and many service industries—are dominated by family firms and individual proprietorships; partnerships

predominate in professional service industries such as law; cooperatives are prominent in some sectors, especially agriculture; despite the privatization trend of the 1990s, state-owned enterprises are highly influential. Saudi Aramco, Indian Railways, China Mobile, China National Petroleum, and Royal Bank of Scotland are all industry leaders that are majority state-owned.

***Notes:***

[a] A. D. Chandler, *The Visible Hand: The Managerial Revolution in American Business* (Cambridge, MA: MIT Press, 1977): Chapter 2.

[b] J. Micklethwait and A. Wooldridge, *The Company: A Short History of a Revolutionary Idea* (New York: Modern Library, 2005).

[c] R. Stark, *Sociology*, 10th edn. (Belmont, CA: Wadsworth, 2006).

[d] A. D. Chandler, *Strategy and Structure* (Cambridge: MIT Press, 1962): 382–3.

[e] A. P. Sloan, *My Years with General Motors* (London: Sidgwick & Jackson, 1963): 42–56.

Despite their diversity, all business enterprises face the same challenge of designing structures and systems that match the particular circumstances of their own situation. In the same way that strategic management is a quest for unique solutions to the matching of internal resources and capabilities to external business opportunity, so organizational design is about selecting structures, systems, and management styles that can best implement such strategies. To establish principles, guidelines, and criteria for designing business organizations we need to consider the fundamental challenges of organizing.

To design a firm we must first recognize what it is supposed to do. According to Henry Mintzberg:

> Every organized human activity—from making pots to placing a man on the moon—gives rise to two fundamental and opposing requirements: the division of labor into various tasks, and the coordination of these tasks to accomplish the activity. The structure of the organization can be defined simply as the ways in which labor is divided into distinct tasks and coordination is achieved among these tasks.[7]

## Specialization and Division of Labor

Firms exist because of their efficiency advantages in producing goods and services. The fundamental source of efficiency is *specialization* through the *division of labor* into separate tasks. Consider Adam Smith's description of pin manufacture:

> One man draws out the wire, another straightens it, a third cuts it, a fourth points it, a fifth grinds it at the top for receiving the head; to make the head requires two or three distinct operations; to put it on is a peculiar business, to whiten the pins is another; it is even a trade by itself to put them into the papers.[8]

Smith's pin makers produced about 4800 pins per person each day. "But if they had all wrought separately and independently, and without any of them having been educated to this peculiar business, they certainly could not each have made 20, perhaps not one pin, in a day." Henry Ford's assembly-line system introduced in 1913 was based on the same principle. Between the end of 1912 and early 1914 the time taken to assemble a Model T fell from 106 hours to six hours.

But specialization comes at a cost. The more a production process is divided between different specialists, the more complex is the challenge of integrating their separate efforts. The more volatile and unstable the external environment, the greater the number of decisions that need to be made and the greater are the coordination costs. Hence, the more stable the environment, the greater the optimal division of labor. This is true both for firms and for entire societies. Civilizations are built on increased divisions of labor, which is only possible through stability. As the recent histories of Somalia, Haiti, and the Congo have demonstrated so tragically, once chaos reigns, societies regress toward subsistence mode, where each family unit must be self-sufficient.

## The Cooperation Problem

Integrating the efforts of specialist individuals involves two organizational problems: there is the cooperation problem—that of aligning the interests of individuals who have divergent goals—and the coordination problem—even in the absence of goal conflict, how do individuals harmonize their different activities?

The economics literature analyzes cooperation problems arising from goal misalignment as the **agency problem**.[9] An agency relationship exists when one party (the principal) contracts with another party (the agent) to act on behalf of the principal. The problem is ensuring that the agent acts in the principal's interest. Within the firm, the major agency problem is between owners (shareholders) and managers. The problem of ensuring that managers operate companies to maximize shareholder wealth is at the center of the corporate governance debate. During the 1990s, changes in top management remuneration—in particular the increasing use of stock options—were intended to align the interests of managers with those of shareholders.[10] However, it seems that bonus and stock option plans offer perverse incentives: encouraging either an emphasis on short-term over long-term profitability or even the manipulation of reported earnings (e.g., Enron, WorldCom).

Agency problems exist throughout the hierarchy. For individual employees, systems of incentives, monitoring, and appraisal encourage them to pursue organizational goals rather than doing their own thing or simply shirking. However, the organization structure itself may be part of the problem. Each department tends to create its own subgoals that conflict with those of other departments. The classic conflicts are between different functions: sales wishes to please customers, production wishes to maximize output, R & D wants to introduce mind-blowing new products, while finance worries about profit and loss.

Several mechanisms are available to management for achieving goal alignment within organizations:

- *Control mechanisms* typically operate through hierarchical supervision. Managers supervise the behavior and performance of subordinates who must seek approval for actions that lie outside their defined area of discretion. Control is enforced through positive and negative incentives: the primary positive incentive is the opportunity for promotion up the hierarchy; negative incentives are dismissal and demotion.

- *Performance incentives* link rewards to output: they include piece rates for production workers and profit bonuses for executives. Such performance-related incentives have two main benefits: first, they are high powered—they relate rewards directly to output—and, second, they economize on the need for costly monitoring and supervision of employees. Pay-for-performance becomes more difficult when employees work in teams or on activities where output is difficult to measure.

- *Shared values.* Some organizations are able to achieve high levels of cooperation and low levels of goal conflict without extensive control mechanisms or performance-related incentives. Churches, charities, clubs, and voluntary organizations typically display a commonality of values among members that supports common purpose. Among firms the presence of shared core values has long been recognized as an ingredient of sustained success.[11] Shared values encourage the perceptions and views of organizational members to converge, which facilitates consensus and avoids conflict. In doing so shared values can act as a control mechanism that is an alternative to bureaucratic control or financial incentives—Bill Ouchi refers to this as *clan control*.[12] An organization's values are one component of its culture. Strategy Capsule 6.2 discusses the role of organizational culture for aligning individual actions with company strategy.

**STRATEGY CAPSULE 6.2**
# Organizational Culture as an Integrating Device

Corporate culture comprises the beliefs, values, and behavioral norms of the company, which influence how employees think and behave.[a] It is manifest in symbols, ceremonies, social practices, rites, vocabulary, and dress. While shared values are effective in aligning the goals of organizational members, culture as a whole exercises a wider influence on an organization's capacity for purposeful action. Organizational culture is a complex phenomenon. It is influenced by the external environment—in particular the national and ethnic cultures within which the firm is embedded. It may also be influenced by the social and professional cultures of organizational members. Most of all, it is a product of the organization's history: the founder's personality and beliefs tend to be especially influential. For example, the corporate culture of Walt Disney Company continues to reflect the values, aspirations, and personal style of Walt Disney. A corporate culture is seldom homogeneous: different cultures may be evident in the research lab, in sales, and within the accounting department.

Culture can facilitate both cooperation and coordination. In companies such as Starbucks, Shell, Nintendo, and Google, strong corporate cultures create a sense of identity among employees that supports communication and organizational routines. However, culture can also impede strategy implementation. Cultures can also be divisive and dysfunctional. At the British bank NatWest during the 1990s, John Weeks identified a "culture of complaining" which was a barrier to top-down strategy initiatives.[b] A culture is likely to support some types of corporate action but handicap others. Salomon Brothers (now part of Citigroup) was renowned for its individualistic, internally competitive culture that reinforced drive and individual effort but did little to support cooperation. The culture of the British Broadcasting Corporation reflects internal politicization, professional values, internal suspicion, and a

dedication to the public good, but without a strong sense of customer focus.[c]

Cultures take a long time to develop and cannot easily be changed. As the external environment changes, a highly effective culture may become dysfunctional. The Los Angeles Police Department's culture of professionalism and militarism, which made it one of the most admired and effective police forces in America, later contributed to problems of isolation and unresponsiveness to community needs.[d]

While recognizing the importance of corporate culture—according to Merck's CEO, "Culture eats strategy for lunch!"[e] —it is far from being a flexible management tool at the disposal of chief executives. Culture is a property of the organization as a whole, which is not amenable to top management manipulation. CEOs inherit rather than create the culture of their organizations. The key issue is to recognize the culture of the organization and to ensure that structure and systems work with the culture and not against it. Where organizational culture supports strategy, it can be very valuable. First, it is cheap: as a control device it saves on the costs of monitoring and financial incentives; second, it permits flexibility: when individuals internalize the goals and principles of the organization, they can be allowed to use their initiative and creativity in their work.

**Notes:**

[a] E. H. Schein, "Organizational Culture," *American Psychologist* 45 (1990): 109–19.

[b] J. Weeks, *Unpopular Culture: The Ritual of Complaint in a British Bank* (Chicago: University of Chicago Press, 2004).

[c] T. Burns, *The BBC: Public Institution and Private World* (London: Macmillan, 1977).

[d] LAPD: Storming the Rampart," *Economist* (December 2, 2000): 72.

[e] J. Weeks, "On Management: Culture Eats Strategy," *Management Today* (June 2006).

## The Coordination Problem

The desire to cooperate is not enough to ensure that organizational members integrate their efforts—it is not a lack of a common goal that causes Olympic relay teams to drop the baton. Unless individuals can find ways of coordinating their efforts, production doesn't happen. As we have already seen in our discussion of organizational capabilities, the exceptional performance of Wal-Mart, the Cirque du Soleil, and the US Marine Corps Band derives less from the skills of the individual members as from superb coordination between them. Among the mechanism for coordination, the following can be found in all firms:

- *Rules and directives*: A basic feature of the firm is the existence of general employment contracts under which individuals agree to perform a range of duties as required by their employer. This allows managers to exercise authority by means of general rules ("Secret agents on overseas missions will have essential expenses reimbursed only on production of original receipts") and specific directives ("Miss Moneypenny, show Mr Bond his new cigarette case with 4G communication and a concealed death ray").
- *Routines*: Where activities are performed recurrently, coordination based on mutual adjustment and rules becomes institutionalized within organizational routines. As we noted in the previous chapter, these "regular and predictable sequences of coordinated actions by individuals" are the foundation of organizational capability. If organizations are to perform complex activities efficiently and reliably, rules, directives, and mutual adjustments are not enough—coordination must become embedded in routines.
- *Mutual adjustment*: The simplest form of coordination involves the mutual adjustment of individuals engaged in related tasks. In soccer or doubles tennis, players coordinate their actions spontaneously without direction or established routines. Such mutual adjustment occurs in leaderless teams and is especially suited to novel tasks where routinization is not feasible.

The relative roles of these different coordination devices depend on the types of activity being performed and the intensity of collaboration required. Rules are highly efficient for activities where standardized outcomes are required—most quality-control procedures involve the application of simple rules. Routines are essential for activities where close interdependence exists between individuals, be the activity a basic production task (supplying customers at Starbucks) or more complex (performing a heart bypass operation). Mutual adjustment works best for non-standardized tasks (such as problem solving) where those involved are well informed of the actions of their co-workers, either because they are in close visual contact (a chef de cuisine and his/her sous chefs) or because of information exchange (designers using interactive CAD software).

## Hierarchy in Organizational Design

Hierarchy is the fundamental feature of organizational structure. It is the primary means by which companies achieve specialization, coordination, and cooperation. Despite the negative images that hierarchy often stimulates, it is a feature of all complex human organizations and is essential for efficiency and flexibility. The critical issue is not whether to organize by hierarchy—there is little alternative—but how the hierarchy should be structured and how the various parts should be linked.

*Hierarchy as Control: Bureaucracy*   Hierarchy is an organizational form in which members of the organization are arranged in vertical layers; at intermediate layers each individual reports to a superior, and has subordinates to supervise and monitor. Hierarchy offers a solution to the problem of cooperation through the imposition of top-down control.

As an administrative mechanism for exercising centralized power, hierarchy was a feature of the government system of the Ch'in dynasty of China in the late third century BC and has been a feature of all large organizations in the fields of public administration, religion, and the military. For Max Weber, "the father of organizational theory," hierarchy was the central feature of his system of bureaucracy which involved: "each lower office under the control and supervision of a higher one"; a "systematic division of labor"; formalization in writing of "administrative acts, decisions, and rules"; and work governed by standardized rules and operating procedures, where authority is based on "belief in the legality of enacted rules and the right of those elevated to authority under such rules to issue commands."[13]

Weber's preference for rationality and efficiency over cronyism and personal use of hierarchical authority typical of his time encouraged organizational designs that sought safeguards against human traits such as emotion, creativity, fellowship, and idiosyncrasies of personality. As a result bureaucratic organizations have been referred to as *mechanistic*[14] or as *machine bureaucracies.*[15]

*Hierarchy as Coordination: Modularity*   In a general sense, hierarchy is a feature of almost all complex systems:[16]

- The human body comprises subsystems such as the respiratory system, nervous system, and digestive system, each of which consists of organs, each of which is made up of individual cells.
- The physical universe is hierarchy with galaxies at the top, below them are solar systems and we can continue down all the way to atoms and further to of subatomic particles.
- Social systems comprise individuals, families, communities, and nations.
- A book consists of letters, words, sentences, paragraphs, and chapters.

Viewing organizations as natural hierarchies rather than as systems of vertical control points to the advantages of hierarchical structures in coordinating:

- *Economizing on coordination*: Suppose we launch a consulting firm with five partners. If we structure the firm as a "self-organized team" where coordination is by mutual adjustment (Figure 6.3a), 10 bilateral interactions must be managed. Alternatively, if we appoint the partner with the biggest feet as managing partner (Figure 6.3b), there are only four relationships to be managed. Of course, this says nothing about the quality of the coordination: for routine tasks such as assigning partners to projects, the hierarchical structure is clearly advantageous; for complex problem solving, the partners are better reverting to a self-organizing team to thrash out a solution. The larger the number of organizational members, the greater the efficiency benefits from

**FIGURE 6.3**   How hierarchy economizes on coordination

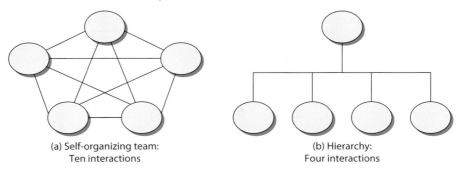

(a) Self-organizing team:
Ten interactions

(b) Hierarchy:
Four interactions

organizing hierarchically. Microsoft's Windows 8 development team involved about 3200 software development engineers, test engineers, and program managers. These were organized into 35 "feature teams," each of which was divided into a number of component teams. As a result, each engineer needed to coordinate only with the members of his or her immediate team. The modular structure of the Windows 8 development team mirrors the modular structure of the product.

● *Adaptability*: Hierarchical, modular systems can evolve more rapidly than unitary systems. This adaptability requires *decomposability*: the ability of each component subsystem to operate with some measure of independence from the other subsystems. Modular systems that allow significant independence for each module are referred to as *loosely coupled*.[17] The modular structure of Windows 8 allows a single feature team to introduce innovative product features and innovative software solutions without the need to coordinate with all 34 other teams. The key requirement is that the different modules must fit together—this requires a standardized interface. The multidivisional firm is a modular structure. At Procter & Gamble, decisions about developing new shampoos can be made by the Global Hair Care division without involving the Global Fabric Care, Global Health Care, or Duracell divisions. A divisional structure also makes it easier for P&G to add new businesses (Gillette, Wella) or to divest them (Folgers Coffee, Pringles).[18]

## Contingency Approaches to Organization Design

Like strategy, organizational design has been afflicted by the desire to find the "best" way of organizing. During the first half of the 20th century, bureaucracy and scientific management were believed to be the best way of organizing. During the 1950s and 1960s, the human relations school recognized that cooperation and coordination within organizations was about social relationships, which bureaucracy stifled through inertia and alienation: Theory X had been challenged by Theory Y.

However, empirical studies pointed to different organizational characteristics being suited to different circumstances. Among Scottish engineering companies, Burns and Stalker found that firms in stable environments had *mechanistic forms*, characterized by bureaucracy; those in less stable markets had *organic forms* that were less formal and more flexible. Table 6.2 contrasts key characteristics of the two forms.

**TABLE 6.2** Mechanistic versus organic organizational forms

| Feature | Mechanistic forms | Organic forms |
|---|---|---|
| Task definition | Rigid and highly specialized | Flexible and broadly defined |
| Coordination and control | Rules and directives vertically imposed | Mutual adjustment, common culture |
| Communication | Vertical | Vertical and horizontal |
| Knowledge | Centralized | Dispersed |
| Commitment and loyalty | To immediate superior | To the organization and its goals |
| Environmental context | Stable with low technological uncertainty | Dynamic with significant technological uncertainty and ambiguity |

*Source:* Adapted from Richard Butler, *Designing Organizations: A Decision-Making Perspective* (London: Routledge, 1991): 76, by permission of Cengage Learning.

By the 1970s, *contingency theory*—the idea there was no one best way to organize; it depended upon the strategy being pursued, the technology employed, and the surrounding environment—had become widely accepted.[19] Although Google and McDonald's are of similar sizes in terms of revenue, their structures and systems are very different. McDonald's is highly bureaucratized: high levels of job specialization, formal systems, and a strong emphasis on rules and procedures. Google emphasizes informality, low job specialization, horizontal communication, and the importance of principles over rules. These differences reflect differences in strategy, technology, human resources, and the dynamism of the business environments that each firm occupies. In general, the more standardized goods or services (beverage cans, blood tests, or haircuts for army inductees) are and the more stable the environment is, the greater are the efficiency advantages of the bureaucratic model with its standard operating procedures and high levels of specialization. Once markets become turbulent, or innovation becomes desirable, or buyers require customized products—then the bureaucratic model breaks down.

These contingency factors also cause functions within companies to be organized differently. Stable, standardized activities such as payroll, treasury, taxation, customer support, and purchasing activities tend to operate well when organized along bureaucratic principles; research, new product development, marketing, and strategic planning require more organic modes of organization.

As the business environment has become increasingly turbulent, the trend has been toward organic approaches to organizing, which have tended to displace more bureaucratic approaches. Since the mid-1980s, almost all large companies have made strenuous efforts to restructure and reorganize in order to achieve greater flexibility and responsiveness. Within their multidivisional structures, companies have decentralized decision making, reduced their number of hierarchical layers, shrunk headquarters staffs, emphasized horizontal rather than vertical communication, and shifted the emphasis of control from supervision to accountability.

However, the trend has not been one way. The financial crisis of 2008 and its aftermath have caused many companies to reimpose top-down control. Greater awareness of the need to manage financial, environmental, and political risks in sectors such as financial services, petroleum, and mining have also reinforced centralized control and reliance on rules. It is possible that the cycles of centralization and decentralization that many companies exhibit are a means by which they balance the tradeoff between integration and flexible responsiveness.[20]

Developments in ICT have worked in different directions. In some cases the automation of processes has permitted their centralization and bureaucratization (think of the customer service activities of your bank or telecom supplier). In other areas, ICT has encouraged informal approaches to coordination. The huge leaps in the availability of information available to organizational members and the ease with which they can communicate with one another has increased vastly the capacity for mutual adjustment without the need for intensive hierarchical guidance and leadership.

# Organizational Design: Choosing the Right Structure

We have established that the basic feature of organizations is hierarchy. In order to undertake complex tasks, people need to be grouped into organizational units, and cooperation and coordination need to be established among these units. The key organizational questions are now:

- On what basis should specialized units be defined?
- How should decision-making authority be allocated?
- How should the different organizational units be assembled for the purposes of coordination and control?

In this section we will tackle two central issues in the design of organizations. First, on what basis should individuals be grouped into organizational units? Second, how should organizational units be configured into overall organizational structures?

## Defining Organizational Units

In creating a hierarchical structure, on what basis are individuals assigned to organizational units within the firm? This issue is fundamental and complex. Multinational, multiproduct companies are continually grappling with the issue of whether they should be structured around product divisions, country subsidiaries, or functional departments, and periodically they undergo the disruption of changing from one to another. Employees can be grouped on the basis of:

- common tasks: cleaners will be assigned to maintenance services and teachers will assigned to a unit called a faculty;
- products: shelf fillers and customer services assistants will be assigned to one of the following departments: kitchen goods, tableware, bedding, or domestic appliances;
- location: the 141,000 associates that work in Starbucks stores are organized by location: each store employs an average of 16 people;
- process: in most production plants, employees are organized by process: assembly, quality control, warehousing, shipping. Processes tend to be grouped into functions.

How do we decide whether to use task, product, geography, or process to define organizational units? The fundamental issue is *intensity of coordination needs*: those individuals who need to interact most closely should be located within the same organizational unit. In the case of Starbucks, the individual stores are the natural units: the manager, the baristas, and the cleaners at a single location need to form a single organizational unit. British Airways needs to be organized by processes and functions: the employees engaged in particular processes—flying, in-flight services, baggage handling, aircraft maintenance, and accounts—need to be working in the same organizational units. These process units then can be combined into broader functional groupings: flight operations, engineering, marketing, sales, customer service, human resources, information, and finance.

This principle of grouping individuals according to the intensity of their coordination needs was developed by James Thompson in his analysis of interdependence within organizations. He distinguished three levels of interdependence: *pooled interdependence* (the loosest), where individuals operate independently but depend on one another's performance; *sequential interdependence*, where the output of one individual is the input of the other; and *reciprocal interdependence* (the most intense), where individuals are mutually dependent. At the first level of organization, priority should be given to creating organizational units for reciprocally interdependent employees (e.g., members of an oilfield drilling team or consultants working on a client assignment).[21]

In general, the priorities for the first level of organization tend to be clear: it is usually fairly obvious whether employees need to be organized by task, process, or location. How the lower-level organizational units should be grouped into broader organizational units tends to be less clear. In 1921 it was far from obvious as to whether DuPont would be better off with its functional structure or reorganized into product divisions. In taking over as Procter & Gamble's CEO in 2000, A. G. Lafley needed to decide whether to keep P&G's new-product divisional structure or revert to the previous structure in which the regional organizations were dominant.

In deciding how to organize the upper levels of firm structure the same principle applies. At Nestlé, it is more important for the managers of the chocolate plants to coordinate with the marketing and sales executives for chocolate than with the plant manager for Evian bottled water: Nestlé is better organized around product divisions than around functions. Hyundai Motor produces a number of different models of car and is present in many countries of the world; however, given its global strategy and the close linkages between its different models, Hyundai is better organized by function rather than by product or geography.

Over time, the relative importance of these different coordination needs changes, causing firms to change their structures. The process of globalization has involved easier trade and communication between countries and growing similarities in consumer preferences. As a result multinational corporations have shifted from geographically based structures to worldwide product divisions.

## Alternative Structural Forms: Functional, Multidivisional, Matrix

On the basis of these alternative approaches to grouping tasks and activities we can identify three basic organizational forms for companies: the **functional structure**, the **multidivisional structure**, and the **matrix structure**.

*The Functional Structure*  Single-business firms tend to be organized along functional lines. Grouping together functionally similar tasks is conducive to exploiting scale economies, promoting learning and capability building, and deploying standardized control systems. Since cross-functional integration occurs at the top of the organization, functional structures are conducive to a high degree of centralized control by the CEO and top management team.

However, even for single-product firms, functional structures are subject to the problems of cooperation and coordination. Different functional departments develop their own goals, values, vocabularies, and behavioral norms, which makes cross-functional integration difficult. As the size of the firm increases, the pressure on top management to achieve effective integration increases. Because the different functions of the firm tend to be tightly coupled rather than loosely coupled, there is limited scope for decentralization. In particular, it is very difficult to operate individual functions as semi-autonomous profit centers.

The real problems arise when the firm grows its range of products and businesses. As we noted with DuPont, during the early 20th century, once a functionally organized company expands its product range, coordination within each product area becomes difficult.

However, as companies and their industries mature, the need for efficiency, centralized control, and well-developed functional capabilities can cause companies to revert to functional structures. For example:

- When John Scully became CEO of Apple in 1984, the company was organized by product: Apple II, Apple III, Lisa, and Macintosh. Cross-functional coordination within each product was strong, but there was little integration across products: each had a different operating system, applications were incompatible, and scale economies in purchasing, manufacturing, and distributions could not be exploited. Scully's response was to reorganize Apple along functional lines to gain control, reduce costs, and achieve a more coherent product strategy.
- General Motors, pioneer of the multidivisional structure, has moved toward a more functional structure. As cost efficiency became its strategic priority, it maintained its brand names (Cadillac, Chevrolet, Buick) but merged these separate divisions into a more functionally based structure to exploit scale economies and faster technical transfer (compare Figure 6.4 with Figure 6.2).

*The Multidivisional Structure*   We have seen how the product-based, multidivisional structure emerged during the 20th century in response to the coordination problems caused by diversification. The key advantage of divisionalized structures (whether product based or geographically based) is the potential for decentralized decision making. The multidivisional structure is the classic example of a loose-coupled, modular organization where business-level strategies and operating decisions can be made at the divisional level, while the corporate headquarters concentrates on corporate planning, budgeting, and providing common services.

Central to the efficiency advantages of the multidivisional corporation is the ability to apply a common set of corporate management tools to a range of different businesses. At ITT, Harold Geneen's system of "managing by the numbers" allowed him to cope with over 50 divisional heads reporting directly to him. At BP, John Browne's system of "performance contracts" allowed direct reporting by over 20 "strategic performance units." Divisional autonomy also fosters the development of leadership capability among divisional heads—an important factor in grooming candidates for CEO succession.

**FIGURE 6.4**  General Motors Corporation: Organizational structure, 1997

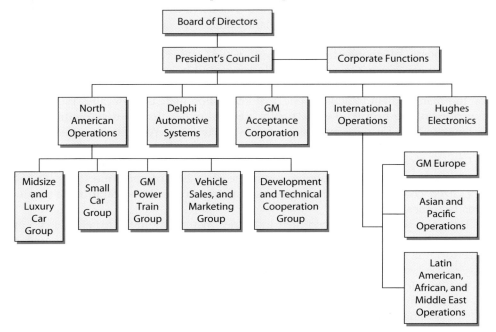

**FIGURE 6.5**  General Electric: Organizational structure, 2009

*Source:* Based on information in General Electric's Annual Report, 2008.

The large, divisionalized corporation is typically organized into three levels: the corporate center, the divisions, and the individual business units, each representing a distinct business for which financial accounts can be drawn up and strategies formulated. Figure 6.5 shows General Electric's organizational structure at the corporate and divisional levels.

In Chapter 14, we shall look in greater detail at the organization of the multi-business corporation.

*Matrix Structures*   Whatever the primary basis for grouping, all companies that embrace multiple products, multiple functions, and multiple locations must coordinate across all three dimensions. Organizational structures that formalize coordination and control across multiple dimensions are called *matrix structures.*

Figure 6.6 shows the Shell management matrix (prior to reorganization in 1996). Within this structure, the general manager of Shell's Berre refinery in France reported to his country manager, the managing director of Shell France, but also to his business sector head, the coordinator of Shell's refining sector, as well as having a functional relationship with Shell's head of manufacturing.

Many diversified, multinational companies, including Philips, Nestlé, and Unilever, adopted matrix structures during the 1960s and 1970s, although in all cases one dimension of the matrix tended to be dominant in terms of authority. Thus, in the old Shell matrix the geographical dimension, as represented by country heads and regional coordinators, had primary responsibility for budgetary control, personnel appraisal, and strategy formulation.

**FIGURE 6.6**   Royal Dutch Shell Group: Pre-1996 matrix structure

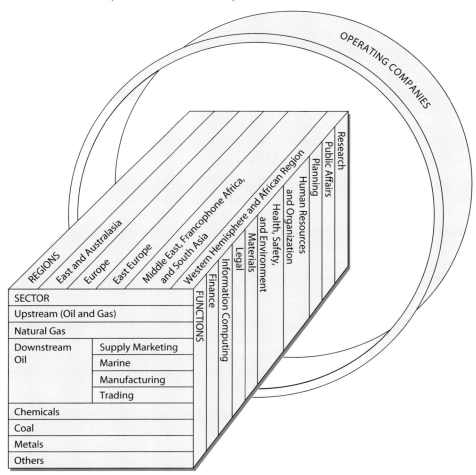

Since the 1980s, most large corporations have dismantled or reorganized their matrix structures. Shell abandoned its matrix during 1995–1996 in favor of a structure based on four business sectors: upstream, downstream, chemicals, and gas and power. During 2001–2002, the Swiss/Swedish engineering giant ABB abandoned its much-lauded matrix structure in the face of plunging profitability and mounting debt. In fast-moving business environments companies have found that the benefits from formally coordinating across multiple dimensions have been outweighed by excessive complexity, larger head-office staffs, slower decision making, and diffused authority. Bartlett and Ghoshal observe that matrix structures "led to conflict and confusion; the proliferation of channels created informational logjams as a proliferation of committees and reports bogged down the organization; and overlapping responsibilities produced turf battles and a loss of accountability."[22]

Yet, all complex organizations that comprise multiple products, multiple functions, and multiple geographical markets need to coordinate within each of these dimensions. The problem of the matrix organization is not attempting to coordinate across multiple dimensions—in complex organizations such coordination is essential. The problem is when this multidimensional coordination is over-formalized, resulting in a top-heavy corporate HQ and over-complex systems that slow decision making and dull entrepreneurial initiative. The trend has been for companies to focus formal systems of coordination and control on one dimension, then allowing the other dimensions of coordination to be mainly informal. Thus, while Shell is organized primarily around four business sectors and these sectors exercise financial and strategic control over the individual operating companies, Shell still has country heads, responsible for coordinating all Shell's activities in relation to legal, taxation, and government relations within each country, and functional heads, responsible for technical matters and best-practice transfer within their particular function, be it manufacturing, marketing, or HR.

## Trends in Organizational Design

Consultants and management scholars have proclaimed the death of hierarchical structures and the emergence of new organizational forms. Two decades ago, two of America's most prominent scholars of organization identified a "new organizational revolution" featuring "flatter hierarchies, decentralized decision making, greater tolerance for ambiguity, permeable internal and external boundaries, empowerment of employees, capacity for renewal, self-organizing units, [and] self-integrating coordination mechanisms."[23]

In practice, there has been more organizational evolution than organizational revolution. Certainly major changes have occurred in the structural features and management systems of industrial enterprises, yet there is little that could be described as radical organizational innovation or discontinuities with the past. Hierarchy remains the basic structural form of almost all companies, and the familiar structural configurations—functional, divisional, and matrix—are still evident. Nevertheless, within these familiar structural features, change has occurred:

- *Delayering*: Companies have made their organizational hierarchies flatter. The motive has been to reduce costs and to increase organizational responsiveness. Wider spans of control have also changed the relationships between managers and their subordinates, resulting in less supervision and greater decentralization of initiative. At Tata Steel, the management hierarchy was reduced from 13 layers to five. In briefing the McKinsey lead consultant, the CEO, Dr Irani, observed: "We are over-staffed, no doubt, but more damaging is the lack of responsiveness to fleeting opportunities . . . Our decision making is not as fast as it should be with everyone looking over their shoulder for approval . . . The objective is to redesign job content more meaningfully. The purpose is to rejuvenate the organization by defining richer jobs with fewer hierarchical layers of reporting.[24]

- *Adhocracy and team-based organization*: Adhocracies, according to Henry Mintzberg, are organizations that feature shared values, high levels of participation, flexible communication, and spontaneous coordination. Hierarchy, authority, and control mechanisms are largely absent.[25] Adhocracies tend to exist where problem solving and other non-routine activities predominate and where expertise is prized. Individual teams involved in research, consulting, engineering, entertainment, and crisis response tend to be adhocracies. At a larger organizational scale, companies such as Google, W. L. Gore & Associates, and some advertising agencies have adopted team-based structures with many of the features of adhocracies.

- *Project-based organizations*: Closely related to team-based organizations are project-based organizations. A key feature of the project-based organization is recognition that work assignments are for a finite duration, hence the organization structure needs to be dynamically flexible. Project-based organizations are common in sectors such as construction, consulting, oil exploration, and engineering. Because every project is different and involves a sequence of phases, each project needs to be undertaken by a closely interacting team that is able to draw upon the know-how of previous and parallel project teams. As cycle times become compressed across more and more activities, companies are introducing project-based organization into their conventional divisional and functional structures—for example new product development, change management, knowledge management, and research are increasingly organized into projects.

- *Network structures*: A common feature of the many descriptions of new approaches to company organization is use of the term *network*. Bartlett and Ghoshal present the *transnational organization* as a multinational corporation organized as an integrated global network;[26] Goold and Campbell propose an organizational design that they call the *structured network*.[27] Viewing organizational structures in terms of networks derives from social network analysis where organizations (and other social institutions) are conceptualized in terms of the social relationships between the individuals and organizational units within them. This emphasis on patterns of communication and interaction rather than the formal relationships puts emphasis on the informal mechanisms through which coordination occurs and work gets done within organizations. Advances in information and communications technology have greatly increased the scope for coordination to occur outside of the formal structure, leading many observes to advocate the dismantling of much of the formal structures that firms have inherited.

- *Permeable organizational boundaries*: The benefits of specialization accrue to organizations as well as to individuals; at the same time, the complexity of most products has been increasing. As a result, firms have sought to narrow their corporate scope through outsourcing and refocusing upon core business activities, while relying on close relationships with partner firms to access a wider range of expertise. As we shall when we look more closely at strategic alliances (Chapter 15), localized networks of closely interdependent firms have been a feature of manufacturing for centuries. Such networks are a traditional feature of the industrial structure of much of northern Italy.[28] Hollywood and Silicon Valley also feature specialized firms that coordinate to design and produce complex products.[29]

These emerging organizational phenomena share several common characteristics:

- A focus on coordination rather than on control: In contrast to the command-and-control hierarchy, these structures focus almost wholly on achieving coordination. Financial incentives, culture, and social controls take the place of hierarchical control.
- Reliance on informal coordination where mutual adjustment replaces rules and directives: Central to all non-hierarchical structures is their dependence on voluntary coordination through bilateral and multilateral adjustment. The capacity for coordination through mutual adjustment has been greatly enhanced by information technology.
- Individuals in multiple organizational roles: Reconciling complex patterns of coordination with high levels of flexibility and responsiveness is difficult if job designs and organizational structures are rigidly defined. Increasingly, individual employees are required to occupy multiple roles simultaneously. For example, in addition to a primary role as a brand manager for a particular product category, a person might be a member of a committee that monitors community engagement activities, part of a task force to undertake a benchmarking study, and a member of a community of practice in web-based marketing.

## Summary

Strategy formulation and strategy implementation are closely interdependent. The formulation of strategy needs to take account of an organization's capacity for implementation; at the same time, the implementation process inevitably involves creating strategy. If an organization's strategic management process is to be effective then its strategic planning system must be linked to actions, commitments and their monitoring, and the allocation of resources. Hence, operational plans and capital expenditure budgets are critical components of a firm's strategic management system.

Strategy implementation involves the entire design of the organization. By understanding the need to reconcile specialization with cooperation and coordination, we are able to appreciate the fundamental principles of organizational design.

Applying these principles, we can determine how best to allocate individuals to organizational units and how to combine these organizational units into broader groupings—in particular the choice between basic organizational forms such as functional, divisional, or matrix organizations.

We have also seen how company's organizational structures have been changing in recent years, influenced both by the demands of their external environments and the opportunities made available by advances in information and communication technologies.

The chapters that follow will have more to say on the organizational structures and management systems appropriate to different strategies and different business contexts. In the final chapter (Chapter 16) we shall explore some of the new trends and new ideas that are reshaping our thinking about organizational design.

 Quizzes and flashcards to test yourself further are available in your interactive e-book at **www.wileyopenpage.com**

## Self-Study Questions

1. It has been argued that traditional approaches to strategic planning (as represented in Figure 6.1) are good systems for exercising control but are not much good for developing strategy, especially for organizations that are facing radical changes in their environment. What do you think some of the strengths and weaknesses of the traditional strategic planning system might be?

2. Referring to Strategy Capsule 6.1, as DuPont expanded its product range (from explosives into paints, dyes, plastics, and synthetic fibers) why do you think the functional structure (organized around manufacturing plants and other functions such as sales, finance, and R & D) became unwieldy? Why did the multidivisional structure based on product groups improve management effectiveness?

3. Within your own organization (whether a university, company, or not-for-profit organization), which departments or activities are organized mechanistically and which organically? To what extent does the mode of organization fit the different environmental contexts and technologies of the different departments or activities?

4. In 2008, Citigroup announced that its Consumer business would be split into Consumer Banking, which would continue to operate through individual national banks, and Global Cards, which would form a single global business (similar to Citi's Global Wealth Management division). On the basis of the arguments relating to the "Defining Organizational Units" section above, why should credit cards be organized as a global unit and all other consumer banking services as national units?

5. The examples of Apple Computer and General Motors (see "Functional Structure" section above) point to the evolution of organizational structures over the industry life-cycle. During the growth phase, many companies adopt multidivisional structures; during maturity and decline, many companies revert to functional structures. Why might this be? (Note: you may wish to refer to Chapter 8, which outlines the main features of the life-cycle model.)

6. Draw an organizational chart for a business school that you are familiar with. Does the school operate with a matrix structure (for instance, are there functional/discipline-based departments together with units managing individual programs)? Which dimension of the matrix is more powerful, and how effectively do the two dimensions coordinate? How would you reorganize the structure to make the school more efficient and effective?

# Notes

1. L. Bossidy and R. Charan, *Execution: The Discipline of Getting Things Done* (New York: Random House, 2002): 71.

2. H. Mintzberg, "Patterns of Strategy Formulation," *Management Science* 24 (1978): 934–48; "Of Strategies: Deliberate and Emergent," *Strategic Management Journal* 6 (1985): 257–72.

3. *MCI Communications: Planning for the 1990s* (Harvard Business School Case No. 9-190-136, 1990): 1.

4. R. M. Grant, "Strategic Planning in a Turbulent Environment: Evidence from the Oil Majors," *Strategic Management Journal* 24 (2003): 491–518.

5. P. F. Drucker, *The Practice of Management* (New York: Harper, 1954).

6. L. Bossidy and R. Charan, *Execution: The Discipline of Getting Things Done* (New York: Random House, 2002): 227.

7. H. Mintzberg, *Structure in Fives: Designing Effective Organizations* (Englewood Cliffs, NJ: Prentice Hall, 1993): 2.

8. A. Smith, *The Wealth of Nations* (London: Dent, 1910): 5.

9. S. Ross, "The Economic Theory of Agency," *American Economic Review*, 63 (1973): 134–9; K. Eisenhardt, "Agency Theory: An Assessment and Reviews," *Academy of Management Review*, 14 (1989): 57–74.

10. I. T. Kay and S. Van Ritten, *Myths and Realities of Executive Pay* (Cambridge: Cambridge University Press, 2007): Chapter 6.

11. T. Peters and R. Waterman, *In Search of Excellence* (New York: Harper & Row, 1982).

12. W. G. Ouchi, *Theory Z* (Reading, MA: Addison-Wesley, 1981).

13. M. Weber, *Economy and Society: An Outline of Interpretive Sociology* (Berkeley, CA: University of California Press, 1968).

14. T. Burns and G. M. Stalker, *The Management of Innovation* (London: Tavistock Institute, 1961).

15. H. Mintzberg, *Structure in Fives: Designing Effective Organizations* (Englewood Cliffs: Prentice Hall, 1993): Chapter 9.

16. H. A. Simon, "The Architecture of Complexity," *Proceedings of the American Philosophical Society* 106 (1962): 467–82.

17. J. D. Orton and K. E. Weick, "Loosely Coupled Systems: A Reconceptualization," *Academy of Management Review* 15 (1990): 203–23.

18. On organizational modularity, see R. Sanchez and J. T. Mahoney, "Modularity, Flexibility, and Knowledge Management in Product and Organizational Design," *Strategic Management Journal* 17 (Winter 1996): 63–76; M. A. Schilling, "Toward a General Modular Systems Theory and its Application to Interfirm Product Modularity," *Academy of Management Review* 25 (2000): 312–334; and C. Baldwin and K. Clark, "Managing in an Age of Modularity," *Harvard Business Review* (September/October 1997): 84–93.

19. "The Contingency Theory of Organizational Design: Challenges and Opportunities," in R. M. Burton, B. Eriksen, D. D. Hakenssen, and C. C. Snow (eds), *Organization Design: The Evolving State of the Art* (New York: Springer-Verlag, 2006): 19–42.

20. J. Nickerson and T. Zenger refer to this as *structural modulation*: "Being Efficiently Fickle: A Dynamic Theory of Organizational Choice," *Organization Science* 13 (2002): 547–67.

21. J. D. Thompson, *Organizations in Action* (New York: McGraw-Hill, 1967). The nature of interdependence in organizational processes is revisited in T. W. Malone, K. Crowston, J. Lee, and B. Pentland, "Tools for Inventing Organizations: Toward a Handbook of Organizational Processes," *Management Science* 45 (March 1999): 489–504.

22. C. A. Bartlett and S. Ghoshal, "Matrix Management: Not a Structure, a Frame of Mind," *Harvard Business Review* (July/August 1990): 138–45.

23. R. Daft and A. Lewin, "Where are the theories for the new organizational forms?" *Organization Science* 3 (1993): 1–6.

24. R. Kumar, "De-Layering at Tata Steel," *Journal of Organizational Behavior Education* 1 (2006): 37–56.

25. H. Mintzberg, *Structure in Fives: Designing Effective Organizations* (Englewood Cliffs, NJ: Prentice Hall, 1993): Chapter 12.

26. C. Bartlett and S. Ghoshal, *Managing across Borders: The Transnational Solution*, 2nd edn (Boston, Harvard Business School, 1998).

27. M. Goold and A. Campbell, *Designing Effective Organizations* (San Francisco: Jossey-Bass, 2002).

28. M. H. Lazerson and G. Lorenzoni, "The Firms that Feed Industrial Districts: A Return to the Italian Source," *Industrial and Corporate Change* 8 (1999): 235–66; A. Grandori, *Interfirm Networks* (London: Routledge, 1999).

29. R. J. DeFilippi and M. B. Arthur, "Paradox in Project-based Enterprise: The Case of Film Making," *California Management Review* 42 (1998): 186–91.

# III

# BUSINESS STRATEGY AND THE QUEST FOR COMPETITIVE ADVANTAGE

# 7 The Sources and Dimensions of Competitive Advantage

SEARS MOTOR BUGGY: $395

For car complete with rubber tires, Timken roller bearing axles, top, storm front, three oil-burning lamps, horn, and one gallon of lubricating oil. Nothing to buy but gasoline.

. . . We found there was a maker of automobile frames that was making 75 percent of all the frames used in automobile construction in the United States. We found on account of the volume of business that this concern could make frames cheaper for automobile manufacturers than the manufacturers could make themselves. We went to this frame maker and asked him to make frames for the Sears Motor Buggy and then to name us prices for those frames in large quantities. And so on throughout the whole construction of the Sears Motor Buggy. You will find every piece and every part has been given the most careful study; you will find that the Sears Motor Buggy is made of the best possible material; it is constructed to take the place of the top buggy; it is built in our own factory, under the direct supervision of our own expert, a man who has had fifteen years of automobile experience, a man who has for the past three years worked with us to develop exactly the right car for the people at a price within the reach of all.

—EXTRACT FROM AN ADVERTISEMENT IN THE SEARS ROEBUCK & CO. CATALOG, 1909: 1150

If the three keys to selling real estate are location, location, location, then the three keys of selling consumer products are differentiation, differentiation, differentiation.

—ROBERT GOIZUETA, FORMER CHAIRMAN, COCA-COLA COMPANY

## OUTLINE

## Introduction and Objectives

In this chapter, we integrate and develop the elements of competitive advantage that we have analyzed in previous chapters. Chapter 1 noted that a firm can earn superior profitability either by locating in an attractive industry or by establishing a competitive advantage over its rivals. Of these two, competitive advantage is the more important. As competition has intensified across almost all industries, very few industry environments can guarantee secure returns; hence, the primary goal of a strategy is to establish a position of competitive advantage for the firm.

Chapters 3 and 5 provided the two primary components of our analysis of competitive advantage. The last part of Chapter 3 analyzed the external sources of competitive advantage: customer requirements and the nature of competition determine the key success factors within a market. Chapter 5 analyzed the internal sources of competitive advantage: the potential for the firm's resources and capabilities to establish and sustain competitive advantage.

This chapter looks more deeply at competitive advantage. We look first at the dynamics of competitive advantage, examining the processes through which competitive advantage is created and destroyed. This gives us insight into how competitive advantage can be attained and sustained. We then look at the two primary dimensions of competitive advantage: cost advantage and differentiation advantage and develop systematic approaches to their analysis.

By the time you have completed this chapter, you will be able to:

- identify the circumstances in which a firm can create and sustain competitive advantage over a rival and recognize how resource conditions create imperfections in the competitive process that offer opportunities for competitive advantage;

- distinguish the two primary types of competitive advantage: cost advantage and differentiation advantage;

- identify the sources of cost advantage in an industry, apply cost analysis to assess a firm's relative cost position, and recommend strategies to enhance cost competitiveness;

- appreciate the potential for differentiation to create competitive advantage, analyze the sources of differentiation, and formulate strategies that create differentiation advantage.

## How Competitive Advantage Emerges and Is Sustained

To understand how **competitive advantage** emerges, we must first understand what competitive advantage is. Most of us can recognize competitive advantage when we see it: Wal-Mart in discount retailing, Singapore Airlines in long-haul air travel, Google in online search, Embraer in regional jets. Yet, defining competitive advantage is troublesome. At a basic level we can define it as follows: *When two or more* *firms compete within the same market, one firm possesses a competitive advantage over its rivals when it earns (or has the potential to earn) a persistently higher rate of profit.*

The problem here is that if we identify competitive advantage with superior profitability, why do we need the concept of competitive advantage at all? A key distinction is that competitive advantage may not be revealed in higher profitability—a firm may forgo current profit in favor of investing in market share, technology, customer loyalty, or executive perks.[1]

In viewing competitive advantage as the result of matching internal strengths to external success factors, I may have conveyed the notion of competitive advantage as something static and stable. In fact, as I acknowledged in Chapter 4 with the discussion of hypercompetition, competitive advantage is a disequilibrium phenomenon: it is created by change and, once established, it sets in motion the competitive process that leads to its destruction.

## The Emergence of Competitive Advantage

The changes that generate competitive advantage can be either internal or external. Figure 7.1 depicts the basic relationships.

*External Sources of Change*   For an external change to create competitive advantage, the change must have differential effects on companies because of their different resources and capabilities or strategic positioning. For example, in the six years prior to 2005, the average price of Brent crude was $22 a barrel. Between 2005 and 2011 it averaged $87 a barrel. The result was to shift the balance of competitive advantage in the European car industry. During 2005–2011, Fiat, Renault, and VW, all of which emphasized small, fuel-efficient cars, improved their profitability relative to that of Daimler and BMW, both of which emphasized larger cars.

The greater the magnitude of the external change and the greater the difference in the strategic positioning of firms, the greater the propensity for external change to generate competitive advantage, as indicated by the dispersion of profitability within

**FIGURE 7.1**   The emergence of competitive advantage

the industry. The world's tobacco industry has a relatively stable external environment and the leading firms pursue similar strategies with similar resources and capabilities. Competitive advantages, as reflected in interfirm profit differentials, tend to be small. The toy industry, on the other hand, comprises a heterogeneous group of firms that experience unpredictable shifts in consumer preferences and technology. As a result, profitability differences are wide and variable.

The competitive advantage that arises from external change also depends on firms' ability to respond to change. Any external change creates entrepreneurial opportunities that will accrue to the firms that exploit these opportunities most effectively. Entrepreneurial responsiveness involves one of two key capabilities:

- The ability to anticipate changes in the external environment. IBM has displayed a remarkable ability to renew its competitive advantage through anticipating, and then taking advantage of, most of the major shifts in the IT sector: the rise of personal computing, the advent of the internet, the shift in value from hardware to software, and the development of cloud computing.
- Speed. As markets become more turbulent and unpredictable, quick-response capability has become increasingly important as a source of competitive advantage. Quick responses require information. As conventional economic and market forecasting has become less effective, so companies rely increasingly on "early-warning systems" through direct relationships with customers, suppliers, and even competitors. Quick responses also require short cycle times so that information can be acted upon speedily. In fashion retailing, quick response to fashion trends is critical to success. Zara, the retail clothing chain owned by the Spanish company Inditex, has built a vertically integrated supply chain that cuts the time between a garment's design and retail delivery to under three weeks (against an industry norm of three to six months.[2] This emphasis on speed as a source of competitive advantage was popularized by the Boston Consulting Group's concept of *time-based competition*.[3] Advances in IT—the internet, real-time electronic data exchange, and wireless communication—have greatly enhanced response capabilities throughout the business sector.

*Internal Sources of Change: Competitive Advantage from Innovation*
Competitive advantage may also be generated internally through innovation which creates competitive advantage for the innovator while undermining the competitive advantages of incumbents—the process Schumpeter refers to as "creative destruction."[4] Although innovation is typically thought of as new products or processes that embody new technology, a key source of competitive advantage is *strategic innovation*—new approaches to doing business, including new business models.

Strategic innovation typically involves creating value for customers from novel products, experiences, or modes of product delivery. Thus, in the retail sector, competition is driven by a constant quest for new retail concepts and formats. This may take the form of big-box stores with greater variety (Toys "R" Us, Home Depot), augmented customer service (Nordstrom), novel approaches to display and store layout (Sephora in cosmetics), or completely new systems of supplying customers that reconfigure the entire value chain (IKEA).

In other sectors, too, competitive advantage typically goes to firms that have developed innovative strategies that have challenged conventional wisdom and conceptualized the way of doing business:

- Southwest Airlines' point-to-point, no-frills airline service using a single type of plane and flexible working methods has made it not only the only consistently profitable airline in North America but also a model for budget airlines throughout the world.
- Nike built its large and successful business on a business system that totally redesigned the shoe industry's traditional value chain—notably by outsourcing manufacturing and concentrating upon design and marketing, and orchestrating a vast global network of producers, logistics providers, and retailers.
- Metro International is a Swedish company that publishes *Metro* newspapers—free, daily newspapers distributed to commuters in major cities. By October 2009, there were 56 daily editions in 19 countries in 15 languages across Europe, North and South America, and Asia with 17 million daily readers.
- SixDegrees.com, launched in 1997, pioneered web-based social networking paving the way first for MySpace then Facebook.

Strategic innovations tend to involve pioneering along one or more dimensions of strategy:

- New industries: Some companies launch products which create a whole new market. Xerox created the plain-paper copier industry, Freddie Laker pioneered budget air travel, and Craig McCaw and McCaw Communications launched the mass market for wireless telephony. For Kim and Mauborgne, creating new markets is the purest form of **blue-ocean strategy**—the creation of "uncontested market space."[5]
- New customer segments: Creating new customer segments for existing product concepts can also open up vast new market spaces. Apple did not invent the personal computer, but it launched the home market for computers. So too with the videocassette recorder (VCR): it was developed by Ampex for use in television studios but introduced into the home by Sony and Matsushita. The success of the Nintendo Wii video games console was based upon extending video gaming into new customer segments.
- New sources of competitive advantage: Most successful blue-ocean strategies do not launch whole new industries—they introduce novel approaches to creating customer value. Dell created an integrated system for ordering, assembling, and distributing PCs, which permitted unprecedented customer choice and speed of fulfillment. Cirque de Soleil reinvented the circus as a multimedia entertainment spectacle. McKinsey & Company identify a key element of strategic innovation that it calls *new game strategy* as it involves reconfiguring the industry value chain in order to change the "rules of the game."[6] (Southwest Airlines and Nike, mentioned above, are examples.) In their study of rejuvenation among mature firms, Charles Baden-Fuller and John Stopford observe that strategic innovation often involves combining performance dimensions that were previously viewed as conflicting.

For example, Richardson, a UK kitchen knife producer, used an innovative design, process innovation, and a lean, entrepreneurial management to supply kitchen knives that combined price competitiveness, durability, sharpness, and responsive customer service.[7] However, Gary Hamel argues that firms need to go beyond strategic innovation: *management innovations* such as Procter & Gamble's brand management system and Toyota's lean production are likely to offer a more sustainable basis for competitive advantage.[8]

## Sustaining Competitive Advantage

Once established, competitive advantage is eroded by competition. The speed with which competitive advantage is undermined depends on the ability of competitors to challenge either by imitation or innovation. Imitation is the most direct form of competition; thus, for competitive advantage to be sustained over time, *barriers to imitation* must exist. Rumelt uses the term **isolating mechanisms** to describe "barriers that limit the ex post equilibration of rents among individual firms."[9] The more effective these isolating mechanisms are, the longer competitive advantage can be sustained against the onslaught of rivals. In most industries, competitive advantage erodes slowly: interfirm profit differentials persist for a period of a decade or more.[10] However, as discussed in Chapter 4 (see the "Dynamic Competition" section), the advent of hypercompetition may have accelerated the process.

To identify the sources of isolating mechanisms, we need to examine the process of competitive imitation. For one firm to successfully imitate the strategy of another, it must meet four conditions: it must identify the competitive advantage of a rival, it must have an incentive to imitate, it must be able to diagnose the sources of the rival's competitive advantage, and it must be able to acquire the resources and capabilities necessary for imitation. At each stage the incumbent can create isolating mechanisms to impede the would-be imitator (Figure 7.2).

**FIGURE 7.2**  Sustaining competitive advantage: Types of isolating mechanism

| REQUIREMENT FOR IMITATION | ISOLATING MECHANISM |
|---|---|
| Identification | —*Obscure* superior performance |
| Incentives for imitation | —*Deterrence*: signal aggressive intentions to imitators<br>—*Preemption*: exploit all available investment opportunities |
| Diagnosis | —Rely on multiple sources of competitive advantage to create "causal ambiguity" |
| Resource acquisition | —Base competitive advantage on resources and capabilities that are *immobile* and *difficult to replicate* |

*Identification: Obscuring Superior Performance*  A simple barrier to imitation is to obscure the firm's superior profitability. According to George Stalk of the Boston Consulting Group: "One way to throw competitors off balance is to mask high performance so rivals fail to see your success until it's too late."[11] In the 1948 movie classic *The Treasure of the Sierra Madre*, Humphrey Bogart and his partners went to great lengths to obscure their find from other gold prospectors.[12]

For firms that dominate a niche market, one of the attractions of remaining a private company is to avoid disclosing financial performance. Few food processors realized the profitability of canned cat and dog food until the UK Monopolies Commission revealed that the leading firm, Pedigree Petfoods (a subsidiary of Mars Inc.), earned a return on capital employed of 47%.[13]

The desire to avoid competition may be so strong as to cause companies to forgo short-run profits. The *theory of limit pricing*, in its simplest form, postulates that a firm in a strong market position sets prices at a level that just fails to attract entrants.[14]

*Deterrence and Preemption*  A firm may avoid competition by undermining the incentives for imitation. If a firm can persuade rivals that imitation will be unprofitable, it may be able to avoid competitive challenges. In Chapter 4 we discussed strategies of deterrence and the role of signaling and commitment in supporting them.[15] For deterrence to work, threats must be credible. Brandenburger and Nalebuff show how NutraSweet's aggressive price war against the Holland Sweetener Company gave it a reputation that deterred other would-be entrants into the aspartame market.[16]

A firm can also deter imitation by *preemption*—occupying existing and potential strategic niches to reduce the range of investment opportunities open to the challenger. Preemption can take many forms:

- Proliferation of product varieties by a market leader can leave new entrants and smaller rivals with few opportunities for establishing a market niche. Between 1950 and 1972, for example, the six leading suppliers of breakfast cereals introduced 80 new brands into the US market.[17]

- Large investments in production capacity ahead of the growth of market demand also preempt market opportunities for rivals. Monsanto's heavy investment in plants for producing NutraSweet ahead of its patent expiration was a clear threat to would-be producers of generic aspartame.

- Patent proliferation can protect technology-based advantage by limiting competitors' technical opportunities. In 1974, Xerox's dominant market position was protected by a wall of over 2000 patents, most of which were not used. When IBM introduced its first copier in 1970, Xerox sued it for infringing 22 of these patents.[18]

*Diagnosing Competitive Advantage: Causal Ambiguity and Uncertain Imitability*  If a firm is to imitate the competitive advantage of another, it must understand the basis of its rival's success. Consider Wal-Mart's success in discount retailing. For Wal-Mart's struggling competitor, Sears Holdings (owner of the Kmart chain of discount stores), it is easy to point to the differences between

Wal-Mart and itself. As one Wal-Mart executive commented: "Retailing is an open book. There are no secrets. Our competitors can walk into our stores and see what we sell, how we sell it, and for how much." The difficult task is to identify which differences are the critical determinants of superior profitability. Is it Wal-Mart's store locations (typically in small towns with little direct competition)? Its tightly integrated supply chain? Its unique management system? The information system that supports Wal-Mart's logistics and decision-making practices? Or is it a culture built on traditional rural American values of thrift and hard work? Similarly, problems face Sony or Nokia should they wish to imitate Apple's incredible success in smartphones and consumer electronics.

Lippman and Rumelt identify this problem as **causal ambiguity**: when a firm's competitive advantage is multidimensional and is based on complex bundles of resources and capabilities, it is difficult for rivals to diagnose the success of the leading firm. The outcome of causal ambiguity is *uncertain imitability*: if the causes of a firm's success cannot be known for sure, success is uncertain.[19]

Recent research suggests that the problems of strategy imitation may run even deeper. We observed in Chapter 5 that capabilities are the outcome of complex combinations of resources and that multiple capabilities interact to confer competitive advantage. Research into complementarity among an organization's activities suggests that these interactions extend across the whole range of management practices.[20] Strategy Capsule 7.1 describes Urban Outfitters as an example of a unique "activity system." Where activities are tightly linked, complexity theory—NK modeling in particular—predicts that, within a particular competitive environment, a number of *fitness peaks* will appear, each associated with a unique combination of strategic variables.[21] The implications for imitation is that to locate on the same fitness peak as another firm not only requires recreating a complex configuration of strategy, structure, management systems, leadership, and business processes but also means that getting it just a little bit wrong may result in the imitator missing the fitness peak and finding itself in an adjacent valley.[22]

One of the challenges for the would-be imitator is deciding which management practices are generic best practices and which are *contextual*—complementary with other management practices. For example, if we consider Sears Holdings' deliberation of which of Wal-Mart's management practices to imitate in its Kmart stores, some practices (e.g., employees required to smile at customers, point-of-sale data transferred direct to the corporate database) are likely to be generically beneficial. Others, such as Wal-Mart's "everyday low prices" pricing policy, low advertising sales ratio, and hub-and-spoke distribution are likely to be beneficial only when combined with other practices.

*Acquiring Resources and Capabilities*   Having diagnosed the sources of an incumbent's competitive advantage, the imitator's next challenge is to assemble the necessary resources and capabilities for imitation. As we saw in Chapter 5, a firm can acquire resources and capabilities in two ways: it can buy them or it can build them. The imitation barriers here are limits to the *transferability* and *replicability* of resources and capabilities. (See Chapter 5's "Sustaining Competitive Advantage" section for a discussion of these resource characteristics.) Strategy Capsule 7.2 looks at competitive advantage in different market settings.

### STRATEGY CAPSULE 7.1
## Urban Outfitters

During the three years to January 2009, Urban Outfitters Inc., which comprises 130 Urban Outfitters stores (together with Anthropologie and Free People chains), has grown at an average of 20% annually and earned a return on equity of 21%. The company describes itself as targeting well-educated, urban-minded, young adults aged 18 to 30 through its unique merchandise mix and compelling store environment: "We create a unified environment in our stores that establishes an emotional bond with the customer. Every element of the environment is tailored to the aesthetic preferences of our target customers. Through creative design, much of the existing retail space is modified to incorporate a mosaic of fixtures, finishes and revealed architectural details. In our stores, merchandise is integrated into a variety of creative vignettes and displays designed to offer our customers an entire look at a distinct lifestyle."

According to Michael Porter and Nicolaj Siggelkow, Urban Outfitters offers a set of management practices that is both distinctive and highly interdependent. The urban-bohemian-styled product mix, which includes clothing, furnishings, and gift items, is displayed within bazaar-like stores, each of which has a unique design. To encourage frequent customer visits, the layout of each store is changed every two weeks, creating a new shopping experience whenever customers return. Emphasizing community with its customers, it forgoes traditional forms of advertising in favor of blogs and word-of-mouth transmission. Each practice makes little sense on its own, but together they represent a distinctive, integrated strategy. Attempts to imitate Urban Outfitters' competitive advantage would most likely fail because of the difficulty of replicating every aspect of the strategy before integrating them in the right manner.

*Source:* Urban Outfitters Inc. 10-K Report to January 31, 2009 (Washington: Sec, 2008); M. E. Porter and N. Siggelkow, "Contextuality within Activity Systems and Sustainable Competitive Advantage," *Academy of Management Perspectives* 22 (May 2008): 34–56.

## Types of Competitive Advantage: Cost and Differentiation

A firm can achieve a higher rate of profit (or potential profit) over a rival in one of two ways: either it can supply an identical product or service at a lower cost or it can supply a product or service that is differentiated in such a way that the customer is willing to pay a price premium that exceeds the additional cost of the differentiation. In the former case, the firm possesses a cost advantage; in the latter, a differentiation advantage. In pursuing cost advantage, the goal of the firm is to become the cost leader in its industry or industry segment. Cost leadership requires the firm to "find and exploit all sources of cost advantage [and] sell a standard, no-frills product."[23] Differentiation by a firm from its competitors is achieved "when it provides something unique that is valuable to buyers beyond simply offering a low price."[24] Figure 7.3 illustrates these two types of advantage. By combining the two types of competitive advantage with the firm's choice of scope—broad market versus narrow segment—Michael Porter has defined three generic strategies: cost leadership, differentiation, and focus (Figure 7.4).

## STRATEGY CAPSULE 7.2
# Competitive Advantage in Different Market Settings

The forces which create and destroy competitive advantage will operate differently in different types of market. Competitive advantage depends critically upon the existence of imperfections in the competitive process, which in turn are the result of the conditions under which the resources and capabilities needed to compete in the industry are supplied. The key distinction is between the two types of value-creating activity: *trading* and *production*. Trading involves arbitrage across space (trade) and time (speculation). Production involves the physical transformation of inputs into outputs.

In trading markets the limiting case is *efficient markets*, which correspond closely to perfectly competitive markets. The key condition is that prices reflect all available information (examples include the markets for securities, foreign exchange, and commodity futures). Because prices adjust instantaneously to newly available information, no market trader can expect to earn more than any other. Any differences in returns reflect either different levels of risk or random factors (luck). It is not possible to beat the market on any consistent basis—in other words competitive advantage is absent. This absence of competitive advantage reflects the conditions of resource. Both of the resources needed to compete—finance and information—are equally available to all traders. There is no basis for one to gain competitive advantage over another.

Competitive advantage in trading markets requires imperfections in the competitive process:

- Where there is an imperfect availability of information. Competitive advantage results from superior access to information—hence the criminal penalties for insider trading in most advanced economies.

- Where transaction costs are present, competitive advantage accrues to the traders with the lowest transaction costs. John Bogle has used this principle as the basis for creating his Vanguard mutual funds. The Vanguard S&P 500 Index fund with transaction and operating costs of 0.5% annually has outperformed 90% of US equity mutual funds.

- If markets are subject to systematic behavioral trends (e.g., the *small firm effect* or the *January effect*), competitive advantage accrues to traders who understand market psychology or utilize knowledge of systematic price patterns (chart analysis). Overshooting is a common aberration caused by imitative trading and converging expectations. This implies competitive advantage can be gained in the short term by following the herd (momentum trading) and longer term by recognizing the likelihood of correction (a contrarian strategy). The world's most successful investor is a prominent contrarian who is "fearful when others are greedy, and greedy when others are fearful."

In production markets the potential for competitive advantage is much greater because of the complex combinations of the resources and capabilities required, the highly differentiated nature of these resources and capabilities, and the imperfections in their supply. Within an industry, the more heterogeneous are firms' endowments of resources and capabilities, the greater the potential for competitive advantage. In the European electricity-generating industry, the growing diversity of players—utilities (EDF, ENEL), gas distributors (Gaz de France, Centrica), oil and gas majors (Shell, ENI), independent power producers (AES, E.ON), and wind generators—has expanded opportunities for competitive advantage and widened the profit differentials between them.

Differences in resource endowments also influence the erosion of competitive advantage. Where competitors possess similar bundles of resources and capabilities, imitation is easy. Where resource bundles are highly differentiated, competition is more likely to be through distinctive strategies.

**FIGURE 7.3**  Sources of competitive advantage

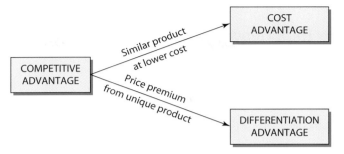

**FIGURE 7.4**  Porter's generic strategies

## Cost Analysis

Historically, strategic management has emphasized cost advantage as the primary basis for competitive advantage in an industry. This focus on cost reflected the traditional emphasis by economists on price as the principal medium of competition. It also reflected the quest by large industrial corporations during the last century to exploit economies of scale and scope through investments in mass production and mass distribution. During the 1970s and 1980s, this preoccupation was reflected in the widespread interest in the experience curve as a tool of strategy analysis (Strategy Capsule 7.3).

In recent decades, companies have been forced to think more broadly and radically about cost efficiency. Growing competition from emerging market countries has created intense cost pressures for Western and Japanese firms, resulting in novel approaches to cost reduction, including outsourcing, offshoring, process re-engineering, lean production, and organizational delayering.

### The Sources of Cost Advantage

There are seven principal determinants of a firm's unit costs (cost per unit of output) relative to its competitors; we refer to these as *cost drivers* (Figure 7.5).

The relative importance of these different cost drivers varies across industries, between firms within an industry, and across the different activities within a firm. By examining each of these different cost drivers in relation to a particular firm, we can analyze a firm's cost position relative to its competitors', diagnose the sources

## STRATEGY CAPSULE 7.3
# BCG and the Experience Curve

The experience curve has its basis in the systematic reduction in the time taken to build airplanes and Liberty ships during World War II.[25] In a series of studies, ranging from bottle caps and refrigerators to long-distance calls and insurance policies, the Boston Consulting Group (BCG) observed a remarkable regularity in the reductions in unit costs with increased cumulative output. Its *law of experience* states: the unit cost of value added to a standard product declines by a constant percentage (typically between 20 and 30%) each time cumulative output doubles (where "unit cost of value added" is the unit cost of production less the unit cost of bought-in components and materials).

The relationship between unit cost and production volume may be expressed as follows:

$$C_n = C_1 . n^{-a}$$

where $C_1$ is the cost of the first unit of production

$C_n$ is the cost of the nth unit of production

$n$ is the cumulative volume of production

$a$ is the elasticity of cost with regard to output.

The experience curve has important implications for strategy. If a firm can expand its output faster than its competitors can, it can move down the experience curve more rapidly and open up a widening cost differential.[26] BCG concluded that a firm's primary strategic goal should be driving volume growth through maximizing market share. BCG identified Honda in motorcycles as an exemplar of this strategy.[27] The quest for market share was supported by numerous studies confirming a positive relationship between profitability and market share.[28] However, association does not imply causation—it seems likely that market share and profitability are both outcomes of some other source of competitive advantage—product innovation, or superior marketing.[29]

The weaknesses of the experience curve as a strategy tool are, first, it fails to distinguish several sources of cost reduction (learning, scale, process innovation); second, it presumes that cost reductions from experience are automatic—the reality is that they must be managed.

of inefficiency, and make recommendations as to how a firm can improve its cost efficiency.

*Economies of Scale*   The predominance of large corporations in most manufacturing and service industries is a consequence of economies of scale. Economies of scale exist wherever proportionate increases in the amounts of inputs employed in a production process result in lower unit costs. Economies of scale have been conventionally associated with manufacturing. Figure 7.6 shows a typical relationship between unit cost and plant capacity. The point at which most scale economies are exploited is the *minimum efficient plant size* (MEPS).

Scale economies arise from three principal sources:

- Technical input–output relationships: In many activities, increases in output do not require proportionate increases in input. A 10000-barrel oil storage tank does not cost five times as much as a 2000-barrel tank. Similar volume-related economies exist in ships, trucks, and steel and petrochemical plants.

**FIGURE 7.5**   The drivers of cost advantage

| ECONOMIES OF SCALE | • Technical input–output relationships<br>• Indivisibilities<br>• Specialization |

| ECONOMIES OF LEARNING | • Increased individual skills<br>• Improved organizational routines |

| PRODUCTION TECHNIQUES | • Process innovation<br>• Re-engineering of business processes |

| PRODUCT DESIGN | • Standardization of designs and components<br>• Design for manufacture |

| INPUT COSTS | • Location advantages<br>• Ownership of low-cost inputs<br>• Nonunion labor<br>• Bargaining power |

| CAPACITY UTILIZATION | • Ratio of fixed to variable costs<br>• Fast and flexible capacity adjustment |

| RESIDUAL EFFICIENCY | • Organizational slack/X-inefficiency<br>• Motivation and organizational culture<br>• Managerial effectiveness |

**FIGURE 7.6**   The long-run average cost curve for a plant

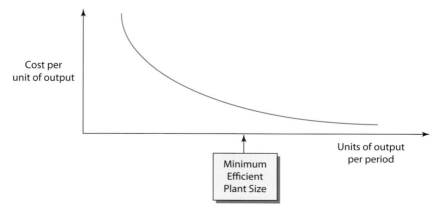

Cost per unit of output

Units of output per period

Minimum Efficient Plant Size

● Indivisibilities: Many resources and activities are "lumpy"—they are unavailable in small sizes. Hence, they offer economies of scale as firms are able to spread the costs of these items over larger volumes of output. A national TV advertising campaign or a research program into fuel cell technology will cost much the same whether it is being undertaken by Toyota or Mazda. However, the costs as a percentage of sales will be much lower for Toyota because it has almost eight times the sales of Mazda.

● Specialization: Increased scale permits greater task specialization that is manifest in greater division of labor. Mass production—whether in Adam Smith's pin factory or Henry Ford's auto plants (see Chapter 6)—involves breaking down the production process into separate tasks performed by specialized workers using specialized equipment. Specialization promotes learning, avoids time loss from switching activities, and assists mechanization and automation. Similar economies are important in knowledge-intensive industries such as investment banking, management consulting, and design engineering, where large firms are able to offer specialized expertise across a broad range of know-how.

Scale economies are a key determinant of an industry's level of concentration (the proportion of industry output accounted for by the largest firms). In many consumer goods industries, scale economies in marketing have driven industry consolidation. Figure 7.7 shows how soft drink brands with the greatest sales volume tend to have the lowest unit advertising costs for different brands. In other industries—especially aerospace, automobiles, software, and communication systems—the need to amortize the huge costs of new product development has forced consolidation (Table 7.1). Where product development is very costly, volume is essential to profitability: the Boeing 747 was hugely profitable because 1415 were built. Concorde, with only 20 planes built, was a financial disaster.

Despite the prevalence of scale economies, small and medium-sized companies continue to survive and prosper in competition with much bigger rivals. In automobiles, some medium-sized companies such as Peugeot, Renault, and BMW have been more profitable than industry leaders. In commercial banking, there is no

**FIGURE 7.7** Economies of scale in advertising: US soft drinks

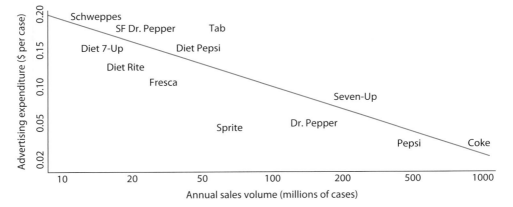

**TABLE 7.1**   Some of the world's most expensive new product development projects

| Product | Lead company | Estimated development cost | Launch date |
|---------|-------------|---------------------------|-------------|
| F-35 Lightning II joint strike fighter | Lockheed Martin | $240 billion[a] | 2012[b] |
| B-2 Spirit "stealth bomber" | Northrup Grumman | $23 billion | December 1993[b] |
| A380 "super-jumbo" | Airbus Industrie | $19 billion | October 2007[b] |
| 787 Dreamliner | Boeing | $16–$18 billion | 3rd Quarter 2010[b] |
| Windows Vista | Microsoft | $7 billion | January 2007 |
| PlayStation 3 | Sony | $7 billion[c] | November 2006 |
| Iridium wireless satellite communication system | Motorola/Iridium Satellite LLC | $6 billion | July 1999 |
| Ford Contour/Mondeo | Ford Motor Company | $6 billion[d] | October 1992 |

**Notes:**
[a] Total program cost over 50 years estimated at $1.5 trillion.
[b] Date of entering service.
[c] Including development of Blu-ray DVD.
[d] Including costs of tooling.

evidence that big banks outperform smaller players either on profitability or costs.[30] How do small and medium-sized firms offset the disadvantages of small scale? First, by exploiting superior flexibility; second, by outsourcing activities where scale is critical to efficiency (e.g., specialist car makers typically license product designs and buy in engines); third, by avoiding the motivational and coordination problems that often afflict large organizations.[31]

*Economies of Learning*   The experience curve has its basis in learning-by-doing. Repetition develops both individual skills and organizational routines. In 1943, it took 40,000 labor-hours to build a B-24 Liberator bomber. By 1945, it took only 8000 hours.[32] The more complex a process or product, the greater the potential for learning. LCD flat screens are notoriously difficult to manufacture—a single defective chip may render an entire screen useless. The dominant position of Sharp and Samsung in flat screens is primarily a result of volume-based learning resulting in exceptionally high yields.[33] Learning occurs both at the individual level through improvements in dexterity and problem solving and at the group level through the development and refinement of organizational routines.[34]

*Process Technology and Process Design*   Superior process technologies can be a source of huge cost economies. Pilkington's float glass process gave it (and its licensees) an unassailable cost advantage in producing flat glass. Ford's moving assembly line reduced the time taken to assemble a Model T from 106 hours in 1912 to six hours in 1914. When process innovation is embodied in new capital equipment, diffusion is likely to be rapid. However, the full benefits of new process technologies typically require system-wide changes in job design, employee incentives, product design, organizational structure, and management controls. Between 1979 and 1986, General Motors spent $40 billion on new process technology with the goal of becoming the world's most efficient manufacturer of automobiles. Yet, in the absence of fundamental changes in organization and management, the productivity gains were meager. After a tour of Cadillac's state-of-the-art Hamtramck plant in Detroit, Toyota chairman Eiji Toyoda told a colleague, "It would have been embarrassing to comment on it."[35] By contrast, the system of lean production pioneered by Toyota involves an integrated combination of work practices including just-in-time scheduling, total quality management, continuous improvement (kaizen), teamwork, job flexibility, supplier partnerships, as well as improvement in capital equipment and IT.[36]

*Business process re-engineering* (BPR) is an approach to redesigning operational processes that gained massive popularity during the 1990s. "Re-engineering gurus" Michael Hammer and James Champy define BPR as: "the fundamental rethinking and radical redesign of business processes to achieve dramatic improvements in critical contemporary measures of performance, such as cost, quality, service, and speed."[37] BPR recognizes that operational and commercial processes evolve over time without consistent direction or systematic appraisal. Information technology typically automates existing processes—"paving over cowpaths."[38] BPR begins with the question: "If we were starting afresh, how would we design this process?" Hammer and Champy identify "commonalities, recurring themes, or characteristics" that can guide BPR:

- Combine several jobs into one.
- Allow workers to make decisions.
- Perform the steps of a process in a natural order.
- Recognize the need for variability in process to cope with different situations.
- Perform processes where it makes the most sense: if the accounting department needs pencils, don't insist on using the firm's purchasing department—allow purchases from the retail store down the street.
- Only require checks and controls where they are essential to efficiency.
- Minimize reconciliation.
- Appoint a case manager to provide a single point of contact at the interface between processes.
- Decentralized decisions: permit overall coordination simply through information sharing.

BPR has led to major gains in efficiency, quality, and speed (Strategy Capsule 7.4), but where business processes are complex and embedded in organizational routines (see "From Resources to Capabilities" section in Chapter 5), it is likely that no one in the organization fully understands the operation of existing processes. In such circumstances, Hammer and Champy's recommendation to "obliterate" existing processes and start with a "clean sheet of paper" runs the risk of destroying organizational capabilities that have been nurtured over a long period. While BPR had lost much of the popularity it had 20 years ago, firms continue to engage in *business process management*, where the emphasis has shifted form workflow management to the broader application of information technology (web-based applications in particular) to the redesign and enhancement of organizational processes.[39]

## STRATEGY CAPSULE 7.4
# Process Re-Engineering at IBM Credit

Michel Hammer and James Champy describe how business process re-engineering resulted in IBM reducing the time taken to approve requests by sales personnel for new customer credit approval from six days to four hours. Under the old system, five stages were involved:

1   an IBM salesperson telephoned a request for financing, which was logged on a piece of paper;

2   the request was sent to the credit department, which checked the customer's creditworthiness;

3   the request and credit check were sent to the business practices department where a loan covenant was drawn up;

4   the paperwork was passed to a pricer, who determined the interest rate;

5   the clerical group prepared a quote letter that was sent to the salesperson.

Frustrated by the delays and resulting lost sales, two managers undertook an experiment. They took a financing request and walked it through all five steps. They discovered that all five stages could be completed within 90 minutes!

The problem was that the process had been designed for the most complex credit requests that IBM received, whereas in the vast majority of cases no specialist judgment was called for: all that was needed was to check credit ratings and to plug numbers into standard algorithms. The credit approval process was redesigned by replacing the specialists (credit checkers, pricers, and so on) with generalists who undertook all five processes. Only where the request was non-standard or unusually complex were specialists called in. Not only was processing time reduced by 94%, but the number of employees involved was reduced and the total number of customer approvals greatly increased.

**Source:** Adapted from M. Hammer and J. Champy, *Re-engineering the Corporation: A Manifesto for Business Revolution* (New York: HarperBusiness, 1993): 36–9.

*Product Design*   *Design-for-manufacture*—designing products for ease of production rather than simply for functionality and esthetics—can offer substantial cost savings, especially when linked to the introduction of new process technology.

- Volkswagen cut product development and component costs by redesigning its 30 different models around just four separate platforms. The VW Beetle, Audi TT, Golf, and Audi A3, together with several Seat and Skoda models, all share a single platform.
- The IBM "Proprinter," one of the most successful computer printers of the 1980s, owed its low costs (and reliability) to an innovative design that:
  - reduced the number of parts from 150, found in the typical PC printer, to 60;
  - designed the printer in layers so that robots could build it from the bottom up;
  - eliminated all screws, springs, and other fasteners that required human insertion and adjustment and replaced them with molded plastic components that clipped together.[40]

Service offerings, too, can be designed for ease and efficiency of production. Motel 6, cost leader in US budget motels, carefully designs its product to keep operating costs low. Its motels occupy low-cost, out-of-town locations; it uses standard motel designs; it avoids facilities such as pools and restaurants; and it designs rooms to facilitate easy cleaning and low maintenance. However, efficiency in service design is compromised by the tendency of customers to request deviations from standard offerings ("I'd like my hamburger with the bun toasted on one side only, please"). This requires a clear strategy to manage variability either through accommodation or restriction.[41]

*Capacity Utilization*  Over the short and medium terms, plant capacity is more or less fixed and variations in output cause capacity utilization to rise or fall. Underutilization raises unit costs because fixed costs must be spread over fewer units of production; pushing output beyond normal full capacity also creates inefficiencies. Boeing's efforts to boost output during 2006–2011 resulted in increased unit costs due to overtime pay, premiums for night and weekend shifts, increased defects, and higher levels of maintenance. Hence, the ability to speedily adjust capacity to downturns in demand can be a major source of cost advantage. During the 2008–2009 recession, survival in hard-hit sectors such as house building, construction equipment, and retailing required moving early to cut capacity through shedding jobs and closing units. The key was to make adjustments in advance of downturns in demand: Caterpillar announced it was cutting 20,000 jobs on January 28, 2008, the same day it revealed that its sales in the previous quarter had increased from the previous year.[42]

*Input Costs*  The firms in an industry do not necessarily pay the same price for identical inputs. There are several sources of lower input costs:

- Locational differences in input prices: The prices of inputs, and wage rates in particular, vary between locations. In the US, software engineers earned an average of $94,000 in 2011. In India, the average was $34,000. In less-skilled occupations, differentials are much wider: in auto assembly the hourly rate in Chinese plants was about $3 an hour in 2011 compared with $70 in the US (inclusive of benefits).[43]
- Ownership of low-cost sources of supply: In raw-material-intensive industries, ownership of low-cost sources of material can offer a massive cost advantage. In petroleum, lifting costs for the three "supermajors" (ExxonMobil, Royal Dutch Shell, and BP) were over $14 per barrel in 2007; for Saudi Aramco they were about $5.
- Non-union labor: Labor unions result in higher levels of pay and benefits and work restrictions that lower productivity. In the US airline industry, non-union AirTran had average salary and benefit cost per employee of $60,863 in 2007 compared with $87,245 for United (80% unionized).
- Bargaining power: The ability to negotiate preferential prices ad discounts can be a major source of cost advantage for industry leaders, especially in retailing.[44] Wal-Mart's UK entry (with its acquisition of Asda) was greeted with dismay by other British supermarket chains: they feared that Wal-Mart's massive bargaining power would allow Asda to gain preferential discounts from suppliers.

*Residual Efficiency*   Even after taking account of the basic cost drivers—scale, technology, product and process design, input costs, and capacity utilization—unexplained cost differences between firms typically remain. These residual efficiencies relate to the extent to which the firm approaches its efficiency frontier of optimal operation which depends on the firm's ability to eliminate "organizational slack"[45] or "X-inefficiency."[46] These surplus costs that keep the firm from maximum-efficiency operation are the inevitable result of employees—both in management and on the shop floor—maintaining some margin of slack in preference to the rigors of operating at maximum efficiency. Eliminating these excess costs often requires a threat to a company's survival, which then creates the impetus for rooting out institutionalized inefficiencies. When faced with bankruptcy or a precipitous fall in profitability, companies can demonstrate a remarkable capacity for paring costs—in his first year as CEO, Carlos Ghosn cut Nissan Motor's operating costs by 20%.[47] At firms such as Wal-Mart, Ryanair, and Air Asia, high levels of residual efficiency are the result of management systems and company values that are intolerant of unnecessary costs and glorify frugality.

## Using the Value Chain to Analyze Costs

To analyze a firm's cost position, we need to look at individual activities. Chapter 5 introduced the *value chain* as a way of seeing the sequence of activities that a company or business unit performs. Each activity tends to be subject to a different set of cost drivers, which give it a distinct cost structure. A value chain analysis of a firm's costs seeks to identify:

1  the relative importance of each activity with respect to total cost;
2  the cost drivers for each activity and the comparative efficiency with which the firm performs each activity;
3  how costs in one activity influence costs in another;
4  which activities should be undertaken within the firm and which activities should be outsourced.

A value chain analysis of a firm's cost position comprises the following stages:

1  Disaggregate the firm into separate activities: Determining the appropriate value chain activities is a matter of judgment. It requires understanding the chain of processes involved in the transformation of inputs into output and its delivery to the customer. Very often, the firm's own divisional and departmental structure is a useful guide. Key considerations are:
   a  the separateness of one activity from another;
   b  the importance of an activity;
   c  the dissimilarity of activities in terms of cost drivers;
   d  the extent to which there are differences in the way competitors perform the particular activity.
2  Establish the relative importance of different activities in the total cost of the product: Our analysis needs to focus on the activities that are the major sources of cost. In disaggregating costs, Michael Porter suggests the detailed assignment

of operating costs and assets to each value activity. [48] Though the adoption of activity-based costing has made such cost data more available, detailed cost allocation can be a major exercise.[49] Even without such detailed cost break-down, it is usually possible to identify which activities are the principal sources of total cost and establish which activities are performed relatively efficiently or inefficiently.

3 Identify cost drivers: For each activity, what factors determine the level of cost relative to other firms? For some activities, cost drivers can be deduced simply from the nature of the activity and the types of cost incurred. For capital-intensive activities such as the operation of a body press in an auto plant, the principal factors are likely to be capital equipment costs, weekly production volume, and downtime between changes of dies. For labor-intensive assembly activities, critical issues are wage rates, speed of work, and defect rates.

4 Identify linkages: The costs of one activity may be determined, in part, by the way in which other activities are performed. Xerox discovered that its high service costs relative to competitors' reflected the complexity of design of its copiers, which required 30 different interrelated adjustments.

5 Identify opportunities for reducing costs: By identifying areas of comparative inefficiency and the cost drivers for each, opportunities for cost reduction become evident. If scale economies are a key cost driver, can volume be increased? If wage costs are excessive, will employees accept productivity-increasing measures; alternatively, can production be relocated? If an activity cannot be performed efficiently within the firm, can it be outsourced?

Figure 7.8 shows how the application of the value chain to automobile manufacture can yield suggestions for possible cost reductions.

## Differentiation Analysis

A firm differentiates itself from its competitors "when it provides something unique that is valuable to buyers beyond simply offering a lower price."[50] Differentiation advantage occurs when a firm is able to obtain from its differentiation a price premium in the market that exceeds the cost of providing the differentiation.

Every firm has opportunities for differentiating its offering to customers, although the range of differentiation opportunities depends on the characteristics of the product. An automobile or a restaurant offers greater potential for differentiation than cement, wheat, or memory chips. These latter products are called *commodities* precisely because they lack physical differentiation. Yet, according to Tom Peters, even commodities can be differentiated to create customer value: "Anything can be turned into a value-added product or service."[51] Consider the following:

● Cement is the ultimate commodity product, yet Cemex, based in Mexico, has become a worldwide supplier of cement and ready-mix concrete through emphasizing "building solutions"—one aspect of which is ensuring that 98% of its deliveries are on time (compared to 34% for the industry as a whole).[52]

● Online bookselling is inherently a commodity business—any online bookseller has access to the same titles and same modes of distribution. Yet

**FIGURE 7.8**  Using the value chain in cost analysis: An automobile manufacturer

SEQUENCE OF ANALYSIS

1. IDENTIFY ACTIVITIES
Establish the basic framework of the value chain by identifying the principal activities of the firm.

2. ALLOCATE TOTAL COSTS
For a first-stage analysis, a rough estimate of the breakdown of total cost by activity is sufficient to indicate which activities offer the greatest scope for cost reductions.

3. IDENTIFY COST DRIVERS
(See diagram.)

4. IDENTIFY LINKAGES
Examples include:
1. Consolidating purchase orders to increase discounts increases inventories.
2. High-quality parts and materials reduce costs of defects at later stages.
3. Reducing manufacturing defects cuts warranty costs.
4. Designing different models around common components and platforms reduces manufacturing costs.

5. IDENTIFY OPPORTUNITIES
COST REDUCTION
For example:
*Purchasing*: Concentrate purchases on fewer suppliers to maximize purchasing economies. Institute just-in-time component supply to reduce inventories.

*R & D/Design/Engineering*: Reduce frequency of model changes. Reduce number of different models (e.g., single range of global models). Design for commonality of components and platforms.

*Component manufacture*: Exploit economies of scale through concentrating production of each component on fewer plants. Outsource wherever scale of production or run lengths are suboptimal or where outside suppliers have technology advantages. For labor-intensive components (e.g., seats, dashboards, trim), relocate production in low-wage countries. Improve capacity utilization through plant rationalization or supplying components to other manufacturers.

VALUE CHAIN

PURCHASING COMPONENTS AND MATERIALS

R & D, DESIGN, AND ENGINEERING

COMPONENT MANUFACTURE

ASSEMBLY

TESTING AND QUALITY CONTROL

INVENTORIES OF FINISHED PRODUCTS

SALES AND MARKETING

DISTRIBUTION AND DEALER SUPPORT

COST DRIVER

Prices of bought-in components depend upon:
• Order sizes
• Average value of purchases per supplier
• Location of suppliers

Size of R & D commitment
Productivity of R & D
Number and frequency of new models
Sales per model

Scale of plants
Run length per component
Capacity utilization
Location of plants

Scale of plants
Number of models per plant
Degree of automation
Level of wages
Location of plants

Level of quality targets
Frequency of defects

Predicatability of sales
Flexibility of production
Customers' willingness to wait

Size of advertising budget
Strength of existing reputation
Sales volume

Number of dealers
Sales per dealer
Desired level of dealer support
Frequency of defects requiring repair under warranty of recalls

Amazon has exploited the information generated by its business to offer a range of value-adding services: best-seller lists, reviews, and customized recommendations.

The lesson is this: differentiation is not simply about offering different product features; it is about identifying and understanding every possible interaction between the firm and its customers and asking how these interactions can be enhanced or changed in order to deliver additional value to the customer. This requires looking at both the firm (the supply side) and its customers (the demand side). While *supply-side analysis* identifies the firm's potential to create uniqueness, the critical issue is whether such differentiation creates value for customers and whether the value created exceeds the cost of the differentiation. Only by understanding what customers want, how they choose, and what motivates them can we identify opportunities for profitable differentiation.

Thus, differentiation strategies are not about pursuing uniqueness for the sake of being different. Differentiation is about understanding customers and how we can best meet their needs. To this extent, the quest for differentiation advantage takes us to the heart of business strategy. The fundamental issues of differentiation are also the fundamental issues of business strategy: Who are our customers? How do we create value for them? And how do we do it more effectively and efficiently than anyone else?

Because differentiation is about uniqueness, establishing differentiation advantage requires creativity: it cannot be achieved simply through applying standardized frameworks and techniques. This is not to say that differentiation advantage is not amenable to systematic analysis. As we have observed, there are two requirements for creating profitable differentiation. On the supply side, the firm must be aware of the resources and capabilities through which it can create uniqueness (and do it better than competitors). On the demand side, the key is insight into customers and their needs and preferences. These two sides form the major components of our analysis of differentiation.

## The Nature and Significance of Differentiation

The potential for differentiating a product or service is partly determined by its physical characteristics. For products that are technically simple (a pair of socks, a brick), that satisfy uncomplicated needs (a corkscrew, a nail), or must meet rigorous technical standards (a spark plug, a thermometer), differentiation opportunities are constrained by technical and market factors. Products that are technically complex (an airplane), that satisfy complex needs (an automobile, a vacation), or that do not need to conform to particular technical standards (wine, toys) offer much greater scope for differentiation.

Beyond these constraints, the potential in any product or service for differentiation is limited only by the boundaries of the human imagination. For seemingly simple products such as shampoo, toilet paper, and bottled water, the proliferation of brands on any supermarket's shelves is testimony both to the ingenuity of firms and the complexity of customers' preferences. Differentiation extends beyond the physical characteristics of the product or service to encompass everything about the product or service that influences the value that customers derive from it. This means that differentiation includes every aspect of the way in which a company relates to its customers. Starbucks' ability to charge up to $5 for a cup of coffee (compared to a US average price of $1.38) rests not just on the characteristics of the coffee but also on the overall "Starbucks Experience" which encompasses the retail environment, the sense of community in which customers participate, and the values that Starbucks projects. Differentiation activities are not specific to particular functions such as design and marketing; they infuse all aspects of the relationship between an organization and its customers, including the identity and culture of a company.

Differentiation includes both tangible and intangible dimensions. *Tangible differentiation* is concerned with the observable characteristics of a product or service that are relevant to customers' preferences and choice processes, for example size, shape, color, weight, design, material, and performance attributes such as reliability, consistency, taste, speed, durability, and safety. Tangible differentiation also extends to products and services that complement the product in question: delivery, after-sales services, and accessories.

Opportunities for *intangible differentiation* arise because the value that customers perceive in a product is seldom determined solely by observable product features or objective performance criteria. Social, emotional, psychological, and esthetic considerations are present in most customer choices. For consumer goods and services the desire for status, exclusivity, individuality, security, and community are powerful motivational forces. Where a product or service is meeting complex customer needs, differentiation choices involve the overall image of the firm and its offering. Image differentiation is especially important for those products and services whose qualities and performance are difficult to ascertain at the time of purchase (so-called experience goods). These include cosmetics, medical services, and education.

*Differentiation and Segmentation*   Differentiation is different from segmentation. Differentiation is concerned with how a firm competes—the ways in which it can offer uniqueness to customers. Such uniqueness might relate to consistency (McDonald's), reliability (Federal Express), status (American Express), quality (BMW), and innovation (Apple). Segmentation is concerned with where a firm competes in terms of customer groups, localities, and product types.

Whereas segmentation is a feature of market structure, differentiation is a strategic choice made by a firm. Differentiation tends to lead to focusing upon particular market segments, but this is not necessarily so. Firms may locate within a segment without differentiating themselves from competitors within the same segment: Ameritrade, E-Trade, and Scottrade are all located within the online segment of the brokerage industry and yet are not significantly differentiated from one another. Conversely, IKEA, McDonald's, Honda, and Starbucks all pursue differentiation, but position themselves within the mass market spanning multiple demographic and socioeconomic segments.[53]

*The Sustainability of Differentiation Advantage*   Differentiation offers a more secure basis for competitive advantage than low cost does. A position of cost advantage is vulnerable to the emergence of new competitors from low-cost countries and to adverse movements in exchange rates. Cost advantage can also be overturned by innovation: discount brokerage firms were undercut by internet brokers, discount stores by online retailers. Differentiation advantage would appear to be more sustainable. Large companies that consistently earn above-average returns on capital—such as Colgate-Palmolive, Diageo, Johnson & Johnson, Kellogg's, Procter & Gamble, 3M, and Wyeth—tend to be those that have pursued differentiation through quality, branding, and innovation.

## Analyzing Differentiation: The Demand Side

Analyzing customer demand enables us to determine which product characteristics have the potential to create value for customers, customers' willingness to pay for differentiation, and a company's optimal competitive positioning in terms of differentiation variables. Analyzing demand begins with understanding why customers buy a product or service. Market research systematically explores customer preferences and customer perceptions of existing products. However, the key to successful differentiation is to understand customers. To gain insight into customer requirements and preferences, simple, direct inquiry into the purpose of a product and the needs of its customers can often be far more illuminating than statistically validated market research (Strategy Capsule 7.5).

Virtually all products and services serve multiple customer needs. As a result, understanding customer needs requires the analysis of multiple attributes. Market research has developed several techniques for analyzing customer preferences in relation to product attributes which can guide decisions over product positioning and design:

- *Multidimensional scaling* (MDS) permits customers' perceptions of competing products to be represented graphically in terms of key product attributes.[54] For example, a survey of consumer ratings of competing pain relievers resulted in the mapping shown in Figure 7.9. Multidimensional scaling has also been used to classify 109 single-malt Scotch whiskies according to the characteristics of their color, nose, palate, body, and finish.[55]

- *Conjoint analysis* measures the strength of customer preferences for different product attributes. The technique requires, first, an identification of the underlying attributes of a product and, second, market research to rank hypothetical products that contain alternative bundles of attributes. The results can then be used to estimate the proportion of customers who would prefer a hypothetical new product to competing products already available in the market.[56] Conjoint analysis has been used to predict market shares of forthcoming new models of personal computer, to analyze windsurfer preferences, and to design new products—including Marriott's Courtyard hotel chain and nature tourism in the Amazon basin.

- *Hedonic price analysis* views products as bundles of underlying attributes.[57] Hedonic price analysis uses regression to estimate the implicit market price for each attribute. For example, price differences among European automatic washing machines can be related to differences in capacity, spin speed, energy consumption, number of programs, and reliability. A machine that spins at 1000 rpm sold at about a $200 price premium to one that spins at 800 rpm.[58] Similarly, price differences between models of personal computer reflect differences in processor speed, memory, and hard drive capacity.[59] The results of this analysis can then be used to make decisions as to what levels of each attribute to include within a new product and the price point for that product.

- *Value curve analysis* maps the performance characteristics of competing products, indicating the potential for new products that offer superior combinations of product characteristics. Kim and Mauborgne show how, in book retailing, applying value metrics—such as price, knowledge levels of staff, selection of books, store ambiance, store hours, and additional facilities to

## Understanding What a Product Is about

Getting back to strategy means getting back to a deep understanding of what a product is about. Some time ago, for example, a Japanese home appliance company was trying to develop a coffee percolator. Should it be a General Electric-type percolator, executives wondered? Should it be the same drip type that Philips makes? Larger? Smaller? I urged them to ask a different kind of question: Why do people drink coffee? What are they looking for when they do? If your objective is to serve the customer better, then shouldn't you understand why that customer drinks coffee in the first place? Then you would know what kind of percolator to make.

The answer came back: good taste. Then I asked the company's engineers what they were doing to help the consumer enjoy good taste in a cup of coffee. They said they were trying to design a good percolator. I asked them what influences the taste in a cup of coffee. No one knew. That became the next question we had to answer. It turns out that lots of things can affect taste—the beans, the temperature, the water. We did our homework and discovered all the things that affect taste . . .

Of all the factors, water quality, we learned, made the greatest difference. The percolator in design at the time, however, didn't take water quality into account at all . . . We discovered next that grain distribution and the time between grinding the beans and pouring in the water were crucial. As a result we began to think about the product and its necessary features in a new way. It had to have a built-in dechlorinating function. It had to have a built-in grinder. All the customer should have to do is pour in water and beans . . .

To start you have to ask the right questions and set the right kinds of strategic goals. If your only concern is that General Electric has just brought out a percolator that brews coffee in 10 minutes, you will get your engineers to design one that brews it in seven minutes. And if you stick to that logic, market research will tell you that instant coffee is the way to go . . . Conventional marketing approaches won't solve the problem. If you ask people whether they want their coffee in 10 minutes or seven, they will say seven, of course. But it's still the wrong question. And you end up back where you started, trying to beat the competition at its own game. If your primary focus is on the competition, you will never step back and ask what the customers' inherent needs are, and what the product really is about.

**Source:** Reprinted by permission of Harvard Business Review. From "Getting Back to Strategy," Kenichi Ohmae, November/ December 1988, p. 154, Copyright © 1988 by the Harvard Business School Publishing Corporation; all rights reserved.

position existing book stores—reveals opportunities for new approaches (such as that offered by Barnes & Noble).[60]

*The Role of Social and Psychological Factors*   Analyzing product differentiation in terms of measurable performance attributes tends to ignore customers' underlying motivations. Few goods or services only satisfy physical needs: most buying is influenced by social and psychological motivations, such as the desire to find community with others and to reinforce one's own identity. Psychologist Abraham Maslow proposed a hierarchy of human needs that progress from basic survival needs to security needs, to belonging needs, to esteem needs, up to the desire for self-actualization.[61] For most goods, brand equity has more to do with

**FIGURE 7.9** Consumer perceptions of competing pain relievers: A multidimensional scaling mapping

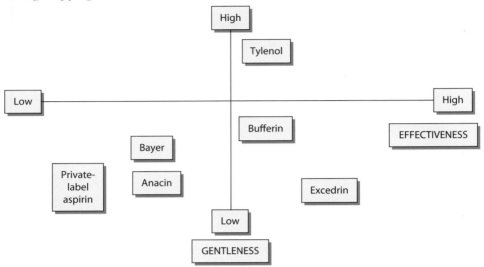

status and identity than with tangible product performance. The disastrous introduction of "New Coke" in 1985 was the result of Coca-Cola giving precedence to tangible differentiation (taste preferences) over intangible differentiation (authenticity).[62] Harley-Davidson harbors no such illusions: it recognizes quite clearly that it is in the business of selling lifestyle, not transportation.

If the dominant customer needs that a product satisfies are identity and social affiliation, the implications for differentiation are far reaching. In particular, to identify profitable differentiation opportunities requires that we analyze not only the product and its characteristics but also customers, their lifestyles and aspirations, and the relationship of the product to those lifestyles and aspirations. Market research that focuses upon traditional demographic and socioeconomic factors may be less useful than a deep understanding of consumers' relationships with a product. Tom Peters extols the merits of "naïve listening"[63] to customers. In practice a deeper understanding of consumers' lifestyles and perceptions may be necessary to interpret their words. Before opening its Fresh and Easy chain of food stores in California, British supermarket giant Tesco sent a team of executives to live with local families.[64] And going beyond functionality to explore the emotional and esthetic aspects of consumers' relationships with products has been central to Japanese approaches to marketing.[65]

Figure 7.10 summarizes the key points of this discussion by posing some basic questions that explore the potential for demand-side differentiation.

## Analyzing Differentiation: The Supply Side

Demand analysis identifies customers' demands for differentiation and their willingness to pay for it, but creating differentiation advantage also depends on a firm's ability to offer differentiation. This in turn depends upon the activities that the firm performs and the resources it has access to.

**FIGURE 7.10**   Identifying differentiation potential: The demand side

*The Drivers of Uniqueness*   Differentiation is concerned with the provision of uniqueness. A firm's opportunities for creating uniqueness in its offerings to customers are not located within a particular function or activity but can arise in virtually everything that it does. Michael Porter identifies several sources of uniqueness:

- product features and product performance;
- complementary services (such as credit, delivery, repair);
- intensity of marketing activities (such as rate of advertising spending);
- technology embodied in design and manufacture;
- quality of purchased inputs;
- procedures that influence the customer experience (such as the rigor of quality control, service procedures, frequency of sales visits);
- skill and experience of employees;
- location (such as with retail stores);
- degree of vertical integration (which influences a firm's ability to control inputs and intermediate processes).[66]

Differentiation can also occur through *bundling*—offering a combination of complementary products and services.[67] As markets mature, so products tend to go through phases of *unbundling*: products become commoditized while complementary services become provided by specialist suppliers. Electronic commerce has enabled customers to assemble their own bundles of goods and services with few transaction costs. The business of European tour operators has shrunk as most vacationers now use online travel and reservations systems to create their own customized vacations. The unbundling of products has encouraged the unbundling of companies.[68]

There are also trends in the opposite direction: the quest for new opportunities for differentiation has encouraged a *rebundling* of products and services into new systems. One of the major developments in business-to-business transactions in recent years has been the emphasis on "providing customer solutions"—producing a combination of goods and services that are tailored to the specific needs of the client. This involves a radical rethink of the business models in most companies.[69]

*Product Integrity*   Differentiation decisions cannot be made on a piecemeal basis. Establishing a coherent and effective differentiation position requires the firm to assemble a complementary package of differentiation attributes. If Burberry, the British fashion house, wants to expand its range of clothing and accessories, it needs to ensure that every new product offering is consistent with its overall image as a quality-focused brand that combines traditional British style with contemporary edginess. *Product integrity* refers to the consistency of a firm's differentiation; it is the extent to which a product achieves:

> total balance of numerous product characteristics, including basic functions, esthetics, semantics, reliability, and economy . . . Product integrity has both internal and external dimensions. Internal integrity refers to consistency between the function and structure of the product—e.g., the parts fit well, components match and work well together, layout achieves maximum space efficiency. External integrity is a measure of how well a product's function, structure, and semantics fit the customer's objectives, values, production system, lifestyle, use pattern, and self-identity.[70]

Simultaneously achieving internal and external integrity is a complex organizational challenge: it requires a combination of close cross-functional collaboration and intimate customer contact.[71] This integration of internal and external product integrity is especially important to those supplying "lifestyle" products, where differentiation is based on customers' social and psychological needs. Here, the credibility of the image depends critically on the consistency of the image presented. One element of this integration is a linked identity between customer and company employees. For instance:

- Harley-Davidson's image of ruggedness, independence, individuality, and community is supported by a top management team that dons biking leathers and rides its "hogs" to owners' group rallies, and a management system that empowers shop-floor workers and fosters quality, initiative, and responsibility.
- MTV's capacity to stay at the leading edge of popular culture and still be cool after 30 years on the air owes much to a human resource strategy that involves recruiting and giving responsibility to young people.

This need for internal/external consistency explains why brand-conscious companies such as Nike, Levi-Strauss, and Apple have been so vigilant over issues of employee exploitation among their offshore suppliers.

*Signaling and Reputation*   Differentiation is only effective if it is communicated to customers. But information about the qualities and characteristics of products is not always readily available to potential customers. The economics literature distinguishes between *search goods*, whose qualities and characteristics can be ascertained by inspection, and *experience goods*, whose qualities and characteristics are only recognized after consumption. This latter class of goods includes medical services, baldness treatments, frozen TV dinners, and wine. Even after purchase, performance attributes may be slow in revealing themselves. Bernie Madoff established Bernard L. Madoff Investment Securities LLC in 1960—it took almost half a century before the renowned investment house was revealed as a "giant Ponzi scheme."[72]

In the terminology of game theory (see Chapter 4), the market for experience goods corresponds to a classic prisoners' dilemma. A firm can offer a high-quality or a low-quality product. The customer can pay either a high or a low price. If quality cannot be detected, then equilibrium is established, with the customer offering a low price and the supplier offering a low-quality product, even though both would be better off with a high-quality product sold at a high price. The resolution of this dilemma is for producers to find some credible means of signaling quality to the customer. The most effective signals are those that change the payoffs in the prisoners' dilemma. Thus, an extended warranty is effective because providing such a warranty would be more expensive for a low-quality producer than a high-quality producer. Brand names, warranties, expensive packaging, money-back guarantees, sponsorship of sports and cultural events, and a carefully designed retail environment in which the product is sold are all signals of quality. Their effectiveness stems from the fact that they represent significant investments by the manufacturer that will be devalued if the product proves unsatisfactory to customers.

The more difficult it is to ascertain performance prior to purchase, the more important signaling is.

- A perfume can be sampled prior to purchase and its fragrance assessed, but its ability to augment the identity of the wearer and attract attention remains uncertain. Hence, the key role of branding, packaging, advertising, and lavish promotional events in establishing an identity for the perfume in terms of the implied personality, lifestyle, and aspirations of the user.
- In financial services, the customer cannot easily assess the honesty, financial security, or competence of the supplier. Hence, financial service companies emphasize symbols of security and stability: imposing head offices, conservative office decor, smartly dressed employees, and trademarks such as Prudential's rock and Travelers' red umbrella. Bernie Madoff's multibillion investment swindle was sustained by his close association with leading figures among New York's Jewish community, his prominent role in cultural and charitable organizations, and the aura of exclusivity around his investment club.

*Brands*  Brands fulfill multiple roles. Most importantly, a brand provides a guarantee by the producer to the consumer of the quality of the product. It does so in several ways. At its most basic, a brand identifies the producer of a product. This ensures that the producer is legally accountable for the products supplied to market. Further, the brand represents an investment that provides an incentive to maintain quality and customer satisfaction. It is a credible signal of quality because of the disincentive of its owner to devalue it. As a result, a brand acts as a guarantee to the customer that reduces uncertainty and search costs. The more difficult it is to discern quality on inspection, and the greater the cost to the customer of purchasing a defective product, the greater the value of a brand: a trusted brand name is more important to us when we purchase mountaineering equipment than when we buy a pair of socks.

The traditional role of the brand as a guarantor of reliability is particularly significant in e-commerce. Internet transactions are characterized by the anonymity of buyers and sellers and lack of government regulation. As a result, well-established players in e-commerce—Amazon, Microsoft, eBay, and Yahoo!—can use their brand to reduce consumers' perceived risk.

By contrast, the value conferred by consumer brands such as Red Bull, Harley-Davidson, Mercedes-Benz, Gucci, Virgin, and American Express is less a guarantee of reliability and more an embodiment of identity and lifestyle. Traditionally, advertising has been the primary means of influencing and reinforcing customer perceptions. Increasingly, however, consumer goods companies are seeking new approaches to brand development that focus less on product characteristics and more on "brand experience," "tribal identity," "shared values," and "emotional dialogue." Traditional mass-market advertising is less effective for promoting this type of brand identity as word-of-mouth promotion deploying web-based social networks—what has been referred to as *viral marketing* or *stealth marketing*.[73]

*The Costs of Differentiation*   Differentiation adds cost. The direct costs of differentiation include higher-quality inputs, better-trained employees, higher advertising costs, and better after-sales service. The indirect costs of differentiation arise through the interaction of differentiation variables with cost variables. If differentiation narrows a firm's segment scope, it also limits the potential for exploiting scale economies. If differentiation requires continual product redesign, it hampers the exploitation of learning economies.

One means of reconciling differentiation with cost efficiency is to postpone differentiation to later stages of the firm's value chain. Economies of scale and the cost advantages of standardization are frequently greatest in the manufacturing of basic components. Modular design with common components permits scale economies while maintaining considerable product variety. All the major automakers have reduced the number of platforms and engine types and increased the commonality of components across their model ranges, while offering customers a greater variety of colors, trim, and accessory options.

New manufacturing technology and the internet have redefined traditional trade-offs between efficiency and variety. Flexible manufacturing systems and just-in-time scheduling have increased the versatility of many plants, made model changeovers less costly, and made the goal of an "economic order quantity of one" increasingly realistic. Automobile and domestic appliance plants increasingly produce multiple models on a single assembly line.[74] Internet communication allows consumers to design their own products and quickly communicate their requirements to manufacturers.

## Bringing It All Together: The Value Chain in Differentiation Analysis

There is little point in identifying the product attributes that customers value most if the firm is incapable of supplying those attributes. Similarly, there is little purpose in identifying a firm's ability to supply certain elements of uniqueness if these are not valued by customers. The key to successful differentiation is matching the firm's capacity for creating differentiation to the attributes that customers value most. For this purpose, the value chain provides a particularly useful framework. Let's begin with the case of a producer good i.e., one that is supplied by one firm to another.

*Value Chain Analysis of Producer Goods*   Using the value chain to identify opportunities for differentiation advantage involves three principal stages:

1  Construct a value chain for the firm and its customer. It may be useful to consider not just the immediate customer but also firms further downstream in the value chain. If the firm supplies different types of customers, it's useful to draw separate value chains for each major category of customer.

2  Identify the drivers of uniqueness in each activity of the firm's value chain. Figure 7.11 identifies some possible sources of differentiation within Porter's generic value chain.

3  Locate linkages between the value chain of the firm and that of the buyer. What can the firm do with its own value chain activities that can reduce the cost or enhance the differentiation potential of the customer's value chain activities? The amount of additional value that the firm creates for its customers through exploiting these linkages represents the potential price premium the firm can charge for its differentiation. Strategy Capsule 7.6 demonstrates the identification of differentiation opportunities by lining the value chains of a firm and its customers.

**FIGURE 7.11**   Using the value chain to identify differentiation potential on the supply side

STRATEGY CAPSULE 7.6

# Using the Value Chain to Identify Differentiation Opportunities for a Manufacturer of Metal Containers

The metal container industry is a highly competitive, low-growth, low-profit industry. Cans lack much potential for differentiation, and buyers (especially beverage and food canning companies) are very powerful. Cost efficiency is essential, but can we also identify opportunities for profitable differentiation? Following the procedure outlined above, we can construct a value chain for a firm and its customers, and then identify linkages between the two. Figure 7.12 identifies five such linkages:

1  Distinctive can designs (e.g., Sapporo's beer can) can support the customer's efforts to differentiate its product.

2  Manufacturing cans to high tolerances can minimize breakdowns on customers' canning lines.

3  Reliable, punctual can deliveries allow canners to economize on their can inventories.

4  An efficient order-processing system reduces canners' ordering costs.

5  Speedy, proficient technical support allows customers to operate their canning lines with high-capacity utilization.

**FIGURE 7.12**  Identifying differentiation opportunities by linking the firm's value chain to that of the customer

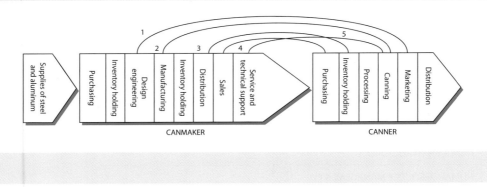

*Value Chain Analysis of Consumer Goods*  Value chain analysis of differentiation opportunities can also be applied to consumer goods. Few consumer goods are consumed directly: typically, consumers engage in a chain of activities that involve search, acquisition, and use of the product. In the case of consumer durables, the value chain may include search, purchase, financing, acquisition of complementary products and services, operation, service and repair, and eventual disposal. Such complex consumer value chains offer many potential linkages with the manufacturer's value chain, with rich opportunities for innovative differentiation. Harley-Davidson has built its strategy around the notion that it is not supplying motorcycles; it is supplying a customer experience. This has encouraged it to expand the scope of its contact with its customers to provide a wider range of services than any other motorcycle company. Even nondurables involve the consumer in a chain of activities. Consider a frozen TV dinner: it must be purchased, taken home, removed from the package, heated, and served before it is consumed. After eating, the consumer must clean any used dishes, cutlery, or other utensils. A value chain analysis by a frozen foods producer would identify ways in which the product could be formulated, packaged, and distributed to assist the consumer in performing this chain of activities.

## Implementing Cost and Differentiation Strategies

The two primary sources of competitive advantage define two fundamentally different approaches to business strategy. A firm that is competing on low cost is distinguishable from a firm that competes through differentiation in terms of market positioning, resources and capabilities, and organizational characteristics. Table 7.2 outlines some of the principal features of cost and differentiation strategies.

Porter views cost leadership and differentiation as mutually exclusive strategies. A firm that attempts to pursue both is "stuck in the middle":

The firm stuck in the middle is almost guaranteed low profitability. It either loses the high-volume customers who demand low prices or must bid away its profits to get this business from the low-cost firms. Yet it also loses high-margin business—the cream—to the firms who are focused on high-margin targets or have achieved differentiation overall. The firm that is stuck in the middle also probably suffers from a blurred corporate culture and a conflicting set of organizational arrangements and motivation system.[75]

**TABLE 7.2**  Features of cost leadership and differentiation strategies

| Generic strategy | Key strategy elements | Resource and organizational requirements |
|---|---|---|
| Cost leadership | Scale-efficient plants | Access to capital |
| | Design for manufacture | Process engineering skills |
| | Control of overheads and R & D | Frequent reports |
| | Process innovation | Tight cost control |
| | Outsourcing (especially overseas) | Specialization of jobs and functions |
| | Avoidance of marginal customer | Incentives linked to quantitative target accounts |
| Differentiation | Emphasis on branding, advertising, design, service, quality, and new product development | Marketing abilities |
| | | Product engineering skills |
| | | Cross-functional coordination |
| | | Creativity |
| | | Research capability |
| | | Incentives linked to qualitative performance targets |

In practice, few firms are faced with such stark alternatives. Differentiation is not simply an issue of "to differentiate or not to differentiate." All firms must make decisions as to which customer requirements to focus on and where to position their product or service in the market. A cost leadership strategy typically implies limited-feature, standardized offerings, but this does not necessarily imply that the product or service is an undifferentiated commodity. Southwest Airlines and AirAsia are budget airlines with a no-frills offering yet have clear market positions with unique brand images. The VW Beetle shows that a utilitarian, mass-market product can achieve cult status.

In most industries, market leadership is held by a firm that maximizes customer appeal by reconciling effective differentiation with low cost—Toyota in cars, McDonald's in fast food, Nike in athletic shoes. The simultaneous pursuit of cost efficiency, quality, innovation, and brand building was a feature of Japanese suppliers of cars, motorcycles, consumer electronics, and musical instruments during the late 20th century. In many industries, the cost leader is not the market leader but a smaller competitor with minimal overheads, non-union labor and cheaply acquired assets. In oil refining, the cost leaders tend to be independent refining companies rather than integrated giants such as ExxonMobil or Shell. In car rental, the cost leader is more likely to be Rent-A-Wreck (a division of Bundy American Corporation) rather than Hertz or Avis. Reconciling cost efficiency with differentiation has been facilitated by management technique: total quality management has refuted the perceived tradeoff between quality and cost; flexible manufacturing systems have reconciled scale economies with variety.

## Summary

Making money in business requires establishing and sustaining competitive advantage. Identifying opportunities for competitive advantage requires insight into the nature and process of competition within a market. Our analysis of the imperfections of the competitive process takes us back to the resources and capabilities needed to compete in a particular market and conditions under which these are available. Similarly, the isolating mechanisms that sustain competitive advantage are dependent primarily upon the ability of rivals to access the resources and capabilities needed for imitation.

Competitive advantage has two primary dimensions: cost advantage and differentiation advantage. The first of these, cost advantage, is the outcome of seven primary cost drivers. We showed that by applying these cost drivers and by disaggregating the form into a value chain of linked activities we can appraise a firm's cost position relative to competitors and identify opportunities for cost reduction. The principal message of this section is the need to look behind cost accounting data and beyond simplistic approaches to cost efficiency, and to analyze the factors that drive relative unit costs in each of the firm's activities in a systematic and comprehensive manner.

The appeal of differentiation is that it offers multiple opportunities for competitive advantage with a greater potential for sustainability than does cost advantage. The vast realm of differentiation opportunity extends beyond marketing and design to encompass all aspects of a firm's interactions with its customers. Achieving a differentiation advantage requires the firm to match its own capacity for creating uniqueness to the requirements and preferences of customers. The value chain offers firms a useful framework for identifying how they can create value for their customers by combining demand-side and supply-side sources of differentiation.

Finally, the basis of a firm's competitive advantage has important implications not just for the design of its strategy but for the design of its organizational structure and systems. Typically, companies that are focused on cost leadership design their organizations differently from those that pursue differentiation. However, the implications of competitive strategy for organizational design are complicated by the fact that, for most firms, cost efficiency and differentiation are not mutually exclusive—in today's intensely competitive markets, firms have little choice but to pursue both.

Quizzes and flashcards to test yourself further are available in your interactive e-book at
**www.wileyopenpage.com**

## Self-Study Questions

1.  Figure 7.1 implies that stable industries, where firms have similar resources and capabilities, offer less opportunity for competitive advantage than industries where change is rapid and firms are heterogeneous. Think of an example of each of these two types of industry. Is there any evidence that interfirm profit differences are wider in the more dynamic, heterogeneous industry than in the more stable, homogeneous industry?

2.  Apple has successfully established itself as the market leader in smartphones with its iPhone. Can Apple sustain its leadership in this market? How?

3.  Illy, the Italian-based supplier of quality coffee and coffee-making equipment, is launching an international chain of gourmet coffee shops. What advice would you offer Illy for how it can best build competitive advantage in the face of Starbucks' market leadership?

4.  Which drivers of cost advantage (Figure 7.5) does Sears exploit in order to offer its Sears Motor Buggy "at a price within the reach of all"? (See quotation that opens this chapter.)

5.  Target (the US discount retailer), H&M (the Swedish fashion clothing chain), and Primark (the UK discount clothing chain) have pioneered *cheap chic*—combining discount store prices with fashion appeal. What are the principal challenges of designing

and implementing a cheap chic strategy? Design a cheap chic strategy for a company entering another market e.g., restaurants, sports shoes, cosmetics, or office furniture.

6. To what extent are the seven cost drivers shown in Figure 7.5 relevant in analyzing the costs per student at your business school or educational institution? What recommendations would you make to your dean for improving the cost efficiency of your school?

7. Bottled water sells at least 200 times the price of tap water, with substantial price differentials between different brands. What are the key differentiation variables that determine the price premium that can be obtained for bottled water?

8. Advise a chain of movie theaters on a differentiation strategy to restore its flagging profitability. Use the value chain framework outlined in Strategy Capsule 7.6 to identify potential linkages between the company's value chain and that of its customers in order to identify differentiation opportunities.

# Notes

1. Richard Rumelt argues that competitive advantage lacks a clear and consistent definition ("What in the World is Competitive Advantage?" Policy Working Paper 2003-105, Anderson School, UCLA, August, 2003).

2. K. Ferdows, M. A. Lewis, and J. Machuca, "Rapid-Fire Fulfillment," *Harvard Business Review* (November 2004): 104–10.

3. G. Stalk Jr., "Time: The Next Source of Competitive Advantage," *Harvard Business Review* (July/August, 1988): 41–51.

4. J. A. Schumpeter, *Capitalism, Socialism and Democracy* (London: Routledge, 1994, first published 1942): 82–3.

5. C. Kim and R. Mauborgne, "Blue Ocean Strategy," *Harvard Business Review* (October 2004).

6. R. Buaron, "New Game Strategies," *McKinsey Quarterly Anthology* (2000): 34–6.

7. C. Baden-Fuller and J. M. Stopford, *Rejuvenating the Mature Business* (London and New York: Routledge, 1992).

8. G. Hamel, "The Why, What, and How of Management Innovation," *Harvard Business Review* (February 2006).

9. R. P. Rumelt, "Toward a Strategic Theory of the Firm," in R. Lamb (ed.), *Competitive Strategic Management* (Englewood Cliffs, NJ: Prentice Hall, 1984): 556–70.

10. R. Jacobsen, "The Persistence of Abnormal Returns," *Strategic Management Journal* 9 (1988): 415–30; R. R. Wiggins and T. W. Ruefli, "Schumpeter's Ghost: Is Hypercompetition Making the Best of Times Shorter?" *Strategic Management Journal* 26 (2005): 887–911.

11. G. Stalk, "Curveball: Strategies to Fool the Competition," *Harvard Business Review* (September 2006): 114–22.

12. The film was based on the book by B. Traven, *The Treasure of the Sierra Madre* (New York: Knopf, 1947).

13. Monopolies and Mergers Commission, *Cat and Dog Foods* (London: Her Majesty's Stationery Office, 1977).

14. S. Martin, *Advanced Industrial Economics*, 2nd edn (Oxford: Blackwell Publishing, 2001): Chapter 8.

15. T. C. Schelling, *The Strategy of Conflict*, 2nd edn (Cambridge, MA: Harvard University Press, 1980): 35–41.

16. A. Brandenburger and B. Nalebuff, *Co-opetition* (New York: Doubleday, 1996): 72–80.

17. R. Schmalensee, "Entry Deterrence in the Ready-to-Eat Breakfast Cereal Industry," *Bell Journal of Economics* 9 (1978): 305–27.

18. Monopolies and Mergers Commission, *Indirect Electrostatic Reprographic Equipment* (London: Her Majesty's Stationery Office, 1976): 37, 56.

19. S. A. Lippman and R. P. Rumelt, "Uncertain Imitability: An Analysis of Interfirm Differences in Efficiency under Competition," *Bell Journal of Economics* 13 (1982): 418–38. See also: R. Reed and R. DeFillippi, "Causal Ambiguity, Barriers to Imitation, and Sustainable Competitive Advantage," *Academy of Management Review* 15 (1990): 88–102.

20. P. R. Milgrom and J. Roberts, "Complementarities and Fit: Strategy, Structure and Organizational Change in Manufacturing," *Journal of Accounting and Economics* 19 (1995): 179–208.

21. J. W. Rivkin, "Imitation of Complex Strategies," *Management Science* 46 (2000): 824–44.

22. M. E. Porter and N. Siggelkow, "Contextuality within Activity Systems and Sustainable Competitive Advantage," *Academy of Management Perspectives* 22 (May 2008): 34–56.

23. M. E. Porter, *Competitive Advantage* (New York: Free Press, 1985): 13.

24. M. E. Porter, *Competitive Advantage* (New York: Free Press, 1985): 120.

25. L. E. Yelle, "The Learning Curve: Historical Review and Comprehensive Survey," *Decision Sciences* 10 (1979): 302–28.

26. D. Ross, "Learning to Dominate," *Journal of Industrial Economics* 34 (1986): 337–53.

27. Boston Consulting Group, *Strategy Alternatives for the British Motorcycle Industry* (London: Her Majesty's Stationery Office, 1975).

28. R. Jacobsen and D. Aaker, "Is market share all that it's cracked up to be?" *Journal of Marketing* 49 (Fall 1985): 11–22.

29. R. Wensley, "PIMS and BCG: New Horizons or False Dawn?" *Strategic Management Journal* 3 (1982): 147–58.

30. M. Venzin, *Building an International Financial Services Firm: How Successful Firms Design and Execute Cross-border Strategies* (Oxford: Oxford University Press, 2009).

31. R. P. McAfee and J. McMillan, "Organizational Diseconomies of Scale," *Journal of Economics and Management Strategy* 4 (1996): 399–426.

32. L. Rapping, "Learning and World War II Production Functions," *Review of Economics and Statistics* (February 1965): 81–6.

33. G. Linden, J. Hart, S. A. Lenway, and T. P. Murtha, "Flying Geese as Moving Targets," *Industry and Innovation* 5 (June 1998): 11–34.

34. L. Argote, S. L. Beckman, and D. Epple, "The Persistence and Transfer of Learning in Industrial Settings,"*Management Science* 36 (1990): 140–54; M. Zollo and S. G. Winter, "Deliberate Learning and the Evolution of Dynamic Capabilities," *Organization Science* 13 (2002): 339–51.

35. M. Keller, *Collision* (New York: Doubleday, 1993): 169–71.

36. J. Womack and D. T. Jones, "From Lean Production to Lean Enterprise," *Harvard Business Review* (March/April 1994); J. Womack and D. T. Jones, "Beyond Toyota: How to Root Out Waste and Pursue Perfection," *Harvard Business Review* (September/October, 1996).

37. M. Hammer and J. Champy, *Re-engineering the Corporation: A Manifesto for Business Revolution* (New York: HarperBusiness, 1993): 32.

38. M. Hammer, "Re-engineering Work: Don't Automate, Obliterate," *Harvard Business Review* (July/August, 1990).

39. V. Glover and M. L. Marcus, "Business Process Transformation," *Advances in Management Information Systems* 9 (M. E. Sharpe, March 2008); R. Merrifield, J. Calhoun, and D. Stevens, "The Next Revolution in Productivity," *Harvard Business Review* (November 2006): 72–9.

40. R. E. Gomory, "From the Ladder of Science to the Product Development Cycle," *Harvard Business Review* (November/December 1989): 103.

41. F. X. Frei, "Breaking the Tradeoff between Efficiency and Service," *Harvard Business Review* (November 2006): 92–103.

42. "Caterpillar to Cut 20,000 Jobs as Downturn Worsens," *Wall Street Journal* (January 28, 2009).

43. J. W. Plunkett, *Plunkett's Automotive Almanac* 2011 (Houston, TX: Plunkett's Research).

44. "Buying Power of Multiproduct Retailers," *OECD Journal of Competition Law and Policy* 2 (March, 2000).

45. R. Cyert and J. March, *A Behavioral Theory of the Firm* (Englewood Cliffs, NJ: Prentice Hall, 1963).

46. H. Leibenstein, "Allocative Efficiency versus X-Efficiency," *American Economic Review* 54 (June 1966): 392–415.

47. K. Kase, F. J. Saez, and H. Riquelme, *The New Samurais of Japanese Industry* (Cheltenham: Edward Elgar, 2006).

48. M. E. Porter, *Competitive Advantage* (New York: Free Press, 1985): 87.

49. R. S. Kaplan and S. R. Anderson, "Time-Driven Activity-based Costing," *Harvard Business Review* (November 2004): 131–8; J. Billington, "The ABCs of ABC: Activity-based Costing and Management," *Harvard Management Update* (Boston: Harvard Business School Publishing, May 1999).

50. M. E. Porter, *Competitive Advantage* (New York: Free Press, 1985): 120.

51. T. Peters, *Thriving on Chaos* (New York: Knopf, 1987): 56.

52. "Cemex: Cementing a Global Strategy," Insead Case No. 307-233-1 (2007).

53. The distinction between segmentation and differentiation is discussed in P. R. Dickson and J. L. Ginter, "Market Segmentation, Product Differentiation and Marketing Strategy," *Journal of Marketing* 51 (April 1987): 1–10.

54. S. Schiffman, M. Reynolds, and F. Young, *Introduction to Multidimensional Scaling: Theory, Methods, and Applications* (Cambridge, MA: Academic Press, 1981).

55. F.-J. Lapointe and P. Legendre, "A Classification of Pure Malt Scotch Whiskies," *Applied Statistics* 43 (1994): 237–57. On the principles of MDS, see I. Borg and P. Groenen, *Modern Multidimensional Scaling: Theory and Application*(New York: Springer-Verlag, 1997).

56. P. Cattin and D. R. Wittink, "Commercial Use of Conjoint Analysis: A Survey," *Journal of Marketing* 46 (Summer 1982): 44–53.

57. K. Lancaster, *Consumer Demand: A New Approach* (New York: Columbia University Press, 1971).

58. P. Nicolaides and C. Baden-Fuller, *Price Discrimination and Product Differentiation in the European Domestic Appliance Market* (London: Center for Business Strategy, London Business School, 1987).

59. A. Pates, "A Reconsideration of Hedonic Price Indexes with an Application to PCs," *American Economic Review* 93 (2003): 1578–96.

60. C. Kim and R. Mauborgne, "Creating New Market Space," *Harvard Business Review* (January/February 1999): 83–93.

61. A. Maslow, "A Theory of Human Motivation," *Psychological Review* 50 (1943): 370–96.

62. "Coke Lore: The Real Story of New Coke," www.thecocacolacompany.com/heritage/cokelore_newcoke.html, accessed February 8, 2012.

63. T. Peters, *Thriving on Chaos* (New York: Knopf, 1987): 149.

64. "Fresh, but far from Easy," *Economist* (June 21, 2007).

65. J. K. Johansson and I. Nonaka, *Relentless: The Japanese Way of Marketing* (New York: HarperBusiness, 1996).

66. M. E. Porter, *Competitive Advantage* (New York: Free Press, 1985): 124–5.

67. S. Mathur, "Competitive Industrial Marketing Strategies," *Long Range Planning* 17, no. 4 (1984): 102–9.

68. J. Hagel and M. Singer, "Unbundling the Corporation," *McKinsey Quarterly* 3 (2000): 148–61.

69. K. R. Tuli, A. K. Kohli, and S. G. Bharadwaj, "Rethinking Customer Solutions: From Product Bundles to Relational Processes," *Journal of Marketing* 71, no. 3 (2007): 1–17.

70. K. Clark and T. Fujimoto, *Product Development Performance* (Boston: Harvard Business School Press, 1991): 29–30.

71. K. B. Clark and T. Fujimoto, "The Power of Product Integrity," *Harvard Business Review* (November/December, 1990): 107–18.

72. "The Madoff Affair: Going Down Quietly," *Economist* (March 14, 2009).

73. D. J. Watts and J. Peretti, "Viral Marketing for the Real World," *Harvard Business Review* (May 2007): 22–3.

74. J. Pine, B. Victor, and A. Boynton, "Making Mass-customization Work," *Harvard Business Review* (September/October 1993): 108–16.

75. M. E. Porter, *Competitive Strategy* (New York: Free Press, 1980): 42.

# 8 Industry Evolution and Strategic Change

No company ever stops changing . . . Each new generation must meet changes—in the automotive market, in the general administration of the enterprise, and in the involvement of the corporation in a changing world. The work of creating goes on.

—ALFRED P. SLOAN JR., PRESIDENT OF GENERAL
MOTORS 1923–37, CHAIRMAN 1937–56

It is not the strongest of the species that survive, nor the most intelligent, but the one that is most responsive to change.

—CHARLES DARWIN

You keep same-ing when you ought to be changing.

—LEE HAZLEWOOD, THESE BOOTS ARE MADE FOR WALKING,
RECORDED BY NANCY SINATRA, 1966

## OUTLINE

# Introduction and Objectives

Everything is in a state of constant change—the business environment especially. One of the greatest challenges of strategic management is to ensure that the firm keeps pace with changes occurring within its environment.

Change in the industry environment is driven by the forces of technology, consumer needs, politics, economic development, and a host of other influences. In some industries, these forces for change combine to create massive, unpredictable changes. For example, in telecommunications new digital and wireless technologies combined with regulatory changes have resulted in the telecom industry of 2012 being almost unrecognizable from that which existed 25 years ago. In other industries—food processing, aircraft production, and car rental—change is more gradual and more predictable. Change is not just the result of external forces. As we have seen, competition is a dynamic process in which firms vie for competitive advantage, only to see it eroded through imitation and innovation by rivals. The outcome is that industries are continually recreated by competition.

The purpose of this chapter is to help us to understand and manage change. To do this we shall explore the forces that drive change and look for patterns that can help us to predict how industries are likely to evolve over time. While recognizing that every industry follows a unique development path, there are common drivers of change that can help us to recognize similar patterns, thereby helping us to identify opportunities for competitive advantage.

Understanding, even predicting, change in an industry's environment is the easy part. By far the greatest challenge is ensuring the adaptation of the firm to that change. For individuals change is disruptive, costly, and uncomfortable. For organizations the forces of inertia are even stronger. As a result, the life cycles of firms tend to be much shorter than the life cycles of industries: changes at the industry level tend to occur through the death of existing firms and the birth of new firms rather than through continuous adaptation by a constant population of firms. We need to understand these sources of inertia in organizations to see how resistance to change can be overcome. Going beyond adaptation, some firms become initiators of change. What determines the ability of these firms to become game-changers in their industries?

Whether a firm is adapting to or initiating change, competing in a changing world requires the development of new capabilities that can help renew competitive advantage. How difficult can this be? The short answer is "Very." We will look not just at the difficulties of building new capabilities but also at the approaches that organizations can take to overcome these difficulties.

By the time you have completed this chapter, you will be able to:

◆ recognize the different stages of industry development and understand the factors that drive the process of industry evolution;

◆ identify the key success factors associated with industries at different stages of their development and recommend strategies, organizational structures, and management systems appropriate to these stages;

◆ appreciate the sources of organizational inertia, the challenges of managing strategic change, and be familiar with different approaches to strategic change—including the use of scenario analysis and the quest for ambidexterity;

◆ become familiar with the different approaches that firms have taken in developing organizational capabilities—and the merits and pitfalls of each;

◆ recognize the principal tools of knowledge management and the roles they can play in developing organizational capability.

# The Industry Life Cycle

One of the best-known and most enduring marketing concepts is the *product life cycle*.[1] Products are born, their sales grow, they reach maturity, they go into decline, and they ultimately die. If products have life cycles, so the industries that produce them experience an **industry life cycle**. To the extent that an industry produces multiple generations of a product, the industry life cycle is likely to be of longer duration than that of a single product.

The life cycle comprises four phases: *introduction* (or *emergence*), *growth*, *maturity*, and *decline* (Figure 8.1). Let us first examine the forces that drive industry evolution, and then let us look at the features of each of these stages. Two factors are fundamental: demand growth and the production and diffusion of knowledge.

## Demand Growth

The life cycle and the stages within it are defined primarily by changes in an industry's growth rate over time. The characteristic profile is an S-shaped growth curve.

- In the *introduction stage*, sales are small and the rate of market penetration is low because the industry's products are little known and customers are few. The novelty of the technology, small scale of production, and lack of experience mean high costs and low quality. Customers for new products tend to be affluent, innovation-oriented, and risk-tolerant.

- The *growth stage* is characterized by accelerating market penetration as technical improvements and increased efficiency open up the mass market.

- Increasing market saturation causes the onset of the *maturity stage*. Once saturation is reached, demand is wholly for replacement.

- Finally, as the industry becomes challenged by new industries that produce technologically superior substitute products, the industry enters its *decline stage*.

**FIGURE 8.1**   The industry life cycle

## Creation and Diffusion of Knowledge

The second driver of the industry life cycle is knowledge. New knowledge in the form of product innovation is responsible for an industry's birth, and the dual processes of knowledge creation and knowledge diffusion exert a major influence on industry evolution.

In the introduction stage, product technology advances rapidly. There is no dominant product technology, and rival technologies compete for attention. Competition is primarily between alternative technologies and design configurations:

- The first 30 years of steam ships featured competition between paddles and propellers, wooden hulls and iron hulls, and, eventually, between coal and oil.
- The beginnings of the home computer industry during 1978–1982 saw competition between different data storage systems (audiotapes versus floppy disks), visual displays (TV receivers versus dedicated monitors), operating systems (CPM versus DOS versus Apple II), and microprocessors.

*Dominant Designs and Technical Standards*   The outcome of competition between rival designs and technologies is usually convergence by the industry around a **dominant design**—a product architecture that defines the look, functionality, and production method for the product and becomes accepted by the industry as a whole. Dominant designs have included:

- The Underwood Model 5 introduced in 1899 established the basic architecture and main features of typewriters for the 20th century: a moving carriage, the ability to see the characters being typed, a shift function for upper-case characters, and a replaceable inked ribbon.[2]
- Leica's Ur-Leica camera developed by Oskar Barnack and launched in Germany in 1924 established key features of the 35 mm camera, though it was not until Canon began mass-producing cameras based on the Leica original that this design of 35 mm camera came to dominate still photography.
- When Ray Kroc opened his first McDonald's hamburger restaurant in Illinois in 1955, he established what would soon become a dominant design for the

**FIGURE 8.2**   Product and process innovation over time

fast-food restaurant industry: a limited menu, no waiter service, eat-in and take-out options, roadside locations for motorized customers, and a franchising model of business system licensing.

The concepts of *dominant design* and **technical standard** are closely related. Dominant design refers to the overall configuration of a product or system. A technical standard is a technology or specification that is important for compatibility. A dominant design may or may not embody a technical standard. IBM's PC established the MS-DOS operating system and Intel x86 series of microprocessor as standards for personal computing that later evolved into the "Wintel" standard. Conversely, the Boeing 707 was a dominant design for large passenger jets but did not set industry standards in aerospace technology that would dominate subsequent generations of airplanes. Technical standards emerge where there are **network effects**—the need for users to connect in some way with one another. Network effects cause each customer to choose the same technology as everyone else to avoid being stranded. Unlike a proprietary technical standard, which is typically embodied in patents or copyrights, a firm that sets a dominant design does not normally own intellectual property in that design. Hence, except for some early-mover advantage, there is not necessarily any profit advantage from setting a dominant design.

Dominant designs also exist in processes. In the flat glass industry there has been a succession of dominant process designs from glass cylinder blowing to continuous ribbon drawing to float glass.[3] Dominant designs are present, too, in business models. In many new markets, competition is between rival *business models*. In home grocery delivery, dotcom start-ups such as Webvan and Peapod soon succumbed to competition from "bricks 'n' clicks" retailers such as Giant, and Wal-Mart (and Tesco in the UK).

*From Product to Process Innovation*   The emergence of a dominant design marks a critical juncture in an industry's evolution. Once the industry coalesces around a leading product design, there's a shift from radical to incremental product innovation. This transition may be necessary to inaugurate the industry's growth phase: greater standardization reduces risks to customers and encourages firms to invest in production capacity. The shift in emphasis from design to manufacture typically involves increased attention to process innovation as firms seek to reduce costs and increase product reliability through large-scale production methods (Figure 8.2). The combination of process improvements, design modifications, and scale economies results in falling costs and greater availability, which in turn drives rapidly increasing market penetration. Strategy Capsule 8.1 uses the history of the automobile industry to illustrate these patterns of development.

Knowledge diffusion is also important on the customer side. Over the course of the life cycle, customers become increasingly informed. As they become more knowledgeable about the performance attributes of rival manufacturers' products, so they are better able to judge value for money and become more price sensitive.

## STRATEGY CAPSULE 8.1
# Evolution of the Automobile Industry

The period 1890–1912 was one of rapid product innovation in the auto industry. After 1886, when Karl Benz received a patent on his three-wheel motor carriage, a flurry of technical advances occurred in Germany, France, the US, and the UK. Developments included:

- the first four-cylinder four-stroke engine (by Karl Benz in 1890);
- the honeycomb radiator (by Daimler in 1890);
- the speedometer (by Oldsmobile in 1901);
- automatic transmission (by Packard in 1904);
- electric headlamps (by General Motors in 1908);
- the all-steel body (adopted by General Motors in 1912).

Ford's Model T, introduced in 1908, with its front-mounted, water-cooled engine and transmission with a gearbox, wet clutch, and rear-wheel drive, acted as a dominant design for the industry. During the remainder of the 20th century, automotive technology and design converged. A key indicator of this was the gradual elimination of alternative technologies and designs. Volkswagen's Beetle was the last mass-produced car with a rear-mounted, air-cooled engine. Citroen abandoned its distinctive suspension and braking systems. Four-stroke engines with four or six inline cylinders became dominant. Distinctive national differences eroded as American cars became smaller and Japanese and Italian cars became bigger. The fall of the Iron Curtain extinguished the last outposts of nonconformity: by the mid-1990s, East German two-stroke Wartburgs and Trabants were collectors' items.

As product innovation slowed, so process innovation took off. In October 1913, Ford opened its Highland Park Assembly Plant, with its revolutionary production methods based on interchangeable parts and a moving assembly line. In the space of one year, chassis assembly time was cut from 12 hours and 8 minutes to 1 hour and 33 minutes. The price of the Model T fell from $628 in 1908 to $260 in 1924. Between 1908 and 1927, over 15 million Model T's had been produced.

The second revolutionary process innovation in automobile manufacturing was Toyota's system of *lean production*, involving a tightly integrated "pull" system of production embodying just-in-time scheduling, team-based production, flexible manufacturing, and total quality management. During the 1970s and 1980s, lean production diffused throughout the world's vehicle industry in the same way that Ford's mass-production system had transformed the industry half a century before.

**Sources:** www.ford.com; http://en.wikipedia.org/wiki/History_of_the_automobile.

## How General Is the Life-Cycle Pattern?

To what extent do industries conform to this life-cycle pattern? To begin with, the duration of the life cycle varies greatly from industry to industry:

- The introduction phase of the US railroad industry extended from the building of the first railroad, the Baltimore and Ohio in 1827, to the growth phase of the 1870s. With the growth of road transport, the industry entered its decline phase during the late 1950s.

- The introduction stage of the US automobile industry lasted about 25 years, from the 1890s until growth took off in 1913–1915. Maturity set in during the mid-1950s, followed by decline during the past decade.

- In personal computers, the introduction phase lasted only about four years before growth took off in 1978. Between 1978 and 1983, a flood of new and established firms entered the industry. Toward the end of 1984, the first signs of maturity appeared: growth stalled, excess capacity emerged, and the industry began to consolidate around fewer companies; however, growth remained strong until the end of the 1990s.

- Digital audio players (MP3 players) were first introduced by Seehan Information Systems and Diamond Multimedia in 1997. With the launch of Apple's iPod in 2001, the industry entered its growth phase. By 2009, slackening growth indicated entry into the mature phase.

Over time, industry life cycles have become increasingly compressed. This is especially evident in e-commerce. Businesses such as online gambling, business-to-business online auctions, and online travel services went from initial introduction to maturity within a few years. Social networking was launched in 1997 by www.sixde grees.com. By 2005, a number of sites were rapidly building their networks, including MySpace, Orkut (Google), Badoo, and LinkedIn. However, it was Facebook that broke away from the pack, achieving 12 million users by the end of 2006, 100 million in August 2008, and 600 million at the beginning of 2011. Since then, monthly growth has slowed to a modest 3.5%. Cusumano and Yoffie argue that "competing on internet time" requires a radical rethink of strategies and management processes.[4]

Patterns of evolution also differ. Industries supplying basic necessities such as residential construction, food processing and clothing may never enter a decline phase because obsolescence is unlikely for such needs. Some industries may experience a rejuvenation of their life cycle. In the 1960s, the world motorcycle industry, in decline in the US and Europe, re-entered its growth phase as Japanese manufacturers pioneered the recreational use of motorcycles. The market for TV receivers has experienced multiple revivals: color TVs, computer monitors, flat-screen TVs, and, most recently, HDTVs. Similar waves of innovation have revitalized retailing (Figure 8.3). These rejuvenations of the product life cycle are not natural phenomena—they are typically the result of companies resisting the forces of maturity through breakthrough product innovations or developing new markets.

An industry is likely to be at different stages of its life cycle in different countries. Although the automobile markets of the EU, Japan, and the US have entered their decline phase, those of China, India, and Russia are in their growth phases. Multinational companies can exploit such differences: developing new products and

**FIGURE 8.3** Innovation and renewal in the industry life cycle: Retailing

introducing them into the advanced industrial countries, then shifting attention to other growth markets once maturity sets in.

A further feature of industry evolution is shifting boundaries of industries—some industries converge (handheld consumer electronic devices such as wireless phones, portable game players, cameras, and calculators increasingly compete in a single market); other industries, such as computers and mortgage banking, tend to fragment. Jacobides argues that, to understand the dynamics of industry change, we need to look at broad sectors that comprise clusters of related industries.[5]

## Implications of the Life Cycle for Competition and Strategy

Changes in demand growth and technology over the cycle have implications for industry structure, the population of firms, and competition. Table 8.1 summarizes the principal features of each stage of the industry life cycle.

*Product Differentiation*    The introduction stage typically features a wide variety of product types that reflect the diversity of technologies and designs—and the lack of consensus over customer requirements. Convergence around a dominant design is often followed by commoditization during the mature phase unless producers develop new dimensions for differentiation. Personal computers, credit cards, online financial services, wireless communication services, and internet access have all become commodity items which buyers select primarily on price. However, the trend toward commoditization also creates incentives for firms to create novel approaches to differentiation.

*Organizational Demographics and Industry Structure*    The number of firms in an industry changes substantially over the life cycle. The field of **organizational ecology**, founded by Michael Hannan, John Freeman, and Glen Carroll, analyzes the population of industries and the processes of founding and selection that determine entry and exit.[6] Some of the main findings of the organizational ecologists in relation to industry evolution are:

- The number of firms in an industry increases rapidly during the early stages of an industry's life. Initially, an industry may be pioneered by a few firms. However, as the industry gains legitimacy, failure rates decline and the rate

**TABLE 8.1**   The evolution of industry structure and competition over the life cycle

|  | Introduction | Growth | Maturity | Decline |
|---|---|---|---|---|
| *Demand* | Limited to early adopters: high-income, avant-garde | Rapidly increasing market penetration | Mass market, replacement/ repeat buying. Customers knowledgeable and price sensitive | Obsolescence |
| *Technology* | Competing technologies, rapid product innovation | Standardization around dominant technology, rapid process innovation | Well-diffused technical know-how: quest for technological improvements. | Little product or process innovation |
| *Products* | Poor quality, wide variety of features and technologies, frequent design changes | Design and quality improve, emergence of dominant design | Trend to commoditization. Attempts to differentiate by branding, quality, and bundling | Commodities the norm: differentiation difficult and unprofitable |
| *Manufacturing and distribution* | Short production runs, high-skilled labor content, specialized distribution channels | Capacity shortages, mass production, competition for distribution | Emergence of overcapacity, deskilling of production, long production runs, distributors carry fewer lines | Chronic overcapacity, reemergence of specialty channels |
| *Trade* | Producers and consumers in advanced countries | Exports from advanced countries to rest of world | Production shifts to newly industrializing then developing countries | Exports from countries with lowest labor costs |
| *Competition* | Few companies | Entry, mergers, and exits | Shakeout, price competition increases | Price wars, exits |
| *Key success factors* | Product innovation, establishing credible image of firm and product | Design for manufacture, access to distribution, brand building, fast product development, process innovation | Cost efficiency through capital intensity, scale efficiency, and low input costs | Low overheads, buyer selection, signaling commitment, rationalizing capacity |

of new firm foundings increases. The US automobile industry comprised 272 manufacturers in 1909,[7] while in TV receivers there were 92 companies in 1951.[8] New entrants have very different origins. Some are start-up companies (*de novo* entrants); others are established firms diversifying from related industries (*de alio* entrants).

●  With the onset of maturity, the number of firms begins to fall. Very often, industries go through one or more *shakeout* phases during which the rate of firm failure increases sharply. After this point, rates of entry and exit decline and the survival rate for incumbents increases substantially.[9] The shakeout phase of intensive acquisition, merger, and exit occurs, on average, 29 years into the life cycle and results in the number of producers being halved.[10] In the US tire industry, the number of firms grew from one (Goodrich) in 1896 to 274 in 1922 before shakeout reduced the industry to 49 firms in 1936.[11]

●  As industries become increasingly concentrated and the leading firms focus on the mass market, so a new phase of entry may take place as new firms create niche positions in the market. An example of this *resource partitioning* is the

US brewing industry: as the mass market became dominated by a handful of national brewers, so opportunities arose for new types of brewing companies—microbreweries and brew pubs—to establish themselves in specialist niches.[12]

However, in different industries structural change follows very different evolutionary paths. In most industries maturity is associated with increasing concentration, but in industries where scale economies are unimportant and entry barriers are low, maturity and commoditization may cause concentration to decline (as in credit cards, television broadcasting, and frozen foods). Some industries, especially where the first mover achieves substantial patent protection, may start out as near-monopolies, and then become increasingly competitive. Plain-paper copiers were initially monopolized by the Xerox Corporation and it was not until the early 1980s that the industry was transformed by a wave of new entry. Seemingly stable mature industries can be transformed within a few years by a wave of mergers. The world petroleum industry consolidated considerably during 1998–2001, as did the world steel industry during 2001–2007.

*Location and International Trade*   Industries move internationally during their life cycles as a result of shifts in demand decreasing dependence on advanced knowledge. New industries begin in the advanced industrial countries because of the presence of affluent consumers and the availability of technical and scientific resources. As demand grows in other countries, they are serviced initially by exports, but a reduced need for sophisticated labor skills makes production attractive in newly industrialized countries. The advanced industrialized countries begin to import. With maturity, commoditization, and deskilling of production processes, production eventually shifts to developing countries where labor costs are lowest.

At the beginning of the 1990s, the production of wireless handsets was concentrated in the US, Japan, Finland, and Germany. By the end of the 1990s, South Korea had joined this leading group. Between 2005 and 2012, production in North America, Western Europe, and Japan was in rapid decline as manufacturing shifted to China, India, Brazil, Vietnam, Hungary, and Romania.

*The Nature and Intensity of Competition*   These changes in industry structure over the life cycle—commoditization, new entry, and international diffusion of production—have implications for competition: first, a shift from non-price competition to price competition; second, margins shrink as the intensity of competition grows.

During the introduction stage, the battle for technological leadership means that price competition may be weak, but heavy investments in innovation and market development depress profitability. The growth phase is more conducive to profitability as market demand outstrips industry capacity, especially if incumbents are protected by barriers to entry. With the onset of maturity, increased product standardization and excess capacity stimulate price competition, especially during shakeout. How intense this is depends a great deal on the balance between capacity and demand and the extent of international competition. In food retailing, airlines, motor vehicles, metals, and insurance, maturity was associated with strong price competition and slender profitability. In household detergents, breakfast cereals, cosmetics, and cigarettes, high seller concentration and strong brands have limited price rivalry and supported high margins. The decline phase is almost always associated with strong price competition (often degenerating into destructive price wars) and dismal profit performance.

*Key Success Factors and Industry Evolution*   These same changes in structure together with changes in demand and technology over the industry life cycle also have important implications for the sources of competitive advantage at each stage of industry evolution:

1 During the introductory stage, product innovation is the basis for initial entry and for subsequent success. Soon, however, other requirements for success emerge. In moving from the first generation of products to subsequent generations, investment requirements grow and financial resources become increasingly important. Capabilities in product development also need to be supported by capabilities in manufacturing, marketing, and distribution.

2 Once the growth stage is reached, the key challenge is scaling up. As the market expands, the firm needs to adapt its product design and its manufacturing capability to large-scale production. As Figure 8.4 shows, investment in R & D, plant and equipment, and sales tends to be high during the growth phase. To utilize increased manufacturing capability, access to distribution becomes critical. The transition to the growth stage of development imposes massive managerial and organizational challenges for young firms resulting from the need to develop new capabilities and establish more complex structures.

3 With the maturity stage, competitive advantage is increasingly a quest for efficiency, particularly in industries that tend toward commoditization. Cost efficiency through scale economies, low wages, and low overheads becomes the key success factor. Figure 8.4 shows that R & D, capital investment, and marketing are lower in maturity than during the growth phase.

4 The transition to decline intensifies pressures for cost cutting. It also requires maintaining stability by encouraging the orderly exit of industry capacity and capturing residual market demand. We consider the strategic issues presented by mature and declining industries more fully in Chapter 10.

## Managing Organizational Adaptation and Strategic Change

We have established that industries change. But what about the companies within them? Let us turn our attention to business enterprises and consider both the impediments to change and the means by which change takes place.

### Why is Change so Difficult? The Sources of Organizational Inertia

At the heart of all approaches to change management is the recognition that organizations find change difficult. Why is this so? Different theories of organizational and industrial change emphasize different barriers to change:

- *Organizational routines*: Evolutionary economists emphasize the fact that capabilities are based on organizational routines—patterns of coordinated interaction among organizational members that develop through continual repetition. The more highly developed are an organization's routines, the

**FIGURE 8.4**  Differences in strategy and performance between businesses at different stages of the industry life cycle

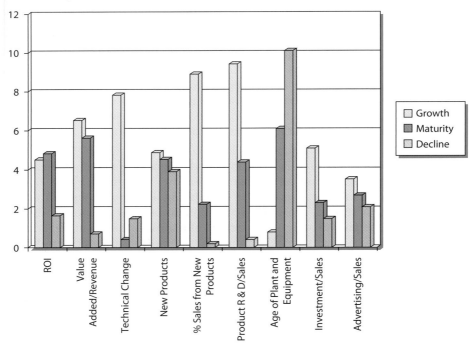

**Note:** The figure shows standardized means for each variable for businesses at each stage of the life cycle.
**Source:** C. Anderson and C. Zeithaml, "Stage of the Product Life Cycle, Business Strategy and Business Performance," *Academy of Management Journal* 27 (1984): 5–24.

more difficult it is to develop new routines. Hence, organizations get caught in **competency traps**[13] where "core capabilities become core rigidities."[14]

- *Social and political structures*: Organizations are both social systems and political systems. As social systems, organizations develop patterns of interaction that make organizational change stressful and disruptive.[15] As political systems, organizations develop stable distributions of power; change represents a threat to the power of those in positions of authority. Hence, both as social systems and political systems, organizations tend to resist change.

- *Conformity*: Institutional sociologists emphasize the propensity of firms to imitate one another in order to gain legitimacy. The process of **institutional isomorphism** locks organizations into common structures and strategies that make it difficult for them to adapt to change.[16] The pressures for conformity can be external—governments, investment analysts, banks, and other resource providers encourage the adoption of similar strategies and structures. Isomorphism also results from voluntary imitation— risk aversion encourages companies to adopt similar strategies and structures to their peers.[17]

- *Limited search*: The Carnegie School of organizational theory (associated with Herbert Simon, Jim March, and Richard Cyert) views *search* as the primary driver of organizational change. Organizations tend to limit search to areas close to their existing activities—they prefer *exploitation* of existing knowledge over *exploration* for new opportunities.[18] Limited search is reinforced, first, by **bounded rationality**—human beings have limited information processing capacity, which constrains the set of choices they can consider and, second, *satisficing*—the propensity for individuals (and organizations) to terminate the search for better solutions when they reach a satisfactory level of performance rather than to pursue optimal performance. The implication is that organizational change is triggered by declining performance.

- *Complementarities between strategy, structure, and systems*: Organizational economics,[19] sociotechnical systems,[20] and complexity theory[21] have all emphasized the importance of *fit* between an organization's strategy, structure, management systems, culture, employee skills—indeed, all the characteristics of an organization. Organizations struggle to establish complex, idiosyncratic combinations of multiple characteristics during their early phases of development in order to match the conditions of their business environment. However, once established, this complex configuration becomes a barrier to change. To respond to a change in its external environment, it is not enough to make incremental changes in few dimensions of strategy—it is likely that the firm will need to find a new configuration that involves a comprehensive set of changes (Strategy Capsule 8.2).[22] The implication is that organizations tend to evolve through a process of *punctuated equilibrium*, involving long periods of stability during which the widening misalignment between the organization and its environment ultimately forces radical and comprehensive change on the company.[23] Systematic changes that involve establishing a new configuration of activities that better matches the requirements of the external environment may require the appointment of a CEO from outside who is not wedded to the previous configuration.

## Organizational Adaptation and Industry Evolution

Thinking about industrial and organizational change has been strongly influenced by ideas from evolutionary biology. Evolutionary change is viewed as an adaptive process that involves *variation*, *selection*, and *retention*.[24] The key issue is the level at which these evolutionary processes occur:

- *Organizational ecology* has been discussed in relation to changes in the number of firms in an industry over time. However, organizational ecology is a broader theory of economic change based on the assumption of organizational inertia. As a result, industry evolution occurs through changes in the population of firms rather than by adaptation of firms themselves. Industries develop and grow through new entry spurred by the imitation of initial successful entrants. The competitive process is a *selection mechanism*, in which organizations whose characteristics match the requirements of their environment can attract resources; those that do not are eliminated.[25]

- *Evolutionary economics* focuses upon individual organizations as the primary agents of change. The process of variation, selection, and retention takes place at the level of the *organizational routine*—unsuccessful routines are

### STRATEGY CAPSULE 8.2
## A Tight-Fitting Business System Makes Change Perilous: The Liz Claiborne Story

During the 1980s, Liz Claiborne became a highly successful designer, manufacturer, and retailer of clothes for professional women. Liz Claiborne's success was based upon a strategy that combined a number of closely linked choices concerning functions and activities.

◆ Design was based around a "color by the numbers" approach involving "concept groups" of different garments that could be mixed and matched.

◆ In department stores, Liz Claiborne encouraged the retailers to provide dedicated space to present Liz Claiborne's concept collections. Liz Claiborne also created a team of consultants whose jobs were to train retail staff at department stores and to ensure that the collections were being displayed correctly.

◆ Retailers could not purchase individual garment lines; they were required to purchase the entire concept group and had to submit a single order for each season—they could not reorder.

◆ Most manufacturing was contracted out to garment makers in SE Asia.

◆ To create close contact with customers, Liz Claiborne offered fashion shows at department stores, "breakfast clinics" where potential customers could see the latest collection, and introduced a point-of-sale data collection system to track customer preferences.

◆ Rather than the conventional four-season cycle of product introduction, Liz Claiborne operated a six-season cycle.

During the 1990s, Liz Claiborne performance went into a sharp decline. The key problem was the trend toward more casual clothes in the workplace. Moreover, financial pressures on department store chains made them less willing to buy complete collections. In response to retailer pressure, Liz Claiborne allowed reordering by retailers. However, once retailers could split orders into smaller, more frequent orders, the entire Liz Claiborne system began to break down since it could not adapt to the quick-response, fast-cycle model that was increasingly dominant within the garment trade. In 1994, Liz Claiborne appointed a new CEO who systematically rebuilt the business around a more casual look, with more flexibility within its collections (although still with a common "color card"), and around a shorter supply chain, with most production in North and Central America.

*Source:* N. Siggelkow, "Change in the Presence of Fit: The Rise, the Fall, and the Renaissance of Liz Claiborne," *Academy of Management Journal* 44 (2001): 838–57.

abandoned; successful routines are retained and replicated within the organization.[26] As we discussed in Chapter 5, these patterns of coordinated activity are the basis for organizational capability. While evolutionary theorists view firms as adapting to external change through the search for new routines, replication of successful routines, and abandonment of unsuccessful routines, such adaptation is neither fast nor costless.

Empirical evidence points to the importance of both processes. The ability of some companies to adapt is indicated by the fact that many have been leaders in

**TABLE 8.2**  World's biggest companies in terms of market capitalization, 1912 and 2012

| 1912 | $billion | 2012 | $billion |
|------|----------|------|----------|
| US Steel | 0.74 | Apple | 429 |
| Standard Oil NJ (Exxon) | 0.39 | ExxonMobil | 407 |
| J&P Coates | 0.29 | Microsoft | 254 |
| Pullman | 0.20 | IBM | 228 |
| Royal Dutch Shell | 0.19 | Wal-Mart | 212 |
| Anaconda | 0.18 | Chevron | 210 |
| General Electric | 0.17 | China Mobile | 204 |
| Singer | 0.17 | General Electric | 201 |
| American Brands | 0.17 | China Construction Bank | 198 |
| Navistar | 0.16 | Google | 194 |
| British American Tobacco | 0.16 | Nestlé | 191 |
| De Beers | 0.16 | Johnson & Johnson | 179 |

*Sources:* L. Hannah "Marshall's 'Trees' and the Global 'Forest': Were 'Giant Redwoods' Different?" in N. Lamoreaux, D. Raff, and P. Temin (eds), *Learning by Doing in Markets, Firms and Nations*, Chicago: University of Chicago Press, 1999: 253–94; *Financial Times* (February 6, 2012).

their industries for a century or more—BASF, the world's largest chemical company, has been a leader in chemicals since it was founded in 1865 as a producer of synthetic dyes. ExxonMobil and Royal Dutch Shell have led the world's petroleum industry for over a century.[27] Budweiser Budvar, the Czech beer company (that has a long-running trademark dispute with Anheuser-Busch) traces its origins to 1785. Mitsui Group, a Japanese conglomerate, is even older—its first business, a retail store, was established in 1673. GKN, the UK-based supplier of auto and aerospace components began as an ironworks in 1767.

Yet these companies are exceptions. Among the companies forming the original Dow Jones Industrial Average in 1896, only General Electric remains in the index today. Of the world's 12 biggest companies in 1912, just two were in the top 12 a century later (Table 8.2). And life spans are shortening: the average period in which companies remained in the S&P 500 was 90 years in 1935; by 2005 it was down to 15 years.

The changing identity of the world's biggest companies over the past century partly reflects the rise of new industries—notably the information and communications technology (ICT) sector, but also the failure of established firms to adapt successfully to the life cycles of their industries.

Even though the industry life cycle involves changes that are largely predictable, the changes in key success factors that we have already identified imply that the different stages of the life cycle require different resources and capabilities. Markides and Geroski show that the "innovators" that pioneer the creation of a new industry are typically different companies from the "consolidators" that develop it:

> The fact that the firms that create new product and service markets are rarely the ones that scale them into mass markets has serious implications for the modern corporation. Our research points to a simple reason for this phenomenon: the skills, mind-sets, and competences needed for discovery and invention are not

only different from those needed for commercialization; they conflict with the needed characteristics. This means that the firms good at invention are unlikely to be good at commercialization and vice versa.[28]

In plant biotechnology, the pioneers were research-based start-ups such as Calgene, Cetus Corporation, DNA Plant Technologies, and Mycogen. By 2012, the leading suppliers of genetically modified seeds were DuPont, Monsanto, Syngenta, and Dow Chemical—all long-established chemical firms. In US wireless telephony the pioneer was McCaw Communications; the current market leaders are AT&T and Verizon.

The typical pattern is that technology-based start-ups that pioneer new areas of business are acquired by companies that are well established in closely related industries, and these established incumbents offer the financial resources and functional capabilities needed to grow the start-up. Of course, some start-ups do survive both industry shakeouts and acquisition to become industry leaders: Google, Cisco Systems, and McDonald's are examples. Geoffrey Moore refers to this ability to make the transition from a start-up serving early adopters to an established business serving mainstream customers as "crossing the chasm."[29]

In most new industries we find a mixture of start-up companies (*de novo* entrants) and established companies that have diversified from other sectors (*de alio* entrants). Which firms are likely to be more successful? The basic issue is whether the flexibility and entrepreneurial advantages of start-ups outweigh the superior resources and capabilities of established firms. This further depends upon whether the resources and capabilities required in the new industry are similar to those present in an existing industry. Where these resource linkages are close, diversifying entrants are likely to have an advantage over new start-ups. Thus:

- In the US automobile industry, former bicycle, carriage, and engine manufacturers tended to be the best performers.[30]
- The US television manufacturing industry was dominated by former producers of radios.[31]

However, viewing this situation as competition between entrepreneurial, resource-poor start-ups and well-endowed established firms is over-simplistic. Start-up companies often possess some important resources. Many new firms are spinoffs from existing companies within the same industry—several studies show that a high proportion of new ventures are established by former employees of incumbent firms. In Silicon Valley most of the leading semiconductor firms, including Intel, trace their origins to Shockley Semiconductor Laboratories, the pioneer of integrated circuits.[32] A similar pattern is evident in the Akron tire industry.[33] These start-up entrepreneurs will carry with then know-how from their former employers.

## Coping with Technological Change

Competition between new start-ups and established firms is not just a feature of the early phases of an industry's life cycle: it is ongoing. Any form of change in the external environment of an industry offers opportunities for newcomers to challenge incumbents. In vacuum cleaners, Dyson displaced established leaders Hoover and Electrolux in several countries' markets. In financial information services, Bloomberg took leadership from Reuters and Dow Jones. The major stumbling block for established firms is technological change. What does research tell us about why technological change is such a problem for established firms?

*Competence enhancing and competence destroying technological change* Tushman and Anderson argue that some technological changes are "competence destroying"—they render obsolete the resources and capabilities of established firms. Other changes are "competence enhancing"—they preserve, even strengthen, the resources add capabilities of incumbent firms.[34] The quartz watch radically undermined the competence base of mechanical watchmakers, requiring transformation of the Switch watch industry. Conversely, the turbofan, a major advance in jet engine technology, extended rather than weakened the capability base of existing jet engine manufacturers.

To determine the impact of a new technology on the competitive position of incumbent firms, it is necessary to look in detail at the implications of new technology for the individual resources and capabilities possessed by established firms. In the typesetting industry, the ability of incumbent firms to withstand the transition to radically new technologies rested upon their strengths in certain key resources that were not undermined by new technology: customer relationships, sales and service networks, and font libraries.[35]

*Architectural and Component Innovation* A key factor determining the success of established firms in adapting to technological change is whether the technological innovation occurs at the *component* or the *architectural* level. Henderson and Clark argue that innovations which change the overall architecture of a product create great difficulties for established firms because an architectural innovation requires a major reconfiguration of a company's strategy and organizational structure.[36] In automobiles, the hybrid engine was an important innovation, but it did not require a major reconfiguration of car design and engineering. The battery-powered electric motor is an architectural innovation—it requires redesign of the entire car and involves carmakers in creating systems for recharging. In many sectors of e-commerce—online grocery purchases and online banking—the internet involved innovation at the component level (it provided a new channel of distribution for existing products). Hence, existing supermarket chains and established retail banks with their clicks 'n' bricks business models have dominated online groceries and online financial services. Similarly with the transistor radio: although a single component, it was an architectural innovation since it required established radio producers to radically change their approaches to product design, manufacturing, and marketing:

> In the mid-1950s engineers at RCA's corporate R & D center developed a prototype of a portable, transistorized radio receiver. The new product used technology in which RCA was accomplished (transistors, radio circuits, speakers, tuning devices), but RCA saw little reason to pursue such an apparently inferior technology. In contrast, Sony, a small, relatively new company, used the small transistorized radio to gain entry into the US market. Even after Sony's success was apparent, RCA remained a follower in the market as Sony introduced successive models with improved sound quality and FM capability. The irony of the situation was not lost on the R & D engineers: for many years Sony's radios were produced with technology licensed from RCA, yet RCA had great difficulty matching Sony's product in the marketplace.[37]

*Disruptive Technologies* Clay Christiansen of Harvard Business School has also questioned why established firms find it so difficult to adapt to new technology. He distinguishes between new technology that is *sustaining*—it augments existing performance attributes—and new technology that is *disruptive*—it incorporates different performance attributes than the existing technology.[38]

In the disk-drive industry, some technological innovations—such as thin-film heads and more finely dispersed ferrous oxide disk coatings—have enhanced the dominant performance criterion: recording density. Such innovation has typically been led by established industry leaders. Other disk-drive technologies, notably new product generations with smaller diameters, were disruptive in their impact: established companies were, on average, two years behind newcomers in launching the new disk sizes and typically lost their industry leadership.[39] Incumbents' resistance to the new disk sizes reflected two factors: inferior initial performance and customer resistance. In 1987, Connor Peripherals began shipping a 3.5-inch disk drive. Industry leader Seagate had developed a 3.5-inch drive but halted its development for two reasons: first, it was inferior to the existing 5.25-inch disk in terms of capacity and cost per megabyte of memory; second, Seagate's main customers, the manufacturers of desktop PCs, showed no interest in the 3.5-inch disks. The 3.5-inch disks were adopted by Compaq and laptop makers. By 1990, the rapid development of the 3.5-inch disk had rendered the 5.25-disk obsolete.[40]

Similarly with other technologies. Steam-powered ships were initially slower, more expensive, and less reliable than sailing ships. The leading shipbuilders failed to make the transition to steam power because their leading customers, the trans-oceanic shipping companies, remained loyal to sail until after the turn of the 20th century. Steam power was used mainly for inland waters, which lacked constant winds. After several decades of gradual development for these niche markets, stream-powered ships were able to outperform sailing ships on ocean routes.

## Managing Strategic Change

Given the many barriers to organizational change and the difficulties that companies experience in coping with disruptive technologies and architectural innovation, how can companies adapt to changes in their environment?

Just as the sources of organizational inertia are many, so too are the theories and methods of organizational change. Traditionally, the management of organizational change has been viewed as a distinct area of management. *Organizational development* (OD) comprises a set of methodologies through which an internal or external consultant acts as a catalyst for systemic change within a team or organizational unit.[41] Organizational development draws upon theories of psychology and sociology and is based upon a set of humanistic values. It emphasizes group processes (e.g., "T-groups") as vehicles for organizational change. The emphasis of organizational development is upon individual organizational units and bottom-up change in larger organizations. Because our emphasis is on strategic change—the redirection and adaptation of the whole organization—our emphasis will be on top-down change processes. Nevertheless, as the recent revolutions in Tunisia, Egypt, and Libya confirm, the power of bottom-up change should not be underestimated.

## Dual Strategies and Organizational Ambidexterity

In Chapter 1 we learned that strategy has two major dimensions: positioning for the present and adapting to the future. As we observed then, reconciling the two is difficult. Derek Abell argues that "managing with dual strategies" is the most challenging dilemma that senior managers face:

> Running a successful business requires a clear strategy in terms of defining target markets and lavishing attention on those factors which are critical to success; changing a business in anticipation of the future requires a vision of how the future will look and a strategy for how the organization will have to adapt to meet future challenges.[42]

Abell argues that dual strategies require dual planning systems: short-term planning that focuses on strategic fit and performance over a one- or two-year period; and longer-term planning to develop vision, reshape the corporate portfolio, redefine and reposition individual businesses, develop new capabilities, and redesign organizational structures over periods of five years or more. Given the observation that companies are biased toward the exploitation of current resources and capabilities in relation to known opportunities, rather than exploration for new opportunities, most firms will emphasize short-term over long-term planning.

The challenges of reconciling "mastering the present" with "pre-empting the future" extend well beyond strategy formulation and the design of strategic planning systems. In recent years, Charles O'Reilly and Michael Tushman have stimulated interest in the **ambidextrous organization**, which is "capable of simultaneously exploiting existing competences and exploring new opportunities."[43] Two types of organizational ambidexterity have been identified:

- *Structural ambidexterity*: exploration and exploitation are undertaken in separate organizational units. It is usually easier to foster change initiatives in new organizational units rather than within the existing organization. For example, faced with the challenge of disruptive technologies, Christensen and Overdorf suggest that established companies develop products and businesses that embody the new technologies in organizationally separate units.[44] Such efforts show mixed results. IBM developed its PC in a separate unit in Florida—a thousand miles from IBM's corporate headquarters in New York. Its leader, Bill Lowe, claimed that this separation was critical to the team's creation of a product design and business system that was radically different from those of IBM's mainframes.[45] Xerox's Palo Alto Research Center (PARC) pioneered many of the technologies that formed the basis of the micro-computer revolution of the 1980s. However, few of these innovations were exploited by Xerox's New York-based establishment. Most flowed to nearby competitors Hewlett-Packard, Apple, Microsoft, and Sun Microsystems.[46] Similarly, GM's Saturn subsidiary set up in Tennessee to pioneer new approaches to manufacturing and marketing did little to revitalize the parent organization.[47] Attempts by Continental, United, British Airways, and several other legacy airlines to adapt to change by establishing budget airline subsidiaries were also costly failures.

- *Contextual ambidexterity* involves the same organizational units and the same organizational members pursuing both exploratory and exploitative activities. At Oticon, the Danish hearing aid company, employees were encouraged to sustain existing products while pursuing innovation and creativity.[48] Under the slogan "Innovation from Everyone, Everywhere" Whirlpool sought to embed innovation throughout its existing organization: "Innovation had been the responsibility of a couple of groups, engineering and marketing. Now, you have thousands of people involved."[49]

## Tools of Strategic Change Management

If organizational change follows a process of punctuated equilibrium in which periods of stability are interspersed by periods of intense organizational upheaval, it follows that top management must play an active role in managing these interludes of strategic change. Most large companies exhibit periodic restructuring, involving simultaneous changes in strategy, structure, management systems, and top management personnel. Such restructuring typically follows declining performance caused either by a major external shock or by a growing misalignment between the firm and its external environment. For example, the oil and gas majors all underwent far-reaching restructuring during 1986–1992 following the oil price decline of 1986.[50] A challenge for top management is to undertake large-scale change before the company is pressured by declining performance.

*Creating Perceptions of Crisis*   Change initiatives frequently fail because they become overwhelmed by the forces of inertia. A crisis sets up the conditions for strategic change by loosening the organization's attachment to the status quo. The problem is that by the time the organization is engulfed in crisis it is already too late, hence the merits of the CEO creating the perception of impending crisis within the company so that necessary changes can be implemented well before the real crisis emerges. At General Electric, even when the company was reporting record profits, Jack Welch was able to convince employees of the need for change in order to defend against emerging threats. Andy Grove's effectiveness at communicating his dictum "Only the paranoid survive" helped Intel to maintain a continual striving for improvement and development despite its dominance of the market for PC microprocessors.

*Establishing Stretch Targets*   Another approach to weakening the powers of organizational inertia is to continually pressure the organizations by means of ambitious performance targets. The idea is that performance targets that are achievable but only with an extension of employee effort can motivate creativity and initiative while attacking complacency. Stretch targets are normally associated with short- and medium-term performance goals for individuals and organizational units. However, they also relate to long-term strategic goals. A key role of vision statements and ambitious strategic intent is to create a sustained sense of ambition and organizational purpose. These ideas are exemplified by Collins and Porras' notion of "Big Hairy Ambitious Goals" that I discussed in Chapter 1.

*Creating Organizational Initiatives*   Among the tools deployed by organizational leaders to influence their members, a potent one is an organization-wide initiative endorsed and communicated by the chief executive. Corporate initiatives sponsored by the CEO are effective for disseminating strategic changes, best practices, and management innovations. At General Electric Jack Welch was an especially effective exponent of using corporate initiatives to drive organizational change. These were built around communicable and compelling slogans such as "Be number 1 or number 2 in your industry," "GE's growth engine," "boundarylessness," "six-sigma quality," and "destroy-your-business-dot-com."

*Reorganization and New Blood*    By reorganizing the company structure top management can create an opportunity for redistributing power, reshuffling top management, and introducing new blood. Periodic changes in organizational structure can stimulate decentralized search and local initiatives while encouraging more effective exploitation of the outcomes of such search.[51] A typical pattern is to oscillate from periods of decentralization to periods of centralization.[52]

Organizational change is also stimulated by recruiting new managers from outside the organization. Externally recruited CEOs result in more strategic change than those promoted from within.[53] In many cases, boards of directors seek out an external CEO for the explicit purpose of leading strategic change—e.g., George Fisher (from Motorola) and Antonio Perez (from HP) at Eastman Kodak, Lou Gerstner (from RJR Nabisco) at IBM, and Stephen Hester (from British Land) at Royal Bank of Scotland. Other members of the top management teams may also act as drivers of change: newcomers to top management hired outside the firms have been shown to be especially effective.[54]

## Dynamic Capabilities

The ability of some firms—IBM, General Electric, 3M, Shell, and Toyota—to adapt to new circumstances while others ossify and fail implies differences in the capability base of different companies. David Teece and his colleagues introduced the term **dynamic capabilities** to refer to a "firm's ability to integrate, build, and reconfigure internal and external competences to address rapidly changing environments."[55]

The precise definition of a dynamic capability has proved contentious. Eisenhardt and Martin consider dynamic capabilities to be any capabilities that allow an organization to reconfigure its resources in order to adapt and change.[56] Winter and Zollo are more precise: a dynamic capability is a "higher level" process through which the firm modifies its operating routines.[57] These differences are important. If dynamic capabilities are simply those that allow change to occur they include product development capability, acquisition capability, research capability, and HR recruitment capabilities. But if dynamic capability is restricted to higher-level capabilities that manage change in lower-level capabilities, we are referring to capabilities that are more strategic and embedded in top management practices. Winter emphasizes that these higher-order change capabilities are not simply ad hoc problem solving: they are approaches to strategic change that are routine, highly patterned, and repetitious.[58]

IBM offers an example of these higher-level dynamic capabilities. Under the leadership of three CEOs—Lou Gerstner, Sam Palmisano, and Ginni Rometty—IBM has developed a system for managing strategic change that comprises its Business Leadership Model, strategy processes such as its "deep dive" and Emerging Business Opportunities methodologies, its Strategic Leadership Forum, and the Corporate Investment Fund (see Strategy Capsule 14.4 in Chapter 14 for additional information).[59]

*Using Scenarios to Prepare for the Future* A company's ability to adapt to changes in its environment depends on its capacity to anticipate such changes. Yet predicting the future is hazardous, if not impossible. "Only a fool would make predictions . . . especially about the future," remarked movie mogul Samuel Goldwyn. But the inability to predict does not mean that it is not useful to think about what might happen in the future. *Scenario analysis* is a systematic way of thinking about how the future might unfold that builds on what we know about current trends and signals. Scenario analysis is not a forecasting technique, but a process for thinking and communicating about the future.

Herman Kahn, who pioneered their use first at the Rand Corporation and subsequently at the Hudson Institute, defined scenarios as "hypothetical sequences of events constructed for the purpose of focusing attention on causal process and decision points."[60] The multiple-scenario approach constructs several distinct, internally consistent views of how the future may look five to 25 years ahead (shorter in the case of fast-moving sectors). Its key value is in combining the interrelated impacts of a wide range of economic, technological, demographic, and political factors into a few distinct alternative stories of how the future might unfold. Scenario analysis can be either qualitative or quantitative or involve some combination of the two. Quantitative scenario analysis models events and runs simulations to identify likely outcomes. Qualitative scenarios typically take the form of narratives and can be particularly useful in engaging the insight and imagination of decision makers.

For the purposes of strategy making, scenario analysis is used to explore likely paths of industry evolution, to examine developments in particular country markets, to think about the impact of new technologies, and to analyze prospects for specific investment projects. Applied to industry evolution, scenarios can clarify and develop alternative views of how changing customer requirements, emerging technologies, government policies, and competitor strategies might have an impact on industry structure and what the implications for competition and competitive advantage might be.

However, as with most strategy techniques, the value of scenario analysis is not in the results but in the process. Scenario analysis is a powerful tool for bringing together different ideas and insights, for surfacing deeply held beliefs and assumptions, for identifying possible threats and opportunities, for generating and evaluating alternative strategies, for encouraging more flexible thinking by managers, and for building consensus. Evaluating the likely performance of different strategies under different scenarios can help identify which strategies are most robust and can assist in contingency planning by forcing managers to address "what if?" questions. Strategy Capsule 8.3 outlines the use of scenarios at Shell.

*Shaping the Future* A succession of management gurus from Tom Peters to Gary Hamel have argued that the key to organizational change is not to adapt to external change but to create the future. Companies that adapt to change are doomed to playing catch-up; competitive advantages accrue to those companies that act as leaders and initiate change. Hamel and Prahalad's *new strategy paradigm* emphasizes the role of strategy as a systematic and concerted approach to redefining both the company and its industry environment in the future.[61]

According to Gary Hamel, in an age of revolution, "the company that is evolving slowly is already on its way to extinction."[62] The only option is to give up incremental improvement and adapt to a nonlinear world—revolution must be met by revolution. Achieving internal revolution requires changing the psychological and sociological norms of an organization that restricts innovation (Table 8.3).

## STRATEGY CAPSULE 8.3

# Multiple-Scenario Development at Shell

Royal Dutch Shell has pioneered the use of scenarios as a basis for long-term strategic planning in an industry where the life of investment projects (up to 50 years) far exceeds the time horizon for forecasting (two to three years). In 1967, a "Year 2000" study was inaugurated and scenario development soon became fundamental to Shell's planning process. Mike Pocock, Shell's former chairman, observed: "We believe in basing planning not on single forecasts, but on deep thought that identifies a coherent pattern of economic, political, and social development."

Shell views its scenarios as critical to its transition from planning toward strategic management, in which the role of the planning function is not so much to produce a plan but to manage a process, the outcome of which is improved decision making by managers. This involves continually challenging current thinking within the group, encouraging a wider look at external influences on the business, promoting learning, and forging coordination among Shell's 200-odd subsidiaries.

Shell's global scenarios are prepared about every four years by a team comprising corporate planning staff, executives, and outside experts. Economic, political, technological, and demographic trends are analyzed 20 years into the future. Shell's 2005–2025 scenarios were based on three sets of forces—market incentives, community, and coercion and regulation—and three objectives—efficiency, social cohesion, and security. Their interactions produced three scenarios, each embodying different social, political, and economic conditions:

- *Low Trust Globalization*: A legalistic world where emphasis is on security and efficiency at the expense of social cohesion.

- *Open Doors*: A pragmatic world emphasizing social cohesion and efficiency with the market providing built-in solutions to crises of security and trust.

- *Flags*: A dogmatic world where community and security values are emphasized at the expense of efficiency.

Once approved by top management, the scenarios are disseminated by reports, presentations, and workshops, where they form the basis for long-term strategy discussion by business sectors and operating companies.

Shell is adamant that its scenarios are not forecasts. They represent carefully thought-out stories of how the various forces shaping the global energy environment of the future might play out. Their value is in stimulating the social and cognitive processes through which managers envisage the future. Then CEO Jeroen van der Veer commented: "the imperative is to use this tool to gain deeper insights into our global business environment and to achieve the cultural change that is at the heart of our group strategy . . . I know that they broaden one's mindset and stimulate discussions."

**Sources:** P. Wack, "Scenarios: Uncharted Waters Ahead," *Harvard Business Review* (September/October, 1985): 72 and "Scenarios: Shooting the Rapids," *Harvard Business Review* (November/December 1985): 139; A. de Geus, "Planning as Learning," *Harvard Business Review* (March/April 1988): 70–4; P. Schoemacher, "Multiple Scenario Development: Its Conceptual and Behavioral Foundation," *Strategic Management Journal* 14 (1993): 193–214; *Shell Global Scenarios to 2025* (Shell International, 2005).

**TABLE 8.3**  Shaking the foundations

| OLD BRICK | NEW BRICK |
| --- | --- |
| Top management is responsible for setting strategy | Everyone is responsible for setting strategy |
| Getting better, getting faster is the way to win | Rule-busting innovation is the way to win |
| IT creates competitive advantage | Unconventional business concepts create competitive advantage |
| Being revolutionary is high risk | More of the same is high risk |
| We can merge our way to competitiveness | There's no correlation between size and competitiveness |
| Innovation equals new products and new technology | Innovation equals entirely new business concepts |
| Strategy is the easy part; implementation the hard part | Strategy is the easy part only if you're content to be an imitator |
| Change starts at the top | Change starts with activists |
| Our real problem is execution | Our real problem is incrementalism |
| Big companies can't innovate | Big companies can become gray-haired revolutionaries |

*Source:* Adapted by permission of Harvard Business School Press from *Leading the Revolution* by Gary Hamel. Boston, MA, 2000, pp. 280–1. Copyright © 2000 by the Harvard Business School Publishing Corporation; all rights reserved.

Hamel's challenge for managers to cast off their bureaucratic chains and become revolutionaries is invigorating and inspiring. But is revolutionary change among established companies either feasible or desirable? Some established companies have achieved radical change:

- Nokia underwent a metamorphosis from a manufacturer of paper and rubber goods to become a world leader in wireless handsets.
- BP transformed itself from a bureaucratic, state-owned UK-based oil company into a flexible, innovative (and accident-prone) global supermajor.
- Microsoft has successfully ridden a series of disruptive changes in the world's computer industry, including the transition, first, to object-oriented computing, then to internet-based networking, and currently to cloud computing.

However, for most established companies, efforts at radical change have resulted in disaster:

- Enron's transformation from a utility and pipeline company to a trader and market-maker in energy futures and derivatives ended in its demise in 2001;
- Vivendi's multimedia empire built on the base of a French water and waste utility fell apart in 2002;
- GEC's reincarnation as Marconi, a telecom equipment supplier, was swiftly followed by bankruptcy in 2002;
- RBS Group's transformation from a Scottish retail bank to the world's biggest commercial bank (as measured by total assets) through a series of cross-border acquisitions culminated in its rescue by the British government in 2008;

● Skandia's quest to become one of the world's most innovative insurance companies ended in a top management scandal and the sale of most of the company's businesses outside of Sweden.

The perils of radical strategic change are not difficult to understand. At their core is the difficulty that established companies experience in developing the new organizational capabilities needed by new circumstances or a new area of business. Let us turn to that issue now.

## Developing New Capabilities

Ultimately, adapting to a changing world is about developing the necessary capabilities to renew competitive advantage. To get a glimpse into the challenges this presents, consider the distinctive capabilities (or core competences) of some of today's leading companies and ask, "Where did these capabilities come from?"

*Early Experiences and Path Dependency*    In many, many instances distinctive capabilities can be traced back to the circumstances which prevailed during the founding and early development of these companies. In other words, organizational capability is subject to **path dependency**—a company's capabilities today are the result of its history.[63] For example:

● How did Wal-Mart Inc., the world's biggest retailer, develop its outstanding capability in supply chain logistics? This superefficient system of warehousing, distribution, and vendor relationships was not the result of careful planning and design; it evolved from the circumstances that Wal-Mart faced during its early years of existence. Its small-town locations in Arkansas and Oklahoma resulted in unreliable delivery from its suppliers; consequently, Wal-Mart established its own distribution system. What about the other capabilities that contribute to Wal-Mart's remarkable cost efficiency? These too can be traced back to Wal-Mart's origins in rural Arkansas and the values of its founder, Sam Walton.

● Similarly with the world's leading oil and gas majors (Table 8.4). Despite long histories of competing together in the same markets, with near-identical products and similar strategies, the majors display very different capability profiles. Industry leaders ExxonMobil and Royal Dutch Shell exemplify these differences. ExxonMobil is known for its outstanding financial management capabilities exercised through rigorous investment controls and unrelenting cost efficiency. Royal Dutch Shell is known for its decentralized, international management capability, which allows it to adapt to different national environments and to become an "insider" wherever it does business. These differences can be traced back to the company's 19th-century origins. ExxonMobil (then Standard Oil New Jersey) acted as a holding company for Rockefeller's Standard Oil Trust, exercising responsibility for overall financial management. Shell was established to sell Russian oil in China and the Far East, while Royal Dutch was created to exploit Indonesian oil reserves. With head offices thousands of miles away in Europe, both parts of the group developed a decentralized, adaptable management style.

These observations are troubling for managers in established companies: if a firm's capabilities are determined during the early stages of its life, is it really possible to

**TABLE 8.4**  Distinctive capabilities as a consequence of childhood experiences: The oil majors

| Company | Distinctive capability | Early history |
|---------|------------------------|---------------|
| ExxonMobil | Financial management | ExxonMobil's predecessor, Standard Oil (NJ), was the holding company for Rockefeller's Standard Oil Trust |
| Royal Dutch Shell | Coordinating a decentralized global network of 200 operating companies | Shell Transport & Trading headquartered in London and founded to sell Russian oil in China and the Far East<br>Royal Dutch Petroleum headquartered in The Hague; founded to exploit Indonesian reserves |
| BP | Elephant hunting | Discovered huge Persian reserves, went on to find Forties field (North Sea) and Prudhoe Bay (Alaska) |
| ENI | Deal making in politicized environments | The Enrico Mattei legacy; the challenge of managing government relations in post-war Italy |
| Mobil | Lubricants | Vacuum Oil Co. founded in 1866 to supply patented petroleum lubricants |

develop the new capabilities needed to adapt to current changes and the challenges of tomorrow? The presence of established capabilities and their embedding within organizational structure and culture present formidable barriers to building new capabilities. Indeed, the more highly developed a firm's organizational capabilities, the greater the barrier they create. Because Dell Computer's direct sales model was so highly developed, Dell found it difficult to adapt to selling through retail outlets as well. Hence the argument that core capabilities are simultaneously core rigidities.[64]

*Integrating Resources to Create Capability*   The encouraging fact is that companies do develop new capabilities—all companies that have survived over periods of multiple decades have done so by creating capabilities that they did not possess before. To appreciate how this is done let us look once more at the structure of organizational capability. In Chapter 5 (Strategy Capsule 5.3) we observed that organizational capability results from the combination of different resources, most importantly the skills of different organizational members. The effectiveness of this integration depends upon the presence of suitable processes, an appropriate organizational structure, motivation, and overall organizational alignment, especially with the organization's culture.

Using each of these components, organizations can put in place the building blocks for developing new capabilities:

- *Processes*: Without processes, organizational capability will be completely dependent on individual skills. With processes (or *organizational routines*) we can ensure that task performance is efficient, repeatable, and reliable. When Whirlpool launched its innovation drive, the emphasis was on creating processes: processes for training employees in the tools of innovation, processes for idea generation, and processes for idea selection and development.[65] Once processes are in place they are developed through routinization and learning—essential to capability development is the creation of mechanisms that facilitate learning-by-doing and ensure the retention and sharing of learning.

● *Structure*: The people and processes that contribute to an organizational capability need to be located within the same organizational unit if they are to achieve the coordination needed to ensure a high performance capability. When Royal Dutch Shell wanted to develop capability in breakthrough innovation, it created a new organizational unit: Gamechanger. When Ducati wanted to create the capabilities needed for a successful MotoGP racing team, it established Ducati Corse as a separate subsidiary. At several of the business schools I have worked, a common complaint among students has been the lack of integration across courses while a common aspiration of several MBA course directors has been to introduce multidisciplinary courses that involve students in cross-functional problem solving. However, little can be achieved if faculty members are located within specialist, discipline-defined departments and coordination across courses is limited to a single teachers' meeting held each semester.

● *Motivation*: Again we come back to the fundamental driver of performance in organizations: without motivation not only will individuals give less than their best but also, equally important, they will not set aside their personal preferences and prejudices to integrate as a team. At Honda Motor, the development of automotive capabilities, especially in engine design, was driven by the passion of its founder Soichiro Honda (Strategy Capsule 8.4)

● *Organizational alignment*: Finally, there is the issue of fit. Excellent capabilities require the components of capability to fit with one another and with the broader organizational context. Harley-Davidson's capabilities in delivering the "Harley Experience" are the result of a close fit between the human resources, the brand, the traditions, and the company's Milwaukie location. Imperfect alignment can stunt capability development: the failure of established airlines to launch low-cost subsidiaries (BA's Go, United's Ted, Continental's Continental Lite) reflects a misfit between the capabilities needed by a budget airline and the culture and management systems of legacy carriers. Corporate culture is a critical ingredient in this fit: in the privatized, competitive, deregulated telecom markets of the 21st century, former national monopolies such as British Telecom (BT), Deutsche Telecom, and Verizon have had difficulty developing the capabilities needed to compete successfully outside their home markets.

*Developing Capabilities Sequentially*   Developing new capabilities requires a systematic and long-term process of development that integrates the four components described above. For most organizations, the key challenge is not obtaining the underlying resources—indeed, many examples of outstanding capabilities have resulted from the pressures of resource shortage. Toyota's lean production capability was born during a period of acute resource shortage in Japan.

If integrating resources into capabilities requires establishing processes, developing these processes through routinization and learning, putting in place the right structure, motivating the people involved, and aligning the new capability with other aspects of the organization, the demands upon management are considerable. An organization must limit the number and scope of the capabilities that it is attempting

## STRATEGY CAPSULE 8.4
# Soichiro Honda and the Isle of Man TT

On March 20, 1954, when Honda Motor Company was still a tiny company of less than six years old, company president Soichiro Honda announced his intention to compete in the Isle of Man TT, which was then the world's premier motorcycle race:

Since I was a small child, one of my dreams has been to compete in motor vehicle races all over the world . . . I have reached the firm decision to enter the TT Races next year.

I will fabricate a 250 cc (medium class) racer for this race, and as the representative of our Honda Motor Co., I will send it out into the spotlight of the world. I am confident that this vehicle can reach speeds exceeding 180 km/h . . .

I address all employees! Let us bring together the full strength of Honda Motor Co. to win through to this glorious achievement. The future of Honda Motor Co. depends on this, and the burden rests on your shoulders. I want you to turn your surging enthusiasm to this task, endure every trial, and press through with all the minute demands of work and research, making this your own chosen path. The advances made by Honda Motor Co. are the growth you achieve as human beings, and your growth is what assures our Honda Motor Co. its future.

Honda's entry was delayed until 1958. In that year Honda won the manufacturer's prize.

to create at any point in time. One implication is that capabilities need to be developed sequentially rather than all at once.

The task of capability development is also complicated by the fact that we have limited knowledge about how to manage capability development. Hence, it may be helpful to focus not on the organizational capabilities themselves but on developing and supplying the products that use those capabilities. A trajectory through time of related, increasingly sophisticated products allows a firm to develop the "integrative knowledge" that is at the heart of organizational capability.[66] Panasonic utilized this approach in developing operational capabilities in countries when establishing manufacturing in new countries:

In every country batteries are a necessity, so they sell well. As long as we bring a few advanced automated pieces of equipment for the processes vital to final product quality, even unskilled labor can produce good products. As they work on this rather simple product, the workers get trained, and this increased skill level then permits us to gradually expand production to items with increasingly higher technology levels, first radios, then televisions.[67]

Where a company is developing an entirely new area of business, such a sequential approach can be effective. The key here is for each stage of development to be linked not just to a specific product (or part of a product) but also to a clearly defined set of capabilities. Strategy Capsule 8.5 looks at the sequential approach to capability development followed by Hyundai Motor.

# Hyundai Motor: Developing Capabilities through Product Sequencing

Hyundai's emergence as a world-class automobile producer is a remarkable example of capability development over a sequence of compressed phases (Figure 8.5). Each phase of the development process was characterized by a clear objective in terms of product outcome, a tight time deadline, an empowered development team, a clear recognition of the capabilities that needed to be developed in each phase, and an atmosphere of impending crisis should the project not succeed. The first phase was the construction of an assembly plant in the unprecedented time of 18 months in order to build Hyundai's first car—a Ford Cortina imported in semi-knocked down (SKD) form. Subsequent phases involved products of increasing sophistication and the development of more advanced capabilities.

**FIGURE 8.5**  Phased development at Hyundai Motor, 1968–1995

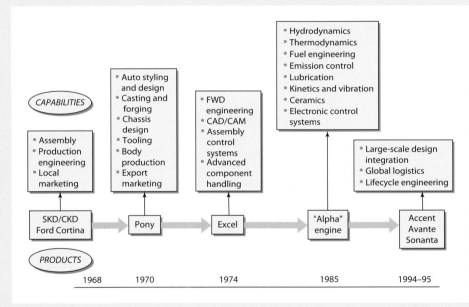

**Source:** L. Kim, "Crisis construction and organizational learning: Capability building and catching up at Hyundai Motor," *Organizational Science* 9 (1998): 506–21. © 1998 by the Institute for Operations Research and the Management Sciences. Reproduced with permission of the Institute for Operations Research and the Management Sciences via the Copyright Clearance Center.

## The Contribution of Knowledge Management and the Knowledge-Based View

Since the early 1990s, our thinking about resources and capabilities and their management has been extended greatly by a set of concepts and practices referred to as *knowledge management*. Knowledge management is an umbrella term that comprises a range of organizational processes and practices whose common feature is their concern with generating value from knowledge. The term is of recent vintage but much of its content is not: it includes many long-established organizational functions such as R & D, management information systems, employee training, and managing intellectual property; even strategic planning can be regarded as a knowledge management activity. Initially, knowledge management was primarily concerned with information technology, especially the use of databases, intranets, expert systems, and groupware for storing, analyzing, and disseminating information. Subsequent developments in knowledge management have been concerned less with data and more with *organizational learning*, especially the transfer of best practices and the derivation of "lessons learned" from ongoing activities. Knowledge management has attracted its share of skepticism and ridicule. Lucy Kellaway of the *Financial Times* observed that it has "attracted more needless obfuscation and wooly thinking by academics and consultants than any other [area]."[68]

*Explicit and Tacit Knowledge*   At the foundation of knowledge management is a set of concepts concerning the nature of knowledge and its role within the firm. These concepts have combined into what is known as the **knowledge-based view of the firm**—a conception of the firm as an assemblage of knowledge assets where value is created by deploying this knowledge.[69]

A key feature of knowledge that is critical to its role in creating organizational capability is the distinction between knowing *how* and knowing *about*:

- *Knowing about* is explicit: it comprises facts, theories, and sets of instructions. *Explicit knowledge* can be communicated at negligible marginal cost between individuals and across space and time. This ability to disseminate knowledge such that any one person's use does not limit anyone else's access to the same knowledge means that explicit knowledge has the characteristic of a public good: once created, it can be replicated among innumerable users at low cost. The digital revolution and the internet have further reduced the costs of disseminating explicit knowledge.
- *Know-how* is tacit in nature: it involves skills that are expressed through their performance (riding a bicycle, playing the piano). Such *tacit knowledge*, on the other hand, cannot be directly articulated or codified. It can only be observed through its application and acquired through practice. Hence, its transfer between people is slow, costly, and uncertain.

If explicit knowledge can be transferred so easily, it is seldom the foundation of sustainable competitive advantage. It is only secure from rivals when it is protected, either by intellectual property rights (patents, copyrights, trade secrets) or by secrecy ("The formula for Coca-Cola will be kept in a safe in the vault of our Atlanta headquarters guarded by heavily-armed Coca-Cola personnel."). The challenge of tacit knowledge is the opposite. If the culinary skills of award-winning chef Daniel Boulud have been acquired through intuition and learning-by-doing, how does he transfer this know-how to the chefs and managers of his six restaurants in New York, Las Vegas, and Palm Beach, Florida? To build organizational capability it is essential that the individual know-how can be shared within the organization. For consulting companies, the distinction between tacit (personalized) and explicit (systematized) knowledge defines their business model and is a central determinant of their strategy.[70]

The result is a "paradox of replication." In order to utilize knowledge to build organizational capability we need to replicate it; and replication is much easier if the knowledge is in explicit form. Yet, in doing so, we also make it easier for rivals to imitate our knowledge. Facilitating internal replication, while limiting external replication, is a key challenge for firms.[71]

*Knowledge Management Activities that Contribute to Capability Development*   Knowledge management can be represented as a series of activities that contribute to capability development by building, retaining, accessing, transferring, and integrating knowledge. Table 8.5 lists several knowledge-management practices.

**TABLE 8.5**   Knowledge-management practices

| Knowledge process | Contributing activities | Explanation and examples |
|---|---|---|
| Knowledge identification | Intellectual property management | During recent decades companies have devoted much greater attention to identifying their intellectual property, and patents especially, with a view to better exploiting its value |
| | Corporate yellow pages | BP's Connect is a corporate yellow pages comprising personnel data that allows each employee to identify the skills and experience of other employees in the organization |
| Knowledge measurement | Intellectual capital accounting | The measurement and valuation of a firm's stock of knowledge was pioneered by Skandia, a Swedish insurance company, with its system of intellectual capital accounting. Dow Chemical uses intellectual capital metrics to link its intellectual property portfolio to shareholder value |
| Knowledge retention | Lessons learned | The US Army's Center for Lessons Learned distils the results of practice maneuvers, simulated battles, and actual operations into tactical guidelines and recommended procedures. All management consulting firms have post-project reviews to recognize and capture the knowledge produced in operational activities |
| Knowledge transfer and sharing | Databases | Project-based organizations typically store knowledge generated in client assignments in searchable databases. Accenture's Knowledge Xchange is an IT system that comprises a database, groupware, dedicated search engine, and an intranet that permits employees to input and access information |
| | Communities-of-practice | Communities of practice are informal, self-organizing networks for transferring experiential knowledge among employees engaged in the same occupation. These are increasingly being deliberately established and managed as a means of facilitating knowledge sharing and group learning |
| | Best practice transfer | Where operations are geographically dispersed, different units are likely to develop local innovations and improvements. Best practice methodology aims to identify then transfer superior practices |

During its early development, knowledge management was heavily orientated toward information technology with the main emphasis on storing organizational knowledge within searchable databases. Growing recognition of the importance of tacit knowledge and the difficulties of articulating and codifying such experiential knowledge has shifted the focus more toward people-to-people modes of knowledge transfer.

### STRATEGY CAPSULE 8.6
## Knowledge Conversion and Knowledge Replication

Nonaka's theory of knowledge creation distinguishes between types of knowledge (tacit and explicit) and levels of knowledge (individual and organizational). Nonaka argues that knowledge conversion between tacit and explicit forms and between individual and organizational levels produces a "knowledge spiral" in which the organization's stock of knowledge broadens and deepens (Figure 8.6). For example, explicit knowledge is internalized into tacit knowledge in the form of intuition, know-how, and routines, while tacit knowledge is externalized into explicit knowledge through articulation and codification. Knowledge also moves

**FIGURE 8.6**    Knowledge conversion

**Source:** Based upon I. Nonaka, "A Dynamic Theory of Organizational Knowledge Creation," *Organization Science* 5 (1994): 14–37.

However, the contribution of knowledge management to capability development in organizations may be less about specific techniques and more about the insight that the knowledge-based view has given to organizational performance and the role of management. For example, Ijiro Nonaka's model of knowledge creation offers penetrating insights into the organizational processes through which knowledge is created and value is created from knowledge (Strategy Capsule 8.6)

between levels: individual knowledge is combined into organizational knowledge; individuals are socialized into organizational knowledge.

Nonaka's knowledge conversion framework can be used to illustrate the transformation of the *craft enterprise* based upon individual, tacit knowledge, to the *industrial enterprise* based upon explicit, organizational knowledge. This is a key stage in firm development that also marks the emergence of industrial society. This transition is depicted in Figure 8.6 and is illustrated by the following examples:

◆ Henry Ford's Model T was initially produced on a small scale by skilled workers, one car at a time. Ford's assembly line mass-production technology systematized that tacit knowledge and built it into machines and processes. The Ford industrial system was no longer dependent upon skilled craftsmen: the assembly lines could be operated by former farm workers and immigrants straight off the boat.

◆ When Ray Kroc discovered the McDonald brothers' hamburger stand in Riversdale, California, he quickly recognized the potential for systematizing and replicating their process. The result was a global fast-food empire in which the McDonald's business model was replicated through operating manuals and training programs, and now 400,000 employees serve 68 million customers daily. Most employees' culinary skills are rudimentary: the relevant knowledge is embedded within the McDonald's business system.

This systematization of knowledge offers massive potential for value creation. The craft enterprise is typically small scale, and skilled employees appropriate a major share of the value that is created. Systematization allows replication and deskilling. Ford and McDonald's were able to expand worldwide. The transformation of craft industries through systematization has been a key feature of the evolution of service industries led by Hilton in hotels, Hertz in car rental, Andersen Consulting (now Accenture) in IT consulting, and Starbucks in coffee shops.

This replication of knowledge is a powerful and lucrative source of scale economy. Its power is well recognized by venture capitalists: a key criterion for evaluating a new business proposal is: "Is it scalable?" Low-cost replication requires systematization: the translation of a business concept and operating system into a set of rules and procedures that provide programmed instructions for the creation of new business units. In some cases the knowledge embedded in a business system may be too complex to be fully articulated. In this case replication can still occur through imitation. In the case of microprocessors, fabrication processes are so complex and the know-how involved so deeply embedded that the only way that Intel can replicate its production capabilities is by replicating its lead plant in every detail—a process called *copy exactly*.[a]

**Note:**
[a]"Copy Exactly Factory Strategy" (www.intel.com/design/quality/mq_ce.htm). See also G. Szulanski and S. G. Winter, "Getting It Right the Second Time," *Harvard Business Review* (January 2002): 62–9.

# Summary

A vital task of strategic management is to navigate the crosscurrents of change. But how can we manage change if we cannot predict it? Despite the failure of almost every forecasting method, help is available from two sources. First, some regularities are evident in the ways in which business environments evolve over time. Second, there is a large body of evidence that the difficulties firms experience in adapting to industrial and technological changes are the result of common factors. By understanding the sources of these barriers to adaptation, we can learn how to overcome them.

The life-cycle model allows us to understand some of the forces driving industry evolution and their impact on industry structure and the basis of competitive advantage. By identifying the stage of development of an industry, we can recognize the forces driving change and anticipate some of the likely directions of development.

Identifying regularities in the patterns of industry evolution is of little use if firms are unable to adapt to these changes. The challenge of adaptation is huge: the presence of organizational inertia means that industry evolution occurs more through the birth of new firms and the death of old ones rather than through adaptation by established firms. Established firms also experience problems in coping with new technologies—the technological changes that are especially devastating are those that are "competence destroying," "disruptive," or embody "architectural innovation."

A key challenge of managing change is the need for managers to operate in two time zones: they must optimize for today while preparing the organization for the future. The concept of the ambidextrous organization is an approach to resolving this dilemma. Other tools for managing strategic change include: creating perceptions of crisis, establishing stretch targets, corporate-wide initiatives, recruiting external managerial talent, dynamic capabilities, and scenario planning.

Whatever approach or tools are adopted to manage change, strategic change requires building new capabilities. To the extent that an organization's capabilities are a product of its entire history, building new capabilities is a formidable challenge. To understand how organizations build capability we need to understand how resources are integrated into capability—in particular, the role of processes, structure, motivation, and alignment. The complexities of capability development and our limited understanding of how capabilities are built point to the advantages of sequential approaches to developing capabilities.

Ultimately, capability building is about harnessing the knowledge which exists within the organization. For this purpose knowledge management offers considerable potential for increasing the effectiveness of capability development. In addition to specific techniques for identifying, retaining, sharing, and replicating knowledge, the knowledge-based view of the firm offers penetrating insights into the challenges of and potential for the creation and exploitation of knowledge by firms.

In the next two chapters, we discuss strategy formulation and strategy implementation in industries at different stages of their development: *emerging industries*, which are characterized by rapid change and technology-based competition, and *mature industries*.

Quizzes and flashcards to test yourself further are available in your interactive e-book at
**www.wileyopenpage.com**

# Self-Study Questions

1.  Consider the changes that have occurred in a comparatively new industry (e.g., wireless communication services, wireless handsets, video game consoles, online auctions, bottled water, online book retailing). To what extent has the evolution of the industry followed the pattern predicted by the industry life-cycle model? What particular features does the industry have that have influenced its pattern of evolution? At what stage of development is the industry today? How is the industry likely to evolve in the future?

2.  Select a product that has become a *dominant design* for its industry (e.g., the IBM PC in personal computers, McDonald's in fast food, Harvard in MBA education, Southwest in budget airlines). What factors caused one firm's product architecture to become dominant? Why did other firms imitate this dominant design? To what extent has the dominant design evolved or been displaced?

3.  The *resource partitioning* model argues that as industries become dominated by a few major companies whose strategies and products converge so opportunities open for new entrants to build specialist niches. Identify an opportunity for establishing a specialist new business in an industry dominated by mass-market giants.

4.  Consider an industry facing fundamental technology change (e.g., the recorded music industry and digital technology, computer software and open-source, newspapers and the internet, automobiles and alternative fuels, corporate IT services and cloud computing). Develop two alternative scenarios for the future evolution of your chosen industry. In relation to one leading player in the industry, identify the problems posed by the new technology and develop a strategy for how the company might adapt to and exploit the changes you envisage.

5.  Identify two sports teams: one that is rich in resources (such as talented players) but whose capabilities (as indicated by performance) have been poor; one that is resource-poor but has displayed strong team capabilities. What clues can you offer as to the determinants of capabilities among sports teams?

6.  In 2006, Disney completed its acquisition of the film animation company Pixar for $7.4 billion. The high purchase price reflected Disney's eagerness to gain Pixar's animation capabilities, its talent (animators, technologists, and storytellers), and its culture of creativity. What risks does Disney face in achieving the goals of this acquisition?

7.  The dean of your business school wishes to upgrade the effectiveness with which the school designs and delivers its educational programs and increase the effectiveness of its graduates in their subsequent careers. Advise your dean on what tools and systems of knowledge management might be deployed in order to support these goals.

# Notes

1. T. Levitt, "Exploit the Product Life Cycle," *Harvard Business Review* (November/December 1965): 81–94; G. Day, "The Product Life Cycle: Analysis and Applications," *Journal of Marketing* 45 (Autumn 1981): 60–7.

2. J. M. Utterback and F. F. Suarez, "Patterns of Industrial Evolution, Dominant designs, and Firms' Survival," Sloan Working Paper no. 3600-93 (MIT, 1993).

3. P. Anderson and M. L. Tushman, "Technological Discontinuities and Dominant Designs," *Administrative Science Quarterly* 35 (1990): 604–33.

4. M. A. Cusumano and D. B. Yoffie, *Competing on Internet Time: Lessons from Netscape and Its Battle with Microsoft* (New York: Free Press, 1998).

5. M. G. Jacobides, "Industry Change through Vertical Disintegration: How and Why Markets Emerged in Mortgage Banking," *Academy of Management Journal* 48, no. 3 (2005): 465–98; M. G. Jacobides, C. Y. Baldwin, and R. Dizaji, "From the Structure of the Value Chain to the Strategic Dynamics of Industry Sectors," Academy of Management Presentation (Philadelphia, August 7, 2007).

6. G. Carroll and M. Hannan, *The Demography of Corporations and Industries* (Princeton, MA: Princeton University Press, 2000). For a survey see J. Baum, "Organizational Ecology," in S. R. Clegg, C. Hardy, and W. R. Nord (eds), *The SAGE Handbook of Organizational Studies* (Thousand Oaks, CA: SAGE Publications, 1996); and D. Barron, "Evolutionary Theory," in D. O. Faulkner and A. Campbell (eds), *The Oxford Handbook of Strategy* (Oxford: Oxford University Press, 2003), vol. 1: 74–97.

7. G. R. Carroll, L. S. Bigelow, M.-D. Seidel, and B. Tsai, "The Fates of de novo and de alio Producers in the American Automobile Industry, 1885–1981," *Strategic Management Journal* 17 (Summer 1996): 117–137.

8. S. Klepper and K. L. Simons, "Dominance by Birthright: Entry of Prior Radio Producers and Competitive Ramifications in the US Television Receiver Industry," *Strategic Management Journal* 21 (2000): 997–1016.

9. High rates of entry and exit may continue well into maturity. See T. Dunne, M. J. Roberts, and L. Samuelson, "Patterns of Firm Entry and Exit in US Manufacturing Industries," *Rand Journal of Economics* 19 (1988): 495–515.

10. S. Klepper and E. Grady, "The Evolution of New Industries and the Determinants of Industry Structure," *Rand Journal of Economics* 21 (1990): 27–44.

11. S. Klepper and K. Simons, "The Making of an Oligopoly: Firm Survival and Technological Change in the Evolution of the US Tire Industry," *Journal of Political Economy* 108 (2000): 728–60.

12. G. Carroll and A. Swaminathan, "Why the Microbrewery Movement? Organizational Dynamics of Resource Partitioning in the American Brewing Industry," *American Journal of Sociology* 106 (2000): 715–62.

13. B. Levitt and J. G. March, "Organizational Learning," *Annual Review of Sociology* 14 (1988): 319–40.

14. D. Leonard-Barton, "Core Capabilities and Core Rigidities: A Paradox in Managing New Product Development," *Strategic Management Journal* 13 (Summer 1992): 111–25.

15. M. T. Hannan, L. Polos, and G. R. Carroll, "Structural Inertia and Organizational Change Revisited III: The Evolution of Organizational Inertia," *Stanford GSB Research Paper* 1734 (April 2002).

16. P. J. DiMaggio and W. Powell, "The Iron Cage Revisited: Institutional Isomorphism and Collective Rationality in Organizational Fields," *American Sociological Review* 48 (1983): 147–60.

17. J.-C. Spender, *Industry Recipes* (Oxford: Blackwell Publishing, 1989).

18. J. G. March, "Exploration and Exploitation in Organizational Learning," *Organizational Science* 2 (1991): 71–87.

19. P. R. Milgrom and J. Roberts, "Complementarities and Fit: Strategy, Structure, and Organizational Change in Manufacturing," *Journal of Accounting and Economics* 19 (1995): 179–208; M. E. Porter and N. Siggelkow, "Contextual Interactions within Activity Systems," *Academy of Management Perspectives* 22 (May 2008): 34–56.

20. E. Trist, "The Sociotechnical Perspective," in A. H. Van de Ven and W. H. Joyce (eds), *Perspectives on Organization Design and Behavior* (New York: John Wiley & Sons, Inc., 1984).

21. J. W. Rivkin, "Imitation of Complex Strategies," *Management Science* 46 (2000): 824–44.

22. M. E. Porter and N. Siggelkow, "Contextual Interactions within Activity Systems," *Academy of Management Perspectives* 22 (May 2008): 34–56.

23. M. L. Tushman and E. Romanelli, "Organizational Evolution: A Metamorphosis Model of Convergence and Reorientation," in L. L. Cummins and B. M. Staw (eds), *Research in Organizational Behavior* 7 (1985): 171–222; E. Romanelli and M. L. Tushman, "Organizational Transformation as Punctuated Equilibrium: An Empirical Test," *Academy of Management Journal* 37 (1994): 1141–66.

24. H. E. Aldrich, *Organizations and Environments* (Stanford, CA: Stanford University Press, 2007).

25. For an introduction to organizational ecology, see M. T. Hannan and G. R. Carroll, "An introduction to organizational ecology," in G. R. Carroll and M. T. Hannan (eds), *Organizations in Industry* (Oxford: Oxford University Press, 1995): 17–31.

26. For a survey of evolutionary approaches, see R. R. Nelson, "Recent Evolutionary Theorizing about Economic Change," *Journal of Economic Literature* 33 (March 1995): 48–90.

27. ExxonMobil Corporation is a descendent of Standard Oil; Royal Dutch Shell was created in 1907 by Royal Dutch Petroleum Co. and Shell Transport and Trading Co.

28. C. Markides and P. Geroski, "Colonizers and Consolidators: The Two Cultures of Corporate Strategy," *Strategy and Business* 32 (Fall 2003).

29. G. A. Moore, *Crossing the Chasm* (New York: HarperCollins, 1991).

30. S. Klepper, "The Capabilities of New Firms and the Evolution of the US Automobile Industry," *Industrial and Corporate Change* 11 (2002): 645–66.

31. S. Klepper and K. L. Simons, "Dominance by Birthright: Entry of Prior Radio Producers and Competitive Ramifications in the US Television Receiver Industry," *Strategic Management Journal* 21 (2000): 997–1016.

32. D. A. Kaplan, *The Silicon Boys and Their Valley of Dreams* (New York: Morrow, 1999).

33. G. Buenstorf and S. Klepper, "Heritage and Agglomeration: The Akron Tyre Cluster Revisited," *Economic Journal* 119 (2009): 705–33.

34. M. L. Tushman and P. Anderson, "Technological Discontinuities and Organizational Environments," *Administrative Science Quarterly* 31 (1986): 439–65.

35. M. Tripsas, "Unravelling the Process of Creative Destruction: Complementary Assets and Incumbent Survival in the Typesetter Industry," *Strategic Management Journal* 18 (Summer 1997): 119–142.

36. R. M. Henderson and K. B. Clark, "Architectural Innovation: The Reconfiguration of Existing Systems and the Failure of Established Firms," *Administrative Science Quarterly* (1990): 9–30.

37. R. M. Henderson and K. B. Clark, "Architectural Innovation: The Reconfiguration of Existing Systems and the Failure of Established Firms," *Administrative Science Quarterly* (1990): 9–30.

38. J. Bower and C. M. Christensen, "Disruptive Technologies: Catching the Wave," *Harvard Business Review* (January/February 1995): 43–53.

39. C. M. Christensen, *The Innovator's Dilemma* (Boston: Harvard Business School Press, 1997).

40. C. M. Christensen, *The Innovator's Dilemma* (Boston: Harvard Business School Press, 1997).

41. T. G. Cummins and C. G. Worley, *Organization Development and Change*, 8th edn (Cincinnati, OH: Southwestern College Publishing: 2005).

42. D. F. Abell, *Managing with Dual Strategies* (New York: Free Press, 1993): 3.

43. C. A. O'Reilly and M. L. Tushman, "The Ambidextrous Organization," *Harvard Business Review* (April 2004): 74–81.

44. C. M. Christensen and M. Overdorf, "Meeting the Challenge of Disruptive Change," *Harvard Business Review* (March/April 2000): 66–76.

45. T. Elder, "Lessons from Xerox and IBM," *Harvard Business Review* (July/August 1989): 66–71.

46. "Xerox PARC: Innovation without Profit?" ICMR Case Study, 2004.

47. J. O'Toole, *Forming the Future: Lessons from the Saturn Corporation* (New York: Harper, 1996).

48. G. Verona and D. Ravasi, "Unbundling dynamic capabilities: An exploratory study of continuous product innovation," *Industrial and Corporate Change* 12 (2002): 577–606.

49. Interview with Nancy Snyder, Whirlpool's vice-president of leadership and strategic competency development, *Business Week* (March 6, 2006), http://www.businessweek.com/innovate/content/mar2006/id20060306_287425.htm?.

50. R. Cibin and R. M. Grant, "Restructuring among the World's Leading Oil Companies," *British Journal of Management* 7 (1996): 283–308.

51. N. Siggelkow and D. A. Levinthal, "Escaping Real (Non-benign) Competency Traps: Linking the Dynamics of Organizational Structure to the Dynamics of Search," *Strategic Organization* 3 (2005): 85–115.

52. J. Nickerson and T. Zenger, "Being Efficiently Fickle: A Dynamic Theory of Organizational Choice," *Organization Science* 13 (September/October 2002): 547–67.

53. M. F. Wiersema, "Strategic Consequences of Executive Succession within Diversified Firms," *Journal of Management Studies* 29 (1992): 73–94.

54. R. Agarwal, P.-L. Chen, and C. Williams, "Renewal through Rookies: The Growth Effects of Top Management Recruits from Different Levels, Organizations, and Industries," Working Paper, Bocconi University, Milan (2011).

55. D. J. Teece, G. Pisano, and A. Shuen, "Dynamic Capabilities and Strategic Management," *Strategic Management Journal* 18 (1997): 509–33.

56. K. M. Eisenhardt and J. A. Martin, "Dynamic Capabilities: What Are They?" *Strategic Management Journal* 21 (2000): 1105–21. See also H. Volberda, *Building the Flexible Firm* (Oxford: Oxford University Press, 1998).

57. M. Zollo and S. G. Winter, "Deliberate Learning and the Evolution of Dynamic Capabilities," *Organization Science* 13 (2002): *339–51;* S. G. Winter, "Understanding Dynamic Capabilities," *Strategic Management Journal* 24 (2003): 991–5.

58. S. G. Winter, "Understanding Dynamic Capabilities," *Strategic Management Journal* 24 (2003): 991–95.

59. J. B. Harreld, C. A. O'Reilly, and M. L. Tushman, "Dynamic Capabilities at IBM: Driving Strategy into Action," *California Management Review* 49, no. 4 (2007): 21–43.

60. H. Kahn, *The Next 200 Years: A Scenario for America and the World* (New York: William Morrow, 1976). For a guide to the use of scenarios in strategy making, see K. van der Heijden, *Scenarios: The Art of Strategic Conversation* (Chichester: John Wiley & Sons, Ltd, 2005).

61. G. Hamel and C. K. Prahalad, Competing for the Future (Boston: Harvard Business School Press, 1995).

62. G. Hamel, *Leading the Revolution* (Boston: Harvard Business School Press, 2000): 5.

63. B. Wernerfelt, "Why Do Firms Tend to Become Different?" in C. E. Helfat (ed.), *Handbook of Organizational Capabilities* (Oxford: Blackwell, 2006): 121–33.

64. D. Leonard-Barton, "Core Capabilities and Core Rigidities," *Strategic Management Journal* 13 (Summer 1992): 111–26.

65. N. T. Snyder and D. L. Duarte, *Unleashing Innovation: How Whirlpool Transformed an Industry* (San Francisco: Jossey-Bass, 2008).

66. C. E. Helfat and R. S. Raubitschek, "Product Sequencing: Co-evolution of Knowledge, Capabilities and Products," *Strategic Management Journal* 21 (2000): 961–79. The parallel development of capabilities and products has also been referred to as "dynamic resource fit." See: H. Itami, *Mobilizing Invisible Assets* (Boston: Harvard University Press, 1987): 125.

67. A. Takahashi, *What I Learned from Konosuke Matsushita* (Tokyo: Jitsugyo no Nihonsha, 1980); in Japanese, quoted by H. Itami, *Mobilizing Invisible Assets* (Boston: Harvard University Press, 1987): 25.

68. L. Kellaway, "Lucy Kellaway Column," *Financial Times* (June 23, 1999): 13.

69. R. M. Grant, "Toward a Knowledge-based Theory of the Firm," *Strategic Management Journal* 17 (Winter 1996): 109–22.

70. M. Hansen, N. Nohria, and T. Tierney, "What's Your Strategy for Managing Knowledge?" *Harvard Business Review* (March 1999): 106–16.

71. B. Kogut and U. Zander, "Knowledge of the Firm, Combinative Capabilities, and the Replication of Knowledge," *Organization Science* 3 (1992): 383–97; J. Rivkin, "Reproducing Knowledge: Replication without Imitation at Moderate Complexity," *Organization Science* 12 (2001): 274–93.

# 9 Technology-based Industries and the Management of Innovation

> Whereas a calculator on the ENIAC is equipped with 18000 vacuum tubes and weighs 30 tons, computers in the future may have only 1000 vacuum tubes and perhaps weigh only 1.5 tons.
>
> —POPULAR MECHANICS, MARCH 1949

> I can think of no conceivable reason why an individual should wish to have a computer in his own home.
>
> —KENNETH OLSEN, CHAIRMAN, DIGITAL EQUIPMENT CORPORATION, 1977

## OUTLINE

# Introduction and Objectives

In the previous chapter we saw that technology is the primary force that creates new industries and transforms existing ones. In the past four decades, new technologies have created many new industries: wireless telephony, biotechnology, photovoltaic power, fiber optics, robotics, and digital imaging. Other industries have been transformed by new technology: telecommunications equipment by internet protocols; the securities industry by online trading; the logistics industry by electronic data interchange (EDI), radio frequency identification (RFID), and global position systems (GPS). New technology is a source of opportunity, especially for new enterprises, but, as we saw in the previous chapter, adapting to new technologies presents major problems for many established companies.

Our focus in this chapter is on business environments where technology is a key driver of change and an important source of competitive advantage. These technology-intensive industries include both emerging industries (those in the introductory and growth phases of their life cycle) and established industries where technology continues to be the major driver of competition (such as pharmaceuticals, chemicals, telecommunications, and electronics). The issues we examine, however, are also relevant to a much broader range of industries where technology has the potential to create competitive advantage.

In the last chapter, we viewed technology as an external force that drove industrial change. In this chapter our primary concern will be the use of technology as a tool of competitive strategy. How can an enterprise best exploit the opportunities that technology offers in order to establish a competitive advantage?

By the time you have completed this chapter, you will be able to:

◆ analyze how technology is likely to affect industry structure and competition;

◆ identify the factors that determine the returns to innovation, and evaluate the potential for an innovation to establish competitive advantage;

◆ formulate strategies for exploiting innovation and managing technology, including:

  • assessing the relative advantages of being a leader or a follower in innovation

  • identifying and evaluating strategic options for exploiting innovation

  • designing strategies and tactics for winning standards wars

  • managing risk;

◆ design the organizational conditions needed to implement innovation and technology strategies.

This chapter is organized as follows. First, we examine the links between technology and competition in technology-intensive industries. Second, we explore the potential for innovation to establish sustainable competitive advantage. Third, we deal with key issues in designing technology strategies, including timing (to lead or to follow), alternative strategies for exploiting an innovation, setting industry standards, and managing risk. Finally, we examine the organizational conditions for the successful implementation of technology-based strategies.

# Competitive Advantage in Technology-intensive Industries

Innovation forms the key link between technology and competitive advantage. It is the quest for competitive advantage that causes firms to invest in innovation; it is innovation that is responsible for new industries coming into being; and it is innovation that allows some firms to dominate their industries. Let us begin by exploring the conditions under which innovation generates profit.

## The Innovation Process

**Invention** is the creation of new products and processes through the development of new knowledge or from new combinations of existing knowledge. Most inventions are the result of novel applications of existing knowledge. Samuel Morse's telegraph, patented in 1840, was based on several decades of research into electromagnetism from Ben Franklin to Ørsted, Ampère, and Sturgeon. The compact disk embodies knowledge about lasers developed several decades previously.

**Innovation** is the initial commercialization of invention by producing and marketing a new good or service or by using a new method of production. Once introduced, innovation diffuses: on the demand side, through customers purchasing the good or service; on the supply side, through imitation by competitors. An innovation may be the result of a single invention (most product innovations in chemicals and pharmaceuticals involve discoveries of new chemical compounds) or it may combine many inventions. The first automobile, introduced by Karl Benz in 1885, embodied a multitude of inventions, from the wheel, invented some 5000 years previously, to the internal combustion engine, invented nine years earlier. Not all invention progresses into innovation: among the patent portfolios of most technology-intensive firms are inventions that have yet to find a viable commercial application. Many innovations may involve little or no new technology: the personal computer was a new configuration of existing technologies; most new types of packaging, including the vast array of tamper-proof packages, involve novel designs but no new technology.

Figure 9.1 shows the pattern of development from knowledge creation to invention and innovation. Historically, the lags between knowledge creation and innovation have been long:

- Chester F. Carlson invented xerography in 1938 by combining established knowledge about electrostatics and printing. The first patents were awarded in 1940. Xerox purchased the patent rights and launched its first office copier in 1958. By 1974, the first competitive machines were introduced by IBM, Kodak, Ricoh, and Canon.
- The jet engine, employing Newtonian principles, was patented by Frank Whittle in 1930. The first commercial jet airliner, the De Havilland Comet, flew in 1957. Two years later, the Boeing 707 was introduced.

Recently, the innovation cycle has speeded up:

- The mathematics of *fuzzy logic* was developed by Lofti Zadeh at Berkeley during the 1960s. By the early 1980s, Dr Takeshi Yamakawa of the Kyushu Institute of Technology had patented integrated circuits embodying fuzzy

**FIGURE 9.1**   The development of technology: From knowledge creation to diffusion

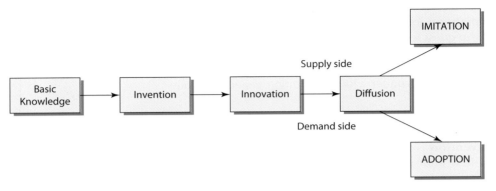

logic, and in 1987 Omron of Kyoto introduced fuzzy logic controllers for industrial machines. By 1991, the world market for fuzzy logic controllers was estimated at $2 billion.[1]

- The use of satellite radio signals for global positioning was developed by physicists at Johns Hopkins University in late 1950s. In 1978, the US Air Force launched its first experimental GPS satellite; the GPS system was fully operational by 1995. Commercial applications began in the early 1990s: Garmin launched its first GPS satellite navigation product in 1991. Car sat-nav systems were offered by Garmin in 1998 and TomTom in 2002.

- MP3, the audio file compression software, was developed at the Fraunhofer Institute in Germany in 1987; by the mid-1990s, the swapping of MP3 music files had taken off in US college campuses, and in 1998 the first MP3 player, Diamond Multimedia's *Rio*, was launched. Apple's iPod was introduced in 2001.

## The Profitability of Innovation

"If a man can . . . make a better mousetrap than his neighbor, though he build his house in the woods, the world will make a beaten path to his door," claimed Emerson. Yet the inventors of new mousetraps, and other gadgets too, are more likely to be found at the bankruptcy courts than in the millionaires' playgrounds of the Caribbean. Certainly, innovation is no guarantor of fame and fortune, either for individuals or for companies. There is no consistent evidence that either R & D intensity or frequency of new-product introductions is positively associated with profitability.[2]

The profitability of an innovation to the innovator depends on the value created by the innovation and the share of that value that the innovator is able to appropriate. The value created by an innovation is distributed among a number of different parties. As Strategy Capsule 9.1 shows, different innovations result in very different distributions of value. In the case of aspartame, the innovator G. D. Searle with NutraSweet was the primary beneficiary. In the case of the personal computer, suppliers and consumers were the primary beneficiaries. In the case of smartphones, followers such as RIM, Apple, and Samsung have appropriated most of the value.

# How the Returns on Innovation Are Shared

The value created by an innovation is distributed among a number of different parties (Figure 9.2).

◆ *Aspartame*: Aspartame, the artificial sweetener, was discovered in 1965 by the drug company G. D. Searle & Co. In 1981, after FDA approval, it was launched as NutraSweet. NutraSweet was sold to soft drink producers and food processors at $200 a kilo: twenty times the price of saccharin and by 1986 was generating sales of $711 million. In 1985, Searle was acquired by Monsanto. In 1992, the main US patent on aspartame expired. Competition from rival producers began in Europe in 1986 and in the US in December 1992. In the first two decades of aspartame's market presence, the innovator, Searle/Monsanto, has appropriated a major part of the value created.

◆ *Personal computers*: The innovators—MITS, Tandy, Apple, and Xerox—earned modest profits from their innovation. The imitators—IBM, Dell, Compaq, Acer, Toshiba, and a host of other later

entrants—did somewhat better, but their returns were overshadowed by the huge profits earned by the suppliers to the industry: Intel in microprocessors, Microsoft in operating systems, Seagate in disk drives, Sharp in flat-panel displays. However, because of strong competition in the industry, the greatest beneficiaries from the invention of the personal computer were consumers, who typically paid prices for their PCs that were far below the value that they derived.[3]

◆ *Smartphones*: These are wireless handsets with enhanced computing capability and internet access. The first were the IBM Simon (1993) and the Nokia 9000 series (1996). During 2000–2002, a host of followers entered the market, including Ericsson, Sony, Palm, and RIM. In 2007, the Apple iPhone was launched. While the pioneers all lost money, among the followers Apple and RIM (until recently) were highly profitable. Several suppliers have also been big winners, including ARM (microprocessors) and application suppliers such as Zynga.

**FIGURE 9.2**   Appropriation of value: Who gets the benefits from innovation?

The term **regime of appropriability** is used to describe the conditions that influence the distribution of returns to innovation. In a strong regime of appropriability, the innovator is able to capture a substantial share of the value created: Pilkington's float glass process, Pfizer's Viagra, and Dyson's dual-cyclone vacuum cleaner—like Searle's NutraSweet—all generated huge profits for their owners. In a weak regime of appropriability, other parties derive most of the value. In e-book readers, the diversity of rivals, the prevalence of open standards, and competition from substitute products such as tablet computers suggest that no players are likely to earn massive profits.

The regime of appropriability comprises four key components which determine the innovator's ability to profit from innovation: property rights, the tacitness and complexity of the technology, lead time, and complementary resources.

*Property Rights in Innovation*   Appropriating the returns on innovation depends, to a great extent, on the ability to establish property rights in the innovation. It was the desire to protect the returns to inventors that prompted the English Parliament to pass the 1623 Statute of Monopolies, which established the basis of patent law. Since then, the law has been extended to several areas of **intellectual property**, including:

- *Patents*: Exclusive rights to a new and useful product, process, substance, or design. Obtaining a patent requires that the invention is novel, useful, and not excessively obvious. Patent law varies from country to country. In the US, a patent is valid for 17 years (14 for a design).
- *Copyrights*: Exclusive production, publication, or sales rights to the creators of artistic, literary, dramatic, or musical works. Examples include articles, books, drawings, maps, photographs, and musical compositions.
- *Trademarks*: Words, symbols, or other marks used to distinguish the goods or services supplied by a firm. In the US and the UK, they are registered with the Patent Office. Trademarks provide the basis for brand identification.
- *Trade secrets*: Offer a modest degree of legal protection for recipes, formulae, industrial processes, customer lists, and other knowledge acquired in the course of business.

The effectiveness of intellectual property law depends on the type of innovation being protected. For new chemical products (a new drug or plastic), patents can provide effective protection. For products that involve new configurations of existing components or new manufacturing processes, patents may fail to prevent rivals from innovating around them. The scope of the patent law has been extended to include life forms created by biotechnology, computer software, and business methods. Business method patents have generated considerable controversy, especially Amazon's patent on "one-click-to-buy" internet purchasing.[4] While patents and copyright establish property rights, their disadvantage (from the inventor's viewpoint) is that they make information public. Hence, companies often prefer secrecy to patenting as a means of protecting innovations.

In recent decades, companies have devoted increasing attention to protecting and exploiting the economic value of their intellectual property. When Texas Instruments began exploiting its patent portfolio as a revenue source during the 1980s, the technology sector as a whole woke up to the value of its knowledge assets. During the 1990s, TI's royalty income exceeded its operating income from other sources. One outcome has been an upsurge in patenting. An average of 231,000 patents were granted by the US Patent Office each year from 2009 to 2011; during 1980–1985 it was 67,000 annually.

*Tacitness and Complexity of the Technology*   In the absence of effective legal protection the extent to which an innovation can be imitated by a competitor depends on the ease with which the technology can be comprehended and replicated. This depends, first, on the extent to which the technical knowledge is codifiable. Codifiable knowledge, by definition, is that which can be written down. Hence, if it is not effectively protected by patents or copyright, diffusion is likely to be rapid and the competitive advantage not sustainable. Financial innovations such as mortgage-backed securities and credit default swaps embody readily codifiable knowledge that can be copied very quickly. Similarly, Coca-Cola's recipe is codifiable and, in the absence of trade-secret protection, is easily copied. Intel's designs for advanced microprocessors are codified and can be copied; however, the processes for manufacturing these integrated circuits are based on deeply tacit knowledge.

The second key factor is *complexity*. Every new fashion, from the Mary Quant miniskirt of 1962 to Jimmy Choo's wedge-heel espadrilles of 2012, involves simple, easy-to-copy ideas. Conversely, Airbus's A380 and Altera Corporation's Stratix V FPGA chip (possibly the world's most complex integrated circuit) present entirely different challenges for the would-be imitator.

*Lead Time*   Tacitness and complexity do not provide lasting barriers to imitation, but they do offer the innovator *time*. Innovation creates a temporary competitive advantage that offers a window of opportunity for the innovator to build on the initial advantage.

The innovator's *lead time* is the time it will take followers to catch up. The challenge for the innovator is to use initial lead-time advantages to build the capabilities and market position to entrench industry leadership. Microsoft, Intel, and Cisco Systems were brilliant at exploiting lead time to build advantages in efficient manufacture, quality, and market presence. Conversely, innovative British companies are notorious for having squandered their lead-time advantage in jet planes, radars, CT scanners, and genomics.

Lead time allows a firm to move down its learning curve ahead of followers. In new generations of microprocessors, Intel has traditionally been first to market, allowing it to move quickly down its experience curve, cut prices, and so pressure the profit margins of its rival, AMD.

*Complementary Resources*   Bringing new products and processes to market requires not just invention; it also requires the diverse resources and capabilities needed to finance, produce, and market the innovation. These are referred to as *complementary resources* (Figure 9.3). Chester Carlson invented xerography but was unable for many years to bring his product to market because he lacked the complementary resources needed to develop, manufacture, market, distribute, and service his invention. Conversely, Searle (and its later parent, Monsanto) was able to provide almost all the development, manufacturing, marketing, and distribution resources needed to exploit its NutraSweet innovation. As a result, Carlson was able

**FIGURE 9.3**   Complementary resources

to appropriate only a tiny part of the value created by his invention of the plain-paper Xerox copier, whereas Searle/Monsanto was successful in appropriating a major part of the value created by its new artificial sweetener.

Complementary resources may be accessed through alliances with other firms, for example biotech firms ally with large pharmaceutical companies for clinical trials, manufacture, and marketing.[5] When an innovation and the complementary resources that support it are supplied by different firms, the division of value between them depends on their relative power. A key determinant of this is whether the complementary resources are *specialized* or *unspecialized*. Fuel cells may eventually displace internal combustion engines in many of the world's automobiles. However, the problem for the developers of fuel cells is that their success depends on automobile manufacturers making specialized investments in designing a whole new range of cars, service station owners providing specialized refueling facilities, and repair firms investing in training and new equipment. For fuel cells to be widely adopted will require that the benefits of the innovation are shared widely with the different providers of these complementary resources. Where complementary resources are generic, the innovator is in a much stronger position to capture value. Because Adobe Systems' Acrobat Portable Document Format (PDF) works with files created in almost any software application, Adobe is well positioned to capture most of the value created by its innovatory software product. However, one advantage of co-specialized complementary resources is that they raise barriers to imitation. Consider the threat that Linux presents to Microsoft Window's dominance of PC operating systems. Intel has adapted its microprocessors to the needs of Windows and most applications software is written to run on Windows, so the challenge for the Linux community is not just to develop a workable operating system but also to encourage the development of applications software and hardware that are compatible with the Linux operating system.

## Which Mechanisms Are Effective at Protecting Innovation?

How effective are these different mechanisms in protecting innovations? Table 9.1 shows that, despite considerable variation across industries, patent protection is of limited effectiveness as compared with lead time, secrecy, and complementary manufacturing and sales/service resources. Indeed, since the late 1980s, the effectiveness of patents appeared to have declined despite the strengthening of patent law. Although patents are effective in increasing the lead time before competitors are able to bring imitative products to market, these gains tend to be small. The great majority of patented products and processes are duplicated within three years.[6]

Given the limited effectiveness of patents, why do firms continue to engage in patenting? Table 9.2 shows that, while protection from imitation is the principal motive, several others are also very important. In particular, much patenting activity appears to be strategic; it is directed toward blocking the innovation efforts of other companies and establishing property rights in technologies that can then be used in bargaining with other companies for access to their proprietary technologies. In semiconductors and electronics, cross-licensing arrangements—where one company gives access to its patents across a field of technology in exchange for access to another company's patents—are critical in permitting "freedom to design": the ability to design products that draw on technologies owned by different companies.[7]

**TABLE 9.1**  The effectiveness of different mechanisms for protecting innovation

|  | Secrecy (%) | Patents (%) | Lead-time (%) | Sales/service (%) | Manufacturing (%) |
|---|---|---|---|---|---|
| **Product innovations** | | | | | |
| Food | 59 | 18 | 53 | 40 | 51 |
| Drugs | 54 | 50 | 50 | 33 | 49 |
| Electronic components | 34 | 21 | 46 | 50 | 51 |
| Telecom equipment | 47 | 26 | 66 | 42 | 41 |
| Medical equipment | 51 | 55 | 58 | 52 | 49 |
| All industries | 51 | 35 | 53 | 43 | 46 |
| **Process innovations** | | | | | |
| Food | 56 | 16 | 42 | 30 | 47 |
| Drugs | 68 | 36 | 36 | 25 | 44 |
| Electronic components | 47 | 15 | 43 | 42 | 56 |
| Telecom equipment | 35 | 15 | 43 | 34 | 41 |
| Medical equipment | 49 | 34 | 45 | 32 | 50 |
| All industries | 51 | 23 | 38 | 31 | 43 |

*Note:*
These data show the percentage of companies reporting that the particular mechanism, their sales and service, and their manufacturing capabilities were effective in protecting their innovations.
*Source:* W. M. Cohen, R. R. Nelson, and J. P. Walsh, "Protecting Their Intellectual Assets: Appropriability Conditions and Why US Manufacturing Firms Patent (Or Not)," NBER Working Paper No. W7552 (February 2000). © 2000. Reprinted by permission of the authors.

**TABLE 9.2** Why do companies patent? (Responses by 674 US manufacturers)

|  | Product Innovations (%) | Process Innovations (%) |
| --- | --- | --- |
| To prevent copying | 95 | 77 |
| For licensing revenue | 28 | 23 |
| To prevent law suits | 59 | 47 |
| To block others | 82 | 64 |
| For use in negotiations | 47 | 43 |
| To enhance reputation | 48 | 34 |
| To measure performance | 6 | 5 |

*Source:* W. M. Cohen, R. R. Nelson, and J. P. Walsh, "Protecting Their Intellectual Assets: Appropriability Conditions and Why US Manufacturing Firms Patent (Or Not)," NBER Working Paper No. W7552 (February 2000). © 2000. Reprinted by permission of the authors.

## Strategies to Exploit Innovation: How and When to Enter

Having established some of the key factors that determine the returns to innovation, let us consider some of the main questions concerning the formulation of strategies to manage technology and exploit innovation.

### Alternative Strategies to Exploit Innovation

How should a firm maximize the returns to its innovation? A number of alternative strategies are available. Figure 9.4 orders them according to the size of the commitment of resources and capabilities that each requires. Thus, licensing requires little involvement by the innovator in subsequent commercialization, hence is a limited investment. Internal commercialization, possibly through creating a new enterprise or business unit, involves a much greater investment of resources and capabilities. In between there are various opportunities for collaboration with other companies. Joint ventures and strategic alliances typically involve substantial resource sharing between companies. On a more limited scale, specific activities may be outsourced to other companies.

Which mode of innovation is chosen by the firm depends on two sets of factors: the characteristics of the innovation and the resources and capabilities of the firm.

*Characteristics of the Innovation*    The extent to which a firm can establish clear property rights in an innovation is a critical determinant of its innovation strategy. Licensing is only viable where ownership in the innovation is protected by patent or copyrights. Thus, in pharmaceuticals, licensing is widespread because patents are clear and defensible. Many biotech companies engage only in R & D and license their drug discoveries to large pharmaceutical companies that possess the necessary complementary resources. Royalties from licensing its sound-reduction technologies accounted for 82% of Dolby Laboratories' 2011 revenues. Conversely, when Steve Jobs and Steve Wozniak developed their Apple I and Apple II computers, they had little option other than to go into business themselves: the absence of proprietary technology ruled out licensing as an option.

**FIGURE 9.4**   Alternative strategies for exploiting innovation

| | Licensing | Outsourcing certain functions | Strategic alliance | Joint venture | Internal commercialization |
|---|---|---|---|---|---|
| **Risk and return** | Little investment risk but returns also limited. Risk that the licensee either lacks motivation or steals the innovation | Limits capital investment, but may create dependence on suppliers/partners | Benefits of flexibility. Risks of informal structure | Shares investment and risk. Risk of partner disagreement and culture clash | Biggest investment requirement and corresponding risks. Benefits of control |
| **Resource requirements** | Few | Permits external resources and capabilities to be accessed | Permits pooling of the resources and capabilities of more than one firm | | Substantial requirements in terms of finance, production capability, marketing capability, distribution, etc. |
| **Examples** | Ericsson with its Bluetooth wireless technology; Dolby Labs with its sound reduction technology; Qualcomm and CDMA | Microsoft's XBox was largely designed by other companies and Flextronics does the manufacturing | Ballard's strategic alliance with DaimlerChrysler to develop fuel cells | Psion created Symbian as a joint venture with Ericsson, Nokia, and Motorola to develop the Symbian mobile phone operating system | Larry Page and Sergey Brin established Google Inc. to develop and market their internet search technology |

The advantages of licensing are, first, that it relieves the company of the need to develop the full range of complementary resources and capabilities needed for commercialization and, second, that it can allow the innovation to be commercialized quickly. If the lead time offered by the innovation is short, multiple licensing can allow for a fast global rollout. The problem, however, is that the success of the innovation in the market is totally dependent on the commitment and effectiveness of the licensees. James Dyson, the British inventor of the bagless vacuum cleaner, created his own company to manufacture and market his "dual cyclone" vacuum cleaners after failing to interest any major appliance company in a licensing deal for his technology.

*Resources and Capabilities of the Firm*   As Figure 9.4 shows, different strategies require very different resources and capabilities. Hence, the choice of how to exploit an innovation depends critically upon the resources and capabilities that the innovator brings to the party. Start-up firms possess few of the complementary resources and capabilities needed to commercialize their innovations. Inevitably, they will be attracted to licensing or to accessing the resources of larger firms through outsourcing, alliances, or joint ventures. As we noted in the previous chapter, new industries often follow a two-stage evolution where "innovators" do the pioneering and "consolidators" with their complementary resources do the developing.

These established corporations with a wealth of resources and capabilities are better placed than start-ups for internal commercialization. Companies such as Sony, DuPont, Siemens, Hitachi, and IBM have strong traditions of pursuing basic research, then internally developing the innovations that arise.

However, even these companies have been forced into more technological collaborations with other companies. Ron Adner observes that innovation increasingly requires coordinated responses by multiple companies. Innovating firms need to identify and map their *innovation ecosystem*, then manage the interdependencies within it. The delayed introduction of HDTV can be attributed to inadequate coordination among TV manufacturers, production studios, and broadcasters.[8]

## Timing Innovation: To Lead or to Follow?

To gain competitive advantage in emerging and technologically intensive industries, is it better to be a leader or a follower in innovation? As Table 9.3 shows, the evidence is mixed: in some products the leader has been the first to grab the prize; in others, the leader has succumbed to the risks and costs of pioneering. Optimal timing of entry into an emerging industry and the introduction of new technology are complex issues. The advantage of being an early mover depends on the following factors:

- *The extent to which innovation can be protected by property rights or lead-time advantages*: If an innovation is appropriable through a patent, copyright, or lead-time advantage, there is advantage in being an early mover. This is especially the case where patent protection is important, as in pharmaceuticals. Notable patent races include that between Alexander Bell and Elisha Gray to patent the telephone (Bell got to the Patent Office a few hours before Gray),[9] and between Celera Inc. and the National Institutes of Health to patent the sequence of the human genome.[10]

- *The importance of complementary resources*: The more important complementary resources are in exploiting an innovation, the greater the costs and risks of pioneering. Several firms—from Sir Clive Sinclair with a

**TABLE 9.3**   Leaders, followers, and success in emerging industries

| Product | Innovator | Follower | The winner |
|---|---|---|---|
| Jet airliner | De Havilland (Comet) | Boeing (707) | Follower |
| Float glass | Pilkington | Corning | Leader |
| X-ray scanner | EMI | General Electric | Follower |
| Office PC | Xerox | IBM | Follower |
| VCRs | Ampex/Sony | Matsushita | Follower |
| Instant camera | Polaroid | Kodak | Leader |
| Microwave oven | Raytheon | Samsung | Follower |
| Video games player | Atari | Nintendo/Sony | Followers |
| Disposable diaper | Procter & Gamble | Kimberley-Clark | Leader |
| Compact disk | Sony/Philips | Matsushita, Pioneer | Leader |
| Web browser | Netscape | Microsoft | Follower |
| Web search engine | Lycos | Google | Follower |
| MP3 music players | Diamond Multimedia | Apple (iPod) | Follower |
| Operating systems for mobile phones | Symbian | Microsoft | Leader (until 2010) |
| Laser printer | Xerox, IBM | Canon | Follower |
| Flash memory | Toshiba | Samsung, Intel | Followers |
| E-book reader | Sony (Digital Reader) | Amazon (Kindle) | Follower |
| Social networking | SixDegrees.com | Facebook | Follower |

*Source:* Based in part on D. Teece, *The Competitive Challenge: Strategies for Industrial Innovation and Renewal* (Cambridge: Ballinger, 1987): 186–8.

battery-driven car to General Motors with its fuel-cell car and Chevrolet Volt—failed commercially with their electric automobiles. The problem for the pioneer is that the development costs are huge because of the need to orchestrate multiple technologies and establish self-sufficiency across a range of business functions. Followers are also favored by the fact that, as an industry develops, specialist firms emerge as suppliers of complementary resources. Thus, in pioneering the development of the British frozen foods industry, Unilever's Bird's Eye subsidiary had to set up an entire chain of cold stores and frozen distribution facilities. Later entrants were able to rely on the services of public cold stores and refrigerated trucking companies.

● *The potential to establish a standard*: As we shall see later in this chapter, some markets converge toward a technical standard. The greater the importance of technical standards, the greater the advantages of being an early mover in order to influence those standards and gain the market momentum needed to establish leadership. Once a standard has been set, displacing it becomes exceptionally difficult. IBM had little success with its OS/2 operating system against the entrenched position of Microsoft Windows. Linux has succeeded in taking market share from Windows. However, the main reason for this is that Linux is free!

Optimal timing depends also on the resources and capabilities that the individual firm has at its disposal. Different companies have different *strategic windows*—periods in time when their resources and capabilities are aligned with the opportunities available in the market. A small, technology-based firm may have no choice but to pioneer innovation: its opportunity is to grab **first-mover advantage** and then develop the necessary complementary resources before more powerful rivals appear. For the large, established firm with financial resources and strong production, marketing, and distribution capabilities, the strategic window is likely to be both longer and later. The risks of pioneering are greater for an established firm with a reputation and brands to protect, while to exploit its complementary resources effectively typically requires a more developed market. Consider the following examples:

● In personal computers, Apple was a pioneer, IBM a follower. The timing of entry was probably optimal for each. Apple's resources were the vision of Steve Jobs and the technical genius of Steve Wozniak; only by pioneering could it hope to be successful. IBM had enormous strengths in manufacturing, distribution, and reputation. It could build competitive advantage even without a clear technological advantage. The key for IBM was to delay its entry until the time when the market had developed to the point where IBM's strengths could have their maximum impact.

● In the browser war between Netscape and Microsoft, Microsoft had the luxury of being able to follow the pioneer, Netscape. Microsoft's huge product development, marketing, and distribution capabilities, and, most important, its vast installed base of the Windows operating system allowed it to overhaul Netscape's initial lead.

● Although General Electric entered the market for CT scanners some four years after EMI, it was able to overtake EMI within a few years because of its ability to apply vast technological, manufacturing, sales, and customer service capabilities within the field of medical electronics.

The most effective follower strategies are those that initiate a new product's transition from niche market to mass market. According to Markides and Geroski, successful first movers pioneer new products that embody new technologies and new functionality.[11] The opportunity for the fast-second entrant is to grow the niche market into a mass market by lowering cost and increasing quality. Timing is critical. Don Sull argues that a successful follower strategy requires "active waiting": a company needs to monitor market developments and assemble resources and capabilities while it prepares for large-scale market entry.[12]

## Managing Risks

Emerging industries are risky. There are two main sources of uncertainty:

- *Technological uncertainty* arises from the unpredictability of technological evolution and the complex dynamics through which technical standards and dominant designs are selected. Hindsight is always 20/20, but *ex ante* it is difficult to predict how technologies and the industries that deploy them will evolve.

- *Market uncertainty* relates to the size and growth rates of the markets for new products. When Xerox introduced its first plain-paper copier in 1959, Apple its first personal computer in 1977, or Sony its Walkman in 1979, none had any idea of the size of the potential market. Forecasting demand for new products is hazardous—most forecasting techniques are based on past data. Demand forecasts for new products tend to rely either on analogies[13] or expert opinion—e.g., combining expert insight and experience using the *Delphi technique*.[14]

If managers are unable to forecast technology and demand, then to manage risk they must be alert to emerging trends while limiting their exposure to risk through avoiding large-scale commitments. Useful strategies for limiting risk include:

- *Cooperating with lead users*: During the early phases of industry development, careful monitoring of and response to market trends and customer requirements is essential to avoid major errors in technology and design. Von Hippel argues that lead users provide a source of leading market indicators, can assist in developing new products and processes, and offer an early cash flow to fund development expenditures.[15] In computer software, *beta versions* are released to computer enthusiasts for testing. Nike has two sets of lead users: professional athletes who are trendsetters for athletic footwear and gang members and hip-hop artists who are at the leading edge of urban fashion trends. In communications and aerospace, government defense contracts play a crucial role in developing new technologies.[16]

- *Limiting risk exposure*: The financial risks of emerging industries can be mitigated by financial and operational practices that minimize a firm's exposure to adversity. By avoiding debt and keeping fixed costs low, a firm can lower its financial and operational gearing. Outsourcing and strategic alliance can also hold down capital investment and fixed costs.

- *Flexibility*: Uncertainty necessitates rapid responses to unpredicted events. Achieving such flexibility means keeping options open and delaying commitment to a specific technology until its potential becomes clear. Large, well-resourced companies have the luxury of pursuing multiple strategic options (Strategy Capsule 9.2).

## Competing for Standards

In the previous chapter, we noted that the establishment of standards is a key event in industry evolution. With the emergence of the digital, networked economy, more and more markets are affected by standards. For companies, the ability to influence or even own a standard is critical to establishing a competitive advantage. Indeed, ownership of an industry standard has the potential to offer returns that are unmatched by any other type of competitive advantage. Table 9.4 lists several companies which own key technical standards within a particular product category.

### STRATEGY CAPSULE 9.2

## Keeping Your Options Open: Microsoft in Operating Systems

♦ In 1988, as I wandered about the floor of Comdex, the computer industry's vast annual trade show, I could feel the anxiety among the participants. Since the birth of the IBM PC six years earlier, Microsoft's Disk Operating System (DOS) had been the de facto standard for PCs. But DOS was now starting to age. Everyone wanted to know what would replace it.

♦ Apple Computer, at the peak of its powers, had one of the largest booths showcasing the brilliantly graphical Macintosh operating system . . . Two different alliances of major companies, including AT&T, HP, and Sun Microsystems, offered graphical versions of Unix . . . And IBM was touting its new OS/2.

♦ Amid the uncertainty, there was something very curious about the Microsoft booth which resembled a Middle Eastern bazaar. In one corner, the company was previewing its highly criticized Windows system . . . In another, Microsoft touted its latest release of DOS. Elsewhere it was displaying OS/2, which it had developed with IBM. In addition, Microsoft was demonstrating new releases of Word and Excel that ran on Apple's Mac. Finally, in a distant corner, Microsoft displayed SCO Unix . . .

♦ "What am I supposed to make of this?" grumbled a corporate buyer standing next to me. Columnists wrote that Microsoft was adrift, that its chairman and COO, Bill Gates, had no strategy.

♦ Although the outcome of this story is now well known, to anyone standing on the Comdex floor in 1988 it wasn't obvious which operating system would win. In the face of this uncertainty, Microsoft followed the only robust strategy: betting on every horse.

**Source:** E. D. Beinhocker, "Robust Adaptive Strategies," *Sloan Management Review* (Spring 1999): 95–106. © 1999 from MIT Sloan Management Review/Massachusetts Institute of Technology. All rights reserved. Distributed by Tribune Media Services.

**TABLE 9.4** Examples of companies that own de facto industry standards

| Company | Product category | Standard |
| --- | --- | --- |
| Microsoft | PC operating systems | Windows |
| Intel | PC microprocessors | x86 series |
| Sony/Philips | Compact disks | CD-ROM format |
| ARM (Holdings) | Microprocessors for mobile devices | ARM architecture |
| Oracle Corporation | Programming language for web apps | Java |
| Rockwell and 3Com | 56K modems | V90 |
| Qualcomm | Digital cellular wireless communication | CDMA |
| Adobe Systems | Common file format for creating and viewing documents | Acrobat Portable Document Format |
| Adobe Systems | Web page animation | Adobe Flash |
| Adobe Systems | Page description language for document printing | Post Script |
| Bosch | Antilock braking systems | ABS and TCS (Traction Control System) |
| IMAX Corporation | Motion picture filming and projection system | IMAX |
| Apple | Music downloading system | iTunes/iPod |
| Sony | High definition DVD | Blu-ray |
| NTT DOCOMO | Mobile phone payment system in Japan | Osaifu-Keitai |

A characteristic of most of these companies is the fact that these standards have generated considerable profits and shareholder value.

## Types of Standard

A *standard* is a format, an interface, or a system that allows interoperability. Adhering to standards allows us to browse millions of different web pages, ensures the light bulbs made by any manufacturer will fit any manufacturer's lamps, and keeps the traffic moving in Los Angeles (most of the time). Standards can be *public* or *private*.

- Public (or *open*) standards are those that are available to all either free or for a nominal charge. Typically, they do not involve any privately owned intellectual property, or the intellectual-property owners make access free (such as Linux). Public standards are set by public bodies and industry associations. Thus, the GSM mobile phone standard was set by the European Telecom Standards Institute. Internet protocols (standards governing internet addressing and routing) are mostly public. They are governed by several international bodies, including the Internet Engineering Task Force.

- Private (*proprietary*) standards are those where the technologies and designs are owned by companies or individuals. If I own the technology that becomes a standard, I can embody the technology in a product that others buy (Microsoft Windows) or license the technology to others who wish to use it (Qualcomm's CDMA).

Standards can also be classified according to who sets them. *Mandatory standards* are set by government and have the force of law behind them. They include standards relating to automobile safety and construction specifications and to TV broadcasting. *De facto standards* emerge through voluntary adoption by producers and users. Table 9.4 gives examples.

A problem with *de facto* standards is that they may take a long time to emerge, resulting in a duplication of investments and delaying the development of the market. It was 40 years before a standard railroad gauge was agreed in the US.[17] One reason for the slow transition of wireless telecoms in the US from analog to digital technology was continuing competition between TDMA and CDMA standards. By contrast, Europe officially adopted GSM (a close relative of TDMA) in 1992.[18] Delayed emergence of a standard may kill the technology altogether. The failure of quadraphonic sound to displace stereophonic sound during the 1970s resulted from incompatible technical standards, which inhibited audio manufacturers, record companies, and consumers from investing in the technology.[19]

## Why Standards Appear: Network Externalities

Standards emerge in markets that are subject to **network externalities**. A network externality exists whenever the value of a product to an individual customer depends on the number of other users of that product. The classic example of network externality is the telephone. Since there is little satisfaction to be gained from talking to oneself on the telephone, the value of a telephone to each user depends on the number of other users connected to the same telephone system. This is different from most products. When I pour myself a glass of Glenlivet after a couple of exhausting MBA classes, my enjoyment is independent of how many other people in the world are also drinking Glenlivet. Indeed, some products may have *negative* network externalities—the value of the product is less if many other people purchase the same product. If I spend $3000 on an Armani silver lamé tuxedo and find that half my colleagues at the faculty Christmas party are wearing the same jacket, my satisfaction is lessened.

Network externalities do not require everyone to use the same product or even the same technology, but rather that the different products are *compatible* with one another through some form of common interface. In the case of wireless telephone service, it doesn't matter (as far as network access is concerned) whether I purchase service from AT&T, Nextel, or T-Mobile, because compatibility between each network allows connectivity. Similarly with railroads: if I am transporting coal from Wyoming to Boston, my choice of railroad company is not critical. Unlike in the 1870s, every railroad company now uses a standard gauge and is required to give "common carrier" access to other companies' rolling stock.

Network externalities arise from several sources:

- *Products where users are linked to a network*: Telephones, railroad systems, and email instant messaging groups are networks where users are linked together. Applications software, whether spreadsheet programs or video games, also links users—they can share files and play games interactively. User-level externalities may also arise through social identification. I watch *American Idol* and the Hollywood Oscar presentations on TV not because I enjoy them but so that I have something to talk to my colleagues about in the faculty common room.[20]

- *Availability of complementary products and services*: Where products are consumed as systems, the availability of complementary products and services depends on the number of customers for that system. Apple's key problem in the computer market is that, because the Macintosh accounts for only 9% of the installed base of personal computers, few leading software firms are writing Mac-based applications. I choose to drive a Ford Focus rather than a Ferrari Testarossa because I know that, should I break down 200 miles from Bismarck, North Dakota, spare parts and a repair service will be more readily available.

● *Economizing on switching costs*: By purchasing the product or system that is most widely used, there is less chance that I shall have to bear the costs of switching. By using Microsoft Office rather than Lotus SmartSuite, it is more likely that I will avoid the costs of retraining and file conversion when I become a visiting professor at another university.

The implication of network externalities is that they create *positive feedback*. Once a technology or system gains market leadership, it attracts a growing proportion of new buyers. Conversely, once market leadership is lost, a downward spiral is likely. This process is called *tipping*: once a certain threshold is reached, cumulative forces become unstoppable.[21] The result is a tendency toward a *winner-takes-all* market. Those markets subject to significant network externalities tend to be dominated by a single supplier (e.g., Microsoft in PC operating systems and office applications, eBay in internet auctions).

Once established, technical and design standards tend to be highly resilient. Standards are difficult to displace due to learning effects and collective lock-in. Learning effects cause the dominant technology and design to be continually improved and refined. Even where the existing standard is inherently inferior, switching to a superior technology may not occur because of collective lock in. The classic case is the QWERTY typewriter layout. Its 1873 design was based on the need to *slow* the speed of typing to prevent typewriter keys from jamming. Although the jamming problem was soon solved, the QWERTY layout has persisted, despite the patenting in 1932 of the more ergonomic Dvorak Simplified Keyboard (DSK).[22]

## Winning Standards Wars

In markets subject to network externalities, control over standards is the primary basis for competitive advantage. Sony and Apple are unusual in that they lost their standards wars (in VCRs and personal computers, respectively) but returned as winners in other markets. Most losers in standards wars—Lotus in spreadsheet software, Netscape in browsers, WordPerfect in word processing software—become mere footnotes in the history of technology. What can we learn from these and other standards wars about designing a winning strategy in markets subject to network externalities?

The first key issue is to determine whether we are competing in a market that will converge around a single technical standard. This requires a careful analysis of the presence and sources of network externalities.

The second strategic issue in standards setting is recognizing the role of positive feedback: the technology that can establish early leadership will rapidly gain momentum. Building a "bigger bandwagon" according to Shapiro and Varian[23] requires the following:

- *Before you go to war, assemble allies*: You'll need the support of consumers, suppliers of complements, even your competitors. Not even the strongest companies can afford to go it alone in a standards war.

- *Preempt the market*: Enter early, achieve fast-cycle product development, make early deals with key customers, and adopt penetration pricing.

- *Manage expectations*: The key to managing positive feedback is to convince customers, suppliers, and the producers of complementary goods that you will emerge as the victor. These expectations become a self-fulfilling prophecy. The massive pre-launch promotion and publicity built up by Sony prior to the American and European launch of PlayStation 2 in October 2000 was an effort to convince consumers, retailers, and game developers that the product would be the blockbuster consumer electronics product of the new decade, thereby stymieing Sega's and Nintendo's efforts to establish their rival systems.

The lesson that has emerged from the classic standards battles of the past is that in order to create initial leadership and maximize positive feedback effects a company must share the value created by the technology with other parties (customers, competitors, complementors, and suppliers). If a company attempts to appropriate too great a share of the value created, it may well fail to build a big enough bandwagon to gain market leadership (Strategy Capsule 9.3). Thus, recent standards battles involve broad alliances, where the owner enlists the support of complementors and would-be competitors. In the 2006–2008 struggle between Sony (Blu-ray) and Toshiba (HD-DVD), each camp recruited movie studios, software firms, and producers of computers and consumer electronics using various inducements, including direct cash payments. The defection of Warner Brothers to the Sony camp was critical to the market tipping suddenly in Sony's favor. However, it appears that all the financial gains from owning the winning DVD standard were dissipated by the costs of the war.[24]

Achieving compatibility with existing products is a critical issue in standards battles. Advantage typically goes to the competitor that adopts an *evolutionary strategy* (i.e., offers backward compatibility) rather than one that adopts a *revolutionary strategy*.[25] A key advantage of the Sony PlayStation 2 over Microsoft Xbox and Nintendo Cube was its compatibility with the PlayStation 1. However, the limited compatibility of PlayStation 3 with PlayStation 2 was one of the many problems that limited the success of PlayStation 3.

What are the key resources needed to win a standards war? Shapiro and Varian emphasize the following:

- control over an installed base of customers;
- owning intellectual property rights in the new technology;
- the ability to innovate in order to extend and adapt the initial technological advance;
- first-mover advantage;
- strength in complements (e.g., Intel has preserved its standard in microprocessors by promoting standards in buses, chipsets, graphics controllers, and interfaces between motherboards and CPUs);
- reputation and brand name.[26]

## STRATEGY CAPSULE 9.3

# Building a Bandwagon by Sharing Value: Lessons from VCRs and PCs

Profiting from standards requires, first, setting the standard and, second, retaining a proprietary interest in the standard in order to appropriate part of its value. There is a tradeoff between the two—the more value a company tries to appropriate, the greater the difficulty in building early support for its technology. Consider the standards wars in VCRs and PCs:

In VCRs, Matsushita's VHS format won against Sony's Betamax format not because of the technical superiority of VHS but because—in contrast to Sony's tight proprietary control of Betamax—Matsushita licensed its VHS system to Sharp, Philips, GE, RCA, and others, allowing it to gain market leadership.

In personal computers, IBM was highly successful in setting the standard, partly because it did not restrict access to its technology. Its product specifications were openly available to "clone makers," and its suppliers (including Microsoft and Intel) were free to supply them with microprocessors and the MS-DOS operating system. IBM was remarkably successful at setting the standard, but failed to appropriate much value

because it retained no significant proprietary interest in the standard—it was Intel and Microsoft that owned the key intellectual property. For Apple, the situation was the reverse. It kept tight control over its Macintosh operating system and product architecture, it earned high margins, but it forfeited the opportunity to set the industry standard.

The tradeoff between market acceptance of a technology and appropriating the returns to a technology is shown in Figure 9.5. Realizing the lessons of these two epic contests, the owners of technical standards have forfeited more and more value to complementors, competitors, and customers in order to establish market leadership. In the browser war of 1995–1998, both Netscape (Navigator) and Microsoft (Explorer) ended up giving away their products.

Companies are now seeking ways to reconcile market acceptance with value appropriation. Adobe gives away its Acrobat Reader to broaden the user base, but charges for the software needed to create PDF documents.

**FIGURE 9.5** Standard wars of the 1970s and 1980s: Video cassette recorders and personal computers

As companies become more familiar with the dynamics of standards competition, they are launching their strategic initiatives earlier, long before product release dates. As a result, standards wars are increasingly about the management of expectations. Companies are also more alert to the emergence of tipping points. As a result, standards wars are being resolved quicker: in high definition DVDs a mere 19 months elapsed between Toshiba's launch of its HD-DVD and its withdrawal from the market.

## Implementing Technology Strategies: Creating the Conditions for Innovation

As we have noted previously, strategy formulation cannot be separated from its implementation. Nowhere is this more evident than in technology-intensive businesses.

Our analysis so far has taught us about the potential for generating competitive advantage from innovation and about the design of technology-based strategies but has said little about the conditions under which innovation is achieved. Incisive strategic analysis of how to make money out of innovation is of little use if we cannot generate innovation in the first place. We know that innovation requires certain resources—people, facilities, information, and time—but, like other capabilities, there is no predetermined relationship between R & D input and innovation output.[27] The productivity of R & D depends critically on the organizational conditions that foster innovation. What are these conditions and how do we create them?

Let's begin with the critical distinction between invention and innovation. While these activities are complementary, they require different resources and different organizational conditions. While invention depends on creativity, innovation requires collaboration and cross-functional integration.

### Managing Creativity

*The Conditions for Creativity*   Invention is an act of creativity requiring knowledge and imagination. The creativity that drives invention is typically an individual act that establishes a meaningful relationship between concepts or objects that had not previously been related. This reconceptualization can be triggered by accidents: an apple falling on Isaac Newton's head or James Watt observing a kettle boiling. Creativity is associated with particular personality traits. Creative people tend to be curious, imaginative, adventurous, assertive, playful, self-confident, risk taking, reflective, and uninhibited.[28]

Individual creativity also depends on the organizational environment in which they work—this is as true for the researchers and engineers at Amgen and Google as it was for the painters and sculptors of the Florentine and Venetian schools. Few great works of art or outstanding inventions are the products of solitary geniuses. Creativity is stimulated by human interaction: the productivity of R & D laboratories depends critically on the communication networks that the engineers and scientists establish.[29] An important catalyst of interaction is *play*, which creates an environment of inquiry, liberates thought from conventional constraints, and provides the opportunity to establish new relationships by rearranging ideas and structures at a safe distance from reality. The essence of play is that it permits unconstrained forms of experimentation.[30] The potential for low-cost experimentation has expanded vastly thanks to advances in computer modeling and simulation that permit prototyping and market research to be undertaken speedily and virtually.[31]

*Organizing for Creativity*  Creativity requires management systems that are quite different from those that are appropriate for efficiency. In particular, creatively oriented people tend to be responsive to distinctive types of incentive. They desire to work in an egalitarian culture with enough space and resources to provide the opportunity to be spontaneous, experience freedom, and have fun in the performance of a task that, they feel, makes a difference to the strategic performance of the firm. Praise, recognition, and opportunities for education and professional growth are also more important than assuming managerial responsibilities.[32] Nurturing the drive to create may require a degree of freedom and flexibility that conflicts with conventional HR practices. At Google engineers have considerable discretion as to which project they join.

Organizational environments conducive to creativity tend to be both nurturing and competitive. Creativity requires a work context that is secure but not cozy. Dorothy Leonard points to the merits of *creative abrasion* within innovative teams—fostering innovation through the interaction of different personalities and perspectives. Managers must resist the temptation to clone in favor of embracing diversity of cognitive and behavioral characteristics within work groups—creating *whole brain teams*.[33] Exploiting diversity may require constructive conflict. Microsoft's development team meetings are renowned for open criticism and intense disagreement. Such conflict can spur progress toward better solutions.

Table 9.5 contrasts some characteristics of innovative organizations compared with those designed for operational efficiency.

## From Invention to Innovation: The Challenge of Integration

*Balancing Creativity and Commercial Direction*  For creativity to create value, both for the company and for society, it must be directed and harnessed. Balancing creative freedom with discipline and integration is a key issue to companies such as Apple and Google, which position themselves on the leading edge of innovation. The problem is especially acute in media companies: "The two cultures—of the ponytail and the suit—are a world apart, and combustible together."[34] Many creative companies have been formed by frustrated innovators leaving established companies. Disney's 2006 acquisition of Pixar was motivated by its desire to reinvigorate its animated movies. Yet Pixar's John Lasseter, who was appointed creative head of Disney's animation studio had been fired from Disney 20 years earlier for his advocacy of computer animation![35] Conversely, HBO's remarkable run of successful TV series between 1999 and 2007 (*The Sopranos, Sex in the City, The Wire, Six Feet*

**TABLE 9.5**  The characteristics of "operating" and "innovating" organizations

|  | Operating organization | Innovating organization |
|---|---|---|
| *Structure* | Bureaucratic<br>Specialization and division of labor<br>Hierarchical control<br>Defined organizational boundaries | Flat organization without hierarchical<br>  control<br>Task-oriented project teams<br>Fuzzy organizational boundaries |
| *Processes* | Emphasis on eliminating variation<br>  (e.g., six-sigma)<br>Top-down control<br>Tight financial controls | Emphasis on enhancing variation<br>Loose controls to foster idea<br>  generation<br>Flexible strategic planning and financial<br>  control |
| *Reward systems* | Financial compensation<br>Promotion up the hierarchy<br>Power and status symbols | Autonomy<br>Recognition<br>Equity participation in new ventures |
| *People* | Recruitment and selection based<br>  on the needs of the organization<br>  structure for specific skills: functional<br>  and staff specialists, general<br>  managers, and operatives | Key need is for idea generators who<br>  combine required technical knowl-<br>  edge with creative personality traits<br>Managers must act as sponsors and<br>  orchestrators. |

*Source:* Adapted from J. K. Galbraith and R. K. Kazanjian, *Strategy Implementation: Structure, Systems and Processes,* 2nd edn (St. Paul, MN: West, 1986).

*Under, Empire Boardwalk*—to mention just a few) reveals a remarkable ability to mesh creativity with commercial acuity.

Creative flair can lead to commercial success if it is focused upon *market need*. Few important inventions have been the result of spontaneous creation by technologists; almost all have resulted from grappling with practical problems. The invention of the Xerox copying process (xerography) by Chester Carlson, a patent attorney, was inspired by his frustration with the tedious task of making multiple copies of patent applications for submission to the US Patent Office. The old adage that "necessity is the mother of invention" explains why customers are such fertile sources of innovation—they are most acutely involved with matching existing products and services to their needs.[36] Involving customers in the innovation process is an initial stage in the move toward *open innovation* (which I will say more about below).

*Organizational Approaches to the Management of Innovation*  Reconciling creativity with commercial effectiveness is a major challenge for organizational design—as Table 9.5 shows, the organizational requirements of the two are very different. The organizational solution (as we explored in Chapter 6) comes from reconciling *differentiation* and *integration*. The creative and operational functions of the organization need different structures and systems. Yet, the key to successful innovation is in integrating creativity and technological expertise with capabilities in production, marketing, finance, distribution, and customer support. Achieving such integration is difficult. Tension between the operating and the innovating parts of organizations is inevitable. Innovation upsets established routines and threatens the status quo. The more stable the operating and administrative side of the organization, the greater the resistance to innovation. The opposition of the US naval establishment to continuous-aim firing, an innovation offering huge improvements in gunnery accuracy, illuminates this resistance to innovation.[37]

As innovation has become an increasing priority for established corporations, so chief executives have sought to emulate the flexibility, creativity, and entrepreneurial spirit of technology-based start-ups. Organizational initiatives aimed at stimulating new product development and the exploitation of new technologies include the following:

- *Cross-functional product development teams*: These have proven highly effective mechanisms for integrating creativity with functional effectiveness. Conventional approaches to new product development involved a sequential process that began in the corporate research lab then went "over the wall" to engineering, manufacturing, finance, and so on. Japanese companies pioneered autonomous product development teams staffed by specialists seconded from different departments with leadership from a "heavyweight" team manager who was able to protect the team from undue corporate influence.[38] Such teams have proven effective in deploying a broad range of specialist knowledge and, most importantly, integrating that knowledge flexibility and quickly, for example through rapid prototyping and concurrent engineering.[39]

- *Product champions*: These provide a means, first, for incorporating individual creativity within organizational processes and, second, for linking invention to subsequent commercialization. The key is to permit the individuals who are sources of creative ideas to lead the teams which develop those ideas—but also to allow this leadership to continue through into the commercialization phases. Companies that are consistently successful in innovation have the ability to design organizational processes that capture, direct, and exploit individuals' drive for achievement and success and their commitment to their innovations. The rationale for creating product champions is that these committed individuals can overcome resistance to change within the organization and generate the enthusiasm that attracts the involvement of others and forges cross-functional integration. Schön's study of 15 major innovations concludes that: "the new idea either finds a champion or dies."[40] A British study of 43 matched pairs of successful and unsuccessful innovations similarly concluded that a key factor distinguishing successful innovation was the presence of a "business innovator" to exert entrepreneurial leadership.[41] 3M Corporation has a long tradition of using product champions to develop new product ideas and grow them into new businesses (Strategy Capsule 9.4).

- *Buying innovation*: Recognition that small, technology-intensive start-ups have advantages in the early stages of the innovation process, while large corporations have superior capabilities, has encouraged large companies to enhance their technological performance by acquiring innovation from other firms. Such acquisition may involve licensing, outright purchase of patents, or acquiring the whole company. In biotechnology, pharmaceutical companies have pioneered this outsourcing of innovation. In addition to licensing drug patents, signing marketing agreements, and acquiring specialist biotech firms (these include Genentech by Roche in 2009, ICOS by Eli Lily in 2007, Chiron by Novartis in 2006, Scious by Johnson & Johnson in 2003), pharmaceutical companies have formed research alliances with biotech specialists.[42] In telecom equipment, Cisco Systems built its leading position in internet protocol switching technologies through acquiring small technology-intensive firms—55 of them between 1993 and 2000 alone.[43]

- **Open innovation**: The shift from vertically integrated systems of innovation, where companies develop their own technologies in-house and then exploit them internally, to more market-based systems, where companies buy in technology while also licensing out their own technologies, has given way to ideas of *open innovation*. As innovation increasingly requires the integration of multiple technologies often from traditionally separate scientific areas, so firms have been forced to look more widely in their sourcing technology and in sharing know-how. Evidence that external linkages promote innovation has reinforced firms' desire to seek technological knowledge from beyond their own borders.[44] Open innovation requires creating a network of collaborative relationships that comprises licensing deals, component outsourcing, joint research, collaborative product development, and informal problem solving and exchanges of ideas. Strategy Capsule 9.5 outlines Procter & Gamble's approach to open innovation.

- *Corporate incubators*: These are business developments established to fund and nurture new businesses based upon technologies that have been developed internally but have limited applications within a company's established businesses. Corporate incubators became very popular during the IT boom at the end of the 1990s, when companies saw the potential to generate substantial value from establishing then spinning off new tech-based ventures.[45] Despite a sound strategic and organizational logic, few major companies have achieved sustained success from the incubator units that they established and among the successful ones many have been sold to venture capital firms. A key problem, according to Hamel and Prahalad, is that: "Many corporate incubators became orphanages for unloved ideas that had no internal support or in-house sponsorship."[46] Despite their uneven track record, several leading companies have experienced considerable success in introducing company-wide processes for developing new businesses based upon internally generated innovations. Strategy Capsule 9.6 outlines the approaches of IBM and Cisco Systems.

## STRATEGY CAPSULE 9.4
# Innovation at 3M: The Role of the Product Champion

### START LITTLE AND BUILD

We don't look to the president or the vice-president for R & D to say, all right, on Monday morning 3M is going to get into such-and-such a business. Rather, we prefer to see someone in one of our laboratories, or marketing, or manufacturing units bring forward a new idea that he's been thinking about. Then, when he can convince people around him, including his supervisor, that he's got something interesting, we'll make him what we call a "project manager" with a small budget of money and talent, and let him run with it. Throughout all our 60 years of history here, that has been the mark of success. Did you develop a new business? The incentive? Money, of course. But that's not the key. The key . . . is becoming the general manager of a new business . . . having such a hot project that management just has to become involved whether it wants to or not. (Bob Adams, Vice-President for R & D, 3M Corporation)

### SCOTCHLITE

Someone asked the question, "Why didn't 3M make glass beads, because glass beads were going to find increasing use on the highways?" . . . I had done a little working in the mineral department on trying to color glass beads and had learned a little about their reflecting properties. And, as a little extra-curricular activity, I'd been trying to make luminous house numbers.

Well, this question and my free-time lab project combined to stimulate me to search out where glass beads were being used on the highway. We found a place where beads had been sprinkled on the highway and we saw that they did provide a more visible line at night . . . From there, it was only natural for us to conclude that, since we were a coating company, and probably knew more than anyone else about putting particles onto a web, we ought to be able to coat glass beads very accurately on a piece of paper.

So, that's what we did. The first reflective tape we made was simply a double-coated tape—glass beads sprinkled on one side and an adhesive on the other. We took some out here in St. Paul and, with the cooperation of the highway department, put some down. After the first frost came, and then a thaw, we found we didn't know as much about adhesives under all weather conditions as we thought . . .

We looked around inside the company for skills in related areas. We tapped knowledge that existed in our sandpaper business on how to make waterproof sandpaper. We drew on the expertise of our roofing people who knew something about exposure. We reached into our adhesive and tape division to see how we could make the tape stick to the highway better.

The resulting product became known as "Scotchlite." Its principal application was in reflective signs; only later did 3M develop the market for highway marking. The originator of the product, Harry Heltzer, interested the head of the New Products Division in the product, and he encouraged Heltzer to go out and sell it. Scotchlite was a success and Heltzer became the general manager of the division set up to produce and market it.

*Source:* "The Technical Strategy of 3M: Start More Little Businesses and More Little Businesses," *Innovation* 5 (1969).

STRATEGY CAPSULE 9.5
# Procter & Gamble's Open Innovation Initiative

In 2000, it became clear that P&G's internally focused approach to innovation and new product development was incapable of delivering the growth targets that the company had set itself. Despite a research staff numbering 7500, P&G estimated that for every one of its own research scientists there were probably 200 outside the company with the potential to contribute to P&G's development efforts. When CEO A. G. Laffey challenged the company to obtain 50% of its innovations from outside the company, the quest for a new innovation model began.

P&G's *Connect and Develop* innovation model seeks to "identify promising ideas throughout the world and apply our own R & D, manufacturing, marketing and purchasing capabilities to them to create better and cheaper products, faster."

The starting point is to identify what P&G is looking for. The approach was to avoid "blue sky" innovation and seek ideas that had already been successfully embodied in a product, a prototype or a technology. To focus the search each business was asked to identify its top ten customer needs. These included: "reduce wrinkles, improve skin texture and tone...softer paper products with higher wet strength." These needs were then translated into specific technical requirements: for example biotechnology solutions that permit detergents to perform well at low temperatures. Priorities are then reordered by identifying initiatives which fit with existing areas of brand strength ("adjacencies") and those which have permitted strengthening of P&G's strategically important areas of technology ("technology game boards").

P&G's innovation network comprises a number of organizations:

◆   Within P&G, 70 *technology entrepreneurs* are responsible for developing external contacts and exploring for innovation in particular localities and with a focus around particular product or technology areas.

◆   *Suppliers*. P&G has an IT platform that allows it to share technology briefs with its suppliers. This is complemented by regular meetings between senior P&G executives and senior executives at individual suppliers which explore mutual development opportunities.

◆   *Technology brokers*. P&G is a member (in some cases a founder member) of several prominent technology brokering networks. These include *NineSigma* which links companies with universities, private labs, government bodies, consultants and other potential solutions providers; *Innocentive*, which brokers solutions to science-based problems; *YourEncore*, a network of retired scientists and engineers; and Yet2.com, an online marketplace for intellectual capital.

These networks generate an enormous flow of suggestions and proposals that are initially screened and disseminated through P&G's *Eureka* online catalog. It is then up to executives within the business groups to identify interesting proposals, to pursue these with the external provider through P&G's External Business Development group, and to then move the initiative into their own product development process.

By 2005, 35% of P&G's new product launches had their origins outside the company. Some of P&G's most successful new products—including Swiffer cleaning cloths, Olay Regeneration, and Crest Spinbrush—had been initiated by outsiders.

**Source:** Reprinted by permission of Harvard Business Review. From "Connect and Develop: Inside Procter & Gamble's New Model for Innovation," L. Huston and N. Sakkab, March 2006, pp. 58–66, Copyright © 2006 by the Harvard Business School Publishing Corporation; all rights reserved.

## STRATEGY CAPSULE 9.6
# Incubating Innovation at IBM and Cisco Systems

IBM uses *Innovation Jam*—a massive online brainstorming process—to generate, select, and develop new business ideas. The 2006 Jam was based upon an initial identification of 25 technology clusters grouped into six broad categories. Web sites were built for each technology cluster and, for a 72-hour period, IBM employees, their families and friends, and suppliers and customers from all around the world were invited to contribute ideas for innovations based on these technologies. The 150,000 participants generated vast and diverse sets of suggestions that were subject to text mining software and review by 50 senior executives and technical specialists who worked in nine separate teams to identify promising ideas. The next phase of the Jam subjected the selected innovation ideas to comments and review by the online community. This was followed by a further review process in which the 10 best proposals were selected and a budget of $100 million was allocated to their development. The selected business ideas included a real-time foreign language translation service, smart healthcare payment systems, IT applications to environmental projects, and 3-D internet. The new businesses were begun as incubator projects and were then transferred to one

or other of IBM's business groups. As well as divisional links, the new ventures were also subject to monthly review by IBM's corporate top management.

Cisco Systems created its *Emerging Technology Business Group* with the goal of creating 20 new ventures by 2012. Within 18 months, 400 ideas for new businesses had been posted on the Cisco wiki and the Emerging Technology Business Group had begun developing several of these suggestions, including *TelePresence*, a video surveillance security system and an IP interoperability and collaboration systems server for emergency services. By 2008, *TelePresence* was established as a regular business group. Like IBM's *Innovation Jam* a key feature of Cisco's incubator model is its close linkage with the rest of the company: the Emerging Technology Group is part of Cisco's R & D organization and is subject to close involvement by Cisco's senior management, including CEO John Chambers.

**Sources:** O. M. Bjelland and R. C. Wood, "An Inside View of IBM's Innovation Jam," *MIT Sloan Management Review* (Fall 2008): 32–43; T. Sanders, "Cisco Reinvents the Corporate Incubator," (July 27, 2007): http://www.vnunet.com/vnunet/news/2194961/cisco-reinvents-corporate, accessed 6 July, 2009.

## Summary

In emerging and technology-based industries, nurturing and exploiting innovation is the fundamental source of competitive advantage and the focus of strategy formulation. Yet the basic tools of strategy analysis are the same as those that we have already encountered in this book. The fundamental strategic issues we are concerned with include the drivers of competition in these markets, the resources and capabilities through which a firm can establish competitive advantage, and the design of structures and systems to implement strategy.

Yet, the unpredictability and instability of these industries mean that strategic decisions in technology-driven industries have a very special character. The remarkable dynamics of these industries mean that difference between massive value creation and ignominious failure may be the result of small errors of timing or technological choices.

In technology-based industries, traditional approaches to strategy based upon forecasting and detailed planning are inadequate. The combination of speed and unpredictability of change means that effective strategies are those which combine clarity of vision with flexibility and responsiveness. The companies that have succeeded in emerging and technology-based industries are those that recognized most clearly the strategic characteristics of their industries and adapted most effectively to them. In industries that have been turned upside-down by technological change—whether telecommunications equipment, medical imaging, information storage, or sports equipment—it is companies that have understood the sources of competitive advantage and assembled the resources and capabilities needed to exploit them that have emerged as winners.

Our learning about how to compete in emerging and technology-based industries has included:

◆ understanding the innovation process, in particular the progression from knowledge creation to invention to innovation to diffusion, and some of the characteristics of these different stages;

◆ the determinants of the profitability of innovation, in particular the role of intellectual-property rights, the complexity and tacitness of the innovation, lead time, and complementary resources;

◆ the design of innovation strategies, including the choice between being an early mover or a follower; the relative merits of licensing, alliances, joint ventures, and internal development exploiting an innovation; and the management of risk;

◆ competing for standards requires recognizing the presence of network externalities and exploiting positive feedback mechanisms to gain market leadership; and the management of identifying the factors that determine the comparative advantages of being a leader or a follower in innovation.

Finally, we addressed strategy implementation in emerging and technology-based industries—creating the structure, management systems, and organizational climate conducive to innovation. Here we recognized some of the challenges of reconciling the conditions for creativity with those required for operational efficiency and commercial effectiveness.

Such dilemmas are central challenges for the managers of technology-intensive firms. A fundamental dilemma is that innovation is an unpredictable process requiring flexibility and market responsiveness, while strategy is about irreversible resource-allocation decisions involving long-term commitments. How can a company create the conditions for nurturing innovation while planning the course of its development? John Scully, a former CEO of Apple, observed: "Management and creativity might even be considered antithetical states. While management demands consensus, control, certainty, and the status quo, creativity thrives on the opposite: instinct, uncertainty, freedom, and iconoclasm."[47]

Fortunately, the experiences of companies such as Cisco Systems, 3M, Amgen, and IBM point to solutions to these dilemmas. The role of cross-functional development teams, product champions, and open innovation are examples of organizational initiatives that have assisted large, established firms in maintaining impressive records of innovation.

Quizzes and flashcards to test yourself further are available in your interactive e-book at
**www.wileyopenpage.com**

## Self-Study Questions

1. Trevor Baylis, a British inventor, submitted a patent application in November 1992 for a wind-up radio for use in Africa in areas where there was no electricity supply and people were too poor to afford batteries. He was excited by the prospects for radio broadcasts as a means of disseminating health education in areas of Africa devastated by AIDS. After appearances on British and South African TV, Baylis attracted a number of entrepreneurs and companies interested in manufacturing and marketing his clockwork radio. However, Baylis was concerned by the fact that his patent provided only limited protection for his invention: most of the main components—a clockwork generator and transistor radio—were long-established technologies. What advice would you offer Baylis as to how he can best protect and exploit his invention?

2. Table 9.1 shows that:
   a. patents have been more effective in protecting product innovations in drugs and medical equipment than in food or electronic components;
   b. patents are more effective in protecting product innovations than process innovations.
   Can you suggest reasons why?

3. Page 255 refers to James Dyson's difficulties in licensing his innovative vacuum cleaner (see http://www.cdf.org/issue_journal/dyson_fills_a_vacuum.html for further information). What lessons would you draw from Dyson's experience concerning the use of licensing by small firms to exploit innovation?

4. From the evidence presented in Table 9.3, what conclusions can you draw regarding the factors that determine whether leaders or followers win out in the markets for new products?

5. In the battle for dominance of the e-book reader market, Amazon with Kindle 2 was ahead of Sony with its Reader Digital Book. Kindle 2 had the biggest number of recent titles available, but thanks to a deal with Google, Sony had a huge number of out-of-copyright titles. What are the sources of network externalities in this market? Will e-book readers become a winner-takes-all market? Why has Amazon been able to gain a lead over Sony (and Samsung)? What can Sony do to fight back?

## Notes

1. "The Logic that Dares Not Speak Its Name," *Economist* (April 16, 1994): 89–91.

2. In the US, the return on R & D spending was estimated at between 3.7% and 5.5%. See M. Warusawitharana, "Research and Development, Profits and Firm Value: A

Structural Estimation," Discussion Paper (Washington, DC: Federal Reserve Board, September, 2008).

3. The excess of the benefit received by the consumer over the price they paid is called *consumer surplus*. See: D. Besanko, D. Dranove, and M. Shanley, *Economics*

*of Strategy* (New York: John Wiley & Sons, Inc., 1996): 442–3.

4. "Knowledge Monopolies: Patent Wars," *Economist* (April 8, 2000): 95–9; "Amazon Loses 1-Click Patent," *Forbes* (July 7, 2011).

5. F. T. Rothermael, "Incumbent Advantage through Exploiting Complementary Assets via Interfirm Cooperation," *Strategic Management Journal* 22 (2001): 687–99.

6. R. C. Levin, A. K. Klevorick, R. R. Nelson, and S. G. Winter, "Appropriating the Returns from Industrial Research and Development," *Brookings Papers on Economic Activity* 18, no. 3 (1987): 783–832.

7. P. Grindley and D. J. Teece, "Managing Intellectual Capital: Licensing and Cross-Licensing in Semiconductors and Electronics," *California Management Review* 39 (Winter 1997): 8–41.

8. R. Adner, "Match your Innovation Strategy to your Innovation Ecosystem," *Harvard Business Review* (April 2006): 17–37.

9. S. Shulman, *The Telephone Gambit* (New York: Norton, 2008).

10. "The Human Genome Race," *Scientific American* (April 24, 2000).

11. C. Markides and P. A. Geroski, *Fast Second* (San Francisco: Jossey-Bass, 2005).

12. D. Sull, "Strategy as Active Waiting," *Harvard Business Review* (September 2005): 120–129.

13. For example, data on penetration rates for electric toothbrushes and CD players were used to forecast the market demand for HDTVs in the United States (B. L. Bayus, "High-Definition Television: Assessing Demand Forecasts for the Next Generation Consumer Durable," *Management Science* 39 (1993): 1319–333).

14. See B. C. Twiss, *Managing Technological Innovation*, 2nd edn (New York: Longman, 1980).

15. E. Von Hippel, "Lead Users: A Source of Novel Product Concepts," *Management Science* 32 (July, 1986).

16. In electronic instruments, customers' ideas initiated most of the successful new products introduced by manufacturers. See E. Von Hippel, "Users as Innovators," *Technology Review* 5 (1976): 212–239.

17. A. Friedlander, *The Growth of Railroads* (Arlington, VA: CNRI, 1995).

18. C. Shapiro and H. R. Varian, *Information Rules: A Strategic Guide to the Network Economy* (Boston: Harvard Business School Press, 1999): 264–7.

19. S. Postrel, "Competing Networks and Proprietary Standards: The Case of Quadraphonic Sound," *Journal of Industrial Economics* 24 (December 1990): 169–86.

20. S. J. Liebowitz and S. E. Margolis ("Network Externality: An Uncommon Tragedy," *Journal of Economic Perspectives* 8 (Spring 1994): 133–50) refer to these user-to-user externalities as *direct externalities*.

21. M. Gladwell, *The Tipping Point* (Boston: Little, Brown and Company, 2000).

22. P. David, "Clio and the Economics of QWERTY," *American Economic Review* 75 (May 1985): 332–7; S. J. Gould, "The Panda's Thumb of Technology," *Natural History* 96, no. 1 (1986): 14–23. For an alternative view

see S. J. Liebowitz and S. Margolis, "The Fable of the Keys," *Journal of Law and Economics* 33 (1990): 1–26.

23. C. Shapiro and H. R. Varian, "The Art of Standards Wars," *California Management Review* 41 (Winter 1999): 8–32.

24. R. M. Grant "The DVD War of 2006–8: Blu-Ray vs. HD-DVD," *Cases to Accompany Contemporary Strategy Analysis*, 7th edn (Chichester: John Wiley & Sons, Ltd, 2010).

25. C. Shapiro and H. R. Varian, "The Art of Standards Wars," *California Management Review* 41 (Winter 1999): 15–16.

26. C. Shapiro and H. R. Varian, "The Art of Standards Wars," *California Management Review* 41 (Winter 1999): 16–18.

27. S. Ahn, "Firm Dynamics and Productivity Growth: A Review of Micro Evidence from OECD Countries," Economics Department Working Paper 297 (OECD, 2001).

28. J. M. George, "Creativity in Organizations," *Academy of Management Annals* 1 (2007): 439–77.

29. M. L. Tushman, "Managing Communication Networks in R & D Laboratories," *Sloan Management Review* 20 (Winter 1979): 37–49.

30. D. Dougherty and C. H. Takacs, "Team Play: Heedful Interrelating as the Boundary for Innovation," *Long Range Planning* 37 (December 2004): 569–90.

31. S. Thomke, "Enlightened Experimentation: The New Imperative for Innovation," *Harvard Business Review* (February 2001): 66–75. L. Grundy, J. Kickel, and C. Prather, "Building the Creative Organization," *Organizational Dynamics* (Spring 1994): 22–37.

32. R. Florida and J. Goodnight, "Managing for Creativity," *Harvard Business Review* (July/August 2005): 124–31.

33. D. Leonard and S. Straus, "Putting Your Company's Whole Brain to Work," *Harvard Business Review* (July/August 1997): 111–21; D. Leonard and P. Swap, *When Sparks Fly: Igniting Creativity in Groups* (Boston: Harvard Business School Press, 1999).

34. "How to Manage a Dream Factory," *Economist* (January 16, 2003).

35. "Lunch with the FT: John Lasseter," *Financial Times* (January 17, 2009).

36. E. Von Hippel (*The Sources of Innovation*, New York: Oxford University Press, 1988) provides strong evidence of the dominant role of users in the innovation process.

37. E. Morrison, "Gunfire at Sea: A Case Study of Innovation," in M. Tushman and W. L. Moore (eds), *Readings in the Management of Innovation* (Cambridge, MA: Ballinger, 1988): 165–78.

38. K. Clark and T. Fujimoto, *Product Development Performance: Strategy, Organization, and Management in the World Auto Industry* (Boston: Harvard Business School Press, 1991).

39. K. Imai, I. Nonaka, and H. Takeuchi, "Managing the New Product Development Process: How Japanese Companies Learn and Unlearn," in K. Clark, R. Hayes, and C. Lorenz (eds), *The Uneasy Alliance* (Boston: Harvard Business School Press, 1985).

40. D. A. Schön, "Champions for Radical New Inventions," *Harvard Business Review* (March/April, 1963): 84.

41. R. Rothwell, C. Freeman, A. Horlsey, V. T. Jervis, A. B. Robertson, and J. Townsend, "SAPPHO Updated: Project SAPPHO Phase II," *Research Policy* 3 (1974): 258–91.

42. G. P. Pisano, *Science Business: The Promise, the Reality, and the Future of Biotech* (Boston: Harvard Business School Press, 2006).

43. "Cisco's Chambers: The Route Ahead," ICFASI Case Study No. 306-172-1 (Chennai, 2006).

44. A. Arora, A. Fosfur, and A. Gambardella, *Markets for Technology* (Cambridge, MA: MIT Press, 2001); S. Breschi and F. Malerba, *Clusters, Networks and Innovation* (Oxford: Oxford University Press, 2005).

45. M. T. Hansen, H. W. Chesborough, N. Nohria and D. N. Sull, "Networked Incubators: Hothouse of the New Economy," *Harvard Business Review* (September/October 2000): 74–88; "How to Make the Most of a Brilliant Idea," *Financial Times* (December 6, 2000): 21.

46. G. Hamel and C. K. Prahalad, "Nurturing Creativity: Putting Passions to Work," *Shell World* (Royal Dutch Shell, September 14, 2007): 1–12.

47. J. Scully, *Odyssey* (Toronto: Fitzhenry and Whiteside, 1987): 18.

# 10 Competitive Advantage in Mature Industries

We are a true "penny profit" business. That means that it takes hard work and attention to detail to be financially successful—it is far from being a sure thing. Our store managers must do two things well: control costs and increase sales. Cost control cannot be done by compromising product quality, customer service, or restaurant cleanliness, but rather by consistent monitoring of the "vital signs" of the business through observation, reports, and analysis. Portion control is a critical part of our business. For example, each Filet-O-Fish sandwich receives 1 fluid ounce of tartar sauce and 0.5 ounces of cheese. Our raw materials are fabricated to exacting tolerances, and our managers check them on an ongoing basis. Our written specification for lettuce is over two typewritten pages long. Our French fries must meet standards for potato type, solid and moisture content, and distribution of strand lengths.

—EDWARD H. RENSI, PRESIDENT AND CHIEF OPERATING OFFICER, MCDONALD'S USA[1]

## OUTLINE

## Introduction and Objectives

Despite the infatuation of both the media and the stock market with technology-based companies such as Google, Facebook, and Twitter, the fact remains that companies where most of us earn our living and spend most of our income are comparatively mature. The leading members of the Fortune Global 500 all belong to industries that have been with us for over a hundred years: petroleum, retailing, automobiles, financial services.

Despite their heterogeneity—they range from beauty parlors to steel production—mature industries present several similarities from a strategic perspective. The purpose of this chapter is to explore these characteristics of mature industries, identify strategies through which competitive advantage can be established within them, and recognize the implications of these strategies for structure, systems, and leadership style. As we shall see, maturity does not imply lack of opportunity. Companies such as H&M (fashion clothing), AirAsia (airlines), Starbucks (coffee shops), and Nucor (steel) have successfully deployed novel strategies in mature sectors. Mature sectors are typically inhabited by mature companies—Coca-Cola, ExxonMobil, and HSBC Holdings were founded in the 19th century, yet, over the past two decades, have achieved combinations of profitability and growth that would make most high-tech companies envious. Nor does maturity mean lack of innovation: as we shall see, many mature industries have been transformed by new technologies and new strategies.

By the time you have completed this chapter, you will be able to:

◆ recognize the principal strategic characteristics of mature industries;

◆ identify key success factors within mature industries and formulate strategies directed toward their exploitation;

◆ design organizational structures and management systems that can effectively implement such strategies;

◆ recognize the characteristics of declining industries, the opportunities for profit they may offer, and the strategy options available to firms.

## Competitive Advantage in Mature Industries

Our analysis of the industry life cycle (Chapter 8) suggests that maturity has two principal implications for competitive advantage: first, it tends to reduce the number of opportunities for establishing competitive advantage; second, it shifts these opportunities from differentiation-based factors to cost-based factors.

Diminishing opportunities for sustainable competitive advantage in mature industries stem from:

● Less scope for differentiation advantage resulting from better informed buyers, product standardization, and lack of technological change.

- Diffusion of process technology means that cost advantages are difficult to obtain and sustain. Once a cost advantage is established, it is vulnerable to exchange rate movements and the emergence of low-cost overseas competitors.

- A highly developed industry infrastructure together with the presence of powerful distributors makes it easier for new entrants to attack established firms.

Warren Buffett, The Sage of Omaha, uses different words to convey a similar idea. He categorizes businesses into "franchises" and "businesses" and views the process of maturity as one of value destruction in which franchises degenerate into businesses:

> An economic franchise arises from a product or service that (1) is needed or desired; (2) is thought by customers to have no close substitute; and (3) is not subject to price regulation. Franchises earn high rates of return on capital . . . [and] can tolerate mismanagement . . . In contrast, "a business" earns exceptional profits only if it is a low-cost operator or if supply of its product or service is tight. And a business, unlike a franchise, can be killed by poor management.[2]

This trend toward deteriorating industry attractiveness is a constant threat in mature industries. The propensity toward overinvestment in capacity, internationalization, and commoditization exacerbates price competition and makes competitive advantage difficult to attain and even harder to sustain.

## Cost Advantage

To the extent that differentiation advantages erode in many mature industries, cost emerges as the key success factor. What are the primary sources of low cost? Three cost drivers tend to be especially important:

- *Economies of scale*: In capital-intensive industries, or where advertising, distribution, or new product development is an important element of total cost, economies of scale are important sources of interfirm cost differences. The increased standardization that accompanies maturity greatly assists the exploitation of such scale economies. In automobiles, as with many other manufacturing industries, industry evolution has been driven by the quest for scale economies. The significance of scale economies in mature industries is indicated by the fact that the association between return on investment and market share is stronger in mature industries than in emerging industries.[3]

- *Low-cost inputs*: The quest for low-cost inputs explains the migration of maturing industries from the advanced to the newly industrializing countries of the world. But accessing low-cost inputs does not necessarily mean establishing operations in India or Vietnam. Established firms can become locked into high salaries and benefits, inefficient working practices, and bloated overheads inherited from more prosperous times. New entrants into mature industries may gain cost advantages by acquiring plant and equipment at bargain-basement levels and by cutting labor costs. Valero Energy Corporation is the largest oil refiner in the US: it acquired loss-making refineries from the majors at below-book prices then operated them with rigorous cost efficiency. Convenience stores throughout North America and Western Europe are increasingly owned and operated by Asian immigrants. These businesses are typically operated by family members who are willing to work long hours without the usual employee fringe benefits and overtime pay.

- *Low overheads*: Some of the most profitable companies in mature industries are those able to slash overhead costs. In discount retailing, Wal-Mart is famous for its parsimonious approach to costs. Among the oil majors, Exxon is known for its rigorous control of overhead costs. Exxon's headquarters cost (relative to net worth) was estimated at less than one-quarter that of Mobil's.[4] When Exxon merged with Mobil, it was able to extract huge cost savings from Mobil. In newspaper and magazine publishing, newcomers such as EMAP in the UK and Media News Group in the US (run by "Lean" Dean Singleton) have deployed a strategy of acquiring titles then pruning overheads.

As cost inefficiencies tend to become institutionalized within mature enterprises, cost reduction may require drastic interventions. **Corporate restructuring**—intensive periods of structural and strategic change—typically involves cost reduction through outsourcing, headcount reduction, and downsizing, especially at corporate headquarters.[5] Successful turnaround strategies typically involve aggressive cost cutting. Empirical research among mature US businesses has identified three successful approaches:

- *Asset and cost surgery*: Aggressive cost reduction through reduction of excess capacity; halting of new investment in plant and equipment; and cutbacks in R & D, marketing expenditures, receivables, and inventories.
- *Selective product and market pruning*: Refocusing on segments that were most profitable or where the firm possessed distinctive strength.
- *Piecemeal productivity moves*: Adjustments to current market position rather than comprehensive refocusing or reorganizing, including reductions in marketing and R & D expenditures, higher capacity utilization, and increased employee productivity.[6]

## Segment and Customer Selection

Sluggish demand growth, lack of product differentiation, and international competition tend to depress the profitability of mature industries. Yet, even unattractive industries may offer attractive niche markets with strong growth of demand, few competitors, and abundant potential for differentiation. As a result, segment selection can be a key determinant of differences in the performance of companies within the same industry. Wal-Mart's profitability was boosted by locating its stores in small and medium-sized towns where it faced little competition. In the auto industry, there is a constant quest to escape competition by creating new market segments with "crossover" vehicles that span existing segments. Opportunities for establishing new segments can arise from the strategies of market leaders. The more that incumbents focus on the mass market, the more likely it is that new entrants can carve out new market niches by supplying underserved customer needs—what Chapter 8 refers to as "resource partitioning."[7]

The logic of segment focus implies further disaggregation of markets—down to the level of the individual customer. Information technology permits new approaches to **customer relationship management** (CRM), making it possible to analyze individual characteristics and preferences, identify individual customers' profit contribution to the firm, and organize marketing around individualized, integrated approaches to customers. In the same way that Las Vegas casinos have long recognized that the major part of their profits derives from a tiny minority of customers—the "high rollers"—so banks, supermarkets, credit card companies, and hotels increasingly use transaction data to identify their most attractive customers, and those that are a drag on profitability.

The next stage in this process is to go beyond customer selection to actively target more attractive customers and transform less valuable customers into more valuable customers. For example, credit card issuer Capital One uses data warehousing, experimentation, simulation, and sophisticated statistical modeling to adjust the terms and features of its credit card offers to the preferences and characteristics of individual customers. Capital One estimates the lifetime profitability of each customer and analyzes the four key events in the credit card life cycle: acquiring the customer, stimulating the customer's card use, retaining the customer, and managing default.[8]

## The Quest for Differentiation

Cost leadership, as we noted in Chapter 7, is difficult to sustain, particularly in the face of international competition. Hence, differentiating to attain some insulation from the rigors of price competition is particularly attractive in mature industries. The problem is that the trend toward commoditization narrows the scope for differentiation and reduces customer willingness to pay a premium for differentiation:

- In tires and domestic appliances, companies' investments in differentiation through product innovation, quality, and brand reputation have generated disappointing returns. Vigorous competition, price-sensitive customers, and strong, aggressive retailers have limited the price premium that differentiation will support.
- Attempts by airlines to gain competitive advantage through offering more legroom, providing superior in-flight entertainment, and achieving superior punctuality have met little market response from consumers. The only effective differentiators appear to be frequent-flier programs and services offered to first- and business-class travelers.

Standardization of the physical attributes of a product and convergence of consumer preferences constrains, but does not eliminate, opportunities for meaningful and profitable differentiation. Product standardization is frequently accompanied by increased differentiation of complementary services—financing terms, leasing arrangements, warranties, after-sales services and the like. In consumer goods, maturity often means a shift from physical differentiation to image differentiation. Entrenched consumer loyalties to specific brands of cola or cigarettes are a tribute to the capacity of brand promotion over long periods to create distinct images among near-identical products.

The intensely competitive retail sector produces particularly interesting examples of differentiation strategies. The dismal profitability earned by many retail chains (Toys "R" Us, Foot Locker, Rite Aid, and J.C. Penny in the US; Carrefour, Metro, and Royal Ahold in Europe) contrasts sharply with the sales growth and profitability of stores that have established clear differentiation through variety, style, and ambiance (Target, TJX, Limited Brands, and Costco in the US; Inditex from Spain; H&M and IKEA from Sweden). A further lesson from highly competitive mature sectors such as retailing is that competitive advantage is difficult to sustain. Most of the outstandingly successful retailers of the previous decade—Best Buy, Body Shop, and Marks & Spencer—have slipped into mediocrity.

## Innovation

We have characterized mature industries as industries where the pace of technical change is low. In many mature industries—steel, textiles, food processing, insurance, and hotels—R & D expenditure is below 1% of sales revenue, while in US manufacturing as a whole just three sectors—computers and electronics, pharmaceuticals, and aerospace—account for 65% of R & D spending.[9] Nevertheless, measured by patenting activity, there is evidence that some mature industries are as innovative as emerging industries.[10] Even in mature low-tech products such as tires, brassieres, and fishing rods, continuing inventiveness is indicated by a steady flow of new patents (Strategy Capsule 10.1).

Despite an increased pace of technological change in many mature industries, the most opportunities for establishing competitive advantage are likely to arise from *strategic innovation*—including *new game strategies* and *blue-ocean strategies* that we discussed in Chapter 7. Indeed, as identified in Chapter 8, it may be that strategic innovation constitutes a third phase of innovation that becomes prominent once product and process innovation slacken. In addition to the *value chain reconfiguration* approach discussed in Chapter 7,[11] firms can seek strategic innovation by redefining markets and market segments. This may involve:

- *Embracing new customer groups*: Harley-Davidson has created a market for expensive motorcycles among the middle-aged, while in the maturing market for video game consoles Nintendo achieved remarkable success with its Wii by appealing to consumers outside the core market of young males. The most rapidly growing churches—for example Jehovah's Witnesses in Russia and Amway Christian Fellowship in America—tend to be those that recruit among non-church-going social and demographic groups.

- *Augmenting, bundling, and theming*: Some of the most successful approaches to differentiation in mature industries involve bundling additional products or services with the core offering. In book retailing, Barnes & Noble offers not only a wide range of titles but also Starbucks coffee shops within its stores. Neighborhood bookstores that have survived competition from the megastores and Amazon.com are often those that have added poetry readings, live music, and other recreational services. This augmenting and bundling of the product offering may extend to involve the customer

## STRATEGY CAPSULE 10.1
# Innovation in Mature Industries: Brassiere Technology

The first patent for a "breast-supporting device" was issued in the US in 1864. However, the first patent relating to an undergarment named "brassiere" was issued to Mary Phelps Jacob in 1913. By 1940, over 550 US patents for brassieres and related breast supporters had been issued.

The technological quest for a better bra continued into the 21st century—between January 2000 and March 2012, the US Patent Office issued 727 patents relating to brassieres. Design innovations include:

◆ Wonderbra (owned by Sara Lee) introduced a "variable cleavage" bra equipped with a system of pulleys;

◆ the Airotic bra designed by Gossard (also owned by Sara Lee) features "twin air bags as standard"—these are inflatable by a "unique G-pump system";

◆ Charnos's Bioform bra replaces underwiring with soft molded polypropylene around a rigid ring—a design inspired by the Frisbee and engineered by Ove Arup, who also engineered London's Millennium Bridge (which had to be closed because of excessive wobbling);

◆ A team at University of Wollongong's Intelligent Polymer Research Institute is developing the world's first "smart-bra"—a sports bra that will adjust for breast movement during exercise.

*Source:* "Bra Wars," *Economist* (December 2, 2000): 112; USTPO Patent Database; "The Physics of Bras," *Discover Magazine* (November 2005).

---

in an entire experience. Theming by retail stores (such as Disney Stores and American Girl) and restaurants (such as Hard Rock Café and Planet Hollywood) reflects the desire to involve customers in an experience that goes beyond the products being sold.[12]

● *Customer solutions*: Another approach to differentiation through bundling products and services is to offer *customer solutions*—an integrated bundle of products and support services that are offered as a customized package. For example, Alstom's rail transport division has transitioned from "being a supplier of goods to a system and service provider": rather than supplying locomotives, rolling stock, and signaling systems as standalone items, it offers "complete transport solutions for train availability during the life cycle of the product."[13] However, as a senior manager from the Italian engineering firm, Bonfiglioli, explained to me (interview, June 2008): "Supplying customer solutions is an appealing strategy, but execution is far from easy. Once we had sales representatives who visited customers carrying a product directory. Now the sales representative has to visit the customer with a team comprising product and maintenance engineers and a financial analyst."

● *Liberation from the maturity mindset*: The ability to create competitive advantage requires managers to free themselves from the cognitive limits associated with notions of maturity. Baden-Fuller and Stopford argue that maturity is a state of mind, not a state of the business—every enterprise has the potential for rejuvenation. The key to strategic innovation is for managers to prevent industry conventions from imprisoning their companies into conventional thinking about strategy. This means cultivating an entrepreneurial organization where middle managers are encouraged to experiment and learn.[14]

Costas Markides identifies several firms that have successfully broken away from conventional wisdom to establish a unique positioning within mature industries:

- Edward Jones, with 2000 offices, mostly in the US but also in Canada and the UK, has rejected the conventional wisdom that successful brokerage firms require scale economies, product diversification, e-commerce, and integration with investment banks. Each Edward Jones' office has just one investment adviser who is motivated to grow local business through face-to-face relationships; there are no proprietary investment products and no online investing.
- Enterprise Rent-A-Car has adopted a location strategy that is quite different from its major competitors, Hertz and Avis. Rather than concentrate on serving the business traveler through locating at airports and downtown, Enterprise concentrates on suburban locations, where it caters primarily to the consumer market.[15]

How do companies break away from the pack and achieve strategic innovation? The problem is that breaking with industry conventions requires confronting industry-wide systems of belief—what J.-C. Spender refers to as *industry recipes*."[16] This is likely to require that managers find ways of altering their *cognitive maps*—the mental frameworks through which they perceive and understand their industry environments.[17] This may explain why strategic innovation in mature industries is so often associated with firms that are either outsiders or peripheral players.

According to Gary Hamel, the role of strategy should be to foster revolution through reorganizing the strategy-making process. This means breaking top management's monopoly over strategy formulation, bringing in younger people from further down the organization, and gaining involvement from those on the periphery of the organization.[18] Ultimately, strategic innovation is likely to require a process of organization-wide change—a "journey of strategic renewal."[19]

## Strategy Implementation in Mature Industries: Structure, Systems, and Style

Across most mature industries, the primary basis for competitive advantage is operational efficiency; however, as we have seen, cost efficiency must be reconciled with innovation and customer responsiveness. What kinds of organizational structures, management systems, and leadership styles do mature businesses need to adopt in order to achieve these multiple performance goals?

## Efficiency through Bureaucracy

As we observed in Chapter 6, the conventional prescription for stable environments was *mechanistic* organizations characterized by centralization, precisely defined roles, and predominantly vertical communication.[20] Henry Mintzberg describes this formalized type of organization dedicated to the pursuit of efficiency as the *machine bureaucracy*.[21] Efficiency is achieved through standardized routines, division of labor, and close management control based on bureaucratic principles. Division of labor extends to management as well as operatives—high levels of vertical and horizontal specialization are typical among managers. Vertical specialization is evident in the concentration of strategy formulation at the apex of the hierarchy, while middle and junior management supervise and administer through the application of standardized rules and procedures. Horizontal specialization takes the form of functional structures.

The machine bureaucracy as described by Mintzberg is a caricature of actual organizations—probably the closest approximations are found in government departments performing highly routine administrative duties (e.g., the Internal Revenue Service or departments of motor vehicle licensing). However, in most mature industries, the features of mechanistic organizations are evident in highly routinized operations controlled by detailed rules and procedures. McDonald's is far from being a typical bureaucracy—in particular, the majority of outlets are franchises operated by independent companies—however, the cost efficiency and consistency that characterizes its performance is achieved through highly standardized and detailed operating procedures that govern virtually every aspect of how it does business (see the quotation that introduces this chapter). Similarly, in Marriott Hotels, HSBC, Toyota Motor Company, and Wal-Mart the ability of these huge organizations to achieve efficiency and consistent high quality is the result of management systems that draw heavily upon the principles of bureaucracy. The key features of these mature organizations are summarized in Table 10.1.

## Trends in Strategy Implementation among Mature Businesses

When competitive advantage in mature industries was all about cost advantage through scale and division of labor, management practices based upon standardized processes, elaborately defined rules, hierarchical control, quantitative performance targets, and incentives closely linked to individual performance work well. However, as we have discussed, the requirements for success in mature industries and the strategies needed to achieve success given these requirements have become much more complex. In terms of cost efficiency, scale advantages have become less important than the flexibility to exploit low-cost inputs and to outsource to low-cost specialists, and creating an organizational environment that constantly strives to eliminate waste and discover new sources of efficiency.

The efficiency leaders in mature industries are not necessarily the biggest firms that are able to exploit scale benefits to the maximum: they are more likely to be companies that have dedicated themselves to efficiency through implementing performance-oriented management systems. Top-performing companies in mature businesses—UPS in delivery services, Wal-Mart in discount retailing, Nucor in steel, ExxonMobil in petroleum—are characterized by management systems that comprise integrated systems where performance goals are the centerpiece of strategy and

**TABLE 10.1** Strategy implementation in mature industries: The conventional model

| | |
|---|---|
| STRATEGY | The primary goal is cost advantage through economies of scale and capital-intensive production of standardized products/services |
| | Strategy formulation primarily the realm of top managers |
| | Middle managers responsible for strategy implementation |
| STRUCTURE | Functional departments (e.g., production, marketing, customer service, distribution) |
| | Distinction between line and staff |
| | Clearly defined job roles with strong vertical reporting/delegation relationships |
| CONTROLS | Performance targets are primarily quantitative and short term and are specified for all members of the organization |
| | Performance is closely monitored by well-established, centralized management information systems and formalized reporting requirements |
| | Financial controls through budgets and profit targets particularly important |
| INCENTIVES | Incentives are based on achievement of individual targets and take the form of financial rewards and promotion up the hierarchy |
| | Penalties exist for failure to attain quantitative targets, for failure to adhere to the rules, and for lack of conformity to company norms |
| COMMUNICATION | Primarily vertical for the purposes of delegation and reporting |
| | Lateral communication limited, often achieved through interdepartmental committees |
| LEADERSHIP | Primary functions of top management: control and strategic direction |
| | Typical CEO profiles include the *administrator*, who guides the organization through establishing and operating organizational systems and principles and building consensus (e.g., Alfred Sloan Jr. of General Motors); the *autocrat*, who uses top-down decision making and leads through centralization of power and force of personality (Lee Iacocca of Chrysler and Steve Jobs at Apple); and the *strategic leader*, who combines clear strategic direction with considerable decentralization of decision making (Sam Palmisano at IBM, Carlos Ghosn at Renault-Nissan, Jeff Immelt at GE). |

these goals are implemented through financial controls, HR policies, and operating practices which are closely integrated with these goals.

Unifying an organization around the pursuit of efficiency requires management systems that allow disaggregation of company-wide goals into specific performance targets for departments and individuals—the *balanced scorecard* is one of the most widely used techniques for achieving this (see Chapter 2). Most important, however, is embedding performance goals within the company's organizational culture:

- Central to UPS's performance-driven management style is a corporate culture that simultaneously embraces high levels of employee autonomy and the company's "obsessive-compulsive personality."[22]

- Wal-Mart's culture of frugality reflects the values of founder Sam Walton. According to Wal-Mart executive Ron Loveless: "Sam valued every penny. People say that Wal-Mart is making $10 billion a year, or whatever. But that's not how people within the company think of it. If you spent a dollar, the question was: 'How many dollars of merchandise would you need to sell to make that dollar?'"[23]

- Ryanair has mastered the art of managing for cost efficiency. From a simple strategic goal of being Europe's lowest-cost airline, Ryanair's route structure, choice of airports, fleet, ticketing system, and HR practices are meticulously aligned to cost minimization. Ryanair's obsession with cost cutting is reflected in the large proportion of employees that are on temporary contracts, the requirement that crews pay for their own uniforms and training, and a heavy emphasis on incentive pay (cabin crew receive a commission on inflight sales).[24]

Reconciling differentiation and innovation with a relentless drive for cost efficiency creates difficult challenges for designing management systems that promote these goals without blunting the imperatives for cost minimization. The conventional model for reconciling efficiency with innovation in mature companies is *internal differentiation*: innovation and entrepreneurship are the responsibility of specialist R & D, new product development, and business development units. However, some established companies in mature industries, including Toyota and Whirlpool, have embraced dispersed innovation, encouraging initiative and ideas from all employees.[25]

## Strategies for Declining Industries

The transition from maturity to decline can be a result of technological substitution (typewriters, photographic film), changes in consumer preferences (canned food, men's suits), demographic shifts (children's toys in Europe), or foreign competition (textiles in the advanced industrialized countries). Shrinking market demand gives rise to acute strategic issues. Among the key features of declining industries are:

- excess capacity;
- lack of technical change (reflected in a lack of new product introduction and stability of process technology);
- a declining number of competitors, but some entry as new firms acquire the assets of exiting firms cheaply;
- high average age of both physical and human resources;
- aggressive price competition.

Despite the inhospitable environment offered by declining industries, research by Kathryn Harrigan has uncovered declining industries where at least some participants earned surprisingly high profits. These included electronic vacuum tubes, cigars, and leather tanning. However, elsewhere—notably in prepared baby foods, rayon, and meat processing—decline was accompanied by aggressive price competition, company failures, and instability.[26]

What determines whether or not a declining industry becomes a competitive bloodbath? Two factors are critical: the balance between capacity and output, and the nature of the demand for the product.

## Adjusting Capacity to Declining Demand

The smooth adjustment of industry capacity to declining demand is the key to stability and profitability during the decline phase. In industries where capacity exits from the industry in an orderly fashion, decline can occur without trauma. Where substantial excess capacity persists, as has occurred among the oil refineries of America and Europe, in the bakery industry, in coal mining, and in long-haul bus transportation, the potential exists for destructive competition. The ease with which capacity adjusts to declining demand depends on the following factors:

- *The predictability of decline*: If decline can be forecast, it is more likely that firms can plan for it. The decline of traditional photography with the advent of digital imaging was anticipated and planned for. Conversely, the decline in sales of personal computers which began in 2011 was largely unexpected. The more cyclical and volatile the demand, the more difficult it is for firms to perceive the trend of demand, even after the onset of decline.
- *Barriers to exit*: Barriers to exit impede the exit of capacity from an industry. The major barriers are:
  - durable and specialized assets. Just as capital requirements impose a barrier to entry into an industry, those same investments also discourage exit. The longer they last and the fewer the opportunities for using those assets in another industry are, the more companies are tied to that particular industry.
  - costs incurred in plant closure. Apart from the accounting costs of writing off assets, substantial cash costs may be incurred in redundancy payments to employees, compensation for broken contacts with customers and suppliers, decommissioning the plant, and environmental cleanup.
  - managerial commitment. In addition to financial considerations, firms may be reluctant to close plants for a variety of emotional and moral reasons. Resistance to plant closure and divestment arises from pride in company traditions and reputation, managers' unwillingness to accept failure, and loyalties to employees and the local community.
- *The strategies of the surviving firms*: Smooth exit of capacity ultimately depends on the willingness of the industry players to close plants and divest assets. The sooner companies recognize and address the problem, the more likely it is that independent and collective action can achieve capacity reduction. In European gasoline retailing, for example, the problem of excess capacity was partially solved by bilateral exchanges of service stations among the major oil companies. Stronger firms in the industry can facilitate the exit of weaker firms by offering to acquire their plants and take over their after-sales service commitments. A key strategy among private equity firms has been initiating *roll-ups* in declining industries—consolidating multiple acquisitions. Between 1989 and 2010, KKR, a private equity firm, spent over $2 billion acquiring magazine titles and other print media businesses and created Primedia Inc. to manage them.[27]

## Strategy Alternatives for Declining Industries

Conventional strategy recommendations for declining industries are either to divest or to harvest (i.e., to generate the maximum cash flow from existing investments without reinvesting). However, these strategies assume that declining industries are inherently unprofitable. If profit potential exists, then other strategies may be attractive. Harrigan and Porter identify four strategies that can profitably be pursued either individually or sequentially in declining industries:[28]

- *Leadership*: By gaining leadership, a firm is well placed to outstay competitors and play a dominant role in the final stages of an industry's life cycle. Once leadership is attained, the firm is in a good position to switch to a harvest strategy and enjoy a strong profit stream from its market position. Establishing leadership can be done by acquiring competitors, but a cheaper way is to encourage competitors to exit (and then acquire their plants). Inducements to competitors to exit may include showing commitment to the industry, helping to lower their exit costs, releasing pessimistic forecasts of the industry's future, and raising the stakes, for example by supporting more stringent environmental controls that make it costly for them to stay in business.

- *Niche*: Identify a segment that is likely to maintain a stable demand and that other firms are unlikely to invade, then pursue a leadership strategy to establish dominance within the segment. The most attractive niches are those that offer the greatest prospects for stability and where demand is most inelastic. In products facing technological obsolescence, established firms have often been successful in cultivating a lucrative high-price, high-quality segment. For example, Richemont has created a very profitable business based upon mechanical watches (Lange & Söhne, Baume et Mercier, Cartier, Piaget, Vacheron Constantin) and luxury fountain pens (Montblanc).

- *Harvest*: By harvesting, a firm maximizes its cash flow from existing assets, while avoiding further investment. A harvesting strategy seeks to boost margins wherever possible through raising prices and cutting costs by rationalizing the number of models, number of channels, and number of customers. Note, however, that a harvest strategy can be difficult to implement. In the face of strong competition, harvesting may accelerate decline, particularly if employee morale is adversely affected by a strategy that offers no long-term future for the business.

- *Divest*: If the future looks bleak, the best strategy may be to divest the business in the early stages of decline before a consensus has developed as to the inevitability of decline. Once industry decline is well established, it may be extremely difficult to find buyers.

Choosing the most appropriate strategy requires a careful assessment both of the profit potential of the industry and the competitive position of the firm. Harrigan and Porter pose four key questions:

- Can the structure of the industry support a hospitable, potentially profitable decline phase?

- What are the exit barriers that each significant competitor faces?
- Do your company strengths fit the remaining pockets of demand?
- What are your competitors' strengths in these pockets? How can their exit barriers be overcome?

Selecting an appropriate strategy requires matching the opportunities remaining in the industry to the company's competitive position. Figure 10.1 shows a simple framework for strategy choice.

**FIGURE 10.1**   Strategic alternatives for declining industries

|  | | COMPANY'S COMPETITIVE POSITION | |
|---|---|---|---|
|  | | Strengths in remaining demand pockets | Lacks strength in remaining demand pockets |
| INDUSTRY STRUCTURE | Favorable to decline | LEADERSHIP or NICHE | HARVEST or DIVEST |
|  | Unfavorable to decline | NICHE or HARVEST | DIVEST QUICKLY |

## Summary

Mature industries present challenging environments for the formulation and implementation of business strategies. Competition, and price competition in particular, is usually strong, and competitive advantage is often difficult to build and sustain: cost advantages are vulnerable to imitation; differentiation opportunities are limited by the trend to standardization.

Stable positions of competitive advantage in mature industries are traditionally associated with cost advantage from economies of scale or experience, with selecting the most attractive market segments and customers to serve, with creating differentiation advantage, and with pursuing technological and strategic innovation.

Implementing these strategies, especially those associated with rigorous cost efficiency, typically requires management systems based upon standardized processes and relentless performance management. However, as mature industries become increasingly complex and turbulent, so the pursuit of cost efficiency needs to be matched with flexibility, responsiveness, and innovation. Companies such as Wal-Mart, Coca-Cola, McDonald's, Banco Santander, and Toyota show remarkable capacity to reconcile vigorous cost efficiency with adaptability.

Declining industries present special challenges to companies: typically, they are associated with intense competition and low margins. However, such environments also present profitable opportunities for those firms that can orchestrate orderly decline from a position of leadership, establish a niche, or generate cash from harvesting assets.

Quizzes and flashcards to test yourself further are available in your interactive e-book at
**www.wileyopenpage.com**

## Self-Study Questions

1. Consider Table 3.1 in Chapter 3. Most of the least profitable US industries are mature industries. Yet at the top of the table are tobacco, personal and household products, and food consumer products, all mature industries. What is it about this latter group of industries that has allowed them to escape the intense price competition and low profitability often associated with mature sectors?

2. Established airlines are cutting costs to compete with the increasing number of budget airlines. Yet, it is unlikely that they will ever match the costs of Southwest, Ryanair, or AirAsia. Which, if any, of the strategies outlined in this chapter offers the best opportunity for the established airlines to improve their competitive position vis-à-vis the budget airlines?

3. Department stores (e.g., Federated Department Stores and Mays in the US, Selfridges and House of Fraser in the UK) face increasing competition from specialized chain retailers and discount stores. What innovative strategies might department stores adopt to revitalize their competitiveness?

4. Book retailing is in decline. From the strategy options identified in the section "Strategy Alternatives for Declining Industries," what recommendations would you offer to (a) Barnes & Noble and (b) an independent book retailer located in your vicinity?

## Notes

1. E. H. Rensi, "Computers at McDonald's," in J. F. McLimore and L. Larwood (eds), *Strategies, Successes: Senior Executives Speak Out* (New York: Harper & Row, 1988): 159–60.

2. Letter to Shareholders, Annual Report of Berkshire Hathaway Inc., 1991.

3. R. D. Buzzell and B. T. Gale, *The PIMS Principles* (New York: Free Press, 1987): 279.

4. T. Copeland, T. Koller, and J. Murrin, *Valuation: Measuring and Managing the Value of Companies*, 3rd edn (New York: John Wiley & Sons, Inc., 2000): 305.

5. R. Cibin and R. M. Grant, "Restructuring among the World's Leading Oil Companies," *British Journal of Management* 7 (December 1996): 283–308.

6. D. C. Hambrick and S. M. Schecter, "Turnaround Strategies for Mature Industrial-Product Business Units," *Academy of Management Journal* 26, no. 2 (1983): 231–48.

7. G. R. Carroll and A. Swaminathan, "Why the Microbrewery Movement? Organizational Dynamics of Resource Partitioning in the American Brewing Industry," *American Journal of Sociology* 106 (2000): 715–762; C. Boone, G. R. Carroll, and A. van Witteloostuijn, "Resource Distributions and Market Partitioning: Dutch Daily Newspapers 1964–94," *American Sociological Review* 67 (2002): 408–31.

8. *Capital One Financial Corporation*, Harvard Business School Case No. 9-700-124 (2000).

9. National Science Foundation, *Research and Development in Industry*: 2002 (www.nsf.gov/statistics/industry).

10. A. M. McGahan and B. S. Silverman, "How Does Innovative Activity Change as Industries Mature?" *International Journal of Industrial Organization* 19, no. 7 (2001): 1141–60.

11. See section entitled: "Internal Sources of Change: Competitive Advantage from Innovation," Chapter 7.

12. B. J. Pine and J. Gilmore, "Welcome to the Experience Economy," *Harvard Business Review* (July/August 1998): 97–105.

13. A. Davies, T. Brady, and M. Hobday, "Organizing for Solutions: System Seller vs. System Integrator," *Industrial Marketing Management* 36 (2007): 183–93.

14. C. Baden-Fuller and J. Stopford, *Rejuvenating the Mature Business* (Boston: HBS Press, 1994): especially Chapters 3 and 4.

15. C. C. Markides, *All the Right Moves* (Boston: Harvard Business School Press, 1999).

16. J.-C. Spender, *Industry Recipes: The Nature and Sources of Managerial Judgment* (Oxford: Blackwell Publishing, 1989). On a similar theme, see also A. S. Huff, "Industry Influences on Strategy Reformulation," *Strategic Management Journal* 3 (1982): 119–131.

17. P. S. Barr, J. L. Stimpert, and A. S. Huff, "Cognitive Change, Strategic Action, and Organizational Renewal," *Strategic Management Journal* 13 (Summer 1992): 15–36.

18. G. Hamel, "Strategy as Revolution," *Harvard Business Review* 96 (July/August 1996): 69–82.

19. H. Volberda, C. Baden-Fuller, and F. van den Bosch, "Mastering Strategic Renewal," *Long Range Planning* 34 (April, 2001): 159–78.

20. T. Burns and G. M. Stalker, *The Management of Innovation* (London: Tavistock Institute, 1961).

21. H. Mintzberg, *Structure in Fives: Designing Effective Organizations* (Englewood Cliffs, NJ: Prentice Hall, 1983): Chapter 9.

22. G. Nieman, *Big Brown: The Untold Story of UPS* (Chichester: John Wiley & Sons, Ltd, 2007): 70.

23. C. Fishman, *The Wal-Mart Effect: The High Cost of Everyday Low Prices* (Harmondsworth: Penguin, 2006).

24. *Ryanair: Defying Gravity*, IMD Case No. 3-1633 (2007). Available from www.ecch.com.

25. "How Whirlpool Defines Innovation," *Business Week* (March 6, 2006).

26. K. R. Harrigan, *Strategies for Declining Businesses* (Lexington, MA: D. C. Heath, 1980).

27. "KKR and Primedia," *Adweek* (May 31, 2011).

28. K. R. Harrigan and M. E. Porter, "End-Game Strategies for Declining Industries," *Harvard Business Review* (July/August 1983): 111–120.

# IV
# CORPORATE STRATEGY

# 11 Vertical Integration and the Scope of the Firm

The idea of vertical integration is anathema to an increasing number of companies. Most of yesterday's highly integrated giants are working overtime at splitting into more manageable, more energetic units—i.e., de-integrating. Then they are turning around and re-integrating—not by acquisitions but via alliances with all sorts cf partners of all shapes and sizes.

—TOM PETERS, LIBERATION MANAGEMENT

Bath Fitter has control of the product from raw material to installation. This control allows them to better guarantee the quality by knowing exactly how it is made, not outsourcing it to someone that could take shortcuts to manufacture the product without Bath Fitter knowing. Also, they control the measuring, installation, and customer facing representative. By doing this, Bath Fitter would be able to get accurate and fast feedback about how the product is being used, quality issues, or the ease of installation.

—"BATH FITTER HAS VERTICAL INTEGRATION," HTTP://BEYONDLEAN.WORDPRESS.COM/2011/08/29/

## OUTLINE

# Introduction and Objectives

Chapter 1 introduced the distinction between corporate strategy and business strategy. Corporate strategy is concerned primarily with the decisions over the scope of the firm's activities, including:

*Product scope*: How specialized should the firm be in terms of the range of products it supplies? Coca-Cola (soft drinks), SABMiller (beer), Gap (fashion retailing), and SAP (software) are specialized companies: each is engaged in a single industry sector. Sony Corporation, Berkshire Hathaway, and Tata Group are diversified companies—they span multiple industries.

*Geographical scope*: What is the optimal geographical spread of activities for the firm? In the restaurant business, Clyde's Restaurant Group owns 13 restaurants in the Washington DC area, Popeye's Chicken and Biscuits has outlets throughout the US, McDonald's Corporation operates in 121 different countries.

*Vertical scope*: What range of vertically linked activities should the firm encompass? Walt Disney is a vertically integrated company: it produces its own movies, distributes them to cinemas and through its own TV networks (ABC and Disney Channel), and uses the movies' characters in its retail stores and theme parks. Nike is much more vertically specialized: it designs and markets footwear and apparel but outsources most activities in its value chain, including manufacturing, distribution, and retailing.

The distinction between business and corporate strategy may be summarized as follows: *corporate strategy* is concerned with *where* a firm competes; *business strategy* is concerned with *how* a firm competes within a particular area of business.[1] So far, the primary focus of the book has been business strategy. In this final part, we shift our attention to corporate strategy: decisions that define the scope of the firm. I devote separate chapters to the different dimensions of scope—vertical scope (*vertical integration*), geographical scope (*multinationality*) and product scope (*diversification*). However, as we shall discover, the key underlying concepts for analyzing these different dimensions—economies of scope in resources and capabilities, transaction costs, and costs of corporate complexity—are common to all three.

In this chapter we begin by considering the overall scope of the firm. We then focus specifically on vertical integration. This takes us to the heart of the determinants of firm boundaries, in particular the role of *transaction costs*. As we shall discover, vertical integration has been a hot topic in corporate strategy. Opportunities for outsourcing, alliances, and electronic commerce have caused companies to rethink which of their activities should remain within their organizational boundaries.

By the time you have completed this chapter, you will be able to:

- ◆ recognize the role of firms and markets in organizing economic activity and apply the principles of *transaction cost economics* to explain why boundaries between firms and markets shift over time;

- ◆ understand the relative advantages of vertical integration and outsourcing in organizing vertically related activities, the factors that determine the relative efficiency of each, understand the circumstances that influence these relative advantages, and apply this understanding to decisions over whether a particular activity should be undertaken internally or outsourced;

◆ identify alternative ways of organizing vertical transactions—including spot market transactions, long-term contracts, franchise agreements, and alliances—and advise a firm on the most advantageous transaction mode given the characteristics and circumstances of the transaction.

## Transaction Costs and the Scope of the Firm

In Chapter 6 (Strategy Capsule 6.1), we traced the development of the business corporation. Firms came into existence because of their efficiency advantages in organizing production. Let us explore this issue and consider the determinants of firm boundaries.

### Firms, Markets, and Transaction Costs

Although the capitalist economy is frequently referred to as a "market economy," it actually comprises two forms of economic organization. One is the *market mechanism*, where individuals and firms, guided by market prices, make independent decisions to buy and sell goods and services. The other is the *administrative mechanism* of firms, where decisions concerning production and resource allocation are made by managers and imposed through hierarchies. The market mechanism was characterized by Adam Smith, the 18th century Scottish economist, as the "invisible hand" because its coordinating role does not require conscious planning. Alfred Chandler has referred to the administrative mechanism of firms as the "visible hand" because coordination involves active planning.[2]

Firms and markets may be viewed as alternative institutions for organizing production. Firms are distinguished by the fact that they comprise a number of individuals bound by employment contracts with a central contracting authority. But firms are not essential for organizing production. When I remodeled my basement, I contracted with a self-employed builder to undertake the work. He in turn subcontracted parts of the work to a plumber, an electrician, a joiner, a drywall installer, and a painter. Although the job involved the coordinated activity of several individuals, these self-employed specialists were not linked by employment relations but by market contracts ("$4,000 to install wiring, lights, and sockets").

Firms and markets coexist, but their relative roles vary. If we compare the supply of mainframe computers with that of the personal computer industry, the administrative mechanisms of firms predominate in the former, and markets are more important in the latter. Thus, in mainframes, IBM's System z computers comprise IBM's microprocessors, IBM's z/OS operating system, and IBM's applications software; IBM also undertakes distribution, marketing, and customer support. Personal computers, by contrast, involve a network of firms linked by market contracts: design and marketing is undertaken by firms such as HP, Acer, and Lenovo. Components are produced by firms such as Intel, Seagate, and Samsung. Assembly is outsourced to contract manufactures such as Asustek, Quanta Computer, and Foxconn. Customer support is also outsourced to specialist suppliers, often located in India or Eastern Europe.

What determines which activities are undertaken within a firm and which through the market? Ronald Coase's answer was *relative cost*.[3] Markets are not costless: making a purchase or sale involves search costs, the costs of negotiating and drawing up a contract, the costs of monitoring to ensure that the other party's side of the contract is being fulfilled, and the enforcement costs of arbitration or litigation should a dispute arise. All these costs are types of **transaction costs**.[4] If the transaction costs associated with organizing across markets are greater than the *administrative costs* of organizing within firms, we can expect the coordination of productive activity will be internalized within firms.

Consider the packaging business (Figure 11.1). With regard to vertical scope, which is more efficient: three independent companies—one producing raw materials (e.g., steel), the next producing semi-finished packaging materials (e.g., steel strip), and the third producing finished packaging (e.g., steel cans)—or having all three stages undertaken by a single company? In the case of product scope, should metal cans, plastic packaging, and domestic appliances be produced by three separate companies or are there efficiencies to be gained by merging all three into a single company? In the case of geographical scope, which is more efficient: three independent companies producing cans in the US, the UK, and Italy, or a single multinational company owning and operating the can-making plants in all three countries?

**FIGURE 11.1** The scope of the firm: Specialization versus integration

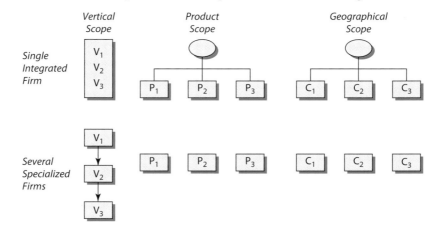

**Note:** In the integrated firm there is an administrative interface between the different vertical units (V), product units (P), and country units (C). Where there is specialization, each unit is a separate firm linked by market interfaces.

## The Shifting Boundary between Firms and Markets

The answers to these questions have changed over time. During the 19th, and for most of the 20th century, companies grew in size and scope, absorbing transactions that had previously taken place across markets. Companies that were once small, specialized, and localized became large, integrated, diversified, and multinational. Applying Ronald Coase's principle, can we attribute this trend to a fall in the administrative costs of firms relative to the transaction costs of markets? Two factors have greatly increased the efficiency of firms in organizing economic activity:

- *Technology*: The telegraph, telephone, and computer have played an important role in facilitating communications within firms and expanding the decision-making capacity of managers.
- *Management techniques*: Developments in the principles and techniques of management have greatly expanded the organizational and decision-making effectiveness of managers. Beginning with the dissemination of double-entry bookkeeping in the 19th century,[5] and the introduction of scientific management in the early 20th century,[6] the past six decades have seen rapid advances in all areas of management theory and methods.

By the late 1960s, the growth in large corporations and the impressive achievements of the new tools of management science and corporate planning encouraged a widespread view that the *market economy* had been replaced by a *corporate economy*. The economist J. K. Galbraith predicted that the inherent advantages of firms over markets in deploying technology and planning production would result in capitalist economies becoming dominated by a small number of giant corporations.[7]

Yet, by the end of the 1990s, these predictions had been refuted by a sharp reversal of the trend toward increased corporate scope. Although large companies continued to expand internationally, the dominant trends of the past three decades have been "downsizing" and "refocusing," as large industrial companies reduced both their product scope through focusing on their core businesses and their vertical scope through outsourcing. As a result, the Forbes 500s share of total US private sector employment fell from 21.2% in 1980 to 14.9% in 1995.[8]

The contraction of corporate boundaries points to markets increasing their efficiency relative to firms' administrative processes. A key factor is greater turbulence of the business environment in recent decades. During periods of instability, the costs of administration within large, complex firms tend to rise as the need for flexibility and speed of response overwhelms traditional management systems. A second factor is the development of information and communications technology (ICT). The advent of computers reinforced the advantages of the giant corporation—only large organizations could afford them. But with the PC, internet, and mobile communication revolution, the benefits of leading-edge ICT have diffused to small firms and individuals, and the creation of virtual digital markets and electronic data interchange have revolutionized market transactions.

Let us focus now on just one dimension of corporate scope: vertical integration. The question we will consider is this: is it better to be vertically integrated or vertically specialized? With regard to a specific activity, the simple question for the firm is: *to make or to buy*? To answer this question, we shall draw in particular on Oliver

Williamson's analysis of transaction costs, which forms the basis for a theory of economic organization that is particularly useful in designing vertical relationships.[9]

## The Benefits and Costs of Vertical Integration

*Vertical integration* refers to a firm's ownership of vertically related activities. The greater a firm's ownership extends over successive stages of the value chain for its product, the greater its degree of vertical integration. The extent of a firm's vertical integration is indicated by the ratio of its value added to its sales revenue: the more a firm makes rather than buys, the greater is its value added relative to its sales revenue.

Vertical integration can be either *backward* (or upstream) into its suppliers' activities or *forward* (or downstream) into its customers' activities. Vertical integration may also be *full* or *partial*. Some California wineries are fully integrated: they produce wine only from the grapes they grow, and sell it all through direct distribution. Most are partially integrated: their homegrown grapes are supplemented with purchased grapes; they sell some wine through their own tasting rooms, but most through independent distributors.

Strategies toward vertical integration have been subject to shifting fashions. For most of the 20th century the prevailing wisdom was that vertical integration was beneficial because it allowed superior coordination and reduced risk. During the past 25 years, there has been a profound change of opinion: outsourcing, it is claimed, enhances flexibility and allows firms to concentrate on those activities where they possess superior capabilities. Moreover, many of the coordination benefits associated with vertical integration can be achieved through collaboration between vertically related companies.

However, as in other areas of management, fashion is fickle. In the media sector, vertical integration between content and distribution has become viewed as a critical advantage in the face of rapid technological change. The resulting wave of mergers between content producers and distributors (TV broadcasters, cable companies, and internet portals) has transformed the industry (Strategy Capsule 11.1).

Our task is to go beyond fads and fashions to uncover the factors that determine whether vertical integration enhances or weakens performance.

### The Benefits from Vertical Integration

*Technical Economies from the Physical Integration of Processes*    Proponents of vertical integration have often emphasized the *technical economies* it offers: cost savings that arise from the physical integration of processes. Thus, most steel sheet is produced by integrated producers in plants that first produce steel, then roll hot steel into sheet. Linking the two stages of production at a single location reduces transportation and energy costs. Similar technical economies arise in integrating pulp and paper production and from linking oil refining with petrochemical production.

However, although these considerations explain the need for the co-location of plants, they do not explain why vertical integration in terms of *common ownership* is necessary. Why can't steel and steel strip production or pulp and paper production be undertaken by separate firms that own facilities which are physically integrated

# Vertical Integration in the Media Sector: Value Creating or Value Destroying?

Considerable vertical integration has occurred between *content* producers (film studios, music publishing, newspapers) and distribution companies (TV broadcasters, cable, satellite TV, internet):

◆ News Corp. expanded from newspapers into movie production (Twentieth Century Fox), broadcast TV (Fox), satellite TV (Sky) and internet services (MySpace);

◆ Viacom owns cable TV channels (MTV, BET, Nickelodeon) and acquired studios (Paramount and DreamWorks).

◆ Time Warner is mainly involved in producing content (Warner Brothers studios, New Line Cinema, Time magazines, CNN news); its distribution mainly comprises cable channels (HBO, Turner Broadcasting, Cartoon Network). The merger of AOL and Time Warner, a vertically integrated content-internet distribution company was a disaster from the outset, and in 2009 AOL was spun off.

◆ Vivendi Universal was the result of the transformation of Compagnie Générale des Eaux, a water and waste management company, into a diversified, vertically integrated, media company led by Jean-Marie Messier which was subsequently broken up between 2002 and 2005 following massive losses.

◆ Disney's content production includes Walt Disney Studios, Pixar, Disney Theatrical Productions, Walt Disney Records, and Disney Publishing Worldwide. Distribution includes film distribution (Walt Disney Pictures, Disney Home Entertainment), broadcast TV (ABC), cable TV (ESPN, Disney Channel), radio (Radio Disney Network), and internet (Disney Online).

The question of whether vertical integration between media content and media distribution creates value was stimulated by the $54 billion hostile takeover bid made by Comcast, America's biggest cable operator, of Walt Disney in 2004. Here are two contrasting views.

## STEVE ROSENBUSH

"Buying Disney shouldn't be a surprise. It's the logical next step," Comcast CEO Brian Roberts said at his February 11 press conference announcing his bid for the Mouse House.

It isn't enough to be just a media company, either. Most content providers benefit from having a certain amount of distribution, which helps lower their costs. That's why, in the future, media and communications will be dominated by hybrids such as News Corp. which recently acquired satellite-TV operator DirecTV.

Comcast's Roberts has embraced this future. The question now is whether Disney CEO Michael Eisner—who spurned an offer for a friendly deal—can accept the same future . . . Now that DirecTV is under Rupert Murdoch's control, it would be folly for Disney to pretend that it can still compete without a distribution partner of comparable stature. Comcast fits the bill. (*Business Week*, February 11, 2004).

## JOHN KAY

Media content needs delivery, and vice versa . . . But this old idea is frequently rediscovered by visionary chief executives, excitable consultants, and greedy investment bankers: the people who proclaimed the AOL–Time Warner deal a marriage made in heaven. And it was revealed with Damascene force to Jean-Marie Messier, a humble French water carrier.

But activities can converge without requiring that the companies that undertake them converge. The erstwhile *maître du monde* might have drawn a useful lesson from his experience at Compagnie Générale des Eaux before his apotheosis as chief executive of Vivendi Universal: sewers and the stuff that goes down them do not need common ownership. (*Financial Times*, March 3, 2004) with one another? To answer this question, we must look beyond technical economies and consider the implications of linked processes for *transaction costs*.

## The Sources of Transaction Costs in Vertical Exchanges

Consider the value chain for steel cans, which extends from mining iron ore to the use of cans by food-processing companies (Figure 11.2). There is vertical integration between some stages; between others there is mostly market contracts between specialist firms. In the final linkage—between can producing and canning—most cans are produced by specialist packaging companies (such as Crown Holdings and Ball Corporation); others are produced by food processors (such as Campbell's Soup and H.J. Heinz) that have backward integrated into can-making.[10]

The predominance of market contracts between steel strip production and can production is the result of low transaction costs in the market for steel strip: there are many buyers and sellers, information is readily available, and the switching costs for buyers and suppliers are low. The same is true for many other commodity products: few jewelry companies own gold mines; few flour-milling companies own wheat farms.

To understand why vertical integration predominates across steel production and steel strip production, let us see what would happen if the two stages were owned by separate companies. Because there are technical economies from hot-rolling steel as soon as it is poured from the furnace, steel makers and strip producers must invest in integrated facilities. A competitive market between the two stages is impossible; each steel strip producer is tied to its adjacent steel producer. In other words, the market becomes a series of *bilateral monopolies*.

Why are these relationships between steel producers and strip producers problematic? To begin with, where a single supplier negotiates with a single buyer, there is no market price: it all depends on relative bargaining power. Such bargaining is likely to be costly: the mutual dependency of the two parties is likely to give rise to *opportunism* and *strategic misrepresentation* as each company seeks to enhance and exploit its bargaining power at the expense of the other. Hence, once we move from a competitive market situation to one where individual buyers and sellers are locked together in close bilateral relationships, the efficiencies of competitive markets are lost.

**FIGURE 11.2** The value chain for steel cans

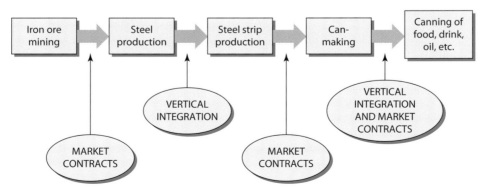

The culprits in this situation are *transaction-specific investments*. When a can-maker buys steel strip, neither the steel strip producer nor the can-maker needs to invest in equipment or technology that is specific to the needs of the other party. In the case of the steel producer and the steel roller, each company's plant is built to match the other party's plant. Once built, the plant's value depends upon the availability of the other party's complementary facilities—each seller is tied to a single buyer, which gives each the potential to *hold up* the other.

Thus, transaction-specific investments result in transaction costs arising from the difficulties of framing a comprehensive contract and the risks of disputes and opportunism that arise from contracts that do not cover every possible eventuality. Empirical research confirms the likelihood of vertical integration where transaction-specific investments are required:[11]

- Among automakers, specialized components are more likely to be manufactured in-house than commodity items such as tires and spark plugs.[12] Similarly, in aerospace, company-specific components are more likely to be produced in-house rather than purchased externally.[13]
- In the semiconductor industry, some companies specialize either in semiconductor design or in fabrication; others are vertically integrated across both stages (e.g., Intel, STMicroelectronics). The more technically complex the integrated circuit and, hence, the greater the need for the designer and fabricator to invest in close technical collaboration, the better the relative performance of integrated producers.[14]

The problem of hold-up could be eliminated by contracts that fully specify prices, quality, quantities, and other terms of supply under all possible circumstances over the entire life of the assets involved. But given uncertainty, it is impossible to anticipate every eventuality, and contracts are inevitably incomplete.

## The Costs of Vertical Integration

The presence of transaction costs in intermediate markets does not mean that vertical integration is necessarily an efficient solution. Vertical integration avoids the costs of using the market, but internalizing a transaction imposes administrative cost. The size of this cost depends on several factors.

*Differences in Optimal Scale between Different Stages of Production*
Suppose that Federal Express requires delivery vans that are designed to meet its particular needs. To the extent that the van manufacturer must make transaction-specific investments, there is an incentive for Federal Express to avoid the ensuing transaction costs by building its own vehicles. Would this be an efficient solution? Almost certainly not: the transaction costs avoided by Federal Express are likely to be trivial compared with the inefficiencies incurred in manufacturing its own vans. Federal Express purchases about 40,000 trucks and vans each year, well below the 200,000 minimum efficient scale of an assembly plant.

The same logic explains why specialist brewers such as Anchor Brewing of San Francisco or Adnams of Suffolk, England are not backward integrated into cans like Anheuser-Busch InBev or SABMiller. Small brewers simply do not possess the scale needed for scale efficiency in can-making.

*Developing Distinctive Capabilities*   A key advantage of a company that is specialized in a few activities is its ability to develop distinctive capabilities in those activities. Even large, technology-based companies such as Xerox, Rolls-Royce, and Philips cannot maintain IT capabilities that match those of IT services specialists such as EDS, IBM, and Accenture. An important advantage of these IT specialists is the learning they gain from working with multiple clients. If General Motors' IT department only serves the in-house needs of GM, this limits the development of its IT capabilities.

However, this assumes that capabilities in different vertical activities are independent of one another and the required capabilities are generic rather than highly customized. Where one capability is closely integrated with capabilities in adjacent activities, vertical integration may help develop these integrated, system-wide capabilities. Thus, Wal-Mart keeps its IT in-house. The reason is that real-time information is central to Wal-Mart's supply chain management, in-store operations, and upper-level managerial decision making. Wal-Mart's need for tightly integrated information and communication services customized to meet its unique business systems inclines it toward in-sourcing.

*Managing Strategically Different Businesses*   These problems of differences in optimal scale and developing distinctive capabilities may be viewed as part of a wider set of problems—that of managing vertically related businesses that are strategically very different. A major disadvantage to FedEx of owning a truck-manufacturing company is that the management systems and organizational capabilities required for truck manufacturing are very different from those required for express delivery. These considerations may explain the lack of vertical integration between manufacturing and retailing. Firms that are integrated across design, manufacturing, and retailing, such as Zara and Gucci, are rare. Most of the world's leading retailers—Wal-Mart, Gap, Carrefour—do not manufacture. Similarly, few manufacturing companies retail their own products. Not only do manufacturing and retailing require very different organizational capabilities, they also require different strategic planning systems, different approaches to control and human resource management, and different top-management styles and skills.

These strategic dissimilarities are a key factor in the trend to vertically de-integrate. Marriott's split into two separate companies, Marriott International and Host Marriott, was influenced by the belief that *owning* hotels is a strategically different business from *operating* hotels. Similarly, the Coca-Cola Company spun off its bottling activities as Coca-Cola Enterprises Inc. partly because managing local bottling and distribution operations is very different from managing the global Coca-Cola brand and the production and distribution of concentrates.

*Incentive Problems*   Vertical integration changes the incentives between vertically related businesses. Where a market interface exists between a buyer and a seller, profit incentives ensure that the buyer is motivated to secure the best possible deal and the seller is motivated to pursue efficiency and service in order to attract and retain the buyer—these are termed *high-powered incentives*. With vertical integration, internal supplier–customer relationships are subject to *low-powered incentives*. When my office computer malfunctions, I call the university's IT department. The incentives for the in-house technicians to respond promptly to my email and voice messages are weak. If I were free to use an outside IT specialist, that specialist would only get the business if they were able to offer same-day service and would only get paid once the problem was resolved.

One approach to creating stronger performance incentives within vertically integrated companies is to open internal divisions to external competition. As we shall examine more fully in Chapter 14, many large corporations have created *shared service organizations*, where internal suppliers of corporate services—such as IT, training, and engineering—compete with external suppliers of the same services to serve internal operating divisions.

*Competitive Effects of Vertical Integration*   Vertical integration can be used to extend a monopoly position at one stage of an industry's value chain to adjacent stages: classic cases are Standard Oil and Alcoa. However, such cases are rare. Economists have shown that there is no additional monopoly profit to be extracted by extending a monopoly to adjacent stages of the value chain.[15]

A more likely risk is that, by vertically integrating, a company damages its competitive position in its original business because it now must compete with its customers or suppliers. When Disney forward integrated by acquiring the ABC TV network, this adversely affected Disney's relationships with other TV networks that were customers for Disney's TV productions, and made other studios (e.g., DreamWorks) more reluctant to collaborate with ABC in developing new TV productions.

*Flexibility*   Both vertical integration and market transactions can claim advantage with regard to different types of flexibility. Where the required flexibility is rapid responsiveness to uncertain demand, there may be advantages in market transactions. The lack of vertical integration in the construction industry reflects, in part, the need for flexibility in adjusting both to cyclical patterns of demand and to the different requirements of each project. Vertical integration may also be disadvantageous in responding quickly to new product development opportunities that require new combinations of technical capabilities. Some of the most successful new electronic products of recent years—Apple's iPod, Microsoft's Xbox, Dell's range of notebook computers—have been produced by contract manufacturers. Extensive outsourcing has been a key feature of fast-cycle product development throughout the electronics sector.

Yet, where system-wide flexibility is required, vertical integration may allow for speed and coordination in achieving simultaneous adjustment throughout the vertical chain. American Apparel is a rare example of a successful US *manufacturer* of apparel. Its tightly coordinated vertical integration from its Los Angeles design and manufacturing base to its 160 retail stores across 10 countries allows a super-fast design-to-distribution cycle. Vertical integration can also reinforce brand identity. Figure 11.3 shows an advertisement for American Apparel.

*Compounding Risk*   To the extent that it ties a company to its internal suppliers and internal customers, vertical integration represents a compounding of risk: problems at any one stage of production threaten production and profitability at all other stages. When union workers at a General Motors brake plant went on strike in 1998, GM's 24 US assembly plants were soon brought to a halt. If Disney animation studios fail to produce blockbuster animation movies that introduce new characters, then the knock-on effects are felt through plummeting DVD sales, lack of spin-off shows on the Disney Channel, reduction of merchandise sales in Disney Stores, and shortage of new attractions at Disney theme parks.

**FIGURE 11.3** An American Apparel advertisement

## Assessing the Pros and Cons of Vertical Integration

We have seen that vertical integration is neither good nor bad. As with most questions of strategy, it all depends upon the specific context. The value of our analysis is that we can identify the factors that determine the relative advantages of the market transactions *versus* internalization. Table 11.1 summarizes some of the key criteria. However, our analysis is not yet complete; we must consider some additional factors that influence the choice of vertical strategy, and in particular the fact that vertical relationships are not limited to the simple choice of make or buy.

## Designing Vertical Relationships

Our discussion so far has compared vertical integration with arm's-length market contracts. In practice buyers and sellers can interact and coordinate their interests

**TABLE 11.1**   Vertical integration (VI) versus outsourcing: Some key considerations

| Characteristics of the vertical relationship | Implication |
| --- | --- |
| How many firms are there in the vertically adjacent activity? | The fewer the number of firms, the greater the transaction costs and bigger the advantages of VI |
| Do transaction-specific investments need to be made by either party? | Transaction-specific investments are the primary source of transaction costs and increase the advantages of VI |
| How evenly distributed is information between the vertical stages? | The greater the information asymmetries, the more likely is opportunistic behavior and the greater the advantages of VI |
| How uncertain are the circumstances of the transactions over the period of the relationship? | The greater the uncertainties concerning costs, technologies, and demand, the greater the difficulty of writing contracts and the greater the advantages of VI |
| Are two stages similar in terms of the optimal scale of operation? | The greater the dissimilarity, the greater the advantages of market contracts as compared with VI |
| Are the two stages strategically similar (e.g., similar key success factors, common resources/capabilities)? | The greater the strategic similarity, the greater the advantages of VI over outsourcing |
| How great is the need for continual investment in upgrading and extending capabilities within individual activities? | The greater the need to invest in capability development, the greater the advantages of outsourcing over VI |
| How great is the need for entrepreneurial flexibility and drive in the separate vertical activities? | The greater the need for entrepreneurship and flexibility, the greater the advantages of high-powered incentives provided by market contracts and the greater the administrative disadvantages of VI |
| How uncertain is market demand? | The greater the unpredictability of demand, the greater the flexibility advantages of outsourcing |
| Does vertical integration compound risk, exposing the entire value chain risks affecting individual stages? | The heavier the investment requirements and the greater the independent risks at each stage, the more risky is VI |

through a variety of relationships. Figure 11.4 shows a number of different types of relationship between buyers and sellers. These relationships may be classified in relation to two characteristics. First, the extent to which the buyer and seller commit resources to the relationship: arm's-length, spot contracts involve no resource commitment beyond the single deal; vertical integration typically involves a substantial investment. Second, the formality of the relationship: long-term contracts and franchises are formalized by the complex written agreements they entail; spot contracts typically involve little or no documentation and are governed by common law; collaborative agreements between buyers and sellers are usually informal—they are trust based; vertical integration allows management discretion to replace legal formality.

## Different Types of Vertical Relationship

These different types of vertical relationship offer different combinations of advantages and disadvantages. For example:

- *Long-term contracts*: Market transactions can be either *spot contracts*—buying a cargo of crude oil on the Rotterdam petroleum market—or *long-term*

**FIGURE 11.4** Different types of vertical relationship

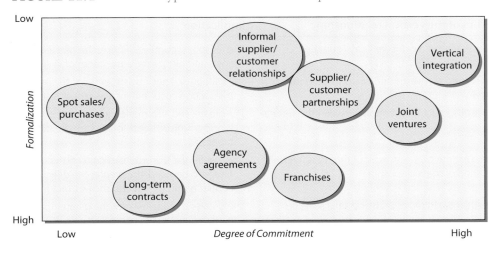

contracts—a series of transactions over a period of time that specify the terms of sales and the responsibilities of each party. Spot transactions work well under competitive conditions (many buyers and sellers and a standard product) where there is no need for transaction-specific investments by either party. Where closer supplier–customer ties are needed, particularly when one or both parties need to make transaction-specific investments, a longer-term contract can help avoid opportunism and provide the security needed to make the necessary investment. However, long-term contracts face the problem of anticipating the circumstances that may arise during the life of the contract: either they are too restrictive or so loose that they give rise to opportunism and conflicting interpretation. Long-term contracts often include provisions for the arbitration of contract disputes.

- *Vendor partnerships*: The greater the difficulties of specifying complete contracts for long-term supplier–customer deals, the greater the advantage of vertical relationships based on trust and mutual understanding. Such relationships can provide the security needed to support transaction-specific investments, the flexibility to meet changing circumstances, and the incentives to avoid opportunism. Such arrangements may be entirely *relational contracts*, with no written contract at all. The model for vendor partnerships has been the close collaborative relationships that many Japanese companies have with their suppliers. Japanese automakers have been much less backward integrated than their US or European counterparts but have also achieved close collaboration with component makers in technology, design, quality, and production scheduling.[16]

- *Franchising*: A franchise is a contractual agreement between the owner of a business system and trademark (the franchiser) that permits the franchisee to produce and market the franchiser's product or service in a specified area. Franchising brings together the brand, marketing capabilities, and business systems of the large corporation with the entrepreneurship and local knowledge of small firms. The franchising systems of companies such as

McDonald's, Century 21 Real Estate, Hilton Hotels, and 7-Eleven convenience stores facilitate the close coordination and investment in transaction-specific assets that vertical integration permits with the high-powered incentives, flexibility, and cooperation between strategically dissimilar businesses that market contracts make possible.

## Choosing between Alternative Vertical Relationships

The criteria listed in Table 11.1 establish the basic features of the vertical relation that favor either market transactions or vertical integration. However, the availability of other types of vertical relationships, such as vendor partnerships and franchises, mean that vertical integration is not the sole solution to problems of transaction costs. Moreover, many of these relational contracts and hybrid arrangements have the capacity to combine the advantages of both vertical integration and market contracts.

Choosing the optimal vertical relationships needs to take account of additional factors to those listed in Table 11.1. In particular:

- *Resources, capabilities, and strategy*: Within the same industry, different companies will choose different vertical arrangements according to their reactive resource and capability strengths and the strategies they pursue. Thus, in fashion clothing, Zara's high level of vertical integration compared to H&M's or Gap's reflects strategy based upon fast-cycle new-product development and tight integration between its retail stores, designers, and manufacturers. While most fast-food chains have expanded through franchising, California-based In-N-Out Burger seeks to maintain its unique culture and distinctive business practices by directly owning and managing its restaurants. While most banks have been outsourcing IT to companies such as IBM and EDS, US credit card group Capital One sees IT as a key source of competitive advantage: "IT is our central nervous system . . . if we outsourced tomorrow we might save a dollar or two on each account, but we would lose flexibility and value and service levels."[17]

- *Allocation of risk*: Any arrangement beyond a spot contract must cope with uncertainties over the course of the contract. A key feature of any contract is that its terms allocate (often implicitly) risks between the parties. How risk is shared is dependent partly on bargaining power and partly on efficiency considerations. In franchise agreements, the franchisee (as the weaker partner) bears most of the risk—it is the franchisee's capital that is at risk and the franchisee pays the franchiser a flat royalty based on sale revenues. In oil exploration, outsourcing agreements between the oil majors (such as Chevron, ExxonMobil, and ENI) and drilling companies (such as Schlumberger or Halliburton) have moved from fixed-price contracts to risk-sharing agreements where the driller often takes an equity stake in the project.

- *Incentive structures*: Incentives are central to the design of vertical relationships. Incentives for opportunistic behavior are the bugbear of market contacts, while weak (low-powered) incentives for performance are the central problem of vertical integration. It seems possible that hybrid and intermediate governance modes offer the best solutions to the design of incentives. Toyota, Benetton, Boeing, and Marks & Spencer have relationships with their vendors that may involve formal contracts, but their essence is that they are long-term and trust based. The key to these relationships is that the promise of a long-term, mutually beneficial relationship trumps short-term opportunism.

## Recent Trends

The main feature of recent years has been a growing diversity of hybrid vertical relationships that have attempted to combine the flexibility and incentives of market transactions with the close collaboration provided by vertical integration. Although collaborative vertical relationships are viewed as a recent phenomenon—associated with microelectronics, biotechnology, and other hi-tech sectors—local clusters of vertically collaborating firms are a long-time feature of the craft industries of Europe. This is especially true of northern Italy, both in traditional sectors such as textiles[18] and newer sectors such as packaging equipment[19] and motorcycles.[20]

The supplier networks of Japanese manufacturers with their knowledge sharing and collaborative new product development have become models for many large American and European companies.[21] There has been a massive shift from arm's-length supplier relationships to long-term collaboration with fewer suppliers. In many instances, competitive tendering and multiple sourcing have been replaced by single-supplier arrangements. These long-term vendor relationships often involve supplier certification, quality assurance programs, and technical collaboration.

The mutual dependence that results from close, long-term supplier–buyer relationships creates vulnerability for both parties. While trust may alleviate some of the risks of opportunism, companies can also reinforce their vertical relationships and discourage opportunism through equity stakes and profit sharing arrangements. For example: Commonwealth Bank of Australia took an equity stake in its IT supplier EDS Australia; pharmaceutical companies often acquire equity stakes in the biotech companies that undertake much of their R & D; and, as already noted, oilfield services companies are increasingly equity partners in upstream projects.

However, in this world of closer vertical relationships, some trends have been in the opposite direction. The internet has radically reduced the transaction costs of markets, particularly in pruning search costs and facilitating electronic payments. The result has been a revival in arm's-length competitive contracting through business-to-business e-commerce hubs such as Covisint (auto parts), Elemica (chemicals), and Rock & Dirt (construction equipment).[22] The incentives to disperse the value chain internationally, particularly to take advantage of low labor costs in emerging countries, has intensified and so has encouraged arm's-length outsourcing. In many sectors, manufacturing is outsourced to China and Southeast Asian countries; services (including call centers and software development) are outsourced to India. We shall return to these international dimensions of outsourcing in Chapter 12 (see "Location and the Value Chain").

The scope of outsourcing has extended from basic components to a wide range of business services, including payroll, IT, training, and customer service and support. Increasingly, outsourcing involves not just individual components and services but whole chunks of the value chain. In electronics, the design and manufacture of entire products are often outsourced to contract manufacturers such as Hon Hai Precision Industry Co., which makes Apple iPods, Nokia phones, and Sony's PlayStation.

Extreme levels of outsourcing have given rise to the concept of the *virtual corporation*: a firm whose primary function is to coordinate the activities of a network of suppliers and downstream partners.[23] In this organizational form the hub company has the role of *systems integrator*. The critical issue is whether a company that outsources most functions can retain the *architectural capabilities* needed to manage the *component capabilities* of the various partners and contractors. The risk is that the virtual corporation may degenerate into a "hollow corporation," where it loses the capability to evolve and adapt to changing circumstances.[24] If, as Prahalad and Hamel argue, core competences are embodied in "core products," then the more these core products are outsourced, the greater is the potential for the erosion of core competence.[25] Andrea Prencipe's research into aero engines points to the complementarity between architectural capabilities and component capabilities. Thus, even when the aero engine manufacturers outsource key components, they typically maintain R & D into those component technologies.[26] The problems experienced by Boeing in managing the outsourced network model it adopted for its 787 Dreamliner point to the complexity of the system integrator role.[27]

## Summary

Our discussion of the shifting boundaries between markets and firms in the organization of economic activity introduced us to some of the important ideas concerning the relative efficiencies of markets and firms: the transaction cost of markets versus the administrative costs of firms. The tendency over the past 200 years for firms to grow in size and scope and to encompass more and more of the economic activity of society reflects the fall in the administrative costs of firms relative to the transactions costs of markets.

In relation to vertical integration decisions, transaction costs also play an important role. The presence of transaction-specific investments, small numbers of firms, and other sources of market inefficiency create important incentives for vertical integration.

However, transaction costs are only one factor to be taken into account when a firm decides which parts of its value chain to engage in. Among the other factors, the role of capabilities is critical: the most persuasive argument for vertical specialization is that firms need to focus on those activities they are best at. For most companies, their IT capabilities are inferior to those of IBM and their logistics capabilities inferior to those of Federal Express. Hence, it makes sense to outsource these activities. But this fails to take account of the linkages among capabilities in different value chain activities. If my product-development capabilities are dependent upon achieving real-time information on customer-buying patterns and my manufacturing capabilities require a highly flexible and responsive distribution capability, then I may need my IT services and logistics system to be tightly integrated with other functions and customized to their needs.

Moreover, vertical integration decisions are not simply make-or-buy choices: there is a wide variety of ways in which a company can structure vertical relationships. Vertical relationships between independent firms do not need to be arm's-length contracts: the recent growth in outsourcing has involved medium- and long-term relationships which are governed partly by contract, but also trust and mutual commitment. In a number of industries specialized types of vertical relationship have appeared such as franchising, dealership arrangements, and agency agreements. Such vertical forms can reconcile the coordination benefits of vertical integration with the capability advantages of vertical specialization. Similarly with internalization: vertical integration may involve a range of relationships between vertically related internal units, including quasi-market contracts.

Ultimately, vertical integration decisions revolve around two key questions. First, which activities will we undertake internally and which will we outsource? Second, how do we design our vertical arrangements with both external and internal suppliers and buyers?

Quizzes and flashcards to test yourself further are available in your interactive e-book at **www.wileyopenpage.com**

## Self-Study Questions

1. "The Shifting Boundary between Firms and Markets" section above argues that developments in information and communication technology (e.g., regarding telephones and computers) during most of the 20th century tended to lower the costs of administration within the firm relative to the costs of market transactions, thereby increasing the size and scope of firms. What about the internet? How has this influenced the efficiency of large integrated firms relative to small, specialized firms coordinated by markets?

2. "The Shifting Barrier between Firms and Markets" section notes that the large US companies account for a smaller percentage of total employment—a development that is attributed to a more turbulent business environment. Explain why external turbulence encourages outsourcing and increased focus on core business.

3. A large proportion of major corporations outsource their IT functions to specialist suppliers of IT services such as IBM, EDS (now owned by Hewlett-Packard), Accenture, and Capgemini. What transaction costs are incurred by these outsourcing arrangements and why do they arise? What are the offsetting benefits from IT outsourcing?

4. In Strategy Capsule 11.1, Steve Rosenbush argues that integration between media content and media distribution companies (and, specifically, between Disney and Comcast) is strategically advantageous. John Kay suggests that there is little need for common ownerships between distribution channels and the content they carry. Explain the arguments of each. Who do you agree with? As more content is being viewed via the internet and on mobile devices, how does this affect the arguments?

5. For its Zara brand, Inditex manufactures the majority of the garments it sells and undertakes all of its own distribution from manufacturing plants to its directly managed retail outlets. Benetton outsources most of its production, and most of its retail outlets are owned and operated by franchisees. Which is the superior system?

# Notes

1. M. J. Piskorski ("A Note on Corporate Strategy," Harvard Business School 9-705-449, 2005) defines *corporate strategy* as: "a set of choices that a corporation makes to create value through configuration and coordination of its multimarket activities." In practice, determining the boundary between business strategy and corporate strategy depends on where we draw the boundaries of industries and markets.

2. A. Chandler Jr., *The Visible Hand: The Managerial Revolution in American Business* (Cambridge, MA: MIT Press, 1977).

3. R. H. Coase, "The Nature of the Firm," *Economica* 4 (1937): 386–405.

4. The term *interaction costs* has also been used to describe "the time and money expended whenever people and companies exchange goods, services or ideas." See J. Hagel and M. Singer, "Unbundling the Corporation," *Harvard Business Review* (March/April 1999): 133–44.

5. Double-entry bookkeeping has its origins in 14th-century Italy and was developed in Venice in the 16th century. See L. Zan, "Accounting and Management Discourse in Preindustrial Settings: The Venice Arsenal at the Turn of the Sixteenth Century," *Accounting and Business Research* 32 (2004): 145–75.

6. F. W. Taylor, *The Principles of Scientific Management* (New York: Bulletin of the Taylor Society, 1916).

7. J. K. Galbraith, *The New Industrial State* (Harmondsworth: Penguin, 1969).

8. L. J. White, "Trends in Aggregate Concentration in the United States," *Journal of Economic Perspectives* 16 (Fall 2002): 137–60.

9. O. E. Williamson, *Markets and Hierarchies: Analysis and Antitrust Implications* (New York: Free Press, 1975); O. E. Williamson, *The Economic Institutions of Capitalism: Firms, Markets and Relational Contracting* (New York: Free Press, 1985).

10. The situation is different in aluminum cans, where aluminum producers such as Alcoa and Pechiney are major producers of beverage cans.

11. For a review of empirical evidence on transaction costs and vertical integration see J. T. Macher and B. D. Richman, "Transaction Cost Economics: An Assessment of Empirical Research in the Social Sciences," *Business and Politics* 10 (2008): Article 1; and M. D, Whinston, "On the Transaction Cost Determinants of Vertical Integration," *Journal of Law Economics and Organization* 19 (2003): 1–23.

12. K. Monteverde and J. J. Teece, "Supplier Switching Costs and Vertical Integration in the Automobile Industry," *Bell Journal of Economics* 13 (Spring 1982): 206–13.

13. S. Masten, "The Organization of Production: Evidence from the Aerospace Industry," *Journal of Law and Economics* 27 (October 1984): 403–17.

14. J. T. Macher, "Technological Development and the Boundaries of the Firm: A Knowledge-based Examination in Semiconductor Manufacturing," *Management Science* 52 (2006): 826–43; K. Monteverde, "Technical Dialogue as an Incentive for Vertical Integration in the Semiconductor Industry," *Management Science* 41 (1995): 1624–38.

15. R. Rey and J. Tirole, "A Primer on Foreclosure," Chapter 33 in M. Armstrong and R. H. Porter (eds), *Handbook of Industrial Organization: Vol. 3* (Amsterdam: Elsevier, 2007).

16. J. H. Dyer, "Effective Interfirm Collaboration: How Firms Minimize Transaction Costs and Maximize Transaction Value," *Strategic Management Journal* 18 (1997): 535–56; J. H. Dyer, "Specialized Supplier Networks as a Source of Competitive Advantage: Evidence from the Auto Industry," *Strategic Management Journal* 17 (1996): 271–92.

17. L. Willcocks and C. Sauer, "High Risks and Hidden Costs in IT Outsourcing," *Financial Times* (May 23, 2000): 3.

18. N. Owen and A. C. Jones, *A Comparative Study of the British and Italian Textile and Clothing Industries,* Department of Trade and Industry (London: HMSO, 2003).

19. G. Lorenzoni and A. Lipparini, "The Leveraging of Interfirm Relationships as Distinctive Organizational Capabilities: A Longitudinal Study," *Strategic Management Journal* 20 (1999): 317–338.

20. G. Lorenzoni and A. Lipparini, "Organizing around Strategic Relationships: Networks of Suppliers in the Italian Motorcycle Industry," in K. O. Cool, J. E. Henderson, and R. Abate (eds), *Restructuring Strategy* (Oxford: Blackwell, 2005): 44–67.

21. J. H. Dyer and K. Nobeoka, "Creating and Managing a High-performance Knowledge-sharing Network: The Toyota Case," *Strategic Management Journal* 21 (2000): 345–68.

22. See www.covisint.com; www.elemica.com; www.rockanddirt.com.

23. "The Virtual Corporation," *Business Week* (February 8, 1993): 98–104; W. H. Davidow and M. S. Malone, *The Virtual Corporation* (New York: HarperCollins, 1992).

24. H. W. Chesborough and D. J. Teece, "When is Virtual Virtuous? Organizing for Innovation," *Harvard Business Review* (May/June 1996): 68–79.

25. C. K. Prahalad and G. Hamel, "The Core Competences of the Corporation," *Harvard Business Review* (May/June 1990): 79–91.

26. S. Brusoni, A. Prencipe, and K. Pavitt, "Knowledge Specialization, Organizational Coupling and the Boundaries of the Firm: Why Do Firms Know More Than They Make?" *Administrative Science Quarterly* 46 (2001): 597–621.

27. "Boeing's Dreamliner Delays Are a Nightmare," *Seeking Alpha*, http://seekingalpha.com/article/110735-boeing-s-dreamliner-delays-are-a-nightmare, accessed July 7, 2009.

# 12 Global Strategy and the Multinational Corporation

Soccer attracts limited interest in cricket-obsessed Pakistan. Yet, the Pakistan city of Sialkot produces the majority of the world's hand-sewn footballs. The world's leading supplier, Adidas, contracts with the major local producer, Forward Sports, which outsources to over 100 local stitching centers. Under pressure from new technology and activists opposing child labor, Sialkot's share of global football production has fallen from over 70% to under 25%. The Adidas' Tango 12 ball used in the Euro 2012 tournament is machine-made with no hand stitching. It is based on research done at Loughborough University in the UK, was lab tested in Germany, field tested in seven countries, and produced in China from materials sourced from China, Taiwan, and South Korea.

## OUTLINE

# Introduction and Objectives

There have been two primary forces driving change in business environment during the past half century. One is technology; the other is internationalization. Internationalization is a source of huge opportunity. In 1981, Infosys, with just six employees, was established in Pune, India. By supplying IT services to corporations throughout the world, Infosys had become the world's eighth-biggest IT services company (just behind its close neighbor, Wipro) with 145,000 employees. Internationalization is also a potent destroyer. For centuries, Sheffield, England was the world's leading center of cutlery manufacture. By 2012, only a few hundred people were employed making cutlery in Sheffield. The industry had been devastated by cheap imports first from South Korea and then from China. Nor is it just the industries in the mature industrial nations that have been ravaged by imports. Bulk imports of second-hand clothing from Europe and North America (much of it from charities and churches) has been ruinous for Kenya's textile and apparel sector.

Internationalization occurs through two mechanisms: trade and direct investment. The growth of world trade has consistently outstripped the growth of world output, increasing export/sales and import penetration ratios for all countries and all industries. For the OECD countries, total trade (imports and exports) rose from 11% of GDP in 1960 to 51% in 2010. Flows of foreign direct investment have risen even faster, reaching $1.5 trillion in 2011.[1]

The forces driving both trade and direct investment are, first, the quest to exploit market opportunities in other countries and, second, the desire to exploit resources and capabilities located in other countries. The resulting "**globalization** of business" has created vast flows of international transactions comprising payments for trade and services, flows of factor payments (interest, profits, and licensing fees), and flows of capital.

What does the internationalization of the world economy mean for our strategy analysis? As we have already noted, internationalization is both a threat and an opportunity. However, in terms of analysis, the primary implication of introducing the international dimension is that it adds considerable complexity to our strategy analysis—not just in broadening the scope of markets (and competition) but also in complicating the analysis of competitive advantage.

> By the time you have completed this chapter, you will be able to:
>
> ◆ use the tools of industry analysis to examine the impact of internationalization on industry structure and competition;
>
> ◆ analyze the implications of a firm's national environment for its competitive advantage;
>
> ◆ formulate strategies for exploiting overseas business opportunities, including overseas market entry strategies and overseas production strategies;
>
> ◆ shape international strategies that achieve an optimal balance between global integration and national differentiation;
>
> ◆ design organizational structures and management systems appropriate to the pursuit of international strategies.

We begin by exploring the implications of international competition, first for industry analysis and then for the analysis of competitive advantage.

## Implications of International Competition for Industry Analysis

### Patterns of Internationalization

Internationalization occurs through *trade*—the sale and shipment of goods and services from one country to another—and *direct investment*—building or acquiring productive assets in another country. On this basis we can identify different types of industry according to the extent and mode of their internationalization (Figure 12.1):

- *Sheltered industries* are served exclusively by indigenous firms. They are sheltered from both imports and inward direct investment by regulation, trade barriers, or because of the localized nature of the goods and services they offer. The forces of internationalization have made this category progressively smaller over time. Sheltered industries are primarily fragmented service industries (dry cleaning, hairdressing, auto repair,), some small-scale production industries (handicrafts, residential construction), and industries producing products that are non-tradable because they are perishable (fresh milk, bread) or difficult to move (beds, garden sheds).

- *Trading industries* are those where internationalization occurs primarily through imports and exports. If a product is transportable, if it is not nationally differentiated, and if it is subject to substantial scale economies, exporting from a single location is the most efficient means to exploit overseas markets. This is the case with commercial aircraft, shipbuilding, and defense equipment. Trading industries also include products whose inputs are available only in a few locations: rare earths from China; caviar from Iran and Azerbaijan.

**FIGURE 12.1**   Patterns of industry internationalization

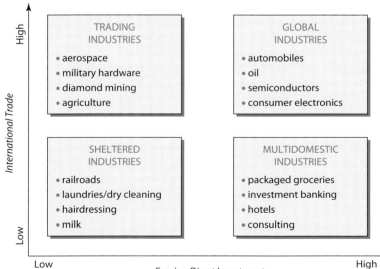

- *Multidomestic industries* are those that internationalize through direct investment—either because trade is not feasible (e.g., service industries such as banking, consulting, or hotels) or because products are nationally differentiated (e.g., frozen ready meals, book publishing).
- *Global industries* are those in which both trade and direct investment are important. These include most major manufacturing industries: automobiles, consumer electronics, semiconductors, pharmaceuticals, petroleum, and beer have high levels of both trade and direct investment.

By which route does internationalization typically occur? In the case of manufacturing companies, internationalization normally begins with exports, typically to countries with the least "psychic distance" from the home country. Later, a sales and distribution subsidiary is established in the overseas country. Eventually, the company develops a more integrated overseas subsidiary that undertakes manufacturing and product development as well.[2] In service industries, internationalization may involve replication (McKinsey & Co.), acquisition (HSBC), or franchising (McDonald's).[3]

## Implications for Competition

Internationalization usually means more competition and lower industry profitability. In 1976, the US automobile market was dominated by GM, Ford, and Chrysler, with 84% of the market. By 2011, there were 14 companies with auto plants within the US; GM and Ford were the remaining indigenous producers accounting for just 35.7% of auto sales.

We can use Porter's five forces of competition framework to analyze the impact of internationalization on competition and industry profitability. If we define the industry in terms of the national market, internationalization directly influences three of the five forces of competition:

- *Competition from potential entrants*: Internationalization is a cause and a consequence of falling barriers to entry into most national markets. Tariff reductions, falling real costs of transportation, foreign-exchange convertibility, the removal of exchange controls, internationalization of standards, and convergence between customer preferences have made it much easier for producers in one country to supply customers in another. Entry barriers that are effective against domestic entrants may be ineffective against potential entrants that are established producers overseas.
- *Rivalry among existing firms*: Internationalization increases internal rivalry primarily because it increases the number of firms competing within each national market—it *lowers seller concentration*. The European market for motor scooters was once dominated by Piaggio (Vespa) and Innocenti (Lambretta). There are now over 25 suppliers of scooters to the European market, including BMW from Germany; Honda, Yamaha, and Suzuki from Japan; Kymco and Kwang Yang from Taiwan; BenZhou/Yiying, Baotian, Zhejiang, and Xingyue from China; Bajaj from India, and Baron and Vectrix from the US. Although internationalization has involved a massive wave of mergers and acquisitions, Ghemawat and Ghadar show that global concentration has declined as a result of national producers entering the global

market.[4] In addition internationalization stimulates competition by increasing investments in capacity and increasing the diversity of competitors.

● *Increasing the bargaining power of buyers*: The option of sourcing from overseas greatly enhances the power of industrial buyers. It also allows distributors to engage in international arbitrage: pharmaceutical distributors have become adept at searching the world for low-price pharmaceuticals then importing them for the domestic market.

## Analyzing Competitive Advantage in an International Context

The growth of international competition over the past 20 years has been associated with some stunning reversals in the competitive positions of different companies. In 1989, US Steel was the world's biggest steel company; in 2012, ArcelorMittal based in Luxemburg and India was the new leader. In 1990, Motorola, Ericsson, and Siemens were the world leaders in wireless handsets. By 2012, Nokia, Samsung, and Apple were leaders.

To understand how internationalization has shifted the basis of competition, we need to extend our framework for analyzing competitive advantage to include the influence of firms' national environments. Competitive advantage, we have noted, is achieved when a firm matches its internal strengths in resources and capabilities to the key success factors of the industry. In international industries, competitive advantage depends not just on a firm's internal resources and capabilities but also on their national environments, in particular the availability of resources within the countries where they do business. Figure 12.2 summarizes the implications of

**FIGURE 12.2**   Competitive advantage in an international context internationalization for our basic strategy model in terms of the impact both on industry conditions and firms' access to resources and capabilities.

## National Influences on Competitiveness: Comparative Advantage

The effect of national resource availability on international competitiveness is the subject of the *theory of comparative advantage*. The theory states that a country has a comparative advantage in those products which make intensive use of those resources available in abundance within that country. Thus, Bangladesh has an abundant supply of unskilled labor. The US has an abundant supply of technological resources: trained scientists and engineers, research facilities, and universities. Bangladesh has a comparative advantage in products that make intensive use of unskilled labor, such as clothing, handicrafts, leather goods, and assembly of consumer electronic products. The US has a comparative advantage in technology-intensive products such as microprocessors, computer software, pharmaceuticals, medical diagnostic equipment, and management consulting services.

The term **comparative advantage** refers to the *relative* efficiencies of producing different products. So long as exchange rates are well behaved (do not deviate far from their purchasing power parity levels), then comparative advantage translates into competitive advantage. Comparative advantages are revealed in trade performance. Table 12.1 shows revealed comparative advantages for several product categories and several countries. Positive values show comparative advantage; negative values show comparative disadvantage.

Trade theory initially looked to natural resource endowments, labor supply, and capital stock as the main determinants of comparative advantage. Emphasis has shifted to the central role of knowledge (including technology, human skills, and management capability) and the resources needed to commercialize that knowledge (capital markets, communications facilities, and legal systems).[5] For industries where

**TABLE 12.1** Indexes of revealed comparative advantage for certain broad product categories

| | US | UK | Japan | Switzerland | Canada | Australia | Taiwan |
|---|---|---|---|---|---|---|---|
| Cereals | +0.83 | −0.24 | −0.99 | −0.99 | +0.80 | +0.97 | −0.78 |
| Mineral fuels | −0.82 | −0.11 | −0.93 | −0.50 | +0.41 | +0.26 | −0.54 |
| Pharmaceuticals | −0.25 | +0.19 | −0.51 | +0.34 | −0.32 | −0.34 | −0.78 |
| Vehicles | −0.41 | −0.25 | +0.81 | −0.68 | +0.04 | −0.69 | +0.31 |
| Aerospace | +0.58 | −0.14 | −0.44 | −0.13 | +0.26 | −0.70 | −0.50 |
| Electrical and electronic equipment | −0.26 | +0.08 | +0.41 | −0.02 | −0.30 | −0.74 | +0.25 |
| Optical, photo, medical, and scientific equipment | +0.09 | −0.02 | +0.21 | +0.37 | −0.36 | −0.46 | +0.20 |
| Apparel (woven) | −0.92 | −0.61 | −0.96 | −0.40 | −0.59 | −0.92 | −0.29 |
| Finance and insurance | −0.10 | +0.56 | +0.08 | +0.69 | −0.08 | +0.05 | −0.85 |

*Note:*
Revealed comparative advantage for each product group is measured as: (exports − imports)/(exports + imports).
*Source:* OECD.

scale economies are important, a large home market is an additional source of comparative advantage (e.g., the US in aerospace).[6]

## Porter's National Diamond

Michael Porter has extended our understanding of international competitive advantage by emphasizing the dynamics through which resources and capabilities are developed.[7] Porter's *national diamond* framework identifies four key factors that determine a country's competitive advantage within a particular sector (Figure 12.3).[8]

1  *Factor conditions*: Whereas the conventional analysis of comparative advantage focuses on endowments of broad categories of resource, Porter emphasizes the role of highly specialized resources many of which are "home-grown" rather than "endowed." For example, in analyzing Hollywood's preeminence in film production, Porter points to the local concentration of highly skilled labor, including the roles of UCLA and USC schools of film. Also, resource constraints may encourage the development of substitute capabilities: in post-war Japan, raw material shortages spurred miniaturization and low-defect manufacturing; in Italy, restrictive labor laws have stimulated automation.

2  *Related and supporting industries*: One of Porter's most striking empirical findings is that national competitive strengths tend to be associated with "clusters" of industries. Silicon Valley's cluster comprises semiconductor, computer, software, and venture capital firms. For each industry, closely related industries are sources of critical resources and capabilities. Denmark's global leadership in wind power is based upon a cluster comprising wind turbine manufacturers, offshore wind farm developers and operators, and utilities.

3  *Demand conditions*: in the domestic market these provide the primary driver of innovation and quality improvement. For example:

   a  Switzerland's preeminence in watches is supported by the obsessive punctuality of the Swiss.

   b  Japanese dominant share of the world market for cameras by companies owes much to Japanese enthusiasm for amateur photography and customers' eager adoption of innovation in cameras.

**FIGURE 12.3**   Porter's national diamond framework

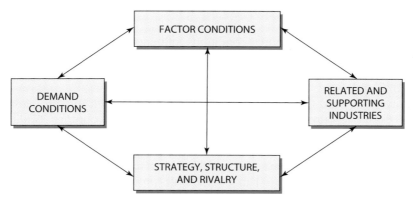

c German dominance of the high-performance segment of the world automobile industry through Daimler, BMW, Porsche, and VW-Audi reflects German motorists' love of quality engineering and their irrepressible urge to drive on autobahns at terrifying speeds.

4 *Strategy, structure, and rivalry*: National competitive performance in particular sectors is inevitably related to the strategies and structures of firms in those industries. Porter puts particular emphasis on the role of intense domestic competition in driving innovation, efficiency, and the upgrading of competitive advantage. The international success of the Japanese in autos, cameras, consumer electronics, and office equipment is based upon domestic industries that feature at least six major producers, all strongly competitive with one another. Conversely, European failure in many hi-tech industries may be a result of European governments' propensity to kill domestic competition by creating *national champions*.

## Consistency between Strategy and National Conditions

Establishing competitive advantage in global industries requires congruence between business strategy and the pattern of the country's comparative advantage. In wireless handsets, it is sensible for Chinese producers, such as ZTE and Huawei, to use their cost advantages to concentrate on the mass market and supply under distributors' brands; for Apple, Samsung, Sony, and RIM the emphasis needs to be differentiation through technology and design.

Achieving congruence between firm strategy and national conditions also extends to the embodiment of national culture within strategy and management systems. The success of US companies in many areas of high technology, including computer software and biotechnology, owes much to a business system of entrepreneurial capitalism which exploits a national culture that emphasizes individuality, opportunity, and wealth acquisition. The global success of Korean corporate giants such as Samsung and LG reflects organizational structures and management systems that embody Korean cultural characteristics such as loyalty, respect for authority, conformity to group norms, commitment to organizational goals, and work ethic—what Professor Young-Ryeol Park refers to as *dynamic collectivism*.[9]

## Applying the Framework: International Location of Production

To examine how national resource conditions influence international strategies, we will look at two types of strategic decision in international business: first, where to locate production activities and, second, how to enter a foreign market. Let us begin with the first of these.

Firms move beyond their national borders not only to seek foreign markets but also to access the resources and capabilities available in other countries. Traditionally, multinationals established plants to serve local markets. Increasingly, decisions concerning where to produce are being separated from decisions over where to sell. For example, ST Microelectronics, the world leader in application-specific integrated circuits (ASICs), is headquartered in Switzerland; production is mainly in France, Italy, and Singapore; R & D is conducted mainly in France, Italy, and the US; and the biggest markets are the US, Japan, Netherlands, and Singapore.

## Determinants of Geographical Location

The decision of where to manufacture requires consideration of three sets of factors:

- *National resource availability*: Firms should produce where they can benefit from favorable supplies of resource. For the petroleum industry this means exploring where the prospects of finding hydrocarbons are high. In assembly-based manufacturing it is a quest for low-cost labor. Table 12.2 shows differences in employment costs between countries. For the technology sector, access to specialist technical know-how is essential.
- *Firm-specific competitive advantages*: For firms whose competitive advantage is based on internal resources and capabilities, optimal location depends on where those resources and capabilities are situated and how mobile they are. Wal-Mart has experienced difficulty recreating its capabilities outside of the US. Conversely, Toyota and IKEA have successfully transferred their operational capabilities to their overseas subsidiaries.
- *Tradability*: The more difficult it is to transport a product and the more it is subject to trade barriers (such as tariffs and quotas), the more production will need to take place within the local market. Services—hairdressing, restaurant meals, banking, and the like—need to be produced in close proximity to where they are consumed.

## Location and the Value Chain

The production of most goods and services comprises a vertical chain of activities where the input requirements of each stage vary considerably. Hence, different countries offer advantage at different stages of the value chain. Table 12.3 shows the pattern of international specialization within textiles and apparel. Similarly with consumer electronics: component production is research- and capital-intensive and is concentrated in the US, Japan, Korea, and Taiwan; assembly is labor-intensive and is concentrated in China, Thailand, and Latin America.

**TABLE 12.2**   Hourly compensation costs for production workers in manufacturing (US$)

|             | 1975 | 2000  | 2010  |
|-------------|------|-------|-------|
| Switzerland | 6.09 | 21.24 | 53.20 |
| Germany     | 6.31 | 24.42 | 43.76 |
| Australia   | 5.62 | 14.47 | 40.60 |
| France      | 4.52 | 15.70 | 40.55 |
| US          | 6.36 | 19.76 | 34.74 |
| Italy       | 4.67 | 14.01 | 33.41 |
| Japan       | 3.00 | 22.27 | 31.99 |
| UK          | 3.37 | 16.45 | 29.44 |
| Spain       | 2.53 | 10.78 | 26.60 |
| Korea       | 0.32 | 8.19  | 16.62 |
| Taiwan      | 0.40 | 5.85  | 8.36  |
| Mexico      | 1.47 | 2.08  | 6.23  |
| Philippines | 0.62 | 1.30  | 1.90  |

**Source:** US Department of Labor, Bureau of Labor Statistics. Reproduced with permission.

**TABLE 12.3** Comparative advantages in textiles and clothing by vertical stage

|  | Fiber production | Spun yarn | Textiles | Apparel |
|---|---|---|---|---|
| Hong Kong | −0.96 | −0.81 | −0.41 | +0.75 |
| Italy | −0.54 | +0.18 | +0.14 | +0.72 |
| Japan | −0.36 | +0.48 | +0.78 | −0.48 |
| US | +0.96 | +0.64 | +0.22 | −0.73 |

**Note:**
Fiber production includes both natural and synthetic fibers. Revealed comparative advantage is measured as (exports − imports)/(exports + imports).
**Source:** United Nations.

**TABLE 12.4** Where does the iPhone4 come from?

| Item | Supplier | Location |
|---|---|---|
| Design and operating system | Apple | US |
| Flash memory | Samsung Electronics | S. Korea |
| DRAM memory | Samsung Electronics | S. Korea |
|  | Micron Technology | US |
| Application processor | Murata | Japan/Taiwan |
| Baseband | Infineon | Taiwan |
|  | Skyworks | US |
|  | TriQuint |  |
| Power management | Dialog Semiconductor | Taiwan |
| Audio | Texas Instruments | US |
| Touchscreen control | Cirrus Logic | US |
| Accel and gyroscope | STMicroelectronics | Italy |
| E-compass | AKM Semiconductor | Japan |
| Assembly | Foxconn | China |

**Source:** "Slicing an Apple," *Economist* (August 10, 2011), http://www.economist.com/node/21525685.

A key feature of recent internationalization has been the international fragmentation of value chains as firms seek to locate countries whose resource availability and cost best match each stage of the value chain.[10] Table 12.4 shows the international composition of Apple's iPhone; Figure 12.4 shows a similar breakdown of the Boeing 787 Dreamliner.

However, cost is just one factor in offshoring decisions. Cost advantages are vulnerable to exchange rate changes and inflationary pressures, so it is important to consider underlying issues concerning the availability and quality of resources and capabilities. Locational decisions are driven more by the potential for overall operational efficiency than by local wage rates.

As the examples of the iPhone and Boeing Dreamliner show, global sourcing is not only about cost efficiency: for technologically advanced products and services the location of sophisticated know-how is more important. Yet, even for knowledge-intensive goods and services, Western companies are finding that China, India, and other emerging market countries can offer world-class skills. For example, Jim Breyer, managing partner of Accel Partners, a Silicon Valley venture capitalist, observed: "Taiwan and China have some of the world's best designers of wireless chips and wireless software." In certain types of precision manufacturing, including

**FIGURE 12.4** The globally dispersed production of the Boeing 787 Dreamliner

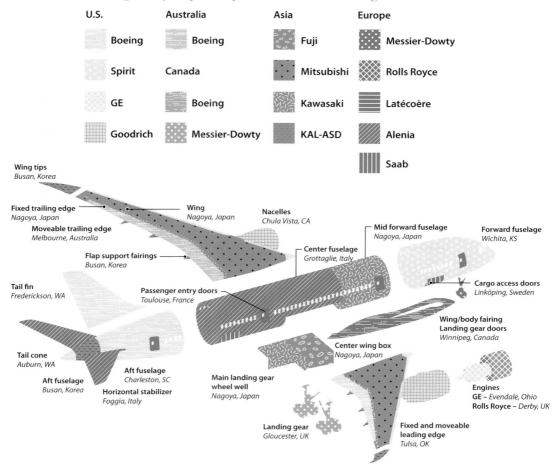

*Source:* Boeing Images, © 2010 Boeing Inc. Reprinted with permission.

the processes that produce magnesium alloy casing for notebook computers, companies such as Waffer in Taiwan offer some of the most sophisticated technology in the world. Most of the leading Indian IT outsourcing companies operate at level 5 (the highest level of expertise) of the Capability Maturity Model (CMM), an international measure of technical skill, while most internal IT departments in Western companies operate at level 2 or 3. Call centers, such as those operated by eTelecare, a Manila-based outsourcing provider, offer better average handling times and customer satisfaction relative to leading companies in the US.[11]

The benefits from fragmenting the value chain must be traded off against the added costs of coordinating globally dispersed activities. Apart from costs of transportation and higher inventories, a key cost of dispersed activities is time. Just-in-time scheduling often necessitates that production activities are carried out in close proximity to one another. Companies that compete on speed and reliability of delivery (e.g., Inditex and Dell) typically forsake the cost advantages of a globally dispersed value chain in favor of integrated operations with fast access to the final market.[12]

Figure 12.5 summarizes the relevant criteria in location decisions.

**FIGURE 12.5** Determining the optimal location of value chain activities

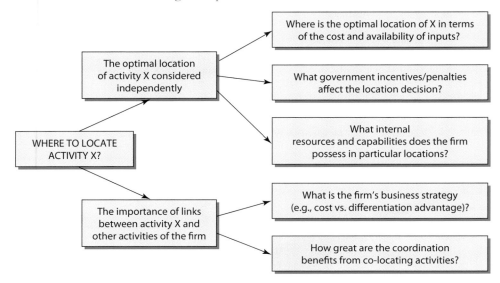

## Applying the Framework: Foreign Entry Strategies

Firms enter foreign markets in pursuit of profitability. The profitability of entering a foreign market depends upon the attractiveness of that market and whether the firm can establish a competitive advantage within it. While market attractiveness can be a magnet for foreign multinationals—the size and growth of the Chinese economy has been irresistible to many Western companies—over the longer term, the key determinant of profitability is likely to be ability to establish competitive advantage vis-à-vis local firms and other multinationals.

A firm's potential for establishing competitive advantage has important implications for the means by which it enters a foreign market. The basic distinction is between market entry by means of *transactions* and market entry by means of *direct investment*. Figure 12.6 shows a spectrum of market entry options arranged according to the degree of resource commitment by the firm. Thus, at one extreme, there is exporting through individual spot-market transactions; at the other, there is the establishment of a wholly owned, fully integrated subsidiary.

How does a firm weigh the merits of different market entry modes? Five key factors are relevant:

1 *Is the firm's competitive advantage based on firm-specific or country-specific resources?* If the firm's competitive advantage is country-based, the firm must exploit an overseas market by exporting. Thus, to the extent that Shanghai Auto's competitive advantage in Western car markets is its low domestic cost base, it must produce in China and export to foreign markets. If Toyota's competitive advantage is its production and management capabilities, then as long as it can transfer these capabilities Toyota can exploit foreign markets either by exports or by direct investment.[13]

**FIGURE 12.6**  Alternative modes of overseas market entry

2  *Is the product tradable and what are the barriers to trade?* If the product is not tradable because of transportation constraints or import restrictions, then accessing that market requires entry either by investing in overseas production facilities or by licensing the use of key resources to local companies within the overseas market.

3  *Does the firm possess the full range of resources and capabilities for establishing a competitive advantage in the overseas market?* Competing in an overseas market is likely to require the firm to acquire additional resources and capabilities, particularly those related to marketing and distributing in an unfamiliar market. Accessing such country-specific resources is most easily achieved by collaborating with a firm in the overseas market. The form of the collaboration depends, in part, on the resources and capabilities required. If a firm needs marketing and distribution, it might appoint a distributor or agent with exclusive territorial rights. If a wide range of manufacturing and marketing capabilities is needed, the firm might license its product and/or its technology to a local manufacturer. In technology-based industries, licensing technology to local companies is common. In marketing-intensive industries, firms with strong brands can license their trademarks to local companies. Alternatively, a joint venture might be sought with a local manufacturing company. Danone, the French dairy products and drinks company, operates joint ventures in Russia, China, Indonesia, Iran, Mexico, Argentina, Saudi Arabia, and South Africa.

4  *Can the firm directly appropriate the returns to its resources?* Whether a firm licenses the use of its resources or chooses to exploit them directly (either through exporting or direct investment) depends partly on appropriability considerations. In chemicals and pharmaceuticals, the patents protecting product innovations tend to offer strong legal protection, in which case patent licenses to local producers can be an effective means of appropriating their returns. In computer software and computer equipment the protection offered by patents and copyrights is looser, which encourages exporting rather than licensing as a means of exploiting overseas markets. With all licensing arrangements, key considerations are the capabilities and reliability of the local licensee. This

is particularly important in licensing brand names, where the licenser must carefully protect the brand's reputation. Cadbury (now owned by Kraft Foods) licenses its trademarks and product recipes to Hershey for the production and sale of its Cadbury chocolate bars in the US. This arrangement reflects the fact that Hershey has production and distribution facilities in the US that Cadbury cannot match, and that Cadbury views Hershey as a reliable business partner.

5 *What transaction costs are involved?* A key issue that arises in the licensing of a firm's trademarks or technology concerns the transaction costs of negotiating, monitoring, and enforcing the terms of such agreements as compared with internationalization through a fully owned subsidiary. In overseas markets, Starbucks owns and operates its coffee shops, while McDonald's franchises its burger restaurants. McDonald's competitive advantage depends primarily upon the franchisee faithfully replicating the McDonald's system. This can be enforced effectively by means of franchise contracts. Starbucks believes that its success is achieved through creating the "Starbucks experience," which is as much about ambiance as it is about coffee. It is difficult to articulate the ingredients of this experience, let alone write it into a contract.

Issues of transaction costs are fundamental to the choices between alternative market entry modes. Barriers to exporting in the form of transport costs and tariffs are types of transaction costs; other costs include exchange rate risk and information costs. Transaction cost analysis has been central to theories of the existence of multinational corporations. In the absence of transaction costs in the markets either for goods or for resources, companies exploit overseas markets either by exporting their goods and services or by selling the use of their resources to local firms in overseas markets.[14] Thus, multinationals tend to predominate in industries where:

- firm-specific intangible resources such as brands and technology are important (transaction costs in licensing the use of these resources favor direct investment);
- exporting is subject to transaction costs (e.g., through tariffs or import restrictions);
- customer preferences are reasonably similar between countries.

## Multinational Strategies: Global Integration versus National Differentiation

So far, we have viewed international expansion, whether by export or by direct investment, as a means by which a company can extend its competitive advantages from its home market into foreign markets. However, international scope may itself be a source of competitive advantage over geographically focused competitors. In this section, we explore whether, and under what conditions, firms that operate on an international basis are able to gain a competitive advantage over nationally focused firms. What is the potential for such "global strategies" to create competitive advantage? In what types of industry are they likely to be most effective? And how should they be designed and deployed in order to maximize their potential?

# The Benefits of a Global Strategy[15]

A **global strategy** is one that views the world as a single, if segmented, market. There are five major sources of value from operating internationally.

*Cost Benefits of Scale and Replication*   Fifty years ago, Ted Levitt pointed out the advantage that companies that compete globally have over their local rivals.[16] Supplying the world market allows access to scale economies in product development, manufacturing, and marketing. (Ghemawat refers to these as benefits from *cross-border aggregation*.)[17] Exploiting these scale economies has been facilitated by the growing uniformity imposed by technology, communication, and travel: "Everywhere everything gets more and more like everything else as the world's preference structure is relentlessly homogenized," observed Levitt.[18] In many industries—commercial aircraft, semiconductors, consumer electronics, video games—firms have no choice: they must market globally to amortize the huge costs of product development. In service industries, the cost efficiencies from international operation derive primarily from economies in the replication of knowledge-based assets, including organizational capabilities.[19] Once a company has created a knowledge-based asset or product—whether a recipe, a piece of software, or an organizational system—it can be replicated in additional national markets at a fraction of the cost of creating the original. Disneyland theme parks in Tokyo, Paris, Hong Kong, and Shanghai replicate the rides and management systems that Disney develops for its parks in Anaheim and Orlando. This is the appeal of franchising: if you create a brilliantly innovative business offering dental care for dogs, why limit yourself to Santa Monica, California? Why not try to emulate McDonald's with its 67,000 outlets across 200 countries of the world?

*Serving Global Customers*   In several industries—for example investment banking, audit services, and advertising—the primary driver of globalization has been the need to service global customers.[20] Hence, auto-parts manufacturers have internationalized as they follow the major of the automobile producers. Law firms such as Baker & McKenzie, Clifford Chance, and Linklaters have internationalized mainly to better serve their multinational clients.

*Exploiting National Resources: Arbitrage Benefits*   As we have already seen, global strategy does not necessarily involve production in one location and then distributing globally. Global strategies also involve exploiting the efficiencies from locating different activities in different places. As we have seen, companies internationalize not just in search of market opportunities but also in search of resource opportunities. Traditionally, this has meant a quest for raw materials and low-cost labor. Increasingly, it means a quest for knowledge. For example, among semiconductor firms, a critical factor determining the location of overseas subsidiaries is the desire to access knowledge within the host country.[21] Ghemawat refers to this exploitation of differences between countries as *arbitrage*.[22] Arbitrage strategies are conventionally associated with exploiting wage differentials by offshoring production to low-wage locations; increasingly arbitrage is about exploiting the distinctive knowledge available in different locations.

*Learning Benefits*   The learning benefits of multinational operations go beyond *accessing* localized knowledge but extend to the *transfer* and *integration* of knowledge from different locations and the *creation* of new knowledge through interacting with different national environments. IKEA's expansion in Japan has required it to adjust to Japanese style and design preferences, Japanese modes of living, and the Japanese's fanatical quality-consciousness. As a result, IKEA has developed its capabilities with regard to both quality and design that it believes will enhance its competitiveness worldwide. According to the CEO of IKEA Japan, "One reason for us to enter the Japanese market, apart from hopefully doing very good business, is to expose ourselves to the toughest competition in the world. By doing so, we feel that we are expanding the quality issues for IKEA all over the world."[23]

Recent contributions to the international business literature suggest that this ability of multinational corporations (MNCs) to develop knowledge in multiple locations, to synthesize that knowledge, and to transfer it across national borders may be their greatest advantage over nationally focused companies.[24] The critical requirement for exploiting these learning benefits is that the company possesses some form of global infrastructure for managing knowledge that permits new experiences, new ideas, and new practices to be diffused and integrated.

*Competing Strategically*  A major advantage of the Romans over the Gauls, Goths, and other barbarian tribes was their ability to draw upon the military and economic resources of the Roman Empire to fight local wars. Similarly, multinational companies possess a key strategic advantage over their nationally focused rivals when engaging in competitive battles in individual national markets: they can use resources from other national markets. At its most simple, this *cross-subsidization* of competitive initiatives in one market using profits from other markets involves *predatory pricing*—cutting prices to a level that drives competitors out of business. Such pricing practices are likely to contravene both the World Trade Organization's anti-dumping rules and national antitrust laws. More usually, cross-subsidization involves using cash flows from other markets to finance aggressive sales and marketing campaigns.[25] Evidence of firms charging lower prices in overseas than in domestic markets and lower export prices to overseas subsidiaries than those charged to third parties supports the argument that firms use domestic profits to subsidize price competition in overseas markets.[26]

Strategic competition between MNCs can result in complex patterns of attack, retaliation, and containment.[27] Fuji Film's sponsorship of the 1984 Olympic Games in Los Angeles was seen by Kodak as an aggressive incursion into its backyard; it responded by expanding its marketing efforts in Japan.[28]

## The Need for National Differentiation

For all the advantages of global strategy, national market differences persist: with a few notable exceptions (Apple's iPod and iPad), most products designed to meet the needs of the "global customer" have lacked global appeal. Ford has struggled in its efforts to introduce a standardized global car: its Mondeo/Contour model was a disappointment; its 2012 Focus, produced at five plants throughout the world, is its latest attempt at a global car. The experience of most auto firms is that their global models become differentiated to meet the needs and preferences of different national markets.[29]

In some industries efforts toward globalization have met with little success. In washing machines, national preferences have shown remarkable resilience: French and US washing machines are primarily top loading, elsewhere in Europe they are mainly front loading; the Germans prefer higher spin speeds than the Italians do; US machines feature agitators rather than revolving drums; and Japanese machines are small. The pioneers of globalization in domestic appliances—Electrolux and Whirlpool—struggle to outperform national and regional specialists.[30] Similarly in retail banking, despite some examples of successful internationalization (Banco Santander, HSBC), most of the evidence points to few economies from cross-border integration and the critical need to adapt to local market conditions.[31]

Every nation represents a unique combination of a multitude of distinctive characteristics. How can we recognize and assess the extent of similarities and differences between countries for the purposes of international strategy formulation? Pankaj Ghemawat proposes four key components of distance between countries: *cultural, administrative and political, geographical,* and *economic*—his *CAGE* framework (Table 12.5).

Ghemawat's broad categories are only a starting point for exploring the national idiosyncrasies that make international expansion such a minefield. For consumer products firms, the structures of national distribution channels are critical. Procter & Gamble must adapt its marketing, promotion, and distribution of toiletries and household products to take account of the fact that, in the US, a few chains account for a major share of its US sales; in southern Europe, most sales are through small, independent retailers, while in Japan, P&G must sell through a multi-tiered hierarchy of distributors. The closer an industry to the final consumer, the more important cultural factors are likely to be. Strategy Capsule 12.1 considers some dimensions of national culture. It is notable that so few retailers have been successful outside their domestic markets. Al-Mart, IKEA, H&M, and the Gap, are among the few retailers that are truly global. Even fewer have been as successful overseas as at home. For many, franchising has provided a lower-risk internationalization strategy.

**TABLE 12.5**  Ghemawat's CAGE framework for assessing country differences

| | Cultural distance | Administrative and political distance | Geographical distance | Economic differences |
|---|---|---|---|---|
| *Distance between two countries increases with* | Different languages, ethnicities, religions, social norms<br>Lack of connective ethnic or social networks | Absence of shared political or monetary association<br>Political hostility<br>Weak legal and financial institutions | Lack of common border, water-way access, adequate transportation or communication links<br>Physical remoteness | Different consumer incomes<br>Different costs and quality of natural, financial, and human resources<br>Different information or knowledge |
| *Industries most affected by source of distance* | Industries with high linguistic content (TV, publishing) and cultural content (food, wine, music) | Industries viewed by government as strategically important (e.g., energy, defense, telecoms) | Products with low value-to-weight (cement), are fragile or perishable (glass, milk), or dependent upon communications (financial services) | Products whose demand is sensitive to consumer income levels (luxury goods)<br>Labor-intensive products (clothing) |

**STRATEGY CAPSULE 12.1**

# How Do National Cultures Differ?

Do people differ between countries with regard to beliefs, norms, and value systems? The answer from a series of research studies is yes.

The best-known study of national cultural differences is by Geert Hofstede. The principal dimensions of national values he identified were:

- *Power distance*: The extent to which inequality, and decision-making power in particular, is accepted within organizations and within society. Power distance was high in Malaysia, and most Latin American and Arab countries; low in Austria and Scandinavia.

- *Uncertainty avoidance*: Preference for certainty and established norms was high in most southern European and Latin American countries; tolerance for uncertainty and ambiguity was high in Singapore, Sweden, the UK, the US, and India.

- *Individualism*: Concern for individual over group interests was highest in the US, the UK, Canada, and Australia. Identification with groups and the collective interest was strongest in Latin America and Asia (especially Indonesia, Pakistan, Taiwan, and South Korea).

- *Masculinity/femininity*: Hofstede identifies emphasis on work and material goals and demarcation of gender roles as *masculine*; emphasis on personal relationships rather than efficiency and belief in gender equality was viewed as *feminine*. Japan, Austria, Venezuela, and Italy scored high on masculinity; Scandinavia and the Netherlands scored very low.

Other studies have used different measures for characterizing national cultures. Other scholars emphasize different dimensions of national cultures. Fons Trompenaars (another Dutchman) identifies the US, Australia, Germany, Sweden and UK as *universalist societies*—relationships are governed by standard rules—Brazil, Italy, Japan, and Mexico are *particularist* societies—social relationships are strongly influenced by contextual and personal factors. In *affective* cultures, such as Mexico and the Netherlands, people display their emotions; in *neutral* cultures, such as Japan and the UK, people hide their emotions.

***Sources:*** G. Hofstede, *Culture's Consequences: International Differences in Work-related Values* (Thousand Oaks, CA: SAGE Publications, 1984); F. Trompenaars, *Riding the Waves of Culture* (London: Economist Books, 1993).

## Reconciling Global Integration with National Differentiation

Choices about internationalization strategy have been viewed as a tradeoff between the benefits of global integration and those of national adaptation (Figure 12.7).[32] Industries where scale economies are huge and customer preferences homogeneous call for a global strategy (e.g., jet engines). Industries where national preferences are pronounced and meeting them does not impose prohibitive costs favor multi-domestic strategies (e.g., retail banking). Indeed, in industries where there are few benefits from global integration, multinational firms may be absent (as in funeral services and laundries). Some industries may be low on both dimensions—car repair and office maintenance services are fairly homogeneous worldwide but lack significant

**FIGURE 12.7**   Benefits of global integration versus national differentiation

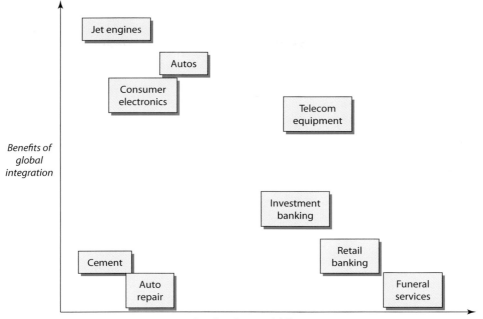

benefits from global integration. Conversely, other industries offer substantial benefits from operating on a global scale (telecommunications equipment, military hardware, cosmetics, and toiletries), but national preferences and standards may also necessitate considerable adaptation to the needs of specific national markets.

Reconciling conflicting forces for global efficiency and national differentiation represents one of the greatest strategic challenges facing MNCs. Achieving *global localization* involves standardizing product features and company activities where scale economies are substantial, and differentiating where national preferences are strongest and where achieving them is not over-costly. Thus, a global car such as the Honda Civic (introduced in 1972 and sold in 110 countries) now embodies considerable local adaptations, not just to meet national safety and environmental standards but also to meet local preferences for legroom, seat specifications, accessories, color, and trim. McDonald's, too, meshes global standardization with local adaptation (Strategy Capsule 12.2).

Reconciling global efficiency with national differentiation involves disaggregating the company by product and function. In retail banking, different products and services have different potential for globalization. Credit cards and basic savings products such as certificates of deposit tend to be globally standardized; checking accounts and mortgage lending are much more nationally differentiated. Similarly with business functions: R & D, purchasing, IT, and manufacturing have strong globalization potential; sales, marketing, customer service, and human resource management need to be much more nationally differentiated. These differences have important implications for how the MNC is organized.

**STRATEGY CAPSULE 12.2**

# McDonald's Goes "Glocal"

For anti-globalization activists, McDonald's is a demon of globalization: it crushes national cuisines and independent, family-run restaurants with the juggernaut of US fast-food corporate imperialism. In reality, its global strategy is a careful blend of global standardization and local adaptation.

McDonald's menus include a number of globally standardized items—the Big Mac and potato fries are international features—however, in most countries McDonald's menus feature an increasing number of locally developed items. These include:

◆ Australia: A range of wraps including Seared Chicken, Tandoori Chicken, and Crispy Sweet Chili Chicken;

◆ France: Croque McDo (a toasted ham and cheese sandwich);

◆ Hong Kong: Grilled Pork Twisty Pasta and Fresh Corn Cup;

◆ India: Shahi Paneer McCurry Pan, McAloo Tikki, Veg Pizza McPuff;

◆ Saudi Arabia: McArabia Kofta, McArabia Chicken;

◆ Switzerland: Shrimp Cocktail, Chickenburger Curry;

◆ UK: A range of deli sandwiches including Spicy Veggie Deli (chickpea patty with coriander and cumin), and Sweet Chili Chicken Deli;

◆ US: Fruit & Maple Oatmeal, Frappes.

There are differences too in restaurant decor, service offerings (internet access in the UK; home delivery in India), and market positioning (outside the US McDonald's is more upmarket). In Israel, many McDonald's are kosher: they do not offer dairy products and are closed on Saturdays. In India, neither beef nor pork is served. In Germany, France, and Spain, McDonald's serves beer. A key reason that almost all of McDonald's non-US outlets are franchised is to

# Strategy and Organization within the Multinational Corporation

These same factors—the benefits from global integration and need for national differentiation—that determine international strategies also have critical implications for the design of organizational structures and management systems to implement these strategies. As we shall see, one of the greatest challenges facing the senior managers of MNCs is aligning organizational structures and management systems to fit with the strategies being pursued.

## The Evolution of Multinational Strategies and Structures

Over the past hundred years, the forces driving internationalization strategies have changed considerably. Yet, the structural configurations of MNCs have tended to persist. We discussed organizational inertia in Chapter 6; it seems likely that, because of their complexity, MNCs face particular difficulties in adapting their structures and systems to change. Chris Bartlett and Sumantra Ghoshal view MNCs as captives of facilitate adaptation to national environments and access to local know-how.

Yet, the principal features of the McDonald's business system are identical throughout the world. McDonald's values and business principles are seen as universal and invariant. Its emphasis on families and children is intended to identify McDonald's with fun and family life wherever it does business. Community involvement and the Ronald McDonald children's charity are also worldwide. Corporate trademarks and brands are mostly globally uniform, including the golden arches logo and "I'm lovin' it" tag line. The business system itself—the franchising, the training of managers and franchisees through Hamburger University, restaurant operations, and supplier relations—is also highly standardized.

McDonald's international strategy was about adapting its US model to local conditions. Now, as new menu items and business concepts are transferred between countries, it is using local differentiation to drive worldwide adaptation and innovation. For example, the McCafé gourmet coffeehouses within McDonald's restaurants were first developed in

Australia. By 2003, McCafés had become established in 30 countries. In responding to growing concern over nutrition and obesity McDonald's has drawn upon country initiatives with regard to ingredients, menus, and information labeling to support global learning.

Has McDonald's got the balance right between global standardization and local adaptation? Simon Anholt, a British marketing expert, argues: "By putting local food on the menu, all you are doing is removing the logic of the brand, because this is an American brand. If McDonald's serves what you think is a poor imitation of your local cuisine, it's going to be an insult." But according to McDonald's CEO Jim Skinner: "We don't run our business from Oak Brook. We are a local business with a local face in each country we operate in." His chief marketing manager, Mary Dillon, adds: "McDonald's is much more about local relevance than a global archetype. Globally we think of ourselves as the custodian of the brand, but it's all about local relevance."

*Source:* www.mcdonalds.com.

---

their history: their strategy-structure configurations today reflect choices they made at the time of their international expansion. Radical changes in strategy and structure are difficult: once an international distribution of functions, operations, and decision-making authority has been determined, reorganization is slow, difficult, and costly, particularly when host governments become involved. This *administrative heritage* of an MNC—its configuration of assets and capabilities, its distribution of managerial responsibilities, and its network of relationships—is a critical determinant of its current capabilities and a key constraint upon its ability to build new strategic capabilities.[33]

Bartlett and Ghoshal identify three eras in the development of the MNC (Figure 12.8):

●  *The early 20th century* was the era of the European multinational. Companies such as Unilever, Shell, ICI, and Philips were pioneers of multinational expansion. Because of the conditions at the time of internationalization—poor transportation and communications, highly differentiated national markets— the companies created *multinational federations*: each national subsidiary was operationally autonomous and undertook the full range of functions, including product development, manufacturing, and marketing.

**FIGURE 12.8** The development of the multinational corporation: Alternative parent–subsidiaries relations

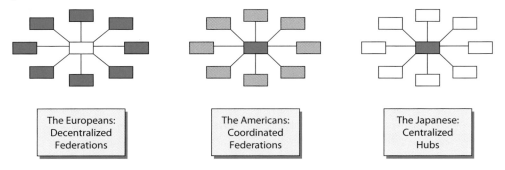

The Europeans:
Decentralized
Federations

The Americans:
Coordinated
Federations

The Japanese:
Centralized
Hubs

**Note:**
The density of shading indicates the concentration of decision making.
**Source:** C. A. Bartlett and S. Ghoshal, *Managing Across Borders: The Transnational Solution* (Boston: Harvard Business School Press, 1998). Copyright © 1989 by the Harvard Business School Publishing Corporation, all rights reserved.

- *After the Second World War* came the era of the American multinational. US dominance of the world economy was reflected in the pre-eminence of US multinationals such as GM, Ford, IBM, Coca-Cola, Caterpillar, and Procter & Gamble. While their overseas subsidiaries were allowed considerable autonomy, this was within the context of the dominant position of their US parent in terms of capital, new product and process technology, management capabilities, and management systems. Their US-based resources and capabilities provided the foundation for their international competitive advantages.

- *The 1970s and 1980s* saw the Japanese challenge. Honda, Toyota, Matsushita, NEC, and YKK pursued global strategies from centralized domestic bases. R & D and manufacturing were concentrated in Japan; overseas subsidiaries undertook sales and distribution. Globally standardized products manufactured in large-scale plants provided the basis for unrivalled cost and quality advantages. Over time, manufacturing and R & D were dispersed, initially because of trade protection by consumer countries and the rising value of the yen against other currencies.

The different administrative heritages of these different groups of MNCs continue to shape their strategies and organizational capabilities. The strength of European multinationals is adaptation to the conditions and requirements of individual national markets. The strength of the US multinationals is their ability to transfer technology and proven new products from their domestic strongholds to their national subsidiaries. Japanese MNCs are notable for the efficiency of global production and new product development. Yet, these core capabilities are also core rigidities. The challenge for European MNCs has been to achieve greater integration of their sprawling international empires; for Shell and Philips this has involved reorganizations over a period of more than two decades. For US MNCs such as Ford and Procter & Gamble it has involved nurturing the ability to tap their foreign subsidiaries for technology, design, and new product ideas. For Japanese MNCs such as Nomura, Hitachi, and

NEC the challenge is to become true insiders in the overseas countries where they do business.

## Reconfiguring the MNC: The Transnational Corporation

*Changing Organization Structure*   For North American and European-based MNCs, the principal structural changes of recent decades have been a shift from organization around national subsidiaries and regional groupings to the creation of worldwide product divisions. For most MNCs, country and regional organizations are retained, but primarily for the purposes of national compliance and customer relationships. Thus, Hewlett-Packard, the world's biggest IT company, conducts its business through five global product groups: Enterprise Servers, Storage and Networking; Enterprise Services; Software; Personal Systems Group; and Imaging and Printing Group. Each of these product groups and each of HP's functions have activities in multiple countries. For example, HP Labs are in Palo Alto, California; Singapore; Bristol, UK; Haifa, Israel; St Petersburg, Russia; Bangalore, India; and Beijing, China. To assist geographical coordination, HP has regional headquarters for the Americas (in Houston), for Europe, the Middle East, and Africa (in Geneva), and for Asia Pacific (in Singapore). Because of the special importance of China and India, its head of the Personal Systems Group also has special responsibility for China and the head of the Imaging and Printing Group has special responsibility for India.

*Reconciling Global Integration and National Differentiation: The Transnational*   However, the formal changes in structure are less important than the changes in responsibilities, decision powers, and modes of coordination within these structures. The fundamental challenge for MNCs has been reconciling the advantages of global integration with those of national differentiation. Escalating costs of research and new product development have made global strategies with global product platforms essential. At the same time, meeting consumer needs in each national market and responding swiftly to changing local circumstances requires greater decentralization. Accelerating technological change further exacerbates these contradictory forces: despite the cost and "critical mass" benefits of centralizing research and new-product development, innovation occurs at multiple locations within the MNC and requires nurturing creativity and initiative throughout the organization. "It's the corporate equivalent of being able to walk, chew gum, and whistle at the same time," notes Chris Bartlett.

Bartlett argues that the simultaneous pursuit of responsiveness to national markets and global coordination requires "a very different kind of internal management process than existed in the relatively simple multinational or global organizations. This is the *transnational organization*."[34] The distinguishing characteristic of the transnational is that it becomes an integrated network of distributed and interdependent resources and capabilities (Figure 12.9). This necessitates that:

- Each national unit is a source of ideas, skills, and capabilities that can be harnessed for the benefit of the total organization.
- National units access global scale economies by designating them the company's world source for a particular product, component, or activity.

**FIGURE 12.9** The transnational corporation

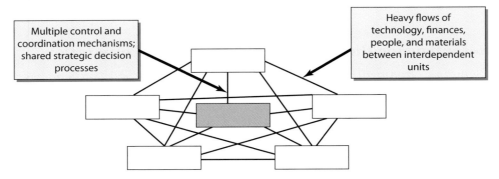

- The center must establish a new, highly complex managing role that coordinates relationships among units but in a highly flexible way. The key is to focus less on managing activities directly and more on creating an organizational context that is conducive to the coordination and resolution of differences. Creating the right organizational context involves "establishing clear corporate objectives, developing managers with broadly based perspectives and relationships, and fostering supportive organizational norms and values."[35]

Balancing global integration and national differentiation requires a company to adapt to the differential requirements of different products, different functions, and different countries. Procter & Gamble adopts global standardization for some of its products (e.g., Pringles potato chips and high-end perfumes); for others (e.g., hair care products and laundry detergent), it allows significant national differentiation. Across countries, P&G organizes global product divisions to serve most of the industrialized world because of the similarities between their markets, while for emerging market countries (such as China and India) it operates through country subsidiaries in order to adapt to the distinctive features of these markets. Among functions, R & D is globally integrated, while sales are organized by national units that are differentiated to meet local market characteristics.

The transnational firm is a concept and direction of development rather than a distinct organizational archetype. It involves convergence of the different strategy configurations of MNCs. Thus, companies such as Philips, Unilever, and Siemens have reassigned roles and responsibilities to achieve greater integration within their traditional "decentralized federations" of national subsidiaries. Japanese global corporations such as Toyota and Matsushita have drastically reduced the roles of their Japanese headquarters. American multinationals such as Citigroup and IBM are moving in two directions: reducing the role of their US bases while increasing integration among their different national subsidiaries.

Multinational corporations are increasingly locating management control of their global product divisions outside their home countries. When Philips adopted a product division structure, it located responsibility for medical electronics in its US subsidiary and leadership in consumer electronics in Japan. Nexans, the world's biggest manufacturer of electric cables, has moved the head office of five of its 20 product divisions outside of France. For example, the head of ships' cables is based in South Korea, the world leader in shipbuilding.[36] Aligning structure, strategy, and national resources may even require shifting the corporate headquarters—HSBC moved from Hong Kong to London; Tetra Pak from Lund, Sweden to Lausanne, Switzerland.[37]

A recent McKinsey study discovered that successful multinationals underperformed successful "national champions." The study identifies a "globalization penalty" reflecting the difficulties which MNCs experienced in:

- setting a shared vision and engaging employees around it;
- maintaining professional standards and encouraging innovation;
- building government and community relationships and business partnerships.

The interviews conducted for the study highlighted the challenges that MNCs faced in reconciling the challenges of local differentiation and global integration:

> Almost everyone we interviewed seemed to struggle with this tension, which often plays out in heated internal debates. Which organizational elements should be standardized? To what extent does managing high-potential emerging markets on a country-by-country basis make sense? When is it better, in those markets, to leverage scale and synergies across business units in managing governments, regulators, partners, and talent?[38]

*Organizing R & D and New Product Development*   Organizing for innovation represents one of the greatest challenges in reconciling local initiative with global integration. The traditional European decentralized model is conducive to local initiatives, but not to their global exploitation. Philips has an outstanding record of innovation in consumer electronics. In its TV business, its Canadian subsidiary developed its first color TV; its Australian subsidiary developed its first stereo sound TV and its British subsidiary developed teletext TVs. However, lack of global integration constrained its success on a worldwide scale. Conversely, many US multinationals have been effective at globally rolling out products and technologies developed at their US cores.

Transnational organizations assign national subsidiaries with global mandates that allow them to take advantage of local resources and capabilities while exploiting globally the results of their initiatives.[39] For example, P&G, recognizing Japanese obsessiveness over cleanliness, assigned increasing responsibility to its Japanese subsidiary for developing household cleaning products. Its Swiffer dust-collecting products were developed in Japan (using technology developed by other firms) then introduced into other markets. Where a local unit possesses unique capabilities, designating it a *center of excellence* can facilitate the dissemination of these capabilities throughout the multinational firm.[40]

## Summary

Moving from a national to an international business environment represents a quantum leap in complexity. In an international environment, a firm's potential for competitive advantage is determined not just by its own resources and capabilities but also by the conditions of the national environment in which it operates, including input prices, exchange rates, and a host of other factors. The extent to which a firm is positioned across multiple national markets also influences its economic power.

Our approach in this chapter has been to simplify the complexities of international strategy by applying the same basic tools of strategy analysis that we developed in earlier chapters. For example, to determine whether a firm should enter an overseas market, our focus has been the profit implications of such an entry. This requires an analysis of (a) the attractiveness of the overseas market using the familiar tools of industry analysis and (b) the potential of the firm to establish competitive advantage in that overseas market, which depends on the firm's ability to transfer its resources and capabilities to the new location and their effectiveness in conferring competitive advantage.

However, establishing the potential for a firm to create value from internationalization is only a beginning. Subsequent analysis needs to design an international strategy: do we enter an overseas market by exporting, licensing, or direct investment? If the latter, should we set up a wholly owned subsidiary or a joint venture? Once the strategy has been established, a suitable organizational structure needs to be designed.

That so many companies that have been outstandingly successful in their home market have failed so miserably in their overseas expansion demonstrates the complexity of international management. In some cases, companies have failed to recognize that the resources and capabilities that underpinned their competitive advantage in their home market could not be readily transferred or replicated in overseas markets. In others, the problems were in designing the structures and systems that could effectively implement the international strategy.

As the lessons of success and failure from international business become recognized and distilled into better theories and analytical frameworks, so we advance our understanding of how to design and implement strategies for competing globally. We are at the stage where we recognize the issues and the key determinants of competitive advantage in an international environment. However, there is much that we do not fully understand. Designing strategies and organizational structures that can reconcile critical tradeoffs between global scale economies versus local differentiation, decentralized learning and innovation versus worldwide diffusion and replication, and localized flexibilities versus international standardization remains a key challenge for senior managers.

Quizzes and flashcards to test yourself further are available in your interactive e-book at
**www.wileyopenpage.com**

## Self-Study Questions

1. With reference to Figure 12.1, identify a *sheltered industry*—one that has been subject to little penetration either by imports or foreign direct investment. Explain why the industry has escaped internationalization. Explore whether there are opportunities for profitable internationalization within the industry and, if so, the strategy that would offer the best chance of success.

2. With reference to Table 12.1, what characteristics of national resources explain the different patterns of comparative advantage for the US and Japan?

3. According to Michael Porter's *Competitive Advantage of Nations*, some of the industries where British companies have an international advantage are: advertising, auctioneering of antiques and artwork, distilled alcoholic beverages, hand tools, and chemical preparations for gardening and horticulture. Some of the industries where US companies have an international competitive advantage are: photo film, aircraft and helicopters, computer hardware and software, oilfield services, management consulting, cinema films and TV programs, healthcare products and services, and financial services. For either the UK or the US, use Porter's national diamond framework (Figure 12.3) to explain the observed pattern of international competitive advantage.

4. When Porsche decided to enter the SUV market with its luxury Cayenne model, it surprised the auto industry by locating its new assembly plant in Leipzig in Eastern Germany. Many observers believed that Porsche should have located the plant either in Central or Eastern Europe where labor costs were very low or (like Mercedes and BMW) in the US where it would be close to its major market. Using the criteria outlined in Figure 12.5, can you explain Porsche's decision?

5. British expatriates living in the US frequently ask friends and relatives visiting from the UK to bring with them bars of Cadbury chocolate on the basis that the Cadbury chocolate available in the US (manufactured under license by Hershey's) is inferior to "the real thing." Should Kraft Foods continue Cadbury's licensing agreement with Hershey or should it seek to supply the US market itself, either by export from the UK or by establishing manufacturing facilities in the US?

6. Has McDonald's got the balance right between global standardization and national differentiation (Strategy Capsule 12.3)? Should it offer its franchisees in overseas countries greater initiative in introducing products that meet national preferences? Should it also allow greater flexibility for its overseas franchisees to adapt store layout, operating practices, and marketing? What aspects of the McDonald's system should McDonald's top management insist on keeping globally standardized?

# Notes

1. Global Investment Trends (UNCTAD, 2011).
2. This process was proposed by J. Johanson and J.-E. Vahlne, "The Internationalization Process of the Firm," *Journal of International Business Studies* 8 (1977): 23–32.
3. S. L. Segal-Horn, "Globalization of service industries," in J. McGee (ed.), *The Blackwell Encyclopedia of Management: Strategic Management* (Oxford: Blackwell Publishing, 2005): 147–54.
4. P. Ghemawat and F. Ghadar, "Global Integration: Global Concentration," *Industrial and Corporate Change* 15 (2006): 595–624.
5. A key finding was that human capital (knowledge and skills) was more important than physical capital (plant and equipment) in explaining US comparative advantage. See W. W. Leontief, "Domestic Production and Foreign Trade," in R. E. Caves and H. Johnson (eds), *Readings in International Economics* (Homewood, IL: Irwin, 1968).
6. P. Krugman, "Increasing Returns, Monopolistic Competition, and International Trade," *Journal of International Economics* (November 1979): 469–79.
7. M. E. Porter, *The Competitive Advantage of Nations* (New York: Free Press, 1990).
8. For a review of the Porter analysis, see R. M. Grant, "Porter's Competitive Advantage of Nations: An Assessment," *Strategic Management Journal* 12 (1991): 535–48.
9. Y.-R. Park, "Korean Business Culture," Presentation, December 15, 2005, http://gc.sfc.keio.ac.jp/class/2005_14969/slides/10/, accessed July 7, 2009.
10. The linking of value-added chains to national comparative advantages is explained in B. Kogut, "Designing Global Strategies and Competitive Value-Added Chains," *Sloan Management Review* (Summer 1985): 15–38.
11. J. Hagel and J. S. Brown, "Thinking Global, Acting Local," *Financial Times* (August 9, 2005).
12. "Sum of the Parts," *Financial Times* (November 17, 2008).
13. The role of firm-specific assets in explaining the multinational expansion is analyzed in R. Caves, "International Corporations: The Industrial Economics of Foreign Investment," *Economica* 38 (1971): 127.
14. D. J. Teece, "Transactions Cost Economics and Multinational Enterprise," *Journal of Economic Behavior and Organization* 7 (1986): 21–45.
15. This section draws heavily upon G. S. Yip, *Total Global Strategy II* (Upper Saddle River, NJ: Prentice Hall, 2003).
16. T. Levitt, "The Globalization of Markets," *Harvard Business Review* (May/June 1983): 92–102.
17. P. Ghemawat, *Redefining Global Strategy: Crossing Borders in a World Where Differences Still Matter* (Boston: Harvard Business School, 2007).
18. T. Levitt, "The Globalization of Markets," *Harvard Business Review* (May/June 1983): 94.
19. S. G. Winter and G. Szulanski, "Replication as Strategy," *Organization Science* 12 (2001): 730–743.
20. D. B. Montgomery, G. S. Yip, and B. Villalonga, "Explaining Supplier Behavior on Global Account Management," Stanford Research Paper No. 1767 (November 2002). Abstract available at SSRN: http://ssrn.com/abstract=355240, accessed July 7, 2009.
21. P. Almeida, "Knowledge Sourcing by Foreign Multinationals: Patent Citation Analysis in the US Semiconductor Industry," *Strategic Management Journal* 17 (Winter 1996): 155–65.
22. P. Ghemawat, "The Forgotten Strategy," *Harvard Business Review* (November 2003): 76–84.
23. Comments by Tommy Kullberg (IKEA Japan) in "The Japan Paradox," conference organized by the European Commission, Director General for External Affairs (December 2003): 62–3, available at http://www.deljpn.ec.europa.eu/data/current/japan-paradox.pdf, accessed July 7, 2009.
24. A. K. Gupta and P. Govindarajan, "Knowledge Flows within Multinational Corporations," *Strategic Management Journal* 21 (April 2000): 473–96; P. Almeida, J. Song, and R. M. Grant, "Are Firms Superior to Alliances and Markets? An Empirical Test of Cross-Border Knowledge Building," *Organization Science* 13 (March/April 2002): 147–61.
25. G. Hamel and C. K. Prahalad, "Do You Really Have a Global Strategy?" *Harvard Business Review* (July/August 1985): 139–48.
26. B. Y. Aw, G. Batra, and M. J. Roberts, "Firm Heterogeneity and Export: Domestic Price Differentials: A Study of Taiwanese Electrical Products," *Journal of International Economics* 54 (2001): 149–69; A. Bernard, J. B. Jensen, and P. Schott, "Transfer Pricing by US Based Multinational Firms," Working Papers 08-29, Center for Economic Studies, US Census Bureau, 2008.
27. I. C. Macmillan, A. van Ritten, and R. G. McGrath, "Global Gamesmanship," *Harvard Business Review* (May 2003): 62–71.
28. R. C. Christopher, *Second to None: American Companies in Japan* (New York: Crown, 1986).
29. The Ford Mondeo/Contour is a classic example of a global product that failed to appeal strongly to any national market. See M. J. Moi, "Ford Mondeo: A Model T World Car?" Working Paper, Rotterdam School of Management, Erasmus University (2001); C. Chandler, "Globalization: The Automotive Industry's Quest for a World Car," *GlobalEdge Working Paper*, Michigan State University (1997).
30. C. Baden-Fuller and J. Stopford, "Globalization Frustrated," *Strategic Management Journal* 12 (1991): 493–507.
31. R. M. Grant and M. Venzin, "Strategic and Organizational Challenges of Internationalization in Financial Services," *Long Range Planning* 42 (October 2009).

32. P. Ghemawat (P. Ghemawat, *Redefining Global Strategy: Crossing Borders in a World Where Differences Still Matter*, Boston: Harvard Business School, 2007) proposes a three-way rather than a two-way analysis. In his Adaptation–Aggregation–Arbitrage (AAA) framework he divides integration into aggregation and arbitrage.

33. C. A. Bartlett and S. Ghoshal, *Managing across Borders: The Transnational Solution*, 2nd edn (Boston: Harvard Business School Press, 1998): 34.

34. C. Bartlett, "Building and Managing the Transnational: The New Organizational Challenge," in Michael E. Porter (ed.), *Competition in Global Industries* (Boston: Harvard Business School Press, 1986): 377.

35. C. Bartlett, "Building and Managing the Transnational: The New Organizational Challenge," in Michael E. Porter (ed.), *Competition in Global Industries* (Boston: Harvard Business School Press, 1986): 388.

36. "The Country Prince Comes of Age," *Financial Times* (August 9, 2005).

37. J. Birkinshaw, P. Braunerhjelm, U. Holm, and S. Terjesen, "Why Do Some Multinational Corporations Relocate Their Headquarters Overseas?" *Strategic Management Journal* 27 (2006): 681–700.

38. M. Dewhurst, J. Harris, and S. Heywood, "Understanding your globalization penalty," *McKinsey Quarterly* (June 2011).

39. J. Birkinshaw, N. Hood, and S. Jonsson, "Building Firm-specific Advantages in Multinational Corporations: The Role of Subsidiary Initiative," *Strategic Management Journal* 19 (1998): 221–42.

40. T. S. Frost, J. M. Birkinshaw, and P. C. Ensign, "Centers of Excellence in Multinational Corporations," *Strategic Management Journal* 23 (2002): 997–1018.

# 13 Diversification Strategy

> Telephones, hotels, insurance—it's all the same. If you know the numbers inside out, you know the company inside out.
>
> —HAROLD SYDNEY GENEEN, CHAIRMAN OF ITT, 1959–1978, AND
> INSTIGATOR OF 275 COMPANY TAKEOVERS

> Creating three independent, public companies is the next logical step for Tyco. . . the new standalone companies will have greater flexibility to pursue their own focused strategies for growth than they would under Tyco's current corporate structure. This will allow all three companies to create significant value for shareholders.
>
> —ED BREEN, CHAIRMAN AND CEO, TYCO INTERNATIONAL LTD, ANNOUNCING
> THE COMPANY'S BREAKUP, SEPTEMBER 19, 2011

## OUTLINE

## Introduction and Objectives

Answering the question "What business are we in?" is the starting point of strategy and the basis for defining the firm's identity. In their statements of vision and mission, some companies define their businesses broadly. Shell's objective is "to engage efficiently, responsibly, and profitably in oil, oil products, gas, chemicals, and other selected businesses." Other companies define their businesses more narrowly: McDonald's vision is "to be the world's best quick-service restaurant chain"; Caterpillar will "be the leader in providing the best value in machines, engines, and support services for companies dedicated to building the world's infrastructure and developing and transporting its resources."

The business scope of firms changes over time. The dominant trend of the past two decades has been "refocusing on core businesses." Philip Morris Companies, Inc. (now renamed Altria Group, Inc.) sold off 7-Up, Miller Brewing, and Kraft Foods and became a specialist tobacco company. Most widely diversified groups—US and European conglomerates such as ITT, Hanson, Gulf & Western, Cendant, Vivendi Universal, and Tyco—have broken up altogether.

Some companies have moved in the opposite direction. Microsoft, once a supplier of operating systems, expanded into application and networking software, information services, entertainment systems, and video games consoles. Google is no longer simply a search engine company; it supplies a wide array of information products, advertising management services, applications software, operating systems (including its Android mobile platform), and, most recently, wireless handsets.

Diversification is a conundrum. The quest to enter new fields of business has probably caused more value destruction than any other type of strategic decision. Yet, diversification also permits a firm to free itself of the restrictions of a single industry and access new growth opportunities.

Our goal in this chapter is to establish the basis on which companies can make corporate strategy decisions that create rather than destroy value. Is it better to be specialized or diversified? Is there an optimal degree of diversification? What types of diversification are most likely to create value?

In practice, we make these types of decision every day in our personal lives. If my car doesn't start in the morning, should I try to fix it myself or have it towed directly to the garage? There are two considerations. First, is repairing a car an attractive activity to undertake? If the garage charges $85 an hour but I can earn $600 an hour consulting, then car repair is not attractive to me. Second, am I any good at car repair? If I am likely to take twice as long as a skilled mechanic then I possess no competitive advantage in car repair.

Diversification decisions by firms involve the same two issues:

◆ How attractive is the industry to be entered?
◆ Can the firm establish a competitive advantage?

These are the very same factors we identified in Chapter 1 (Figure 1.5) as determining a firm's profit potential. Hence, no new analytic framework is needed for appraising diversification decisions: diversification may be justified either by the superior profit potential of the industry to be entered or by the ability of the firm to create competitive advantage in the new industry. The first issue draws on the industry analysis developed in Chapter 3; the second draws on the analysis of competitive advantage developed in Chapters 5 and 7.

Our primary focus will be the latter question: under what conditions does operating multiple businesses assist a firm in gaining a competitive advantage in each? This leads into exploring linkages between different businesses within the diversified firm—a phenomenon often referred to as *synergy*.

By the time you have completed this chapter, you will be able to:

◆ comprehend the factors causing the trends, first, toward diversification and, subsequently, toward refocusing;

◆ recognize the corporate goals that have motivated diversification and the tendency for growth and risk reduction to conflict with value creation;

◆ understand the conditions under which diversification creates value for shareholders, and assess the potential for value creation from economies of scope, internalizing transactions, and corporate parenting;

◆ appreciate the implications of different types of business relatedness for the success of diversification and the management of diversification.

## Trends in Diversification over Time

As a background to our analysis of diversification decisions, let's begin by examining the factors that have influenced diversification strategies in the past.

### The Urge to Diversify, 1950–1980

In Chapter 11, while discussing "The Shifting Boundary between Firms and Markets," I identified diversification as a major contributor to the widening scope of firms during the 20th century. Between 1950 and 1980, the expansion of companies into different product markets was a major source of corporate growth in all the advanced industrial nations.[1] The 1970s saw the peak of the diversification boom, with the emergence of a new corporate form—the *conglomerate*—represented in the US by ITT, Textron, and Allied Signal, and in the UK by Hanson, Slater-Walker, and BTR. These highly diversified enterprises were created from multiple, unrelated acquisitions. Their existence reflected the view that senior management no longer needed industry-specific experience; corporate management simply needed to deploy the new techniques of financial and strategic management.[2] Figure 13.1 shows changing patterns of diversification strategy during the latter part of the 20th century.

### Refocusing, 1980–2009

After 1980, the diversification trend went into sharp reverse. Between 1980 and 1990, the average index of diversification for the Fortune 500 declined from 1.00 to

0.67.[3] Unprofitable "noncore" businesses were divested and many diversified companies fell prey to acquirers, who promptly restructured them.[4] Acquisition activity was extremely heavy during the 1980s—some $1.3 trillion in assets were acquired, including 113 members of the Fortune 500—but, unlike the previous decade, only 4.5% of acquisitions represented unrelated diversification.[5] Moreover, acquisitions by the Fortune 500 were outnumbered by dispositions. By the end of 2010 there were only 22 conglomerates left in the US of which three had announced their intention to split up.[6] The refocusing trend was strongest in the US, but was also evident in Canada and Europe and, to a lesser extent, in Japan.[7]

This trend toward specialization was the result of three principal factors.

*Emphasis on Shareholder Value*   The primary driver of refocusing was the reordering of corporate goals from growth to profitability. Sluggish growth and high interest rates during the early 1980s and from 1989 to 1990 exposed the inadequate profitability of many large, diversified corporations. Institutional shareholders, including pension funds such as California's Public Employees' Retirement system, became more active in pressuring top management for better shareholder returns—this led to increased CEO turnover.[8]

The surge in leveraged buyouts put further pressure on executives to boost shareholder returns. Kohlberg Kravis Roberts' $31 billion takeover of the tobacco and food giant RJR Nabisco in 1989 demonstrated that even the largest US companies were vulnerable to attack from corporate raiders.[9] The result was a rush by diversified giants to restructure before leveraged buyout specialists did it for them. Evidence of "conglomerate discounts"—that the stock market was valuing diversified companies at less than the sum of their parts—provided a further incentive for breakups.[10]

*Turbulence and Transaction Costs*   In Chapter 11, we observed that the relative costs of organizing transactions within firms and across markets depend on

**FIGURE 13.1**   Diversification strategies of large US and UK companies during the late 20th century

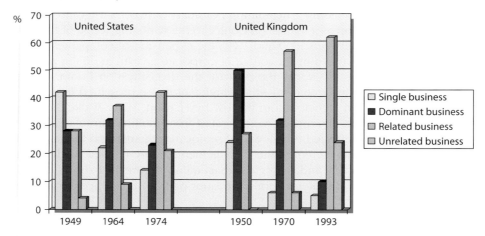

*Sources:* R. P. Rumelt, "Diversification Strategy and Profitability," *Strategic Management Journal* 3 (1982): 359–70; R. Whittington, M. Mayer, and F. Curto, "Chandlerism in Post-war Europe: Strategic and Structural Change in France, Germany and the UK: 1950–1993," *Industrial and Corporate Change* 8 (1999): 519–50; D. Channon, *The Strategy and Structure of British Enterprise* (Cambridge: Harvard University Press, 1973).

the conditions in the external environment. Administrative hierarchies are very efficient in processing routine transactions, but in turbulent conditions the pressure of decision making on top management results in stress, inefficiency, and delay. As the business environment has become more volatile, specialized companies are more agile than large diversified corporations where strategic decisions require approval at divisional and corporate levels. At the same time, external markets for resources, and capital markets especially, have become increasingly efficient. Many diversified companies have spun off their growth businesses because of the greater potential of external capital markets to fund their development.

Outside the mature industrialized countries, the situation is very different. Highly diversified business groups dominate the industrial sectors of many emerging countries: Tata Group and Reliance in India, Charoen Pokphand (CP) in Thailand, Astra International in Indonesia, Sime Darby in Malaysia, Grupo Alfa and Grupo Carso in Mexico. One reason for the continued dominance of large conglomerates in emerging market countries may be the higher transaction costs associated with their less sophisticated markets for finance, information, and labor that offer diversified companies advantages over their specialized competitors.[11]

*Trends in Management Thinking*   Optimism that new tools and systems of financial and strategic management would enable companies to span many different businesses has been replaced by recognition that competitive advantage requires focusing on key strengths in resources and capabilities. Deploying core resources and capabilities across different product markets can support profitable diversification. Hence, the focus of diversification analysis has been to identify the circumstances in which multibusiness activity can create value. Analysis of economies of scope, the transferability of resources and capabilities across industry boundaries,

**FIGURE 13.2**   The evolution of diversification strategies, 1960–2012

and the role of transaction costs have allowed us to be more precise about these circumstances. Mere linkages between businesses are not enough: the key to creating value is the ability of the diversified firm to share resources and transfer capabilities more efficiently than alternative institutional arrangements can. Moreover, it is essential that the benefits of these linkages are not outweighed by the additional management costs of exploiting them. Figure 13.2 summarizes some of the key developments in diversification strategy over the past 50 years.

## Motives for Diversification

A critical development in the transition from diversification to refocusing was the reordering of corporate objectives. Corporate diversification for most of the 20th century was driven by two key objectives: *growth* and *risk reduction*. During the last two decades of the 20th century, decisions over firms' business portfolios were increasingly dominated by a third objective: *creating shareholder value*.

### Growth

In the absence of diversification, firms are prisoners of their industry. For firms in stagnant or declining industries this is a daunting prospect, especially for top management. The urge to achieve corporate growth that outstrips that of a firm's primary industry is an appealing prospect for managers. Companies in low-growth, cash-flow-rich industries such as tobacco and oil have been especially susceptible to the temptations of diversification. During the 1980s, Exxon diversified into copper and coal mining, electric motors, and computers and office equipment; RJR Nabisco transformed itself from a tobacco company into a diversified consumer products company. In both cases diversification destroyed shareholder value. The leveraged buyout of RJR Nabisco by Kohlberg Kravis Roberts was followed by its breakup. Reynolds American, Inc. is now a specialist tobacco company.

### Risk Reduction

If the cash flows of different businesses are imperfectly correlated, then bringing them together under common ownership reduces the variance of the combined cash flow. However, such risk reduction appeals to managers more than to owners. Shareholders can diversify risk by holding diversified portfolios. Hence, what advantage can there be in companies diversifying for them? The only possible advantage could be if firms can diversify at lower cost than individual investors. In fact, the reverse is true: the transaction costs to shareholders of diversifying their portfolios are far less than the transaction costs to firms diversifying through acquisition. Not only do acquiring firms incur the heavy costs of using investment banks and legal advisers, they must also pay an acquisition premium to gain control of an independent company.

The *capital asset pricing model* (CAPM) formalizes this argument. The theory states that the risk that is relevant to determining the price of a security is not the overall risk (variance) of the security's return but the *systematic risk*—that part of the variance of the return that is correlated with overall market returns. This is measured by the security's *beta coefficient*. Corporate diversification does not reduce systematic risk: if three separate companies are brought under common ownership, in the absence of any other changes, the beta coefficient of the combined company is simply the weighted average of the beta coefficients of the constituent companies. Hence, the simple act of bringing different businesses under common ownership does not create shareholder value through risk reduction.[12]

Empirical studies are generally supportive of the absence of shareholder benefit from diversification that simply combines independent businesses under a single corporate umbrella.[13] Unrelated diversification may even fail to lower unsystematic risk.[14]

Special issues arise once we consider the risk of bankruptcy. For a marginally profitable firm, diversification can help avoid cyclical fluctuations of profits that can push it into insolvency. However, diversification that reduces the risk of bankruptcy is beneficial to bondholders (and other creditors) rather than shareholders.[15]

Are there circumstances in which reductions in unsystematic risk can create shareholder value? If there are economies to the firm from financing investments internally rather than resorting to external capital markets, the stability in the firm's cash flow that results from diversification may reinforce independence from external capital markets. For ExxonMobil, BP, and the other major oil companies, one of the benefits of extending across upstream (exploration and production), downstream (refining and marketing), and chemicals is that the negative correlation of the returns from these businesses increases the overall stability of their cash flows. This in turn increases their capacity to undertake huge, risky investments in offshore oil production, transcontinental pipelines, and natural gas liquefaction. These benefits also explain why firms pursue hedging activities that only reduce unsystematic risk.[16]

The financial turmoil of 2008–2009 has created a new appreciation of the risk-spreading benefits of diversification. The seizing-up of credit markets toward the end of 2008 was less serious for large firms with diversified cash flows that were less dependent on banks providing working capital.

## Value Creation: Porter's "Essential Tests"

If we return to the assumption that corporate strategy should be directed toward the interests of shareholders, what are the implications for diversification strategy? At the beginning of the chapter, we revisited our two sources of superior profitability: industry attractiveness and competitive advantage. In establishing the conditions for profitable diversification, Michael Porter refines these into "three essential tests" which determine whether diversification will truly create shareholder value:

- *The attractiveness test*: The industries chosen for diversification must be structurally attractive or capable of being made attractive.
- *The cost-of-entry test*: The cost of entry must not capitalize all the future profits.
- *The better-off test*: Either the new unit must gain competitive advantage from its link with the corporation or vice versa.[17]

*The Attractiveness and Cost-of-Entry Tests*   A critical realization in Porter's "essential tests" is that industry *attractiveness* is insufficient on its own. Although diversification allows a firm to access more attractive investment opportunities than are available in its own industry, it faces the challenge of entering a new industry. The second test, *cost of entry*, recognizes that for outsiders the cost of entry may counteract the attractiveness of the industry. Pharmaceuticals, corporate legal services, and defense contracting offer above-average profitability precisely because they are protected by barriers to entry. Firms seeking to enter these industries have a choice. They may acquire an established player, in which case the acquisition price will almost certainly fully capitalize the target firm's profit prospects (especially given the need to pay an acquisition premium over the market price of the target).[18] Alternatively, entry may occur through establishing a new corporate venture. In this case, the diversifying firm must directly confront the barriers to entry protecting that industry.[19]

Hewlett-Packard has diversified into IT services primarily because it views IT services as a more attractive industry than IT hardware. However, building an IT service business was expensive for HP: its $13.9 billion acquisition of EDS in 2008 was at a 30% premium over EDS's market value; its $10.3 billion acquisition of Autonomy in 2011 involved a 60% premium.

*The Better-Off Test*   Porter's third criterion for successful diversification—*the better-off test*—addresses the basic issue of competitive advantage: if two businesses producing different products are brought together under the ownership and control of a single enterprise, is there any reason why they should become any more profitable? Combining different, but related, businesses can enhance the competitive advantages of the original business, the new business, or both. For example:

● Procter & Gamble's 2005 acquisition of Gillette was intended to boost the competitive position of both companies through combining the two companies' global marketing and distribution networks, transferring Gillette's new product development capabilities to P&G, and increasing both companies' bargaining power relative to retail giants such as Wal-Mart.
● The spate of mergers between banks and insurance companies (Citigroup acquired Travelers, Allianz acquired Dresdner Bank, and Credit Suisse acquired Winterthur) was based upon the belief that cross-selling of banking and insurance products would benefit both sides of the new *bancassurance* companies.

*Primacy of the Better-Off Test*   In most normal circumstances it is only the better-off test that matters. In the first place, industry attractiveness is rarely a source of value from diversification—in most cases, cost-of-entry cancels out advantages of industry attractiveness.

The second reason why the better-off test normally dominates is that it can make sense for a company to enter an unattractive industry so long as the cost of entry is sufficiently discounted and the better-off test is met. When private equity firm Golden Gate Capital bought Eddie Bauer, Inc. in August 2009, the deal was motivated not by the attractiveness of the retail clothing sector but by Golden Gate's ability to buy the 400-store chain for a mere $286 million, then apply its financial and strategic management capabilities to revitalizing the sportswear chain. Sony Corporation's acquisition of CBS Records, Bertelsmann Music Group (BMG), and EMI Records, took Sony into the spectacularly unattractive music publishing industry. The attraction for Sony was building its integrated position in entertainment.

So, let us now further explore the ways in which diversification can make businesses "better off" through analyzing the relationship between diversification and competitive advantage.

## Competitive Advantage from Diversification

If the primary source of value creation from diversification is exploiting linkages between different businesses, what are these linkages and how are they exploited? The critical linkages are those that arise through the sharing of resources and capabilities across different businesses.

### Economies of Scope

The most general argument concerning the benefits of diversification focuses on the presence of **economies of scope** in common resources: "Economies of scope exist when using a resource across multiple activities uses less of that resource than when the activities are carried out independently."[20]

Economies of scope exist for similar reasons as economies of scale. The key difference is that economies of scale relate to cost economies from increasing output of a *single product*; economies of scope are cost economies from increasing the output of *multiple products*.[21] The nature of economies of scope varies between different types of resources and capabilities.

*Tangible Resources*   Tangible resources—such as distribution networks, information technology systems, sales forces, and research laboratories—offer economies of scope by eliminating duplication between businesses through creating a single shared facility. The greater the fixed costs of these items, the greater the associated economies of scope are likely to be. Entry by cable TV companies into telephone services and telephone companies into cable TV are motivated by the desire to spread the costs of networks and billing systems over as great a volume of business as possible. Common resources such as customer data bases, customer service centers, and billing systems have encouraged Centrica, Britain's biggest gas utility, to diversify into supplying electricity, fixed-line and mobile telephone services, broadband internet connections, home security systems, home insurance, and home-appliance repair.

Economies of scope also arise from the centralized provision of administrative and support services to the different businesses of the corporation. Within diversified companies, accounting, legal services, government relations, and information technology tend to be centralized, often through *shared service organizations* that supply common administrative and technical services to the operating businesses. Similar economies arise from centralizing research activities in a corporate research lab.

*Intangible Resources*   Intangible resources such as brands, corporate reputation, and technology offer economies of scope from the ability to extend them to additional businesses at low marginal cost.[22] Exploiting a strong brand across additional products is called *brand extension*. Starbucks has extended its brand to ice cream, packaged cold drinks, home espresso machines, audio CDs, and books.

*Organizational Capabilities*   Organizational capabilities can also be transferred within the diversified company. For example:

- LVMH is the world's biggest and most diversified supplier of branded luxury goods. Its distinctive capability is the management of luxury brands. This capability comprises market analysis, advertising, promotion, retail management, and quality assurance. These capabilities are deployed across Louis Vuitton (accessories and leather goods); Hennessey (cognac); Moët & Chandon, Dom Pérignon, Veuve Clicquot, and Krug (champagne); Céline, Givenchy, Kenzo, Christian Dior, Guerlain, and Donna Karan (fashion clothing and perfumes); TAG Heuer and Chaumet (watches); Sephora and La Samaritaine (retailing); Bulgari (jewelry); and some 25 other branded businesses.

- Sharp Corporation—originally established to manufacture metal products and the Ever Sharp Pencil—developed capabilities in the miniaturization of electronic products. It has introduced a stream of innovative products, beginning with the world's first transistor calculator (1964), the first LCD pocket calculator (1973), LCD color TVs, PDAs, internet viewcams, ultraportable notebook computers, mobile telephones, and photovoltaic cells.

Some of the most important capabilities in influencing the performance of diversified corporations are *general management capabilities*. General Electric possesses strong technological and operational capabilities at business level and it is good at sharing these capabilities between businesses (e.g., turbine know-how between jet engines and electrical generating equipment). However, its core capabilities are in general management and these reside primarily at the corporate level. They include its ability to motivate and develop its managers, its outstanding strategic and financial management that reconciles decentralized decision making with strong centralized control, and its international management capability. Similar observations could be made about 3M. While 3M's capabilities in technical know-how, new product development, and international marketing reside within the individual businesses, it is the corporate management capabilities and the systems through which they are exercised that maintain, nourish, coordinate, and upgrade these competitive advantages.[23]

## Economies from Internalizing Transactions

Although economies of scope provide cost savings from sharing and transferring resources and capabilities, does a firm have to diversify across these different businesses to exploit those economies? The answer is no. Economies of scope in resources and capabilities can be exploited simply by selling or licensing the use of the resource or capability to another company. In Chapter 9, we observed that a firm can exploit proprietary technology by licensing it to other firms. In Chapter 12, we noted how technology and trademarks are licensed across national frontiers as an alternative to direct investment. Similarly across industries: Starbucks' extension of its brand to other products has been achieved primarily through licensing: Pepsi produces and distributes Starbucks Frappuccino; Unilever produces Tazo Tea beverages, Dreyer's produces Starbucks ice cream. Walt Disney exploits the enormous value of its trademarks, copyrights, and characters partly through diversification into theme parks, live theater, cruise ships, and hotels; but it also licenses the use of these assets to producers of clothing, toys, music, comics, food, and drinks, as well as to the franchisees of Disney's retail stores. Disney's income from licensing fees and royalties was over $2 billion in 2005.

Even tangible resources can be shared across different businesses through market transactions. Airport and railroad station operators exploit economies of scope in their facilities not by diversifying into catering and retailing but by leasing out space to specialist retailers and restaurants.

Are economies of scope better exploited internally within the firm through diversification or externally through market contracts with independent companies? The key issue is *relative efficiency*—what are the transaction costs of market contracts compared with the administrative costs of diversified activities? Transaction costs include the costs involved in drafting, negotiating, monitoring, and enforcing a contract, plus the costs of protecting against exploitation by the partner. The costs of internalization consist of the management costs of establishing and coordinating the diversified business.[24]

Consider the following:

- In the case of Walt Disney Company, it licenses Donald Duck trademarks to Florida's Natural Growers rather than setting up its own orange-juice company; it owns and operates Disneyland and Disney World theme parks but licenses its trademarks and technology to Oriental Land Company, the owner and operator of Tokyo Disneyland.
- Both Mars and Cadbury used their confectionary brands to enter the European ice cream market. Cadbury decided to license its brands to Nestlé. Mars entered the business itself by setting up production and distribution facilities, competing with Unilever and Nestlé. The result was that Cadbury made significant profits from its licenses whereas Mars experienced years of losses or low returns on its investment.

Finding the right answer is complex. It depends on the nature of the resource or capability that is generating the "better off" benefits. If the resource can be traded or licensed out for anything close to its real value, as in the case of the Donald Duck trademark or the confectionary brands, then it is not necessary to enter another business in order to capture the extra profitability. Cadbury captured more profitability by not entering the ice-cream business. If, on the other hand, the resource is one that cannot easily be traded, such as general management capabilities, then it will be necessary to enter the new business in order to create the extra profitability. There is little scope for 3M to deploy its new product development capabilities other than within its own business. Similarly, for Apple the only way for it to exploit its capabilities in user-friendly design was to diversify outside of its core computer business.

Virgin has a separate licensing company but it licenses its brand mainly to companies within the Virgin group. So why doesn't Virgin license its brand to companies it does not have an equity interest in? The answer presumably is that the brand is part of a package of benefits that Virgin offers, some of which could not be traded or licensed. For example, Virgin has developed special marketing skills around its brand, often using the brand and Richard Branson to gain press comment in place of expensive advertising.

## Parenting Advantage

The recognition that it is only certain kinds of economies of scope that justify diversification led Goold, Campbell, and Alexander to propose the concept of *parenting value added* (an alternative to Porter's better-off test).[25] Parenting value comes from deploying the resources and general management skills possessed by the parent company. In Virgin's case they include the brand, Richard Branson's skill at attracting media coverage, and Virgin's business partnering capabilities. If these skills add value to a new business, then Virgin should think of entering that business. While Porter's better-off test focuses on the potential to share resources, Goold and his colleagues focus on the role of corporate managers in identifying and exploiting such linkages. Hence, they argue that parenting value added explains nearly all successful diversification because parenting is the central capability that is difficult to imitate and lies at the heart of the efficiency and effectiveness of the diversified corporation.

A further insight that arises from the parenting approach is that the criterion for diversification should not be the potential to add value from a diversification but whether the firm can *add more value than could any other parent*. General Electric's sale of NBC Universal to Comcast in 2011 reflected the fact that, irrespective of GE's capacity to add value to NBC Universal, Comcast (because of its other media interests) could add more value.

## The Diversified Firm as an Internal Market

We see that economies of scope on their own do not provide an adequate rationale for diversification: they must be supported by potential to economize on transaction costs. In fact, the lower costs of managing transactions internally can offer "better off" efficiencies, even when no economies of scope are present.

*Internal Capital Markets*    Consider the case of financial capital. The diversified firm represents an internal capital market: the corporate allocating capital between the different businesses through the capital expenditure budget. Which is more efficient, the internal capital markets of diversified companies or the external capital market? Diversified companies have two key advantages:

- By maintaining a balanced portfolio of cash-generating and cash-using businesses, diversified firms can avoid the costs of using the external capital market, including the margin between borrowing and lending rates and the heavy costs of issuing new debt and equity.
- Diversified companies have better access to information on the financial prospects of their different businesses than that typically available to external financiers.[26]

Against these advantages is the critical disadvantage that investment allocation within the diversified company is a politicized process in which strategic and financial considerations are subordinated to turf battles and ego building. Evidence suggests that diversified firms' internal capital markets tend to cross-subsidize poorly performing divisions and are reluctant to transfer cash flows to the divisions with the best prospects.[27] However, the efficiency of capital allocation varies greatly across companies. Marakon Associates identified several conglomerates with exceptional performance in terms of ten-year shareholder returns. They included GE and Berkshire Hathaway of the US, Hutchison Whampoa of Hong Kong, Bouygues and Lagardère of France, Wesfarmers of Australia, ITC of India, and Grupo Carso of Mexico. These companies were characterized by: "Strict financial discipline, rigorous analysis and valuation, a refusal to overpay for acquisitions, and a willingness to close or sell existing businesses."[28]

Another form of organization that reduces the transaction costs of external capital markets is the *private equity firm*. These firms raise money creating a fund that is then used to buy businesses. Instead of raising money each time they want to buy a business, they do the money raising once. Moreover, they have developed ways of avoiding the agency problems of self-seeking managers. Each fund has to be closed and returned to investors within a set number of years, often 10–14 years. This encourages the managers in the private equity firm to take particular care when allocating money from the fund. They want to make sure that each allocation will produce a good return before the fund is closed. They also give equity stakes to the managers in charge of each business that will pay out when the business is sold. This reduces the motivation for playing politics. Finally, the managers leading the individual businesses do not participate in the management decisions of the private equity firm. Many corporations, in contrast, have the heads of the biggest divisions sitting on the corporate-level management committee (more on this in the next chapter).

*Internal Labor Markets*  Efficiencies also arise from the ability of diversified companies to transfer employees, especially managers and technical specialists, between their divisions, and to rely less on hiring and firing. As companies develop and encounter new circumstances, so different management skills are required. The costs associated with hiring include advertising, time spent in interviewing and selection, and the costs of head-hunting agencies. The costs of dismissing employees can be very high where severance payments must be offered. A diversified corporation has a pool of employees and can respond to the specific needs of any one business through transfer from elsewhere within the corporation.

The broader set of career opportunities available in the diversified corporation may attract a higher caliber of employee. Graduating students compete intensely for entry-level positions with diversified corporations such as Canon, General Electric, Unilever, and Nestlé in the belief that these companies can offer richer career development than more specialized companies.

The informational advantages of diversified firms are especially important in relation to internal labor markets. A key problem of hiring from the external labor market is limited information. A résumé, references, and a day of interviews are poor indicators of how a new hire will perform in a particular job. The diversified firm that is engaged in transferring employees between different positions and different internal units can build detailed information on the competencies and characteristics of its employees. This informational advantage exists not only for individual employees but also for groups of individuals working together as teams. Hence, in exploiting a new business opportunity an established firm is at an advantage over the new firm, which must assemble its team from scratch.

## Diversification and Performance

Where diversification exploits economies of scope in resources and capabilities in the presence of transaction costs, it has the potential to create value for shareholders. Diversification that seeks only growth or risk reduction is likely to destroy value. How do these predictions work in practice?

### The Findings of Empirical Research

Empirical research into diversification has concentrated on two major issues: first, how do diversified firms perform relative to specialized firms and, second, does related diversification outperform unrelated diversification?

*The Performance of Diversified and Specialized Firms*   Despite many empirical studies since the 1960s, consistent, systematic relationships between diversification and performance are lacking. Beyond a certain threshold, high levels of diversification appear to be associated with lower profitability, probably because of the organizational complexity that diversification creates. Among British companies, diversification was associated with increased profitability up to a point, after which further diversification was accompanied by declining profitability.[29] Several other studies have detected a similar curvilinear relationship between diversification and profitability.[30] McKinsey & Company points to the benefits of moderate diversification: "a strategic sweet spot between focus and broader diversification." Diversification, McKinsey argues, makes most sense when a company has exhausted growth opportunities in its existing markets and can match its existing capabilities to emerging external opportunities.[31] However, McKinsey also notes that "conglomerates have underperformed more focused companies . . . From 2002 to 2010, the revenues of conglomerates grew by 6.3% those of focused companies by 9.2%." Their return on capital and their total shareholder returns were also lower.

A key problem is distinguishing *association* from *causation*. If moderately diversified companies are generally more profitable than specialized firms, is it because diversification increases profitability or because profitable firms channel their cash flows into diversifying investments?

The performance effects of diversification depend on the mode of diversification. Mergers and acquisitions involving companies in different industries appear to perform especially poorly.[32]

More consistent evidence concerns the performance results of refocusing initiatives by North American and European companies: when companies divest diversified businesses and concentrate more on their core businesses, the result is, typically, increased profitability and higher stock-market valuation.[33] These findings may reflect a changing relationship between diversification and profitability over time: the growing turbulence of the business environment may have increased the costs of managing widely diversified corporations.

*Related and Unrelated Diversification*   Given the importance of economies of scope in shared resources and capabilities, it seems likely that diversification into *related* industries should be more profitable than diversification into *unrelated* industries. Empirical research initially supported this prediction. Rumelt discovered that companies that diversified into businesses closely related to their core activities were significantly more profitable than those that pursued unrelated diversification.[34] By 1982, Tom Peters and Robert Waterman were able to conclude: "virtually every academic study has concluded that unchanneled diversification is a losing proposition."[35] This observation supported one of their "golden rules of excellence":

> *Stick to the Knitting.* Our principal finding is clear and simple. Organizations that do branch out but stick very close to their knitting outperform the others. The most successful are those diversified around a single skill, the coating and bonding technology at 3M for example. The second group in descending order, comprise those companies that branch out into related fields, the leap from electric power generation turbines to jet engines from GE for example. Least successful are those companies that diversify into a wide variety of fields. Acquisitions especially among this group tend to wither on the vine.[36]

Subsequent studies have clouded the picture: the superiority of related diversifiers may be the result of risk factors and industry influences;[37] unrelated may even outperform related diversification.[38] Several factors may be confusing the relationship. First, related diversification offers greater potential benefits than unrelated but the linkages it involves also create more difficult management problems. (I shall address this issue in the next chapter.) Second, the apparently poor results from unrelated diversification might be the result of poorly performing companies seeking to get far away from their existing businesses.[39] Finally, the distinction between "related" and "unrelated" diversification is not always clear: it may depend upon the strategy and characteristics of individual firms. Champagne and luggage are not obviously related products, but LVMH applies similar brand management capabilities to them both. Let us consider this issue further.

## The Meaning of Relatedness in Diversification

If *relatedness* refers to the potential for sharing and transferring resources and capabilities between businesses, there are no unambiguous criteria to determine whether two industries are related; it all depends on the company undertaking the diversification. Empirical studies have defined relatedness in terms of similarities between industries in technologies and markets. These similarities emphasize relatedness at the *operational* level—in manufacturing, marketing, and distribution—typically activities where economies from resource sharing are small and achieving them is costly in management terms. Conversely, one of the most important sources of value creation within the diversified firm is the ability to apply common general management capabilities, strategic management systems, and resource allocation processes to different businesses. Such economies depend on the existence of *strategic* rather than *operational* commonalities among the different businesses within the diversified corporation.[40]

- Berkshire Hathaway is involved in insurance, candy stores, furniture, kitchen knives, jewelry, and footwear. Despite this diversity, all these businesses have been selected on the basis of their ability to benefit from the unique style of corporate management established by chairman Warren Buffett and CEO Charles Munger.

- Richard Branson's Virgin Group covers a huge array of businesses from airlines to health clubs. Yet they share certain strategic similarities: almost all are start-up companies that benefit from Branson's entrepreneurial zeal and expertise; almost all sell to final consumers and are in sectors that offer opportunities for innovative approaches to differentiation.

The essence of such strategic-level linkages is the ability to apply similar strategies, resource allocation procedures, and control systems across the different businesses within the corporate portfolio.[41] Table 13.1 lists some of the strategic factors that determine similarities among businesses in relation to corporate management activities.

Unlike operational relatedness, where the opportunities for exploiting economies of scope in joint inputs are comparatively easy to identify—even to quantify— strategic relatedness is more elusive. It necessitates an understanding of the overall strategic approach of the company and recognition of its corporate-level management capabilities.

Ultimately, the linkage between the different businesses within a company may depend upon the strategic rationale of the company. Prahalad and Bettis use the term *dominant logic* to refer to managers' cognition of the rationale that unifies the different parts of the company.[42] Such a common view of a company's identity and raison d'être is a critical precondition for effective integration across its different businesses. However, dominant logic needs to be underpinned by economic synergies. Otherwise, an appealing dominant logic—such as Allegis Corporation's desire to meet travelers' needs by combining airlines and hotels or General Mills meeting "the needs and wants of the homemaker" by diversifying into toys, fashion clothing, specialty retailing, and restaurants—will fail to translate into real value creation.

**TABLE 13.1** The determinants of strategic relatedness between businesses

| Corporate Management Tasks | Determinants of Strategic Similarity |
| --- | --- |
| Resource allocation | Similar sizes of capital investment projects<br>Similar time spans of investment projects<br>Similar sources of risk<br>Similar general management skills required for business unit managers |
| Strategy formulation | Similar key success factors<br>Similar stages of the industry life cycle<br>Similar competitive positions occupied by each business within its industry |
| Performance management and control variables | Targets defined in terms of similar performance<br>Similar time horizons for performance targets |

***Source:*** R. M. Grant, "On Dominant Logic, Relatedness, and the Link between Diversity and Performance," *Strategic Management Journal* 9 (1988): 641. Reused by permission of John Wiley & Sons, Ltd.

# Summary

Diversification is like sex: its attractions are obvious, often irresistible, yet the experience is often disappointing. For top management it is a minefield. The diversification experiences of large corporations are littered with expensive mistakes: Exxon's attempt to build Exxon Office Systems as a rival to Xerox and IBM; Vivendi's diversification from water and environmental services into media, entertainment, and telecoms; Royal Bank of Scotland's quest to transform itself from a retail bank into a financial services giant. Despite so many costly failures, the urge to diversify continues to captivate senior managers. Part of the problem is the divergence between managerial and shareholder goals. While diversification has offered meager rewards to shareholders, it is the fastest route to building vast corporate empires. A further problem is hubris. A company's success in one line of business tends to result in the top management team becoming overconfident of its ability to achieve similar success in other businesses.

Nevertheless, for companies to survive and prosper over the long term they must change; inevitably, this involves redefining the businesses in which they operate. The world's two largest IT companies—IBM and Hewlett-Packard—are both over six decades old. Their longevity is based on their ability to adapt their product lines to changing market opportunities. Essentially, they have applied existing capabilities to developing new products, which have provided new growth trajectories. Similarly with most other long-established companies: for 3M, Canon, Samsung, and DuPont, diversification has been central to the process of evolution. In most cases, this diversification was not a major discontinuity, but an initial incremental step in which existing resources and capabilities were deployed to exploit a perceived opportunity.

If companies are to use diversification as part of their long-term adaptation and avoid the many errors that corporate executives have made in the past, then better strategic analysis of diversification decisions is essential. The objectives of diversification need to be clear and explicit. Shareholder value creation has provided a demanding and illuminating criterion with which to appraise investment in new business opportunities. Rigorous analysis also counters the tendency for diversification to be a diversion—corporate escapism resulting from the unwillingness of top management to come to terms with difficult conditions within the core business.

The analytic tools at our disposal for evaluating diversification decisions have developed greatly in recent years. In the late 1980s, diversification decisions were based on vague concepts of synergy that involved identifying linkages between different industries. We are now able to be much more precise about the need for economies of scope in resources and capabilities *and* the economies of internalization that are prerequisites for diversification to create shareholder value. Recognizing the role of these economies of internalization has directed attention to the role of top management capabilities and effective corporate management systems in determining the success of diversification.

Quizzes and flashcards to test yourself further are available in your interactive e-book at
**www.wileyopenpage.com**

## Self-Study Questions

1. An ice-cream manufacturer is proposing to acquire a soup manufacturer on the basis that, first, its sales and profits will be more seasonally balanced and, second, from year to year, sales and profits will be less affected by variations in weather. Will this risk spreading create value for shareholders? Under what circumstances could this acquisition create value for shareholders?

2. Tata Group is one of India's largest companies, employing 424,000 people in many different industries, including steel, motor vehicles, watches and jewelry, telecommunications, financial services, management consulting, food products, tea, chemicals and fertilizers, satellite TV, hotels, motor vehicles, energy, IT, and construction. Such diversity far exceeds that of any North American or Western European company. What are the conditions in India that might make such broad-based diversification both feasible and profitable?

3. Giorgio Armani S.p.A. is an Italian private company owned mainly by the Armani family. Most of its clothing and accessories are produced and marketed by the company (some are manufactured by outside contractors). For other products, notably fragrances, cosmetics, and eyewear, Armani licenses its brand names to other companies. Armani is considering expanding into athletic clothing, hotels, and bridal shops. Advise Armani on whether these new businesses should be developed in-house, by joint ventures, or by licensing the Armani brands to specialist companies already within these fields.

4. General Electric, Berkshire Hathaway, and Richard Branson's Virgin Group each comprise a wide range of different businesses that appear to have few close technical or customer linkages. Are these examples of unrelated diversification and do the corporate and ownership links within each of the groups result in the creation of any value? If so, what are the sources of this value creation?

## Notes

1. A. D. Chandler Jr., *Strategy and Structure: Chapters in the History of the Industrial Enterprise* (Cambridge, MA: MIT Press, 1962); R. P. Rumelt, *Strategy, Structure and Economic Performance* (Cambridge, MA: Harvard University Press, 1974); H. Itami, T. Kagono, H. Yoshihara, and S. Sakuma, "Diversification Strategies and Economic Performance," *Japanese Economic Studies* 11, no. 1 (1982): 78–110.

2. M. Goold and K. Luchs, "Why Diversify? Four Decades of Management Thinking," *Academy of Management Executive* 7, no. 3 (August 1993): 7–25.

3. G. F. Davis, K. A. Diekman, and C. F. Tinsley, "The Decline and Fall of the Conglomerate Firm in the 1980s: A Study in the De-Institutionalization of an Organizational Form," *American Sociological Review* 49 (1994): 547–70.

4. R. E. Hoskisson and M. A. Hitt, *Downscoping: How to Tame the Diversified Firm* (New York: Oxford University Press, 1994).

5. A. Shleifer and R. W. Vishny, "The Takeover Wave of the 1980s," *Science* 248 (July/September 1990): 747–9.

6. J. Cyriac, T. Koller, and J. Thomsen, "Testing the Limits of Diversification," *McKinsey Quarterly* (February 2012).

7. L. G. Franko, "The Death of Diversification: The Focusing of the World's Industrial Firms, 1980–2000," *Business Horizons* (July/August, 2004): 41–50.

8. During 2004–2006, CEO turnover reached an all-time high. See Booz Allen Hamilton, "CEO Succession 2006: The Era of the Inclusive Leader," *strategy+business* (Summer 2007), http://www.boozallen.com/media/file/Era_of_the_Inclusive_Leader_.pdf, accessed August 22, 2012.

9. B. Burrough, *Barbarians at the Gate: The Fall of RJR Nabisco* (New York: Harper & Row, 1990).

10. L. Laeven and R. Levine, "Is there a Diversification Discount in Financial Conglomerates?" *Journal of Financial Economics* 82 (2006): 331–67.

11. T. Khanna and K. Palepu, "Why Focused Strategies May Be Wrong for Emerging Markets," *Harvard Business Review* (July/August, 1997): 41–51; D. Kim, D. Kandemir, and S. T. Cavusgil, "The Role of Family Conglomerates in Emerging Markets," *Thunderbird International Business Review* 46 (January 2004): 7–20.

12. See any standard corporate finance text, for example R. A. Brealey, S. Myers, and F. Allen, *Principles of Corporate Finance*, 8th edn (New York: McGraw-Hill, 2006): Chapter 8.

13. See, for example, H. Levy and M. Sarnat, "Diversification, Portfolio Analysis and the Uneasy Case for Conglomerate Mergers," *Journal of Finance* 25 (1970): 795–802; R. H. Mason and M. B. Goudzwaard, "Performance of Conglomerate Firms: A Portfolio Approach," *Journal of Finance* 31 (1976): 39–48; J. F. Weston, K. V. Smith, and R. E. Shrieves, "Conglomerate Performance Using the Capital Asset Pricing Model," *Review of Economics and Statistics* 54 (1972): 357–63.

14. M. Lubatkin and S. Chetterjee, "Extending Modern Portfolio Theory into the Domain of Corporate Strategy: Does It Apply?" *Academy of Management Journal* 37 (1994): 109–36.

15. The reduction in risk that bondholders derive from diversification is termed the *coinsurance effect*. See L. W. Lee, "Coinsurance and the Conglomerate Merger," *Journal of Finance* 32 (1977): 1527–37.

16. S. M. Bartram, "Corporate Risk Management as a Lever for Shareholder Value Creation," *Financial Markets, Institutions and Instruments* 9 (2000): 279–324.

17. M. E. Porter, "From Competitive Advantage to Corporate Strategy," *Harvard Business Review* (May/June 1987): 46.

18. M. Hayward and D. C. Hambrick, "Explaining the Premiums Paid for Large Acquisitions," *Administrative Science Quarterly* 42 (1997): 103–27.

19. A study of 68 diversifying ventures by established companies found that, on average, breakeven was not attained until the seventh and eighth years of operation: R. Biggadike, "The Risky Business of Diversification," *Harvard Business Review* (May/June 1979): 103–111.

20. The formal definition of *economies of scope* is in terms of "subadditivity." Economies of scope exist in the production of goods $x_1, x_2, \ldots, xn$, if $C(X) < RiCi(xi)$ where: $X < Ri(xi)$

$C(X)$ is the cost of producing all $n$ goods within a single firm

$RiCi(xi)$ is the cost of producing the goods in $n$ specialized firms.

See W. J. Baumol, J. C. Panzar, and R. D. Willig, *Contestable Markets and the Theory of Industry Structure* (New York: Harcourt Brace Jovanovich, 1982): 71–2.

21. Economies of scope can arise in consumption as well as in production: customers may prefer to buy different products from the same supplier. See T. Cottrell and B. R. Nault, "Product Variety and Firm Survival in Microcomputer Software," *Strategic Management Journal* 25 (2004): 1005–26.

22. There is some evidence to the contrary. See H. Park, T. A. Kruse, K. Suzuki, and K. Park, "Long-term Performance Following Mergers of Japanese Companies: The Effect of Diversification and Affiliation," *Pacific Basin Finance Journal* 14 (2006); and P. R. Nayyar, "Performance Effects of Information Asymmetry and Economies of Scope in Diversified Service Firms," *Academy of Management Journal* 36 (1993): 28–57.

23. The role of capabilities in diversification is discussed in C. C. Markides and P. J. Williamson, "Related Diversification, Core Competencies and Corporate Performance," *Strategic Management Journal* 15 (Special Issue, 1994): 149–65.

24. This issue is examined more fully in D. J. Teece, "Towards an Economic Theory of the Multiproduct Firm," *Journal of Economic Behavior and Organization* 3 (1982): 39–63.

25. M. Goold, A. Campbell, and M. Alexander, *Corporate-Level Strategy: Creating Value in the Multibusiness Company* (New York: John Wiley & Sons, Inc., 1994).

26. J. P. Liebeskind, "Internal Capital Markets: Benefits, Costs and Organizational Arrangements," *Organization Science* 11 (2000): 58–76.

27. D. Scharfstein and J. Stein, "The Dark Side of Internal Capital Markets: Divisional Rent Seeking and Inefficient Investment," *Journal of Finance* 55 (2000): 2537–64; V. Maksimovic and G. Phillips, "Do Conglomerate Firms Allocate Resources Inefficiently across Industries?" *Journal of Finance* 57 (2002): 721–67; R. Rajan, H. Servaes, and L. Zingales, "The Cost of Diversity: The Diversification Discount and Inefficient Investment," *Journal of Finance* 55 (2000): 35–84.

28. C. Kaye and J. Yuwono, "Conglomerate Discount or Premium? How Some Diversified Companies Create Exceptional Value," Marakon Associates (2003), http://www.nd.edu/~cba/cc/pdf/Doyle_Portfolio%20decision%20making.pdf, accessed August 22, 2012.

29. R. M. Grant, A. P. Jammine, and H. Thomas, "Diversity, Diversification and Performance in British Manufacturing Industry," *Academy of Management Journal* 31 (1988): 771–801.

30. L. E. Palich, L. B. Cardinal, and C. C. Miller, "Curvi-linearity in the Diversification–Performance Linkage:

An Examination of over Three Decades of Research," *Strategic Management Journal* 22 (2000): 155–74.

31. N. Harper and S. P. Viguerie, "Are You Too Focused?" *McKinsey Quarterly* (Special Edition, 2002): 29–37.

32. J. D. Martin and A. Sayrak, "Corporate Diversification and Shareholder Value: A Survey of Recent Literature," *Journal of Corporate Finance* 9 (2003): 37–57.

33. C. C. Markides, "Consequences of Corporate Refocusing: Ex Ante Evidence," *Academy of Management Journal* 35 (1992): 398–412; C. C. Markides, "Diversification, Restructuring and Economic Performance," *Strategic Management Journal* 16 (1995): 101–18.

34. R. P. Rumelt, *Strategy, Structure and Economic Performance* (Cambridge, MA: Harvard University Press, 1974).

35. T. Peters and R. Waterman, *In Search of Excellence* (New York: Harper & Row, 1982): 294.

36. T. Peters and R. Waterman, *In Search of Excellence* (New York: Harper & Row, 1982): 294.

37. H. K. Christensen and C. A. Montgomery, "Corporate Economic Performance: Diversification Strategy versus Market Structure," *Strategic Management Journal* 2 (1981): 327–43; R. A. Bettis, "Performance Differences in Related and Unrelated Diversified Firms," *Strategic Management Journal* 2 (1981): 379–83.

38. See, for example, A. Michel and I. Shaked, "Does Business Diversification Affect Performance?" *Financial Management* 13, no. 4 (1984): 18–24; G. A. Luffman and R. Reed, *The Strategy and Performance of British Industry*: 1970–80 (London: Macmillan, 1984).

39. C. Park, "The Effects of Prior Performance on the Choice between Related and Unrelated Acquisitions," *Journal of Management Studies* 39 (2002): 1003–19.

40. For a discussion of relatedness in diversification, see J. Robins and M. F. Wiersema, "A Resource-Based Approach to the Multibusiness Firm: Empirical Analysis of Portfolio Interrelationships and Corporate Financial Performance," *Strategic Management Journal* 16 (1995): 277–300; J. Robins and M. F. Wiersema, "The Measurement of Corporate Portfolio Strategy: Analysis of the Content Validity of Related Diversification Indexes," *Strategic Management Journal* 24 (2002): 39–59.

41. R. M. Grant, "On Dominant Logic, Relatedness, and the Link between Diversity and Performance," *Strategic Management Journal* 9 (1988): 639–42.

42. C. K. Prahalad and R. A. Bettis, "The Dominant Logic: A New Linkage between Diversity and Performance," *Strategic Management Journal* 7 (1986): 485–502.

# 14 Implementing Corporate Strategy: Managing the Multibusiness Firm

Some have argued that single-product businesses have a focus that gives them an advantage over multibusiness companies like our own—and perhaps they would have, but only if we neglect our own overriding advantage: the ability to share the ideas that are the result of wide and rich input from a multitude of global sources. GE businesses share technology, design, compensation and personnel evaluation systems, manufacturing practices, and customer and country knowledge.

—JACK WELCH, CHAIRMAN, GENERAL ELECTRIC COMPANY, 1981–2001

## OUTLINE

# Introduction and Objectives

A multibusiness firm comprises a number of businesses—organized as business units, divisions, or subsidiaries—coordinated and controlled by a corporate headquarters. These businesses may be different product groups—as in the case of 3M or Samsung; they may be different regional and national businesses—as in the case of McDonald's and Banco Santander; or they may be vertically related businesses—as in the case of ExxonMobil or De Beers. The key feature of the multibusiness firm is that decision making is divided between the individual businesses, each of which is responsible for its own operational decisions, and the headquarters, which is responsible for corporate matters.

In the last chapter, I concluded that the case for diversification depends on whether the diversified company can create value by operating across multiple businesses. Chapters 11 and 12 arrived at the same conclusion in relation to vertical integration and multinational operations. Vertical integration, international expansion, or diversification may have the potential to create value, but value is only realized if these strategies are implemented effectively. This requires answering the following questions: How should the multibusiness corporation be structured? Through what systems and tools should management exercise control and coordination? What roles do the chief executive and top management team need to fulfill and what styles of leadership are likely to be most effective? Our quest to answer these questions requires us to look closely at the activities of the corporate head office and its relationships with the businesses.

The main focus of this chapter will be the mechanisms through which corporate management creates value, namely managing the business portfolio, managing individual businesses, managing linkages between businesses, and leading change. We then consider the problem of corporate governance in the large, multibusiness corporation.

By the time you have completed this chapter, you will be able to:

- ◆ recognize the principal organizational features of the multibusiness corporation;
- ◆ apply the techniques of portfolio analysis to corporate strategy decisions;
- ◆ understand how corporate headquarters manages its individual businesses through strategic planning and financial control and by managing linkages across businesses;
- ◆ analyze the fit between a firm's corporate strategy, organization structure, management systems, and leadership style;
- ◆ analyze the potential for value creation through restructuring a multibusiness corporation;
- ◆ appreciate the governance issues that impact the work of managers within the multibusiness corporation.

## The Role of Corporate Management

For the multibusiness corporation to be viable, the benefits from bringing businesses under common ownership and control must exceed the costs of the corporate overlay. Goold, Campbell, and Alexander go further. They propose a tougher hurdle for multibusiness companies: for each and every business within the corporate portfolio not only must the additional profit from inclusion within the corporate fold exceed the cost of headquarters management but also the net gain should be bigger than that which any other potential corporate parent can offer.[1] (Otherwise, it would be profitable to sell the business.) This concept of *parenting advantage*—that a company must be able to add more value to a business than rivals could—directs our attention to the mechanisms through which multibusiness corporations create value for the businesses they own.

We shall focus on four activities through which corporate management adds value to its businesses:

- managing the overall corporate portfolio, including acquisitions, divestments, and resource allocation;
- managing each individual business;
- managing linkages among businesses;
- managing change.

In the four sections that follow we will consider each of these activities and establish the conditions under which they create value.

## Managing the Corporate Portfolio

The basic questions of corporate strategy are "What businesses should we be in?" and "How should we manage those businesses in order to generate as much value from them as possible?" *Portfolio planning models* can assist help managers with both of these questions.

### General Electric and the Development of Strategic Planning

Portfolio planning techniques were one outcome of the pioneering work in corporate strategy initiated by General Electric at the end of the 1960s.[2] GE comprised 46 divisions and over 190 businesses. To manage this sprawling industrial empire more effectively, GE launched a series of initiatives together with Boston Consulting Group, McKinsey & Company, Arthur D. Little, and Harvard Business School. The result was three key developments in strategic management at the corporate level. The first was the identification of *strategic business units (SBUs)*—businesses that were sufficiently self-contained to formulate a separate competitive strategy.[3] The other two were *portfolio planning models* and the *PIMS database*, which we will discuss below.

### Portfolio Planning: The GE/McKinsey Matrix

The basic idea of a portfolio-planning model is to represent graphically the individual businesses of a multibusiness company in terms of key strategic variables that

**FIGURE 14.1** The GE/McKinsey portfolio planning matrix

determine their potential for profit. These strategic variables typically relate to the attractiveness of their market and their competitive advantage within that market. This analysis can guide:

- allocating resources between the businesses on the basis of each business's market attractiveness and competitive position;
- formulating business unit strategy—by comparing the strategic positioning of each business, opportunities for repositioning (including divestment) can be identified;
- analyzing portfolio balance: a single display of all the company's businesses permits assessment of the overall balance of the portfolio in terms of *cash flow generation* and *growth prospects*;
- setting performance targets on the basis of each business's market attractiveness and its competitive position.

In the GE/McKinsey matrix (Figure 14.1) the industry attractiveness axis combines market size, market growth rate, market profitability (return on sales over three years), cyclicality, inflation recovery (potential to increase productivity and product prices), and international potential (ratio of foreign to domestic sales). Business unit competitive advantage combines market share, return on sales relative to competitors, and relative position with regard to quality, technology, manufacturing, distribution, marketing, and cost.[4] The strategy implications are shown by three regions of Figure 14.1.

## Portfolio Planning: BCG's Growth–Share Matrix

The Boston Consulting Group's *growth–share matrix* also uses industry attractiveness and competitive position to compare the strategic positions of different businesses. However, it uses a single indicator as a proxy for each of these dimensions: industry attractiveness is measured by *rate of market growth* and competitive advantage by *relative market share* (the business unit's market share relative to that of its largest competitor). The four quadrants of the BCG matrix predict patterns of profits and cash flow and indicate strategies to be adopted (Figure 14.2).[5]

The simplicity of the BCG matrix is both its usefulness and its limitation. It can be prepared very easily and offers a clear picture of a firm's business portfolio in

**FIGURE 14.2**  The BCG growth–share matrix

relation to some important strategic characteristics. Moreover, the analysis is versatile: it can be applied to business units and to the positioning of different products, brands, distribution channels, and customers. Though simplistic, it can be useful as a preliminary view before embarking upon a more detailed and rigorous analysis.

However, the simplistic approach of both the BCG and McKinsey business portfolio matrices has resulted in both losing their popularity as analytic tools. Apart from their naive approaches to the determinants of industry attractiveness and competitive advantage, there are problems relating to market definition. For example, in the BCG matrix, is BMW's auto business a dog because it holds less than 2% of the world auto market or a cash cow because it is market leader in the luxury car segment? An even greater problem is the implicit assumption that every business in the portfolio is independent—a direct denial of the basic rational for the multibusiness corporation: the synergistic linkages between businesses.[6]

## Portfolio Planning: The Ashridge Portfolio Display

The Ashridge Portfolio Display is based upon Goold, Campbell and Alexander's concept of *parenting advantage*.[7] It takes account of the fact that the value-creating potential of a business within a company's business portfolio depends not just on the characteristics of the business (as assumed by the McKinsey and BCG matrices) but also on the characteristics of the parent. The focus, therefore, is on the *fit* between a business and its parent company. The positioning of a business along the horizontal axis of Figure 14.3 depends upon the parent's potential to create profit for the business by, for example, applying its corporate-level management capabilities, sharing resources and capabilities with other businesses, or economizing on transaction costs. The vertical axis measures the potential for value destruction by the parent. This can be caused by the costs of corporate overhead or the mismatch between the management needs of the business and the management systems and style of the parent (e.g., bureaucratic rigidity, incompatibility

**FIGURE 14.3** Ashridge portfolio display: The potential for parenting advantage

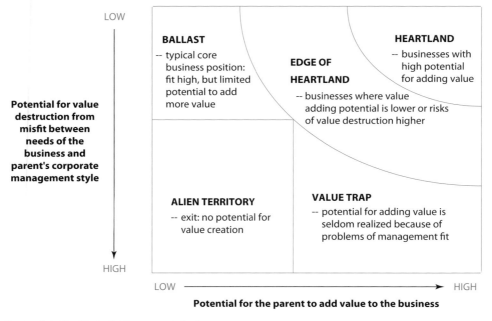

*Source:* Ashridge Strategic Management Centre.

with top management's mindset, politicization of decision making, and inappropriate strategic guidance).

In recognizing that businesses are not independent entities and introducing the role of strategic fit in influencing the potential for value creation and value destruction, the Ashridge matrix introduces the key issues of synergy that are ignored by other portfolio-planning matrices. The problem is complexity: both dimensions of the Ashridge matrix require difficult subjective evaluations that do not lend themselves to quantification.

## Managing Individual Businesses

Some of the most important opportunities for corporate headquarters to create value arise from its ability to improve the strategic and operational management of its businesses, what Goold, Campbell, and Alexander call "standalone influence." This influence is exercised through the corporate parent's ability to:

> Appoint the general manager of each business and influence management development and succession planning within the businesses. It can approve or reject budgets, strategic plans, and capital expenditure proposals and it can influence the shape and implementation of these plans and proposals. It can provide advice and policy guidance to the businesses. The parent also influences the businesses by the hints and pressures passed on through both formal and informal line management meetings and contacts, and, more indirectly, through the corporate culture.[8]

The mechanisms through which the corporate headquarters exercises control over individual businesses can be divided into two types. Corporate management can control decisions, through requiring that certain decisions—typically those involving significant resource commitments—are referred upward for corporate approval. For example, the corporate HQ might require that capital expenditure requests that exceed $5 million are approved by the executive committee. Alternatively, corporate management can control businesses through setting and monitoring performance targets, backed by incentives and penalties to motivate their attainment. The distinction is between *input* and *output* control: the company can control the inputs into strategy (the decisions) or the output from strategy (the performance). Although most companies use a combination of input and output controls, there is an unavoidable tradeoff between the two: more of one implies less of the other. If the corporate HQ micromanages divisional decisions, it must accept the performance outcomes that will result from this. If the corporate HQ imposes rigorous performance targets, it must give divisional managers the freedom to make the decisions necessary to achieve those targets.

## The Strategic Planning System

In Chapter 1, I stated that corporate strategy is set at the corporate level and business strategy is set at the business level. In reality, business strategies are formulated jointly by corporate and divisional managers. In most diversified, divisionalized companies, business strategies are initiated by divisional managers, and the role of corporate managers is to probe, appraise, amend, and approve divisional strategy proposals. The challenge for corporate management is to create a strategy-making process that reconciles the decentralized decision making essential to fostering flexibility, responsiveness, and a sense of ownership at the business level, with the ability of the corporate level to bring to bear its knowledge, perspective, and responsibility for the shareholder interest. Achieving an optimal blend of business-level initiative and corporate-level guidance and discipline is a difficult challenge for the multibusiness corporation. Common to the success of General Electric, ExxonMobil, Samsung, and Unilever is a system of strategic management that has managed this difficult tradeoff between business initiative and corporate control. Strategy Capsule 14.1 describes key elements of the strategic planning process at ExxonMobil.

*Rethinking Strategic Planning*    Since the early 1980s, the strategic planning systems of large firms have been bombarded by criticism from academics and consultants. Two features of corporate strategic planning systems have attracted particular scorn:

- *Strategic planning systems don't make strategy.* Ever since Henry Mintzberg attacked the "rational design" school of strategy (see Chapter 1), strategic planning systems have been castigated as ineffective for formulating strategy. In particular, formalized strategic planning has been viewed as the enemy of flexibility, creativity, and entrepreneurship. Marakon consultants Mankins and Steele observed that "strategic planning doesn't really influence most companies' strategy." The rigidities of formal planning cycles mean that "senior executives … make the decisions that really shape their companies'

## STRATEGY CAPSULE 14.1
# Strategic Planning at ExxonMobil

ExxonMobil is one of the world's biggest and most financially successful companies. Its strategic planning system reconciles long-term strategic planning with rigorous, short-term financial control; and centralized direction with flexible, responsive decision making among the divisions. ExxonMobil's strategic planning process follows an annual cycle that is similar to the generic strategic planning process outlined in Chapter 6 (Figure 6.1).

The principal stages of the planning cycle are as follows:

1    *Economic review and energy review* are forecasts of the economy and energy markets issued in February by the corporate planning department. They provide a basis for strategic planning.

2    *Business plans* are developed during spring and summer by individual businesses' units and are aggregated and refined by the global divisions into *divisional plans*. Their time horizon is ten years for the upstream divisions and five years for downstream divisions and chemicals. With input from the corporate planning department, the divisional plans are discussed, revised, and finally approved by the corporate management committee (during October).

3    *The corporate plan* aggregates the divisional plans. This is undertaken by the corporate-planning department then discussed and revised by the management committee, before submission to the board of directors for approval (during November).

4    *The financial forecast* comprises two-year forecasts of revenues, operating costs, capital expenditures, interest and other expenses, income, and cash flow for divisions and for the company as a whole. These provide the basis for *operating and capital budgets* for the upcoming year.

5    *The stewardship basis* comprises performance targets for the upcoming year. They include financial objectives, operating targets, safety and environmental objectives, and strategy mileposts.

6    *Stewardship reviews*: in February of each year, each division's performance for the previous year is evaluated against its stewardship objectives. These reviews involve presentations by the divisional top management to the management committee.

7    *Investment reappraisals* occur in August and September and involve the divisions reporting back on the outcomes of specific investment projects.

The annual strategic planning cycle is supplemented by *strategic studies*: ad hoc projects by the corporate-planning department that address specific strategic issues involving market, technological, and political changes.

Strategy making also involves informal communication and coordination between the different levels of the corporation. Communication between the management committee (comprising ExxonMobil's executive board members) and the divisional presidents and their management teams is supported by each member of the management committee acting as a contact director for two or three divisions. The dialog between the divisional presidents and members of the management committee is a mechanism for knowledge sharing and initiating strategic changes that adds flexibility to the formal strategic planning process. The result is a system of strategy formulation and performance management that is simultaneously top-down and bottom-up.

Fundamental to ExxonMobil's close integration of financial management with strategic planning is ExxonMobil's emphasis on *stewardship*—a doctrine of managerial accountability that makes each executive personally responsible to the corporation and its shareholders.

strategies … outside the planning process typically in an ad hoc fashion without rigorous analysis or productive debate." [9] They advocate "continuous, decision-oriented planning" of the kind they identify at Microsoft, Boeing, and Textron, where the top management team accepts responsibility for analyzing the critical issues that face the company and then takes strategic decisions.

- *Weak strategy execution.* Achieving more effective strategy execution means linking strategic planning to operational management. Larry Bossidy and Ram Charan argue that introducing *milestones*—specific actions or intermediate performance goals to be achieved at specified dates—can "bring reality to a strategic plan." [10] Thus, to keep Honeywell's strategy for cost cutting in its automotive business on track, managers developed a succession of milestones for shifting production overseas. As we noted in Chapter 2, the *balanced scorecard* offers another approach to cascading high-level strategic plans into specific functional and operational targets for different parts of the organization. Building on their balanced scorecard approach, Kaplan and Norton propose that *strategy maps* be used to plot the relationships between strategic actions and overall goals. [11] To link strategic planning more closely to its implementation, Kaplan and Norton recommend that companies upgrade their strategic planning units into *offices of strategy management*, which are responsible not just for managing the annual strategic planning cycle but also for overseeing the execution of strategic plans. [12]

## Performance Management and Financial Control

Most multidivisional companies have a dual planning process: strategic planning concentrates on the medium and long term, financial planning controls short-term performance. Typically, the first year of the strategic plan includes the performance plan for the upcoming year in terms of an operating budget, a capital expenditure budget, strategy targets relating to market share, output, and employment levels, and specific strategic milestones. Annual performance plans are agreed between senior business-level managers and corporate-level managers. They are monitored on a monthly and quarterly basis. At the end of each financial year, they are probed and evaluated in performance review meetings between business and corporate management.

Performance targets emphasize financial indicators (return on invested capital, gross margin, growth of sales revenue) and include strategic goals (market share, new product introductions, market penetration, quality) and operational performance (output, productivity). Performance targets are usually specified in detail for the next year, with less detailed performance targets set for subsequent years. Monthly and quarterly monitoring focuses on the early detection of deviations from targets.

Performance targets are supported by management incentives and sanctions. Companies whose management systems are heavily orientated toward demanding profit targets typically use powerful individual incentives to create an intensely motivating environment for divisional managers. At ITT, Geneen's obsession with highly detailed performance monitoring, ruthless interrogation of divisional executives, and generous rewards for success developed an intensely competitive cadre of executives. They worked relentless, long hours and applied the same performance demands on their subordinates as Geneen did of them. [13] Creating a performance-driven culture requires unremitting focus on a few quantitative performance targets

## STRATEGY CAPSULE 14.2
## Performance Management at BP

BP's organizational philosophy, established by John Browne (CEO 1995–2007), emphasized three principles:

◆ BP operates in a decentralized manner, with individual business unit leaders (such as refinery managers) given broad latitude for running the business and direct responsibility for delivering performance.

◆ The corporate organization provides support and assistance to the business units through a variety of functions, networks, and peer groups.

◆ BP relies upon individual performance contracts to motivate people.

The group chief executive is responsible for presenting the five-year and annual group plans to the board for approval. The goals, metrics, and milestones in group plans are cascaded down in the plans for each of the segments, functions, and regions. Some of these same goals and metrics are reflected in individual performance contracts. A performance contract outlines the key results and milestones an employee is expected to achieve that year. Progress against targets and milestones in an employee's performance contract plays an integral part in annual bonus determinations. BP regards performance contracts as an essential component in delegating commitments for BP's annual plans to individual leaders. In performance contracts, BP attempts to set the goals high, but not so high that they cannot be reached. The performance contracts include financial, operational, strategic, and HSSE (health, safety, security, and environmental) objectives.

*Source:* Adapted from *The Report of the BP US Refineries Independent Safety Review Panel*, January 2007, with permission from BP International.

that can be monitored on a short-term basis. PepsiCo's obsession with monthly market share nourishes an intense, marketing-oriented culture. Chief executive Indra Nooyi observed: "We are a very objective-driven company. We spend a lot of time up front setting objectives and our guys rise to the challenge of meeting those objectives. When they don't meet the objectives, we don't have to flog them because they do it themselves."[14] One executive put it more bluntly: "The place is full of guys with sparks coming out of their asses."[15]

Even in businesses where interdependence is high and investment gestation periods are long, as in petroleum, short- and medium-term performance targets can be highly effective in driving efficiency and profitability. The performance management system of BP, the UK-based petroleum company, is described in Strategy Capsule 14.2. However, BP's performance-oriented culture has also been identified as a factor in several tragic accidents involving BP including explosions at its Texas City refinery (in 2005) and Deepwater Horizon drilling platform (in 2010).

*Balancing Strategic Planning and Financial Control*   One implication of the tradeoff between *input control* (controlling decisions) and *output control* (controlling performance) is that, in designing their corporate control systems, companies must emphasize either strategic planning or financial control. Michael Goold and

**TABLE 14.1**  Characteristics of different corporate management styles

|  | Strategic planning | Financial control |
|---|---|---|
| *Business strategy formulation* | Businesses and corporate HQ jointly formulate strategy The HQ coordinates strategies of businesses | Strategy formulated at business unit level Corporate HQ largely reactive, offering little coordination |
| *Controlling performance* | Primarily strategic goals with medium- to long-term horizon | Financial budgets set annual targets for ROI and other financial variables with monthly and quarterly monitoring |
| *Advantages* | Effective for exploiting (a) linkages among businesses, (b) innovation, (c) long-term competitive positioning | Business unit autonomy supports initiative, responsiveness, efficiency, and development of business leaders |
| *Disadvantages* | Loss of divisional autonomy and initiative Conducive to unitary strategic view Tendency to persist with failing strategies | Short-term focus discourages innovation and long-term development Limited sharing of resources and capabilities among businesses |
| *Style suited to* | Companies with few closely related businesses Works best in highly competitive, technology-intensive sectors where investment projects are large and long term | Highly diversified companies with low relatedness among businesses Works best in mature, low-tech sectors where investment projects are relatively small and short term |

*Source:* Based on M. Goold and A. Campbell, *Strategies and Styles* (Oxford: Blackwell Publishing, 1987) with permission of John Wiley & Sons, Ltd.

Andrew Campbell found that the corporate management systems of British multi-business companies emphasized one or the other.[16] The *strategic planning companies* emphasized the longer-term development of their businesses and had corporate HQs that were heavily involved in business-level planning. The *financial control companies* had corporate HQs that emphasized short-term budgetary control and rigorously monitored financial performance against ambitious targets, but had limited involvement in business strategy formulation—this was left to divisional and business unit managers. Table 14.1 summarizes key features of the two styles.

Over time, companies have made increasing use of financial control in managing their business units. This has occurred even in capital-intensive sectors with long time horizons, such as petroleum, where strategic planning has become increasingly oriented toward short- and medium-term financial targets.[17] However, one outcome of the financial crisis has been a discrediting of short-term shareholder value maximization and an increasing emphasis of strategic over financial management.

## Managing Linkages across Businesses

As we saw in our chapters on vertical integration, international strategy, and diversification, the main opportunities for creating value in the multibusiness company arise from sharing resources and transferring capabilities among the different businesses within the company. This sharing occurs both through the centralization of common services at the corporate level and through direct linkages between the businesses.

## Common Corporate Services

The simplest form of resource sharing in the multidivisional company is the centralized provision of common services and functions. These include corporate management functions such as strategic planning, financial control, treasury, risk management, internal audit, taxation, government relations, and shareholder relations. They also include business services that are more efficiently provided on a centralized basis, such as research, engineering, human resources management, legal services, management development, purchasing, and any other administrative services subject to economies of scale or learning.[18]

In practice, the benefits of the centralized provision of common services tend to be smaller than many corporate managers anticipate. Centralized provision can avoid costs of duplication but there can be little incentive among headquarters staff and specialized corporate units to meet the needs of their business-level customers. The experience of many companies is that corporate staffs tend to grow under their own momentum with few obvious economies from central provision and few benefits of superior services.

As a result, many companies separated their corporate headquarters into two groups: a *corporate management unit* responsible for supporting the corporate management team in core support activities such as strategic planning, finance, and legal, and a *shared services organization* responsible for supplying common services such as research, engineering, training, and information technology to the businesses. By 2000, shared corporate services accounted for 43% of headquarters staff among large UK corporations. To encourage efficiency and customer-orientation among these shared service organizations, some companies have operated them as profit centers supplying services on an arm's-length basis to internal operating units—sometimes in competition with external suppliers.

Procter & Gamble's Global Business Services organization employs 7,000 people in six "global hubs": Cincinnati (US), San Jose (Puerto Rico), Newcastle (UK), Brussels (Belgium), Singapore, and Manila (Philippines). It offers more than 170 employee and business services, including IT, finance, facilities, purchasing, employee services, and business building solutions to P&G businesses in 170 countries. Through scale economies and standardizing systems, it has cut costs by over $800 million. Its innovations have included virtualization (e.g., replacing physical product mock-ups with virtual reality applications), accelerating internal collaboration (e.g., through video collaboration studios), providing decision support (e.g., its "Decision Cockpits"), and driving digital capabilities through creating a real-time environment.[19]

Deloitte's 2011 survey of global shared services found that:

- companies are structuring their shared service organizations around global hub-and-spoke configurations where the location of different services is determined primarily by labor factors, including cost, availability, language skills, and quality;
- as a result US- and European-based companies were increasingly locating service units in Asia and Latin America;
- as well as established transactional services such as IT, HR, and finance, shared service centers were increasingly being used for other functions, such as supply chain, marketing, real estate, and legal services;
- companies are increasingly blending shared services with the outsourcing of services;

● most companies realize considerable benefits form the shared services model, not only in cost but also in control, data visibility, and as a platform for growth.[20]

## Business Linkages and Porter's Corporate Strategy Types

Exploiting economies of scope doesn't necessarily mean centralizing resources at the corporate level. Resources and capabilities can also be shared between the businesses. Michael Porter has argued that the way in which a company manages these linkages determines its potential to create value for shareholders.[21] He identifies four corporate strategy types:

● *Portfolio management*: The most limited form of resource sharing is where the parent company simply acquires a portfolio of attractive, soundly managed companies, allows them to operate autonomously, and links them through an efficient internal capital market.

● *Restructuring*: Conglomerates, such as Danaher and Textron in the US and Tomkins PLC and Invensys PLC in the UK, create value primarily by restructuring: acquiring poorly managed companies, then intervening to appoint new management, dispose of underperforming businesses, restructure balance sheets, and cut costs. As conglomerates have increasingly restructured themselves into oblivion (either transforming themselves into more focused industrial companies or breaking up entirely) private equity groups—such as Carlyle, KKR, Blackstone, and Texas Pacific in the US and Alchemy and Candover in the UK—have increasingly taken on the same restructuring role. These firms create investment funds organized as limited partnerships that make leveraged buyouts of private and public companies. The finding that, on average, the returns from private equity funds are lower than those on the stock market as a whole suggests that the value created by restructuring is limited.[22]

● *Transferring skills*: Organizational capabilities can be transferred between business units. LVMH transfers brand management and distribution capabilities among its different luxury-brand businesses. Sharp transfers its opto-electronics capabilities across a number of consumer, electronic, and office equipment products. Creating value by sharing skills requires that the same capabilities are applicable to the different businesses and that mechanisms are established to transfer these skills through personnel exchange and best practice transfer. As the opening quotation to this chapter indicates, sharing know-how and capabilities is at the heart of value creation at General Electric.

● *Sharing activities*: Porter argues that the most important source of value arises from exploiting economies of scope in common resources and activities. For these economies to be realized, corporate management must play a key coordinating role, including involvement in formulating business unit strategies and intervention in operational matters to ensure that opportunities for sharing R & D, advertising, distribution systems, and service networks are fully exploited. In some countries, Unilever has a single marketing and distribution organization that handles a wide range of different consumer products.[23] The emergence of Samsung Electronics as a global leader in digital consumer products during the early part of the 21st century owed much to its development of advanced design capabilities. It's centers in London, Tokyo, San Francisco, and Seoul are shared across Samsung's different business units.[24]

## The Role of the Corporate Headquarters in Managing Linkages

The closer the linkages among businesses, the greater the opportunities for creating value from sharing resources and transferring capabilities, and the greater the need for corporate headquarters to coordinate across businesses. We noted earlier that the *financial control* style of management occurs mainly in conglomerates where the independence of each business limits the coordinating role of the head office to manage the budgetary process and establish "framework conditions" for divisional planning.

In more closely related companies, such as the vertically integrated oil companies, or companies with close market or technological links (such as IBM, Procter & Gamble, American Express, and Alcoa), corporate management uses a *strategic planning* style, which is likely to involve not only coordination of strategies but also operational coordination to exploit the economies of scope and transferable skills discussed in Chapter 13. The extent of corporate involvement in interdivisional affairs is a key determinant of the size of the corporate headquarters. Berkshire Hathaway, which has almost no linkages among its businesses, has a corporate staff of about 50. Hewlett-Packard, with about the same sales but much closer linkages between its divisions, has close to 3000 employees at its Palo Alto head office. Where business units are linked through their sharing of a common resource or capability, the corporate headquarters is likely to be closely involved in the development and deployment of that resource or capability. For example, Pfizer and Corning Inc. have strong corporate R & D groups, Dow has a strong corporate manufacturing function, and Virgin's corporate team plays a key role in managing the Virgin brand.[25]

Developing and sharing resources and capabilities may require ad hoc organizational arrangements such as *cross-divisional task forces*. Such task forces might be formed for the introduction and dissemination of total quality management, to reengineer financial management practices, to promote fast-cycle new product development or to coordinate business development in China.

Sharing capabilities and know-how between businesses implies an important role for knowledge management in the multibusiness firm. In industries such as beer, cement, food processing, and telecommunication services international expansion offers few economies of scope in shared resources, the key to creating value from a global presence is through the transfer of innovation and sharing of know-how.

Exploiting linkages between businesses imposes costs. Though Porter may be right that the *potential* for value creation increases as a company moves from a loose, "portfolio management" strategy toward the more integrated "shared activity" strategy, this potential is not always realized. For example, most attempts at exploiting the potential for cross selling across different businesses have yielded disappointing results, especially in financial services.[26] Lorsch and Allen point to some of the management costs incurred in exploiting linkages between businesses. They compare three conglomerates with three vertically integrated paper companies.[27]

The coordination requirements of the paper companies resulted in greater involvement of head office staff in divisional operations, larger head office staffs, more complex planning and control devices, and a lower responsiveness to change in the external environment. By contrast, the conglomerates made little attempt to exploit linkages even if they were present:

> The conglomerate firms we had studied seemed to be achieving appreciable degrees of financial and managerial synergy but little or no operating synergy. Some of the firms saw little immediate payoff in this operating synergy; others met with little success in attempting to achieve it.[28]

The success with which the corporate headquarters manages linkages between businesses depends on top management's understanding of the commonalities among its different businesses. Ultimately, these commonalities have their basis in the underlying rationale for the corporation—what Prahalad and Bettis call *dominant logic*: "the way in which managers conceptualize the business and make critical resource allocation decisions."[29] The success of the multibusiness corporation depends upon strategic similarity among the different businesses that is consistent with an overall dominant logic.

## Managing Change in the Multibusiness Corporation

Conceptions of the role of corporate management in the multibusiness company have shifted greatly over time. These shifting roles have been associated with different priorities with regard to value creation within the multibusiness corporation. During the 1970s and early 1980s, corporate management was concerned with the creation of large business empires. The motivation was partly growth but also the belief in the power of new tools of strategic and financial management to transcend industry boundaries. During the late 1980s, a profound shift in top management priorities occurred, and throughout the 1990s, the dominant theme was applying the logic and principles of shareholder value maximization to restructure diversified corporate empires. The principal sources of value were pruning business portfolios and exercising "standalone" influence to boost the performance of individual businesses. During the present century, the primary challenges have been, first, creating value through exploiting linkages between businesses and improving integration within the corporation and, second, increasing responsiveness to external change and accelerating the pace of organizational evolution. These shifts in strategic priorities have been associated with different leadership styles. Let me address each of these two major transitions.

### Value Creation through Corporate Restructuring

During the late 1980s and 1990s, a large proportion of the largest corporations of North America and Europe underwent intense phases of corporate change typically triggered by declining financial performance or some external threat. Given the tendency for most multibusiness corporations to develop through a series of incremental strategy initiatives, periodic corporate restructuring based upon a comprehensive corporate review that appraises individual businesses and review of the overall business portfolio can be critical to revitalization.

McKinsey & Company's pentagon framework offers a systematic approach to analyzing the potential for increasing the market value of a multibusiness company through corporate restructuring.[30] The analysis comprises five stages—these correspond to the five nodes of Figure 14.4:

1 *The current market value of the company*: The starting point of the analysis is current enterprise value, which comprises the value of equity plus the value of debt. (As we know from Chapter 2, if securities markets are efficient, this equals the net present value of anticipated cash flow over the life of the company.)

2 *The value of the company as is*: Even without any changes to strategy or operations, it may be possible to value simply by managing external perceptions of a company's future prospects. Over the past two decades, companies have devoted increasing attention to managing investor expectations by increasing the quantity and quality of information flow to shareholders and investment analysts and establishing departments of investor relations for this purpose.

3 *The potential value of the company with internal improvements*: As we have seen, corporate management has opportunities for increasing the overall value of the company by making strategic and operational improvements to individual businesses that increase their cash flows. These might include exploiting global expansion opportunities, outsourcing certain activities, and cost-cutting opportunities.

4 *The potential value of the company with external improvements*: Having determined the potential value of its constituent businesses, corporate management needs to determine whether changes in the business portfolio can increase overall company value. The key is to apply the principle of parenting advantage: even after strategic and operating improvements have been made, can a business be sold for a price greater than its value to the company?

**FIGURE 14.4** The McKinsey restructuring pentagon

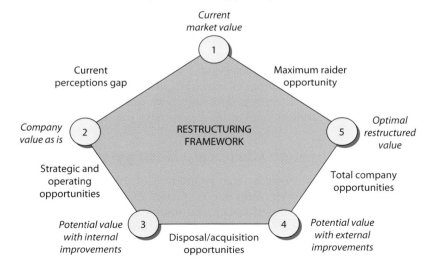

**Source:** T. E. Copeland, T. Koller, and J. Murrin, *Valuation* (New York: John Wiley & Sons, Inc. 1990).

**5** *The optimum restructured value of the company*: The previous four steps establish maximum value potential of a company. Assuming that these changes could also be undertaken by an alternative owner of the company, the difference between the maximum restructured value and the current market value represents the profit potential available to a corporate raider.

This type of analysis has been traditionally associated with leveraged buyout specialists and other corporate raiders. Faced with this threat, comprehensive corporate restructuring became widespread among large multibusiness companies (e.g., the restructuring wave by the oil majors during 1986–1992).[31]

Leadership style associated with corporate restructuring is indicated by the nicknames given to some of the prominent exponents: "Chainsaw Al" Dunlap (at Scott Paper and Sunbeam), "Neutron Jack" Welch (at General Electric), and "Fred-the-Shred" Goodwin (at Royal Bank of Scotland). This points to an emphasis on cost cutting and asset divestment. The leadership mode associated with this approach is characterized by obsessive commitment to the maximization of shareholder value and the bottom-line results needed to achieve it, managing through performance targets and an emphasis on performance incentives (both compensation incentives and the threat of termination for underperformance).

## Beyond Restructuring: How the Headquarters Can Drive Corporate Evolution

Disillusion with the shareholder value maximization model, diminishing returns to cost cutting, and the need to create new sources of corporate value have resulted in profound shifts in the corporate strategies of multibusiness companies. Increasingly, large multibusiness companies have sought to identify opportunities for innovation, for new product development, and for creating value from exploiting new and more sophisticated linkages between companies. Corporate headquarters are concerned less with the problem of control and more with the problem of identifying and implementing the means for creating value within and between their individual businesses. The use of the term *parenting* to describe the corporate role reflects this growing emphasis on corporate development. This emphasis has involved the corporate headquarters in a quest for new sources of value. To get a clearer idea of how this has happened let us look at three examples: GE under Jack Welch, Samsung Electronics, and IBM (see Strategy Capsules 14.3, 14.4, and 14.5). These examples point to three approaches to stimulating corporate adaptation:

- *Adaptive tension*: At General Electric, Jack Welch, CEO from 1981 until 2001, created a corporate management system that decentralized decision making to business-level managers but created a level of internal stress that counteracted complacency and fostered responsiveness to external change and a striving for constant performance improvement. While GE's "pressure cooker" atmosphere stimulated incremental change, Welch led systemic change through periodic corporate initiatives (such as his "boundarylessness," "six-sigma," and "be #1 or #2 in your industry" initiatives).

- *Institutionalizing strategic change*: As we have already noted, companies' strategic planning systems are seldom the sources of major strategic

## STRATEGY CAPSULE 14.3
# Jack Welch's Reinventing of Corporate Management

Jack Welch's 20-year tenure as chairman and CEO of General Electric began with an intensive period of restructuring, which transformed the business's portfolio and slashed costs. From 1984 onwards, however, Welch systematically rebuilt GE's management systems, redefining the role of the corporate headquarters and creating a decentralized system where the pressures of performance improvement and the drive to seize new opportunities fostered continual change. Welch's initiatives included:

◆ *Delayering*: Welch's fundamental criticism of GE's management was that it was slow and unresponsive. Welch eliminated GE's sector level of organization so that the 12 business heads reported directly to him. GE's layers of hierarchy were cut from nine or ten to four or five. The resulting broadening of spans of control meant that each executive was managing more direct reports, forcing executives to delegate decision making.

◆ *Changing the strategic planning system*: Welch replaced the staff-led, document-driven process with more personal, less formal, but very intensive face-to-face discussions. Data-heavy business plans were replaced by a slim "play-book" that summarized key strategic issues facing the business and proposed actions. Discussion of these issues and actions were the basis for a half-day review session where business heads and key executives met with Welch and his top-management team in an open dialogue.[a]

◆ *Redefining the role of headquarters*: The changes in the strategic planning system reflected broader changes in the role of the corporate headquarters. Welch viewed headquarters as interfering too much, generating too much paper, and failing to add value. His objective was to "turn their role 180 degrees from checker, inquisitor, and authority figure to facilitator, helper, and supporter … Our job is to help, it's to assist, it's to make these businesses stronger, to help them grow and be more powerful."[b] The businesses were also expected to help one another: Welch's concept of the "boundaryless company" aimed at permeable internal boundaries allowing "integrated diversity"—the ability to transfer the ideas, business practices, and people freely and easily. "Boundaryless behavior combines 12 huge global businesses—each number one or number two in its markets—into a vast laboratory whose principal product is new ideas, coupled with a common commitment to spread them throughout the company."[c]

◆ *Work-out*: As well as being pressured from above by Welch and his management team, divisional managers were pressured from below. Work-out meetings were offsite meetings where the heads of a business or function were required to respond to criticisms and suggestions from subordinates.

**Notes:**
[a]*General Electric: Jack Welch's Second Wave (A)*, Case No. 9–391–248 (Boston: Harvard Business School, 1991).
[b]Jack Welch, "GE Growth Engine," speech to employees, 1988.
[c]"Letter to Share Owners," General Electric Company 1993 Annual Report (Fairfield, CT, 1994): 2.

## STRATEGY CAPSULE 14.4
# Reformulating Strategic Planning at IBM

IBM has a remarkable history of adapting to change. Its business has successfully transitioned from tabulating machines to mainframe computers, to personal computers, to networked information technology, to cloud computing. Within the space of 15 years it has also changed from a hardware into a software and services company. Under its past three CEOs, IBM's pace of evolution accelerated, assisted by IBM's processes for making and implementing strategy.

In 1999, CEO Lou Gerstner began a series of fundamental changes to IBM's strategic planning system which continued under his successor, Sam Palmisano. The outcome was the IBM Strategic Leadership Model, which linked processes for strategic insight with processes for strategy execution. Strategic insight involved several approaches to sensing new opportunities:

◆ The technology team meets monthly to assess emerging technologies and their market potential.

◆ The strategy team comprising a cross section of general managers, strategy executives, and functional managers meets monthly to review business unit strategies and recommend new initiatives.

◆ The integration and values team comprises 300 key leaders selected by the top management team responsible for integrating IBM through company-wide initiatives called "winning plays."

◆ A "deep dive" is a structured, analytical process conducted by an ad hoc team to explore a specific opportunity or strategic issue. It may result in a recommendation to enter a new area of business or to exit from a particular technology or product market.

The initiatives arising from these processes are then acted on by the three main executing vehicles:

◆ "Emerging business opportunities" is a business development process that recognizes that new business initiatives are likely to require management methods (and investment criteria) that are very different from established ones. Between 1999 and 2005, 18 EBOs were established, including Linux, autonomic computing, blade servers, digital media, network processing, and life sciences.

◆ "Strategic leadership forums" are three- to five-day workshops facilitated by IBM's Global Executive and Organizational Capability Group. Their purpose is to transform strategic initiatives into action plans and to address other pressing strategic issues, such as addressing poor performance in particular area of business. They are initiated by a senior manager and overseen by the strategy team.

◆ The Corporate Investment Fund finances new initiatives identified by the integration and values team or by EBOs. They are used to support winning play initiatives and other projects which aren't included in the annual budgeting process—possibly because that falls between businesses.

*Source:* J. B. Harreld, C. A. O'Reilly, and M. L. Tushman, "Dynamic Capabilities at IBM: Driving Strategy into Action," *California Management Review* 49 (Summer 2007): 21–43.

## STRATEGY CAPSULE 14.5

# Samsung Electronics: Top-Down Initiatives that Drive Corporate Development

Samsung is the biggest of South Korea's *chaebols*—diversified groups of separate companies linked together by cross-shareholdings and controlled by the founding family. The Samsung group comprises 83 companies but has no legal identity; the closest to a parent company is Everland, in which the founding Lee family has a controlling 46% stake. The biggest company is Samsung Electronics, the world's largest electronics company in terms of sales. The head of the group, and chairman of Samsung Electronics, is Lee Kun-hee, son of the founder Lee Byung-chull and father of Jay Y. Lee, president of Samsung Electronics.

Samsung Electronics' rapid development has been the result of a series of large-scale corporate initiatives that are ambitious, focused, long-term, and driven by intense top-down commitment. In 1982, Samsung Electronics resolved to become world leader in memory devices—it achieved this in DRAM chips in 1992, then in 2004 began investing massively in flash memories. In 2000, it began producing batteries for mobile digital devices; by 2009, it was world leader, similarly with flat-panel televisions. These successes involved massive commitments of resources to technology (Samsung receives more US patents than any other company except IBM), manufacturing (for semiconductor production Samsung built the world's biggest fabrication complex), design (with the creation of design centers in five cities of the world), and the Samsung brand. The effectiveness of this resource

mobilization has been supported by a culture and working practices that support high levels of coordination and commitment. Samsung's culture is built around many tales of outstanding endeavor, including building a four-kilometer paved road in a single day to ensure that Samsung's first integrated circuit plant could open on time.

In 2010–2011, based upon its analysis of long-term trends, Samsung established five new corporate initiatives, each of which would represent a major new business.

Samsung's new product development success has been supported by a knowledge management system which aims to exploit the expertise of the entire company. In April 2009, the Visual Display Division of Samsung Electronics' Digital Media Business had just completed work on a high-resolution LED TV when it was assigned a new project: it was required to roll out a high-definition, 3-D television within a year. To achieve this goal, the two task forces assigned to the project turned to Samsung Electronics' Test and Error Management System (TEMS), a knowledge management system containing a vast reservoir of information from every product development project undertaken at the company.

*Source:* "Samsung: The Next Big Bet," *Economist* (October 1, 2011); *Samsung Electronics*, HBS Case 9–705–508 (revised 2009); "Samsung Electronics' Knowledge Management System," *Korea Times* (Wednesday, October 6, 2010).

| Sector | Investment ($billion) | Target sales, 2020 ($billion) | Target jobs, 2020 |
|---|---|---|---|
| Solar panels | 5.1 | 8.5 | 10,000 |
| LED lighting | 7.3 | 15.2 | 17,000 |
| E-vehicle batteries | 4.6 | 8.7 | 7,600 |
| Biotech drugs | 1.8 | 1.5 | 1,000 |
| Medical devices | 1.0 | 8.5 | 10,300 |

initiatives: the impetus for major strategy redirection usually comes from outside formal strategy processes. The IBM case example shows that strategic planning systems can be redesigned as systems for sensing external changes and responding to the opportunities these changes offer.

● *Top-down, large-scale development initiatives*: Throughout this book, we have pointed to the key role of *strategic intent*—top-down strategic goals—in unifying and motivating organizational members. In some companies, linking such strategic intent to specific projects and programs has been an especially powerful vehicle for corporate development. The rise of Samsung Electronics to become the world's largest electronics company has been on the basis of a small number of hugely ambitious development projects that have involved massive commitments of finance and human ingenuity and effort.

Adaptation to changing circumstances also requires timing. Intel's former CEO, Andy Grove emphasizes the importance of CEOs identifying *strategic inflection points*—instances where seismic shifts in a firm's competitive environment require a fundamental redirection of strategy.[32] Grove identifies three such key inflection points at Intel: the transition from DRAM chips to microprocessors as its core business, the choice of its x86 series of microprocessors in preference to a RISC architecture, and its decision to replace its faulty Pentium chips.[33]

Finally, managing change also requires creating the certainty that provides the security that allows people to leap into the unknown. Some of the companies that have been most effective in adapting to change—IBM, Philips, General Electric, Danone, and HSBC—have done so while emphasizing the continuity of their heritage and identity. Creating a sense of identity is more challenging for a company that spans several businesses than for one whose identity is determined by the products it offers (McDonald's or De Beers). It goes beyond "strategic relatedness" and "dominant logic" and embraces vision, mission, and culture. In the previous chapter, I observed that the luxury goods giant LVMH deploys its core brand management capabilities across several different businesses. Its success in doing so depends critically upon establishing a corporate identity that forms a cultural glue between these disparate businesses: "The common cultural trunk is based on the permanent search for quality of the products and the management, human relations based on responsibility and initiative, and rewarding competences and services."[34] It would appear that a stable, well-established organizational identity may support not only the management of diversity but also the management of change.[35]

## Governance of Multibusiness Corporations

So far our discussion of the multibusiness corporation has focused on the means by which the corporate headquarters can create value. What we have not discussed is: value for whom? This takes us to the issue of **corporate governance**.

Corporate governance is the system by which companies are directed and controlled. Corporate governance centers on the role of boards of directors, which have primary responsibility for the governance of companies. The reason corporate governance is an important issue is because of the separation of ownership from control in large companies, especially public companies. Where ownership is highly dispersed, what is to prevent the management of a company from running the company for its own interests?

The challenges of corporate governance are not unique to multibusiness companies. Corporate governance presents problems to all companies where the owners are not directly engaged in managing the company. However, it is large corporations where the problems of separation of ownership and control are most acute, and large corporations also tend to be multibusiness corporations. Even a highly specialized company such as McDonald's is divided into regional groupings (US, Europe, Asia Pacific, and the Middle East), which are further divided into divisions (UK and Northern Europe, Russia and Eastern Europe, West USA, Central USA etc.). Moreover, the separation of decision authority between the corporate HQ and the individual businesses complicates corporate governance.

Let us begin by outlining the key issues of corporate governance in large companies, then deal specifically with the issues that arise in relation to the structures of multibusiness corporations.

## The Challenge of Corporate Governance

Is Williamson right that the corporate head office can be relied upon to act as an "agent of the stockholders whose purpose is to monitor the operations of the constituent parts"? Among diversified firms, it seems that multidivisional structures are more conducive to profitability than alternative structural forms, yet it is also clear that multidivisional structures are no safeguard against agency problems. The most notorious examples of chief executives operating their companies as personal fiefdoms are found among divisionalized, multibusiness corporations—Howard Hughes at Hughes Corporation, Ken Lay at Enron, Dennis Kozlowski at Tyco, Jean-Marie Messier at Vivendi Universal, and Fred Goodwin at Royal Bank of Scotland. While the CEOs of diversified companies may avoid emotional commitment to particular businesses, this does not mean that they are more predisposed to shareholder return over the quest for Napoleonic personal grandeur.

Top management's pursuit of personal goals related to the aggrandizement of wealth, power, influence, and status in preference to owners' goals of value maximization are primarily a problem for public companies.[36] The critical problem is that the ability of shareholders to exercise effective control over management is limited by their large number. This creates, first, a coordination problem and, second, an incentive problem—if each shareholder owns only a small fraction of a company and if that company's shares only account for a small fraction of the shareholder's total wealth, then the costs of active engagement are high relative to the likely returns. Disgruntled shareholders typically sell their shares rather than oppose the incumbent management team.

Given widespread shareholder apathy, boards of directors tend to become tools of top management rather than agents of the shareholders.

*Rights of Shareholders*    Company law relating to the rights of shareholders typically covers shareholders' right to sell their shares, their right to company information (including access to audited financial statements), their right to elect and remove members of the board of directors, and their right to share in the profits of the company.

Although seemingly straightforward, these rights are often abrogated by companies. For example, managers are more likely than shareholders to oppose takeover by another company: while shareholders benefit financially, senior executives often lose their jobs. Hence, companies frequently create impediments to hostile takeover either in the form of special voting rights for certain classes of share or "poison pill" defenses. Yahoo! defended against a 2008 takeover bid from Microsoft through a provision that any hostile bid would trigger the creation of a rights issue to existing shareholders. To resist takeover by Mittal Steel, Arcelor attempted to make itself indigestible by arranging a merger with Russian steel giant Severstal.

In terms of rights to information: managers' desire to manipulate their companies' share prices has resulted in misreporting their financial results. Financial misreporting was at the center of the scandals that engulfed Enron and WorldCom in the US and Parmalat and Royal Ahold in Europe.[37] New standards of financial reporting include America's Sarbanes–Oxley Act.

*Responsibilities of Boards of Directors*   The board of directors, according to *OECD Principles of Corporate Governance*, has the responsibility to "ensure the strategic guidance of the company, the effective monitoring of management by the board, and the board's accountability to the company and the shareholders."[38] This requires that:

- Board members act in good faith, with due diligence and care, in the best interest of the company and its shareholders.
- Board members review and guide corporate strategy, major plans of action, risk policy, annual budgets and business plans; set and monitor performance objectives; and oversee major capital expenditures; select, monitor, and compensate key executives; ensure the integrity of the corporation's accounting and financial reporting systems; and oversee the process of disclosure and communication.

The ability of the board to achieve these goals has been compromised by several impediments:

- The dominance of the board by executive directors: In both the US and UK and some other countries, the top management team (the CEO, CFO and other senior executives) are likely to be made up of board members.
- Combining the roles of board chair and CEO: This is common in the US, less so in most European companies. US opinion suggests that splitting board chair and CEO roles is neither an advantage nor disadvantage: it depends entirely upon the attributes of the person doing the job.[39] However, interlocking boards, where CEOs serve as independent members on one another's boards, does appear to be an unambiguous constraint on board independence.
- Boards have become increasingly preoccupied with compliance issues with the result that their role in guiding corporate strategy has shrunk.

Dominic Barton, global managing director of McKinsey & Company, argues that if boards are to become effective agents of long-term value creation they must devote much more time to their roles and need to have more relevant industry experience, and they need a small analytical staff to support their work.[40]

The harshest criticisms of board oversight have been in relation to management compensation. The escalation of CEO compensation among large public companies since the early 1990s has been little short of staggering. The paradox is that the massive payouts to CEOs have been the result of compensation systems designed to align management goals with those of shareholders, especially through the grant of stock options and emphasis on performance-related bonuses. Yet some of the biggest executive payouts have been by companies that have experienced shareholder returns that have ranged from indifferent to disastrous (Table 14.2). Performance bonuses and options packages have been extended down corporate hierarchies to include middle managers as well as the top management team. In the UK, salary comprised 54% of overall executive compensation as compared with bonuses 24%, and options and long-term incentive plans 22%.[41] Aspects of the poor alignment between executive compensation and shareholder value creation include linking bonuses to short-term performance, a failure to correct for overall stock market movements, and incentives for creating shareholder value not being matched by penalties for its destruction.[42]

The division of decision-making responsibilities between a corporate headquarters with responsibilities for the company as a whole and individual businesses has implications for corporate governance. This separation of powers may mitigate some of the problems of agency; there are also arguments that the multibusiness firm exacerbates agency problems.

**TABLE 14.2**  Highest-paid CEOs of US companies, 2011

| Rank | CEO | Company | Total pay ($million) | Change on 2010 (%) |
| --- | --- | --- | --- | --- |
| 1 | David Simon | Simon Property Group | 137.2 | +458 |
| 2 | Leslie Moonves | CBS | 68.4 | +20 |
| 3 | David Zaslav | Discovery Communications | 52.4 | +23 |
| 4 | Sanjay K. Jha | Motorola Mobility | 47.2 | +262 |
| 5 | Philippe P. Dauman | Viacom | 43.1 | −49 |
| 6 | David M. Cote | Honeywell International | 35.7 | +135 |
| 7 | Robert A. Iger | Walt Disney | 31.4 | +12 |
| 8 | Clarence P. Cazalot Jr | Marathon Oil | 29.9 | +239 |
| 9 | John P. Daane | Altera | 29.6 | +278 |
| 10 | Alan Mulally | Ford Motor | 29.5 | +11 |
| 11 | Gregory Q. Brown | Motorola Solutions | 29.3 | +113 |
| 12 | Richard C. Adkerson | Freeport-McMoRan | 28.4 | −19 |
| 13 | Ian M. Cumming | Leucadia National | 28.2 | +531 |
| 14 | Brian L. Roberts | Comcast | 26.9 | −13 |
| 15 | Jeffrey L. Bewkes | Time Warner | 25.7 | −2 |
| 16 | Rex W. Tillerson | ExxonMobil | 25.2 | +17 |
| 17 | Samuel J. Palmisano | IBM | 24.2 | −4 |
| 18 | William C. Weldon | Johnson & Johnson | 23.4 | +1 |
| 19 | James Dimon | JPMorgan Chase | 23.1 | +11 |
| 20 | Louis R. Chenevert | United Technologies | 22.2 | +17 |

*Source:* "50 Highest-Paid CEOs of 2012: AP Pay Survey," www.therichest.org/business/50-highest-paid-ceos-2012/ (May 26, 2012). Implications of the Multidivisional Form for Corporate Governance

*The Theory of the M-form*   While Alfred Chandler identified diffusion of the multidivisional form as a critical factor in the development of the multibusiness corporation,[43] Oliver Williamson provided its theoretical rationale.[44] Williamson argued that by distributing decision making between a corporate HQ and business divisions, the divisionalized firm (or in his terminology, the *M-form*) facilitated corporate governance in two ways:

- *Allocation of resources*: Resource allocation within any administrative structure is a political process in which power, status, and influence can triumph over purely commercial considerations.[45] To the extent that the multidivisional company can create a competitive internal capital market in which capital is allocated according to financial and strategic criteria, it can avoid much of the politicization inherent in purely hierarchical systems. The multidivisional company does this through operating an internal capital market where budgets are linked to past and projected divisional profitability, and individual projects are subject to a standardized appraisal process.

- *Agency problems*: The basic agency problem is that owners (shareholders) desire maximization of the value of the firm, while their agents (managers) are more interested in salaries, security, and power. Given the limited power of shareholders to discipline and replace managers and the weakness of boards to control management, the corporate head office of a multidivisional firm can act as an interface between shareholders and the divisional managers and enforce adherence to profit goals. With divisions designated as profit centers, financial performance can readily be monitored by the head office and divisional managers can be held responsible for performance failures. According to Williamson, multibusiness companies can be more effective profit maximizers than specialist companies can because of two critical advantages of the corporate head office over the board of directors of a single business company: first, the corporate head office has better access to information about the business and, second, it is easier for a corporate head office to replace business managers than it is for a board of directors.[46] At General Electric, ExxonMobil, and PepsiCo, this capacity for corporate headquarters to create strongly profit-oriented systems is particularly evident.

*Problems of Divisionalized Firms*   Rather than acting as an effective agent of shareholders and operating internal capital markets where resources are allocated to their most profitable uses, there is ample evidence that decision making in multibusiness firms tends to be highly politicized.[47] Moreover, rather than representing shareholders' interests, corporate headquarters are liable to become vehicles of CEO ambition that are divorced both from shareholders and from the realities of the businesses. Some of the most notorious examples of large-scale destruction of shareholder value—from Enron, WorldCom, and Parmalat through to Royal Bank of Scotland, Bank of America, and Kaupthing Bank of Iceland—involved empire-building CEOs of multibusiness companies.

In practice, multidivisional companies may lack the flexibility and responsiveness that their modular should, in principle, be capable of. Henry Mintzberg points to two key rigidities:[48]

● *Constraints on decentralization*: Individual divisions often feature highly centralized power that arises from divisional presidents' personal accountability to the head office. Moreover, the operational freedom of the divisional management exists only so long as the corporate head office is satisfied with divisional performance. Divisional underperformance typically leads to a curtailing of divisional autonomy as the corporate head office intervenes.

---

### STRATEGY CAPSULE 14.6
## Governance in Holding Companies

A holding company is a company that owns a controlling interest in a number of subsidiary companies. The term *holding company* is used to refer both to the parent company and to the group as a whole. Holding companies are common in Japan (notably the traditional *zaibatsu* such as Mitsubishi and Mitsui), in Korea (*chaelbols* such as LG, Hyundai, and SK) and the Hong Kong trading houses (Swire, Jardine Matheson, and Hutchison Whampoa). In the US, holding companies own the majority of US banking assets.

Within holding companies, the parent exercises control over the subsidiary through appointing its board of directors. The individual subsidiaries typically retain high levels of strategic and operational autonomy. Unlike the multidivisional corporation, the holding company lacks financial integration: there is no centralized treasury, profits accrue to the individual operating companies, and there is no centralized budgeting function—each subsidiary is a separate financial entity. The parent company provides equity and debt capital and receives dividends from the subsidiary.

Although the potential for exploiting synergies between businesses is more limited in the holding company than in the divisionalized corporation, the holding company structure has important advantages for large family-owned companies. The attractiveness of holding companies is that they allow family dynasties to retain ownership and control of business empires that diversify family wealth across multiple sectors. At the same time their decentralization allows effective management of the group without the need for the parent company to develop a tremendous depth of management capability.

Thus, the Tata Group, India's biggest business concern with over $60 billion in revenue and 424,000 employees, is controlled by the Tata family through Tata Sons Ltd, parent company of the group. Among the many hundreds of subsidiaries, several are leading companies within their industries, including Tata Steel, Tata Motors (owner of Jaguar and Land Rover), Tata Tea (owner of the Tetley brand), and Tata Consulting Services. Twenty-seven Tata companies are publicly listed.

In contrast to the public corporations where the key governance problem is a tendency for salaried managers to operate the company in their own interests, the problems of holding companies relate to the rights of minority shareholders. At Fiat Group the Agnelli family exerts effective control with just 10% of the total equity. By acting in concert with banks and other leading families, a family can extend its influence with quite small ownership stakes: the Agnelli family was able to gain control of Telecom Italia despite owning a mere 0.6% of total equity.

***Sources:*** M. Granovetter, "Business Groups and Social Organization," in N. J. Smelser and R. Swedberg, *Handbook of Economic Sociology* (Princeton, NJ: Princeton University Press, 2005): 429–50; F. Amatori and A. Colli, "Corporate Governance: The Italian Story," Bocconi University, Milan (December 2000).

● *Standardization of divisional management*: In principle, each division can adapt itself to the requirements of its business sector. In practice, there are powerful forces for standardizing control systems and management styles across the multidivisional corporation. The difficulties that many large, mature corporations experience with new business development often result from applying to new businesses the same management systems designed for existing businesses.[49]

However, we must recognize that, while the multidivisional corporation is the dominant organizational form for multibusiness firms in North America and much of Western Europe, it is not the only way to organize the multibusiness firm. Among family-owned companies and in much of Asia the holding-company structure is widespread. This creates rather different governance issues (Strategy Capsule 14.6).

## Summary

In this chapter we have examined the role of the corporate headquarters in large, complex companies, namely those that manage multiple business units. Our focus has been on how corporate management creates value within these companies. We identified three principal types of value-creating activity:

◆ Managing the business portfolio: reallocating resources from unattractive to attractive industries. This requires the exercise of superior foresight by top management in order to anticipate industries with growing profit potential and exit from industries before the onset of decline.

◆ Managing individual businesses: increasing the performance of individual businesses by enhancing the quality of their decision making, installing better managers, and creating incentives that drive superior performance.

◆ Managing linkages among businesses: exploiting opportunities for sharing resources and transferring capabilities comprises multiple activities ranging from the centralized provision of functions to best practices transfer. The key is to ensure that the potential gains from exploiting such economies of scope are not outweighed by the costs of managing the added complexity.

In addition, the success of the multibusiness company is dependent upon two additional performance dimensions. The first is the capacity for change. While corporate restructuring is typically a periodic process of large-scale strategic and organizational change, typically in response to deteriorating financial performance, a bigger challenge is creating systems and attitudes that permit continuous strategic adaptation.

The second concerns corporate governance. Those who control large, complex companies are well positioned to appropriate the value that these companies create. In the case of public, multidivisional corporations, self-seeking senior managers are the primary culprits. In family-controlled holding companies it is the controlling family that tends to exploit its power at the expense of other owners.

Given multiple sources of value creation and value destruction, it is impossible to offer generic recommendations as to how a multibusiness company should implement its corporate strategy: each firm is unique in terms of its portfolio of products and markets, its resources and capabilities, its corporate culture, its administrative heritage, and the characteristics of its corporate managers. Highly diversified, divisionalized corporations can be superbly managed generators of value (General Electric and LVMH) or they can be vehicles for empire-building, egotistical executives (Vivendi Universal under Jean-Marie Messier and Tyco under Dennis Kozlowski). Family-controlled holding companies can be defensive institutions that pursue family interests at the expense of other share-holders (Parmalat) or creators of world-class businesses (Samsung). Given these factors, it is hardly surprising that empirical research offers limited guidance as to the correlates of superior performance among multibusiness firms. As with so many other aspects of strategic management, *fit* is the key—the consistency with which strategy, the characteristics of the external environment, resources, capabilities, structure, systems, leadership style, culture, and history interlink.

 Quizzes and flashcards to test yourself further are available in your interactive e-book at **www.wileyopenpage.com**

## Self-Study Questions

1. You have been appointed CEO of Procter & Gamble, which owns many businesses ranging from laundry detergents to shaving products, skin care products, hair care products, dental products, and perfumes. Your VP of strategic planning has asked for your advice on which portfolio matrix—the McKinsey matrix, BCG matrix, or Ashridge matrix—she should use for analyzing P&G's portfolio of businesses. What advice would you offer her?

2. Apply the BCG matrix to the different programs that your institution offers. (You will need to make some informed guesses about market growth rates and relative market share.) Does this analysis offer useful strategy implications for the different programs?

3. The discussion of "performance management and financial control" identified two companies where the corporate HQ imposes a strong performance management system on its business units, PepsiCo and BP. For which company do you think a performance management system using financial targets is better suited?

4. Identify a poorly performing multibusiness company (examples might include Sony, Time Warner, Bombardier, Pearson, News International). Using the McKinsey pentagon framework, in which stage do you perceive the greatest opportunities for value creation through restructuring? (Use the company's web site or visit www.hoovers.com to access information on the company.)

5. Which do you think is a better organizational form for the diversified, multinational corporation: the divisionalized corporation (such as General Electric, Philips, and Sony) or the holding company (such as Tata Group, Samsung Group, and the Virgin Group)?

# Notes

1. M. Goold, A. Campbell, and M. Alexander, *Corporate-Level Strategy: Creating Value in the Multibusiness Company* (New York: John Wiley & Sons, Inc., 1994).

2. *General Electric: Strategic Position: 1981*, Case No. 381-174 (Boston: Harvard Business School, 1981): 1.

3. McKinsey & Company has recently reconceptualized SBUs as *value cells*. See M. Giordano and F. Wenger, "Organizing for Value," *Perspectives on Finance and Strategy* 18 (2008).

4. For a fuller discussion of the GE/McKinsey matrix see "Enduring Ideas: The GE–McKinsey Nine-box Matrix," *McKinsey Quarterly* (September 2008).

5. For a fuller discussion of the BCG matrix see B. Henderson,*The Experience Curve Reviewed: IV: The Growth Share Matrix or Product Portfolio*, Boston: Boston Consulting Group (1973).

6. Booz Allen Hamilton claims that "dog" businesses can offer promising potential: H. Quarls, T. Pernsteiner, and K. Rangan, "Love Your Dogs," *strategy+business*, March 15, 2005, http://www.booz.com/media/file/Love_Your_Dogs.pdf, accessed August 23, 2012.

7. M. Goold, A. Campbell, and M. Alexander, *Corporate-Level Strategy: Creating Value in the Multibusiness Company* (New York: John Wiley & Sons, Inc., 1994).

8. M. Goold, A. Campbell, and M. Alexander, *Corporate-Level Strategy: Creating Value in the Multibusiness Company* (New York: John Wiley & Sons, Inc., 1994): 90.

9. M. C. Mankins and R. Steele, "Stop Making Plans; Start Making Decisions," *Harvard Business Review* (January 2006): 76–84.

10. L. Bossidy and R. Charan, *Execution: The Discipline of Getting Things Done* (New York: Crown Business, 2002): 197–201.

11. R. S. Kaplan and D. P. Norton, "Having Trouble with Your Strategy? Then Map It," *Harvard Business Review* (September/October 2000): 67–76.

12. R. S. Kaplan and D. P. Norton, "The Office of Strategy Management," *Harvard Business Review* (October 2005): 72–80.

13. Geneen's style of management is discussed in Chapter 3 of R. T. Pascale and A. G. Athos, *The Art of Japanese Management* (New York: Warner Books, 1982).

14. Tuck School of Business, CEO Speaker Series, September 23, 2002.

15. "Those Highflying PepsiCo Managers," *Fortune* (April 10, 1989): 79.

16. M. Goold and A. Campbell, *Strategies and Styles* (Oxford: Blackwell Publishing, 1987).

17. R. M. Grant, "Strategic Planning in a Turbulent Environment: Evidence from the Oil and Gas Majors," *Strategic Management Journal* 24 (2003): 491–518.

18. M. Goold, D. Pettifer, and D. Young, "Redesigning the Corporate Center," *European Management Review* 19, no. 1 (2001): 83–91.

19. P&G's Global Business Services: Transforming the way business is done, http://www.pg.com/en_US/downloads/company/PG_GBS_Factsheet.pdf, accessed September 7, 2012.

20. Deloitte Consulting LLP, *2011 Global Shared Services Survey Results: Executive Summary* (March 2011).

21. M. E. Porter, "From Competitive Advantage to Corporate Strategy," *Harvard Business Review* (May/June 1987): 46.

22. L. Phalippou and O. Gottschalg, "The Performance of Private Equity Funds," *Review of Financial Studies* 22 (2009): 1747–76; M. Humphery-Jenner, "Private Equity Fund Size, Investment Size, and Value Creation," *Review of Finance* (2011).

23. F. A. Maljers, "Corporate Strategy from a Unilever Perspective," in F. A. J. van den Bosch and A. P. de Man (eds), *Perspectives on Strategy: Contributions of Michael E. Porter* (Boston: Kluwer, 1997): 35–45.

24. "How Samsung Became a Global Champion," *Financial Times* (September 5, 2004).

25. M. Goold, D. Pettifer, and D. Young, "Redesigning the Corporate Center," *European Management Review* 19, no. 1 (2001): 83–91.

26. "Cross-selling's Elusive Charms," *Financial Times* (November 16, 1998): 21.

27. J. W. Lorsch and S. A. Allen III, *Managing Diversity and Interdependence: An Organizational Study of Multi-divisional Firms* (Boston: Harvard Business School Press, 1973).

28. J. W. Lorsch and S. A. Allen III, *Managing Diversity and Interdependence: An Organizational Study of Multi-divisional Firms* (Boston: Harvard Business School Press, 1973): 168.

29. C. K. Prahalad and R. Bettis, "The Dominant Logic: A New Linkage between Diversity and Performance," *Strategic Management Journal* 7 (1986): 485–502.

30. T. Copeland, T. Koller, and J. Murrin, *Valuation: Measuring and Managing the Value of Companies*, 3rd edn (New York: John Wiley & Sons, Inc., 2000).

31. R. Cibin and R. M. Grant, "Restructuring among the World's Largest Oil Companies," *British Journal of Management* 7 (December 1996): 411–28.

32. R. A. Burgelman and A. Grove, "Strategic Dissonance," *California Management Review* 38 (Winter 1996): 8–28.

33. A. Grove, *Only the Paranoid Survive* (New York: Bantam, 1999).

34. R. Calori, "How Successful Companies Manage Diverse Businesses," *Long Range Planning* 21 (June 1988): 85.

35. J. van Rekom, K. Corley, and D. Ravasi, "Extending and Advancing Theories of Organizational Identity," *Corporate Reputation Review* 11 (2008): 183–8.36.

36. Among private companies, the key governance problem is typically one set of owners (e.g., the founding family) enriching themselves at the expense of the other owners. See J. C. Coffee, "A Theory of Corporate Scandals:

Why the US and Europe Differ," Columbia Law School Working Paper No. 274 (March, 2005).

37. R. M. Grant and M. Visconti, "The Strategic Background to Corporate Accounting Scandals," *Long Range Planning* 39 (August 2006): 361–83.

38. *OECD Principles of Corporate Governance* (Paris: OECD, 2004).

39. "Splitting the Chairman and CEO Roles," *Business Week* (January 10, 2008): http://www.businessweek.com/managing/content/jan2008/ca2008018_642807.htm, accessed July 8, 2009.

40. D. Barton, "Capitalism for the Long Term," *Harvard Business Review* (March/April 2011): 84–92.

41. M. J. Conyon, S. I. Peck, L. E. Read, and G. V. Sadler, "The Structure of Executive Compensation Contracts: The UK Evidence," *Long Range Planning* 33 (August 2000): 478–503.

42. See, for example, P. Bolton, J. Scheinkman, and W. Xiong, "Pay for Short-term Performance: Executive Compensation in Speculative Markets," NBER Working Paper 12107 (March 2006); M. C. Jensen and K. J. Murphy, "Remuneration: Where We've Been, How We Got Here, What are the Problems," ECGI-Finance Working Paper 44 (2004).

43. A.D. Chandler, *Strategy and Structure* (Cambridge, MA: MIT Press, 1962).

44. O. E. Williamson, *Markets and Hierarchies: Analysis and Antitrust Implications* (New York: Free Press, 1975); and O. E. Williamson, "The Modern Corporation: Origins, Evolution, Attributes," *Journal of Economic Literature* 19 (1981): 1537–68.

45. J. L. Bower, *Managing the Resource Allocation Process* (Boston: Harvard Business School Press, 1986).

46. O. E. Williamson, "The Modern Corporation: Origins, Evolution, Attributes," *Journal of Economic Literature* 19 (1981): 1537–68.

47. T. R. Eisenmann and J. S. Bower, "The Entrepreneurial M-form: A Case Study of Strategic Integration in Global Media Companies," in J. L. Bower and C. G. Gilbert (eds), *From Resource Allocation to Strategy* (New York: Oxford University Press, 2005): 307–29.

48. H. Mintzberg, *Structure in Fives: Designing Effective Organizations* (Englewood Cliffs, NJ: Prentice Hall, 1983): Chapter 11.

49. J. Birkinshaw and A. Campbell, "Know the Limits of Corporate Venturing," FT Summer School, *Financial Times* (August 10, 2004).

# 15 External Growth Strategies: Mergers, Acquisitions, and Alliances

> When it comes to mergers, hope triumphs over experience.
>
> —IRWIN STELZER, US ECONOMIST AND COLUMNIST

## OUTLINE

- ◆ **Introduction and Objectives**
- ◆ **Mergers and Acquisitions: Causes and Consequences**
  - • The Motives for Mergers and Acquisitions
  - • Empirical Evidence on Mergers and Acquisitions
  - • Post-Merger Integration

- ◆ **Strategic Alliances**
  - • Motives for Alliances
- ◆ **Summary**
- ◆ **Self-Study Questions**
- ◆ **Notes**

## Introduction and Objectives

Mergers, acquisitions, and alliances are key instruments of corporate strategy as they are the principal means by which firms achieve major extensions in the scope of their activities. Mergers, acquisitions, and alliances are not strategies in themselves: they are tools of strategy—the means by which a firm pursues a particular strategic aim.

Mergers and acquisitions also represent one of the great paradoxes of strategic management. A slew of empirical studies have shown that mergers and acquisitions create little or no value overall. However, for *acquiring* firms, the evidence is clear: on average, acquisitions destroy shareholder value for the acquirer. The beneficiaries of mergers and acquisitions are the shareholders of the acquired firm together with the lawyers and investment bankers who arrange them. This being the case, why is acquisition the preferred means of corporate growth for so many companies?

Strategic alliances also raise interesting and important strategic issues. Increasingly firms are competing not independently but in collaboration with other firms. Indeed, some of these collaborators may include a firm's competitors. In exploring strategic alliances we extend our view of strategic management beyond the limits of the single firm.

Our goal is to look at the efficacy of mergers, acquisitions, and alliances as instruments of corporate strategy, the circumstances where they can be successful, and how they should be managed.

By the time you have completed this chapter, you will:

◆ be familiar with the factors that have motivated mergers and acquisitions;

◆ appreciate why so many mergers and acquisitions have generated disappointing results;

◆ be able to assess the potential for a merger or acquisition to create value for the forms involved;

◆ appreciate the challenges of post-merger integration;

◆ be familiar with the different types of strategic alliances and recognize the circumstances in which strategic alliances can create value for the partners.

## Mergers and Acquisitions: Causes and Consequences

An **acquisition** (or takeover) is where one company purchases another. This involves the acquiring company (the acquirer) making an offer for the common stock of the other company (the acquiree) at a fixed price per share. Acquisitions can be "friendly," that is when they are supported by the board of the target company, or "unfriendly," when they are opposed by the target company's board—in the latter case they are known as *hostile takeovers*.

A **merger** is where two companies amalgamate to form a new company. This requires agreement by the shareholders of the two companies who then exchange their shares for shares in the new company. Mergers typically involve companies of similar size (Daimler and Chrysler; Exxon and Mobil), although, as in these two examples, one firm is usually the dominant partner. A higher market capitalization may allow a smaller company to merge with a much larger one (e.g., AOL and Time Warner). Where the companies involved are in different countries, a merger may be preferred to an acquisition for political reasons (e.g., Alcatel and Lucent, Daimler-Benz and Chrysler, Mittal Steel and Arcelor).

The term *merger* is sometimes used to denote both mergers and acquisitions— below I follow this popular convention. (Table 15.1 shows the biggest acquisitions of the current century.)

## The Motives for Mergers and Acquisitions

At the beginning of this chapter I stated that mergers and acquisitions are not strategies in themselves but the tools of strategy. Can acquisition—essentially trading in companies—be a strategy in itself? For such an activity to qualify as a viable strategy, the essential condition is that the acquirer is better at valuing companies than the stock market is. This would allow the acquirer to identify undervalued companies, buy them, and then sell them once the market had corrected its valuation. Such a strategy can work for portfolio investment; for the acquisition of entire companies it does not work because of the costs involved. These comprise the acquisition premium that must be paid to take control of a company (typically 20–60%) and the transaction costs involved (legal and investment bank fees). Even for private equity

**TABLE 15.1**   Top-20 mergers and acquisitions of the 21st century

| Year | Purchaser | Purchased | Value ($billion) |
|---|---|---|---|
| 2000 | Vodafone AirTouch PLC | Mannesmann | 183 |
| 2000 | AOL | Time Warner | 165 |
| 2000 | Pfizer | Warner-Lambert | 90 |
| 2000 | Exxon | Mobil | 85 |
| 2007 | Royal Bank of Scotland, Banco Santander, Fortis | ABN AMRO | 79 |
| 2000 | Glaxo Wellcome PLC | SmithKline Beecham PLC | 76 |
| 2004 | Royal Dutch Petroleum Co. | Shell Transport & Trading Co | 75 |
| 2009 | Gaz de France | Suez | 75 |
| 2006 | AT&T Inc. | BellSouth Corporation | 73 |
| 2001 | Comcast Corporation | AT&T Broadband | 72 |
| 2002 | Bell Atlantic | GTE | 71 |
| 2000 | SBC Communications | Ameritech | 70 |
| 2009 | Pfizer | Wyeth | 68 |
| 2004 | Sanofi-Synthélabo SA | Aventis SA | 60 |
| 2002 | Pfizer | Pharmacia Corporation | 60 |
| 2007 | Enel S.p.A. | Endesa SA | 60 |
| 2004 | JPMorgan Chase & Co | Banc One Corp | 59 |
| 2007 | Procter & Gamble | Gillette | 57 |
| 2008 | InBev | Anheuser-Busch | 52 |
| 2008 | Bank of America | Merrill Lynch | 50 |

firms, which build investment funds comprising portfolios of acquired companies, the key to value creation is not simply buying and selling companies. They create value primarily through financial restructuring and strategic redirection. Hence, the starting point for any assessment of a merger or acquisition proposal has to be a clear recognition of its strategic objectives. These might include:

- acquiring strategically important resources and capabilities;
- seeking cost economies and market power;
- expanding into new geographical markets;
- diversifying into new industries.

*Acquiring Resources or Capabilities*   We discovered in Chapter 5 that the most valuable resources and capabilities are those that are not transferable and not easily replicated. Obtaining such resources and capabilities may require acquisition. The UK-based company Reckitt Benckiser was created by a merger in 1999; since then, it has used acquisition to build a large portfolio of brands that include Clearasil skin products, Dettol disinfectant, Durex contraceptives, Finish dishwashing products, Nurofen analgesics, Scholl footcare products, Woolite laundry products, and dozens more. US-based Fortune Brands has followed a similar strategy.

In technology-based industries, established companies regularly acquire small, start-up firms in order to acquire capabilities in emerging areas of technology. Between March 2005 and December 2011, Google acquired 95 mostly small technology-based companies which provided the basis for most of its new product launches. Over the same period, Microsoft made 71 acquisitions; these have provided Microsoft with the technical capabilities needed for it to build its position in video games, online advertising, internet telephony, and cloud computing. Each year, Microsoft hosts its VC Summit, where venture capitalists from all over the world are invited to market their companies. Walt Disney's 2006 acquisition of Pixar, the animated movie studio founded by John Lasseter and Steve Jobs, is a classic example of a large established company acquiring a small start-up in order to obtain technical and creative capabilities.

Acquisition can short circuit the tortuous process of developing internally a new organizational capability. However, using acquisitions to extend a company's capability base involves major risks. To begin with, acquisitions are expensive. In addition to the acquisition premium that must be paid, the targeted capability comes with a mass of additional resources and capabilities that are most likely surplus to requirements for the acquiring firm. Most importantly, once the acquisition has been made, the acquiring company must find a way to integrate the acquiree's capabilities with its own. All too often, culture clashes, personality clashes between senior managers, or incompatibilities of management systems can result in the degradation or destruction of the very capabilities that the acquiring company was seeking.

*Cost Economies and Market Power from Horizontal Mergers*   The most obvious benefits to acquisition are between companies in the same industry. The mergers between United and Continental Airlines which created the world's biggest airline and between Exxon and Mobil creating the world's biggest listed petroleum company both created massive cost economies by eliminating duplicate functions and exploiting scale economies, as well as increasing market power.

*Geographical Extension*   Acquisition is the most popular means of entry into foreign markets by larger companies. Acquisition allows firms to gain critical mass within an overseas market quickly and to overcome key "liabilities of foreignness"— notably lack of local knowledge, lack of local connections, and barriers to distribution. During the 21st century, geographical extension has been the most important motivation for mergers. Spurred by the trend toward globalization, cross-border mergers as a proportion of all mergers grew from 23% in 1998 to 45% in 2007.[1] In the process many industries have been transformed:

- In automobiles recent cross-border mergers have included Geely (China) and Volvo (Sweden), Tata Motors (India) and Jaguar and Land Rover (UK), Fiat (Italy) and Chrysler (US), GM (US) and Daewoo (South Korea), and Renault (France) and Nissan (Japan).
- Beer—an industry once populated by medium-sized, national companies— is now dominated by multinational giants such as Anheuser-Busch InBev, SABMiller, and Heineken. Each of these was created from scores of acquisitions: Heineken acquired 34 beer companies in 31 countries during 2002–2011.
- Luxottica has become the world's largest supplier of spectacles and sunglasses through a series of cross-border acquisitions, including LensCrafters, Ray-Ban, Sunglass Hut, Oakley, and Grupo Tecnol.

*Diversification*   Acquisition is the predominant mode of diversification for firms. The alternative—diversification by means of new business start-up—tends to be too slow for most companies. While a number of companies have formed internal "business incubators" for developing new business ventures, such start-ups seldom provide the basis for major diversifications (Samsung, 3M, and the Virgin Group are notable exceptions). By contrast, acquisition allows firms to quickly establish a major presence in a different sector. For example:

- IBM's transition from a hardware to a software and services company involved the acquisition of 115 companies between 2000 and 2011, including PwC Consulting, Rational Software Corp., Ascential Software Corp., Internet Security Systems, Cognos, SPSS Inc., and Netezza.
- Comcast, once a US provider of cable TV services, was transformed into a diversified telecommunication and entertainment company with the acquisition of AT&T Broadband, Adelphia Cable, and NBC Universal.

Diversification may also involve small acquisitions which provide a foundation for internal investment. For example, Microsoft's entry into video games with the launch of Xbox in November 2001 was preceded by the acquisition of several small companies, such as RenderMorphics (3-D graphics hardware), Exos (video game controllers), and a number of video game software developers (VGA-Animation Software, Electric Gravity, FASA Interactive, Bungie, and NetGames).

## Empirical Evidence on Mergers and Acquisitions

As a means of strategy execution, the chief attraction of mergers and acquisitions (M&As) is the speed with which they can be put into effect. After spending a decade gradually expanding its range of corporate-banking activities into investment banking, Bank of America's 2009 acquisition of Merrill Lynch catapulted the firm into the ranks of the world's leading investment banks. The decision to acquire Merrill Lynch was made over a single weekend.

Yet these advantages of speed come at a cost. Empirical research into the performance consequences of mergers and acquisitions makes for depressing reading. The performance effects of mergers and acquisitions have been measured using both shareholder returns and accounting data on profitability. The only clear finding is that acquisitions benefit the shareholders of the acquired firms. For acquiring firms, studies show that the returns are, on average, either negative or insignificant from zero. Combining the effects on both acquirers and acquirees, the overall picture is one of small gains to mergers, typically around 2% of the combined market value of the companies involved.[2] Studies that use accounting data to compare post-merger profitability with pre-merger profitability show little consistency in their findings: "results from these accounting-based studies are all over the map."[3]

These findings are hardly surprising. The fact that the sole beneficiaries of M&A activity are the shareholders of the acquired companies is an inevitable result of the large acquisition premiums paid by acquirers. These acquisition premiums are also the main reason why the returns to acquirers are so poor. The inconsistency of findings reflects the heterogeneity of the phenomenon. Acquisitions are motivated by different strategic goals, and each involves a unique combination of circumstances. Even when mergers and acquisitions are grouped into different categories, the performance outcomes remain unclear. For example, one might expect that horizontal mergers (which increase market share and offer gains from scale economies) would be more successful than diversifying mergers; among diversifying mergers, it would be expected that the acquisition of firms in related businesses would outperform unrelated acquisitions. Yet both these highly plausible predictions fail to find robust empirical support.

*When Do Mergers and Acquisitions Make Sense?*   In the absence of strong general findings about the outcomes of mergers, we need to consider each proposed merger or acquisition on its own merits—which means subjecting it to systematic strategic appraisal. Let us start with the strategic goals of mergers and acquisitions.

The reason that shareholders should view acquisitions with extreme skepticism is that they are so appealing to top management, and CEOs in particular. Managerial incentives, both financial and psychic, tend to be associated more with a company's size than with its profitability. Acquisition is certainly the fastest way of growing. Even more dangerous is CEOs' quest for celebrity status; again, large-scale acquisitions are the surest way that a CEO can gain media coverage while projecting an image of power and influence. The combination of these two creates the phenomenon of *empire building*. The "titans of industry" that used multiple acquisitions to pursue ambitious growth—Jean-Marie Messier at Vivendi Universal, Fred Goodwin at Royal Bank of Scotland, Bernie Ebbers at WorldCom—appear to be victims of hubris (exaggerated self-confidence), leading to a distorted judgment and becoming increasingly divorced from reality.

The stock market may collude with such behavior. Michael Jensen suggests that CEOs of companies with overvalued equity will make equity-financed acquisitions to help support their share price.[4] AOL's merger with Time Warner may reflect this motive.

The further factor encouraging M&As that lack a convincing strategic rationale is the propensity for imitation. M&A activity is highly cyclical, with a heavy clustering in specific sectors during specific periods: the petroleum mergers of 1998–2002; the 1990s rush for banks and insurance companies to combine; the telecoms' urge to merge of 1998–2005; and the global consolidation of the beer, pharmaceuticals, and metals sectors during the past decade.[5] This sectoral clustering is associated with shocks affecting particular industries (e.g., deregulation in telecommunications or the repeal of the Glass–Stegall Act in banking). It is also reinforced by the propensity of firms to follow the leader: if firms resist the urge to merge, they risk being alone at the fringes of the dance floor with only unattractive dancing partners left.

The implications is that M&A decisions need to be based, first, upon a clear identification of what the acquirer's strategy is and how the proposed acquisition will contribute to that strategy and, second, upon a detailed and realistic assessment of what the outcome of the acquisition will be. This is easier with some acquisitions than it is with others. In the case of horizontal acquisitions, it is usually possible not just to identify the likely cost savings from integrating the two companies but also to come up with some realistic estimates of what those savings might be. Other sources of synergy are much more elusive. For example, estimates of the potential marketing benefits or the implications for innovation are likely to be much more speculative. Acquiring companies tend to overestimate the gains from mergers. Many diversifying mergers within financial services have been motivated by wildly optimistic forecasts of the potential for cross-selling and customers' desire for one-stop shopping. The risk is that acquirers fall victim to their own propaganda: in seeking to persuade the stock market about the benefits of an acquisition, they believe their own inflated estimates of potential synergies.

A realistic assessment of the potential gains from a merger or acquisition requires intimate knowledge of the target company. This is a bigger problem for hostile takeovers than for agreed acquisitions. However, even friendly takeovers are still prone to information asymmetry (the so-called *lemons problem*)—the seller knows much more about the acquisition target than the buyer, so the acquirer can be hoodwinked into overpaying. One year after its acquisition of Jaguar, a Ford executive commented: "If we had known what a terrible shape Jaguar was in, we would never had paid the price we did."

## Post-Merger Integration

Case-study evidence shows that some of the most carefully planned mergers and acquisitions can end up as failures because of the problems of managing post-merger integration. The combination of Daimler-Benz and Chrysler was exemplary in its pre-merger planning; the outcome was disastrous. Not only did Chrysler's problems appear to be intractable but also Chrysler's demands on the group's top management negatively impacted the core Daimler-Benz business.[6]

Frequently, it appears that where the potential benefits of mergers and acquisitions are large the costs and risks of integrations are also large. Thus, Capron and Anand argue that cross-border acquisitions typically have the strongest strategic logic.[7] Yet, the evidence of DaimlerChrysler, BMW/Rover, and Alcatel-Lucent suggests that when differences in corporate culture are accentuated by differences in national culture the challenge of post-merger integration becomes immense.

A growing body of literature views acquisition as an organizational capability and points to the need for acquisition capabilities to be developed through explicit and experiential learning. Acquisition performance tends to increase with experience... although not at first. A learning threshold appears, after which subsequent acquisitions add value.[8] Explicit learning through the codification of acquisition processes also appears to be conducive to acquisition success.[9]

In common with my approach throughout this book, I consider that it is important to separate issues of pre-acquisition planning and post-acquisition management. In the long and rich history of acquisition disasters, poor post-acquisition management has been identified as the source of the problem. Yet, in many of these cases the integration problems could have been anticipated: the critical problem was going ahead with the acquisition without making an adequate assessment of post-merger management problems. Thus, in the case of Quaker Oats' acquisition of Snapple (universally known as "the billion-dollar blunder"), the critical problem—the impediments to integrating Snapple's distribution system with that of Quaker's Gatorade—were evident to the marketing managers and the franchised distributors of the two companies prior to the takeover.[10]

Conversely, Walt Disney's acquisition of Pixar was preceded by an anticipation of the problems that might arise and a careful and sensitive approach to planning, and then implementing, the integration of Pixar (Strategy Capsule 15.1).

## Strategic Alliances

A **strategic alliance** is a collaborative arrangement between two or more firms to pursue agreed common goals. *Strategic alliances* take many different forms:

- A strategic alliance may or may not involve equity participation: the alliance between General Motors and Peugeot to develop cars together was reinforced by GM taking a 7% equity stake in Peugeot. Other alliances are agreements without any ownership stakes: the agreement between Nokia and Microsoft for Nokia to develop a range of new smartphones based upon the Windows phone-operating system involved no exchange of equity between the companies. A joint venture is a particular form of equity alliance where the partners form a new company that they jointly own: Dow Corning Inc. is a joint venture between Corning and Dow Chemical that produces silicon-based products. Volkswagen, China's leading automobile marque, operates through two main joint ventures, one with SAIC Motor and one with the FAW Group.
- Alliances are created to fulfill specific purposes:
  - Star Alliance is an agreement among 25 airlines (including United, Lufthansa, and Air Canada) to code share flights and link frequent-flier programs
  - Automobili Lamborghini and Callaway Golf Company formed an R & D alliance in 2010 to develop advanced composite materials
  - GlaxoSmithKline and Dr Reddy's Laboratories (a leading Indian pharma company) formed an alliance in 2009 to market Dr Reddy's products in emerging-market countries through GSK's sales and marketing network

## STRATEGY CAPSULE 15.1
# Walt Disney Company and Pixar

Most industry observers were pessimistic about Disney's $7.4-billion acquisition of rival animated movie producer Pixar in 2006. Most acquisitions of movie studios had experienced major difficulties: General Electric's NBC acquisition of Universal Studios and Viacom's of DreamWorks. The worries were that Disney's corporate systems would suppress Pixar's creativity and that Pixar's animators would leave. Although the two companies had allied for several years (Disney distributed Pixar movies), the relationship had not been smooth.

In fact, the acquisition appears to have been highly successful. Several Pixar movies have been massive box office successes—*Cars*, *WallE*, and *Toy Story 3*—and the "Disney machine" has generated massive revenues from DVDs, toys, and licensing. Disney's CEO, Bob Iger, claims that, compared with the earlier alliance between the two companies, ownership of Pixar has facilitated the closer coordination needed to exploit the synergies between the two companies.

Factors contributing to the success of the merger include:

◆ a high level of personal and professional respect among the key personnel at Pixar and Disney. In announcing the acquisition, CEO Iger commented: "We also fully recognize that Pixar's extraordinary record of achievement is in large measure due to its vibrant creative culture, which is something we respect and admire and are committed to supporting and fostering in every way possible";

◆ a rapid and honest communication to Pixar employees about the merger and its implications;

◆ prior to the acquisition, creating an explicit map of which elements of Pixar would remain unchanged and which would be adapted to and integrated with Walt Disney's existing activities and practices;

◆ Pixar's president Edwin Catmull was put in charge of Walt Disney Animation Studios;

◆ Bob Iger's ability to draw upon his personal experience of working for companies that had been acquired;

◆ an explicit list of guidelines to protect Pixar's creative culture: Pixar employees were able to keep their relatively generous health benefits and weren't forced to sign employment contracts;

◆ honoring commitments: according to Edwin Catmull: "Everything they've said they would do they have lived up to."

In one respect, the Disney–Pixar merger flouted conventional wisdom. According to Bob Iger: "There is an assumption in the corporate world that you need to integrate swiftly. My philosophy is exactly the opposite. You need to be respectful and patient."

***Source:*** The Walt Disney Company Press Release, "Disney Completes Pixar Acquisition," Burbank, CA, May 5, 2006; "Disney: Magic restored," *The Economist*, April 17, 2008; "Disney and Pixar: The Power of the Prenup," www.nytimes.com/2008/06/01/business/media/01pixar.html?pagewanted=all.

○ The Rumaila Field Operating Organization is a joint venture among China National Petroleum Company, BP, and South Oil Company to operate Iraq's biggest oilfield;

● Alliances may be purely bilateral arrangements, or they may be a part of a network of interfirm relationships. One form of alliance network is the supplier network, exemplified by that of Toyota. Toyota's supplier network comprises first-level, second-level, and tertiary suppliers bound by long-term relationships with Toyota and supported by a set of routines that permit knowledge sharing and continuous improvement.[11] Clothing companies Inditex (Zara) and Benetton maintain similar networks. Another type of alliance network is the localized industry cluster that characterizes the industrial districts of Italy (e.g., Prato woolen knitwear cluster, Carrara stonecutting cluster, and Sassuolo ceramic tile cluster). The Hollywood film industry represents another such cluster. Relationships within these localized networks are based upon history and proximity and are informal rather than formal.[12]

## Motives for Alliances

Alliances are motivated primarily by opportunities for exploiting complementarities between the resources and capabilities owned by different companies:

- Bulgari Hotels and Resorts is a joint venture that combines Bulgari's reputation for luxury and quality with Marriott International's capabilities in developing and operating hotels;
- Nike's alliance with Apple links Nike's capabilities with athletic shoes with Apple's microelectronics capabilities in order to offer real-time biometric data delivered to an iPod;
- Sasol Chevron Holdings is a 50/50 global joint venture that combines Sasol's gas-to-liquids technology with Chevron's reserves of natural gas and downstream distribution to build plants which convert natural gas into synthetic gasoline.

There has been a debate in the literature as to whether the primary aim of strategic alliances is to *access* the partner's resources and capabilities or to *acquire* them through learning.[13] The strategic alliance between Intel and DreamWorks Animation allows each company to access the other's capabilities in order to jointly develop next-generation 3-D films.[14] Conversely, General Motor's NUMMI joint venture with Toyota was motivated by GM's desire to learn about the Toyota Production System.[15]

In most instances alliances are about accessing rather than acquiring capabilities: for most firms the basic rationale of alliances is that they allow the firm to specialize in a limited range of capabilities while enabling the exploitation of specific opportunities that require a wider range of capabilities.[16] A key advantage of such alliances is the flexibility they offer: especially when making option-type investments.[17] IBM has several programs for funding collaborative research with universities throughout the world. The result is hundreds of projects where IBM commits relatively small amounts of funding to R & D projects with highly uncertain outcomes. Such projects give IBM the option, if successful, to first obtain intellectual property protection and then devote much larger resources to the commercial development of the innovation.[18]

Alliances also permit risk sharing. In petroleum, most upstream projects are joint ventures. Kazakhstan's Kashagan field, the biggest oilfield discovered in the last 30 years, is being developed by a consortium comprising ENI, Shell, Total,

ExxonMobil, KazMunayGas, ConocoPhillips, and Inpex. Most major defense contracts are undertaken by consortia: the F-35 jet fighter has a development cost of $235 billion. It is being built by Lockheed Martin and partners Northup Grumman and BAE Systems.

It is tempting to view a strategic alliance as a quick and low-cost means of extending the capabilities available to a firm. However, managing alliance relationships is itself a critically important organizational capability. *Relational capability* comprises building trust, developing interfirm knowledge sharing routines, and establishing mechanisms for coordination.[19] The more a company outsources its value chain activities to a network of alliance partners, the more it needs to develop the "systems integration capability" to coordinate and integrate the dispersed activities.[20] The delays that have plagued the Boeing 787 Dreamliner are one indicator of the challenges of managing a network of alliances in developing a complex, technologically advanced product.[21]

*International Alliances*   Strategic alliances play a particularly important role in a firm's internationalization strategies. When entering an overseas market, the internationalizing firm will typically lack the local knowledge, political connections, and access to distribution channels that a local firm will possess. At the same time acquiring a local firm may not be an attractive option, either because local regulations or ownership patterns make acquisition difficult or because the internationalizing firm may be reluctant to make a large and irreversible financial commitment to the overseas market. In such circumstances, alliances—either with or without equity— can offer an attractive mode of foreign entry. By sharing resources and capabilities, alliances economize on the investment needed for major international initiatives. The FreeMove alliance formed by Telefónica Móviles (Spain), TIM (Italy), T-Mobile (Germany), and Orange (France) created a seamless third-generation, wireless communication network across Europe at a fraction of the cost incurred by Vodafone; it also allowed each firm access to the mobile network of the leading operator in at least five major European markets.[22]

Some firms have built their internationalization strategies almost entirely on cross-border alliances:

- Gazprom, the Russian gas giant, has alliances relating to pipeline projects with ENI (Italy), CNPC (China), EON (Germany), PDVSA (Venezuela), and MOL (Hungary); liquefied natural gas projects with Petro-Canada and Sonatrach (Algeria); and long-term supply arrangements with Gaz de France.
- General Motors has established a network of strategic alliances, most of them reinforced by equity participation, in order to build its presence in emerging markets and extend its range of small cars (Figure 15.1).

For the local partner, an alliance with a foreign firm can also be an attractive means of accessing resources and capabilities. In many emerging-market countries—notably China and India before their accession to the World Trade Organization—governments often oblige foreign companies to take a local partner in order to encourage the flow of technology and management capabilities to the host country. For example, China's automobile industry has been developed almost entirely through joint ventures with US, Japanese, and European automakers.

**FIGURE 15.1**   General Motors' network of international alliances with other automakers

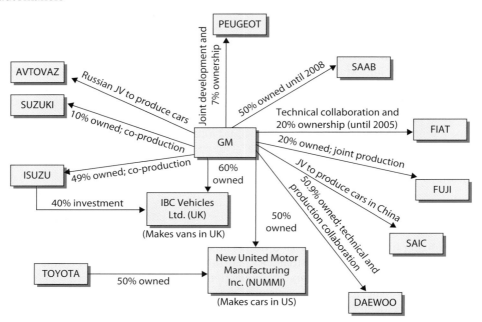

However, for all their attractions, international alliances are difficult to manage: the usual problems that alliances present—those of communication, agreement, and trust—are exacerbated by differences in language, culture, and greater geographical distance. Danone's joint venture with Wahaha created the largest drinks company in China; however, misunderstanding and misaligned incentives resulted in the joint venture collapsing in 2011.[23]

It is tempting to conclude that international alliances are most difficult where national cultural differences are wide (e.g., between Western and Asian companies). However, some alliances between Western and Asian companies have been highly successful (e.g., Fuji/Xerox and Renault/Nissan). Conversely, many alliances between Western companies have been failures: BT and AT&T's Concert alliance, the GM/Fiat alliance, and Swissair's network of airline alliances. Disagreements over the sharing of the contributions to and returns from an alliance are a frequent source of friction, particularly in alliances between firms that are also competitors. When each partner seeks to access the other's capabilities, "competition for competence" results.[24] During the 1980s, Western companies fretted about losing their technological know-how to Japanese alliance partners. In recent years, Western companies have been dismayed by the speed at which their Chinese partners have absorbed their technology and emerged as international competitors. In rail infrastructure, China's state-owned companies have used their partnerships with Germany's Siemens, France's Alstom, Japan's Kawasaki Heavy Industries, and Canada's Bombardier to build homegrown capabilities that are now being exported.[25] The complaints made by Western companies against their Chinese joint-venture partners in 2012 are almost identical to those made against Japanese joint-venture partners in the 1980s.[26]

## Summary

Mergers and acquisitions can be useful tools of several types of strategy: for acquiring particular resources and capabilities, for reinforcing a firm's position within an industry, and for achieving diversification or horizontal expansion.

However, despite the plausibility of most of the stated goals that underlie mergers and acquisitions, most fail to achieve their stated goals. Empirical research shows that the gains flow primarily to the shareholders of the acquired companies.

These disappointing outcomes may reflect the tendency for mergers and acquisitions to be motivated by the desire for growth rather than for profitability. The pursuit of growth through merger is sometimes reinforced by CEO hubris, producing a succession of acquisitions that will ultimately lead to the company failing or restructuring.

A second factor in the poor performance consequences of many mergers are the unforeseen difficulties of post-merger integration. The diversity of mergers and their outcomes makes it very difficult to generalize about the types of merger or the approaches to integration that are associated with success.

Strategic alliances take many forms. In common is the desire to exploit complementarities between the resources and capabilities of different companies. Like mergers and acquisitions, and like relationships between individuals, they have varying degrees of success. Unlike mergers and acquisitions, the consequences of failure are usually less costly. As the business environment becomes more complex and more turbulent, the advantages of strategic alliances both in offering flexibility and in reconciling specialization with the ability to integrate a broad array of resources and capabilities become increasingly apparent.

Quizzes and flashcards to test yourself further are available in your interactive e-book at
**www.wileyopenpage.com**

## Self-Study Questions

1. Most of the mergers and acquisition in Table 15.1 are horizontal (i.e., they are between companies within the same sector). Some of these horizontal M&As are between companies in the same country; some cross national borders. Are there any reasons why horizontal M&A is likely to be more beneficial than other types of M&A (diversifying and vertical) and involve less risk? Among these horizontal M&As, which do you think will be more successful: those between companies in the same country or those that cross borders?

2. All of the CEOs associated with merger-intensive strategies (Jean-Marie Messier at Vivendi Universal, Fred Goodwin at Royal Bank of Scotland, Bernie Ebbers at WorldCom, Steve Case at AOL, Ed Whitacre at AT&T, Jeff Kindler at Pfizer, and Ivan Seidenberg at Verizon) have been male. Does this reflect the predominance of men among the ranks of CEOs, or is there something inherently masculine about the pursuit of growth through merger?

3. Commenting on the Pixar acquisition (Strategy Capsule 15.1), Disney's CEO stated: "You can accomplish a lot more as one company than you can as part of a joint venture." Do you agree? Illustrate your answer by referring to the some of the joint ventures (or alliances) referred to in this chapter. Would these have been more successful as mergers?

4. Different automobile companies have internationalized in different ways. Toyota has expanded organically, establishing subsidiaries in overseas markets. Ford went through a phase of acquisition (buying Volvo, Jaguar, Land Rover, and a major stake in Mazda). General Motors has favored strategic alliances (Figure 15.1). What do you see as the advantages and disadvantages of GM's alliance-based international strategy?

# Notes

1. I. Erel, R. C. Liao, and M. S. Weisbach, *Determinants of Cross-Border Mergers and Acquisitions*, Fisher College of Business, Ohio State University (March 2011).
2. S. N. Kaplan, "Mergers and Acquisitions: A Financial Economics Perspective," University of Chicago, Graduate School of Business Working Paper (February, 2006); P. A. Pautler, *Evidence on Mergers and Acquisitions*, Bureau of Economics, Federal Trade Commission (September 25, 2001).
3. S. N. Kaplan, "Mergers and Acquisitions: A Financial Economics Perspective," University of Chicago, Graduate School of Business Working Paper (February, 2006): 8.
4. M. C. Jensen, "Agency Costs of Overvalued Equity," *Harvard Business School* (May 2004).
5. G. Andrade, M. Mitchell, and E. Stafford, "New Evidence and Perspectives on Mergers," *Journal of Economic Perspectives* 15 (Spring 2001): 103–20.
6. "DaimlerChrysler: Stalled," *Business Week* (September 10, 2003).
7. L. Capron and J. Anand, "Acquisition-based Dynamic Capabilities," in C. E. Helfat, S. Finkelstein, W. Mitchell, M. A. Peteraf, H. Singh, D. J. Teece, and S. G. Winter, *Dynamic Capabilities* (Malden, MA: Blackwell, 2007): 80–99.
8. S. Finkelstein and J. Haleblian, "Understanding Acquisition Performance: The Role of Transfer Effects," *Organization Science* 13 (2002): 36–47.
9. M. Zollo and H. Singh, "Deliberate Learning in Corporate Acquisitions: Post-acquisition Strategies and Integration Capabilities in US Bank Mergers," *Strategic Management Journal* 24 (2004): 1233–56.
10. C. E. Helfat, S. Finkelstein, W. Mitchell, M. A. Peteraf, H. Singh, D. J. Teece, and S. G. Winter, *Dynamic Capabilities* (Malden, MA: Blackwell, 2007): 57–62.
11. J. H. Dyer and K. Nobeoka, "Creating and Managing A High-Performance Knowledge-Sharing Network: The Toyota Case," *Strategic Management Journal* 21 (2000): 345–67.
12. "Local Partnership, Clusters and SME Globalization" Workshop Paper on Enhancing the Competitiveness of SMEs (OECD, June 2000).
13. D. C. Mowery, J. E. Oxley, and B. S. Silverman, "Strategic Alliances and Interfirm Knowledge Transfer," *Strategic Management Journal* 17 (Winter 1996): 77–93.
14. "Intel, DreamWorks Animation Form Strategic Alliance to Revolutionize 3-D Filmmaking Technology," (July 8, 2008), www.intel.com/pressroom/archive/releases/2008/20080708corp.htm, accessed April 2, 2012.
15. J. A. Badaracco, *The Knowledge Link: How Firms Compete through Strategic Alliances* (Boston: Harvard Business School Press, 1991).
16. R. M. Grant and C. Baden-Fuller, "A Knowledge Accessing Theory of Strategic Alliances," *Journal of Management Studies* 41 (2004): 61–84.
17. R. S. Vassolo, J. Anand, and T. B Folta, "Non-additivity in Portfolios of Exploration Activities: A Real Options-based Analysis of Equity Alliances in Biotechnology," *Strategic Management Journal* 25 (2004): 1045–61.
18. www.ibm.com/developerworks/university/collaborativeresearch/projects.html, accessed April 2, 2012.
19. P. Kale, J. H. Dyer, and H. Singh, "Alliance Capability, Stock Market Response and Long Term Alliance

Success," *Strategic Management Journal* 23 (2002): 747–67.

20. A. Prencipe, "Corporate Strategy and Systems Integration Capabilities," in A. Prencipe, A. Davies, and M. Hobday (eds), *The Business of Systems Integration* (Oxford: Oxford University Press, 2003): 114–132.

21. "Dreamliner Becomes a Nightmare for Boeing," *Der Spiegel* (March 3, 2011) http://www.spiegel.de/international/business/0,1518,753891,00.html, accessed March 10, 2011.

22. *Freemove: Creating Value through Strategic Alliance in the Mobile Telecommunications Industry*, IESE Case 0-305-013 (2004).

23. S. M. Dickinson, "Danone v. Wahaha: Lessons for Joint Ventures in China," www.chinalawblog.com/DanoneWahahaLessons.pdf, accessed April 5, 2012.

24. G. Hamel, "Competition for Competence and Inter-partner Learning within International Strategic Alliances," *Strategic Management Journal* 12 (1991): 83–103.

25. "China: A Future on Track," *Financial Times* (September 24, 2010).

26. See R. Reich and E. Mankin, "Joint Ventures with Japan Give Away Our Future," *Harvard Business Review* (March/April 1986).

# 16 Current Trends in Strategic Management

We live in a period of profound transition—and the changes are more radical per-haps than even those that ushered in the "Second Industrial Revolution" of the mid-dle of the 19th century, or the structural changes triggered by the Great Depression and the Second World War.[1]

—PETER F. DRUCKER, MANAGEMENT THINKER AND WRITER, 1909–2005

We are at the very beginning of time for the human race. It is not unreasonable that we grapple with problems. But there are tens of thousands of years in the future. Our responsibility is to do what we can, learn what we can, improve the solutions, and pass them on.

—RICHARD FEYNMAN, 1918–1988; NOBEL PRIZE FOR PHYSICS, 1965

## OUTLINE

## Introduction

With the 21st century only in its second decade, it has become clear that the year 2000 marked a watershed, both in terms of the global economy and in terms of the development of business. Our challenge in this chapter is to assess what has changed in the business environment, whether the extreme turbulence that has characterized the century so far will continue, and, if so, what the implications for strategic management are.

We are in uncharted waters and, unlike the other chapters of this book, this chapter will not equip you with proven tools and frameworks that you can deploy directly in case analysis or in your own companies. Our approach is exploratory. We begin by reviewing the forces that are reshaping the environment of business. We will then draw upon concepts and ideas that are influencing current thinking about strategy and the lessons offered from leading-edge companies about strategies, organizational forms, and management styles that can help us to meet the challenges of this demanding era.

## The New Environment of Business

The 21st century began with the bursting of the dot.com stock market bubble. March 2000 marked the beginning of the NASDAQ's decade-long bear market.[2] The following year saw the terrorist attacks of September 11, which triggered a train of events including the invasions of Afghanistan and Iraq. In November 2001, Enron, one of America's most successful and admired energy companies, entered bankruptcy—the first of a series of financial scandals that engulfed companies on both sides of the Atlantic. Unprecedented market turbulence was evident in commodities and foreign exchange: in one six-month period, NYMEX crude oscillated between $37 and $147 a barrel. The biggest financial trauma was the financial crisis that began with the fall of Lehman Brothers, in September 2008, followed by the collapse of the banking systems of Iceland and Ireland, and culminating in the Greek government's debt default of March 2012. Meanwhile, political turbulence reached new peaks with the overthrow of the Tunisian, Egyptian, and Libyan governments in the Arab Spring of 2011. Nor was instability restricted to the political and economic spheres. There were natural catastrophes, including the Indian Ocean tsunami of December 2004, Hurricane Katrina that devastated New Orleans in 2005, and major earthquakes affecting Iran (2003), Sichuan, China (2008), Haiti (2010), and Japan (2011).

The speed at which the Roaring Nineties (the last decade of the 20th century) turned into the Nightmare Noughties (the first decade of the 21st century) has been a profound shock to business leaders. To understand how companies are adjusting to the new conditions and the strategic options available to them, let us look more carefully at the major characteristics of today's business environment.

### Turbulence

In reviewing the events of the 21st century, my focus was on the turbulence and unpredictability that has characterized the business environment. Almost all the events I listed—from the September 11 attacks of 2001 to the Arab Spring of 2011—were highly improbable and unpredicted, what have been called *black swan events* (Strategy Capsule 16.1).

A key issue is whether the black swan events we have witnessed between 2000 and 2011 simply reflect an unusual preponderance of extreme events or whether we are witnessing systematic changes that have made the business environment more crisis-prone. The latter seems likely. A feature of the global economy, and human society in general, is increasing interconnectedness through trade, financial flows, markets, and communication. Systems theory predicts that increasing levels of interconnectedness within a complex, nonlinear system increase the tendency for small initial movements to be amplified in unpredictable ways.

Shifts in the global balance of economic power will continue to undermine the ability of the leading industrial nations to control these disruptive forces. The rise of the BRIC countries is creating a multipolar world where the Old Order—the US, the EU, Japan, and the institutions they created (the World Bank, IMF, and OECD) are less able to offer global leadership. Looking ahead to 2025, the US National Intelligence Council predicts:

> The international system—as constructed following the Second World War—will be almost unrecognizable . . . owing to the rise of emerging powers, a globalizing economy, an historic transfer of relative wealth and economic power from west to east, and the growing influence of non-state actors.[3]

## STRATEGY CAPSULE 16.1
# Black Swan Events

The term *black swan*, a metaphor popularized by Nassim Taleb, refers to events that are extremely rare, have a major impact, and are unpredicted, despite the fact that they are rationalized retrospectively i.e., they *could* have been predicted. The term derives from the widespread belief that all swans were white until black swans were discovered in Western Australia at the end of the 17th century. Taleb argues that almost all significant events in human history are black swans: despite their rareness, the sources of black swan events are many, and their impact is amplified by the fact that they are not predicted.

Our vulnerability to black swan events is exacerbated by conventional approaches to risk management. These typically assume, first, that past events provide a basis for predicting future events and, second, that the probabilities of these events tend to be normally distributed. Extrapolating the past into the future makes strong assumptions about the stability of the underlying processes that generate uncertain events, while the very rareness of unusual events makes it very difficult to understand their causes. Growing awareness of *long tail* or *power law distributions* has brought into question conventional assumptions about the normal distribution of uncertain events.

Thus, Taleb's conclusion is that managing black swans is essentially about building robustness to reduce vulnerability to negative events and responsiveness to exploit positive ones.

## Competition

Among the wide array of uncertainties that firms face when looking at the immediate future, there is one near certainty: that economic growth, especially in the advanced economies, will remain sluggish throughout the medium term. The aftermath of the consumer-led, debt-fuelled growth and the financial crisis has been the need for massive deleveraging by households, companies, and governments. The corporate sector is the least of the problems: debt/equity ratios are generally modest (indeed, a bigger problem is channeling firms' cash balances into productive investment). However, for the household and government sectors the problems are both serious and long-term. For the governments of the US, Europe, and Japan, expansive fiscal and monetary policies are making the problem increasingly intractable. With the economies of China, India, and Brazil also decelerating, the prospects for robust global growth seem remote.

In most sectors of the global economy, with a few notable exceptions, such as agriculture, excess capacity is the norm. Such conditions will fuel strong price competition and squeeze profit margins.

An additional source of competitive pressure is internationalization by companies from emerging-market countries. In China, India, and other countries, firms that were once contract manufacturers supplying OEM products for sale under their customers' brands are increasingly competing with those customers in final markets.[4] At the beginning of 2012 there were at least 30 Chinese and Indian firms supplying Android smartphones under their own brand names. The entrance of emerging-market firms onto the world stage has been marked by increasing numbers of cross-border acquisitions by companies from emerging countries (Table 16.1).

## Technology

The potential for digital technologies to undermine established positions of competitive advantage and redraw industry barriers appears as great now as it was 20 years ago. Indeed, the pace of creative destruction is accelerating. Just as Netflix sealed the fate of Blockbuster, so Netflix may be a casualty of the displacement of DVDs by video streaming. Such uncertainties are part of a broader picture of disruption within what was once known as the "television industry" which now forms a part of

**TABLE 16.1**  Emerging-market corporations acquiring Western companies

| Year | Acquirer | Country | Target | Country | Value ($million) |
|------|----------|---------|--------|---------|------------------|
| 2011 | HTC | Taiwan | S3 Graphics | US | 300 |
| 2011 | Geely | China | Volvo | Sweden | 1,800 |
| 2008 | Tata Motor | India | Jaguar Land Rover | UK | 2,300 |
| 2007 | CEMEX | Mexico | Rinker Group | US | 14,200 |
| 2007 | United Spirits Ltd | India | Whyte & Mackay Ltd | UK | 1,176 |
| 2006 | Mittal Steel | India | Arcelor | Lux/Fr. | 32,800 |
| 2006 | Tata Steel | India | Corus | UK/Neth. | 7,800 |
| 2006 | Tata Coffee Ltd | India | Eight O'Clock Coffee Co. | US | 220 |
| 2006 | China National Chemical Corp. | China | Adisseo | France | 480 |

a much broader arena of ferment involving the producers of a wide array of digital content for distribution through multiple channels for viewing on a multitude of mobile and home-based digital devices. The impact of technology causing industries to converge then reconfigure is a pervasive feature of the digital landscape. In hand-held devices, Nokia cell phones, Apple iPods, Nintendo Gameboys, Palm PDAs, and RIM's BlackBerry smartphones once competed in different markets. Increasingly, mobile hand-held devices share functions and compete in a shared market space.

## Social Pressures and the Crisis of Capitalism

For organizations to survive and prosper requires that they adapt to the values and expectations of society—what organizational sociologists refer to as *legitimacy*.[5] One fall-out from the 2008/9 financial crisis was the loss of legitimacy that many businesses suffered—financial service firms in particular. This negatively affected their reputations among consumers, the morale of their employees, the willingness of investors and financiers to provide funding, and the government policies toward them. For commercial and investment banks, loss of social legitimacy may be a greater a threat to their survival than their weak balance sheets. Similar legitimacy challenges face Rupert Murdoch's News Corp. media empire following the "phone hacking" scandal at its British newspapers.[6]

The notion that the business enterprise is a social institution that must identify with the goals and aspirations of society has been endorsed by most leading management thinkers, including Peter Drucker, Charles Handy, and Sumantra Ghoshal.[7] The implication is that when the values and attitudes of society are changing so must the strategies and behaviors of companies. While anti-business sentiment has for the most part been restricted to the fringes of the political spectrum—neo-Marxists, environmentalists, and anti-globalization activists—the events of 2001 to 2012, including corporate scandals such as Enron and WorldCom and the financial crisis of 2008–2009, have moved disdain for business corporations and their leaders into the mainstream of public opinion.

A feature of growing disenchantment with market capitalism has been the undermining of the *Washington Consensus*—the widely held view that the competitive market economy based on private enterprise, deregulation, flexible labor markets, and liberal economic policies offers the best basis for stability and prosperity and, according to the World Bank and the IMF, the primary foundation for economic development.

Central to the fraying legitimacy of market capitalism has been widespread dismay over changes in the distribution of income and wealth. Figure 16.1 shows evidence of the growing income disparities that have been characteristic of increasing inequality in almost all countries of the world. One of the few unifying features of Occupy Wall Street—the diverse protest movement that has directed hostility toward financiers and the world's financial centers—is the protesters' identification with "we are the 99%": a reference to the 1% of the population that accounts for 42% of America's personal wealth.[8] The contrast between the massive compensation received by financial service executives and the destruction they have brought to employment and living standards for the mass of the population has undermined faith in market capitalism.

The relative economic decline of the US, Europe, and Japan relative to China and other emerging market countries has reinforced this waning confidence in free market capitalism. Between 2000 and 2011, the number of Global Fortune 500

**FIGURE 16.1** Ratio of average CEO total direct compensation to average production worker compensation, 1965–2009

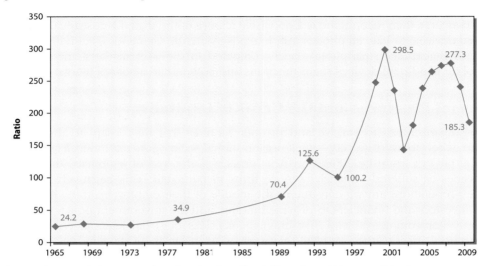

**Sources:** Economic Policy Institute based on data from *The Wall Street Journal*, Mercer, and Hay Group.

companies from the BRIC countries grew from 16 to 83. In 2010, China overtook Japan as the world's second-biggest economy. The growing prominence of Chinese state-owned multinationals in global markets has triggered debate over the merits of state-supported capitalism. As the *Economist* reports:

> the Chinese no longer see state-directed firms as a way-station on the road to liberal capitalism; rather, they see it as a sustainable model. They think they have redesigned capitalism to make it work better, and a growing number of emerging-world leaders agree with them. The Brazilian government, which embraced privatization in the 1990s, is now interfering with the likes of Vale and Petrobras, and compelling smaller companies to merge to form national champions.[9]

Recognition of the merits of **state capitalism** in combining the entrepreneurial drive of capitalism with the long-term orientation and coordinated resource deployment of government planning is one aspect of a growing interest in alternative forms of business enterprise. The United Nations' designation of 2012 as the "International Year of Cooperatives" did much to raise the profile of businesses that are mutually owned by consumers (e.g., credit unions), employees (e.g., the British retailing giant John Lewis Partnership), or by independent producers (e.g., agricultural marketing cooperatives). Cooperatives account for 21% of total production in Finland, 17.5% in New Zealand, and 16.4% in Switzerland. In Uganda and other African countries, cooperatives are the dominant organizational form in agriculture.[10]

Adapting to society's growing demands for fairness, ethics, and sustainability presents challenges for business leaders that extend beyond the problems of reconciling societal demands with shareholder interests. Should a company determine unilaterally the values that will govern its behavior, or does it seek to reflect those of the society in which it operates? Companies that embrace the values espoused by their founders are secure in their own sense of mission and can ensure a long-term consistency in their strategy and corporate identity (e.g., Walt Disney Company and Wal-Mart with respect to founders Walt Disney and Sam Walton). However, there is a risk that these values become out of step with those of society as a whole or with the requirements for business effectiveness. Thus, at British retailer Marks & Spencer and chocolate maker Cadbury, social responsibility and paternalism toward employees became a source of rigidity rather than a competitive advantage. Other companies have experienced the reverse: by taking account of the interests and needs of different stakeholders and of society at large, some companies report a greater responsiveness to their external environment, greater commitment from employees, and enhanced creativity.

# New Directions in Strategic Thinking

The external pressures impacting firms is evident in the worldwide rise in company failures over the past decade. In the US, business bankruptcy filings grew from 19,695 in 2006 to a peak of 60,837 in 2009 before dropping to 47,806 in 2011. Major US bankruptcies of 2011–2012 have included AMR (the parent of American Airlines), Eastman Kodak, MF Global, Dynegy Holdings, Borders Group, and Blockbuster Entertainment. The pressures of a more demanding business environment are forcing companies to rethink their strategies.

## Reorienting Corporate Objectives

The waning appeal of shareholder value maximization during the past decade culminated in the declaration by former GE chairman Jack Welch, a leading exponent of shareholder value maximization, that it was a "dumb idea." Yet adapting corporate goals to accommodate greater social and environmental responsibility restricts the ability of companies to survive increasingly intense competition. Recent efforts to reconcile a broader societal role with the need for profit maximization have emphasized either the need for companies to maintain social legitimacy or the potential for such a broadening of goals to open up new avenues for value creation—the central theme of Porter and Kramer's *shared value* concept.[11] The appeal of this broader concept of the role of the firm is that it maintains the fundamental orientation of the firm toward earning profit or, equivalently, value creation. (The value of the firm is the capitalized value of economic profit, or free cash flows, over its lifetime.)

The key reorientation of the doctrine of shareholder value creation is away from its 1990s preoccupation with stock market valuation towards a refocusing of top management priorities up on the fundamental drivers of enterprise value. This reflects a recognition that management cannot create stock market value: only the stock market can do that. What management can do is to generate the stream of profits that the stock market capitalizes into its valuation of the firm. Indeed, as I argued in Chapter 2, the critical focus of top management should not even be profits; it should be the strategic factors that drive profits: operational efficiency, customer satisfaction, innovation, and new product development.

The implication is not that business leaders abandon shareholder value maximization in favor of some woolly notion of pursuing stakeholder interests or to seek some new model of capitalism, but that they should focus more determinedly on identifying and managing the basic drivers of value creation.[12] Common to most of the corporate disasters of the 21st century from Enron and Parmalat to Royal Bank of Scotland and MF Global has been poor corporate strategies. Hence, to improve corporate performance, it is unlikely that a massive extension of government regulation, a new model of capitalism, or a re-engineering of human nature offer the best solutions. The most useful antidote to the threats of corporate empire building, CEO hubris, and blind faith in new business models is likely to be a stronger emphasis on the basic principles of strategy analysis. As Dick Rumelt has pointed out: "Bad strategy abounds!"[13]

## Seeking More Complex Sources of Competitive Advantage

Focusing on strategy fundamentals does not necessarily lead to simple strategies. As we observed in Chapter 7, in today's dynamic business environment competitive advantages are difficult to sustain. As the rate of technology diffusion increases and new competitors with unassailable cost advantages emerge from newly industrializing countries, so established firms are under increasing pressure to access new sources of competitive advantage. A key feature of companies that have maintained both profitability and market share over many years—for example Toyota, Wal-Mart, 3M, Canon, Swatch, and Samsung—is their development of multiple layers of competitive advantage, including cost efficiency, differentiation, innovation, responsiveness, and global learning. As we shall see, reconciling the different requirements of different performance dimensions imposes highly complex organizational challenges that are pushing companies to fundamentally rethink their structures and management systems.

Thus, the ability of some companies to combine multiple capabilities recalls Isaiah Berlin's classification of intellectuals into foxes and hedgehogs: "The fox knows many things; the hedgehog knows one big thing."[14] Despite Jim Collins' praise for companies that have a single penetrating insight into the complexities of their business environments, it appears that companies that have built their strategy on such insight often have difficulty in adapting to subsequent changes in their markets: Toys "R" Us with big-box retailing, Dell with its direct sales model, General Motors with its multi-brand market segmentation strategy, AOL with dial-up internet access.[15]

## Managing Options

As we observed in the last section of Chapter 2 ("Strategy as Options Management"), the value of the firm derives not only from the present value of its profit stream (cash flows) but also from the value of its options. During turbulent times, real options—growth options, abandonment options, and flexibility options—become increasingly important as sources of value. Taking account of options has typically involved adjustment of investment appraisal methodologies so that option values are incorporated into capital budgeting decisions. However, the implications of option thinking extend to the most fundamental aspects of a firm's strategy—and to the tool of strategy analysis that it employs. To take just one example of how a failure to take account of option value can lead to a misguided strategy, consider conventional approaches to corporate finance. The attraction of leveraged buyout has been to create shareholder value through substituting low-cost debt (the interest payments on which are tax deductible) for high-cost equity. Yet, such reductions in the cost of capital also destroy option value: highly leveraged firms have fewer opportunities to take advantage of unexpected investment opportunities (including acquisition) and have less flexibility in adjusting to an unexpected downturn.

Viewing strategy as the management of a portfolio of options shifts the emphasis of strategy formulation from making resource commitments to the creation of opportunities. Strategic alliances offer a particularly potent tool for creating growth options: they allow a firm to make limited investments in new technological and market opportunities that can be "exercised" through larger investments (possibly in the form of a joint venture or an outright acquisition) as more information emerges.

The adoption of options thinking also has far-reaching implications for our tools and frameworks of strategy analysis. For example:

- Industry analysis has taken the view that decisions about industry attractiveness depend on profit potential. However, if industry structure becomes so unstable that forecasting industry profitability is no longer viable, it is likely that industry attractiveness will depend much more on option value. From an options perspective, an attractive industry is one that is rich in options, for example an industry that produces a number of different products and comprises multiple segments, has many strategic groups, utilizes a diversity of alternative technologies and raw materials, and where internal mobility barriers tend to be low. Thus, consumer electronics, semiconductors, packaging, and investment banking would seem to be more attractive in terms of options than electricity or steel or car rental.

- An options approach also has major implications for the analysis of resources and capabilities. In terms of option value, an attractive resource is one that can be deployed in different businesses and support alternative strategies. A technological breakthrough in nanotechnology is likely to offer greater option value than a new process that increases the energy efficiency of blast furnaces will. A relationship with a rising politician is a resource that has more option value than a coalmine. Similarly with capabilities: a highly specialized capability, such as expertise in the design of petrochemical plants, offers fewer options than expertise in the marketing of fast-moving consumer goods. Dynamic capabilities are important because they generate new options: "Dynamic capabilities are the organizational and strategic routines by which firms achieve new resource combinations as markets emerge, collide, split, evolve, and die."[16]

## Understanding Strategic Fit

Central to just about everything in this book is the notion of *strategic fit*. In Chapter 1, we looked at how strategy must *fit* with the business environment and with the firm's resources and capabilities; we viewed the firm as an *activity system* where all the activities of the firm fit together (Figure 1.3). In Chapter 6, we looked at *contingency approaches* to organizational design: the idea that the structure and management systems of the firm must fit with the firm's business environment.

In Chapter 8, we saw how complementarities between strategy, structure, and management systems can act as a barrier to change. In recent years our understanding of fit (or contingency) has progressed substantially as a result of two major concepts: complementarity and complexity. These concepts offer new insights into linkages within organizations.

*Complementarity Research*  Complementarity research addresses the linkages among a firm's management practices. A key focus has been the transition from mass manufacturing to lean manufacturing where it has been observed that reorganizing production processes tends to be counterproductive without the simultaneous adaptation of a range of human resource practices.[17] Similarly, a six-sigma quality program needs to be accompanied by changes in incentives, recruitment policies, product strategy, and capital budgeting practices.[18]

At one extreme, recognition of complementarities in management practices makes it difficult to make generalizations about strategic management: every firm is unique and must create a unique configuration of strategic variables and management practices. In practice, strategic choices tend to converge on a limited number of *configurations*. Thus, successful adaptation among large European companies was associated with a small number of configurations of organizational structure, processes, and boundaries.[19]

*Complexity Theory*  Organizations—like the weather, ant colonies, and flocks of birds, human crowds, and seismic activity—are *complex systems* whose behavior results from the interactions of a large number of independent agents. This behavior of complex systems has interesting features that have important implications for the management of organizations:

- *Unpredictability*: The behavior of complex adaptive systems cannot be predicted in any precise sense. There is no convergence on stable equilibria; cascades of change are constantly interacting to reshape competitive landscapes. As noted in Strategy Capsule 16.1, the outcomes tend to follow *power law distributions*: small changes typically have minor consequences but may also trigger major movements.[20]

- **Self-organization**: Complex biological and social systems have a capacity for self-organizing. A bee colony or shoal of fish shows coordinated responses to external threats and opportunities without anyone giving orders. Groups of human beings also display coordinated behavior patterns e.g., when walking along crowded sidewalks. Quite sophisticated synchronized behavior can be achieved through adopting just a few simple rules. There are three main requirements for self-organization: *identity* that permits a common sense-making process within the organization, *information* that provides the possibility of synchronized behavior, and *relationships* that are the pathways through which information is transformed into intelligent, coordinated action.[21]

- *Inertia, chaos, and evolutionary adaptation*: Complex systems can stagnate into inertia (stasis) or become disorderly (chaos). In between is an intermediate region where the most rapid evolutionary adaptation occurs. Positioning at this *edge of chaos* results in both small, localized adaptations and occasional evolutionary leaps that allow the system to attain a higher *fitness peak*.[22] Kaufman's *NK model*, which allows the behavior of complex systems to be simulated, has been widely applied to the study of organizations.[23]

*The Contextuality of Linkages within the Firm*   Common to both the complementarity and complexity approaches to analyzing linkages among a firm's activities is the concept of *contextuality*—the extent to which the benefits from any particular activity depend upon which other activities are taking place.[24] Porter and Siggelkow identify two dimensions of this contextuality:

- *Contextuality of activities*: Some management activities are generic: their performance effects are independent of other activities—for example using computers for managing accounting systems is optimal for virtually all firms independently of what business the firm is in or how other activities are organize. The benefits from other activities are dependent upon what other activities are taking place. For example, payments linked to individual employee output only boost productivity if employees work independently.
- *Contextuality of interactions*: Do activities interact in similar ways across firms? Generic interactions are those which are the same for all firms. For example, the benefits from flexibility in manufacturing will always increase with increased product differentiation. Other interactions are context-specific. For example, in the case of Ryanair's activity system (Figure 1.3), the complementarity between a point-to-point route structure and 25-minute aircraft turnarounds in achieving high aircraft utilization is dependent upon the airline's policy of no through ticketing and no baggage transfers.[25]

Acknowledging the different ways in which a firm's activities interact offers insight into some of the complexities of strategic management. In particular, it helps us to understand why a strategy that has worked well for one company is a dismal failure when adopted by a competitor; it points to the risks in attempting to transfer "best practices" either from another firm or even from another part of the same firm; it allows us to see why piecemeal adaptations to external change often make the situation worse rather than better; and it reveals why post-merger integration is so treacherous.

## Redesigning Organizations

A more complex, more competitive business environment requires that companies perform at higher levels with broader repertoires of capabilities. Building multiple capabilities and achieving excellence across multiple performance dimensions requires managing dilemmas. A company must produce at low cost while also innovating; it must deploy the massed resources of a large corporation while showing the entrepreneurial flair of a small start-up; it must achieve reliability and consistency while also making local adaptations to meet individual circumstances. We addressed one of these dilemmas: the challenge of *ambidexterity*—optimizing efficiency and effectiveness for today while adapting to the needs of tomorrow—in Chapter 8. In reality, the problem reconciling incompatible strategic goals is much broader: the challenge of today is reconciling *multiple* dilemmas—this requires *multi-dexterity*.

Implementing complex strategies with conflicting performance objectives takes us to the frontiers of management knowledge. We know how to devise structures and systems that drive cost efficiency; we know the organizational conditions conducive to innovation; we know a good deal about the characteristics of *high-reliability organizations*, we have insights into the sources of entrepreneurship. But how on earth do we achieve all of these simultaneously?

## Multi-Dimensional Structures

Organizational capabilities, we have learned (Chapter 5), need to be embodied in processes and housed within organizational units that provide the basis for coordination between the individuals involved. The traditional matrix organization allows capabilities to be developed in relation to products, geographical markets, and functions. And the more capabilities an organization develops, the more complex its organizational structure becomes.

- The total quality movement of the 1980s resulted in companies creating organizational structures to implement quality management processes.
- The adoption of social and environmental responsibility by companies has resulted in the creation of structures devoted to these activities.
- The dissemination of knowledge management during the 1990s resulted in many companies setting up knowledge management structures and systems.
- The need to develop and exercise capabilities to meet the needs of large global customers has resulted in multi-national corporations establishing organizational units for managing key accounts.[26]
- The quest for innovation and organizational change has resulted in the establishment of organizational units that conduct "exploration" activities (see the discussion on ambidexterity in Chapter 8) these include project teams for developing new products and incubators for developing new businesses. They also include organizational change initiatives such as General Electric's "Work-Out" program and innovation structures such as IBM's online "Innovation Jam," a temporary organization that administers a biannual, 72-hour online session involving tens of thousands of contributors from inside and outside the company, then harvesting the results.[27] Such organizational structures that are outside companies' formal operating structures for the purposes of fostering *dynamic capabilities* have been described as *parallel learning structures*.[28]

## Coping with Complexity: Making Organizations Informal, Self-Organizing, and Permeable

If firms expand their range of capabilities, the implications for organizational complexity are frightening. In Chapter 6, we observed that traditional matrix structures which combined product, geographical, and functional organizations proved unwieldy for many corporations. We are now introducing additional dimensions to the matrix!

*Informal Organization*   The answer to that added complexity is informal rather than formal structures and systems. The organizational requirements for coordination are different from those required for compliance and control. Traditional hierarchies with bureaucratic systems are based upon the need for control. Coordination requires structures that support modularity, but within each module, team-based structures are often most effective in supporting organizational processes; and coordination between modules does not necessarily need to be managed in a directive sense—coordination can be achieved by means of standardized interfaces, mutual adjustment, and horizontal collaboration (see discussion of "The Coordination Problem" and "Hierarchy in Organizational Design" in Chapter 6.

The scope for team-based structures to reconcile complex patterns of coordination with flexibility and responsiveness is enhanced by the move toward project-based organizations. More companies are organizing their activities less around functions and continuous operations and more around time-designated projects where a team is assigned to a specific project with a clearly defined outcome and a specified completion date. While construction companies and consulting firms have always been structured around projects, a wide range of companies are finding that project-based structures featuring temporary cross-functional teams charged with clear objectives are more able to achieve innovation, adaptability, and rapid learning than more traditional structures. A key advantage of such temporary organizational forms is that they can avoid the ossification of structures and concentrations of power that more permanent structures encourage. W. L. Gore, the supplier of Gore-tex and other hi-tech fabric products, is an example of a team-based, project-focused structure that integrates a broad range of highly sophisticated capabilities despite an organizational structure that is almost wholly informal: there are no formal job titles and leaders are selected by peers. Employees ("associates") may apply to join particular teams, and it is up to the team members to choose new members. The teams are self-managed and team goals are not assigned from above but agreed through team commitments. Associates are encouraged to work with multiple teams.[29]

Reducing complexity at the formal level can foster greater variety and sophisticated coordination at the informal level. In general, the greater the potential for reordering existing resources and capabilities in complex new combinations, the greater the advantages of *consensus-based hierarchies*, which emphasize horizontal communication, over *authority-based hierarchies*, which emphasize vertical communication.[30]

*Self-Organization*   When discussing complexity theory, I identified three factors that are conducive to self-organization in complex systems: identity, information, and relationships. There is ample evidence of the role that these can play in substituting for traditional management practices.

- *Identity*: For coordination to be effective in the absence of top-down directives, it requires shared cognition of what the organization is and an emotional attachment toward what it represents. These form *organizational identity*—a collective understanding of what is presumed core, distinctive, and enduring about the character of an organization.[31]

  Organizations lose an enormous organizing advantage when they fail to create a clear and coherent identity. In a chaotic world, organizational identity needs to be the most stable aspect of the endeavor. Structures and programs come and go, but an organization with a coherent center is able to sustain itself through turbulence because of its clarity about who it is. Organizations that are coherent at their core move through the world with more confidence.[32]

A strong consensus around organizational identity provides a powerful basis for coordinated action that permits flexibility and responsiveness to be reconciled with continuity and stability. Of course, organizational identity, because it is permanent, can be an impediment to, rather than a facilitator of, change. The key challenge for organizational leaders is to reinterpret organizational identity in a way that can support and legitimate change. Michael Eisner at Disney, Lou Gerstner at IBM, and Franck Riboud at Danone all initiated major strategic changes, but within the constancy of their companies' identities. Organizational identity creates an important linkage between a firm's internal self-image and its market positioning. With the increase of symbolic influences on consumer choices, the linkage between product design, brand image, and organizational identity becomes increasingly important. For companies such as Apple, Alessi, and Bang & Olufsen, product design is an important vehicle for establishing and interpreting organizational identity.[33]

- *Information*: The information and communication revolution of the past two decades has transformed society's capacity for self-organization, as evident from the role of the BlackBerry Messenger in the London riots of 2011 and the role of Twitter in coordinating the anti-Putin protests in Moscow in 2011–2012. Within companies, information and communication networks support spontaneous patterns of complex coordination with little or no hierarchical direction. Indeed, real-time coordination is increasingly characterized by automated process where human intervention is absent (Strategy Capsule 16.2).

- *Relationships*: According to Wheatley and Kellner-Rogers, "Relationships are the pathways to the intelligence of the system. Through relationships, information is created and transformed, the organization's identity expands to include more stakeholders, and the enterprise becomes wiser. The more access people have to one another, the more possibilities there are. Without connections, nothing happens . . . In self-organizing systems, people need access to everyone; they need to be free to reach anywhere in the organization to accomplish work."[34] There is increasing evidence that a major part of the work of organizations is achieved through informal social networks.[35]

*Breaking Down Corporate Boundaries* Even with informal coordination mechanisms, modular structures, and sophisticated knowledge management systems, there are limits to the range of capabilities that any company can develop internally. Hence, in order to expand the range of capabilities that they can deploy, firms collaborate in order to access the capabilities of other firms. This implies less distinction between what happens within the firm and what happens outside it. Strategic alliances, as we have already seen, permit stable yet flexible patterns for integrating the capabilities of different firms while also sharing risks. While localized networks of firms—such as those that characterize Italy's clothing, furniture, and industrial machinery industries—offer potential for building trust and interfirm routines, web-based technologies permit much wider networks of collaboration. The open innovation efforts described in this book—Procter & Gamble's "Connect & Develop" approach to new product development and IBM's "Innovation Jam"—both point to the power of ICT technologies to enable firms to draw upon ideas

**STRATEGY CAPSULE 16.2**
## The Automated Economy

Management has always been closely identified with the management of people. This reflects the primary role of labor as a factor of production. Yet a growing feature of the modern economy is the replacement of people and human decision making by information technology. The economist Brian Arthur points to the emergence of a "second economy" where economic activity is coordinated entirely by machines. One example is the issuing of boarding cards by self-service machines at airports. On inserting a frequent-flier card or credit card, the machine issues a boarding pass, receipt, and luggage tag within the space of four or five seconds. Within these seconds, observes Arthur, a complex conversation takes place entirely among machines. With your identity established, your flight status is checked with the airline along with your past travel history. Your name is checked with the database of the Transportation Security Administration, and possibly with the National Security Agency. Your seat choice

is confirmed, your frequent-flier status is checked, and mileage is credited. Your seat allocation takes account of the aircraft's loading system which ensures an even weight distribution of the fuselage. The disintermediation of human decision makers by intelligent systems that process information, optimize decisions, and coordinate subsequent activities is an increasingly common feature of distribution systems, financial services, even petroleum reservoir management. When you use a self-service checkout at a supermarket, an integrated information system links your purchases to shelf-filling activity within the store, deliveries from warehouse to store, and production planning and supply logistics by manufacturers.

**Source:** S. Hoover, "Digitized Decision Making and the Hidden Second Economy," Techonomy Conference, October 9, 2011; W. B. Arthur, "The Second Economy," *McKinsey Quarterly* (October 2011).

and expertise across the globe. The collaborative potential of the internet is most strongly revealed in open-source communities that build highly complex products, such as Linux and Wikipedia, through global networks of individual collaborators.[36]

## The Changing Role of Managers

Changing external conditions, new strategic priorities, and different types of organization call for new approaches to management and leadership. The era of restructuring and shareholder focus was associated with *change masters*[37]—highly visible, individualistic, and often hard-driving management styles of CEOs such as Lee Iacocca at Chrysler, John Browne at BP, Michael Eisner at Disney, and Rupert Murdoch at News International. These leaders were, first and foremost, strategic decision makers, charting the direction and redirection of their companies, and making key decisions over acquisitions, divestments, new products, and cost cutting.

In the emerging 21st century organization, this "buck stops here" peak decision-making role may no longer be feasible, let alone desirable. As organizations and their environments become increasingly complex, the CEO is no longer able to access or synthesize the information necessary to be effective as a peak decision maker. Recent contributions to the literature on leadership have placed less emphasis on the role of executives as decision makers and more on their role in guiding organizational evolution. Gary Hamel is emphatic about the need to redefine the work of leadership:

> The notion of the leader as a heroic decision maker is untenable. Leaders must be recast as social-systems architects who enable innovation . . . In Management 2.0, leaders will no longer be seen as grand visionaries, all-wise decision makers, and ironfisted disciplinarians. Instead, they will need to become social architects, constitution writers, and entrepreneurs of meaning. In this new model, the leader's job is to create an environment where every employee has the chance to collaborate, innovate, and excel.[38]

Jim Collins and Jerry Porras also emphasize that leadership is less about decision making and more about cultivating identity and purpose:

> If strategy is founded in organizational identity and common purpose, and if organizational culture is the bedrock of capability, then a key role of top management is to clarify, nurture and communicate the company's purpose, heritage, personality, values, and norms. To unify and inspire the efforts of organizational members, leadership requires providing meaning to people's own aspirations. Ultimately this requires attention to the emotional climate of the organization.[39]

This changing role also implies that senior managers require different knowledge and skills. Research into the psychological and demographic characteristics of successful leaders has identified few consistent or robust relationships—successful leaders come in all shapes, sizes, and personality types. However, research using *competency modeling* methodology points to the key role of personality attributes that have been referred to by Daniel Goleman as *emotional intelligence*.[40] These attributes comprise: *self-awareness*, the ability to understand oneself and one's emotions; *self-management*, control, integrity, conscientiousness, and initiative; *social awareness*, particularly the capacity to sense others' emotions (empathy); and *social skills*, communication, collaboration, and relationship building. Personal qualities are also the focus of Jim Collins' concept of "Level 5 Leadership," which combines personal humility with an intense resolve.[41]

A similar transformation is likely to be required throughout the hierarchy. Informal structures and self-organization have also transformed the role of middle managers from being administrators and controllers into entrepreneurs, coaches, and team leaders.

The insights provided by complexity theory also offer more specific guidance to managers, in particular:

- *Rapid evolution requires a combination of both incremental and radical change*: While stretch targets and other performance management tools can produce pressure for incremental improvement, more decisive intervention may be needed to stimulate radical change. At IBM, Sam Palmisano's leadership between 2002 and 2012 refocused IBM upon research and innovation, expanded IBM's presence in emerging markets, and inaugurated a new era of social and environmental responsibility.[42]

- *Establishing simple rules*: If the coordinated behaviors of complex systems can be simulated with a few simple rules, it seems feasible that companies can be managed by a few simple rules with limited managerial direction. For instance, rather than plan strategy in any formal sense, rules of thumb in screening opportunities (*boundary rules*) can locate the company where the opportunities are richest. Thus, Cisco's acquisition strategy is guided by the rule that it will acquire companies with fewer than 75 employees of which 75% are engineers. Second, rules can designate a common approach to how the company will exploit opportunities (*how-to rules*). Thus, Yahoo! has a few rules regarding the look and functionality of new web pages, but then gives freedom to developers to design new additions.[43]

- *Managing adaptive tension*: If too little tension produces inertia and too much creates chaos, the challenge for top management is to create a level of adaptive tension that optimizes the pace of organizational change and innovation. This is typically achieved through imposing demanding performance targets, but ensuring that these targets are appropriate and achievable.

## Summary

Since I began studying business strategy during the late 1970s, I have heard repeated calls for a revolution in the theory and practice of management. During the 1980s, Tom Peters invited managers to "thrive on chaos" and embrace "liberation management";[44] at the end of the 1990s, Peter Drucker observed that most of the assumptions underlying management had "outlived their usefulness" and needed reformulation;[45] most recently, Gary Hamel has established the Management Innovation Exchange "with the goal of making institutions of all kinds more adaptable, more innovative, more inspiring, and more socially accountable."[46]

The propensity for management theory and management practice to lag behind to reflect the priorities and thinking of an earlier era is a continuing dilemma for management scholars and practicing managers. Accelerating rates of change in the business environment have made this problem more acute. Our review of the changes that have taken place in the business environment since 2000 reveals the new challenges that face firms and their leaders, in particular the need to compete at a higher level along a broader front. A common feature of these challenges is that almost all of them present dilemmas: between competing for the present and adapting to the future, between efficiency and innovation, between centralized resource deployment and decentralized responsiveness, and so on.

In responding to these challenges, business leaders are supported by two developments. The first comprises emerging concepts and theories that offer both insight and the basis for new management tools. Key developments include complexity theory, the principles of self-organization, real option analysis, organizational identity, network analysis, and new concepts of innovation, knowledge management, and leadership.

A second area is the innovation and learning that results from adaptation and experimentation by companies. Long-established companies such as IBM and P&G have embraced open innovation;

technology-based companies such as Google, W. L. Gore, Microsoft, and Facebook have introduced radically new approaches to project management and human resource management, including allowing individuals to choose which projects to work on and giving them autonomy in innovation initiatives. In emerging-market countries we observe novel approaches to government involvement in business (China), new initiatives in managing integration in multibusiness corporations (Samsung), new approaches to managing ambidexterity (Infosys), and novel approaches to encouraging employee engagement (Haier).

At the same time, it is important not to overemphasize either the obsolescence of existing principles or methods of management. Many of the features of today's business environment are extensions of well-established trends rather than fundamental discontinuities. Indeed, it has typically been radically new management concepts and ideas that have been found wanting: the dawning of the "new economy," the new era of "virtual corporations," the revolutionary potential of "knowledge management," and the coordination benefits of the "networked organization" have all failed to convince. Certainly our strategy analysis will need to be adapted and augmented in order to take account of new circumstances; however, the basic tools of analysis—industry analysis, resource and capability analysis, the applications of economies of scope to corporate strategy decisions—remain relevant and robust. One of the most important lessons to draw from the major corporate failures that have scarred the 21st century—Enron, WorldCom, Lehman Brothers, and Royal Bank of Scotland—has been the realization that the rigorous application of the tools of strategy analysis outlined in this book might have helped these firms to avoid their misdirected odysseys.

Quizzes and flashcards to test yourself further are available in your interactive e-book at **www.wileyopenpage.com**

# Notes

1. P. F. Drucker, *Management Challenges for the 21st Century* (New York: HarperCollins, 2001): ix–x.
2. The NASDAQ hit the all-time high of 5132 on March 10, 2000.
3. US National Intelligence Council, *Global Trends 2025: A Transformed World* (Washington DC, November 2008), www.dni.gov/nic/NIC_2025_project.html, accessed July 8, 2009.
4. J. Alceler and J. Oxley, "Learning by Supplying," Harvard Business School Discussion Paper (March 2012).
5. A. Y. Lewin, C. B. Weigelt, and J. D. Emery, "Adaptation and Selection in Strategy and Change," in M. S. Poole and A. H. van de Ven (eds), *Handbook of Organizational Change and Innovation* (New York: Oxford University Press, 2004): 108–60.
6. http://www.thedailybeast.com/articles/2012/03/28/murdoch-hacking-scandal-could-go-global-threaten-news-corp-core-tv-business.html, accessed April 14, 2012.
7. P. F. Drucker, *Managing in the Next Society* (London: St. Martin's Press, 2003); S. Ghoshal, C. A. Bartlett, and P. Moran, "A New Manifesto for Management," *Sloan Management Review* (Spring 1999): 9–20; C. Handy, *The Age of Paradox* (Boston: Harvard University Press, 1995).
8. *The One Percent* is a 2006 documentary produced by Jamie Johnson and Nick Kurzon and premiered on HBO in 2008.
9. "The Rise of State Capitalism," *Economist* (January 21, 2012).
10. http://www.worldwatch.org/membership-co-operative-businesses-reaches-1-billion, accessed April 14, 2012.
11. M. E. Porter and M. R. Kramer, "Creating Shared Value," *Harvard Business Review* (January 2011): 62–77 (see Chapter 2 for a discussion).
12. See, for example, P. Barnes, *Capitalism 3.0* (San Francisco: Berrett-Koehler, 2006); D. Rodrik, *The*

*Globalization Paradox: Democracy and the Future of the World Economy* (New York: W.W. Norton, 2011).

13. R. P. Rumelt, "The Perils of Bad Strategy," *McKinsey Quarterly* (June 2011).

14. I. Berlin, *The Hedgehog and the Fox* (New York: Simon & Schuster, 1953).

15. J. Collins, *Good to Great* (New York: HarperCollins, 2001).

16. K. M. Eisenhardt and J. A. Martin, "Dynamic Capabilities: What Are They?" *Strategic Management Journal* 21 (2000): 1105–21.

17. K. Laursen and N. J. Foss, "New Human Resource Management Practices, Complementarities and the Impact on Innovation Performance," *Cambridge Journal of Economics* 27 (2003): 243–63.

18. Six sigma is a quality management methodology first developed by Motorola in 1986 that aims to reduce defects among products and processes to less than 3.4 per million. See C. Gygi, N. DeCarlo, and B. Williams, *Six Sigma for Dummies* (Hoboken, NJ: John Wiley & Sons, Inc., 2005).

19. R. Whittington, A. Pettigrew, S. Peck, E. Fenton, and M. Conyon, "Change and Complementarities in the New Competitive Landscape," *Organization Science* 10 (1999): 583–600.

20. P. Bak, *How Nature Works: The Science of Self-organized Criticality* (New York: Copernicus, 1996).

21. M. J. Wheatley and M. Kellner Rogers, *A Simpler Way* (San Francisco: Berrett-Koehler, 1996).

22. P. Anderson, "Complexity Theory and Organizational Science," *Organization Science* 10 (1999): 216–232.

23. S. McGuire, B. McKelvey, L. Mirabeau, and N. Oztas, "Complexity Science and Organization Studies," in S. Clegg (ed.), *The SAGE Handbook of Organizational Studies* (Thousand Oaks, CA: SAGE Publications, 2006): 165–214.

24. M. E. Porter and N. Siggelkow, "Contextuality within Activity Systems and Sustainable Competitive Advantage," *Academy of Management Perspectives* 22 (May 2008): 34–56.

25. These issues are discussed in greater depth in M. E. Porter and N. Siggelkow, "Contextuality within Activity Systems and Sustainable Competitive Advantage," *Academy of Management Perspectives* 22 (May 2008): 34–56.

26. G. S. Yip and A. J. M. Bink, *Managing Global Customers: An Integrated Approach* (Oxford: Oxford University Press, 2007).

27. O. M. Bjelland and R. C. Wood, "An Inside View of IBM's 'Innovation Jam,'" *MIT Sloan Management Review* (Fall 2008): 32–40.

28. G. Bushe and A. B. Shani, *Parallel Learning Structures* (Reading, MA: Addison-Wesley, 1991).

29. G. Bushe and A. B. Shani, *Parallel Learning Structures* (Reading, MA: Addison-Wesley, 1991): Chapter 5.

30. J. A. Nickerson and T. R. Zenger, "The Knowledge-based Theory of the Firm: A Problem-solving Perspective," *Organization Science* 15 (2004): 617–632.

31. D. A. Gioia, M. Schultz, and K. G. Corley, "Organizational Identity, Image and Adaptive Instability," *Academy of Management Review* 25 (2000): 63–81.

32. M. J. Wheatley and M. Kellner-Rogers, "The Irresistible Future of Organizing," (July/August 1996), http://margaretwheatley.com/articles/irresistiblefuture.html, accessed August 27, 2012.

33. D. Ravasi and G. Lojacono, "Managing Design and Designers for Strategic Renewal," *Long Range Planning* 38, no. 1 (February 2005): 51–77.

34. M. J. Wheatley and M. Kellner-Rogers, "The Irresistible Future of Organizing," (July/August 1996), http://margaretwheatley.com/articles/irresistiblefuture.html, accessed August 27, 2012.

35. L. L. Bryan, E. Matson, and L. M. Weiss, "Harnessing the Power of Informal Employee Networks," *McKinsey Quarterly* (November 2007).

36. A. Wright, "The Next Paradigm Shift: Open Source Everything," http://www.brighthand.com/default.asp?newsID=14348, accessed July 8, 2009.

37. R. M. Kanter, *The Change Masters* (New York: Simon & Schuster, 1983).

38. G. Hamel, "Moon Shots for Management?" *Harvard Business Review* (February 2009): 91–8.

39. J. C. Collins and J. I. Porras, *Built to Last* (New York: Harper Business, 1996).

40. D. Goleman, "What Makes a Leader?" *Harvard Business Review* (November/December 1998): 93–102. See also J. C. Hayton and G. M. McEvoy, "Developing and Assessing Professional and Managerial Competence," *Human Resource Management* 45 (2006): 291–4.

41. J. Collins, "Level 5 Leadership: The Triumph of Humility and Fierce Resolve," *Harvard Business Review* (January 2001): 67–76.

42. "IBM's Sam Palmisano: A Super Second Act," *Fortune* (March 4, 2011).

43. For discussion of the role of rules in strategy making, see K. M. Eisenhardt and D. Sull, "Strategy as Simple Rules," *Harvard Business Review* (January/February 2001): 107–16.

44. T. Peters, *Thriving on Chaos* (New York: Knopf, 1987); T. Peters, *Liberation Management* (New York: Knopf, 1987).

45. P. F. Drucker, *Management Challenges for the 21st Century* (New York: HarperCollins, 2001): ix–x.

46. www.managementexchange.com.

# GLOSSARY

**acquisition (or takeover)**   The purchase of one company by another.

**activity system**   A conceptualization of the firm as a set of inter-related activities.

**agency problem**   An agency relationship exists when one party (the principal) contracts with another party (the agent) to act on behalf of the principal. The agency problem is the difficulty of ensuring that the agent acts in the principal's interest.

**ambidextrous organization**   An organization that can simultaneously exploit existing competences while exploring new opportunities for future development.

**balanced scorecard**   A tool for linking strategic goals to performance indicators. These performance indicators combine performance indicators relating to financial performance, consumer satisfaction, internal efficiency, and learning and innovation.

**barriers to entry**   Disadvantages that new entrants to an industry face in relation to established firms.

**barriers to exit**   Costs and other impediments which prevent capacity from leaving an industry.

**benchmarking**   A systematic process for comparing the practices, processes, resources and capabilities of other organizations with one's own.

**blue-ocean strategy**   The discovery or creation of uncontested market space.

**bottom of the pyramid**   This refers to the poorest people in the world: typically the 2 billion people who live on less than $2 per day.

**bounded rationality**   The principle that the rationality of human beings is constrained ("bounded") by the limits of their cognition and capacity to process information.

**business model**   The overall logic of a business and the basis upon which it generates revenues and profits.

**business strategy (aka competitive strategy)**   This refers to how a firm competes within a particular industry or market.

**capability**   More precisely referred to as *organizational capability*, is an organization's capacity to perform a particular task or function.

**causal ambiguity**   The difficulty facing any observer of diagnosing the sources of the competitive advantage of a firm with superior performance. It means that potential rivals face the problem of *uncertain imitability.*

**comparative advantage**   A country's ability to produce a particular product at a lower relative cost than other countries.

**competency trap**   The barrier to change which results from an organization developing high levels of capability in particular activities.

**competitive advantage**   A firm possesses a competitive advantage over its direct competitors when it earns (or has the potential to earn) a persistently higher rate of profit.

**consumer surplus**   The value that a consumer receives from a good or service minus the price that he or she paid.

**contingency theory**   Postulates that there is no single best way to design and manage an organization. The optimal structure and management systems for any organization are contingent upon its context—in particular, the features of its business environment and the technologies it utilizes.

**corporate governance**   The system by which companies are directed and controlled.

**corporate planning**   A systematic approach to resource allocation and strategic decisions within a company over the medium to long-term (typically 4 to 10 years).

**corporate restructuring**   Radical strategic and organizational change designed to improve performance through cost reduction, employment reduction, divestment of assets, and internal reorganization.

**corporate social responsibility (CSR)**   The social responsibilities of a business organization.

**corporate strategy**   A firm's decisions and intentions with regard to the scope of its activities (its choices in relation to the industries, national markets, and vertical activities within which it participates) and the resource allocation among these.

**customer relationship management (CRM)**   A set of tools, techniques, and methodologies for understanding the needs and characteristics of customers in order to better serve them.

**dominant design**  A product architecture that defines the look, functionality, and production method for the product and becomes accepted by the industry as a whole.

**dynamic capabilities**  Organizational capabilities that allow an organization to reconfigure its resources and modify its operating capabilities in order to adapt and change.

**economic profit**  Pure profit: it is the surplus of revenues over all the costs of producing that revenue inputs (including the costs of capital).

**economic value added (EVA)**  A measure of economic profit. It is the excess of net operating profit after tax over the cost of the capital used in the business.

**economies of scale**  These exist when increases in the scale of a firm or plant result in reductions in costs per unit of output.

**economies of scope**  These exist when using a resource across multiple products or multiple markets uses less of that resource than when the activities are carried out independently.

**emergent strategy**  The strategy that results from the actions and decisions of different organizational members as they deal with the forces which impinge upon the organization.

**first-mover advantage**  The competitive advantage that accrues to the firm which is first to occupy a new market or strategic niche, or to exploit a new technology. First-mover advantage is a special case of *early-mover advantage*.

**functional structure**  Organization around specialized business functions such as accounting, finance marketing, operations, etc.

**game theory**  This analyzes and predicts the outcomes of competitive (and cooperative) situations where each player's choice of action depends upon the choices made by the other players in the game. Game theory has applications to business, economics, politics, international relations, biology, and social relations.

**global strategy**  A strategy that treats the world as a single, if segmented, market.

**globalization**  The process through which differences between countries diminish and the world becomes increasingly integrated.

**hypercompetition**  Competition that is characterized by rapid and intensive competitive moves where competitive advantage is quickly eroded and firms are continually seeking new sources of competitive advantage.

**industry life cycle**  The pattern of industry evolution from introduction to growth to maturity to decline.

**innovation**   The initial commercialization of invention by producing and marketing a new good or service or by using a new method of production.

**institutional isomorphism**   The tendency for organizations that are subject to common social norms and pressures for legitimacy to develop similar organizational characteristics.

**intellectual property**   Intangible goods that have no physical presence and which are "creations of the mind." It includes ideas, names, symbols, designs, artwork, and writings.

**intended strategy**   The strategy conceived by top management with the intention of implementing it within the organization.

**invention**   The creation of new products and processes through the development of new knowledge or from new combinations of existing knowledge.

**isolating mechanisms**   Barriers that protect the competitive advantage of firms from imitative competition.

**key success factors**   Sources of competitive advantage within an industry.

**knowledge-based view of the firm**   This regards the firm as a pool of knowledge assets. The key challenge of management is to integrate the specialized knowledge of organizational members into the production of goods and services.

**matrix structures**   Hierarchies that comprise multiple dimensions; these typically include product (or business) units, geographical units, and functions.

**merger**   The amalgamation of two or more companies to form a new company. In a merger, the owners of the merging companies exchange their shares for shares in the new company.

**multidivisional structure**   A company structure comprising separate business units, each with significant operational independence, coordinated by a corporate head office that exerts strategic and financial control.

**network effects (or network externalities)**   Linkages between the users of a product or technology that result in the value of that product or technology being positively related to the number of users.

**open innovation**   An approach to innovation where a firm seeks solutions from organizations and individuals outside the firm and shares its technologies with other organizations.

**organizational culture**   An organization's values, traditions, behavioral norms, symbols, and social characteristics.

**organizational ecology (aka organizational demography and the population ecology of organizations)** This studies the organizational population of industries and the processes of founding and selection that determine entry and exit.

**organizational routines** Patterns of coordinated activity through which organizations are able to perform tasks on a regular and predictable basis.

**path dependency** The simple fact that history matters; more specifically, it implies that an organization's strategy and structure and management's options for the future are determined by past decisions.

**prisoner's dilemma** A simple game theory model which shows how lack of cooperation results in an outcome that is inferior to that which could have been achieved with cooperation.

**profit** The surplus of revenues over costs available for distribution to the owners of the firm.

**real option analysis** This identifies and values possibilities for investment in uncertain opportunities. The two major types of real option are investments in flexibility and investment in growth opportunities.

**realized strategy** The actual strategy that the organization pursues; it is the outcome of the interaction of intended strategy with emergent strategy.

**regime of appropriability** The conditions that determine the extent to which a firm is able to capture profits from its innovations.

**resources** The assets of the firm including tangible assets (such as plant, equipment, land, and natural resources), intangible resources (such as technology, brands and other forms of intellectual property) and human resources.

**resource-based view of the firm** A theoretical perspective on the firm that emphasizes the role of resources and capabilities as the basis of competitive advantage and the foundation for strategy.

**scenario analysis** A technique for integrating information and ideas on current trends and future developments into a small number of distinctly different future outcomes.

**segmentation** The process of disaggregating industries and markets into more narrowly defined sub-markets on the basis of product characteristics, customer characteristics or geography.

**self-organization** The tendency for complex systems, both natural and biological, to spontaneously achieve order and adaptation though decentralized interactions without any centralized direction or control.

**seller concentration**   This measures the extent to which a market is dominated by a small number of firms. The concentration ratio measures the market share of the largest firms e.g., the four-firm concentration ratio (CR4) is the combined market share of the four biggest firms.

**stakeholder approach to the firm**   This proposes that the firm operates in the interests of all its stakeholders (owners, employees, customers, suppliers and society). Top management has the task of balancing and integrating these different interests.

**strategic fit**   The consistency of a firm's strategy with its external environment and with its internal environment, especially with its goals and values, resources and capabilities, and structure and systems.

**state capitalism**   A market-based economy where a large proportion of leading enterprises are owned by the government.

**strategic alliance**   A collaborative arrangement between two or more firms involving their pursuit of certain common goals.

**strategic group**   A group of firms within an industry that follow similar strategies.

**strategic intent**   The goal of an organization in terms of a desired future strategic position.

**SWOT framework**   The SWOT framework classifies the factors relevant for a firm's strategic decision making into four categories: strengths, weaknesses, opportunities and threats.

**technical standard**   A specification or requirement or technical characteristic that becomes a norm for a product or process thereby ensuring compatibility.

**transaction costs**   The costs incurred in researching, negotiating, monitoring and enforcing market contracts.

**value**   Within management terminology, value is used to refer to two very different concepts. In its plural form, *values* typically refer to ethical precepts and principles. In its singular form it typically refers to economic value: the monetary worth of a product or asset.

**value added**   Sales revenue minus the cost of bought-in goods and services; it is equal to all the firm's payments to factors of production (i.e., wages and salaries + interest + rent + royalties and license fees + taxes + dividends + retained profit).

**value chain**   A sequence of vertically related activities undertaken by a single firm or by a number of vertically-related firms in order to produce a product or service.

**vertical integration**   A firm's ownership of adjacent vertical activities.

# INDEX

Note: Page numbers in *italics* refer to illustrations and tables.